RELATIONAL PSYCHOANALYSIS

VOLUME 5

RELATIONAL PERSPECTIVES BOOK SERIES

Volume 52

The Relational Perspectives Book Series (RPBS) publishes books that grow out of or contribute to the relational tradition in contemporary psychoanalysis. The term *relational psychoanalysis* was first used by Greenberg and Mitchell (1983) to bridge the traditions of interpersonal relations, as developed within interpersonal psychoanalysis and object relations, as developed within contemporary British theory. But, under the seminal work of the late Stephen Mitchell, the term *relational psychoanalysis* grew and began to accrue to itself many other influences and developments. Various tributaries—interpersonal psychoanalysis, object relations theory, self psychology, empirical infancy research, and elements of contemporary Freudian and Kleinian thought—flow into this tradition, which understands relational configurations between self and others, both real and fantasied, as the primary subject of psychoanalytic investigation.

We refer to the relational tradition, rather than to a relational school, to highlight that we are identifying a trend, a tendency within contemporary psychoanalysis, not a more formally organized or coherent school or system of beliefs. Our use of the term *relational* signifies a dimension of theory and practice that has become salient across the wide spectrum of contemporary psychoanalysis. Now under the editorial supervision of Lewis Aron and Adrienne Harris, the Relational Perspectives Book Series originated in 1990 under the editorial eye of the late Stephen A. Mitchell. Mitchell was the most prolific and influential of the originators of the relational tradition. He was committed to dialogue among psychoanalysts and he abhorred the authoritarianism that dictated adherence to a rigid set of beliefs or technical restrictions. He championed open discussion, comparative and integrative approaches, and he promoted new voices across the generations.

Included in the Relational Perspectives Book Series are authors and works that come from within the relational tradition, extend and develop the tradition, as well as works that critique relational approaches or compare and contrast it with alternative points of view. The series includes our most distinguished senior psychoanalysts along with younger contributors who bring fresh vision.

RELATIONAL PERSPECTIVES BOOK SERIES
LEWIS ARON & ADRIENNE HARRIS
Series Editors

RELATIONAL
PSYCHOANALYSIS

VOLUME 5

Evolution *of* Process

EDITED BY

LEWIS ARON • ADRIENNE HARRIS

Routledge
Taylor & Francis Group

New York   London

LCCN: 2007275272

Routledge
Taylor & Francis Group
711 Third Avenue
New York, NY 10017

Routledge
Taylor & Francis Group
27 Church Road
Hove, East Sussex BN3 2FA

© 2012 by Taylor & Francis Group, LLC
Routledge is an imprint of Taylor & Francis Group, an Informa business

Printed in the United States of America on acid-free paper
Version Date: 20110726

International Standard Book Number: 978-0-415-88826-4 (Hardback) 978-0-415-88827-1 (Paperback)

Visit the Taylor & Francis Web site at
http://www.taylorandfrancis.com

and the Routledge Web site at
http://www.routledgementalhealth.com

*Dedicated to the memory of
Stephen A. Mitchell (1946–2000).
On the 10th anniversary of his passing,
he remains an inspiration.*

Contents

Contributors

Lewis Aron, PhD, is the director of the New York University Postdoctoral Program in Psychotherapy and Psychoanalysis, cochair of the Sándor Ferenczi Center at the New School for Social Research, and an honorary member of the William Alanson White Psychoanalytic Society. He was the founding president of the International Association for Relational Psychoanalysis and Psychotherapy (IARPP). Along with Adrienne Harris, he is the series editor of the Relational Perspectives Book Series for Routledge and the author of *A Meeting of Minds: Mutuality in Psychoanalysis* (Analytic Press, 1996).

Anthony Bass, PhD, is a faculty member and supervising analyst at the New York University Postdoctoral Program in Psychotherapy and Psychoanalysis and is also faculty at the Columbia University Center for Psychoanalytic Training and Research. He is the president of the Steven Mitchell Center for Relational Studies and the founding director of the International Association for Relational Psychoanalysis and Psychotherapy. He is the editor-in-chief of *Psychoanalytic Dialogues.*

Beatrice Beebe, PhD, is a clinical professor of psychology and psychiatry in the College of Physicians and Surgeons at Columbia University. She is coauthor (with Frank Lachmann) of *Infant Research and Adult Treatment* (Analytic Press, 2002).

Philip M. Bromberg, PhD, is a training and supervising analyst and faculty member of the William Alanson White Psychoanalytic Institute and a clinical professor of psychology at the New York University Postdoctoral Program in Psychotherapy and Psychoanalysis. He is author of *Standing in the Spaces: Essays on Clinical Process, Trauma, and Dissociation* (Analytic Press, 1998) and *Awakening the Dreamer: Clinical Journeys* (Analytic Press, 2006) as well as *The Shadow of the Tsunami*, expected to be released by Routledge in late 2011.

Steven H. Cooper, PhD, is a training and supervising analyst at the Boston Psychoanalytic Society and Institute, a supervising analyst and faculty at the Massachusetts Institute for Psychoanalysis, and a clinical associate professor of psychology at Harvard Medical School. A joint editor-in-chief of *Psychoanalytic Dialogues*, he is the author of *Objects of Hope: Exploring Possibility and Limit in Psychoanalysis* (Analytic Press, 2000) and *A Disturbance in the Field: Essays in Transference-Countertransference Engagement* (Routledge, 2010). He has a private practice in Cambridge, Massachusetts.

Jody Messler Davies, PhD, is a supervising analyst and past cochair of the relational track for the New York University Postdoctoral Program in Psychotherapy and Psychoanalysis and is a supervisor at the National Institute for the Psychotherapies. A coeditor of *Psychoanalytic Dialogues*, she is the author of numerous psychoanalytic publications and coauthor (with Mary Gail Frawley-O'Dea) of *Treating the Adult Survivor of Childhood Sexual Abuse: A Psychoanalytic Perspective* (Basic Books, 1994).

Darlene Bregman Ehrenberg, PhD, is a training and supervising analyst at the William Alanson White Psychoanalytic Institute. She serves on the editorial boards of *Contemporary Psychoanalysis, Psychoanalytic Inquiry,* and the *International Forum of Psychoanalysis*; she is also the author of *The Intimate Edge: Extending the Reach of Psychoanalytic Interaction* (W.W. Norton, 1992).

Dianne Elise, PhD, is a supervising analyst and faculty member of the Psychoanalytic Institute of Northern California and training analyst of the International Psychoanalytic Association. She is associate editor of *Studies in Gender and Sexuality* and has served on the editorial board of the *Journal of the American Psychoanalytic Association*.

Glen Gabbard, PhD, is the Brown Foundation Chair of Psychoanalysis and professor of psychiatry at Baylor College of Medicine in Houston, Texas, as well as training and supervising analyst at the Houston/Galveston Psychoanalytic Institute. From 2001 to 2007 he was joint editor-in-chief of the *International Journal of Psychoanalysis*. He is the author or editor of 25 books, including *Love and Hate in the Analytic Setting* (Aronson, 1977) and *Boundaries and Boundary Violations in Psychoanalysis* (Basic Books, 1995).

Adrienne Harris, PhD, is a clinical associate professor at the New York University Postdoctoral Program in Psychotherapy and Psychoanalysis and associate editor of *Psychoanalytic Dialogues* and *Studies in Gender and*

Sexuality. She is a series editor, along with Lewis Aron, of the Relational Perspectives Book Series, and is author of *Gender as Soft Assembly* (Analytic Press, 2005) and coeditor *First Do No Harm: The Paradoxical Encounters of Psychoanalysis, Warmaking, and Resistance* (Routledge, 2010, with Steven Botticelli).

Irwin Z. Hoffman, PhD, is a faculty member and supervising analyst at the Chicago Center for Psychoanalysis and at the National Training Program for Contemporary Psychoanalysis, lecturer in psychiatry at the University of Illinois College of Medicine, and adjunct clinical professor at the New York University Postgraduate Program in Psychotherapy and Psychoanalysis. He is on the editorial board of *Psychoanalytic Dialogues*, is corresponding editor for *Contemporary Psychoanalysis*, and has served on the board of the *International Journal of Psychoanalysis*. He is the author of a series of publications developing his "dialectical constructivist" point of view, including his book *Ritual and Spontaneity in the Psychoanalytic Process: A Dialectical Constructivist View* (The Analytic Press, 1998). Dr. Hoffman is in private practice in Chicago.

Steven Knoblauch, PhD, is a faculty member and supervisor at the New York University Postdoctoral Program in Psychotherapy and Psychoanalysis and the Institute for the Psychoanalytic Study of Subjectivity in New York. He is author of *The Musical Edge of Therapeutic Dialogue* (Analytic Press, 2000) and coauthor of *Forms of Intersubjectivity in Infant Research and Adult Treatment* (Other Press, 2005) as well as *The Return of the Embodied Analyst: From Reich to Relationality* (with John Sletvold), forthcoming from Routledge.

Thomas Ogden, MD, is a supervising and personal analyst at the Psychoanalytic Institute of Northern California and member of the Faculty of the San Francisco Center for Psychoanalysis. His books include *Rediscovering Psychoanalysis: Thinking and Dreaming, Learning and Forgetting* (Routledge, 2008); *This Art of Psychoanalysis: Dreaming Undreamt Dreams and Interrupted Cries* (Routledge, 2005); and *Reverie and Interpretation: Sensing Something Human* (Jason Aronson, 1997).

D. Orfanos, PhD, ABPP, is a clinic director at the New York University Postdoctoral Program in Psychotherapy and Psychoanalysis. He is also on the board of directors of the Stephen Mitchell Center for Relational Studies and is president of the International Association for Relational Psychoanalysis and Psychotherapy. Dr. Orfanos is past president of the Division of Psychoanalysis (39) of the American Psychological Association.

Stuart A. Pizer, PhD, ABPP, is a founding member, faculty member, former president, and supervising analyst at the Massachusetts Institute for Psychoanalysis, assistant clinical professor of psychology in the Department of Psychiatry at Harvard Medical School, and visiting faculty member at the Psychoanalytic Institute of Northern California and the Toronto Institute for Contemporary Psychoanalysis. A past president of the International Association for Relational Psychoanalysis and Psychotherapy, he is also an associate editor for *Psychoanalytic Dialogues* and corresponding editor for *Contemporary Psychoanalysis* as well as the author of *Building Bridges: The Negotiation of Paradox in Psychoanalysis* (Analytic Press, 1998).

Philip Ringstrom, PhD, PsyD, is a senior training and supervising analyst and faculty member at the Institute of Contemporary Psychoanalysis in Los Angeles, California. He is a member of the editorial boards of both the *International Journal of Psychoanalytic Self Psychology* and *Psychoanalytic Dialogues*. He is also a member of the International Council of Self Psychologists and on the board of directors of the International Association of Relational Psychoanalysis and Psychotherapy.

Jill Salberg, PhD, is a faculty member and supervisor at the New York University Postdoctoral Program in Psychotherapy and Psychoanalysis, the Stephen Mitchell Center for Relational Studies, and the Institute for Contemporary Psychotherapy. Her articles on Freud, gender, termination, and Judaism and psychoanalysis have been published in *Psychoanalytic Dialogues* and *Studies in Gender and Sexuality,* and she has chapters in *The Jewish World of Sigmund Freud* (McFarland, 2010) and *Answering a Question with a Question: Judaism and Contemporary Psychoanalysis* (Academic Studies Press, 2010). She is a contributor to and editor of *Good Enough Endings: Breaks, Interruptions, and Terminations from Contemporary Relational Perspectives* (Routledge, 2010).

Stephen Seligman, PhD, is a clinical professor of psychiatry in the Infant–Parent Program at the University of California–San Francisco, training and supervising analyst and faculty at the San Francisco Center for Psychoanalysis and Psychoanalytic Institute of Northern California, and a faculty member at the New York University Postdoctoral Program in Psychotherapy and Psychoanalysis. In addition, he is joint editor-in-chief of *Psychoanalytic Dialogues.*

Joyce Slochower, PhD, is a faculty member at the New York University Postdoctoral Program in Psychotherapy and Psychoanalysis, the Steven Mitchell Center for Relational Studies, the National Training Program of NIP, and the Psychoanalytic Institute of Northern California. She is the author of *Holding and Psychoanalysis: A Relational Perspective* (Analytic Press, 1996) and *Psychoanalytic Collisions* (Analytic Press, 2006).

Donnel B. Stern, PhD, is a training and supervising analyst and faculty member at the William Alanson White Psychoanalytic Institute and faculty and supervisor at the New York University Postdoctoral Program in Psychotherapy and Psychoanalysis. A past editor of *Contemporary Psychoanalysis,* he is currently the editor of the Psychoanalysis in a New Key book series for Routledge and author of two books, *Unformulated Experience: From Dissociation to Imagination in Psychoanalysis* (Analytic Press, 1997) and *Partners in Thought: Working With Unformulated Experience, Dissociation, and Enactment* (Routledge, 2010).

Paul Wachtel, PhD, graduated from and is faculty at the New York University Postdoctoral Program in Psychotherapy and Psychoanalysis and is presently Distinguished Professor of Psychology in the doctoral program in clinical psychology at City College and the City University New York Graduate Center. His books include *Relational Theory and the Practice of Psychotherapy* (Guilford, 2007); *Therapeutic Communication* (Guilford, 1993); *Psychoanalysis, Behavioral Therapy, and the Relational World* (APA, 1997); and *Inside the Session: What Really Happens in Psychotherapy* (APA, 2011).

Foreword: Voyaging the Relational Sea Change

Spyros D. Orfanos

About 37 years ago, I was struggling with the idea of whether to study psychology as an undergraduate. I had taken a few courses and was not particularly impressed with the field, neither its empirical nor Freudian zealots. And the Fordham University Jesuits with whom I was studying at the time had turned me off to ancient philosophy and comparative literature—two particular interests of mine. I considered the Jesuit's approach a serious misunderstanding of text, ideas, and life. I always believed Nietzsche's Zarathustra was right: "God is dead," and I believed that *the gods* were alive in biology, history, culture, the unconscious, and chance.

My state of intellectual melancholia was beginning to take its toll on me. And then things changed. The change was no doubt complex, but it was not complicated. It involved *Eros* and it also involved *Logos*. I decided to give the study of psychology one last try, and I registered for a class in abnormal psychology, which happened to be taught by an unassuming, bearded man named Stephen Mitchell. This young professor had a flair for teaching and a scholarly style that juggled precision, pluralism, and passion. He taught about the suffering and treatment of people by making references to Goethe, the existentialists, and psychiatrists like Harry Stack Sullivan and R. D. Laing. He lectured and discussed the nuances of interaction among psychology, culture, and politics. And he seemed to have a restless spirit of inquiry. His was a psychology that inspired. I switched my college major to psychology.

Stephen A. Mitchell went on to emerge as a central figure in the develop-ment of the relational point of view in psychoanalysis. His ideas and unique contributions will someday be carefully considered and evaluated for their brilliance and creativity. But Mitchell did not stand alone as the sole advo-cate for the relational point of view. A community of like-minded analysts and scholars were already on the job, so to speak.

We often think of Greenberg and Mitchell's (1983) *Object Relations Theory in Psychoanalysis* as the beginning of relational thinking but that is not quite right. There was a "before the beginning" phase that involved creativ-ity, both conceptual and clinical. Contributions from analysts like Heinrich Racker, Merton Gill, Edward Levenson, Darlene Bregman Ehrenberg, Irwin Hoffman, and a number of philosophical (feminism and constructivism) and sociopolitical developments (the demise of the medical model and the insertion of the subject into the clinical narrative) comprised this before the beginning phase. The early contributions and developments that pre-ceded the comparative psychoanalytic opus of Greenberg and Mitchell were necessary for the evolution of the relational point of view. But it is a principle of the relational view that often we cannot tell exactly when something starts and when it exactly finishes. History is construction. We can, however, surmise that the emergence of the relational point of view was revolutionary in psychoanalysis and that it involved a community of clinicians and scholars. This community did not emerge overnight but over time with its individuals engaged in mutual scholarship and nonlinear learning. True, there were leaders, some public and some less public, as is the case with any creative group, but the leaders tended not to be positiv-ists as is so often the implicit demand placed on leaders. The relational perspective was not centered on the ideas of one leader or scholar. Mitchell has often been set up by critics as the solo leader of the relational move-ment, but he would have been the first to dismiss himself in that role. Having studied community psychology for a spell, he was too savvy to feel that one individual could responsibly establish a tradition of innovation—a core collective was needed. Mitchell facilitated the creation of an informal core of relational scholars.

The papers in this volume attest to the success of the unusual profes-sional community that was formed by the relational point of view. The 20 contributors to this volume demonstrate an originality of thinking and action (practice) that taken together demonstrate the continued creative spirit generated by the relational revolution. They write about clinical pro-cess as if they had bodies, were situated in time, space, culture, and society and struggling for credibility and authority (Shapin, 2010). Marx was wrong; not all revolutions are taken over by clerks.

Why refer to the relational perspective as revolutionary? I shall try to out-line an answer to this by way of borrowing from those who study creativity and aesthetics (Sternberg, 1999). But it is understood that there is no *a priori* scale that renders one psychoanalytic model more creative than another. Creative contributions differ not only in their amounts but also in the types of creativity they represent. Sigmund Freud and Anna Freud were highly creative psychoanalysts, but the nature of their contributions was different. Sigmund Freud proposed a radically new theory of human motivation that he called a Copernican revolution in thought, and Anna Freud elaborated on and modified her father's theory. According to Sternberg, creative contributions can be categorized into those that accept current paradigms and attempt to replicate or extend them and those that reject current paradigms and attempt to replace them. Accepting the current paradigm can mean leaving the field as it is with perhaps some redefinition or movement forward in increments (in the direction it is already going). Greenberg and Mitchell describe this as a "preservative" strategy. Rejecting the current paradigm can mean (1) a redirection or (2) a reinitiation in either small steps forward or substantial leaps (reinitiation represents a major paradigm shift). Greenberg and Mitchell describe this as an "alternative" model. In music, Beethoven's work can be viewed as a redirection from the classical style of music that had been used by Mozart and others. He used many of the same classical forms as had his predecessors, but he also showed that a greater level of emotionality could be introduced into the music without sacrificing the classical forms (Kivy, 2001). In psychoanalysis, Lacan (2002) can be seen as redirecting French psychoanalysis by "a return to Freud" and his defining of the unconscious as "the discourse of the Other."

Reinitiation, the second manner by which a current paradigm is rejected, is a bit more complex than redirection. Creative contributors who are engaged in reinitiation suggest that the field or subfield has reached an undesirable point or has exhausted itself moving in the direction that it is moving. But rather than suggesting that the field or subfield move in a different direction from where it is (as in redirection), the creative contributor suggests a different direction from a different point in the multidimensional space of contributions. In effect, the contributor is suggesting that people question their assumptions and "start over" from a point that most likely makes different assumptions. Mitchell (1988, 1997) questioned the assumptions of many of the dominant psychoanalytic models of his day (ego psychology, the Kleinian tradition, and interpersonal psychoanalysis) and argued for a fresh approach. According to Aron and Harris (2005) he described these developments as revolutionary rather than evolutionary but also understood the aesthetic and constructive aspects of such designations as being in the service of theory building. It is unlikely that the relational revolution in theory and action is a Copernican change. Mitchell believed the relational model was "better" and "more useful." He explained in an interview with Rudnytsky (2002), "It explains people–clinicians as well as patients—to themselves much better. It's also more consistent with a whole range of movements in other intellectual disciplines" (p. 118).

In 1983, Greenberg and Mitchell borrowed the term *paradigm shift* from the work of the famed American historian and philosopher of science Thomas Kuhn. In 1963 Kuhn published his highly influential *The Structure of Scientific Revolution*, a book about scientific revolutions and the periods of great upheaval when existing scientific ideas are replaced with radically new ones. The concept of paradigm was a constellation of shared assumptions, beliefs, and values that unite a scientific community and allow normal science to take place. At the time, the dominant philosophical view in the English-speaking world was logical positivism, and Kuhn's ideas challenged the belief in the orderly accumulation of scientific knowledge. In fact, Kuhn argued that adopting a new paradigm involves a certain act of faith. Moreover, he questioned the validity of the concept of objective truth and theory-free observation. But there were problems with the term *paradigm* primarily related to definition. Kuhn's ideas dropped out of favor in numerous intellectual circles. In psychoanalysis, this was partly because the scientific narrative lost its dominance and was now valued as just one narrative choice out of many. Thus, a descriptive method used by a historian of science seemed to fade.

The more current term used by many relationalists to describe the dramatic changes in thinking and action is the metaphor *sea change*. This term is drawn from a phrase in a wonderfully evocative song from Shakespeare's *The Tempest* connoting transformation. Ironically for psychoanalysts, the lines of the song evoke radical change in the presence of the death of a father. Transformation implies a loss. In this case, the father may be Freud and his notions of drive.

While relational studies have been at the center of practically all the major developments and innovations in psychoanalytic psychology for over a quarter of a century (Orfanos, 2006), Greenberg and Mitchell did not originally imagine a relational school of psychoanalysis. But a tradition has indeed evolved over time with a number of women and men having made astonishing contributions to theory and practice under the umbrella term *relational*. This volume does not aspire to offer the final word in an authoritative and definitive voice in a dialogue that is still very much ongoing. Its specific contribution lies in the implicit case it makes for the existence and viability of polyphony.

The tempo and momentum of creativity in relational studies seemed to find its rhythm in the early 1990s and has not slowed down. Relationalists mutually inform each other and transform each other through their writings and public actions in psychoanalytic institutes and at national and international conferences. This is a testimony to the importance of the psychological sense of community that the relational revolution maintains.

The distinguished thinkers and outstanding writers presented in this volume on clinical process tell us stories. All their stories, except for Ehrenberg's, have been published in the first decade of the 21st century. And almost all of the contributors were there during the first sparks of the relational revolution in the 1980s and continue in the present to push the theoretical envelope. Their ideas have not stayed static with just replication of concepts and actions. They continue to redirect and reinitiate. The small miracle of the volume is that there is nothing nostalgic or sentimental about the tone of the papers. The clinical stories told here are enlightening because they are more than their content. They are the kinds of clinical stories relational analysts tell each other when there is time and encouragement and an atmosphere of creativity. There is a healthy intermingling of the theoretical along with the clinical. I am thankful to the editors Lew Aron and Adrienne Harris, both in their own right major innovators of the relational point of view as demonstrated in this volume, for having conceived of the current collection of clinical process stories.

Can a volume of clinical process stories change the way we practice the art of psychoanalysis? Probably not, but it can certainly help us think differently and more deeply. All educators know that learning is nonlinear and that it involves a mutually constructed relationship over time with elements of agency and chance. The papers assembled demonstrate a remarkable inventiveness. A reader can be dazzled by them; she or he can be enriched and even galvanized. But the authors do not always evoke agreement from the reader: That would not be a relational aesthetic. The amazing papers that follow will have concrete elements that can serve as background guides to those who understand that the clinical is learned by way of great study and ongoing disciplined practice of the type that allows for personal expressiveness and spontaneity. I have read just about all the papers previously as journal publications, with the exception being Lew Aron's afterword, but as with any truly good work rereading these papers makes sense in a different way this time around. The selections do not include all the strong clinical articles published under the relational point of view in recent times, but they are some of the best.

While the papers are clinical in nature, they do have wider social implication. Taken as a whole, they form a mutually productive synchrony. Ideas in individual selections build on each other, and there is a steady expansion of the conversation on clinical process. There are echoes here of the individual and collective creative flow found among Athenian philosophers, tragedians, and sculptures in the 5th century B.C.E. and among Parisian painters, poets, and composers in the early part of the 20th century. The independence and the recognition of each other as part of a larger, cocreative project counter the typical Western tradition of the individual scholar as a bounded being. There is nothing more practical and relational than that.

By way of orienting the reader and providing a preview, the papers are arranged in chronological order. They are broadly about clinical engagement, enactment, impasse, nonverbal dimensions, the relational unconscious, and clinical theory. All but three present detailed clinical material. The great wealth of contributions in this collection begins with the trailblazing ideas of Ehrenberg on the therapeutic relationship and its subtle particulars. Her radical work on what we now call intersubjectivity began in the mid-1970s in the "before the beginning" phase of the relational perspective. Her contribution here on psychoanalytic engagement emphasizes the transactional field in which the subjectivities of each in the analytic dyad are influenced by overt and covert reactions of the other. Her clinical emphasis on the intersubjective posits that insight is often the result of change rather than the cause of change.

It should come as no surprise to those who work in the relational tradition that clinical phenomena are implicitly or explicitly constructivist (created by the dyad). Enter Hoffman, whose clinical theory of "dialectical constructivism" is at the core of his relational sensibility. Phenomenologically, he may be the theorists of ambiguity *par excellence*. For him, the radical center of therapeutic action is not the moment of interpretation; it can be located in the dialectic of spontaneous, personal involvement, and critical reflection on the process. Hoffman is also profoundly grounded in the existential believing that life exists against a background of death. With the notion that there is a thin line between the idealization of the analyst and resentment of the analyst for his or her privileged position in the analytic situation and world, he offers two rich clinical vignettes. The vignettes are about the coconstruction of meaning in the face of mortality.

In a creative chapter on psychoanalytic enactments, Slochower tackles questions about clinical misdemeanors and gives numerous examples of such. She distinguishes secret delinquencies from serious ethical violations that disrupt the treatment (i.e., having sex with patients, stealing from them, or exploiting them in other ways). Misdemeanors are about self-interest. In my own clinical practice, I know that I will on occasion bring a cup of coffee into the session, write a note about something on my mind not having to do with the therapy, or emotionally withdraw from a patient who bores me. Obviously, these misdemeanors are not all equal and may involve enactments that are shaped by the emotional quality of my relationship with my patients. I feel guilt about these misdemeanors, and I am less than bold about bringing critical reflection to such events; I am more likely to bring self-judgment to them. My patients tend to ignore such moments perhaps for both conscious and unconscious reasons. No doubt, the power differential in the room plays a role in this. We are committed, argues Slochower, to placing our patients' needs above our own and to addressing whatever resistances interfere with doing this. But this is another instance of a psychoanalytic ideal in collision with the actual.

In a different register, Seligman presents a wealth of material on the developmental perspective, and he does so without resorting to reductionism. While there is no integrated developmental model of relationality, there is ample evidence Seligman writes for thinking about babies as wired for human interaction. Moreover, there is evidence for a clinical theory and technique that places engagement, rather than positivist observation, at the center of therapeutic action. With the decentering of the Oedipus complex and the emergence of dissociation as a defensive organization with varying degrees of rigidity and fragmentation, Seligman builds a developmental view that supports clinical psychoanalysis not as reparenting but as the restoration and integration of aspects of self-experience that are detached or disavowed. A stunningly detailed clinical example of the relevance of infant research and its applicability to adult treatment is offered by Beebe. Her case study of a lengthy, face-to-face psychoanalysis examines moment-to-moment communications, affective climate, and the variety of forms of implicit nonverbal intersubjectivity. Using dual-screen videotaping that shows the faces of both patient and analyst, she allows the reader to see the connections between her groundbreaking research on infants and the swift, subtle, and coconstructed interactions in adult analytic work.

Impasse is a major experience in much of psychoanalytic work, and relationalists have developed various ways to conceptualize it and to work with it. Pizer's paper in this volume is one important example. He is interested in "how impasse can work in the wings like a silent killer." With his usual evocative expressive writing style and moving clinical content, he presents a case study that has two phases with a 14-year break in between (the first phase was a psychotherapy and the second an analysis). He focuses on what makes therapy and analysis relational and concludes that it is "the overarching and ultimate commitment to a thoroughgoing, mutual, open, and explicit reflection in treatment dialogue on the multiple conscious and unconscious meanings of our reciprocal interactions...." His actual analysis of a simple and not uncommon remark by his patient brings to focus not only impasse, dissociation, and distributed self-states but perhaps most importantly also the necessity for joint courageous inquiry.

Knoblauch, in a paper that has not been previously published, compares clinical process to the process of improvisation in jazz. The "talking cure," he explains, is limited. For instance, many traumatic experiences are unspeakable. What makes jazz a particularly good metaphor for psychoanalytic process is that it requires "careful attention to nonverbal embodied dimensions of communication, particularly rhythm, tone and gesture, for recognizing and expressing affect." Knoblauch finds that we pay more attention to "structures" of experience in the subjectivities of analysands and analysts rather than attending to "process." He advocates a shift of analytic attention from the former to the latter. In a *tour de fo*rce writing exercise of a narrative sequence with a patient he calls Denise, Knoblauch discovers 31 points of foci for attention occurring on both symbolic and subsymbolic registers. This type of expansion of attention enables the analyst and ultimately the patient to broaden awareness and thus to make for a more significant clinical experience.

There was profound grief and mourning over the sudden death of Steve Mitchell in 2000. He had been one of the initiators of an international relational membership organization (the International Association for Relational Psychoanalysis and Psychotherapy) that hoped to have its inaugural conference in early 2002. Despite the deep sense of loss, we continued with the planning of the conference, which was dedicated to the memory of Mitchell. The opening plenary presentation was given by Davies. There was an unspoken, perhaps unconscious, group question in the air on the morning of January 19, 2002, as to how the creativity of the relational revolution would be affected by Mitchell's absence. Davies gave us the mesmerizing case of Karen, which broke new ground on the matter of "impasses as enactments that one cannot get out of but one can't get into because of the analyst's dissociated shame-riddled self-states." It is my belief that upon the completion of Davies's presentation all 1,009 members of the audience in the Grand Ballroom of the Waldorf-Astoria Hotel in New York City realized that, while the loss of Mitchell was costly, the creativity of the relational perspective was alive and well.

Among the many innovative theoretical ideas offered by the relational sea change in psychoanalysis is that of the third. What makes it particularly innovative when clarified by Aron is its clinical utility. Clinical utility is a hallmark of the relational approach. Aron rightly argues that impasse often leaves no space for thinking. It creates a closed system. In part, Aron bases his own ideas on Jessica Benjamin's seminal conceptualizations about the third. Thirdness is a way to conceptualize reflection and symbolization so that the analytic dyad can deal with getting stuck in doer and done, tug-of-war interlocking dynamics, and complementary splitting. In a surprising and brilliant turn, Aron goes beyond the clinical in his afterword and applies the notions of thirdness to professional institutions and theories.

Bass takes up the matter of clinical interlocks and enactments in the context of the analytic frame and rules. While the frame has been understood to be a therapeutic structure with boundaries for the process of therapy to unfold, Bass creativity conceptualizes its intersubjective dimensions. Using clinical material that rapidly goes back and forth, he nimbly demonstrates the utility of Ferenczi's "elasticity of technique" and flexibility and argues that the establishment of the frame is, in addition to a boundary structure, an integral part of the process itself and reflects the conscious and unconscious aspects of both patient and analyst. He convincingly explains, "Over time I have come to recognize that any frame for an ever deepening analysis benefits from allowing more play to stretch and fit the unforeseen."

In a shift from the previous clinical themes, the next paper tackles the crucial matter of the relational unconscious. Elise's clinical material highlights a relational approach to oedipal dynamics. She considers maternal subjectivity and desire (including her own self as analyst). Using myth metaphors, she explores the impact of desexualization of the maternal on the development of her female patient's sexuality. She proposes "that an oedipal fantasy where maternal and paternal figures compete for the daughter, as do Demeter and Hades in the Persephone myth, is not truly triangular for the daughter but two dyads split apart." Through a chance encounter, Elise's patient is pressed to contend with her analyst's sexually agentic being—a being that is both maternal and sexual.

Focusing on the analyst's countertransference, Cooper hones in on "analyst disclosure" and particularly analytic reverie (more quieter moments). Influenced by the many contributions of Thomas Ogden, Cooper uses exquisite self-reflection to show how for him, unlike for Ogden, "reverie is more fleeting, imperfect, and a more porous vessel." Odgen focuses on the dialectical interplay of the analysand and analyst states of reverie, bringing forth a third analytic subject. Cooper's manner of reverie, however, leads to private, imagined interpretations of what has been enacted and conscious attempts to reveal the analyst's experience to better understand the transference–countertransference. Cooper reconceptualizes such as "analyst-disclosure" as opposed to "self-disclosure" and as related to the analyst's ethical imagination. Such disclosures allow the patient to see the analyst's mind at work. He gives two strong clinical vignettes that serve to help his patients better understand enactments of the transference–countertransference.

While Philip Bromberg's vitalizing contributions to the relational literature are numerous and highly influential, it may be that his most important explorations have to do with personality functioning (especially but not limited to traumatization). He understands processes such as an "ongoing, nonlinear repatterning of self-state configurations." These configurations are in a continuing dialectic between dissociation and conflict. In this paper he suggests that retaining the notion of unconscious fantasy interferes with the acknowledgment that the clinical process is inherently relational. He believes the same about mental functioning. He argues for a more flowing, impressionistic view of transitional process than that offered by the hard-edged concept of unconscious fantasy.

Next, Salberg explores one of the least written about topics in relational analysis: termination. Given the aim of deep and layered engagement, ending treatment can be a great loss for both participants in the dyad. It is no wonder that "the mutual process of attaching and detaching, of growing closer, and then saying good-bye" pulls for strong feelings and sometimes strong dissociative processes. Offering brutally honest personal material and detailed clinical process notes with patients, Salberg makes an argument for termination as enactment. In the case of her patient Ellen, she knowingly "insisted" on ending the work albeit for good reasons, but later it turns out that it was reparative related to the original trauma—the death of Ellen's brother.

The postmodern self with its multiple realities, varieties, and open systems pulls for chaos and complexity theory and nonlinear dynamic systems (NDS). Harris is one of the most astute relational theorists and clinicians considering NDS development in discussions of analytic change. Whether conceptualizing gender in general or an individual parent mourning the loss of a spouse she is thinking about multiple, deep, and dynamic positions. In her paper here on clinical impasse, Harris writes elegantly about impasse in the analyst, specifically in the process of mourning in the analyst. She opens herself up to the task of mourning. Given that chaos theory holds that small differences are sufficient for transformative movement, she argues that "mutative action is potentiated by virtue of an analytic stance, or rather by shifts in the internal world of the analyst." It is not a question of action or speech. Such dichotomies no longer hold. Clinical momentum, Harris argues, must come from authentic change in the analyst. She knows all too well that authentic change is nonlinear and that our experience of it is speckled with return and repetition.

The social psychologist Kurt Lewin once remarked, "There is nothing as practical as a good theory." Stern, who in the past introduced the highly useful concept of "unformulated experience," has been recently developing a theory of narrative. He holds that narrative does not result from the analyst's objective interventions but is the outcome of emergent and coconstructed clinical process. Like most relationalists, Stern believes that the relationship of patient and analyst "is one of continuous, mutual unconscious influence. Neither the patient nor the analyst has privileged access to the meanings of his own experience." The aim is not interpretation or narrative in the form of text interpretation but the "broadening of the range within which analyst and patient become able to serve as one another's witnesses." He uses case material to show how patient and analysts can become "partners in thought" rather than get stuck in unresolved enactments and their underlying dissociations. The case resolutions often lead to new narratives, ones that are emergent and coconstructed. The stories told then further connect Stern to his patients and the other way around.

Striking a different note on clinical process, Gabbard and Ogden highlight the special ongoing maturational issues for psychoanalysts. After beginning with the admission that "few of us feel that we really know what we are doing when we complete our formal psychoanalytic training," they emphasize that much of analysts' growth and development really takes place after they graduate. They outline eight maturational experiences that can play important roles in the development of analytic identity. These types of experiences range from "developing a voice of one's own" to "working with consultants" to "daring to improvise." The aim is to "keep changing, to be original in their thinking and behavior as analysts," to speak for oneself.

Lastly, if for Hamlet, "The play's the thing," then for Ringstrom improvisational play is the thing. And the thing here is the healing liberation that improvisation can create for an analytic dyad. It is about a kind of mutually enhanced free associational process involving scripts, assigned roles, and dramatic sequences. Improvisation is a way to "cultivate" playing with thoughts, feelings, and interactions that arise both within and between an analytic dyad. For Ringstrom improvisation is "more than just being spontaneous" for it involves moments of mutual surrender to the creation of thirdness (i.e., improvised script) versus submitting to the other's domination. In his work with a patient with a victimized manner, improvisation allowed for the experience to be "refreshing versus stagnating, uplifting versus depressing and expanding versus compressing."

For years now, Paul Wachtel has stood at a slight tilt to the world of psychology and psychoanalysis. His interests in the integration of various forms of psychotherapy, his pluralism, and his emphasis on action in the context of reflection have made for some interesting and innovative ideas. In Chapter 18, Wachtel critiques the linear, archaeological vision implied by "surface and depth" dichotomies and the emphasis in psychoanalysis of two domains: the nursery and the consulting room. Using vivid case material he demonstrates the importance of spending a significant amount of session time discussing patients' daily life as a way of getting at why they are having difficulty in their life. The call to mind the "gap," as he calls it, is not a downgrading of the importance of affect, motivation, or presentation of self and other but rather a rightful placing of focused inquiry and patterned action.

Overall, this volume challenges you, the reader, in what I consider to be a lively and engaging way. It looks at clinical process issues in a way that is enthusiastic and meaningful. We have here a treasure of views about contemporary relational practice. If the art of relational psychoanalysis is action under uncertainty, then the 19 papers presented here stimulate plenty of new ideas for dealing with the suffering of our patients and our own humanity and the ongoing complexities of clinical encounters. With such amazing ideas, clinicians can keep busy learning for another generation. And in the spirit of the relational sensibility, I venture to say that what the reader brings and how she or he voyages "on such a full sea" of clinical process can be what will make this volume a great one.

References

Aron, L., & Harris, A. (Eds.). (2005). Introduction. *Relational psychoanalysis: Innovation and expansion* (pp. xi– xiii). Hillsdale, NJ: The Analytic Press.

Greenberg, J. R., & Mitehell, S. A. (1983). *Object relations in psychoanalytic theory*. Cambridge, MA: Harvard University Press.

Kivy, P. (2001). *The possessor and the possessed: Handel, Mozart, Beethoven and the idea of musical genius*. New Haven, CT: Yale University Press.

Kuhn, T. (1963). *The structure of scientific revolution*. Chicago: University of Chicago Press.

Lacan, J. (2002). *Écrits: A selection* (B. Fink, Trans.). New York: W. W. Norton.

Mitchell, S. A. (1988). *Relational concepts in psychoanalysis*. Hillsdale, NJ: The Analytic Press.

Mitchell, S. A. (1997). *Influence and autonomy in psychoanalysis*. Hillsdale, NJ: The Analytic Press.

Orfanos. S. D. (2006). On such a full sea: Advances in psychoanalytic psychology. *New York State Psychological Association Notebook, 8*(4), 2–8.

Rudnytsky, P. L. (2002). Stephen A. Mitchell: Between philosophy and politics. In *Psychoanalytic conversations*. Hillsdale, NJ: The Analytic Press.

Shapin, S. (2010). *Never pure*. Baltimore, MD: The Johns Hopkins University Press.

Sternberg, R. J. (1999). A propulsion model of types of creative contributions. *Review of General Psychology, 3*(2), 83–100.

Editors' Introduction

Lewis Aron and Adrienne Harris

Relational Psychoanalysis: The Emergence of a Tradition, edited by Steven A. Mitchell and Lewis Aron in 1999, was the first of what was to become a series of books within the Relational Perspectives Book Series (RPBS) published by The Analytic Press and later by Routledge. At that time, Aron and Mitchell were interested in establishing a beachhead in American psychoanalysis, pulling together the early and first theorizing, under a relational rubric, of a number of analysts associated with diverse affiliations. The analysts who contributed to these early volumes can be described in a variety of ways: the immigrant generation, growing up somewhere and journeying to the new relational world; diverse thinkers, grounded in other schools of psychoanalysis, other domains outside psychoanalysis, the world of the activist, the world of the clinic. Now close to two decades later, Lewis Aron and Adrienne Harris (who joined as co-editor with Aron after Mitchell's death in 2000) put together a state-of-the-art assemblage of writers, now seasoned and engaged practitioners of relational psychoanalysis.

A tradition grows in fertile soil, but also strong plants are those that can survive in difficult conditions. One might say that relational psychoanalysis has met both those circumstances. Mitchell set the stage for a rich and very diversified world of theory and practice. He was a man interested in creating landscapes. One might say his vision of relational psychoanalysis was architectural. He wanted individual voices, deeply personal and experience-near encounters with the clinical and theoretical problems that animated the lives and works of the practitioners he drew around him.

Relational psychoanalysis also arose in a climate of deep antagonisms, controversies, and ferment. Turbulent critique from within the field and outside required of relational analysts that they think deeply and carefully and responsibly about the ideas that so fully and vibrantly entered the field. Disclosure and enactment; subjectivity and intersubjectivity; multiplicity of self-states; trauma and fantasy; investigating Thirdness as an aspect of clinical dyads, family patterns—all these problems preoccupied relational analysts over the past several decades. From the initial assumption, following Hoffman and Gill that clinical process was best understood as a social construction, many relational analysts studying gender, sexuality, identities of many sorts found that these terms, while necessary, required exegesis, evolution, enlightenment, and expansion.

We invited two senior analysts in the relational community, Hazel Ipp and Spyros Orfanos, to write more detailed forewords to the specific volumes: Ipp on *Theory* and Orfanos on *Process*.

In introducing the *Theory* volume, Ipp tracks the simultaneous movement toward depth and breadth. She underscores how many relational authors are committed to writing theory in the spirit of uncertainty, of the radically unsettled experiences of self and other, self and culture, self and self. She gives us the felicitous and grace-filled word *ubuntu*, drawn from an African heritage well known to the South Africans in our group (Ipp and Suchet). An ethics of relatedness: *ubuntu* is an inspired organizing term for relational work. In introducing the *Process* volume, Orfanos tracks the relational turn in terms of evolution and revolution, the nature of creative innovation, redirection and reinitiation. He views the wide range of clinical contributions to process as sharing a sensibility in which relational psychoanalysis is understood as therapeutic action under conditions of inevitable uncertainty, and he reviews 19 papers contributing to our understanding of the ongoing complexities of clinical encounters. These are collections of some of the strongest and most articulate and innovative voices in our unfolding tradition.

We have described Mitchell's vision in terms of landscapes and architectural designs, and these capture one aspect of the international growth of the relational psychoanalytic edifice, the institutional structure of a school of thought. In these volumes we might be seen as adding new towers to the relational landscape, but we prefer one of Mitchell's other ubiquitous tropes, that of adding voices to the conversation.

In an incisive doctoral dissertation examining the life and work of Mitchell, Steve Dorse (2010) highlighted the use of "voices" throughout Mitchell's work. Here are a few of the examples highlighted by Dorse: Mitchell (1988) often spoke about the analyst's voice in speaking to a patient, where "the analyst becomes the various figures in the analysand's relational matrix, taking on their attributes and assuming their voices" (p. 296). From his perspective, "the struggle is to find an authentic voice in which to speak to the analysand, a voice more fully one's own" (p. 295). The patient is encouraged "to suspend continuity" (p. 142) and "hear the echoes of other voices, to feel other presences of earlier selves and earlier experiences of others" (p. 142).

In his Editorial Philosophy to the inaugural issue of *Psychoanalytic Dialogues*, Mitchell (1991) wrote that "contemporary psychoanalytic theories can be understood as single voices within a larger discussion, voices that can be more fully grasped and appreciated only when one has access to the other participants in the conversation" (p. 5). Dorse (2010) argues that Mitchell used the metaphor of "voices" interchangeably with "ideas." In using analytic theories, Mitchell focused his attention on how these voices/ideas engaged each other, allowing him a full appreciation of what any individual theory had to offer.

In describing the various analytic writers who had relational sensibilities before the advent of a relational tradition, Mitchell (1999) wrote, "Each one was a voice in the wilderness" (p. 11), and he considered "one of the major projects of [his] own work to be getting people to notice that there were many voices in the wilderness, a veritable chorus, in fact" (p. 11). To develop this point, he offers the following parable to capture "the experience of many people who identify with the term 'relational psychoanalysis'..." (p. 11). We quote it at length because it is one of his less well-known passages:

> Once upon a time, out in the wilderness, lonely relational voices were each singing loudly, oblivious of those around them. Some of those voices were those of the excluded, some of the misunderstood, and some were voices of those who just felt they had a unique song to sing. But, gradually, various relational theorists and clinicians began to look around and discover they were not alone. They found that while their individual voices were faint, their efforts, drawn together in harmony, made a very compelling sound, different from the droning strains of traditional psychoanalysis that they had each, in their own way, left behind. So the excluded formed their own chorus, their own tradition, their own system of notation, their own psychoanalytic subculture. And a lively subculture it has been. Over the years, things started to dry up in the mainstream, and the sounds of vitality that wafted over from the wilderness suddenly became interesting. "I wonder what those guys are singing? Gee, I bet we can sing that way too. In fact, now that I am trying it out, it feels as if we've always been singing that way. Come on back; come on back. We are all really the same." Suddenly, the excluders became gracious hosts. Some of the wilderness choir felt very flattered and returned. Of course, there were all sorts of political problems, because wilderness institutes did not have the right credentials, so that only special wilderness writers could become "honorary" members, and so on. But many of those in the wilderness subculture, originally based partly on exclusion, but now a thriving community, simply did not find returning a terribly interesting or compelling prospect. (p. 11)

Mitchell's use of the voice as a synecdoche emphasizes what is most unique, personal, subjective, and expressive about the individual person as well as what is most characteristic of the theory. But here Mitchell explicitly describes relational psychoanalysis as a chorus, a choir made up of distinct and individual voices. The voices may blend together in harmony but may also be dissonant at times and can sing solos and stand out as distinct, even clashing. This is our vision for these volumes of *Relational Psychoanalysis*. Listen to the voices arrayed in these two volumes. Together they make up a glorious harmonious anthem; individually each voice is rich and distinct with its own timbre. Listen for and enjoy the overtones, the tensions, the consonance and dissonance. Our intention is not to resolve the music to a stable tone but rather to keep it going with more and more voices contributing.

References

Dorse, S. (2010). Constriction as a theme in the life and work of Stephen A. Mitchell. Doctoral dissertation, C. W. Post Campus, Long Island University, NY.

Mitchell, S. A. (1988). *Relational concepts in psychoanalysis: An integration*. Cambridge, MA: Harvard University Press.

Mitchell, S. A. (1991). Editorial philosophy. *Psychoanalytic Dialogues, 1*(1), 1–7.

Mitchell, S. A. (1999). Reply to Richards. *The Round Robin: Newsletter of Section I, Division of Psychoanalysis (39), APA, 14*(1), 10–14.

Mitchell, S. A., & Aron, L. (Eds.) (1999). *Relational psychoanalysis: The emergence of a tradition*. Hillsdale, NJ: The Analytic Press.

1

Psychoanalytic Engagement*

Darlene Bregman Ehrenberg

▼ ▼ ▼ ▼ ▼

I

The Transaction as Primary Data

The interactive dimension of the patient–analyst relationship received considerable attention in the early work of Ferenczi (1916, 1950, 1955) and Rank (1929), and also in the interpersonal literature, particularly in the writings of Sullivan dating from the 1930s (published 1940, 1953, 1954, 1956, 1962), Fromm-Reichmann (1950, 1952), J. Rioch (1943), C. Thompson (1950, 1952), M. J. White (1952), Tauber (1954, 1979), Wolstein (1954, 1959, 1971, 1973), Feiner (1970, 1975, 1979, 1982), Singer (1971, 1977), Levenson (1972, 1974, 1981a, 1981b, 1982a, 1982b, 1983), Ehrenberg (1974, 1975, 1976, 1982), Epstein (1979), and Chrzanowski (1979). Attention to the analytic interaction is also evident in the writings of Lacan (1936, 1952, 1956, 1961), Winnicott (1947, 1963, 1969, 1971), Little (1951, 1957), Fairbairn (1958), Guntrip (1969), and Searles (1965, 1979).

In the classical literature the analytic interaction is considered in essays by Menaker (1942), Gitelson (1952, 1962), Anna Freud (1954), Stone (1954, 1961, 1973, 1981), Tower (1956), Loewald (1960, 1970), Kernberg (1965), Greenson and Wexler (1969), Viderman (1974), Sandler (1976), Lipton (1977), Gill (1979, 1982a, 1982b, 1983) and Klauber (1981).

---

* This chapter is a combined and condensed version of two earlier papers: "Psychoanalytic Engagement I: The Transaction as Primary Data," *Contemporary Psychoanalysis, 18*, 1982, pp. 535–555; and "Psychoanalytic Engagement II: Affective Considerations," *Contemporary Psychoanalysis, 20*, 1984, pp. 560–582. Many of the ideas presented in these early papers are developed more fully in my later work; see especially Ehrenberg (1992, 1995, 1996, 2000, 2003, 2005, 2006, 2010).

Writing from a Kleinian perspective Heimann (1950) noted the analyst's role in provoking the patient's reactions, and Racker (1957) and Baranger and Baranger (1966) elaborated field models of the analytic interaction. Following the Barangers, Langs (1976, 1979, 1981) made this conception the fundamental consideration in his own extensive publications.

Although these authors differ in terms of their theories of personality, their concepts of health and pathology, their perspectives on technique, and their visions of cure, they agree that the analytic interaction constitutes a transactional field.

I believe this has radical implications for a theory of technique. If we accept the concept of the analytic interaction as a transactional field, we are forced to expand the traditional view of the transference as the analytic "playground" (Freud, 1914) and as the "point of urgency" (Strachey, 1934) to recognize that transference and countertransference constitute an interlocking unity, and that all of the transactions in the immediate field of experience constitute primary analytic data. This view also requires recognizing that even the more classical forms of interpretation and intervention have definite interactive meaning and consequences. It also follows that in the choice of whether to address the immediate transaction, and to what degree, or not to address it at all, the analyst exerts leverage on the way the relationship will evolve.

Since within the transactional framework whatever we do must be viewed as having impact and consequence, the analytic transaction, by its very interpersonal nature, provides unique opportunities for new experiences. The question I would like to explore is whether there are ways to intervene deliberately to facilitate the work.

In earlier papers (1974, 1975, 1976, 1982) I pointed out the value of making explicit the subtle cues sent and received out of awareness and the specific responses to them and how this makes it possible to use the interaction as a diagnostic tool as well as a therapeutic medium. My experience has been that focusing on the transactions between patient and analyst, and on what goes on affectively between (and within) each of them, as primary analytic data makes it possible to delineate what is being structured interactively in process. Styles and patterns of bonding, expectations, sensitivities, and patterns of responsiveness, including tendencies to collusion, or to carrying the emotions of the other, can begin to be clarified. This allows for also clarifying vulnerability to confusion as to what is self-generated or what may reflect some pattern of unconscious responsiveness in a moment-by-moment way. Becoming able to comprehend the ways in which one may be contributing to one's own mystification, and one's own resistances to functioning autonomously, allows the sense of helplessness one experiences when one is "mystified" (Laing, 1965) to be mitigated. This allows for disavowed experiences to be reclaimed, and for exploring the motivations for the prior disavowal in the context of a new sense of choice, competence, and responsibility. Emotionally significant associations to the past and memories of relevant historical material not available before often then begin to become accessible, allowing new perspectives on the past. This, in turn, can open a possibility for a necessary and important process of mourning. In this way the immediate interactive process can become a medium of and a locus of therapeutic action.

Nevertheless, there are times when even more may be required to facilitate those reparative (B. Ehrenberg, 1980) and restorative (Feiner, 1982, 1983) or corrective experiences (Loewald, 1960, 1970; Winnicott, 1963; and Gill, 1982b) that may be necessary for further change to occur.

II

The Nature of the Analyst's Engagement

Most of the literature on countertransference (as of 1984) advises that analysts monitor their reactions as a "clue" to better understand the nature of the treatment issues, and as a means of identifying subtle transference phenomena (See Epstein and Feiner, 1979, for an overview). This is in the tradition of Heimann (1950) who warned against the analyst's undisciplined discharge of feelings, to avoid the evident dangers of acting out, wild analysis, manipulation, or the intrusive imposition of the analyst's residual pathology. Such caution seemed warranted in light of the fact that some of the early explorations of more direct participation by the analyst, such as the early radical endeavors of Ferenczi (see Jones, 1957) and Alexander (1956), raised legitimate concern that active participation by the analyst might eventually compromise the integrity of the analytic work. Later efforts in which the analyst participated by assuming a "supplementary" role in relation to the patient's "faulty ego" (see McLaughlin, 1981) helped clarify that this often interfered with achieving analytic goals. For these reasons direct participation came to be considered controversial by analysts of all points of view. (McLaughlin, 1981; and Witenberg, 1976).

Nevertheless, despite the evident potential angers, there is a growing literature from all psychoanalytic schools of thought suggesting the possibility that the analyst's more direct affective engagement can be constructive in advancing the analytic effort without compromising its integrity. Such participation need not involve the "lending of egos," acting out, manipulation, seduction, mystification, nor any other non-analytic gesture. Many authors have also noted that with more disturbed or primitively organized patients the analyst's *active responsiveness* may be essential if any kind of therapeutic change is to be achieved. This body of work includes the papers of J. Rioch (1943), Winnicott (1947, 1969), Little (1951, 1957), Fromm-Reichmann (1952), Tauber (1954, 1979), Stone (1954, 1961), Tower (1956),

Nacht (1957, 1962), Wolstein (1959), Gitelson (1952, 1962), Searles (1965, 1979), Singer (1971, 1977), Levenson (1972, 1983), Bird (1972), Stein (1973), Ehrenberg (1974, 1975, 1976, 1982), Sandler (1976), McDougall (1979), Feiner (1979, 1982, 1983), Bollas (1983) and Hoffman (1983).

In the vanguard emphasizing the value and importance of the analyst's explicit affective reactions was the seminal work of Winnicott (1947). He focused on the importance of knowing that one can evoke the analyst's hatred so that one can work through one's own, and of the opportunity to experience that it is possible for the analyst to withstand and survive one's aggression. Addressing the experience the patient needs with his analyst he wrote: "If the patient seeks objective or justified hate he must be able to reach it, else he cannot feel he can reach objective love" (p. 199).

Winnicott (1947, 1969) also notes that the opportunity to discover that one has an impact, and what that impact is enables the patient to clarify the limits of his or her assumed helplessness as well as his or her assumed omnipotence in relation to the analyst and that the unflappable analyst may be useless when it would have been essential for the patient to know he or she is able to elicit the analyst's responsiveness. He or she also cautions that there are moments when the analyst's assumption of a non-responsive stance may foster the patient's mystification or, at the extreme, provoke a suicide.

I would add that it is also important to be able to *explicitly acknowledge and address* the interactive subtleties of what transpires affectively between patient and analyst, including the ways they connect and the ways they lose each other, in real time and in real ways, as this shifts from moment-to-moment; and just as for some patients the opportunity to experience that one can get into a toxic interaction and *move through it* to a positive place can become a revelation and the medium of "working through," for others, the discovery that neither participant need be damaged or diminished by expressions of *positive* feelings and experiences of closeness is equally important.

Searles (1965) and Singer (1971) note the beneficial consequences a patient derives from the experience of his ability to give to the analyst, to feel useful, relevant, appreciated. Searles (1965) also describes how some patients need consensual validation so as to remain convinced of the reliability of their own perceptions (particularly those perceptions of the therapist). He describes the ego-fragmentation that can occur if this is not provided.

Stern (1983) notes that certain categories of experience "can never even occur unless elicited or maintained by the actions of another and would never exist as a part of known self-experience without another" (p. 74).

What I am stressing is that certain kinds of experiences simply cannot be achieved if the analyst is not affectively engaged and responsive in particular ways.

Several authors have stressed that when the patient's resistance takes the form not simply of detachment, but of an effort to render the work useless, dealing with this in a constructive and effective way is essential if the patient's growth in the analytic relationship is to remain possible (Fromm-Reichmann, 1950; Tower, 1956; Winnicott, 1947, 1969; Nacht 1957; Bird, 1972).

Bird (1972) writes that there are times when "our not confronting the patient becomes in itself not merely an unfriendly act but a destructive one. By not confronting the patient with the actuality of the patient's secret, silent obstruction of analytic progress, the analyst himself silently introduces even greater obstructions" (p. 249).

I agree that, while we cannot always avoid the negation of ourselves, violations of the process, or even our own collusion in these violations, we must be able to address these issues and that there are also times when the analyst must take a stand and set limits to protect the relationship and the work from becoming unduly compromised. Nevertheless, I think that it is not just a matter of setting limits. What is also often crucial is *demonstrating our commitment to the process and to the relationship despite the patient's behavior and despite our own reactions to it.*

In this kind of process the goal is not to stay outside the danger zones, and protect against toxic developments or to simply survive them but to help identify the danger zones and to find ways to safely enter them and deconstruct (and demystify) the interactive subtleties so that the potential time bombs can be defused once and for all. For some patients the *new* experience that the analyst is willing to engage with them even when it is risky and problematic can be profoundly meaningful. The opportunity this can provide to discover that it is possible to touch and be touched in a positive way, even in the context of negative interactions, and that it is possible to move through a toxic interaction and reach a positive outcome, can constitute an experiential kind of insight that throws old assumptions open to question. Fears of contact as being inevitably dangerous to self, to other or to both, or conflicts about contact, can be worked through as they are challenged by the live *new* experience of the moment. If there is no possibility of emotional contact, this kind of process simply cannot occur.

Acknowledging that a patient has been able to scare us or arouse our anger also can be crucial. Some patients have told me explicitly that had I not reacted and shown that I was vulnerable when they threatened me or acted out in destructive ways, they would have kept upping the ante until they were able to provoke my reaction. The point here is that deconstructing and defusing potentials for escalating toxicity in the crucible of the actual lived interactive experience in a moment-by-moment way is not simply a way of creating the conditions for constructive work; in itself it becomes an important medium of the work. This allows for clarifying the ways power and responsibility may be disavowed without conscious awareness and also for discovering that it is possible to make reparations and to have them be accepted when one has failed the other in some way (Fromm-Reichmann,

1950). In addition, establishing that one need not be bound by the limitations of the other, and that one cannot use the limitations and failings of the other to exempt oneself from responsibility for one's own behavior, can also be profoundly important.

What I am stressing is that the analyst's more direct affective engagement not only can be constructive, but may also be essential. Of course, it matters *how* we engage affectively, *how* we work with what goes on affectively between patient and analyst, and whether we deal with this explicitly and constructively.

Clinical Examples

My focus is on the analyst's interventions with regard to the immediate interactive process, particularly as these involve some measure of affective responsiveness and active engagement, and also on ways taking a stand to protect the work from being unduly compromised can be an expression of our commitment to the patient and to the process and how this can become pivotal in the work.

Ronald

Ronald, a young man in his 20s, was referred by a colleague after 2 years of treatment that seemed to have reached a stalemate. Despite acute somatic reactions to stress (including a severe colitis requiring several hospitalizations) and a history of obesity in the past (he was not obese at the time of treatment), Ronald was not aware of great emotional distress except about his physical condition. He was zombie-like and detached. He claimed to have "no feelings," had little to say, and was not sure why he was coming to treatment. He would miss sessions and acted cynically as though he were saying, "What's the difference anyway?" This was his attitude in general, toward work and toward all relationships. Sessions were characterized by a kind of vapidity when he did come. I tried to convey to Ronald his impact on me.

I told him that although he seemed to be reluctant to be concerned as to whether our sessions were useful in any way, I was not. I also said that I did not like to feel useless, which is what I did feel in these sessions. And I wondered if he were aware of his having this impact on me. He seemed quite surprised by this and became curious. Our painstakingly following the minutest vicissitudes of his reactions to me, and mine to him, allowed him to notice that his detachment was itself a reaction to the situation and that instead of making him more invisible this had impact on me. This was a revelation as far as he was concerned and affected him greatly. Gradually he began to get in touch with deep feelings of vulnerability, pain, sadness and anger. This evoked many associations to his childhood, which had been extremely traumatic, including memories of scenes of his father, a chronic alcoholic, physically threatening his mother with a knife and the terror Ronald had experienced. He was able to experience with me emotions he had not experienced then, as he told all this to me. At times I commented how painful some of the experiences he reported sounded, when I felt he was glossing over this. He reported that he was touched by the fact I did not accept his own efforts to minimize the extent of his pain. For the first time he could remember he was able to cry and to admit how hurt, hopeless, and desperate he felt.

The man who was untouchable and "did not care" was now very emotional, even passionate. He was able to describe a decision never to be vulnerable again, made out of anger and despair as a child, and a feeling that he would rather be dead. In the context of a growing sense of hope and possibility based on his actual experience of our relationship, he described with great emotion a desire to someday have a family of his own. He contrasted this with how reluctant he had always been to think about having children or a family due to the pain of his own experience and the wish not to inflict anything similar on a child. Three years after termination (treatment lasted about 6 years), he continues to be free of the somatic symptoms, is successful professionally, and is in a stable and gratifying relationship with a young woman with whom he had become involved during the course of our work.

Dani

Dani, a young woman in her 20s had been anorexic and suicidal. She also suffered from serious colitis and amenorrhea. She was unable to function apart from her family but felt like a "wild maniac" with them. She described experiencing her body as separate from herself, feeling dead inside, like a robot or a machine, unable to enjoy anything including sex, incapable of orgasm, and as experiencing a living death. She was intensely preoccupied with her body and her weight and exercised fanatically. She described herself as knowing she was extremely beautiful (which she was) but, though obsessed with looking beautiful and spending hours putting on makeup and trying on different clothes, she hated how she looked and was often unable to go out because she felt ugly and fat. She was 5 feet 6 inches tall and weighed 100 pounds. She would go on eating binges and then starve herself and take laxatives. She would drink herself into oblivion or eat dog food to make herself sick. She would sleep with men she hated. She would compulsively steal things she did not need or buy things she could not afford. Her explanation was that it was as though forces "beyond her control" took over. She could not distinguish between dreams and hallucinations and found this terrifying. She insisted her behavior had no rhyme or reason and described feeling like a helpless bystander in relation to herself.

Her attitude toward treatment was one of cynicism, pessimism, and despair. She was suspicious of being exploited or manipulated by me. For many months she began every session stating she was going to go to California instead of going through with treatment, but she continued to come three times a week. I focused on the fact that all she felt she was obliged to do was to bring her body to the sessions and the rest was up to me, and how this seemed to characterize her relation to every aspect of her life. This clarified how actively she was attempting to place the major share of the responsibility for the treatment on me and challenged her view of herself as the helpless victim, which she had never grasped before.

As I directed my efforts toward trying to discover the logic of what she experienced as her own incomprehensible radical mood swings, I was able to relate these to specific events in our interaction. She was almost embarrassed to be "caught" as her tantrums in relation to me, her threats to destroy my office and attack other patients, and to "do herself in" to get back at me could be clearly seen as the consequence of her acute sensitivity to any lapses in attention or alertness on my part.

The consequence of all of this was that she could no longer argue that she was a hopeless "maniac" whose behavior was beyond comprehension. She described a sense of coming out of a fog, of feeling the veil or cloud she had been submerged in was lifting. There were shifts back and forth from the new level of functioning to the old. Subsequently, when I was a few minutes late for a session she became distressed and agitated and would not accept my apology. She acted as though I had mortally wounded her in an unforgivable way and refused to speak the whole session.

When I noted, in the following session, how punitive she had been and expressed my own dislike of being treated that way, she acknowledged that I could have apologized till kingdom come but she would not have yielded. There were associations to hearing her parents in their bedroom and feeling excluded and that was how it felt when she was outside in the waiting room and I was inside my office with another patient. She elaborated how she used to make scenes to keep her parents apart and how painful it was when they were together and she was excluded. She then did apologize to me for not accepting my apology and said that her not accepting my apology was the way she used to respond to her mother. She described how she used to "get away with murder" by presenting herself as not responsible and how successfully she had used her tantrums to manipulate and get between her parents.

In one session when it was clear that much was still unresolved and the session was about to end, she raged about how I would leave her this way before a weekend. She expressed a great deal of anger toward me for "opening her up to so much pain." She threatened she would go out and walk in front of a bus and kill herself if I didn't help her that moment. I told her that I did not like to be threatened. I noted also that her inability to endure any frustration seemed to be part of the problem. She became sheepish and said she used to do this kind of thing with her parents and her boyfriends and that usually it worked. She reported after the weekend that she held together without causing any catastrophes but cried that it had been a great strain. She stated that for the first time, however, despite all her prior treatment, she realized she would have to take responsibility for herself.

As we explored further her feelings about our transactions she began to express remorse and regret for how awful she had been to her parents, boyfriends, siblings, and me and to struggle to develop new ways of relating. Her self-esteem increased markedly as she discovered her own capacities to be compassionate and sensitive to me and that I was responsive to her gestures. It also became clear that she had always used herself as an instrument to evoke particular responses from others, often at the expense of her own needs and well-being. We learned, for example, that her body had become a battleground for complicated psychological dramas. Eating and not eating had become ways of pleasing and hurting others. The same applied to sex and to decisions to live or die. These had all been ways of asserting herself and of feeling she had some power. Nevertheless, the sense of desperation and impotence she felt otherwise was now clear. She discovered that she could express her feelings more directly, be even more effective, and avoid the negative repercussions of the acting out.

Her symptoms abated and she stabilized her weight between 110 and 115 pounds. She also developed a romantic relationship with a young man and began to establish herself as a freelance professional.

After 2 years of work on her anxieties about the work and her intensifying relationships with me and with her boyfriend, she felt more confident and less angry and vulnerable. About this time she began to menstruate, and, after a long interval of struggling with a decision regarding whether she wanted to live with her boyfriend, she decided to move in with him.

The new situation of living with a boyfriend intensified all her fears of closeness and of her own vulnerability. She struggled with fears of sexual dependence and of orgasm and was able to link these fears to the dynamics of the anorexia. That is, she resisted taking in anything as a defense against her fear of not being able to control her desires or her dependency needs if allowed expression. Fears of being hurt or disappointed, helplessly at the mercy of the other who might give or withhold, and resentment of her own feelings of intense vulnerability once she allowed herself to care all surfaced now in relation to me. There were associations to her feelings regarding a recent ski injury I had suffered that had left me on crutches for an extended period, as to how vulnerable it made her realize she was. The result of being able to acknowledge all of these feelings was that she was also able to realize the ways in which she was not helpless and could survive disappointment. Following this she reported increasing ability to enjoy sex and to experience orgasm.

At a point when things were going well with her boyfriend, she expressed new fears that continued treatment, which had become the metaphor of her right to be her own person, might pose a threat to her love relationship. She was aware of impulses to resort to earlier patterns of sacrificing her own needs to avoid any risks. At the same time she expressed fears that she could not sustain the love relationship without treatment, fears that treatment would go on forever, and awareness of her resentment of her sense of dependence on me. As she articulated all of this she was able to express how she felt stronger, whole, and more independent than she had ever felt in her life.

Laura

In the third year of treatment Laura learned I was pregnant. She expressed outrage and let loose a torrent of verbal abuse. To get revenge she threatened suicide. I focused on her feelings about the pregnancy and on her behavior now in relation to me. I said if she wanted to talk about her feelings that was fine but challenged her assumptions that she was not accountable for her behavior because she was "too sick" and that the fact she was distressed gave her license to threaten me or to assume she had claims on my private life. These had in fact been a rationalization for all kinds of interpersonal intimidation tactics throughout her life. Things had to be her way "or else."

At first she raged that as her analyst I was supposed to accept her behavior no matter what she did. Her view was that since she paid me this gave her certain rights over me. I insisted that this was not an acceptable definition of our relation as far as I was concerned. I also said that unless she took responsibility for her participation in our work she could not blame me if our work fails. Although she argued strenuously with what I said, I remained firm that it was necessary and important to explore her hateful feelings but not to enact them. In a session sometime later she began to sob as she expressed relief and gratitude that I had stood up to her. She stated that no one had ever related to her in this way before, and expressed fears she had that I wouldn't be able to "handle" her, as her parents had not been able to. There were associations to how she had terrorized her mother with her tantrums when she was a child. She reported that instead of trying to stop her, her mother had let her become "loathsome" and then hated her for being that way. She continued to sob as she stated, "If only she had stopped me," and expressed anger that she had not. She expressed a wish to have control imposed from outside because of her fears of her own destructive potential to herself and to others.

I said that even though it might be true that her mother had had problems setting limits this did not absolve her of her responsibility for her own behavior in response to her mother's limitations, and that the same was true for her behavior now with me. I stated I could not allow her to abuse me sadistically even if I disappointed or failed her in some way.

She was now able to recognize and acknowledge that she had actually enjoyed exploiting other people's vulnerabilities, tyrannizing them while presenting herself as the innocent and self-righteous victim. She described with embarrassment the "pleasure," the almost "sexual pleasure," this gave her.

As she began to recognize and admit her "sadism" as her own, she also began to realize she had the capacity and option for compassion as well. She began to take increasing responsibility for helping me to understand her when I didn't, and to take pleasure and pride in being able to do so.

In the months following she went through a self-conscious and painful exploration of how "outrageous" she had been to me, and to her parents over the years. She elaborated how she had walked all over them. Though now articulate about her anger that they had permitted her to get away with this, she also began to express remorse for having exploited what she began to see with growing compassion as their vulnerability and limitations.

As she became increasingly able to appreciate that she had choices about how she wanted to define herself, there began to develop deep feelings of affection, tenderness and respect between us. In contrast to the long periods of hatefulness that had been so difficult for both of us, our sessions began to be a pleasure. She explored her "attachment" to me and expressed surprise at the intensity of her feelings about sessions ending, about the time she had to wait between sessions, and about the pain of feeling so "vulnerable."

Marilyn

Marilyn, a single woman in her 30s, began a session telling me that she was angry with me because I had left a letter visible in my office and she had been unable to resist reading it. She stated that if a child has a problem stealing and the mother leaves money lying around then the mother is guilty of complicity.

I noted that her reaction seemed similar to her reaction the prior session when she had asked what was the occasion for the flowers that were in my office that day. She had become angry when I would not give the details and had stated self-righteously that if I were not prepared to answer her question I had no business having the flowers in my office.

I had to deal with my own anger and resist the impulse to respond in a hostile way. After some reflection, I remarked that there were two issues that we might want to consider. One had to do with her difficulty dealing with the pain evoked by both incidents, and the other had to do with her behavior and the way she responded to me. I stated that although I felt responsive to her pain I was irritated by her accusations and blame and by her efforts to coerce me to behave according to her dictates. I also added that although it was clear that it was hard for her to take "no" for an answer, or to deal with her disappointment and hurt, I felt she was not allowing me the right to say "no." Having been able to say this, I now felt analytically engaged again myself, no longer angry and actually curious.

She began to cry and said she felt she couldn't do anything right. She elaborated that my comments had made her feel worthless and hopeless, and that all she wanted was my love and approval and she did not know how to get it. I noted that what she wanted seemed very complex. I also said that if she would have been successful in her efforts to coerce me to respond to her as she had wanted me to, this might have foreclosed the possibility of clarifying the extent of her pain when she is disappointed, which was now evident, and the way in which she becomes coercive in response to frustration. She softened and offered associations to an interaction with a man she had dated over the weekend in which he told her about another woman with whom he was involved. She reported that she found this so painful she had to leave.

This was obviously relevant in that in our own interaction the flowers and the letter were indicative of my connections elsewhere. She responded with associations to how excluded she had felt from her parents' relationship as a child. She cried as she elaborated that she couldn't even bear to admit how much it mattered to her then and that she felt the same feelings now toward me and also in relation to this man. She described fights with her father and how he wouldn't talk to her for days if she didn't do things his way. She also described instances where the only way she could get what she wanted from her parents was by bullying them and making them feel guilty, as she had tried to do with me. She stated that I was the first person who had stood up to her when she bullied instead of succumbing or rejecting her altogether. She assumed it was her "love" that turned other people away in that it was "poisonous," "voracious," "demanding," and "coercive." I pointed out that it was not the love that was "poisonous" but her behavior when she felt frustrated. The problem was complicated by her reacting with rage to the feeling that if she cared about another she was dependent, vulnerable, and at that person's mercy. She could not tolerate the fact that she could not control the other's responses when she would have liked to. She was now able to articulate that at times this felt like a life and death issue for her.

In the following sessions she reported with some embarrassment how much this interaction with me had meant to her. In a subsequent session she described an incident with a man she had begun to date. Rather than try to control and manipulate him she was able to tell him how vulnerable she felt as she began to become more seriously interested in him. He told her the thing he liked about her was her honesty and that she was not pushy. She began to cry because it was the first time in her life she felt she had been able to be that way. She said that she felt "great" and elaborated that she now realized she could be "soft" without being a "wimp." She described feeling excited and proud, feeling like an adult (a new feeling for her), and feeling good about herself whether or not the relationship worked out. She stated that it was a breakthrough for her that she could be this open, that she was not frightened of not being able to tolerate or survive frustration, and that she did not become "ugly" and "controlling" as she usually did. She had a new sense of dignity and self-respect.

There is a sequel to this vignette. Many months later when Marilyn had begun to live with the man with whom she had become involved at the time just reported she related the following dream:

> I was woken up by a phone call. A friend wanted to make plans. I was aware it would take me away from lying bed with my boyfriend. While I am lying in bed I am aware that around my vagina are beautiful purple violets with black seeds. The doorbell rings and I have to get out of bed to answer it and make arrangements with the person at the door. I had a sense of not wanting to lose any of the seeds. I try to catch them as I get up but I don't catch all of them.

Her associations were:

> I think it has to do with having babies. I don't want to lose the seeds. I feel like I have to hold on to them for a while though because it's not quite time yet. I think the violets are related to our last session and to my feelings about myself as a woman. I feel a potential for flowering and feeling pleased rather than feeling I am damaged or missing something or inadequate. It's interesting that violets are my mother's favorite flowers. It's interesting that I would choose that flower.

There were associations to her mother and how her mother suffered from the same sense of dependency on a man so as to define her worth and her identity, with which she was struggling. I present this dream because violets were the predominant flower in the bouquet in my office that had been the center of the interaction I reported earlier, and although in the dream there was a sense of things still to work out she had, nevertheless, achieved her own "violets."

In the context of a view of the analytic relationship as a transactional field, I have emphasized the importance of treating the immediate transactional experience as primary analytic data and how this allows for clarifying how the contributions of each participant are influenced by the overt and covert reactions of the other. In addition, I have emphasized ways the analyst's affective participation can be essential to facilitate and advance the analytic work. I have also tried to illustrate how conveying our commitment to the relationship and to maintaining a constructive process, despite negative developments, and our willingness to take a stand to protect the work from being unduly compromised when this is an issue, can be pivotal in expanding the possibilities both in terms of treatable pathology and in terms of achievable results.

References

Alexander, F. (1956). *Psychoanalysis and psychotherapy.* New York: W. W. Norton & Co.

Baranger, M., & Baranger, W. (1966). Insight in the analytic situation. In R. E. Litman (Ed.), *Psychoanalysis in the Americas* (pp. 57–72). New York: International Universities Press.

Bird, B. (1972). Notes on transference: Universal phenomenon and hardest part of analysis. *Journal of the American Psychoanalytic Association, 20,* 267–301.

Bollas, C. (1983). Expressive uses of the countertransference. *Contemporary Psychoanalysis, 19,* 1–34.

Chrzanowski, G. (1979). The transference–countertransference interaction. *Contemporary Psychoanalysis, 15,* 458–471.

Ehrenberg, B. (1980). The repair of the unconscious. *Contemporary Psychoanalysis, 16,* 249–257.

Ehrenberg, D. B. (1974). The intimate edge in therapeutic relatedness. *Contemporary Psychoanalysis, 10,* 423–437.

Ehrenberg, D. B. (1975). The quest for intimate relatedness. *Contemporary Psychoanalysis, 11,* 320–331.

Ehrenberg, D. B. (1976). The "intimate edge" and the "third area." *Contemporary Psychoanalysis, 12,* 489–496.

Ehrenberg, D. B. (1982). Discussion: Approaches in psychotherapy. *Contemporary Psychoanalysis, 18,* 522–534.

Ehrenberg, D. B. (1985). Counter transference resistance. *Contemporary Psychoanalysis, 21,* 563–576.

Ehrenberg, D. B. (1987). Abuse and desire: A case of father–daughter incest. *Contemporary Psychoanalysis, 23,* 593–604.

Ehrenberg, D. B. (1990). Playfulness in the psychoanalytic relationship. *Contemporary Psychoanalysis, 26,* 74–95.

Ehrenberg, D. B. (1992a). *The intimate edge: Extending the reach of psychoanalytic interaction.* New York: Norton.

Ehrenberg, D. B. (1992b). On the question of analyzability. *Contemporary Psychoanalysis, 28,* 16–31.

Ehrenberg, D. B. (1992c). Analytic interaction beyond words. *Contemporary Psychotherapy Review, 7,* 5–24.

Ehrenberg, D. B. (1992d). The role of encounter in the process of working through–. *International Forum of Psychoanalysis, 1,* 1, 44–50.

Ehrenberg, D. B. (1995a). Counter transference disclosure. Discussion: Panel on Self disclosure: Therapeutic tool or self indulgence. *Contemporary Psychoanalysis, 31,* 2, 213–228.

Ehrenberg, D. B. (1995b). The analyst's theorizing. *Journal of the American Psychoanalytic Association, 42*, 1247–1251.

Ehrenberg, D. B. (1996). On the analyst's emotional availability and vulnerability. *Contemporary Psychoanalysis, 32*, 275–286.

Ehrenberg, D. B. (2000). Potential impasse as analytic opportunity: Interactive considerations. *Contemporary Psychoanalysis, 36*, 573–586.

Ehrenberg, D. B. (2001). In the grip of passion: Love or addiction? On a specific kind of masochistic enthrallment. In J. Petrucell & C. Stuart (Eds.), *Hungers and Compulsions: The Psychodynamic treatment of eating disorders and addictions*. Northvale, New Jersey: Jason Aronson Inc.

Ehrenberg, D. B. (2003). A radical shift in thinking about the change-process: Commentary. *Psychoanalytic Dialogues, 13*, 579–603.

Ehrenberg, D. B. (2004). How I become a psychoanalyst. *Psychoanalytic Inquiry, 24*, 4, 490–516.

Ehrenberg, D. B. (2005). Afterword to the intimate edge in therapeutic relatedness. In L. Aron & A. Harris (Eds.), *Relational psychoanalysis, vol. II: Innovation and expansion* (pp. 17–28). Hillsdale, NJ: The Analytic Press.

Ehrenberg, D. B. (2006a). The interpersonal/relational interface: History, context, and personal reflections. *Contemporary Psychoanalysis, 42*, 535–550.

Ehrenberg, D. B. (2006b). La natura dell'azione terapeutica: Un cambiamento radicale di pensiero sul processo di cambiamento e sulla natura della partecipazione dell'analista. *Ricerca Psicolanalitica: Revista Della Relazione in Psicolanalisi, 17*(3), 315–332.

Ehrenberg, D. B. (2010). Working at the "intimate edge." *Contemporary Psychoanalysis, 46*(1), 120–141.

Epstein, L. (1979). The therapeutic function of hate in the countertransference In L. Epstein & A. Feiner (Eds.), *Countertransference: The therapist's contribution to the therapeutic situation*. New York: Jason Aronson.

Epstein, L., & Feiner, A. (1979). *Countertransference: The therapist's contribution to the therapeutic situation*. New York: Jason Aronson.

Fairbairn, W. R. (1958). On the nature and aims of psycho-analytical treatment. *International Journal of Psychoanalysis, 39*, 374–385.

Feiner, A. (1970). Toward an understanding of the experience of inauthenticity. *Contemporary Psychoanalysis, 7*, 64–83.

Feiner, A. (1975). The dilemma of integrity. *Contemporary Psychoanalysis, 11*, 500–509.

Feiner, A. (1979). Countertransference and the anxiety of influence In L. Epstein & A. Feiner (Eds.), *Countertransference: The therapist's contribution to the therapeutic situation*. New York: Jason Aronson.

Feiner, A. (1982). Comments on the difficult patient. *Contemporary Psychoanalysis, 18*, 397–411.

Feiner, A. (1983). On the facilitation of the therapeutic symbiosis. *Contemporary Psychoanalysis, 19*, 673–689.

Ferenczi, S. (1916). *Contributions to psycho-analysis*. London: Hogarth Press, 1952.

Ferenczi, S. (1950). *Further contributions to the theory and technique of psycho-analysis*. London: Hogarth Press.

Ferenczi, S. (1955). *Final contributions to the problems and methods of psycho-analysis*. London: Hogarth Press.

Freud, A. (1954). The widening scope of indications for psychoanalysis. *Journal of the American Psychoanalytic Association, 2*, 607–620.

Freud, S. (1914). Remembering, repeating and working through. In J. Strachey (Ed. & Trans.), *The standard edition of the complete psychological works of Sigmund Freud* (Vol. 12, p. 154). London: Hogarth Press, 1958.

Fromm-Reichmann, F. (1950). *Principles of intensive psychotherapy.* Chicago: University of Chicago Press.

Fromm-Reichmann, F. (1952). Some aspects of psychoanalytic psychotherapy with schizophrenia In E. B. Brody & C. F. Redlich (Eds.), *Psychotherapy with schizophrenics.* New York: International Universities Press.

Gill, M. (1979). The analysis of the transference. *Journal of the American Psychoanalytic Association, 27*(Suppl.), 263–288.

Gill, M. (1982a, April). *The distinction between the interpersonal paradigm and the nature of the interpersonal relationship.* Paper presented at the William Alanson White Institute.

Gill, M. (1982b). *Analysis of transference, vol. 1.* New York: International Universities Press.

Gill, M. (1983). The interpersonal paradigm and the degree of the therapist's involvement. *Contemporary Psychoanalysis, 19,* 200–237.

Gitelson, M. (1952). The emotional position of the analyst in the psycho-analytic situation. *International Journal of Psychoanalysis, 33,* 1–10.

Gitelson, M. (1962). The curative factors in psychoanalysis. *International Journal of Psychoanalysis, 43,* 194–205.

Greenson, R., & Wexler, M. (1969). The non-transference relationship in the psychoanalytic situation. *International Journal of Psychoanalysis, 50,* 27–39.

Guntrip, H. (1969). *Schizoid phenomena, object relations and the self.* New York: International Universities Press.

Heimann, P. (1950). On countertransference. *International Journal of Psychoanalysis, 31,* 81–84.

Hoffman, I. (1983). The patient as interpreter of the analyst's experience. *Contemporary Psychoanalysis, 19,* 389–422.

Jones, E. (1957). *The life and work of Sigmund Freud, vol. 3.* New York: Basic Books.

Kernberg, O. (1965). Countertransference. *Journal of the American Psychoanalytic Association, 13,* 38–56.

Klauber, J. (1981). *Difficulties in the analytic encounter.* New York: Jason Aronson.

Lacan, J. (1936). Au del du principe de ralit l'evolution. *Psychiatrique, 3,* 67–86.

Lacan, J. (1952). Intervention sur le transfert. *Revue Francaise de Psychanalyse, 16,* 154–163.

Lacan, J. (1956). Fonction et champ de la parole et du langage en psychanalyse. In *The language of the self* (A. Wilden, Trans.). Baltimore, MD: Johns Hopkins Press, 1968.

Lacan, J. (1961). The direction of the treatment and the principles of its power (A. Sheridan, Trans.). In *Écrits* (pp. 149–206). New York: W. W. Norton, 1977.

Laing, R. (1965). Mystification, confusion and conflict. In I. Boszormenyi-Nagy & J. L. Framo (Eds.), *Intensive family therapy.* New York: Harper & Row.

Langs, R. (1976). *The bipersonal field.* New York: Jason Aronson.

Langs, R. (1979). The interaction dimension of countertransference In L. Epstein & A. Feiner (Eds.), *Countertransference: The therapist's contribution to the therapeutic situation.* New York: Jason Aronson.

Langs, R. (1981). Modes of "cure" in psychoanalysis and psychoanalytic psychotherapy. *International Journal of Psychoanalysis, 62,* 199–214.

Levenson, E. (1972). *The fallacy of understanding.* New York: Basic Books.

Levenson, E. (1974). Changing concepts of intimacy in psychoanalytic practice. *Contemporary Psychoanalysis, 10,* 359–369.

Levenson, E. (1981). Facts or fantasies: On the nature of psychoanalytic data. *Contemporary Psychoanalysis, 17,* 486–500.

Levenson, E. (1982a). Follow the fox. *Contemporary Psychoanalysis, 18,* 1–15.

Levenson, E. (1982b). Playground or playpen? *Contemporary Psychoanalysis, 18,* 365–372.

Levenson, E. (1983). *The ambiguity of change.* New York: Basic Books.

Lipton, S. D. (1977). The advantage of Freud's technique as shown in his analysis of the Rat Man. *International Journal of Psychoanalysis, 58,* 255–274.

Little, M. (1951). Countertransference and the patient's response to it. *International Journal of Psychoanalysis, 32,* 32–40.

Little, M. (1957). "R": The analyst's response to his patient's needs. *International Journal of Psychoanalysis, 38,* 240–254.

Loewald, H. (1960). On the therapeutic action of psychoanalysis. *International Journal of Psychoanalysis, 41,* 16–33.

Loewald, H. (1970). Psychoanalytic theory and the psychoanalytic process. *Psychoanalytic Study of the Child, 25,* 45–68.

McDougall, J. (1979). Countertransference and primitive communication. In L. Epstein & A. Feiner (Eds.), *Countertransference: The therapist's contribution to the therapeutic situation.* New York: Jason Aronson.

McLaughlin, J. (1981). Transference, psychic reality, and countertransference. *Psychoanalytic Quarterly, 50,* 639–654.

Menaker, E. (1942). The masochistic factor in the psychoanalytic situation. *Psychoanalytic Quarterly, 11,* 171–186.

Nacht, S. (1957). Technical remarks on the handling of the transference neurosis. *International Journal of Psychoanalysis, 38,* 196–203.

Nacht, S. (1962). The curative factors in psycho-analysis. *International Journal of Psychoanalysis, 43,* 206–211.

Racker, H. (1957). The meaning and uses of countertransference. *Psychoanalysis Quarterly, 26,* 303–357.

Rank, O. (1929). *Will therapy and truth and reality* (J. Taft, Trans.). New York: Alfred A. Knopf, 1964.

Rioch, J. M. (1943). The transference phenomenon in psychoanalytic therapy. *Psychiatry, 6,* 147–156.

Sandler, J. (1976). Countertransference and role responsiveness. *International Review of Psychoanalysis, 3,* 43–47.

Searles, H. (1965). *Collected papers on schizophrenia and related subjects.* New York: International Universities Press.

Searles, H. (1979). *Countertransference and related subjects: Selected papers.* New York: International Universities Press.

Singer, E. (1971). The patient aids the analyst: Some clinical and theoretical observations. In B. Landis & E. Tauber (Eds.), *In the name of life.* New York: Holt, Rinehart and Winston.

Singer, E. (1977). The fiction of analytic anonymity. In K. Frank (Ed.), *The human dimension in psychoanalytic practice.* New York: Grune & Stratton.

Stein, M. (1973). Acting out as a character trait: Its relation to transference. *Psychoanalytic Study of the Child, 28,* 347–364.

Stern, D. (1983). The early development of schemas of self, other and self with others. In J. Lichtenberg & S. Kaplan (Eds.), *Reflections on self psychology* (pp. 49–84). Hillsdale, NJ: The Analytic Press.

Stone, L. (1954). The widening scope of indications for psychoanalysis. *Journal of the American Psychoanalytic Association, 2,* 567–594.

Stone, L. (1961). *The psychoanalytic situation.* New York: International Universities Press.

Stone, L. (1973). On resistance to the psychoanalytic process. *Psychoanalysis and Contemporary Science, 2,* 42–73.

Stone, L. (1981). Some thoughts on the "here and now" in psychoanalytic technique and process. *Psychoanalytic Quarterly, 50,* 709–731.

Strachey, J. (1934). The nature of the therapeutic action of psychoanalysis. *International Journal of Psychoanalysis, 15,* 127–159.

Sullivan, H. S. (1940). Conceptions of modern psychiatry. In *Collected works.* New York: W. W. Norton.

Sullivan, H. S. (1953). The interpersonal theory of psychiatry. In *Collected works.* New York: W. W. Norton.

Sullivan, H. S. (1954). The psychiatric interview. In *Collected works.* New York: W. W. Norton.

Sullivan, H. S. (1956). Clinical studies in psychiatry. In *Collected works.* New York: W. W. Norton.

Sullivan, H. S. (1962). Schizophrenia as a human process. In *Collected works.* New York: W. W. Norton.

Tauber, E. (1954). Exploring the therapeutic use of countertransference data. *Psychiatry, 17,* 331–336.

Tauber, E. (1979). Countertransference reexamined. In Epstein & A. Feiner (Eds.), *Countertransference: The therapist's contribution to the therapeutic situation* (pp.). New York: Jason Aronson.

Thompson, C. (1950). *Psychoanalysis: Evolution and development.* New York: Hermitage House.

Thompson, C. (1952). Counter–transference. *Samiksa, 6,* 205–211.

Tower, L. (1956). Countertransference. *Journal of the American Psychoanalytic Association, 4,* 224–255.

Viderman, S. (1974). Interpretation in the analytical space. *International Review of Psychoanalysis, 1,* 467–480.

White, M. J. (1952). Sullivan and treatment. In P. Mullahy (Ed.), *The contributions of Harry Stack Sullivan* (pp. 117–150). New York: Hermitage House.

Winnicott, D. W. (1947). Hate in the countertransference. In *Through paediatrics to psychoanalysis.* London: Tavistock Publications.

Winnicott, D. W. (1963). Dependence in infant-care, in child-care, and in the psychoanalytic setting. In *The maturational processes and the facilitating environment.* New York: International Universities Press, 1965.

Winnicott, D. W. (1969). The use of an object and relating through identifications. In *Playing and reality.* New York: Basic Books, 1971.

Winnicott, D. W. (1971). *Playing and reality.* New York: Basic Books.

Witenberg, E. (1976). To believe or not to believe. *Journal of the Academy of Psychoanalysis, 4,* 433–445.

Wolstein, B. (1954). *Transference.* New York: Grune & Stratton.

Wolstein, B. (1959). *Countertransference.* New York: Grune & Stratton.

Wolstein, B. (1971). *Human psyche in psychoanalysis.* Springfield, IL: Charles C. Thomas.

Wolstein, B. (1973). The new significance of psychoanalytic structure. In E. G. Witenberg (Ed.), *Interpersonal explorations in psychoanalysis.* New York: Basic Books.

2

At Death's Door

*Therapists and Patients as Agents**

Irwin Z. Hoffman

▼　▼　▼　▼　▼

In February 1999, David Feinsilver, my sister's husband and my good colleague and friend, died at the age of 59 of cancer. He had been on the staff at Chestnut Lodge in Rockville, Maryland, for more than 27 years. In October 1999, the annual Chestnut Lodge symposium (focusing that year on the subject of therapeutic action) was dedicated to his memory. As one who had been close to him and with whom David had shared common psychoanalytic interests and—increasingly toward the end of his life—common ideas about the analytic process, I was invited to be one of two plenary speakers. Thus, the context of the original presentation was one in which my sister and her grown children were present along with many others who knew the family well. Presenting the paper was itself a highly personal act of affirmation in the face of loss and mortality, part of a ritual of memorialization and rededication. The reader is invited to consider the context-dependent meaning of that moment, in which aspects of the content of the paper were paralleled by aspects of the process of presenting it.

* This paper originally appeared in *Psychoanalytic Dialogues, 10*(6), 2000, pp. 823–846. Reprinted with permission.

Rising to the Occasion

David Feinsilver was a champ when it came to living to the fullest, whatever the obstacles. He came to Chicago with my sister and both of their grown children in April 1997 to attend my younger son's bar mitzvah. That was a brave and generous feat considering the amount of discomfort, pain, and fatigue that David was experiencing from his cancer and chemotherapy treatment. David always pushed himself, though, to try to do whatever was necessary or, more than that, the maximum that was possible. That attitude generated some outstanding writing in David's last years and months. In one of his last papers, "The Therapist as a Person Facing Death: The Hardest of External Realities and Therapeutic Action" (Feinsilver, 1998), David defined the term *mensch* in a manner that could so readily apply to him: "a person who confronts, clarifies, and overcomes what frustrates him, internally and externally, and then acts morally, ethically, and with compassion, to do what the situation calls for; in essence a person who rises to the occasion on difficult occasions to do 'the right thing'" (p. 1148). So, considered in a secular way, there was David at the bar mitzvah rising to the occasion, despite his illness, to celebrate my son's emergence in the community as a responsible agent, as a contributor to the uniquely human project of socially constructing and maintaining a world of meaning and value against the backdrop of mortality and of a brutally indifferent universe.

Acts of Will and Imagination I:
A Patient at the Analyst's Door

Two and a half weeks after the bar mitzvah, my 18-year-old son stood at the side of my bed. I'd been home from the hospital for just a few hours, recovering from triple coronary bypass surgery, an operation David himself had had more than 20 years earlier. Since David and I were somewhat competitive, perhaps he was right to needle me with the suggestion that some part of me was loath to concede bragging rights to him with regard to dealing with life-threatening illness. It had all happened very fast. A stress test in the course of a routine physical examination revealed an arrhythmia, leading to further tests and an angiogram (6 days after the bar mitzvah) in which the entirely asymptomatic arterial blockages were unmistakably evident. The location of one of the blockages precluded angioplasty and made the surgery several days later the only viable option.

I'm not sure when I was in the most danger—in the presurgery period when I was working out strenuously oblivious to my coronary artery disease; while listening somewhat nervously as my son gave his bar mitzvah speech in the temple; while I gave my own at the reception; during the surgery itself; or recovering in the hospital, when I thought I'd die of starvation, lack of sleep, or boredom. In any case, it was great being home after the 5-day hospital stay. My wife was outdoing herself trying to make me comfortable. She had prepared something for me to eat that I actually enjoyed, and I felt more relaxed than I had since the surgery. But now my son at the side of the bed was saying, "Dad, something very weird just happened. I opened the door for my friend, who was dropping off some flowers and a card for you. An older man was behind her, and, as she left, this fellow approached and asked, 'Where's the body?' I was a little thrown, as you can imagine, but after a moment I said, 'If you mean my Dad, he's upstairs resting.' The guy said, 'OK, please give him this,' and he gave me this check." My son handed it to me, and I was rather startled as I looked at it and at the accompanying note from Manny, an 86-year-old patient I'd been seeing in analytic therapy for 12 years and whom I had written about extensively in the last chapter of my book, which was then nearing completion. The discussion of the work with Manny centers largely on the issue of mortality. In the note, Manny explained that he thought that in this difficult time I might appreciate the payment for recent, not-yet-billed sessions.

I had a mixture of feelings, including amusement, appreciation, and rather intense annoyance. I thought and mumbled something like, "Jeez, this man has been in analysis for over 50 years [encompassing two analysts before me]. He knows better than to show up at the house on a day like this. And what in the world did that remark mean? 'Where's the body?'"

A few days later, I was making phone calls, thanking people, including patients, for their cards and calls and gifts, letting people know I was doing well, and informing them of the time when I'd likely be returning to work. Manny was among the first people I called. Not only had he made the effort to come to the house with that check; he had also come to the hospital and delivered an orchid the first day after the surgery, leaving it with a receptionist in the lobby. So I wanted to thank him. Yet I also knew it was likely that I would express some displeasure about his coming to the house. I knew I was angry about that. It seemed impulsive, intrusive, at least poor judgment on Manny's part. I can't say I remember exactly what my expectations were as I made the call, whether I "planned" to say anything about those negative reactions or just had a readiness to say something and thought I'd play it by ear. I began by thanking Manny for the orchid and for the check and telling him that the surgery was a success and that I was recovering well. At some point, Manny began talking animatedly about the money, why he thought it might be useful for me to have it as soon as possible, and so forth. He said he'd gone to the hospital first but, finding I'd been discharged, decided to just drive straight to my house. At that point I said, "You know, Manny, I don't think coming to the house was such a good idea." I don't recall exactly what was said after that. I know we didn't get into it very much on the phone. He may have asked why, and I believe I said because it was my first day home, I needed a little privacy, he didn't know who he would encounter at the door, and so on. I mentioned that even close relatives and friends were not visiting on that day. He was polite about it, as I recall, and said something like, "OK, sorry, just thought you might be able to use the money. Hope your recovery continues to go well."

We can pause for a moment to consider my comment on the phone. The time to judge it is at this juncture, because we are always acting in the analytic situation (and in life in general, for that matter) without the benefit of hindsight. Moreover, even hindsight hardly tells all that we would like to know, because we can never know just what would have happened had we chosen a different course. Even another similar moment with the same patient, not to mention a different patient, would not afford an opportunity to find out because there are countless factors that would not be the same. So the moment is unique. I could consider the circumstances, the patient's vulnerability, the patient's history, how the patient responded in the past if I said something that might have been narcissistically injurious, the possible unconscious meanings of the patient's gesture. All of these factors undoubtedly "entered my mind" and influenced my choice. But there are other considerations that are simply my own feelings and my wish to relate to Manny in an honest, authentic way. By that time, I had given a lot of thought to the importance of the analyst's authenticity and spontaneity in the process considered in dialectical interplay with psychoanalytic discipline and ritual (Hoffman, 1998). It seemed to me that it was important for the health of the relationship, and therefore for the patient's health, that the analyst or analytic therapist (terms that I am using interchangeably; see Hoffman, 1998, pp. xiii–xvi; Fosshage, 1997) not regularly bury intense countertransferential feelings. Apart from the fact that there is a danger that these feelings will build up and get expressed unconsciously, and apart from all we've learned since Racker (1968) about the "meanings and uses of countertransference" as an avenue for exploring the patient's intrapsychic life, part of the patient's need developmentally is for a real relationship with a real person, notwithstanding the many contrived aspects of the analytic arrangement.

The importance of the analyst's honesty and authenticity, though, is just one major consideration. It doesn't provide a sacrosanct prescription for action any more than does the rule of abstinence. Honesty is not always the best policy. There are times, particularly in our roles as analytic therapists, when other considerations may take precedence. So, there was no way to wring the disturbing element of choice out of my action when I was deciding what to say to Manny. In this instance, what pushed the issue over the edge for me was Manny's elaboration on the value of his visit. He seemed to be protesting too much, thereby seeming to betray a bit of his own conflict.

Meanwhile, his protests made it that much harder for me to go along, since my silence combined with "uh huhs" in a friendly tone could be misconstrued as mere agreement and gratitude.

With regard to the issue of choice on my part, I should add that the counterpart, as I see it, is choice on Manny's part. Whatever the dynamics governing his action, I regard him as a responsible, free agent, not merely an organism responding to internal and external pressures. He did not *have* to come to the house. He could have noted the impulse to do so and, taking the totality of the situation into consideration, he could have decided to put the check in the mail with a note or a card. From my perspective at the time, that would have been the wiser course. We are so used to thinking of anything our patients do as psychically determined that we end up contradicting ourselves whenever we treat them as free, responsible, and not fully predictable agents. Although the ideology of psychic determinism presumably covers all human functioning, including that of the analyst, Freud's paradigmatic "person" was decidedly the patient not the analyst. Thus, the patient's freedom was precluded by the combination of forces acting on his or her ego. But the analyst's freedom was also virtually eliminated by the requirement that he or she follow whatever scientific method was necessary to explore and discover the truth about the patient's unconscious uninfluenced by the analyst. As Otto Rank (1945) wrote, "In Freud's analysis, the will apparently plays no particular part, either on the side of the patient or on the side of the analyst" (p. 11).

Without attempting to solve the conundrum of free will that philosophers have been struggling with for millennia, I would like to offer one philosophical reflection. Determinism is no more satisfying intellectually than is free will, since it merely begs the question of origins. If what I am writing right now is determined *entirely* by causes other than my will, what were the causes of those causes, and so on, ad infinitum? There is nothing any more or less unfathomable about how a person could be a choosing subject or agent than there is about the origin of the universe. Moreover, ultimately, we act *as though* we believe people are responsible agents, and to act differently would create a very different world. Then, the question would be whether we want to "choose" to create that world in which human beings are *not* held responsible for their actions. I think most of us would be averse to creating or living in such an environment.

Regarding the human will as opposed to psychic determinism, Rank (1945) offers the following:

> The causality principle means a denial of the will principle since it makes the thinking, feeling, and acting of the individual dependent on forces outside of himself and thus frees him of responsibility and guilt.... Only in the individual act of will do we have the unique phenomenon of spontaneity, the

establishing of a new primary cause.... So one sees why a natural science psychology denies will and consciousness and in their place must introduce the unconscious Id as a causal factor which morally does not differ at all from the idea of God, just as sexuality as a scapegoat is not different from the idea of the devil. In other words, scientific psychoanalysis gives the individual only a new kind of excuse for his willing and a new release from the responsibility of consciousness. (pp. 44–45)*

So I see Manny as responsible and as capable of having chosen a different course, just as I am responsible for my conduct on the phone. This perspective is important because it has practical consequences for how I relate to the patient and for how I reflect on my own participation. I think there are still many indications that analysts are very much encouraged to think of what they are doing as akin to treating a disease or disorder such that, if only enough were known, there could be a "treatment of choice" for a condition or for a state of mind at a particular moment. The condition or the state of mind and the treatment in this model are, for all practical purposes, homogeneous across all analytic dyads. So, if we had a diagnosis for Manny complete with a developmental assessment or an assessment of his state of mind at the time of the visit to the house, maybe the analyst would know what to do. What is most unlikely in this model is that the patient would become the object of any sort of criticism, since his or her behavior is merely a reflection of an illness that is, of course, not the patient's fault. So, the patient behaves in some way, and the analyst makes the appropriate, prescribed "intervention." Neither party in such an interaction is seen as a freely participating subject, heavily influenced, to be sure, by internal and external factors but free nevertheless. Instead,

---

* Rank's conviction about the central role of the patient's will seems to have developed partly as a reaction to its complete absence from Freud's theorizing and from psychoanalytic theory in general. In the context of that reaction, Rank was zealous about the analytic process fostering the emergence and development of the patient's autonomous self. In that spirit, he abhorred the analyst's moral influence except insofar as it facilitated the patient's autonomy (e.g., see Rank, 1945, pp. 66–68)—a view quite contrary to my own. The perspective I have called *dialectical constructivism* (Hoffman, 1996, 1998) calls for recognition of the inevitability of the analyst's moral influence and the desirability of its being exercised in a reflective, self-critical, and judicious way. In Rank's "constructive therapy," the analyst aspires to promote the patient's achievement of unencumbered agency and freedom that are decidedly in the spirit of an enlightenment, "modern" sensibility and that are wholly lacking in the postmodern appreciation of the individual's inevitable sociocultural embeddedness as well as of the influence of unconscious dimensions of the transference and the countertransference. Those factors, however, can be regarded as powerful *influences* without being wholly determining of the patient's experience and behavior, so that "space" is still left for the individual will as a "primary cause." In effect, I am advocating an integration of modern and postmodern perspectives on human agency (see Margulies, 1999).

both parties are seen as doing what they *must* do, given the pressures that are impinging on them.*

A few days later, I received an e-mail from Manny. Would anyone care to guess what he wrote? By the way, a suspicion that he might say this or that is not the same as knowing what is coming, even though with hindsight we often feel we "knew" all along what was going to happen. The hindsight often transforms the mere "inkling" that was there *before* the fact into an absolute conviction in the way we remember it *after* the fact. "I knew it," we say, "I just knew it!" Here are some excerpts from Manny's e-mail:

> Dear Irwin:
> I trust you are recovering rapidly. I hesitate to even write this because I am angry at your reciting Emily Post to me. I did not deserve it, and it only shows your affection is only skin-deep. I am aware about visiting uninvited and am meticulous in following this because it is the only respectful and decent way to operate—but there is such a thing as extenuating circumstances....
> I always wondered how you could learn to care for clients with troubles, including yours truly.
> You put on a good show, and it probably was helpful. But I am not looking for a "show." I could go on to the reality of my visit and [tell you] that it wasn't to invade your family. In fact, I have tried to keep our relationship in as classical a manner as possible. Perhaps you are too arrogant in your interpretation.
>
> Konfused

My reaction to the letter was one of shock and injury. I was quite hurt by it, considering the years of work and the genuine feelings I had developed for this man. I think he knew how much value I placed on the sincerity of my attitude toward him so he knew he was getting to me at a very deep level. And he knew also that it was a time of heightened vulnerability for me. At the same time, I had to recognize that he must have been incredibly hurt by my remark for his reaction to be so extreme. Was "I don't think coming to the house was such a good idea" *such* a terrible thing to say under those circumstances? Why wasn't Manny more forgiving, or even apologetic himself, or at least more balanced in his response? Was it incumbent upon me now to soul-search, to consider that I should have felt differently or at least handled my feelings differently? Maybe I could have emphasized more how thoughtful his gesture was while still registering some reservation about his "house call," which we could take up when we resumed our regular meetings. If my affect were different, maybe my tone of voice would

---

* The disease model does, of course, apply best to certain conditions in which biological causation of symptoms has been demonstrated—such as manic-depressive illness and schizophrenia. Even in those conditions, however, it is quite possible that the role of the individual's will may be underestimated or denied by both caregivers and patients.

have been different so that both what I said and how I said it would have been different. In any case, I felt it was important to convey to Manny that I was deeply affected by his letter while I also defended the authenticity of my feeling for him and the value of the analytic work, which I felt might be in jeopardy. I responded to Manny's e-mail with a long one of my own several days later. It read, in part, as follows:

> Dear Manny,
> I am very upset by your note. Whatever it means that I objected to your coming to the house, it doesn't mean that my affection for you is only skin-deep. How can years of knowing each other be nullified by one moment like that? You mean a lot to me, and what you feel toward me means a lot to me. And you do have the power to hurt me, as I know I have the power to hurt you. I doubt that would be the case unless we had some pretty strong personal connection.
>
> Our relationship is based on honesty. Ironically, I think it would have been more in an Emily Post spirit of "correct" analyst manners on my part to just say everything was fine when I didn't feel that way....
>
> I can understand your feeling hurt by my saying I didn't think coming to the house was such a good idea, but I really don't think it's fair (or true) to say that it proves that all the rest was "just for show." There's nothing I can do, of course, to "prove" that my feelings for you are sincere. For the moment, all I can do is appeal to you to at least consider that you MIGHT be wrong in your conclusion that they're not.
>
> Maybe there's reason to trust a person's affection MORE when they are also prepared to tell you what bothers them. That's at least another way to look at it.
>
> My thought is that we are really close enough and you know me well enough so that, feeling as hurt as you felt by me, you wanted to say something that you knew would get to me because you know that for me there is hardly anything more important than trying to be honest and genuine. So what would cut to the core more than to call me a phony? Well, you're right. It does.
>
> I do appreciate your writing the note and letting me know how you feel. I realize that you might have been tempted not to bother, to just say "to hell with him" and write me off. So I take your note as expressing something of an interest in trying to develop more mutual understanding and give us a chance to work things out. Like bypass surgery, one wishes it didn't have to happen at all, but once it happens, what's there to do but try to make the best of it? With this event between us, maybe we both wish it didn't happen, either because *I* would have reacted differently or *you* would have reacted differently, or something. But since it did happen maybe we can use it in a way that will actually deepen our relationship and from which we can both learn. I hope so.
>
> Love,
> Irwin

Although the letter is certainly very expressive of my feelings, I think it's important to emphasize that it was also carefully written and consistent with what seemed right to me in my role as Manny's analyst. Among other things, in the letter I try to impress on Manny the importance of keeping an open mind as to the meaning of my response to his coming to the house—a meaning that I appeal to him to regard as at least ambiguous in its implications. While revealing of my personal involvement and vulnerability, the letter also attempts to demonstrate my "survival" (Winnicott, 1971) as the analyst, dedicated to, and even passionate about, the continuation of the analytic work. Thus, even though the e-mail may seem, in the foreground, to illustrate "spontaneity" and "expressiveness," it also reflects, I hope, my understanding of the risks and potentials of the situation and of proportional analytic restraint. In other words, I see it as emerging, not from a striving for "authenticity" viewed in isolation from the analytic context, but from the dialectical interplay of "expressive participation and psychoanalytic discipline" (Hoffman, 1998, Ch. 7).

I heard back from Manny that he was certainly interested in continuing the analytic work and that he looked forward to resuming it when I returned to the office. I did not take for granted that he would continue, and I felt relieved when he indicated that he would. The resumption itself was a generous, forgiving act on Manny's part, responsive perhaps to my very personal letter. If he stopped abruptly by his own choice, or if he fell ill or died, my own action in disapproving of his visit to the house could readily have taken on a much darker coloring in my eyes as well as in the eyes of others. The patient's response coconstructs the meaning of our participation. Therefore, exactly the same actions can become sources of guilt or of pride, or anything in between, depending on what *the patient* decides to do in response or depending on contingencies outside anyone's control. In a sense, a great deal of luck is involved in determining the value we place, perhaps unfairly, on what we have done. In this connection, Thomas Nagel (1979), the philosopher, writes about "moral luck" (following Williams, 1976), suggesting, for example, that exactly the same moment of inattention on the part of a driver of a car can result either in catastrophe (e.g., hitting and killing a child running into the street) or in nothing noteworthy at all (pp. 28–29). Perhaps the inconsequential moment would not even register in the driver's memory.

But as it turned out, with a little bit of luck and Manny's generous effort, we did a lot of useful work on this episode at the house once we resumed our regularly scheduled sessions. Manny was embarrassed about having come to the house, but he also wanted me to appreciate his good intentions, which I did. He was especially mortified by his peculiar question to my son ("Where's the body?") and very apologetic about it. We understood it, at least in part, as an expression of his anxiety about my well-being, a condensed version of a question such as, "Where is your father, who I have been so terrified might die?" Manny had been emphatically opposed to my having the surgery, believing it would surely kill me. He had written to me to say that, because I was asymptomatic, I would be much safer if I resisted the recommendations of the medical authorities whom Manny regarded as engaged in nothing short of a nefarious racket of expensive, unnecessary, and dangerous procedures. Since I didn't follow his advice, perhaps his question could be understood as shorthand for, "Where's that father of yours, who by all rights should be nothing but a corpse by now, since he was fool enough to ignore my wise counsel?"

Manny rightfully pointed out that several factors mitigated, for him, the sense of inappropriateness of his conduct in coming to the house that day. First, his first analyst (of the two before me) was prone to blurring the boundaries between analytic life and everyday social life in that he would often invite Manny and other patients to his house along with other friends. This analyst was well known in Chicago's early period of psychoanalysis, when there was apparently an inner circle composed of devotees of the new discipline—some of them patients, some not. I admitted that I had completely forgotten about this precedent that Manny had for his own inclinations. Second, I myself had done my share to encourage Manny to think of himself as part of my family. Over the years, he had introduced me to his interest in orchids and had given me a couple of them purchased at a huge and nationally known orchid nursery in the Chicago area. I had taken them home and told Manny that my wife's interest had been sparked enough so that she was reading about the subject and had gone to visit this nursery with a friend. So, Manny's feeling that he had a place in my home was not without support from me. When we consider the positions patients are in when confronted with life-threatening illness in their analysts—and some of us have been in that place ourselves as patients—sympathetic understanding is certainly called for. The analytic situation, as I and others have written (e.g., Davies, 1998, 2000), lends itself to being construed as one of seduction and abandonment. And when is that aspect of it more salient than the moment when the analyst is a "person facing death," and the patient, who is so attached and to whom the analyst means so much, is so thoroughly excluded from normal channels of connection, including contacts with others with whom the analyst is close?

Yet we also had to consider other, less benign meanings of the visit. My annoyance was not without foundation. There was something intrusive and entitled about Manny's being at the door at that time. In the background there was the history as I reported it in my earlier account of this case (Hoffman, 1998):

> There is little doubt…that embedded within the existential, universal predicaments of life with which Manny struggles, we can find an idiosyncratic neurosis. Manny was abused as a child, given forced enemas to empty his

bowels, probably before he was old enough to control his sphincters. His mother was overbearing, controlling, intrusive, and even violent. She would beat his father who would cower before her fits of rage. The patient remembers not one single occasion when his father stood up to her. And she would bad-mouth her husband to her son, offering Manny the sense that he was special, at the center of her life, a "gift" that did more to suffocate him than to build his sense of self. (p. 252)

With this background, how could that visit to the house *not* reflect some element of identification that Manny had with his intrusive mother—a readiness, absorbed through his relationship with her, to overstep boundaries, to feel entitled to enter the private space of the other, indeed, especially the private space of the most intensely valued love object, and to do it, that invasive act, under the guise of its being exactly what the loved one needs.

Manny had his own elaborations to confirm this interpretation. When I suggested that perhaps he would have simply dropped the check into the mail slot had the door not been open at the moment he arrived, Manny volunteered that in fact he had the fantasy of visiting me all along—a fantasy that struck him as unrealistic as soon as he saw my son. He thought he was acting very much like his mother, who had a habit of bringing gifts and food to anyone in the neighborhood who was sick, whether they wanted her offerings or not, and always with strings attached. That is, she was frequently angry with others for not extending themselves to her as much as she did to them. Also, Manny wanted me to know that when he delivered the orchid to the hospital he had similarly imagined a visit to my bedside—an admittedly unrealistic fantasy during the recovery period immediately following the surgery. He was brought back to reality—at the same time that he was able to make close contact indirectly—through a conversation on the phone with my wife, who was in the recovery room. She advised him to leave the orchid with the receptionist in the lobby.

Finally, Manny wanted me to know that he was very conflicted about coming to the house and that he was actually "in a sweat" about it as he was driving down. He knew it might not be the best thing to do and had grave misgivings about it. As he anxiously drove around the neighborhood, having difficulty finding the address, he felt a very powerful internal pressure to go through with the plan despite his very strong reservations. His own awareness that his action might not have reflected his best judgment, however, made it not easier (as I would have hoped would be the case) but more difficult to absorb my disapproval because he felt I was failing to take for granted that he *knew* about all those considerations but had come to the house anyway because of a sense of overwhelming inner compulsion.

Reinterpreting a Dream:
The Coconstruction of New Meaning

Manny's visit turned up the volume on a possible meaning of a dream he had reported months before (Hoffman, 1998). At that time, he had returned, temporarily and briefly, from a winter vacation, one that had been open-ended so that it simulated a quasi-termination:

> Manny could be gone a month or two or even more. It did not make sense, therefore, for me to hold his times. He said he'd call me when he returned and take his chances. So we were faced with an ambiguous interruption, neither quite a vacation in the usual sense, nor a full termination. I decided it afforded an opportunity to construct a benign kind of semi-ending, one the patient had never been able to experience before in analysis. In the "last session," I presented him with a gift, two books dealing with questions of origins, the beginnings of the universe and of life, and evolution, all questions I knew Manny was interested in. Accompanying the gift was a card on which I had written, in part, "Congratulations on your 'graduation.' If these books don't answer *all* your remaining questions about the meaning of life, you will definitely need more analysis (the advanced, postgraduate kind of course)." Manny was moved and delighted. He appreciated my turning this juncture into something of an ending, even though he thought he'd surely be back if he didn't die in the interim. He joked that he'd write or call to give me his address and phone number (unknown at the time of the meeting) so that I could call him in Palm Springs if I needed him. The next day he left an envelope for me in the waiting room containing two tickets to a concert in town that he couldn't attend while he was away. Several weeks later, he returned for a few days for business reasons. In the first of two scheduled sessions he spoke with elation about one of the books I had given him (*Shadows of Forgotten Ancestors* by Carl Sagan and Ann Druyan), which he said he was enjoying as much if not more than any he had ever read. He was thrilled with the ideas and conveyed them to me in a manner that was unusually animated. He seemed stronger and healthier than I had ever seen him, reporting that he was having a great time with his wife in Palm Springs, although he missed our meetings. He said he'd be back in Chicago in mid-spring and would like to resume the therapy. But he was rather unfazed when I told him I had given away his times. He said he understood and he'd just take whatever was possible when he got back. In the second of the two sessions, after speaking with some pride and satisfaction about the pile of business matters he had been tackling, he reported the following dream: "I was heading for my first analyst's office. But in front of his building a huge crowd of people had gathered and I had to struggle to get through. A crowd of people was also in the lobby. So I decided I would just scale the outer wall, which I was able to do with ease, like Spider-Man. I went in then through the bathroom window and got to his office. I said, 'I know I'm late.' He replied 'Yes I know. You understand that it will cost you 3 hours at $11 per hour.'" (pp. 259–260)

Continuing now with my original commentary on the dream:

> He said his first analyst reminded him of me, in that he was warm and very
> human. He thought the people in front of the building represented my other
> patients, including whoever had taken his old times, and that his "lateness"
> referred to the duration of his trip, which meant leaving his times open. The
> penalty of three hours at $11 corresponded, he guessed, to what had been our
> frequency of meetings for a long time and to what was an obvious fraction of
> the fee, one-tenth to be exact. In the time-machine of the dream perhaps he
> was taking us back to a pre-inflation era. Being charged for three hours might
> allude to his discomfort and maybe to his guilt over the possibility that I had
> neglected my self-interest in not charging him for any of the missed time. He
> wasn't sure what scaling the wall meant and had no associations that illumi-
> nated that image for us. I suggested that it might be a whimsical way of repre-
> senting his recovery of a sense of youthful vitality. The fact that in the dream
> it's his first analyst who appears, which takes the patient back 50 years, might
> also refer to his sense of himself as having youthful strength and energy. I
> suggested, also, that the image of scaling the wall might refer to his feeling
> special to me, so that he felt confident that he would have access to me even-
> tually, even if something unusual was required and even if it did worry him
> that I might overextend myself. After all, I'd just given him a gift, which is not
> the standard kind of analytic interaction. The scaling of the wall might also
> allude, specifically, to the books on evolution, to his own adaptability, to the
> "survival of the fittest." Although I did not think of it at the time, it might well
> be relevant that the other book I gave him was *Climbing Mount Improbable* by
> Richard Dawkins. What seems evident is that the quasi-termination, buffered
> and enhanced by the use of various transitional objects, was a powerful cata-
> lyst for Manny's development in terms of his capacity to feel confident about
> his own resources as well as the enduring aspects of his connection with me
> and with the analytic process. (pp. 260–261)

Needless to say, it makes no sense to think of events *subsequent* to a
dream as though they were day-residues of the dream, yet possible meanings that are obscured by features of the transference and the countertransference at the time the dream was reported may be illuminated by features
of the analytic relationship that emerge later. These meanings can be understood as also active preconsciously at the earlier time, though resisted by
both participants. And there are contingencies, such as my surgery, that may
evoke feelings that would not have been evoked otherwise. The transference and the countertransference do not simply "unfold" over time according to some predetermined blueprint. Perhaps a kind of blueprint exists,
but it is for many different things, only some of which will emerge in the
course of an analysis. Which facets emerge is decided by a complex interplay of contingency and choice. The choice of either one of the parties,
incidentally, can be construed as a contingency from the point of view of

the other. So, for example, Manny's decision to come to the house is an unpredictable contingency from my point of view, and my disapproving remark is an unpredictable contingency from his point of view. Each of us may be influencing the other and creating part of the context for the other's experience and for the other's choices. But influence is a far cry from total determination. Thus, even if an analyst knew fully the nature of his or her contribution to a patient's experience (which is never possible), he or she could not know—at most could only suspect—how the patient will choose to respond.

Returning to the meaning of the dream, in this instance the interpretations of Manny's sense of entitlement in scaling the walls of my building, of his intrusiveness, and of the element of identification with his invasive mother do not occur to me or to Manny at a juncture when we are both delighted by his progress and eager to recognize how much each of us has contributed and is appreciated by the other. But when Manny comes to my house and I experience some sense of violation of my space, those aspects of his motivation impress themselves on me, and I can reflect retrospectively on their relevance to the dream and on the reasons for missing that interpretation earlier. Neither the positive countertransference nor the negative countertransference promotes grasping the whole truth of the meaning of the dream. An understanding that is more complex and integrative, although still not comprehensive (because none ever is), is one that combines what each quality of countertransference illuminates. On one hand, *against* the current of the positive countertransference at the earlier time, there was probably something grandiose and presumptuous about Manny's idea that he was so special that he could bypass all other patients if he wanted access to me after his winter break. On the other hand, *against* the current of the negative countertransference at the later time, there was something loving, generous, and understandable about his wanting to be close to me after my surgery, his wanting these unusual "extenuating circumstances," as he refers to them in his e-mail, to afford the opportunity to live out the fantasy of being part of my immediate family, like a son, a father, or a wife. In the context of the analysis, the act is hardly reducible to a repetition via identification with his abusively invasive mother. Perhaps it has some of that coloring, but it is also an act of will and of imagination, expressive of vitality, of love, and of intimate connection. In fact, in light of the template of the history, including the forced enemas, Manny's offering could be viewed as akin to the child's freely offering a bowel movement as an act of proud generosity as opposed to either compliant submission or defiant withholding. Rank (1945) writes that we must recognize that the patient in analysis "suffers … from a situation in which a strange will is forced on him and makes him react with accentuation of his own will" and that "this negative reaction of the patient represents the actual therapeutic value, the expression of will as such, which in the analytic situation can only manifest itself as resistance, as protest—that is, only as counter-will" (p. 13).

So, Manny's "counter-will" expresses itself as a spontaneous act of love that defies analytic decorum. The current of repetition is joined by a current of growth, of differentiation of the present from the past. The negative countertransference blinds me to what the positive countertransference illuminates and vice versa. But the dream is irreducibly ambiguous and holds an indeterminate potential for meaning. Just as my surgery and Manny's visit to my house bring out meanings that were unanticipated, so might other eventualities bring out yet additional unanticipated meanings. And for every meaning that is brought out in this way, there are countless others that are left dormant, unknown, and unexplored.

Acts of Will and Imagination II:
An Analyst at the Patient's Door

Now consider this scene as described by my brother-in-law David (Feinsilver, 1998) in his paper "The Therapist as a Person Facing Death." For 6 years, David had been working with Wally, a young man in his early 20s and a patient at Chestnut Lodge. Wally knew of David's cancer and sobbed at learning of its recurrence. The following is excerpted from David's paper:

> One day, before Wally's hour, I began to receive concerned phone calls from various quarters of the hospital saying that Wally was acting strangely and had not shown up for his regular appointments. I became concerned. But when he did not show up for his hour, nor answer his phone, I started to become furious over his pulling his self-destructive routine of abandoning me as he felt I was doing to him. So when I got to his house a block away and he did not respond to my ringing the bell and knocking, I told him that I knew he was in there and he had two choices: either he opened the door or I was calling the police to have him committed back into the in-patient unit because I was not going to let him continue down this self-destructive path of cutting me and everybody off as a way of trying to handle his anger about my illness. I told him I didn't know how suicidal he was but I wasn't about to take any chances (and I meant it). He answered the door immediately and pleaded, as we walked back to my office, that although he was certainly feeling like wanting to do away with himself I didn't have to worry. He wouldn't. (pp. 1136–1137)

A little later in David's paper (Feinsilver, 1998), we learn that, back at the office, Wally began to clarify what had "set him off":

> [He spoke] of his rage at starting to get excited about the prospect of seeing me two times a week but then [started] to think about what good it would do

to increase the time to two times a week if he were just going to lose me soon anyway. In the next session Wally proudly announced that he had worked out with his family that they could afford the increase and he wanted to start as soon as possible.

This sequence turned out to be a turning point in the work with Wally, enabling us to begin to work through the fears underlying his rageful protestations about going forward in life in general and "taking in all that new stuff," while also beginning to articulate the elements of the self-destructive, "negative therapeutic reaction" that has been precipitating his breakdowns and doing him in throughout his life. (p. 1137)

David later comments as follows:

I believe Wally experienced my confrontation of his suicidality as a concrete expression of caring from the person who had abandoned him. He probably heard words to the effect that if somebody who is dying still feels there is "work of noble note" to be done [quoting Tennyson, as David does at the beginning of his paper], then maybe the least he could do was show up. Since this sequence Wally has started to become more involved in working with me psychotherapeutically in our hours on the problem of his retreating from success, as well as working outside the hours on the very practical manifestations of this in developing close friends and maintaining a job. (p. 1137)

Wally comes out of his self-destructive retreat because, as David says, he feels it's "the least he can do" in light of David's illness and effort. I think this aspect of Wally's motivation and of the motivation of the other patients David tells us about is underemphasized by David in his formal discussion of the principles of therapeutic action that emerge in the context of his terminal illness. I believe these patients get better partly because the factor of their malignant envy has been much reduced. The sense that the analyst already has his fill of narcissistic supplies, combined with the sense that what he *offers* is by far too little and too late, can result in patients begrudging the analyst the satisfaction of having the power to make a difference in their lives. But now David is dying. The patient becomes the fortunate one, the "have" rather than the "have not," the one whose situation is enviable. Now the patient is more readily able to "give" David his or her progress as, in effect, a gift. It is "the least [the patient] can do" under the circumstances, to stop withholding on the grounds that David already *has* so much, whereas what he *offers* is barely a drop in the bucket. Now, what David offers to his patients is perceived as *much more*, relatively, because he has so much *less* for himself.

It doesn't always go that way of course. Ann-Louise Silver (1990) beautifully documents a range of different reactions and adaptations that characterized her patients at Chestnut Lodge when she was afflicted with a life-threatening illness in the early 1980s. In terror of abandonment, for example, some patients seemed to become more disturbed and disorganized. But despite the variations, and in keeping with David's experience (Feinsilver, 1998), Silver also writes:

> I do remember vividly that my patients were striving to work with me.... That is, they worked to rebuild the holding environment and I struggled to assist them. I observed their efforts gratefully, and I am confident that they perceived my being grateful. I have special fondness for those patients who saw me through those months. We are like veterans who fought together at the front lines. (p. 164)

So picture now, if you will, David at Wally's door and Manny at mine. Two very different scenes, of course. In one, the therapist is at the door; in the other, the patient. In one, the patient is the object of the therapist's concern; in the other, the therapist is the object of the patient's concern. Yet the points of commonality are also striking. David is facing his own death as is Manny in his old age, and both are at the door of someone they love—someone they fear could die even before they do. Four human beings facing death, their own and each other's. David says, and Manny says, "Look, these are extenuating circumstances. I will not proceed as though this were business as usual. I will do what it takes to offer something. I will try, in accord with David's definition of a *mensch*, "to rise to the occasion on a difficult occasion to do 'the right thing'" (Feinsilver, 1998, p. 1148). To be sure, David's action *seems* the wiser of the two, and it elicits a much more positive response than what Manny gets from me. But Manny's intentions certainly include a desire to reach out, to be close, to offer something. Perhaps he felt, like Wally, that it was "the least he could do" under the circumstances. We are in this together, he and I, "on the front lines." And under these conditions, he has the opportunity to allow his emotional attachment to override the usual constraints of the analytic situation, to show me more directly what he feels about me, and to search out my personal feelings about him. However awkward and stumbling, and even ill-advised, Manny is reaching imaginatively here for something new, for something different. It's no wonder that he experienced my disapproving response as so injurious and as so jeopardizing of his sense of the authenticity of my interest in him. And given how hurt he was, his continuing in the analysis with me and his willingness to collaborate with me in exploring the meaning of this episode, including his own contribution, reflects his effort to integrate his autonomous, creative participation with responsiveness to my needs as his analyst and as a person.

From Idealization to Identification:
The Patient's Progress as a Reparative Gift

David wonders toward the end of his paper whether the catalytic power that his terminal illness seemed to generate "can occur under ordinary circumstances." He asks, "Can we bottle it for export, so to speak, for everyday analytic work?" (Feinsilver, 1998, p. 1148). His answer is definitively yes. He believed that the key factor is the optimal emergence of the analyst as a person to facilitate differentiation of transference-based fantasy and reality. But maybe we need to go further and recognize that the emergence of the particular reality of the analyst's mortality is not just one of many realities that might emerge and facilitate differentiation. It is the ultimate reality, the core of the analyst's being, and at the same time the deepest common ground with the patient. Yet it is the most difficult of realities to bring into the foreground, because, as Ernest Becker (1973) demonstrated so compellingly in his book *The Denial of Death*, its denial is so common and its acknowledgment so universally horrifying. Becker suggests that the disillusioning power of the primal scene inheres in its exposure of the parents' corporeal existence, of their need-driven animality, and of their mortality, at a point when the child has a need to see the parents as superior, as transcending of materiality, as, in effect, more godlike (pp. 42–46).

In continuity with that facet of childhood, therapeutic action depends partly on the jointly constructed impression that the analyst is a superior power—an impression cultivated by the ritualized asymmetry of the analytic situation, even as it is challenged and rendered ironic through the analysis of the transference. With that power, which is associated with a kind of selflessness, the analyst is in a position to affirm the patient as an agent, as a contributor to the coconstruction of the reality of the community, the culture, and the network of relationships in which the patient lives. It's a power that has as its precursor the power of parents in their relationships with children in their innocence. When children absorb, uncritically, *destructive* attitudes that leave them profoundly *flawed* in their capacity as agents, they subsequently, as adults, need a specially designed arrangement to elevate a human authority to a status that can compete with the malignant influence of the original caregivers. In that respect, the analyst, as I've discussed elsewhere (Hoffman, 1998, Ch. 1), inherits functions that used to belong to the gods or to the priestly mediators of divine authority.

But the therapeutic benefits of the analyst's status as a superior, benevolent, relatively selfless being can be offset by the factor of malignant envy referred to earlier along with the deep resentment that, in the cosmic order, what is being offered is much too little too late. The patient feels cheated and withholds the best that he or she could potentially give. He or she holds out for a better deal, for justice in a cosmic court, for a new start, for rebirth.

At some level, the patient, since he or she is indeed *not* a naïve infant but a discerning, interpreting adult, is always aware of what I've referred to as the dark side of the analytic frame—the way the arrangement serves the analyst's all-too-human needs, narcissistic and monetary. It is "a strange will" indeed, as Rank (1945) says, that is forced on the patient through the analytic situation. Money for love hardly comes close to having love bestowed simply in response to one's being born into the world, to the mere fact of one's existence. Moreover, there is a thin line, surely, between the patient's need for an idealized object and the patient's resentment of the analyst's privileged position. If there is to be any therapeutic benefit, in the end the patient must *forgive* the analyst for the reality that he or she is indeed simply a person like the patient. The patient must choose *to forgive* to choose *to take* whatever good the analyst has to offer. What seems anomalous as a basis for that forgiving attitude, the emergence of the reality of the analyst's mortality, refers, of course, to the most common thing in the world, the universal certainty that applies to everyone. It's only denial that keeps that fact of life in the background, hidden from the participants' view.

Overcoming that denial is not easy, and how overcoming it can be translated into a form of action that can practically apply to the analytic situation is not obvious. Unfortunately, life-threatening conditions come into play often enough as catalysts, but, when they don't, we need to find ways to bring ourselves and our patients more in touch with our common humanity. To speak of death could seem contrived at times, but it's also possible that we are not alert enough for occasions when it would be important for the subject to be raised. After all, it is inescapably the case that, in living, however passionately, however expansively, we are, all of us, at every moment, also dying. Some have noted (Cohen, 1983; Garcia-Lawson, 1997) that it is all too rare that the analyst, regardless of age or state of health, explores with the patient how the patient might feel and what he or she might do in the event of the analyst's death. But I think more generally, in keeping with David Feinsilver's (1998) view, what brings the patient into contact with the analyst's mortality, and hence with the sense that the analyst and the patient share a common plight, is attention to the analyst's limitations and vulnerability in all the ways that they may spontaneously come into play in the course of the work. It is then, perhaps, that our patients can integrate the need for idealization with acknowledgment that we, as analysts, are also patients—that we are, indeed, vulnerable enough, threatened enough, suffering enough, deprived enough, bereaved enough, traumatized enough, flawed enough, yet also good enough, to earn the patient's empathic identification and reparative concern. Then, in that reversal recognized by Searles (1975) as essential to therapeutic action, "the patient [becomes] therapist to [the] analyst" and can choose to offer him or her the most meaningful of gifts—evidence of an enhanced capacity for responsive and creative living.

The analyst, in turn, can absorb the patient's movement in that healthy direction as testimony to the analyst's worth, despite all his or her limitations, as a powerfully constructive influence in the patient's life.

References

Becker, E. (1973). *The denial of death*. New York: Free Press.

Cohen, J. (1983). Psychotherapists preparing for death: Denial and action. *American Journal of Psychotherapy, 37*, 223–226.

Davies, J. M. (1998). Thoughts on the nature of desires: The ambiguous, the transitional, and the poetic: Reply to commentaries. *Psychoanalytic Dialogues, 8*, 805–823.

Davies, J. M. (2000). Descending the therapeutic slopes—Slippery, slipperier, slipperiest: Commentary on papers by Barbara Pizer and Glen O. Gabbard. *Psychoanalytic Dialogues, 10*, 219–229.

Feinsilver, D. B. (1998). The therapist as a person facing death: The hardest of external realities and therapeutic action. *International Journal of Psychoanalysis, 79*, 1131–1150.

Fosshage, J. L. (1997). Psychoanalysis and psychoanalytic psychotherapy: Is there a meaningful distinction in the process? *Psychoanalytic Psychology, 14*, 409–425.

Garcia-Lawson, K. A. (1997). Thoughts on termination: Practical considerations. *Psychoanalytic Psychology, 14*, 239–257.

Hoffman, I. Z. (1996). The intimate and ironic authority of the psychoanalyst's presence. *Psychoanalytic Quarterly, 65*, 102–136.

Hoffman, I. Z. (1998). *Ritual and spontaneity in the psychoanalytic process: A dialectical-constructivist view*. Hillsdale, NJ: The Analytic Press.

Margulies, A. (1999). The end of analysis? Or, our postmodern existential situation. A review essay on *Ritual and spontaneity in the psychoanalytic process: A dialectical-constructivist view* by Irwin Z. Hoffman. *Contemporary Psychoanalysis, 35*, 699–712.

Nagel, T. (1979). *Mortal questions*. New York: Cambridge University Press.

Racker, H. (1968). *Transference and countertransference*. New York: International Universities Press.

Rank, O. (1945). *Will therapy and truth and reality* (J. Taft, Trans.). New York: Knopf.

Searles, H. F. (1975). The patient as therapist to his analyst. In P. L. Giovacchini (Ed.), *Tactics and techniques in psychoanalytic therapy, vol. 2: Countertransference* (pp. 95–151). New York: Aronson.

Silver, A.-L. S. (1990). Resuming the work with a life-threatening illness—and further reflections. In H. J. Schwartz & A.-L. S. Silver (Eds.), *Illness in the analyst: Implications for the treatment relationship* (pp. 151–176). Madison, CT: International Universities Press.

Williams, B. (1976). Moral luck. *Proceedings of the Aristotelian Society, 1*(Suppl.), 115–135.

Winnicott, D. W. (1971). *Playing and reality*. New York: Basic Books.

AFTERWORD

One development in my own thinking in the last few years has entailed increased curiosity about the sociopolitical implications of psychoanalytic work (Hoffman, 2009a, 2010; Layton, Hollander, & Gutwill, 2006;

Tolleson, 2009). What are the taken-for-granted values that I am living out in my clinical practice? To what extent is a "normative unconscious" (Layton, 2006) governing the way my patients and I are working
together, the goals that we implicitly or explicitly set, and even the ways
that we are engaged with each other from moment to moment? Is such
awareness and critical thinking conducive to subtle or not-so-subtle
changes in what we do within the constraints of the analytic process? Or
are these things so deeply entrenched in my patients and in me that it's
impractical to imagine how any changes in attitude or perspective could
emerge that would reflect heightened political consciousness and moral
sensibility bearing on a transformed sense of fulfillment in life?

It's interesting to look at earlier papers to see whether I can find precursors of this interest in the clinical work and clinical theory that they
convey or advocate. There are a number of features of this essay, "At
Death's Door," that I think could be regarded as providing fertile ground
for the later development.

First, the emphasis throughout, in keeping with the subtitle of the
essay, is on "therapists and patients as agents." I am viewing Manny as
responsible for whatever he chooses to do or say, and I am similarly
regarding myself as responsible for my choices. To say that is not to deny
that both of us are acting in ways that are heavily influenced by our
personal histories, by our intrapsychic dynamics, by our interpersonal
experience and mutual influence, and, finally, by our embeddedness in a
sociocultural surround that shapes every moment of our encounter. But
I refuse to regard all of those factors as wholly determining of Manny's
or my actions. I feel that there has to be a "space" left that allows our
behavior to reflect, not only all of those influences, but also our personal
freedom. I think consciousness of our responsibility as participants in
the analytic relationship paves the way to raised consciousness about
our responsibility as citizens of the world.

What I am reacting against when I underscore that dimension of our
analytic engagement are very deeply entrenched concepts that reside
at the core of the psychoanalytic tradition. In particular I am thinking
of concepts such as psychic determinism, free association, and evenly
hovering attention (Hoffman, 2006). Psychic determinism, by definition, excludes the factor of individual freedom and will (Rank, 1945,
pp. 44–45). Free association strips the analysand of his or her responsibility for making judgments about what to say and how to say it. The
injunction is not to censor, not to judge, but just to speak of whatever
"comes to mind," and what comes to mind is not something one controls.
In a complementary way, evenly hovering attention entails an injunction directed at the analyst that opposes his or her making judgments
about what is important, what warrants interest, what warrants praise or

criticism. The analytic participants, analyst and analysand, are, in effect, turned into complementary parts of a machine. They aren't real people engaged in a human interaction. All of it could be thought of as under the rubric of "technical rationality," with a scientific apparatus treating, operating on, an organism with a disorder.

Establishing the humanity of the participants while still engaging in an analytic process is transitional to encouraging reflections on both people's political positions as they are enacted within the analytic dyad and as they are expressed outside the office. I want Manny and myself to struggle with what we mean to each other, with what we have done and are doing with each other, and with the whole quality of our relationship as it evolves over time. I feel Manny didn't "have to" come to my house to deliver that check. I want him to take responsibility for that even as we explore the dynamics of that choice. I, in turn, didn't "have to" say on the phone that I didn't think coming to the house was such a good idea. So it's important that I take responsibility for that. I don't take Manny's later return to the therapy for granted but see it as his generous contribution to the survival and growth of our relationship. Eventually, we explore his deciding to bring that check to the house, and different meanings emerge over time.

When I write to Manny in reply to his angry e-mail in which he implies that my interest in him is fake, I am trying to maintain analytic discipline while conveying my perspective as honestly as I can. I've heard it argued that that e-mail borders on malpractice because it entails objections to the feelings Manny expressed based upon their emotional impact on me. In effect, it is argued that Manny is pressured to inhibit his true feeling and its expression to accommodate my sense of vulnerability, allegedly a nonanalytic exchange that violates a tacit analytic contract. My response is that there are no affects that emerge and develop outside of a social context. So whatever Manny feels is context dependent. If I respond to his angry accusations with what I have elsewhere referred to as "that stereotypic, stylized posture of psychoanalytic hyper-unperturbed calm" (Hoffman, 2009b, p. 621), what will emerge will not be some kind of pure culture of Manny's conscious and unconscious affective experience but rather his response to that particular, institutionalized, rather peculiar, "psychoanalytically correct" stance. Meanwhile, an opportunity would be missed for a genuine, very complex encounter, one that I feel is ultimately deeply engaged and loving on my part. In effect, Manny, via the struggle about the wisdom of his visit, finds some of the personal intimacy with me that he craves and that he came to the house hoping the "extenuating circumstances" would permit. A meaning that seems obvious to me now that I missed or didn't value enough originally is that, ironically, Manny's bringing that check to my home could be viewed as "subversive" in that it pushes for a personal encounter with me that is outside of the capitalist ritual of the paid for psychoanalytic session. Had that struck me more forcefully at the time, perhaps my attitude on the phone would have been more generous, although of course there were other considerations.

The whole scene can be treated as an enactment, the multiple meanings of which are eventually explored, at least in part. Appreciating the possible value of manifest interpersonal influence does not preclude, indeed complements, exploration of relevant history and of the transference–countertransference dynamics. Finally, my e-mail includes my imploring Manny to be more open-minded in considering the meaning of my behavior. In effect, I appeal to him to adopt a "constructivist" rather than a "positivist" attitude as he reflects on what I said on the phone and its implications. I have no illusion that such an attempt to persuade and edify will succeed by itself, but it can plant seeds that might bear fruit in the future.

Whatever asymmetry of power is optimal for a transformative psychoanalytic conversation, it is accompanied by a more or less conscious undercurrent of mutual identification with respect to the ultimate vulnerability of the participants. When that vulnerability is denied it can fuel subtle abuses of power on the part of the analyst beginning with a refusal to recognize the patient as a fellow caregiver with power to deeply affect the analyst's sense of worth. Manny learns that he matters to me, not only as one who needs my "analytic love" and expertise and not only as a source of income but as one whose affirmative presence and participation can nurture my survival, indeed my thriving, as an analyst and as a person.

Traditional psychoanalytic thinking promotes a very one-sided arrangement in which the analyst is always, overtly at least, in the role of caregiver. But as a result the patient is deprived of opportunities to have the more caring and generous aspects of himself or herself recognized and affirmed. Tolleson (2009) writes:

> So while we have fundamentalized narcissistic needs, and positioned ourselves clinically in relation to those needs, we have not done the same with morality needs—compassion, responsibility, caring for others (with the exception of Klein's essentializing of guilt and the pursuit of love over hate). Samuels (2004) criticizes the standard—and reifying—psychoanalytic theorizing in which the patient is viewed as an infant whose wellbeing rests on whether it is gratified or failed by the broader society as mother. In a powerful reversal, he suggests we regard the patient as a "citizen" who is caregiver to the baby-world. (p. 199)

There is a bond between Manny and me that is reciprocal and powerful. Our consciousness of our own and each other's mortality and vulnerability is critical to that bond. Awareness of mortality has the potential to promote mutual identification and sense of responsibility for the well-being of the other. But it also has the potential, via denial, to promote hierarchical splitting and abuse of power. The connection between the politics of the analytic relationship and national and international politics becomes clear. Judith Butler (2004) is eloquent and passionate on the interface of intimate interpersonal life and sociopolitical realities. Regarding the vulnerability "that is part of bodily life" Butler writes:

> Mindfulness of this vulnerability can become the basis of claims for non-military political solutions, just as denial of this vulnerability through a fantasy of mastery (an institutionalized fantasy of mastery) can fuel the instruments of war. We must attend to it, even abide by it, as we begin to think about what politics might be implied by staying with the thought of corporeal vulnerability itself, a situation in which we can be vanquished or lose others. (p. 29)

The intra-analytic politics that are seen as governing of the analytic relationship in "At Death's Door," the foregrounding of the vulnerability of the participants and of their responsibility for each other's well-being, stops short of a politically conscious and critical psychoanalysis because its focus remains the analytic dyad considered outside of the context of the sociopolitical realities in which the process is embedded (Botticelli, 2004). It provides fertile ground, however, for movement in that direction. I and others are called upon to confront and act upon our responsibility, as analysts and as citizens of the world, to embrace that difficult—yet I've come increasingly to believe—morally imperative course.

References

Botticelli, S. (2004). The politics of relational psychoanalysis. *Psychoanalytic Dialogues, 14,* 635–651.

Butler, J. (2004). *Precarious life: The powers of mourning and violence.* New York: Verso.

Hoffman, I. Z. (2006). The myths of free association and the potentials of the analytic relationship. *International Journal of Psychoanalysis, 87,* 43–61.

Hoffman, I. Z. (2009a). Doublethinking our way to scientific legitimacy: The desiccation of human experience. *Journal of the American Psychoanalytic Association, 57,* 1043–1069.

Hoffman, I. Z. (2009b). Therapeutic passion in the countertransference. *Psychoanalytic Dialogues, 19,* 617–637.

Hoffman, I. Z. (2010, April). Discussion of papers by Lynne Layton and Malcolm Slavin at invited panel, Dialectical Constructivism: Existential, Sociopolitical, and Clinical Contexts. Meeting of Division of Psychoanalysis (39) of the American Psychological Association, Chicago.

Layton, L. (2006). Racial identities, racial enactments and normative unconscious processes. *Psychoanalytic Quarterly, 75,* 237–269.

Layton, L., Hollander, N. C., & Gutwill, S. (Eds.) (2006). *Psychoanalysis, class and politics: Encounters in the clinical setting.* New York: Routledge.

Rank, O. (1945). *Will therapy and truth and reality* (J. Taft, Trans.). New York: Knopf.

Samuels, A. (2004). Politics on the couch? Psychotherapy and society—some possibilities and some limitations. *Psychoanalytic Dialogues, 14,* 817–835.

Tolleson, J. (2009). Saving the world one patient at a time: Psychoanalysis and social critique. *Psychotherapy and Politics International, 7,* 190–205.

3

The Analyst's Secret Delinquencies*

Joyce Slochower

▼ ▼ ▼ ▼ ▼

Dr. M, a supervisee with whom I have been working for several years, opened our session with a confession that she made with some difficulty. Before I describe it, let me contextualize things a bit. Dr. M is a sensitive, skilled analyst who has been in the field for nearly 2 decades. We had worked together for 5 years, and I knew her to be a serious professional with an impeccable sense of commitment to her patients. For all these reasons, I found Dr. M's confession jarring.

About 10 minutes into a telephone session, Dr. M's patient, Mr. J, interrupted himself to ask about "a weird noise" he heard, saying it sounded like pages in a magazine being turned. Mr. J's guess was correct; Dr. M was, in fact, quietly skimming through magazines and catalogs and giving Mr. J less than her full attention. "On the spot" and feeling intensely guilty, Dr. M said that she was taking notes on the session and had been turning the pages of her notebook. Mr. J seemed to accept her explanation easily and returned to describing other experiences.

Before I address the very complex dynamics embedded in this enactment, let me underscore that Dr. M is far from alone in her secret delinquency. Although rarely acknowledged in public forums, Dr. M's action represents

* Earlier versions of this chapter were presented at the Manhattan Institute of Psychoanalysis, December 2000, New York City; Division of Psychoanalysis (39) American Psychological Association, April 2001, Santa Fe, New Mexico; and the Austin Riggs Center, December 2001, Stockbridge, Massachusetts. A version also appears in my book, *Psychoanalytic Collisions*, Hillsdale, NJ, Analytic Press, 2006. I thank Glen Gabbard, Adrienne Harris, Sue Grand, Margaret Crastnopol, Ruth Gruenthal, Susan Kraemer, and Kristina Schellinski for their very helpful comments on an earlier draft. This chapter originally appeared in *Psychoanalytic Dialogues*, *13*(4), 2003, pp. 451–469. Reprinted with permission.

one example of many common infractions of the analytic contract. Yet, despite a burgeoning literature on serious ethical violations by professionals, analysts have not directly taken up the question of how to understand those less egregious, yet still worrying breaches of our professional role. Probably both because analytic misdemeanors seldom disrupt the treatment on a permanent basis and because they are nevertheless unacceptable, these acts are rarely discussed and, to my knowledge, never written about.

This paper has two aims. The first is to identify and attempt to understand the nature and motivations underlying analysts' tendency to commit small delinquencies. The second is to bring these issues into the arena of dialogue with the explicit intention of changing problematic aspects of our professional behavior. In the course of this paper I describe a variety of analytic delinquencies, including my own. I invite you to join me in directly investigating the nature of professional delinquencies, their dynamics, and their consequences for both analyst and patient.

The Analytic Ideal and the Real Analyst

It is a paradoxical yet crucial professional ideal to which we aspire. We aim to be emotionally and intellectually present for our patients, to use our subjective reactions in the service of the work, to attempt to suspend or, in any case, bracket our self-interest when it is counter or irrelevant to our patient's best interests. This is how we attempt to protect the analytic space and work with a clear focus on our patients' needs. We assume that we will become personally "caught up" with our patients and that we are capable (at least retrospectively) of studying those moments. We use our personhood in the work and endeavor mightily to understand its impact. In line with Winnicott's (1947) conception of countertransference hate, we tend to think of our professional misbehavior in terms of its potential therapeutic *usefulness*. After all, moments of enactment often deepen the work and the analytic relationship. There is not much room in this model for expressions of self-interest that are *not* also useful to our patients. How much more difficult it becomes to consider the impact of our real failures (Kraemer, 1996). Yet I suspect that we are all susceptible to engaging in analytic delinquencies or misdemeanors.

By characterizing some therapeutic actions as delinquencies or misdemeanors, I am deliberately and almost arbitrarily creating a category of professional behavior that is often secretive and usually guiltily enacted. I use the idea of misdemeanors to designate those smaller breaches wherein we relatively momentarily, but with apparently conscious intent, deliberately disengage from the treatment process in the pursuit of a personal agenda. While the bulk of professional misdemeanors are intentionally hidden, committed either when patients are on the couch or during phone sessions, some occur in face-to-face therapy sessions. In minor and more egregious ways, we take advantage of an opportunity temporarily to withdraw affectively, cognitively (or both) from our patients; at the same time, we are aware that we are violating implicit, if not explicit, professional norms.

Let me offer some anecdotal examples of minor and more serious delinquencies. All are uncensored and reported with permission. Some were described by patients, others by analysts about themselves. They include making a note to oneself about a forgotten task, adding to a grocery list, planning an event, filing or painting one's nails, combing hair, putting on makeup, surfing the web, searching a dating website, eating a snack, skimming a magazine or journal, checking e-mail, buying airline tickets online, reading correspondence, pumping breast milk, watching a sports scoreboard online, writing patients' bills, deliberately cutting a session short by a minute or two, and charging for a missed session during a vacation that the patient was unaware the analyst took. Strikingly, in only two of these instances did patients indicate that they were aware of the therapist's breach. One person reported to me that while lying on his analyst's couch he sniffed several times and then asked, "Do I smell nail polish?" He did. Another colleague reported that a patient's previous analyst regularly ate dinner during their sessions until one day the patient exploded with the comment, "What is this, a fucking picnic?"

There is a second group of misdemeanors that are engaged in openly during face-to-face sessions, in full "view" of patients. These include eating or taking long phone calls, using a treatment hour to discuss a matter of personal concern, asking patients to recommend physicians, stocks, discount clothing stores, restaurants, hotels, and so on. In contrast to hidden misdemeanors, these "open" breaches are more clearly located within the relational domain. On one level, they can be understood as a form of indirect communication with one's patient or a reenactment reflective of implicit aspects of the treatment relationship. That we seem to be acting openly may invite, or at least make more possible, the patient's response. Yet these small bits of misbehavior often do not enter the treatment conversation, perhaps because our need to preserve an element of self-interest tends to put enormous pressure on our patients *not* to notice, or at least address, what we are doing. This silent pressure can exclude our action from therapeutic discourse so that "open" misdemeanors may, in fact, function more like the secretive ones that effectively render our patient silent.

Although both the types of breaches and the frequency with which they are committed are variable, it is my sense that only the unusual, or perhaps very young, analyst is altogether innocent in this regard. And because both hidden and explicit misdemeanors remain sequestered, if not split off, from the rest of the analyst's self-experience, these kinds of actions frequently seem to go unnoticed or at least unacknowledged by patients. On those occasions when a delinquency is detected, analysts may commit a second breach by lying or rationalizing in an effort to cover up their action.

In my experience, misdemeanors are usually circumscribed moments within a given treatment that stand in stark contrast to the analyst's ordinarily high level of therapeutic engagement. Because our misdemeanors are so often disavowed, their negative effect on our self-image as caring and committed professionals tends to remain sequestered.

Professional misdemeanors represent another dimension of the malignant underbelly of the analytic position that Irwin Hoffman (1998) describes. He focuses on how analysts can exploit their professional role to feed their narcissism or enjoy a sense of control or power. This "dark side" of the analytic frame may be expressed, for example, in an analyst's potentially exploitative request to publish material about a particular patient.

How is it that otherwise conscientious analysts engage in secret delinquencies? Chessick (1990, 1994) describes the insidious impact of such corruption on psychoanalysis as a profession. He suggests that professional corruption reflects a gradual falling away from the individual and group ego ideal, a deterioration that illustrates the demoralizing impact of life itself. Chessick urges analysts to consciously attend to and resist the "inevitable pressure tending to force us onto a line of development of corruption" (p. 394).

Some support for Chessick's assertion may be found in "off-the-record" conversations I have had with colleagues and supervisees about professional misdemeanors. My younger colleagues in training responded with outrage and shock to the idea that analysts commit these acts. They ascribed misdemeanors to burnout or to a loss of ethical standards, and several declared that they would terminate their analysis were their analysts ever to commit even the smallest of such breaches. In marked contrast, the bulk of the two dozen older analysts with whom I spoke responded with little surprise, and sometimes with amusement, and spontaneously added other examples of professional misdemeanors to my list. And after I presented this paper for the first time,* I received several messages from analysts who asked me to include their confessions in my paper. Some analysts seemed to view their "misbehavior" as a rebellion, more or less conscious, against their own theoretical model, while others saw their actions as purely selfishly motivated. Although I surmised that a sense of shame or guilt lay beneath their amusement, I also heard a tendency to rationalize such actions or avoid addressing their dynamics. Perhaps, as Chessick suggests, a layer of cynicism that had infiltrated the professionalism of senior colleagues had not yet compromised the idealism of younger therapists.

---

* Notably, during its delivery, there was a great deal of laughter.

It is my impression that analysts are less likely to bring misdemeanors into supervision than more emotionally tinged enactments. When we sneakily transgress our own professional standards, supervisors and colleagues can seem to be the moral "police" whose judgment must be sidestepped. Indeed, the clash between these minor acts of psychopathy and the analytic ideal can result in a quasi-conscious disavowal of professional breaches. These misdemeanors then remain sequestered from evenly hovering attention, the process of self-examination, and thus from analytic discourse. Ultimately, of course, such disavowal may result in more egregious misdemeanors—acts—that traverse this permeable boundary between delinquencies and serious analytic crimes.

The extent to which misdemeanors are denied suggests that most of us have a difficult time contending with any evidence of our "delinquent" behavior. Only when we can tolerate this disruption of a positive professional self-image can we easily acknowledge, reflect on, and work with the impact of a breach on our patient and ourselves.

The Analytic Breach: Crime, Misdemeanor, or Enactment?

It is difficult to delineate precisely which aspects of professional behavior constitute misdemeanors, for this category inevitably overlaps with both enactments and more serious analytic crimes. Additionally, such distinctions are subjective, contextual, and open to interpretation. The gravity of a given breach is always colored by the particulars of the patient's experience within the therapeutic dyad and the sociocultural context in which the treatment takes place.*

It is crucial to distinguish deliberate professional breaches from those moments of wandering attention and emotional preoccupation to which we are all vulnerable. Although the latter may reflect a breakdown of the analytic function, more often these moments carry symbolic meanings that can be studied and used, for example, by exploring our personal reverie (Ogden, 1994). When we can locate our breach within the relational configuration and parse its dynamics, that breach may ultimately

---

* For example, in some cultures and at different periods in the history of psychoanalysis, analysts regularly sip tea, knit, crochet, allow their dogs or cats in the consulting room, and so on. It is difficult, if not impossible, to mark an absolute line around the notion of misdemeanors. When such actions are culturally sanctioned, analysts may feel freer to engage in them openly. Whether or not a given action represents a misdemeanor often depends on the meanings of that action for a particular patient and analyst. Is the action openly or implicitly acknowledged by both parties? Is the patient free to express her feelings about the analyst's action? Are even these "acceptable" analytic activities experienced as symbolic thefts by patient or analyst?

be of analytic *use;* that is, it may stimulate a dialogue that opens up or deepens the work. Yet making such distinctions can be self-serving; by attributing an action to relational dynamics we may avoid confronting unpleasant realities that are discrepant with our self-image as caring and committed analysts. Similarly self-serving may be our attempt to categorize a particular breach as a misdemeanor or enactment; what constitutes a misdemeanor or enactment to us may seem like a crime to our patient or colleague, and vice versa.

Smaller bits of deliberate analytic acting out can be contrasted with more serious analytic "crimes," enactments, and moments of reverie wherein the analyst's attention wanders inadvertently. Major boundary violations on the analyst's part effectively destroy the treatment relationship and sometimes the analyst as well. These egregious breaches of the therapeutic contract so seriously compromise the treatment that the analyst may be open to ethical censure, legal suit, or both. Gabbard and Lester (1995), detailing the early history of serious boundary violations beginning with Freud, describe both sexual and nonsexual transgressions.

There is some overlap between major boundary violations and enactments that emerge in the emotional or erotic heat of an analytic encounter, and the line between these two categories is sometimes a fuzzy one. Gabbard and Lester note that boundary violations typically emerge from a slide down a "slippery slope" wherein the analyst's emotional involvement with a patient gradually erodes a clear sense of the boundary between them. They recount a number of contemporary clinical cases in which the analyst's violations of the treatment contract eventually destroyed the therapeutic relationship.

While not all boundary violations reflect countertransference enactments, an analyst who commits serious breaches is frequently under the sway of an intense emotional involvement that overrides awareness of the treatment boundaries. Although enactments can often be addressed in a way that deepens the work, major boundary violations not only are disruptive of the analytic relationship, they are much more likely to derail it permanently. They tend to be highly exploitative of the patient, are committed with more persistence, and are less easily discussed. In contrast, misdemeanors have a more insidious impact on patient and analyst. On one hand, most misdemeanors are committed with more deliberateness than are unconsciously motivated enactments, which seem to "burst out" between patient and analyst. Misdemeanors also appear not to be powered by a strong affective charge; they emerge during periods of analytic quietude more than under the gun of intense affective pressure. Yet these distinctions are far from pristine, for a purposefully committed misdemeanor may embody other, far more unconscious motivations.

Hidden Misdemeanors: Relational and Personal Contributors

Analytic misdemeanors take different forms and have different effects when they are committed secretly, as we saw in Dr. M's secret magazine reading, and when they are open and blatant. Where secretiveness may, in fact, shield a patient from awareness of the analyst's attentional departure, breaches that are openly committed appear to have the patient's tacit and sometimes direct consent. For this reason, explicit misdemeanors tend simultaneously to reflect the analyst's self-interest and a dynamically driven enactment around a core treatment theme.

A patient of mine, Samuel, described his experience in a previous treatment. As an aside, he mentioned that his analyst frequently ate a meal as they talked. Samuel had not been consciously bothered by this behavior and, probably in response to my surprised expression, added that his analyst had asked if he minded and he had said no.

Over time, Samuel and I were able to understand his analyst's actions on several levels. Samuel consciously enjoyed these dinner sessions because he was left with the feeling that things were "comfy" between them; he enjoyed the "special place" accorded to him through this intimacy. Samuel was initially unaware of any more complex feelings about his therapist's actions.

It only gradually emerged that other, more troublesome meanings were embedded in this enactment. Despite Samuel having freely consented to this breach of analytic etiquette, he had, in fact, been quite *unfree* in that interaction. Samuel experienced his analyst's request as an implicit demand that he comply with, and not react negatively to, the analyst's desire to eat. Since Samuel's need to please others was very strong, his response was not surprising. By "not minding" that his therapist ate dinner, Samuel placed himself (and was placed) in a compliant position vis-à-vis the other's needs, a pattern of relatedness reminiscent of Samuel's relationship with both parents. Those experiences had left Samuel with a major difficulty in the area of self-assertion. His analyst's apparent oblivion to the impact of this interaction reinforced Samuel's chronic but still unconscious sense that his needs were less important than those of the other.

Samuel and his analyst both seemed to exclude or deny the reenactment around Samuel's pattern of self-effacement and compliance to the other's needs that was embedded in these dinner sessions. In a sense, analyst and patient together established an emotional context of apparent ease that was contingent on Samuel's participation as a compliant partner and that precluded a dynamic investigation of their interaction.

It is impossible, of course, to ascertain the relative weight of this analyst's conscious self-interest or unconscious participation in a reenactment of Samuel's relational pattern. However, given that the analyst focused on Samuel's needs at other times, I suspect that a key motivational factor involved personal need—in this case, hunger—leading the analyst to override what he knew about Samuel and actually to recreate an exploitative interaction within the treatment context.

On yet another level, Samuel may have unconsciously assimilated a different, equally troublesome message from these dinner sessions. Did his analyst have difficulty meeting his own needs—after all, he regularly deprived himself of a dinner break and "snuck" in time for himself in the context of helping the other. Samuel may well have identified with his analyst's implicit self-deprivation, a pervasive theme in Samuel's own relational pattern.

Analytic Misdemeanors in a Relational Context

In contrast to the explicit impact of overt misdemeanors, hidden misdemeanors may actually or merely apparently shield patients from our actions. It is interesting to note that, although we might assume that analytic breaches are inevitably registered by our patients, most of the analysts with whom I spoke asserted with certainty that their patients were unaware of their temporary withdrawal. It is difficult to ascertain whether or not their patients were subliminally aware of those moments of relative cognitive/emotional absence. Interestingly, in those cases where the analysts' actions were explicit, patients apparently manifested little distress. As Jacobs (2001) notes, patients often suppress, deny, or rationalize their perceptions of their analyst. The result is an unconscious collusion between the two.

How can we understand this collusion? Are those patients with whom analysts "stray" people who are unable to ask for much, who content themselves with a modicum of attention? Are they more narcissistic than not, unaware of the analysts' self-involvement as they are unaware of their own impact? Or do some patients bracket their emotional responses in these situations to protect the illusion of analytic attunement (Slochower, 1996)? Yet, even when these experiences are not consciously assimilated, how could they not subtly alter the affective coloring of the therapeutic moment? Certainly, when we parse a misdemeanor retrospectively, we can relocate our action within the interpersonal field (internally at least) and may be able to examine its intersubjective and personal meanings.

Let us return to Dr. M. She told me about her magazine sneaking with much embarrassment and worry about my censorious reaction, but with strikingly little curiosity. Although I agreed that magazines should not be read during telephone sessions, I made it clear that I was not shocked. I wondered aloud if we could look at her behavior with curiosity rather than simply with censure. We knew her patient to be an earnest and rather intellectualized young man, someone who had considerable difficulty accessing his emotional life. He was deeply committed to his treatment and maintained a friendly although aloof stance vis-à-vis Dr. M. Dr. M was aware that she sometimes struggled against boredom during their sessions; this was especially true during telephone contacts. They had agreed to use the phone to maintain continuity during Mr. J's extended business trips, and, consciously at least, Dr. M felt comfortable with this arrangement.

As Dr. M and I considered her actions within the dyadic context, we wondered if she had unconsciously responded to her patient's emotional withdrawal by reading magazines. Did her action reflect an unconscious hopelessness about making contact with her emotionally disengaged patient? Was Dr. M expressing disowned resentment toward Mr. J for his frequent business trips? As we discussed these possibilities, we realized that Dr. M felt particularly deprived of contact in the absence of the visual stimulation of the "in person" session. Perhaps she had responded to this deprivation by turning to magazines to fill in the missing visual element. It seemed likely that her strong need to make contact, a need already reactive to Mr. J's schizoid style, was further exacerbated during the emotionally remote telephone sessions.

As we discussed these dynamics, Dr. M said, with much embarrassment, that she doubted that her action could be fully explained in this way because she *typically* looked through magazines when doing phone sessions with many of her patients. Although Dr. M knew that her activity compromised her attentiveness, she looked forward to phone sessions because they gave her a chance to relax a bit. Dr. M had been peripherally aware that she was doing something wrong, but she had never allowed herself to think about her actions.

Thus, despite the unique aspects of Dr. M's response to Mr. J, it was clear that her misdemeanors involved more or less chronic expressions of opportunism. Dr. M took advantage of many telephone sessions and sometimes of patients' use of the couch to look through magazines and, in other small ways, satisfy herself while still "playing the role" of good analyst. As she put it, Dr. M made use of her hidden position to take something for herself. It is noteworthy that Dr. M did not commit these breaches with very difficult patients who "demanded" her attention. Instead, it was with patients whom she experienced as having a less demanding presence that she responded with an eruption of personal desire.

Dr. M expressed intense guilt, shame, and anxiety about what she identified as a failure of professionalism and an abandonment of her patients. As we continued to discuss her experience of herself as an analyst, she became increasingly conscious of a heretofore disowned, chronic sense of depletion and strain that pervaded her working life. Dr. M's need to support her family led her to take on a maximum number of patient hours while counterbalancing that strain in little ways. She began to wonder if patients she found easier to work with had picked up on her strain and, recognizing how much difficulty she had had openly taking what she needed, somehow "allowed" her these periods of emotional respite. Dr. M was also aware that there was not a great deal she could do about the ongoing strain in her life. Ultimately, she decided to guard against the danger of taking advantage of her patients: she exercised increased vigilance vis-à-vis her own tendency to sneak what she needed and more concretely, decided to stop doing telephone sessions except in real emergencies. Now that Dr. M was conscious of her tendency to withdraw from him, her emotional involvement with Mr. J gradually intensified, and she began to address the subtle enactment that had been taking place between them.*

The Analyst's Countertransference and the Analyst's Compromise

In contrast to the subtle, yet pervasive underlying strains that impel some analysts to commit misdemeanors with many patients, some delinquencies are driven by factors unique to particular treatment configurations. We react to a treatment moment or to ongoing relational dynamics with an association to unsettled needs and obligations, a sense of rebellion against our own theory or even against the analytic ideal. Those associations may well emerge in moments of reverie within the analytic third (Ogden, 1994).

When we are able to engage and address these associations (whether privately or with our patients), we have an opportunity to deepen and enrich the work. We may, however, also avoid active self-reflection and instead secretly reward ourselves with small "pleasures." Many analysts seem especially vulnerable to committing infractions in treatment configurations characterized by ongoing feelings of boredom or emotional disengagement with patients whom they find ungratifying. During my internship training year, I had such an experience.

Ms. R was a pleasant but extremely self-involved woman who spoke virtually nonstop during our sessions. She was uninterested in hearing anything from me and filled our time with vignettes about herself that seemed

---

* A colleague who read this paper commented that Dr. M's willingness to reveal herself to me within the supervisory context was unusual. I agree. I suspect that the fact that this was a private supervisory relationship *outside* the institute training framework played a large role in creating the open atmosphere that permitted her to take this chance. In addition, such "confessions" are more likely to occur in long-term and intimate supervisory relationships. It is certainly not surprising that these issues so rarely enter the supervisory or peer supervisory processes, for such confessions require a very high degree of trust between colleagues.

devoid of self-reflectiveness. Unable to engage her in exploring either the content or the process of our sessions, I talked to her about how disturbed she became when I entered the therapeutic dialogue. She responded to my interventions with confusion, avoidance, and sometimes disorganization. Eventually my supervisor suggested that Ms. R needed to use much of our time to ventilate in my presence and that I contain my wish to comment on her experience.

Metaphorically sitting on my hands, I became intensely frustrated and bored during these sessions. I was uncomfortable and ashamed of these feelings and avoided discussing them with my supervisor, from whom I anticipated a censorious response. Instead, I sometimes took advantage of Ms. R's prone position to look through my appointment book and make "to-do" notes to myself. I expressed my countertransference by "taking" for myself, compensating for a sense of deprivation and irritation (both at her and at my supervisor) during these hours. On one level, it is possible that my withdrawal actually sustained the treatment, giving my patient plenty of room and protecting her from my excessively ambitious wish to intervene. Yet I suspect that on another level my cognitive and emotional withdrawal inadvertently supported Ms. R's self-involvement without explicitly disrupting the therapeutic frame. Interestingly, Ms. R seemed oblivious to my inattentiveness, and thus I experienced little pressure from the treatment relationship to address my actions.

In certain respects, analysts who withdraw from the treatment context in relatively small ways paradoxically both breach and protect the analytic frame. For patients who cannot tolerate too much engagement on the analyst's part, the analyst's momentary removal reduces the affective tension between patient and analyst and may allow the patient to experience a needed sense of emotional autonomy (Slochower, 1996). The therapist may resort to small misdemeanors in a quasi-unconscious attempt to restore herself and to sustain her involvement in the treatment. As Frankel (2001) noted, misdemeanors are potentially protective of the analyst and may thus also protect the treatment.

It seems to me that my behavior with Ms. R had both effects. I created emotional room for her as I turned to my own interests in a secretive way. Yet, despite the possibility that my action represented a compromise that in part protected Ms. R, my inability to examine my behavior or to take the matter up with my supervisor reflected both avoidance and a breach of therapeutic professionalism. It was not until considerably later in my professional development that I was able to tolerate examining the dynamics underlying this experience, in particular, a disavowed sense of anger about feeling used and unrecognized.

I suspect that most misdemeanors, like my own experience and that of Dr. M, contain an element of inner negotiation on the analyst's part (Pizer,

1998). Delinquencies may camouflage the analyst's unconscious compromise, reflecting a struggle to balance or regulate conflicting need states (see Aron, 1999). In part, at least, this attempt arises directly out of the nature of analytic work. Although most of us derive considerable gratification from our role, it is equally true that we sometimes feel deprived—concretely or symbolically—as we attempt to be fully present for our patients. The strain of focusing on the other is intensified by the relative sensory deprivation of long days in a still and constant consulting room. Inevitably, the struggle to be present for our patients will at times clash with our own needs. Small bits of analytic "theft" may represent our unconscious attempt to balance these two desires in an unsatisfactory internal negotiation between the wish to be a good analyst and to reward ourselves in one way or another.*

These negotiations may represent, to one degree or another, attempts at self-regulation. Many, perhaps most, of these negotiations are minor. While working on this paper, I observed myself in such a moment. I suspect that it would have gone unregistered by me were it not for the fact that I was writing it. I recently found an old photo of my now grown-up daughter. She was about 10 at the time, smiling hugely and looking utterly adorable. I had slipped the picture into a pile on my desk to await a moment when I would have time to put it into an album. During an analytic session with a quiet and very thoughtful patient who works hard and is engaged with me in a low-keyed way, I impulsively pulled out that photo. Smiling at my daughter's aliveness and youthful beauty, I was briefly suffused with a sense of warmth and personal pleasure. This was a "stolen" pleasure; I had briefly but quasi-deliberately removed myself from my patient affectively and enjoyed a private moment of loving pleasure before returning the photo and turning once again to my patient.†

As I think about my experience, I suspect that I unconsciously used that moment of contact with my intensely affective daughter to counterbalance the very quiet, sad (and, on some level, less gratifying) emotionality between my patient and me. In part, the moment reflected an enactment that repeated aspects of my patient's experience with his own self-involved parents. It may also have contained aspects of what Ogden (1994) described as reverie, in that my withdrawal resulted in a renewed awareness of my patient's experience with his parents. I want to emphasize, though, the *deliberateness* with which I turned to that photo in contrast to the unconscious

---

* It is interesting that, despite my colleagues' frequent use of theft as a metaphor to describe their misdemeanors, only one analyst mentioned a financial delinquency. Is the area of financial theft so profoundly, not to mention legally, unacceptable that analysts do not act out in this way? Or, because of these grave implications, can analysts not acknowledge that they overcharge or otherwise steal from patients?

† I chose not to tell my patient about what I had done but instead began to talk with him about where we were emotionally with each other.

flavor of enactments or the peripheral cognitive/emotional phenomena that Ogden describes, wherein we *find* our attention wandering elsewhere. In this instance, I briefly withdrew from an intense but difficult emotional engagement and sought a simpler and more joyous affective moment with my daughter. I offer this vignette to illustrate our very small, often unconscious effort at self-regulation within the treatment frame. It is when those efforts fail in major ways (as they did with my patient Ms. R) that we may find ourselves committing flagrant breaches of the analytic contract.

Analytic Crimes, Misdemeanors, and Object Relatedness

To some extent, the analytic community shares a consensual sense of the nature of the analytic frame. If not psychopathic, analysts who commit smaller or larger infractions of that frame contend with anxiety about being caught as well as guilt when *not* discovered. That guilt often arises even when the patient remains oblivious to the infraction and when awareness that we are doing something sneaky or wrong is kept at the periphery. Analytic crimes and misdemeanors profoundly affect both our professional self-image and our relationships with our patients. Yet it seems to me that there are important distinctions to be made with regard to the quality of the object relationship embodied in analytic infractions versus analytic crimes.

Analysts who commit serious and persistent violations of the treatment contract not only take for themselves while blotting out an awareness of their patients, they also actively *reject or deliberately exploit* the patient's subjecthood. In this process, they unconsciously or purposefully transform the patient into an object.* I believe an important distinction lies here. Whereas the analyst who commits a serious "crime" transforms the patient from subject to object and explicitly takes advantage of the patient's emotional vulnerability, misdemeanors involve the analyst's attentional and affective *withdrawal* from the arena of the patient's needs. Rather than using the patient to further the analyst's own needs, the analyst withdraws from her patient into a state of solipsistic subjecthood, temporarily losing contact with the reality of her *patient as a subject* so that the analyst becomes the single subject in the room (Benjamin, 1995, 1998).

Interestingly, all the analysts with whom I spoke commented that they never committed misdemeanors during emotionally intense or demanding sessions but, instead, during quieter sessions whether on the telephone or in person. I wonder if it is precisely the *absence* of intense emotional demands on the patient's part that creates room for the analyst to experience her

---

* Sue Grand (2000) has powerfully illustrated the dynamics of such exploitative relatedness in her discussion of human malevolence.

self-interest. During these calmer sessions, the analyst who commits a mis-demeanor implicitly turns to her own desire and *away* from her patient's. She attempts to balance personal need with her patient's by "appearing" to be analytically involved. This retreat from the relational field into a self-involved state is, surely, a temporary abandonment of the patient and the analytic task. Nevertheless, hidden misdemeanors are often less abusive than analytic crimes or misdemeanors committed in face-to-face sessions: The latter actions transform the patient *from subject to object* in an explicitly exploitative way.

To some degree, analytic delinquencies represent an expression of burn-out, overwork, or intensified personal strain. When analysts are driven by professional interest, need, or greed to see more patients and work longer days, a sense of increased inner pressure is nearly inevitable. And when analysts do not allow themselves, or are unable to create, other venues for personal restoration, emotional and physical depletion can become chronic. By committing a misdemeanor, the analyst may unconsciously attempt to recapture something for herself and simultaneously express disowned hos-tility toward her patients. Thus, an analyst who struggled to earn enough money to support his family complained to me that he often felt that his patients "sucked him dry." His intense experience of depletion resulted in his hatred of those patients who remained in need even when he felt that he had little left to give. That hatred ultimately found expression in a variety of forms, including (although not limited to) misdemeanors.

The Analytic Ideal and the Analyst's Humanity

There is something ironic about the notion that to do good analytic work we must be present as full and feeling persons in the treatment relationship while always aiming to use our humanity in the service of our patients' needs.* Certainly, the past decade has seen a dramatic shift in our view of that analytic ideal. It is now widely recognized that we exist as *persons* who struggle to function as analysts within the therapeutic encounter and,

---

* This paper was written well before the catastrophe of September 11, 2001. The new context created by the events of that day evoked intense feelings in many of us, and in the New York area many psychotherapists responded to the immense need and crisis with enormous generosity. In the face of that crisis, we set aside personal need in a big way, and I suspect that the kinds of thefts that I describe in this paper had little, if any, place in our work. Yet I do wonder what the long-term effects of this massive strain will be on us. Will it become necessary to balance that strain by committing professional delinquencies? Or will our refreshed awareness of the preciousness of life and our obli-gation and desire to be of use support a movement away from the phenomenon I have spoken about here?

further, that our subjectivity enriches and deepens analytic work. Yet, while there are myriad ways we *do* "get" for ourselves emotionally while we work without committing misdemeanors, at times the press of our own needs may be insufficiently met within the constraints of our analytic role. For despite the potentially therapeutic benefits of our subjectivity, there are times when that subjectivity is transformed into responses that collide with the analytic ideal and override our professional commitment.

Individual analysts may well respond to different dimensions of the professional ideal with a feeling of increased pressure. Some analysts may experience their patients' need for holding or self-preoccupation as a nearly intolerable deletion of their subjectivity and may react by asserting those needs and "stealing" in small ways. Others may find it difficult to respond when the treatment seems to require that they be fully emotionally present, using their experience of their patient to deepen the work. All of us struggle at times with the intensity of emotional demands implicit in this work, particularly during periods of personal life stress, illness, or other crisis.

Winnicott (1947) believed that the analyst expresses her selfishness or hatred of the patient in symbolic ways, for example, in the strict ending of the hour. He suggested that this expression supported the treatment and the analyst, allowing her to work more effectively. But what if these symbolic expressions of personal need are not enough? Are we capable of remaining focused on the patient for much of the working day in a manner far more complete than is required, perhaps, in any other profession? I suggest that, unless we own and consciously struggle with our greed, sense of deprivation, or selfishness—that is, with our very *unideal* humanity—it is almost inevitable that those feelings will ultimately become sequestered and thus expressed illicitly. (See Susan Kraemer's, 1996, discussion of the mother's nonuseful failures and Slavin & Kriegman's, 1998, description of the inherent conflict between the patient's and analyst's self-interests as they play out in the analytic situation.)

The analytic ideal contains within it a disregard for those dimensions of the analyst's humanness that are *not* integral to the treatment relationship. I believe that this is true across the theoretical continuum. Analytic misdemeanors may thus represent an unconscious rebellion against the ideal analytic position, whatever its shape, and an implicit, symbolic assertion of the analyst's subjecthood. These misdemeanors are virtually ubiquitous precisely because we find it so difficult to acknowledge openly and struggle with the clash between our very human selfishness and the still extraordinary demands of this "impossible profession."

Analytic misdemeanors at once disrupt and sustain the treatment contract. They represent a real failure of the analytic function yet also reflect our abiding and immutable humanity, the limits of our ability to fully suspend personal needs in the context of a requirement that we do so. It is essential that we analysts contend with the paradoxical necessity simultaneously to embrace the analytic ideal, its inevitable clash with our own very real and limiting humanity, and the need to sustain an ongoing and conscious struggle against the abandonment of that ideal.

References

Aron, L. (1999). Clinical choices and the relational matrix. *Psychoanalytic Dialogues, 9*, 1–30.

Benjamin, J. (1995). *Like subjects, love objects*. New Haven, CT: Yale University Press.

Benjamin, J. (1998). *Shadow of the other*. London: Routledge.

Chessick, R. (1990). In the clutches of the devil. *Psychoanalytic Psychotherapy, 7*, 142–151.

Chessick, R. (1994). On corruption. *Journal of the American Academy of Psychoanalysis, 22*, 377–398.

Frankel, J. (2001, April). *Pre-existing and emergent thirds: Play, submission, and suffering in the analytic relationship. Discussion of papers by Sue Grand, Phil Ringstrom, and Joyce Slochower*. Presented at Annual Spring Meeting, Division of Psychoanalysis (39), American Psychological Association, Santa Fe, NM.

Gabbard, G. O., & Lester, E. P. (1995). *Boundaries and boundary violations in psychoanalysis*. New York: Basic Books.

Grand, S. (2000). *The reproduction of evil*. Hillsdale, NJ: The Analytic Press.

Hoffman, I. Z. (1998). *Ritual and spontaneity in psychoanalysis*. Hillsdale, NJ: The Analytic Press.

Jacobs, T. J. (2001). On misreading and misleading patients: Some reflections on communications, miscommunications and countertransference enactments. *International Journal of Psychoanalysis, 82*, 653–669.

Kraemer, S. (1996). "Betwixt the dark and the daylight" of maternal subjectivity: Meditations on the threshold. *Psychoanalytic Dialogues, 6*, 765–791.

Ogden, T. (1994). *Subjects of analysis*. Northvale, NJ: Jason Aronson.

Pizer, S. (1998). *Building bridges: The negotiation of paradox in psychoanalysis*. Hillsdale, NJ: The Analytic Press.

Slavin, M., & Kriegman, D. (1998). Why the analyst needs to change: Toward a theory of conflict, negotiation, and mutual influence in the therapeutic process. *Psychoanalytic Dialogues, 8*, 247–284.

Slochower, J. (1996). *Holding and psychoanalysis: A relational perspective*. Hillsdale, NJ: The Analytic Press.

Winnicott, D. W. (1947). Hate in the countertransference. In *Collected papers: Through pediatrics to psychoanalysis* (pp. 194–203). New York: Basic Books, 1958.

4

The Developmental Perspective in Relational Psychoanalysis*

Stephen Seligman

▼ ▼ ▼ ▼ ▼

THE PERSONAL BACKSTORY: THROUGH THE NEW LEFT AND MARX–FREUD TO INTERSUBJECTIVE-DEVELOPMENTAL PSYCHOANALYSIS

My interest in developmental psychoanalysis has been rooted in these orienting principles. That appeal, in turn, has been nested in my own personal development. The editors of this volume have been generous in allowing me to publish a short personal intellectual-historical reminiscence, which seems in keeping with the overall subject. Even as psychoanalysts have been more revealing about the personal roots of their clinical work, we have been less explicit about the sources of our theoretical commitments.

My attention to the relationship between developmental thinking and psychoanalysis focused in the early 1980s. I finished graduate school in 1981, completing a program that included a strong introduction to physical sciences and neuroanatomy and physiology along with analysis and child development. I was impressed with the immediacy of the physically present body and, even as I remained well aware of their limitations, by the methods of the natural sciences. Nonetheless, although my identity as a professional had become prominent and irrevocable, I remained deeply engaged with political and philosophical themes that had animated my own personal and intellectual psychosocial development throughout my own late adolescent college and postcollege years. As a radical New Leftist who was using the movement as a way to sort

* An earlier version of portions of this paper appeared in *Contemporary Psychoanalysis*, 39(3), 2003, pp. 477–508. Reprinted with permission.

out some my own personal concerns along with fighting for what I still regard as very just causes, I had been interested in both sociopolitical theories and psychoanalysis, along with wanting to include a social service and social action agenda in my everyday work.

During my clinical training, I spent a fair amount of time working with children, as there seemed to me more opportunities to intervene into the social environments that were ordinarily neglected in most of the adult treatment settings where I also worked. I found that I enjoyed this and seemed to be good at it.

This practical interest combined with a more theoretical sense that looking at childhood offered an opportunity to examine questions about the comparative effects of environmental and constitutional influences that seemed important in sorting out what one could expect of social movements. Having studied both analysis and radical social theories in college, I was aware of a gap between them: By and large, the critical social theories concerned themselves with power inequalities, but they did not, especially then, propose a strong psychological theory. Psychoanalysis, on the other hand, offered a method suitable to the radical project of unearthing the hidden dynamics by which people collaborate with forces that frustrate, deprive, and even oppress them, but it privileged asocial, individual motivations and personality structures. After college, I had been active in a series of "Marx–Freud" study groups and radical psychology projects and spent some of my first postgraduate year in two seminars: one on Hegel and Marx and the other on British object relations theory featuring Winnicott.

That I developed a specific interest in infancy research was due to the fortunate fact that Selma Fraiberg had brought her infant–parent psychotherapy program to the San Francisco General Hospital outpost of the University of California, at which I was working as a postdoctoral fellow and where I have continued to work since then. Fraiberg and her colleagues (Fraiberg, Adelson, & Shapiro, 1975) devised a novel method of psychodynamic intervention into the problems of infants and their families, best known by their rubric about working with the "Ghosts in the Nursery." This innovation has been pivotal in the growth of a robust, worldwide practice of treatment and support for the emotional development of infants and young children. During these same years, the direct observation of infant–parent interaction was coming of age, as a generation of bold and sensitive researchers provided a new understanding of the baby as active, social, and psychologically alive from birth (Bowlby, 1969; Brazelton, Kozlowski, & Main, 1974; Emde, 1988; Greenspan, 1989; Sander, 2002; Stern, 1985). Since many of them were analysts and their findings contradicted the established orthodoxies about the infant and, indeed, the fundamental human motivations, they were sowing the seeds of a new paradigm that was to transform the broader analytic landscape.

For me, the attention to the vital images of infancy offered the prospect of analytic models rooted in direct experience of the most compelling sort. Watching babies and parents interact has much in common with fine arts like dance, music, and film, where form and motion, varying over time, convey the fundamental effects; here these were articulated in an affectively rich field, conveyed through bodily movements and gestures. Psychoanalysis always seemed to me to live on the edge of this kind of immediacy but distanced from it by its insistence on the primacy of the verbal and its peculiar theory of the "instincts" as something prior to human action.

Meanwhile, the beginnings of what was to become the "Relational Revolution" were taking hold, emerging into prominence with Greenberg and Mitchell's (1983) landmark *Object Relations in Psychoanalytic Theory*. Supported by the more socially oriented tradition of interpersonal analysis as well as by insurgent feminism, critical social theory, and the new developmental research without abandoning the Freudian roots, the relational turn seemed best adapted to provide the overarching framework for the new synthesis in which I was interested and that has since come to seem to be the only way that analysis, as a field, can move forward to adapt to the new knowledge and styles of the current moment.

The iconoclastic and flexible relational approach to clinical work also suited me well, both temperamentally and intellectually, offering an alternative to my complex relationship with certain aspects of the analytic clinical method in which I had been trained. Although my ego-psychologically oriented teachers were impressively dedicated, intelligent, and thoughtful and some could be flexible (especially in practice), there still was widespread adherence to the usual shibboleths about neutrality and the like without querying their real value, along with a surprising lack of cosmopolitan interest in the various currents in the analytic world of which I was becoming aware, including self psychology, Lacanian and other French innovations, and, of course, the British object relations groups. This was all further fueled, as it has been for many, by work with children and especially by my work with infants and their parents. Working with babies washes away blocks to spontaneity and authenticity, especially with the psychosocially and economically compromised such as the largely African American and Latina families who used the program at which I was working.

Inasmuch as I have always loved the great analytic traditions and did usually respect my analytic teachers while skeptical of them, my own long-standing interest in interdisciplinary approaches was reinforced in this moment. I read through the infancy research literature and became involved in both the infant mental health and analytic worlds, especially through The National Center for Clinical Programs (now zero to three) and the Division of Psychoanalysis (39) of the American Psychological Association, where the relational turn was gaining national attention. I began to make a series of presentations in both arenas, bringing analytic ideas to the broader groups involved in infant intervention at the same time that I was integrating infant observation into the analytic area. Overall, I saw myself as a bridge-builder loyal to the Freudian enthusiasms for ambiguity, fantasy, and the ineffability of what can be said and known about oneself. At the same time, I contested the rigidities and orthodoxies that stood in the way of a pragmatic, contemporary approach that could encompass comprehensively what really seemed immediate and experientially compelling in analysis. I still felt that the extraordinary world of infants points us in that direction.

The following paper, then, rests on my conviction that intersubjectively oriented relational analysis, among the analytic orientations, provides the most integrative and comprehensive framework for psychoanalytic developmental thinking. Writing for a special issue of *Contemporary Psychoanalysis* edited by Jay Greenberg in honor of Stephen Mitchell, I worked to reflect Mitchell's own complex and critical approach to this problematic. As was typical, Mitchell sought to preserve and extend what has been valuable in the existing traditions while clarifying their limitations and conceptual and empirical flaws so as to formulate a forward-moving approach. On one hand, the "classical" approaches, including the contemporary Freudian and Kleinian, have been constrained from embracing the new developmental research by their loyalty to the primacy of the endogenous, irrational motives in their theories and clinical work. While these colleagues are sometimes seriously interested in the new developmental ideas, their approach to them is typically conservative and piecemeal, falling short of a generous reconsideration of the issues that are actually raised. From a different vantage point, interpersonalists have also been wary of developmental thinking, as they have noted the risks of overemphasizing the regressive aspects of the analytic situation.

Partly motivated by my interest in updating the traditional theories without jettisoning them, I have been particularly interested in a complex, nonreductionistic mediation between developmental research and theories with analysis, one that does not overlook either the subtleties by which early relationship patterns are transformed into later psychological structures or the intricacies of the adult analytic situation, with all its puzzling twists and turns. In general, the applications of infancy research to analysis have been very valuable, including pointing to serious flaws in the established orthodoxies, bringing lived experience, especially of emotions and the actual body, into psychoanalysis, and calling our attention to the importance of the observable details and patterns of dyadic interaction, especially the nonverbal and affective. Overall, inasmuch as the basic observations have highlighted the dramatic impacts of relationships, interpersonal attention, and recognition processes, they have spurred and buttressed the broad relational move to two-person thinking.

References

Bowlby, J. (1969). *Attachment and loss, vol. 1: Attachment.* New York: Basic Books.

Brazelton, T. B., Kozlowski, B., & Main, M. (1974). The origins of reciprocity: The early mother–infant interaction. In M. Lewis & L. Rosenblum (Eds.), *The effect of the infant on its caregiver.* New York: Wiley.

Emde, R. (1988). Development terminable and interminable: I. Innate and motivational factors from infancy. *International Journal of Psychoanalysis, 69,* 23–42.

Fraiberg, S., Adelson, E., & Shapiro, V. (1975). Ghosts in the nursery: A psychoanalytic approach to the problem of impaired infant–mother relationships. *Journal of the American Academy of Child Psychiatry,* 387–422.

Greenberg, J., & Mitchell, S. (1983). *Object relations in psychoanalytic theory.* Cambridge, MA: Harvard University Press.

Greenspan, S. (1989). *The development of the ego: Implications for personality theory, psychopathology, and the psychotherapeutic process.* Madison, CT: International Universities Press.

Sander, L. W. (2002). Thinking differently: Principles of process in living systems and the specificity of being known. *Psychoanalytic Dialogues, 2,* 11–42.

Stern, D. N. (1985). *The interpersonal world of the infant.* New York: Basic Books.

Key Points of a Psychoanalytic Developmental Perspective[*]

The broad and fundamental context for this paper is as follows:

1. The study of human development is fundamentally interdisciplinary and integrative. It integrates a range of disciplines from genetics and neuroscience to history, economics and sociocultural studies. Developmental psychoanalysis can read at the center of such integration.

2. Studying child development, especially infant development, helps us understand the transactions among sociocultural and economic influences and "biology," especially as they organize at the level of individual people. To the extent that it is possible to talk about, this field helps clarify questions about "nature and nurture."

3. Current developmental research and theory show that relationships between children and the people that care for them—*emotionally as well as physically*—are at the core of the developmental process.

Individual factors cannot be understood sensibly or effectively without reference to their social contexts. (Usually, the converse holds, at least at the level of individuals.) There is a striking consilience among the various disciplines about this.

4. Among the various psychoanalytic orientations, this direction is most consistent with intersubjectively oriented relational psychoanalysis.

5. Psychoanalytic theories rely on accounts of child development to express their basic assumptions and to buttress their arguments about them. Developmental imagery is a prominent factor in how analysts organize clinical data. Analytic theories seek coherence among their theories of early development, motivation, psychic structure, psychopathology, and clinical technique.

Relational Psychoanalysis and Developmental Thinking: An Overview

Psychoanalytic theories rely on accounts of child development to express their basic assumptions and to buttress their arguments about them. Developmental imagery is a prominent factor in how analysts organize clinical data. Analytic theories establish coherence among their theories of early development, motivation, psychic structure, psychopathology, and clinical technique.

Relational psychoanalysis has linked to those developmental models that have seen human contact as primary from the beginning. Within psychoanalysis, British object relationalists, interpersonalists, and self psychologists have highlighted this, while contemporary relationally oriented infant researchers have extended this orientation. They have contradicted the Freudian–Kleinian image of the irrational baby by describing the youngest infants' organizing, interpersonal competences.

Overall, relational analysis provides an acute integration of analytic theory and technique with contemporary developmental psychoanalysis and developmental psychology overall, rooted as it is in the view that people are essentially oriented to human relationships, throughout the life span. But while relational psychoanalysis draws heavily on the infant research image of the adaptive, social infant, it does not subsume its own developmental model to it. While frankly developmentalist, it has synthesized that point of view with a number of other crucial emphases: gender theory, social theory, trauma studies, nonlinear dynamic systems theories, and the irrationalist psychoanalytic orientations, all anchored in a philosophical orientation in contemporary dialectical constructivist hermeneutic epistemologies. In addition, the influence of developmental thinking has been annealed with interpersonal psychoanalysis. The interpersonalists' enthusiasm for the immediacy of direct interactions in the present provides a counterweight to the temptation to cast the analytic situation in the form of the child–parent relationship, at the expense of its other dynamisms.*

Stephen Mitchell's Elaboration of the Role of Developmental Thinking in Analytic Theory and Clinical Work

In addition to proposing and applying an array of brilliant psychoanalytic ideas, Stephen Mitchell was acutely aware of the role of such ideas in shaping analysts' thinking, in both our intellectual discourse and clinical work. His seminal volumes sparking the relational turn, *Object Relations in Clinical Psychoanalysis* (Greenberg & Mitchell, 1983) and *Relational Concepts in Psychoanalysis* (Mitchell, 1988), are remarkable explications of the underlying assumptions and clinical uses of key analytic theories. Throughout his subsequent work, he remains mindful of the consequences of the various applications of developmental thinking and relies heavily on it, both in the clinical explorations of *Hope and Dread in Psychoanalysis* (1993b) and *Influence and Autonomy in Psychoanalysis* (1997) and then even more explicitly in *Relationality*'s (2000) synthesis of Loewald with leading British object relationalists, and finally in the exploration of the implications of attachment theory for erotics and romance in the posthumously published *Can Love Last?* (2002).

In *Relational Concepts in Psychoanalysis*, Mitchell (1988) located the problematics of the legacy of childhood in adult life as a matter of complex tensions and mediations, distinguishing the "relational-conflict" perspective from both the purely developmentalist and the drive-ego oriented models. He acutely identified the value of thinking about early experiences to yield both metaphors for analytic work and direct information about character formation, but he also cautioned against the dual temptations of reducing adult pathology to childhood difficulties and casting therapeutic action as little more than the provision of what was missing in the past; as in his treatment of so many other core issues in the relational project, he was both

---

* In this way, relational psychoanalysis differed in its inception from self psychology, with which it shares a number of assumptions and antecedents; it has been both more inclusive of a variety of influences and less reliant on the direct analogy of the therapeutic dyad to parent–child care. Mitchell took care to distinguish his "relational-conflict" perspective from more purely developmentalist approaches. This gap has narrowed as the original Kohutian model has included a variety of new influences, including the sophisticated intersubjectivism of Stolorow and his many substantial cocontributors and the various efforts to integrate nonlinear systems theories, including developmental systems theories (e.g., Beebe & Lachmann, 2002; Seligman, 2005; Stolorow, 1997).

critical and integrative as he approached established models. The relations between present and past are complex and mediated, by time, will, realities, the immediacies of current situations, and so on.

Mitchell (1988) described how each theory generates its own "metaphor of the baby" that organizes theorizing and clinical data. All things being equal, the self psychologist might pay more attention to the patient's long-ings to be admired while the drive-ego analyst would attend to rivalrous feelings. In addition, the same phenomenon might be interpreted in differ-ent ways: The Kleinian analyst may hear an account of separation anxiety as reflecting the analysand's concerns about destructiveness, whereas an attachment-oriented analyst might hear it as a sign of attachment insecu-rity. Developmental formulations reflect analytic models' core assumptions: What are the core motivations? What are the origins of fantasies and other forms of primitive psychic life? What are the origins of psychopathology? How continuous is adulthood with childhood and with which eras of child-hood? Is the relationship to other people, and to reality in general, innate or acquired? (For further elaboration of this, see Lichtenberg, 1983; Lachmann, 2001; Seligman, 2001; Stern, 1985.)

Implications of the "Relational Baby" for Theories of Early Development, Psychic Structure, Psychopathology, and Clinical Technique

To gloss them quickly, analytic theories of development can be roughly sorted into three groups (which correspond roughly, but not completely, to the groups that Greenberg & Mitchell, 1983, propose): (1) those that emphasize the primacy of irrational solipsistic drive-instincts; (2) those that emphasize relationships; and (3) mixed models. The baby in the drive-instinct model is primitive, motivated to reduce internal tension, with little or no sense of the distinction between herself and other peo-ple. Interest in social relationships is secondary to the primitive motives and is acquired in the course of development. Normal development is thus relatively discontinuous, because this early stage is quite differ-ent from psychological maturity. Primitive psychopathology is analogous with very early development. These models are based, by and large, on retrospective inferences from analyses. For this reason, they might be more properly called genetic models, rather than developmental, because they look backward rather than emphasizing forward movement and growth. (Rapaport & Gill, 1959, made this particular distinction in their seminal paper on the metapsychological perspectives.) Although they differ significantly, Freud's and Klein's models are the most striking examples here.

In contrast, the "relational baby" is oriented to the outside world from the beginning, and particularly prepared for human interaction; social relations are a primary motive. Although very dependent, this baby's mind is organized, becoming increasingly complex and integrated as it meets a supportive caretaking environment. Attachment relationships, selfobject functions, and the various autonomous ego structures are all examples of such phenomena. Thus, early development is continuous with later development, since these same processes organize adult personality. Primitive psychopathology is not the same as infancy, because normal infants are not disorganized or primitive, just less organized and more dependent; psychopathology is a variant of development rather than a fixation to an early developmental stage. Direct observation of infants and children is given more weight. Interpersonal psychoanalysis, self psychology, attachment theory, and the ego-developmental side of Hartmannian and Eriksonian ego psychology (Hartmann, 1956; Erikson, 1950) are all in this camp.

"Mixed models" preserve both images of the baby, to varying degrees and with different integrations. Winnicott's (1960) developmental scheme is the most subtle and extraordinary of these, capturing the distinctive, bodily based frailty and interdependency of infants' worlds without sacrificing a sense of their social nature. Many of the ego psychologists who worked within the structural model continued to maintain the image of babies' primitivity even as they acknowledged their capacities; Hartmann (1956), Mahler, Pine, and Bergman (1975), Kernberg (1991), and Anna Freud and her followers may be included here.

Relational Psychoanalysis and the Consolidation, Extension, and Sophistication of the Developmental Perspective

Historical Backgrounds: Developmental Perspectives Within the Prerelational Analytic Paradigms

When the relational movement emerged in the 1980s, an influential developmentally oriented perspective had already materialized in North American psychoanalysis. Early on, ego psychology had declared an interest in motives and processes that were autonomous of the drives and called for research on child development. In addition, its links to child analytic work were quite substantial. Child analysts like Anna Freud, Erik Erikson, and Margaret Mahler had become very influential, and the direct observation of infants was well under way.

Meanwhile, the extension of psychoanalytic psychotherapy to a broader, "subneurotic" population led analytic therapists to reconceptualize their work in terms of developmental deficits rather than as a matter of drive-defense conflicts alone: Technical constraints were modified to permit more interaction and direct emotional contact. The burgeoning interest in pre-oedipal psychopathology brought further attention to early childhood and dislocated the Oedipus complex as the focal moment in personality organization. This shift had the broader effect of loosening the hold of the psychosexual instinct theory, sustained as it was by the centrality of the oedipal triangle in the dominant analytic models. Attention shifted to the parent–infant dyadic processes at the foundations of ego development, which were less a matter of drives than of care and interpersonal organization. Other factors, including emergent feminism and the beginnings of psychopharmacologic, neuroscientific, and infant observation research, also supported this dislocation.

Many analysts began to move beyond the syntheses of the classical model with the developmental-relationally oriented perspectives that had already emerged. Instead, they declared that the established assumptions were outmoded and should be replaced by new ones that emphasized the fundamental interpersonal processes that organized senses of self and others. Although Sullivan (1953), Erikson (1950), and Bowlby (1969) had already delineated such basic perspectives, Kohut's (1977) self psychology now gathered attention both outside and within the drive-ego hegemony and was a basic challenge to some of its most established theories. As it was augmented and transformed by the intersubjectivist vision of philosophically oriented analysts such as Stolorow and his colleagues (Atwood & Stolorow, 1984) and intersubjectivist infancy researchers like Demos (1988), Emde (1983), and Stern (1985), it was a pillar of the broad relational-intersubjective turn.

Relational Psychoanalysis as an Integrative Paradigm Shift

Thus, by the 1980s, several of the basic assumptions that had organized psychoanalysis' intellectual–political centers were dislocated. Relational analysis in general, and Stephen Mitchell in particular, came along at the right time. The new "relational" innovation took the dislocation of the classical assumptions to its logical and pragmatic conclusion, with the radical declaration that a new paradigm was in order. Relationships were seen as the primary motivators and organizers of psychic life; the dynamic transaction between people, rather than within the individual minds, was the primary context for theory building and clinical technique. Reality was on a par with the intrapsychic, and present and past were in a dynamic interplay rather than either being reducible to the other. In the fundamental intersubjectivist turn, both analysis and development were now described as "two-person" systems, and the analyst's authority was relocated as derived from the analytic setting rather than his or her capacity to be an instrument to discern the facts of the patient's psychic life.

Relational analysis consolidated a number of currents that were filtering into the psychoanalytic arena—feminism, intersubjectivist-phenomenological philosophy, the hermeneutic-constructivist critique of the analyst's authority, research into early development, an overall interest in democratization of psychoanalytic institutions. Relational analytic culture and theorizing declared the virtues of inclusiveness, a strategy and sentiment that Mitchell embodied in both his writing and political style. Thus, relational psychoanalysis drew on a number of antecedents and sought to integrate them under the new paradigm. In this way, it went further at its inception than either the Kohutian self psychology and the established ego psychology. The timing of its emergence was an important factor in this, inasmuch as many of the new influences were more fully visible at the time of its inception.

Developmental Research Supporting the Relational Perspective

Infant development research played a central role in all of this. By the 1980s, the shift to the image of the competent, social infant was well under way, and the effects of this shift in undermining some of the established "one-person" assumptions were already influential. At the same time that these questions were raised within the broader analytic arena, there was an explosion of direct observational research into infancy by developmental psychologists and pediatricians as well as by analysts. Analysts since Freud had been theorizing a passive, primitive, and disorganized infant on the basis of retrospective hypothesizing, but these findings showed that babies, from the beginning, were fundamentally social, oriented to evoke and respond to caregivers, affectively articulate and influential on their environments, and able to distinguish self from others. Taken along with new clinical problems, these new observations dislocated the instinct model's assumptions about infancy and, correspondingly, about the bedrock of human psychology and the corresponding theories of early development, psychic structure, psychopathology, and clinical technique. Instead, the dyad, rather than the individual, was the fundamental unit of development, and dyadic structures organized mental life from the start. Consistent with the broader relational paradigm, the fundamental units of psychic structure were organized in two-person systems that could be manifested internally, externally, or in the intersubjective spaces in between.

Since relational psychoanalysis was consolidating at the same time as these findings, it was in a special position to integrate them from the beginning, and at the most fundamental level. A number of the core concepts from the infant research directly paralleled the relational view of human nature and clinical interaction, including the view of the infant–parent relationship as a mutual influence structure; the transactional systems perspective; the emphases on affect and dyadic internal representations; the attention to interactions and nonverbal communication; the central role of reality in development; the assumption of continuity between earlier and later developmental stages; and the conceptualization of attachment and intersubjectivity as fundamental motivation systems (see, e.g., Lachmann, 2001; Seligman, 1996, 2001; Stern, 1985). In addition, the relational synthesis involved a reading of the new research that highlighted certain dimensions that were not so explicitly developed in it, such that there was a reciprocal relationship between them. The new analytic interest in the development of subjectivity and intersubjectivity and the dynamics of recognition added a crucial dimension (e.g., Benjamin, 1995; Stolorow, Atwood, & Brandchaft, 1994).

Implications for Clinical Theory and Technique I: The Psychoanalytic Relationship as a Dyadic System

Applied to analytic clinical work, the image of the infant and parent as a dyadic mutual influence system supports the emerging relational-intersubjectivist conception of analysis as a fundamentally two-person process. Thus, the image of the detached and "objective" analyst has been dislocated. Engagement, rather than positivist observation, was placed at the center of the therapeutic action. As in early development, analysis depends on the basic human affinity to be activated and changed in a two-person, coconstructed system. Interventions are mediated in the interpersonal-intersubjective process rather than just in the isolated mind. While the direct effects of understanding are not dismissed, the effects of various kinds of interactions have now been taken up by the contemporary relational analysts.

Intersubjectivity as an Orienting Principle: Analytic Dyads and Infant–Parent Relationships as Bidirectional Transactional Systems

Both infancy research and the relational psychoanalytic perspective rest on the assumption of the inextricability of individuals and social surround. Just as the infant's development is dependent on caregivers, the analytic process depends on the analyst–patient relationship. We become aware of ourselves as we are seen by others, and it is in becoming aware of others that we develop our own sense of self. Self and others cannot be understood without reference to one another. The fundamental constructs for understanding development and psychoanalysis are "self-with-other" units.

Overall, the developmental research into early development synergizes with the emerging relational model of analysis as a two-person system, with therapist and patient each affecting one another in myriad ways, verbal and nonverbal, in the rapid flux of moment-to-moment interactions as well as in the broad sweeps of the evolving relationship. The image of the infant–parent relationship as a mutual influence system has clarified and buttressed this perspective. The core research on the infant–parent relationship has defined it as a bidirectional, mutual-influence system, in which babies and their caregivers are essentially inextricable and cannot be conceptualized without reference to one another. Winnicott's (1960) maxim, "There is no infant ... [without the mother]," has been borne out as an observable fact.

In particular, the relational interest in the inseparability of transference and countertransference closely parallels the essentially dyadic focus of the infancy researchers. Just as infants activate the maternal capacities of the mother as they are sustained by them, analysts cannot help but find themselves implicated in the patient's relational dilemmas, and, indeed, will find their own personalities implicated in their response to them. Although crude parallelisms to the infant–parent system have been rejected as the particular asymmetries of the analytic situation were noted, relational psychoanalysis nonetheless made the clearest statement that the analyst and patient are coconstructing a relationship in which neither of them can be seen as distinct from the other. Relationalists have further applied their clinical emphasis on mutual influence in dyads to revisit some of the traditional approaches to infant–parent interactions. Projective identification, for example, has been described as occurring in a bidirectional interpersonal field in which the infant and parent, or patient and analyst, are acting together to construct a dyadic situation, even when one member of the dyad is more influential than the other in the situation and even when the situation is largely experienced internally (Ogden, 1982; Seligman, 1999).

The developmental researchers' "transactional systems perspective" (Sameroff & Chandler, 1975) adds to this. Here, factors in systems are understood as having their effects as they articulate with other factors rather than in a simple linear manner: The various factors transform each other at any given moment, and especially as they interact over time and create new patterns. They cannot be understood in isolation. For example, an infant with a mild constitutional hypersensitivity to stimulation may become overwhelmed with a hypomanic mother but may flourish with a cautious one. The "same" temperamental attribute becomes different depending on its context.

In addition to paralleling the relational clinical perspective, the transactional-mutual influence model also links to its hermeneutic-constructivist epistemological orientation. Taking self-with-other as the basic unit of psychic structure and analytic interaction also implies that analytic knowledge itself cannot be extricated from the intersubjective field. Interventions themselves change the situation into which they are offered, and the analyst's own psychology and countertransference responses are implicated in technique. While various analysts have noted this phenomenon, the relationists have made it a central focus of their clinical model and have differed from many previous observers (although not all) in taking an affirmative approach to such uncertainty. Relational psychoanalysis has made the fullest link among the epistemological, clinical, and developmental aspects of emerging psychoanalytic currents (Hoffman, 1998; Benjamin, 1995; Spezzano, 1996).

Observing Intersubjectivity: Internal Representations, Affect, and Interaction in Developmental and Clinical Process

The infant researchers have carefully and vividly made sense of the nonverbal, affective rhythms and choreographies of infant–parent interactions to show how emotionally influential and expressive they are, thus confirming the ordinary intuitions of parents and most everyone else who takes time to look at babies. From this vantage point, they take for granted that infants create and directly experience actual interactions. They thus extend and confirm the intersubjectivist perspective, rooted as it is in the simultaneity and inextricability of the intrapsychic and interpersonal dimensions.

Implementing and supporting this general perspective, the developmentalists, including both the infant observers and developmentally oriented adult analysts, have generated an array of specific categories that capture how relationships and their internal representations organize internal psychic life and interpersonal interactions. These include both broad, macroanalytic categories, such as empathy, reciprocity, recognition, and the secure-insecure-disorganized attachment classifications, and the microanalytic categories, like contingency, affect attunement, and disruption and repair. Some of these are derived directly from analytic practice while others emerge from the direct observation of infants, but all are presented as salient in both arenas.* In addition, some of the established languages of the object relations models, such as projective identification, have been similarly

---

* An array of convergent concepts have been offered, including generalized representations of interactions (Stern, 1985), internal working models (Bowlby, 1980), forms of constructing intersubjectivity (Seligman, 1999), interpersonal expectancies and implicit relational knowledge (Lyons-Ruth, 1998), model scenes (Lichtenberg, 1989), and other specific formulations of self-development including those of Emde (1983), Demos (1988), and Fast (1985).

understood as descriptions of relational forms that can be observed in both infancy and psychoanalyses. These various forms are often saturated with affect and bodily expressiveness but can encompass verbal language later in life.

Contemporary accounts of clinical interaction draw on these various descriptors. At times, this is quite explicit. For example, the attachment researchers describe the different categories of secure, insecure, and the disorganized attachment (Hesse & Main, 2000). Beebe and Lachmann (2002) describe processes, such as "disruption and repair" or "chase and dodge," in adult therapies, having first noted them in mother–infant interaction. Other clinical accounts are more implicit in their elaboration of various two-person interaction structures. A number of papers describe the mutual interplay of patients' and analysts' interactions, inner states, emotional and behavioral cues, and the like, including careful attention to the moment-to-moment details of how various of the patient's particular gestures and statements affect the analyst's inner experience (Knoblauch, 1997).

Many of these conceptualizations emphasize nondeclarative psychological patterns that operate at a nonreflective level of personality organization: A number of writers have referred to the concept of procedural knowledge to describe the ways that actions can have direct effects without conscious reflection. Interpersonal relations are like riding a bicycle or driving a car: You follow certain patterns without thinking about them at all. Lyons-Ruth (1998) coined the term *implicit relational knowing* to capture such processes in the social arena. Developmental neuropsychoanalytic researchers, such as Schore (1994, 2003a, 2003b), have extended these efforts to show how brain development is directly affected by actual experience, including by psychotherapy.

Implications for Clinical Theory and Technique II: The Intertwining of Action and Reflection, Present and Past and Internal World and External Reality

The Affirmative Approach to Analytic Interaction and the Direct Observation of Actual Interactions in Development

Thus, the relational-developmentalist innovation offers an elaborate and detailed perspective on how internal life is articulated in dyadic interactions in general and therapeutic interactions in particular. Pragmatically, this approach offers a number of specific ways of helping analysands see how their behavior reflects their inner experience. The developmental-interactional descriptors offer detailed ways of talking about both verbal, and especially nonverbal, interactions that can be affectively rich and quite experience near; this is especially relevant in the transference–countertransference dynamics. The potentials of talking about "what is going between us" are affirmed as capturing the meanings and developmental potentials of interactions rather than avoided as resistant distraction.*

More broadly, developmental psychology supports an affirmative approach to interaction in the analytic setting. Relational psychoanalysis synthesizes the developmental perspective with the interactionist-interpersonalist influence that was essential in its inception. Unlike the classical analysts, the interpersonal analysts had always affirmed the direct effects of analytic interaction for therapeutic change. Action is not necessarily seen as regressive or in the way of the analytic process; interaction is not only inevitable but also potentially progressive. As in child development, interactions have both regressive and progressive potentials, and the point is to find the most adaptive way of solving the issues at hand rather than expecting verbal communication. This respect for the actual analytic interaction is supported by the developmental research, and is an aspect of the broader elevation of actual reality in the relational paradigm from its secondary position in the classical instinct models.

An affirmative approach to analytic interaction, however, does not intrinsically devalue interpretive techniques or theories of phantasies or genetic reconstruction, although some have taken it this way.† Once we assume that interaction and interpretation are not intrinsically opposed, the question of how they affect one another can be approached in the context of each specific clinical situation. While it may sometimes be true that understanding, recognition, and self-reflection are obviated by action, there is no particular reason to assume that this should be true in general. In addition, the sense of being understood is a feature of relationships that is often established nonverbally. This is indeed clearest in the observation of infant–parent interactions, where understanding and recognition, including specific interpretations of psychological states, are conveyed in affectively charged interaction sequences. In a compelling elaboration of this, the attachment researchers have shown that secure attachment and the sense of being understood are synergistic (Main, 2000; Fonagy, 2000; see also Seligman, 2000; Slade, 2000).

---

* Along similar lines, Levenson (1983) wrote, "The cardinal question for the patient may not be "What does it mean?" but "What's going on around here?" (p. ix).

† Some approaches to the infant research have directly shown that the phantasy-oriented concepts can be directly observed to a greater extent than has often been thought. In one of my own papers, for example, I have described interactive dynamics between a father and a 3-day-old infant that reflect the patterns of primitive projective identification and can be seen as "structuring" such patterns in the boy's internal world (Seligman, 1999).

Past and Present in Transaction

This approach correlates with another basic emphasis of the relational orientation: that the past is carried into the present so as to be directly expressed and transformed at the same time. Such transactions take many forms. These include both actual reenactments in current situations, along with internal representations of all sorts—images, affects, bodily states, interpersonal expectations, fantasies, dreams, memories, and more. Such representations are not precise, nor are they veridical, but instead reflect subjective experience as it is elaborated in the ongoing transactions through which any given moment in development is taken into the next, and then both transformed and preserved as time goes forward.* This approach differs from the contemporary Freudian emphasis on the resistance of the analytic surface to the expression of underlying psychic reality. In this way, it enhances the possibility of the analyst and patient being on the same side. Just as the "baby watchers" can claim to know a great deal about babies from their observations, analysts can claim to know a lot from what they see, hear, and feel.

In confidently asserting the connections between childhood and adulthood, the psychoanalytic approach to developmental research goes further than the developmental researchers themselves do; the academic developmentalists have generally been quite cautious about this, oriented as they are by their careful empiricist constraints. The ambitious linkage of present and past is particular to psychoanalysis, with its single-case orientation, its reliance on clinical inference, and, currently, its affirmative use of such hermeneutic validity criteria as narrative efficacy and goodness of fit. Psychoanalysis established itself by linking childhood and adulthood and remains the most articulate of all the human sciences in regard to such matters.

Relational Analysis Is Not Reparenting: Mitchell's Constructive Critique of Oversimplification in Developmental Models of Psychopathology and Therapeutic Action

Overall, there is thus a dialectical approach to the problem of the effects of the past in the present. On one hand, the essential effects of affective and cognitive immaturity are taken very seriously, and concepts such as fantasies, drives, or primitive needs and states of minds are not neglected. Although adult events may be given more weight than in some other analytic approaches, childhood is still regarded as the most influential. On the other hand, the relational approach to development and psychopathology

---

* Lachmann (2001) wrote about the "dialectic of repetition and transformation."

does not rely on a conception of child psychology as organized by endogenous, infantile givens that may be preserved directly into adulthood if development goes badly. Similarly, there is no assumption that the psychopathogenic situation is preserved so as to be presented anew in the analytic situation. Instead, there is a dynamic interaction between the repeated past and the current moment.

Mitchell (1988) is explicit about differentiating the relational-clinical principle of finding the resonances of the past in the present, inside and outside of the analytic relationship, from a more reductionist orientation that seeks the infantile part of the patient so as to offer what was not previously provided. He approvingly quotes Levenson's (1983) disparaging characterization of developmental fixation theory looking for something in the patient that is "stuck...like a fishbone in the craw of his maturity" (p. 142).

This is a subtle but important distinction. In *Relational Concepts in Psychoanalysis*, Mitchell (1988) illustrates it by commenting on one of Michael Balint's (1968) clinical illustrations. Balint describes a case in which his patient made the extraordinary move of somersaulting in one of her sessions, which led to striking analytic progress. Mitchell critiques Balint's idea that this remarkable gesture already existed within the patient rather than being created between them. Mitchell instead stresses the coconstruction of the transformative moment. Rather than being "something that has been contained within this woman, repressed, submerged, pushing for release... the act did not simply emerge—it was invited. It was Balint, the adult analyst, who suggested that the patient try a somersault; what was new was her ability to respond to the invitation" (Mitchell, 1988, p. 155).

From this perspective, Mitchell delineated the relational-conflict model by critiquing those earlier developmental-arrest models that specified the provision of what was missing in childhood as the main mode of therapeutic action, such as those of the self psychological and middle schools. At the same time, he enhanced the interpersonalist-interactionist model by including the more sophisticated insights about development, psychic structure, and psychopathology that were emerging from those analytic innovations along with the new developmental research. As he so often did, he relied heavily on the very ideas that he critiqued to create extraordinarily advanced and subtle syntheses (see also Aron, 2003).

Mitchell's (1988) basic statement remains acute and generative. Having already distinguished the relational perspective from those based on drive theories, he goes on to differentiate the relational-conflict and developmental-arrest models:

> Developmental-arrest authors, who draw on relational-model theory skewed by the developmental tilt, tend to view the patient as an infantile self in an adult body, fixed in developmental time and awaiting interpersonal conditions

which will make further development possible. In this view, what was missed and is still missing needs to be provided essentially in the form in which it was missed the first time around. The developmental tilt has collapsed generic relational needs into infantile forms, and the analyst must enter at the point of the so-called environmental failure, providing relational experiences as replacements for those the infant never encountered.

From a relational-conflict perspective, disturbances in early relationships with caretakers seriously distort subsequent relatedness, not by freezing or fixing infantile needs, but by setting in motion a complex process through which the child creates an interpersonal world (or world of object relations) out of what is available.... The analysand enters treatment with a narrowed relational matrix; he seeks connections by projecting and recreating familiar, constricted relational patterns, experiencing all important relationships (especially the one with the analyst) along old lines. He continually reinternalizes and consolidates these relational configurations. The central process in psychoanalytic treatment is the relinquishment of ties to these relational patterns, thereby allowing an openness to new and richer interpersonal relations. (p. 170)

Here, the picture of the internal world is very complex, with various internal representations of relationships dissociated from, or in conflict with, one another and actualized through evoking reactions in important people that further complicate the already difficult thicket of relational opportunities and choices. Despite the misconceptions of its critics, the relational model was never meant as a prescription for reparenting or the simple provision of a replacement for missed infantile experience. Mitchell (1988) stresses the patient's giving up old relational patterns to gain more freedom in the present.

As relational theory evolved, this notion has become more complex, annealed with new ideas such as the restoration and integration of dissociated selfobject experiences. Various modes of therapeutic action may be involved in bringing about these outcomes, and their effects are regarded as synergistic rather than exclusive. These include insight, interrupting old relational patterns, the creation of new conditions of safety against which established expectations can be reviewed (see, e.g., Greenberg, 1996; Weiss, Sampson, & the Mount Zion Psychotherapy Research Group, 1986), containment and holding, empathy and the working through of disruptions in the therapeutic tie (Kohut, 1977; Beebe & Lachmann, 2002), enhancing reflective functioning, interpretation, and such innovative notions as negotiation of paradox (Pizer, 1992), and the transformative "now moment" (Stern, Sander, Nahum, Harrison, Buschweiler-Stern, & Tronick, 1998). This is, of course, a very incomplete list, suggestive rather than comprehensive.

Overall, then, both action and reflection and past and present are seen as having a transactional relationship in the therapeutic process. Just as the past is always immanent in the present without being reducible to it, analytic interaction inevitably reflects the inner world but is simultaneously a new creation. As with the infant and parent, the resonances of the past in the present may be elaborated in interactions, including quite irrational and fantasmatic representations, and, as with older children and adults, they may be articulated in explicitly reflective thinking. There are, of course, many blends and points in between enactment and reflections. Indeed, from the relational point of view, it is those moments where enactment and reflection are in some kind of resonance, rather than where reflection has subsumed action, where the greatest therapeutic gain is likely. Again, the analyst's task is not simply to unearth the past in the present or to attain some idealized provision of a novel experience but to "find a way to be with patients that gives them the greatest opportunity, despite the odds, to make better lives for themselves" (Hoffman, 1998, p. xxxi).

An ordinary vignette from one of my own cases illustrates this approach. Ms. A was a sophisticated and thoughtful attorney and single mother, but she would abruptly end her intimate relationships with men whenever she became close to someone. As her analysis proceeded, we were slowly able to understand how this involved a reaction to her childhood experience of having been the target of ongoing erotic intrusion from her brother and uncles at the same time that her parents were remote and inattentive. She had little confidence in the transformative effects of any close relationship, finding herself overwhelmed with a sense of danger and stimulating, troubling thoughts in the romantic relationships and in analysis.

At one point in our work together, a number of helpful sessions took place shortly before I announced an upcoming summer vacation. Shortly thereafter, Ms. A announced that she would have to stop analysis altogether, beginning with the next week's sessions. With a tone of dismissive irritation, she said that things were getting too hard and "it wasn't worth it."

When she did in fact miss the first meeting of the next week, I was aware that calling to suggest that she come back and talk things through might well be taken as a pressuring invitation to more suffering whereas not calling would be neglectful and dismissive of our close and productive analytic relationship. I did call, and Ms. A agreed to meet, albeit ambivalently. I described the relational-conflict dilemma in which we found ourselves: If she continued, she would be succumbing to a confinement, but if she left, she would be depriving herself once again of something that could be very helpful, following the affective-interpersonal assumption that deep relationships couldn't really make any difference.

Ms. A now went on to talk with full emotion about her intense "separation anxiety" and her sense that something quite bad was about to happen. When I made the amplifying comment that she must find me dangerous, she said that she in fact knew that I was not going to hurt her. I found this very moving and was a bit relieved of my own countertransference anxiety about pressing her to continue in analysis. This made things even more challenging, she explained, since she was finding herself in the grip of anxieties that she knew did not make sense. We could now talk about how no one in her family had responded to her sense that something was wrong, leaving her feeling abandoned and doubting that her own feelings were valid. She now felt freer to consider that it might turn out different here, and the prospect of things going forward increased.

Implications for Clinical Theory and Technique III: Developmental Concepts and Emerging Clinical Emphases

There has been a substantial development in the relational conception of clinical psychoanalysis since Mitchell's original statements, including by Mitchell himself. A complex set of perspectives is evolving rather than a single statement or consensus. In conceptualizing psychopathology and case formulation, developmental thinking has been incorporated in formulations about the subjective experience of key childhood relationships. As in other analytic models, the relational synthesis of clinical and developmental thinking has generated a series of core themes, or master narratives. These include attachment, recognition, mutuality and its failures, trauma and misrecognition, and the interplay of danger and safety, among many others.

At the most basic level, for example, there is an ongoing focus on establishing and maintaining relational ties, internal and external, throughout the lifespan. Attachment and affect regulation provide a sense of basic security. Attachment theory provides a basic slant, both in its general form asserting that relationship security is an essential human motivation and in its specific forms describing the various categories of attachment security, insecurity, and disorganization. The attachment patterns endure over development, even as they are transformed, and the basic motivation remains central.

In addition, the need to maintain such ties is evoked to explain the tenacity of painful, costly relational patterns. These basic modes were the only ones available to the child in the "pathogenic" family, who therefore cannot conceive of alternatives at an affectively meaningful level, even as an apparently thoughtful adult. To consider that things could be otherwise is to risk loss, isolation, shame, and the like, potentially at a catastrophic level.

The relational-intersubjectivist emphasis on recognition dynamics plays a similar role: Being understood by the people that matter to you is especially important for children but remains important at all ages. Kohut's original selfobject (1977) concept placed recognition into the forefront of psychoanalytic discussions, and the issues have been developed with increasing sophistication by an array of intersubjectivist writers, including Benjamin (1995), Stolorow and colleagues (1994), and Ogden (1994). Many of these writers have been influenced by Hegel and other dialectical and phenomenological philosophers. Lacanian (1949) ideas have also had an effect. Overall, the dynamics of recognition have been rendered with increasing complexity, so as to include issues of dominance and submission, excitement and surrender, the tensions between autonomy and dependency in love and hate, and many other forms. Linkages to other psychological domains, such as trauma, gender, and sexual excitement, have been prominently developed.

Current relational thinking has reemphasized trauma in its account of the origins of psychopathology. This draws on the feminist critique of Freud's abandonment of the seduction theory and the current awareness, in both academic research and the popular mind, of the profound effects of actual trauma, along with direct clinical experience (see, e.g., Allison, 1993; Bromberg, 1998; Davies & Frawley, 1994; Herman, 1992; McCourt, 1996). It also correlates with the current interest in trauma in a number of related fields, including psychiatry, developmental neuroscience, and cultural studies. Much of the research about trauma is developmentally oriented, including both detailed psychological accounts and a recent array of findings about the direct effects of abuse and neglect on brain development (see, e.g., Perry, Pollard, Blakly, Baker, & Vigilante, 1995; Schore, 1994, 2003b).

This approach also synergizes with the relational attention to actual experience. Rather than starting with a preconceived set of psychosexual or even psychosocial challenges that must be solved to attain adequate development, this perspective looks at the particular "bad" experiences that derail development, in the problematic childhood realities that lead each patient to the impasses that bring them to analysis in the first place. The concept of trauma is also being more broadly applied to an array of psychopathologies rather than just in more restricted situations. Overall, this has led to a more open and case-specific approach to case formulation and technique as well as to clinical narratives in the relational-clinical literature (see Davies, 2004; Hoffman, 1998; Mitchell, 1993b; Pizer, 2003, for some striking examples).

The emphasis on "what really happened" correlates with the respectful and affirmative attention to the patient's subjective experience of events, including of childhood events. Rather than start from the Freudian position that experience is likely to involve significant distortion, the contemporary approach takes subjective experience as legitimate in itself rather than parsing out the veridical events and the contribution of the irrational unconscious. This basic turn is linked to the contemporary shift to empathy as the basis for the analyst's inquiry as opposed to the effort to approach the analysand's psychology as a matter of objectively ascertainable facts; Kohut (1977) and, especially, the intersubjectivist self psychologists have been crucial in this direction (Bacal, 1985; Stolorow & Atwood, 1992).

This approach also supports the recognition of an aspect of posttraumatic pathology that has not received sufficient attention until recently. In addition to the overwhelming nature of the experience itself, trauma often occurs in contexts that preclude awareness of its meanings (see, e.g., Bromberg, 1998; Davies & Frawley, 1994; Auerhahn & Peskin, 2003). The child suffers the mind-crushing bind of suffering at the hands of someone on whom he or she depends at the most basic levels. In the classic example, the victim of incest will find it nearly impossible to appreciate how awful the sexual approaches are when the same man who molests her may be so kind at other times and is someone on whom she depends. When others act as if nothing untoward is going on, the difficulties are amplified. A stance of "not knowing what one knows" (Bowlby, 1988) must be maintained to keep the crucial relationships intact.

This, in turn, correlates with dissociation coming to play a key role in the emerging relational approach to psychopathology and clinical technique, as central as that of repression in classical theory (see, e.g., Bromberg, 1998; Davies, 1996). Rather than conceptualizing dissociation as indicative of more primitive pathology or severe trauma, this approach sees it as a form of defensive organization with varying rigidity and fragmenting effects at various developmental-pathological levels.

Along these lines, innovative models of a "relational unconscious" have been proposed (see, e.g., Davies, 1996; Stolorow & Atwood, 1992). These emphasize how thoughts may be inaccessible to conscious reflection because of the various dissociative and mind-fragmenting processes rather than the established concepts of a dynamic unconscious maintained by repression. Similar dynamics are described in terms of experience, which is not formulated in terms of ordinary awareness (Stern, 1997) but in less mentalized forms. As I have said, the developmentalists' concept of "procedural knowledge," currently extended from cognitive psychology to interpersonal relations, captures the way that much of what is known is never put into words but instead preserved in affect-interaction schemas (Beebe & Lachmann, 2002; Clyman, 1992; Lyons-Ruth, 1998; Seligman, 1999).

Closely related to dissociation is the emphasis on multiplicity in self-organization. Rather than looking at self-experience in terms of a single "self" or ego, the relational approach starts with a sense of personal experience with varied potentials, linked to various personal-historical events, cultural pressures and opportunities, and the like. Psychological resilience is understood in terms of the flexible integration of a multiplicity of self-experiences, which may become fragmented and disintegrated in traumatic development. Mitchell opened up this discussion in the relational literature, and it has been elaborately developed by many writers. Harris (2005) captured this conceptualization in her phrase "the softly-assembled self." Again, links with a wide range of related emerging fields are conspicuous here, including neuroscience and postmodern theories of culture and gender as well as developmental psychology.

From this perspective, analysis is understood as facilitating the restoration and integration of aspects of self-experience that have been fragmented or detached; these often make themselves known in interactions whose meaning is not explicit, or disavowed. Bromberg (1998), for example, called upon analysts to "stand in the spaces" between the dissociated "selves," bearing them in mind and enduring the anxiety of painful and contradictory experiences coming into the analytic space. Recent articulations of this perspective formulate the therapeutic effect of the analyst's working with the various projections of the analysand in such a way as to support this aim. Davies (2004), for example, described a case in which she found herself absorbing and barely tolerating her patient's projected experience of her as cruel and withholding. Eventually, she and her patient were able to talk about this in an affectively saturated way, which allowed the patient to integrate and transform these various images of selves and others. My example of Ms. A also illustrates such processes.*

Developmental Assumptions and the Dynamics of Gender and Authority: Dislocating the Oedipus Complex

Another crucial feature of the relational approach to development is the dislocation of the Oedipus complex from the center of the analytic narrative. The classical Freudian theories identify the oedipal phase as the crucial phase for successful development. Its prominence is marked by the traditional delineation of development and psychopathology into pre-oedipal and oedipal. Here, the absence of adequate oedipal resolution is a sign of fundamental developmental weakness, correlated with limited ego development, pathology organized around deficits rather than conflicts, and indications for technical compromises involving "support" rather than interpretation. Contemporary models, including many ego psychological models, have

---

* Similarities to other object relations approaches can be noted here. Winnicott's (1960) notion of the analytic integration of the wounded, walled-off "false self" resonates with the contemporary emphases. Along related lines, contemporary Kleinians' conceptualizations of "pathological organizations" suggest a similar perspective, inasmuch as they describe psychic life becoming organized around internal object configurations which take the place of the person's direct experience of his or her unbearable anxieties and authentic motivations and memories (Rosenfeld, 1971). Bion's (1962) conceptualization of what happens in the absence of the reflective capacity for "thinking" contains many parallels to the notion that trauma precludes awareness of the extraordinary confusion and agony that it creates (Britton, 1992; Fonagy & Target, 1996; Seligman, 1999). Attachment theorists are now thinking along similar lines as they explore the links between trauma, psychic disorganization, and the failure of reflective functioning (Hesse & Main, 2000; Slade, 2000).

softened this distinction. But the oedipal/pre-oedipal dichotomy remains in common use, especially by the contemporary Freudians. In addition, the oedipal narrative has traditionally had a normative, prescriptive function: A particular form of oedipal resolution—the heterosexual identification with the same-sex parent—has been treated as the desired outcome, with other outcomes regarded as pathological.

Relational psychoanalysts, along with self psychological and interpersonalist psychoanalysis, are less reliant on these formulations. This is correlated with the assertion of the fundamental supraordinacy of relational motives, with the marginalization of the irrational drives. Because the drive-oriented theories conceptualize the basic motives as asocial, if not antisocial, they require some set of developmental constructs like the Oedipus complex to integrate the uncivilized, natural motivations into the social world. Hence, the Oedipus complex is the moment in which the dual organizers of social life, gender and restraining authority, become part of the personality. Maturity is fundamentally a matter of mastering the conflicts between the irrational, intrinsic, natural forces and the ordering requirements of social life.

The relational developmental models focus on interpersonal, self object dynamics, and thus do not have the same need to rely on the oedipal triangle to integrate the drives into the social world. The earliest and most basic motivations and states do not necessarily come into conflict with the social world as the child moves more fully into it. There is no special theoretical requirement for a transformational moment like the Oedipus complex: Development is more continuous.*

De-centering the Oedipus Complex and the Constructivist Conception of Authority

The deemphasis on the Oedipus complex correlates with the relational reconceptualization of the analyst's authority. Oedipal authority is paternal, oracular, and suppressive. This is eloquently depicted in Sophocles's play: In the absence of vision or restraint, chaos and destruction ensue. The classical

---

* Even as the Kleinian Middle School innovations emphasized dyadic infant development, they never fully abandoned the theory of the irrational instincts. Fairbairn (1952) and Bowlby (1969) were notable exceptions. In parallel, they kept oedipal development as a simultaneous lynchpin along with the dyadic concepts. The Kleinians relocated oedipal development as a basic aspect of the early phantasmatic object configurations, and many in the middle group offered a dual track theory, maintaining the division between basic, pre-oedipal pathology, which was their primary concern, and less severe, neurotic oedipal pathology, which was left to other analytic theorizing. The ego psychologists and mixed-model theorists maintained the pre-oedipal/oedipal hierarchy, even as they sought to integrate developmental models.

analytic conception of the analyst as the observer of emerging psychic facts, bearing the burden and discipline necessary for "objectivity," is rooted in and supported by the oedipal narrative, which is thus simultaneously moral and developmental. Such authority exists by virtue of its moral necessity and its capacity to see the truth clearly. It is an inevitable given, whose absence or distortion manifests in pathology.

In the relational conceptualization, the analyst's authority is itself an emergent, contingent aspect of the analytic relationship that is created as part of establishing the analytic relationship, and as such, is under ongoing "negotiation," both conscious and unconscious. The analyst's authority is not a given but is derived from the transaction between analyst and patient. The analyst may indeed have substantial expertise, but the patient's interest and attribution of various meanings to this expertise charges it with significance, in the broader context of the transference–countertransference and the overall analytic setting.* The decentering of the Oedipus complex in the developmental narrative thus correlates with the constructivist-dialectical view of the analyst's authority and the mutual influence model drawn both from infancy research and the new "two-person" model of the analytic dyad.

Along these lines, superego development is deemphasized in the relational model. Since involvement with others, including concern and empathy, is at the core of development, a restraining agency is not the primary requirement for adequate development, although it may nonetheless be significant. Instead, cooperation and recognition of others are a fundamental source of moral development. Here again, the shift to a relational model parallels developmental research, such as Kohlberg's (Colby, Kohlberg, Gibbs, & Lieberman, 1983) Piagetian reformulation of moral development (see also Emde, Biringen, Clyman, & Oppenheim, 1991), and feminist critiques, such as Gilligan's (1979) reformulation of the gender-specific aspects of feminine development. In addition, feminist object relations-oriented reformulations of the development of gender and sexual orientation support this deemphasis of the superego as they reinterpret the overall problem of the role of the oedipal situation.

These rereadings also synergize with the possibility of new, broader formulations of the oedipal concept (see, e.g., Chodorow, 1978; Cooper, 2003; Davies, 2003; Greenberg, 1991). Along with suggesting that the oedipal narrative reflects a particular, rather than universal, pathway to sexual orientation and gender identity, gender theorists have suggested a more fluid and flexible version of the oedipal complex itself that allows for various outcomes. (Chodorow's, 1994, title, "Heterosexuality as a Compromise

---

* Sullivan (1953) suggested this insight when he took pains to justify the analyst's authority as a matter of "expertise" rather than taking it for granted.

Formation," embodies this direction.) Others have emphasized the ways that oedipal issues evolve in subsequent development, in forms more varied and complex than the basic mother–father–child triangle that has always typified the established account.

Relationality, Maternal Authority, and the Dynamics of Attachment and Recognition

The relational reorientation also implies that the analyst's power and authority are more like the mother's than the father's. In the dyadic, transactional conception of early development, the mother's being a mother is itself dependent on the infant, at the most fundamental level, and, within the intertwined dyad, is inseparable from the infant's influence. This parallels the relational conception of the analyst's authority as cocreated.

The relational conception of the analyst's role emphasizes security, responsiveness, and recognition rather than hegemonic power like that of the (castrating) father or even the analyst's quasi-scientific skill. Instead, dangers of misrecognition and nonrecognition are given more weight, and the effects of the vulnerable child's choice between collaborating with such misrecognitions or being abandoned are attended to. This is paralleled in the concern that authoritarian analytic practice will itself be retraumatizing. Here, the links to feminism become more obvious, as contemporary developmental imagery affirms what has often been devalued as belonging to the marginalized feminine.

Integrating Maternal Subjectivity Into Development Theory

Another effect of the mutual influence of feminism and the relational approach to development is the recognition of the mother's subjectivity and individuality. Although the British object relations theorists recognized the essential place of the maternal function, they did not pay much attention to the specific psychology of the mother herself: Winnicott's (1958b) extraordinary account of "primary maternal preoccupation" is the exception that proves the rule, since it investigates that phase of maternal psychology characterized by immersion into the maternal role. Kohut (1977), Mahler (1972), and the developmental ego psychologist Hartmann (1956) followed the same pattern, configuring the mother from the point of view of the child's developmental needs.

Feminist revisions of the analytic developmental accounts have more fully asserted the independent character of the mother. Chodorow's (1978) pathbreaking accounts of the intergenerational transmission of the mothering role provided a basic description of the internal gratifications and compromises that were organized in the feminine identification with the maternal. Motherhood was no longer taken for granted but was itself a developmental process with its own interiority. Many other contemporary accounts have taken the mother's subjectivity as an essential, rather than peripheral, part of the child development process. Benjamin (1988) characterized the fundamental dynamics of submission and dominance that are involved in the two-person negotiation of infants' establishing their own subjectivity in relation to their dependence on the mother. Clinical infant observers, such as Fraiberg (Fraiberg, Adelson, & Shapiro, 1975) in her seminal "Ghosts in the Nursery," developed complex accounts of how specific events in the parents' pasts led to specific parenting styles. Although this was most apparent when the parents' own histories were traumatic, the general principle of the intergenerational transmission of parenting style is now well established (Seligman, 1994; Stern, 1995).

Polyphonic Narratives of Gender Development and Morality

As I noted already, this shift also synergizes with the feminist-postmodernist assertion of multiple narratives about the development of gender and sexual orientation. In its typical reading, the oedipal structure implies the suppression of polymorphous perversity in service of a single object choice and takes the repudiation of homosexual wishes in the identification with the same-gender parent as essential to mature sexual development. Relationship-oriented theories that give primacy to interpersonal attachment, intimacy, care, and recognition will be more sympathetic to alternate conceptions of gender and erotic patternings. Rather than treating sexuality as a primary, irreducible factor, relational motivational-developmental theory treats it as embedded in the interplay of a variety of affective and relational issues, such as security, excitement, pleasure and pain, delight and disgust.

Here, the relational-developmental perspective synergizes with the postmodern, critical approach to psychoanalysis and gender, which is less concerned with describing normal and abnormal patterns of development than with exposing psychoanalysis' own potentials for being used to impose cultural discipline. Mitchell (1981) anticipated this in an early article in which he argued that analysts who analyze homosexuality as a pathology while not doing the same for heterosexuality are engaged in a nonanalytic practice, since they presume to know the meaning of a phenomenon on the psychological surface without proper data. He focused on issues of love, attachment, and eros in his last book, *Can Love Last?* (2002), informed by an array of subsequent contributions that owed some of their own existence to the open psychoanalytic space that he had created (see, e.g., Benjamin, 1988, 1995; Dimen & Goldner, 1999; Elise, 1997; Layton, 1988.)

Along similar lines, the body is itself regarded as "relational" rather than as autonomous and presocial (see, e.g., Aron & Anderson, 1998). The body and the sense of self-with-others are fundamentally intertwined, evolving in each family and taking on the various constraints and opportunities offered in particular cultures. Consistent with the open, constructivist aesthetic of the relational approaches to general personality development and clinical relationships, the approach to erotics, sexual, and gender development attends to what works out in each particular situation, as the individual interacts with the social surround.

Directions for the Future: Linking With Current and Emerging Knowledge in Developmental Thinking

Overall, one of the great strengths of relational psychoanalysis has been its links with new thinking in other fields. Many of the most recent developments in such adjacent areas synergize with the emerging questions within this field. Without claiming comprehensiveness, I offer a brief, suggestive list of a few current directions.

Much ongoing work regards *trauma*, both within and outside relational psychoanalysis. This includes significant research on the effects of childhood trauma from a variety of sources, including trauma researchers, infant and child clinicians, developmental neuroscientists, historians, and cultural and critical theorists. In the developmental field, there is an increasing convergence between the observations of infants in abusive or neglectful environments and developmental studies of brain anatomy and physiology, and these in turn provide strong conceptual correlations with the assumptions of developmental-relational psychoanalysis.

Similarly, *attachment* researchers have extended Bowlby's original project that emphasized the infant's proximity to the caregiver to include an emphasis on the parents' understanding and reflecting the infant's own internal world: The child's capacity for reflective functioning is synergistic with the overall sense of personal security. This view parallels the relational-intersubjectivist postulate that recognition by others is essential to the development of an integrated sense of self. With the development of the Adult Attachment Interview, some of the most basic contemporary psychoanalytic ideas are finding strong empirical support in developmental psychology research. In addition, processes such as dissociation, procedural rules, and other elements of what has been theorized in terms of the "relational unconscious" have gained increasing attention by those interested in attachment theory.

There may also be opportunities to link the relational-intersubjectivist concepts with other psychoanalytic schools. The reformulation of the oedipal theories to which I have already referred suggests one such direction. Recently, a number of writers have attempted to synthesize Kleinian–Bionian ideas, such as early phantasies, containment, thinking, and projective identification, with findings from infant observation research, attachment theory, and intersubjectivity theory (Alvarez, Fonagy, Grotstein, Seligman); these efforts have generally not overlooked the essential differences. Many syntheses of Winnicottian analysis with infancy research have been offered. Mitchell's own syntheses are exemplary, including in his final theoretical book, *Relationality* (2000), a relational reading of the theories of Loewald, Bowlby, Fairbairn, and others.

Some of the most innovative of the recent developmentally oriented syntheses have relied on *nonlinear dynamic systems theories*. These approaches capture the intricate, multimodal ebb and flow of developmental processes in the complex contexts of families and the broad social surround, affecting and being affected by genetic and physiological factors. Quite recently, there have been a number of applications of this perspective to psychoanalysis, which have drawn heavily on developmental models but extended further to discussions of psychoanalytic metapsychology, motivation, psychopathology, the technique and therapeutic action of psychoanalysis, and the like (Ghent, 2002; Sander, 2002; Seligman, in press; Shane & Coburn, 2003).

There has been relatively little work to apply the relational perspective to child analysis and child psychotherapy. One substantial exception here is to be found in the burgeoning area of infant intervention, and psychodynamic infant–parent psychotherapy in particular. Since Selma Fraiberg proposed the infant–parent psychotherapy model that took the "ghosts in the nursery" into account, a growing array of clinicians have established their intervention with the caregiving relationship as the patient. With regard to child analysis and psychotherapy, there has been a much greater lag.

Similarly, and perhaps of the greatest importance, there is a pressing need to implement public policies that protect the welfare and development of children. Although developmental findings have decisively demonstrated that early caregiving relationships are crucial for subsequent psychological well-being, social and economic conditions are increasingly trying for children and their families. Amid such adversity, psychotherapists in general, and psychoanalysts in particular, are in a position to make a contribution to the public health of children, especially in concert with other advocates (see, e.g., Altman, 1995).

References

Allison, D. (1993). *Bastard out of Carolina*. New York: Plume.

Altman, N. (1995). *The analyst in the inner city: Race, class, and culture through a psychoanalytic lens*. Hillsdale, NJ: The Analytic Press.

Aron, L. (2003). Clinical outbursts and theoretical breakthroughs: A unifying theme in the work of Stephen A. Mitchell. *Psychoanalytic Dialogues, 13*, 259–273.

Aron, L., & Anderson, F. S. (1998). *Relational perspectives on the body*. Hillsdale, NJ: The Analytic Press.

Atwood, G. E., & Stolorow, R. D. (1984). *Structures of subjectivity: Explorations in psychoanalytic phenomenology*. Hillsdale, NJ: The Analytic Press.

Auerhahn, N., & Peskin, H. (2003). Action, knowledge, acknowledgment and interpretive action in work with holocaust survivors. *Psychoanalytic Quarterly, 72*, 615–658.

Bacal, H. (1985). Optimal responsiveness and the therapeutic process. In A Goldberg (Ed.), *Progress in Self Psychology* (Vol. 1). New York: Guilford.

Balint, M. (1968). *The basic fault: Therapeutic aspects of regression*. Evanston, IL: Northwestern University Press.

Beebe, B., & Lachmann, F. M. (1988). The contribution of mother–infant mutual influence to the origins of self- and object-representation. *Psychoanalytic Psychology, 5*, 305–337.

Beebe, B., & Lachmann, F. M. (2002). *Infant research and adult treatment*. Hillsdale, NJ: The Analytic Press.

Benjamin, J. (1988). *The bonds of love: Psychoanalysis, feminism, and the problem of domination*. New York: Pantheon.

Benjamin, J. (1995). *Like subjects, love objects*. New Haven, CT: Yale University Press.

Bion, W. R. (1962). A theory of thinking. *International Journal of Psychoanalysis, 43*, 306–310.

Bowlby, J. (1969). *Attachment and loss, vol. 1: Attachment*. New York: Basic Books.

Bowlby, J. (1980). *Attachment and loss, vol. 3: Loss*. New York: Basic Books.

Bowlby, J. (1988). *A secure base: Parent–child attachment and healthy human development*. New York: Basic Books.

Britton, R. (1992). Keeping things in mind. In R. Anderson (Ed.), *Clinical lectures on Klein and Bion*. London: Routledge.

Bromberg, P. (1998). *Standing in the spaces: Essays on clinical process, trauma, and disassociation*. Hillsdale, NJ: The Analytic Press.

Chodorow, N. (1978). *The reproduction of mothering: Psychoanalysis and the sociology of gender*. Berkeley: University of California Press.

Chodorow, N. (1994). Heterosexuality as a compromise formation. In *Femininities, masculinities, sexualities: Freud and beyond*. Lexington: University Press of Kentucky.

Clyman, R. (1992). The procedural organization of emotions: A contribution from cognitive science to the psychoanalytic theory of therapeutic action. In T. Shapiro & R. Emde (Eds.), *Affect: Psychoanalytic perspectives*. Madison, CT: International Universities Press.

Colby, A., Kohlberg, L., Gibbs, J., & Lieberman, M. (1983). A longitudinal study of moral judgment. *Monographs of the Society for Research in Child Development, 48*(1).

Cooper, S. (2003). You say oedipal, I say postoedipal: A consideration of desire and hostility in the analytic relationship. *Psychoanalytic Dialogues, 1*, 41–64.

Davies, J. M. (1996). Linking the "pre-analytic" with the postclassical: Integration, dissociation, and the multiplicity of unconscious process. *Contemporary Psychoanalysis, 32,* 553–576.

Davies, J. M. (2003). Falling in love with love: Oedipal and postoedipal manifestations of idealization, mourning, and erotic masochism. *Psychoanalytic Dialogues, 13,* 1–27.

Davies, J. M. (2004). Whose bad objects are we anyway? Repetition and our elusive love affair with evil. *Psychoanalytic Dialogues, 14*(1), 711–732.

Davies, J. M., & Frawley, M. G. (1994). *Treating the adult survivor of childhood sexual abuse: A psychoanalytic perspective.* New York: Basic Books.

Demos, E. V. (1988). Affect and the development of the self: A new frontier. In A. Goldberg (Ed.), *Frontiers in self psychology: Progress in self psychology,* Vol. 3. Hillsdale, NJ: The Analytic Press.

Dimen, M., & Goldner, V. (1999). *Gender in psychoanalytic space: Between clinic and culture.* New York: Other Press.

Elise, D. (1997). Primary femininity, bisexuality and the female ego ideal: A re-examination of female developmental theory. *Psychoanalytic Quarterly, 66,* 489–517.

Emde, R. (1983). The prerepresentational self and its affective core. *Psychoanalytic Study of the Child, 38,* 165–192.

Emde, R. (1988). Development terminable and interminable: I. Innate and motivational factors from infancy. *International Journal of Psychoanalysis, 69,* 23–42.

Emde, R. N., Biringen, Z., Clyman, R. B., & Oppenheim, D. (1991). The moral self of infancy: Affective core and procedural knowledge. *Developmental Review, 11,* 251–270.

Erikson, E. H. (1950). *Childhood and society.* New York: Norton, 1963.

Fairbairn, W. R. D. (1952). *An object relations theory of personality.* New York: Basic Books.

Fast, I. (1985). *Event theory: A Piaget-Freud integration.* Hillsdale, NJ: Lawrence Erlbaum Associates.

Fonagy, P. (2000). Attachment and borderline personality disorder. *Journal of the American Psychoanalytic Association, 48,* 1129–1146.

Fonagy, P., & Target, M. (1966). Playing with reality: I. Theory of mind and the normal development of psychic reality. *International Journal of Psychoanalysis, 77,* 217–234.

Fraiberg, S. (Ed.). (1980). *Clinical studies in infant mental health: The first year of life.* New York: Basic Books.

Fraiberg, S., Adelson, E., & Shapiro, V. (1975). Ghosts in the nursery: A psychoanalytic approach to the problem of impaired infant–mother relationships. *Journal of the American Academy of Child Psychiatry, 14,* 387–422.

Ghent, E. (2002). Wish, need, drive: Motive in the light of dynamic systems theory and Edelman's selectionist theory. *Psychoanalytic Dialogues, 12,* 763–808.

Gilligan, C. (1979). Woman's place in man's life cycle. *Harvard Educational Review, 49,* 431–446.

Greenberg, J. (1991). *Oedipus and beyond: A clinical theory.* Cambridge, MA: Harvard University Press.

Greenberg, J. (1996). Psychoanalytic words and psychoanalytic acts: A brief history. *Contemporary Psychoanalysis, 32,* 195–213.

Greenberg, J., & Mitchell, S. (1983). *Object relations in psychoanalytic theory.* Cambridge, MA: Harvard University Press.

Harris, A. (1991). Gender as contradiction. *Psychoanalytic Dialogues, 1,* 197–224.

Harris, A. (2005). *Gender as a soft assembly.* Hillsdale, NJ: The Analytic Press.

Hartmann, H. (1956). Notes on the reality principle. In *Essays on ego psychology*. New York: International Universities Press.

Herman, J. L. (1992). *Trauma and recovery*. New York: Basic Books.

Hesse, E., & Main, M. (2000), Disorganized infant, child, and adult attachment: Collapse in behavioral and attentional strategies. *Journal of the American Psychoanalytic Association, 48*, 1097–1128.

Hoffman, I. Z. (1998). *Ritual and spontaneity in the psychoanalytic process: A dialectical-constructivist view*. Hillsdale, NJ: The Analytic Press.

Kernberg, O. F. (1991). A contemporary reading of "On narcissism." In J. Sandler, E. S. Person, & P. Fonagy (Eds.), *Freud's "On Narcissism": An introduction*. New Haven, CT: Yale University Press.

Klein, M. (1946). Notes on some schizoid mechanisms. In J. Riviere (Ed.), *Developments in psychoanalysis* (pp. 292–320). London: Hogarth Press, 1952.

Knoblauch, S. (1997). Beyond the word in psychoanalysis: The unspoken dialogue. *Psychoanalytic Dialogues, 7*, 491–516.

Kohut, H. (1977). *The restoration of the self*. New York: International Universities Press.

Lacan, J. (1949). The mirror stage as formative of the function of the I as revealed in psychoanalytic experience. In *Ecrits: A selection*. New York: Norton.

Lachmann, F. M. (2001). Some contributions of empirical infant research to adult psychoanalysis: What have we learned? How can we apply it? *Psychoanalytic Dialogues, 2*, 167–185.

Layton, L. (1988). *Who's that girl? Who's that boy?* Northvale, NJ: Aronson.

Levenson, E. (1983). *The ambiguity of change*. New York: Basic Books.

Lichtenberg, J. D. (1983). *Psychoanalysis and infant research*. Hillsdale, NJ: The Analytic Press.

Lichtenberg, J. D. (1989). *Psychoanalysis and motivation*. Hillsdale, NJ: The Analytic Press.

Lyons-Ruth, K. (1998). Implicit relational knowing: Its role in development and psychoanalytic treatment. *Infant Mental Health Journal, 19*, 282–289.

Mahler, M. S. (1972). On the first three subphases of the separation-individuation process. *International Journal of Psychoanalysis, 53*, 333–338.

Mahler, M. S., Pine, F., & Bergman A. (1975). *The psychological birth of the human infant: Symbiosis and individuation*. New York: Basic Books.

Main, M. (1999). Epilogue: Attachment theory, eighteen points with suggestions for future studies. In *Handbook of attachment* (pp. 845–887). New York: Guilford.

Main, M. (2000). The organized categories of infant, child, and adult attachment: Flexible vs. inflexible attention under attachment-related stress. *Journal of the American Psychoanalytic Association, 48*, 1055–1096.

McCourt, F. (1996). *Angela's ashes*. New York: Scribner.

Mitchell, S. A. (1981). The psychoanalytic treatment of homosexuality: Some technical considerations. *International Review of Psychoanalysis, 8*, 63–87.

Mitchell, S. A. (1988). *Relational concepts in psychoanalysis: An integration*. Cambridge, MA: Harvard University Press.

Mitchell, S. A. (1993a). Aggression and the endangered self. *Psychoanalytic Quarterly, 62*, 351–382.

Mitchell, S. A. (1993b). *Hope and dread in psychoanalysis*. New York: Basic Books.

Mitchell, S. A. (1997). *Influence and autonomy in psychoanalysis*. Hillsdale, NJ: The Analytic Press.

Mitchell, S. A. (2000). *Relationality: From attachment to intersubjectivity*. Hillsdale, NJ: The Analytic Press.

Mitchell, S. A. (2002). *Can love last?* New York: W. W. Norton.

Ogden, T. (1982). *Projective identification and psychotherapeutic technique.* New York: Jason Aronson.

Ogden, T. (1994). *Subject of analysis.* Northvale, NJ: Jason Aronson.

Perry, B., Pollard, R. A., Blakly, T. L., Baker, W. L., & Vigilante, D. (1995). Childhood trauma, the neurobiology of adaptation, and "use-dependent" development of the brain: How "stages" become "traits." *Infant Mental Health Journal, 16,* 271–291.

Pizer, S. (1992). The negotiation of paradox n the analytic process. *Psychoanalytic Dialogues, 2,* 215–240.

Pizer, B. (2003). When the crunch is a (k)not: A crimp in relational dialogue. *Psychoanalytic Dialogues, 13,* 171–192.

Rapaport, D., & Gill, M. M. (1959). The point of view and assumptions of metapsychology. *International Journal of Psychoanalysis, 40,* 153–162.

Rosenfeld, H. A. (1971). Contributions to the psychopathology of psychotic patients: The importance of projective identification in the ego structure and object relations of the psychotic patient. In E. B. Spillius (Ed.), *Melanie Klein today* (Vol. 1). London: Routledge, 1988.

Sameroff, A. J., & Chandler, M. J. (1975). Reproductive risk and the continuum of caretaking casualty. In F. D. Horowitz (Ed.), *Review of child development research* (Vol. 4, pp. 184–224). Chicago: University of Chicago Press.

Sander, L. W. (2002). Thinking differently: Principles of process in living systems and the specificity of being known. *Psychoanalytic Dialogues, 2,* 11–42.

Schore, A. N. (1994). *Affect regulation and origin of the self.* Hillsdale, NJ: Lawrence Erlbaum Associates.

Schore, A. N. (2003a). *Affect dysregulation and the disorders of the self.* New York: Norton.

Schore, A. N. (2003b). *Affect regulation and the repair of the self.* New York: Norton.

Seligman, S. (1994). Applying psychoanalysis in an unconventional context: Adapting "infant–parent psychotherapy" to a changing population. *Psychoanalytic Study of the Child, 49,* 481–500.

Seligman, S. (1996). Commentary on "The irrelevance of infant observation for psychoanalysis" by Peter Wolff. *Journal of the American Psychoanalytic Association, 44,* 430–446.

Seligman, S. (1999). Integrating Kleinian theory an intersubjective infant research: Observing projective identification. *Psychoanalytic Dialogues, 9,* 129–159.

Seligman, S. (2000). Clinical implications of current attachment theory. *Journal of the American Psychoanalytic Association, 48,* 1189–1196.

Seligman, S. (2001). The new baby settles in: Commentary on paper by Frank M. Lachmann. *Psychoanalytic Dialogues, 2,* 195–212.

Seligman, S. (2005). Dynamic system theories as a metaframework for psychoanalysis. *Psychoanalytic Dialogues, 15, 2:* 285–319.

Seligman, S., & Shanok, R. S. (1995), Subjectivity, complexity and the social world: Erikson's identity concept and contemporary relational theories. *Psychoanalytic Dialogues, 5,* 537–565.

Slade, A. (2000). The development and organization of attachment: Implications for psychoanalysis. *Journal of the American Psychoanalytic Association, 48,* 1147–1174.

Slochower, J. (1996). *Holding and psychoanalysis: A relational perspective.* Hillsdale, NJ: The Analytic Press.

Sophocles (1972). *Oedipus the king* (A. Burgess, Trans.). Minneapolis: University of Minnesota Press.

Spezzano, C. (1996). The three faces of two-person psychology: Development, ontology, and epistemology. *Psychoanalytic Dialogues, 6*, 599–622.

Stern, D. B. (1997). *Unformulated experience: From dissociation to imagination in psychoanalysis*. Hillsdale, NJ: The Analytic Press.

Stern, D. N. (1985). *The interpersonal world of the infant*. New York: Basic Books.

Stern, D. N. (1989). The representation of relational patterns: Developmental considerations. In A. Sameroff & R. Emde (Eds.), *Relationship disturbances in early childhood: A developmental approach*. New York: Basic Books.

Stern, D. N. (1995). *The motherhood constellation: A unified view of parent–infant psychotherapy*. New York: Basic Books.

Stern, D. N., Sander, L., Nahum, J., Harrison, A., Buschweiler-Stern, N., & Tronick, E. (1998). Non-interpretive mechanisms in psychoanalytic therapy. *International Journal of Psychoanalysis, 79*, 903–921.

Stolorow, R. D. (1997). Dynamic, dyadic, intersubjective systems: An evolving paradigm for psychoanalysis. *Psychoanalytic Psychology, 14*, 337–346.

Stolorow, R. D., & Atwood, G. (1992). *Contexts of being: The intersubjective foundations of psychological life*. Hillsdale, NJ: The Analytic Press.

Stolorow, R. D., Atwood, G. E., & Brandchaft, B. (Eds.) (1994). *The intersubjective perspective*. Northvale, NJ: Jason Aronson.

Sullivan, H. S. (1953). *The interpersonal theory of psychiatry*. New York: Norton.

Thelen, E. (1995). Motor development: A new synthesis. *American Psychologist, 50*, 79–95.

Weiss, J., Sampson, H., & the Mount Zion Psychotherapy Research Group (1986). *The psychoanalytic process: Theory, clinical observation, and empirical research*. New York: Guilford.

Winnicott, D. W. (1958a). The capacity to be alone. *International Journal of Psychoanalysis, 39*, 416–420.

Winnicott, D. W. (1958b). *Through paediatrics to psycho-analysis*. London: Hogarth Press.

Winnicott, D. W. (1960). The theory of parent–infant relationship. In The maturational processes and the facilitating environment. New York: International Universities Press.

Wollheim, R. (1993). *The mind and its depths*. Cambridge, MA: Harvard University Press.

AFTERWORD: DEVELOPMENTS AND DIRECTIONS A DECADE LATER

Since the publication of the original paper, early development research, including about early psychosocial and physical development, trauma, parent–infant interaction, and attachment, has continued to support the shifts within psychoanalysis toward the central role of social motivations, emotions and relationships in motivation, psychological structure, and clinical work. The acceleration of neuroscience research is most striking, as an outpouring of findings demonstrate how the brain both depends on and is the central organizer of each person's relationships with the social world. Overall, the progress I highlighted in this paper has continued at a dramatic pace, and the paradigm shift toward a general view of development and motivation as fundamentally social is well established.

From my point of view, the ongoing project of bringing developmental findings and analysis together involves both the enthusiasms of consilience and the tensions of contradiction. As with the relational advance in general, the new syntheses need not jettison the classical analytic attention to the world of verbal meanings, narrative, and fantasies and its respect for the irrational, turbulent, and unknowable aspects of the mind and of human interaction. This implies the task of rediscovering what remains vital in the grand psychoanalytic traditions—Kleinian–Bionian, British independent-object relations, and Anglo-American ego-developmental psychology traditions—without sacrificing the long overdue orientation toward attachment, protection, caregiving, and love that is taking hold. As I, among others, have written elsewhere, nonlinear dynamic systems theories provide a broad, effective conceptual envelope that can enhance and organize this project. I might add that, among the grand psychoanalytic writers, Erikson and Winnicott still seem to me to be the most prescient and insightful in providing luminous models that encompass both the Freudian genius and the current observations.

In addition, I have come to see phenomenological philosophy and psychology as offering a strong envelope to think about "the feeling of what is really happening" (cf. Damasio, 1999). In keeping with my own pursuit of core elements of experience, sentimental, grandiose, and Sisyphean as it may be, I find myself thinking about what I have learned from direct observation of babies and parents and from my hours with patients to explore the subjective experience of time and other fundamental dimensions, as it varies with age and in different kinds of mental organizations and states of mind (Seligman, 2011). Among the many who have pursued this sort of project, Louis Sander's (2008) syntheses of psychoanalysis, biologically oriented dynamic systems theory and infancy research and Daniel Stern's (1977, 2010) combination of immersion in direct observation of infants with a simultaneously psychoanalytic, aesthetic, scientific, and philosophical sensibility show the potentials in this area.

References

Damasio, A. (1999). *The feeling of what happens: Body and emotion in the consciousness.* New York: Harcourt Brace & Company.
Sander, L. W. (2008). *Living systems, evolving consciousness, and the emerging person: A selection of papers from the life work of Louis Sander* (G. Amadei & I. Bianchi, Eds.). New York: The Analytic Press.
Seligman, S. (2011). *The experience of time: Trauma, non-responsive parenting and the vacuity of the future.* Presentation at the San Francisco Center for Psychoanalysis.
Stern, D. N. (1977). *The first relationship: Infant and mother.* Cambridge, MA: Harvard University Press.
Stern, D. N. (2010). *Forms of vitality: Exploring dynamic experience in psychology, the arts, psychotherapy and development.* New York: Oxford University Press.

5

Faces in Relation

A Case Study[*]

Beatrice Beebe

▼　▼　▼　▼　▼

Although the coconstruction of the intersubjective field is currently of great interest to psychoanalysts, detailed clinical material illustrating the nonverbal and implicit dimension of this process remains rare. As Lyons-Ruth (1999) notes, much remains to be learned about how implicit modes of intimate relating are transformed and about the analyst's specific, collaborative participation in this process as a "new kind of relational partner" (p. 612). This paper details aspects of verbal as well as nonverbal and implicit processes[†] in the 10-year treatment of Dolores, and particularly my collaborative participation.

Dolores suffered early maternal loss and trauma. Many aspects of her traumatic experiences were communicated to me in nonverbal and implicit modes. She was preoccupied with faces, and she clung to the memory of her first mother's lost face as a beacon of her identity. Two themes of the 10-year treatment conducted three times a week, sitting up, merit particular attention: the integration of the "faces" of Dolores herself, her multiple early attachment figures, and my own, particularly as we struggled to regain "face-to-face" relating in the process of developing a deep mutual attachment; and traumatic loss and mourning. (Many other aspects of the treatment were important but will not be addressed here.) Although Dolores wanted to be able to find her own face in mine, she could not look at me, she shut her own face down, and she was often silent or dissociated. My

---

[*] This paper originally appeared in *Psychoanalytic Dialogues*, *14*(1), 2004, pp. 1–51. Reprinted with permission.

[†] See Beebe, Knoblauch, Rustin, and Sorter (2003) for definitions of implicit and nonverbal processes and their complex interrelation.

response to Dolores was shaped by my backgrounds as a psychoanalyst and as an infant researcher, particularly my own work on facial mirroring and vocal rhythm coordination in the mother–infant face-to-face exchange (see Jaffe, Beebe, Feldstein, Crown, & Jasnow, 2001; Beebe & Lachmann, 2002). In this way, we were matched: We both had a preoccupation with facial dialogue. Dolores reminds us how powerfully, and how early, we are affected by the "face dialogue."

The Face in Psychoanalysis

Facial communication operates at a nonsymbolic, implicit/procedural level, largely out of awareness. Research using brain imaging suggests that faces enjoy a special status in the brain, because neural activity in the temporal lobes (fusiform gyrus) surges twice as much when adults watch faces versus other objects (Bower, 2001).

The role of the face in psychoanalysis is directly linked to seeing and being seen. Unless the treatment is organized in a sitting position, the face obviously plays a far diminished role, but it is still important in the interchanges around greeting and separation. Seeing and being seen carry many connotations, from Freud's (1913) view that the therapist's being seen dilutes the transference to Sartre's (1992) view that seeing and being seen can objectify the self and other (see Eigen, 1993) to the view that being seen and responded to by the other is constitutive of the self (see Winnicott, 1965; Bion, 1977; Kohut, 1977).

Winnicott's understanding of mother–infant communication and its analogies in adult treatment has been very influential. One of his most famous descriptions is of facial communication. Winnicott (1974) asks what infants see when they see their mother's face; Winnicott's answer is that infants see themselves. Here we are alerted to the tremendous power of the mother's facial response and its role in shaping the sense of self. However, this famous concept emphasizes the mother's impact on the infant, matching or reflecting back the infant's affective state, but it omits Winnicott's equal appreciation for the role of the infant. The infant's facial/visual responsiveness has a reciprocal power to affect the mother's feeling of being recognized and loved by her baby (see Tronick, 1989).

Eigen (1993) notes that "the centrality of the human face as symbolic of personality permeates the fabric of human experience" (p. 49). He suggests that the human face is the most prominent "organizing principle in the field of meaning" (p. 56). He argues that psychoanalysis must concern itself with the face, particularly with respect to the early disorders of the self, because of the central importance of the face of the other in the formation of self-feeling (see also Weil, 1958; Winnicott, 1965, 1974; Kohut, 1977). Patients with these early disorders are often unable to create an enduring image of the therapist's face, which is a critical aspect of the treatment. Eigen (1993) argues that the therapist's facial behavior plays an essential role in evoking and broadening the patient's capacity to experience. He describes the work of Lévinas (1974), who argues that the birth of the human personality is associated with a positive experience of a face.

A substantial body of experimental adult literature demonstrates that facial action is simultaneously communicative and self-regulatory, modulating physiological arousal and subjective experience. Tomkins (1962, 1963) considered the face central, expressing emotion both to others and to the self, through feedback from the tongue and facial muscles, the sound of one's own voice, and changes in blood flow and temperature of the face. Changes in facial action are associated with subjective changes, either intensifying or inhibiting the experience of the emotion (Tomkins, 1962). Facial action can influence subjective experience of emotion without awareness (Izard, 1971; Ekman, Friesen, & Ancoli, 1980; Ekman, Levenson, & Friesen, 1983; Adelmann & Zajonc, 1989; Levenson, Ekman, & Friesen, 1990).

Because a particular facial expression is associated with a particular pattern of physiological arousal (Ekman, 1983), matching the expression of the partner produces a similar physiological state in the onlooker. Thus matching of expressions is an important way the emotional state of the individual can be transmitted to the partner (see Izard, 1971; Laird, 1984; Winton, 1986; Adelmann & Zajonc, 1989). Other research shows that, even without matching of facial expression, *the mere perception of emotion in the partner creates a resonant emotional state in the perceiver*, for infants as well as adults (Davidson & Fox, 1982). Positive as well as negative emotional "matching" reactions can be evoked out of awareness, so that important aspects of face-to-face communication occur on a nonconscious level (Dimberg, Thunberg, & Elmehed, 2000). The Heller and Haynal (1997) study ("A Doctor's Face: Mirror of His Patient's Suicidal Projects") dramatically illustrates this nonconscious facial communication.

Introduction to Dolores

Dolores is a brilliant and accomplished professional woman, capable at times of highly articulate self-reflection. She is very gifted at language. Preoccupied with very early, nonverbal experiences, she nevertheless possesses a remarkable ability to put her experiences into words. Her descriptions are often poetic. She is very interested in mothers and infants and has read widely. Because of her own remarkable abilities and resources, aided by three previous treatments, Dolores has been able to maintain a high level of professional functioning while simultaneously participating in an intense, difficult, and at times terrifying and destabilizing treatment with me. Aspects of the treatment described are disquieting.

Despite Dolores's language gifts, because of her long periods of profound dissociation and because of her very early maternal loss, much of the early progress of the treatment occurred through the "action-dialogue" of our nonverbal communication. I used all modalities to try to reach her: the rhythm and intonation of our voices, our breathing rhythms, our head and bodily orientation, as well as my steady gaze, the dampening of my bodily activity, and my facial response. Although I was aware of some of my own nonverbal behavior, most of it was out of my awareness. Only after reviewing in detail the videotaped interactions I describe later, in preparation for writing this paper, did I become aware of the full range of my nonverbal behavior with Dolores.

In the second year of treatment, I made an unusual intervention derived from my research background with videotape microanalysis of mother–infant interactions. I took a series of videotapes of Dolores and me together and of my face only while I interacted with her. I was familiar with using videotape viewing to facilitate understanding of nonverbal communication patterns in the treatment of mother–infant pairs (see Downing, 2001; Cohen & Beebe, 2002; Beebe, 2003). I became interested in videotaping as a possible aid to reaching Dolores because, despite her gifts, in very central ways she was deeply shut down and difficult to engage. This paper describes some of these videotaped interactions and their impact on the treatment. By analyzing the videotapes I came to understand a great deal more about the nonverbal and implicit aspects of my own collaborative participation. I hope in this paper to find a language to describe our experiences together as we struggled with the sequelae of Dolores's early trauma and to stay as close as possible to the actual words and actions of the two partners. Although most of this 10-year treatment was conducted as an ordinary psychoanalytic exchange, sitting up, in this paper I focus on the unusual videotaping rather than the background of usual therapeutic exchange.

The paper is organized with two intersecting goals. The first is a description of clinical material, from various points across the 10-year treatment, selected particularly as it is relevant to Dolores's concerns about the face and her traumatic loss and mourning. Some of the material is based on notes taken during sessions and some from videotapes taken of my face only, as I was interacting with Dolores. The videotaped sessions occur a year and a half into the treatment. Whereas the material taken from notes describes the verbal interaction, the material taken from videotapes depicts the nonverbal and implicit process as well.

The second goal of the chapter is an ongoing commentary on this clinical material to illustrate the concepts from Beebe, Rustin, Sorter, and Knoblauch

(2003), "An Expanded View of Forms of Intersubjectivity in Infancy and Their Application to Psychoanalysis." Through this clinical material we revisit the central concepts of Meltzoff, Trevarthen, and Stern: the dialogic origin of mind, the role of correspondences, and the idea that symbolic forms of intersubjectivity are built on presymbolic forms. In addition, we revisit various concepts offered to broaden a definition of the presymbolic origins of intersubjectivity: interactive regulation, the role of self-regulation, the role of difference, distress regulation, and the "balance model" of self- and interactive regulation.

Dolores is a 40-year-old biology professor, very attractive, and sociable with students. An early marriage ended very unhappily. Since then she has had some long friendships with men, including a long relationship with a boyfriend that did not work out, but she never remarried. Despite a few close and devoted friends, overall she is isolated and spends a great deal of time alone. Her primary mode of adaptation is to withdraw. Although she has been successful in her teaching career, she has difficulty thinking and writing alone. This is her fourth attempt at treatment.

For the first year of the treatment, Dolores and I lived in the same city. However, when she obtained a teaching job 3 hours away in a neighboring state, where there were no adequate mental health facilities, Dolores and I decided to continue the treatment. Every other week she came into the city for two double sessions in person, on two successive days; otherwise the treatment took place on the telephone.

For the first 2 years of her life, Dolores had a foster mother with whom she had a close and affectionate relationship. Then her biological mother reclaimed her, and she never saw the "good" foster mother again. During the period with her biological mother, when she was approximately 2 to 4 years old, Dolores was emotionally, physically, and sexually abused. At 4 years old, she became mute, which precipitated a year-long hospitalization. A photograph taken at this time shows a child with a swollen, bruised face and a sullen stare. After the year in the hospital, Dolores was adopted by a loving family. She thus had multiple abrupt, total changes of her attachment systems, including the early disruption of the bond to the original biological mother.

In treatment, Dolores was preoccupied with faces and particularly the face of her first, good foster mother. She used the metaphors of the "good face" and the "bad face" for her foster mother and her abusive biological mother, respectively. She longed for an attachment to me, yet she could not look at me and often could not talk. Her facial and bodily expressiveness was inhibited, shut down. For the first portion of every session, she wore her sunglasses, which she took off only after considerable prodding. She appeared shy, hesitant, wary, low key. At times she was severely dissociated. The treatment was a struggle to regain face-to-face relating and to create a secure attachment. Now, a decade later, she does look at me with a reasonably normal gaze pattern, most of the time. The attachment is progressively more secure, but much remains to be done.

At the beginning of the treatment Dolores and I sat face to face at the usual psychotherapy distance. The following process is based on notes taken during the first 6 sessions at the very beginning of the treatment. She glanced intermittently during these sessions but made no sustained eye contact. Dolores had discussed some good memories of the good foster mother.

The "Good Face" of the First Mother: A Fragment From the First Session

> Dolores: [*speaking slowly, in a childlike voice*] I do have the good face. It made me survive. I know that face, looking at me. I make that face happy; I know how her face goes. When I get so isolated, I'm missing someone I can give this to.
> BB: Yes.

Her comment that she can make the face happy, and that when she is isolated she is missing someone she can "give this to," illustrates the bidirectional model of influence that is central in infant research on face-to-face interaction. She describes the experience of the child who makes the mother's face come alive. This is the other side of the usual description of the mother's echoing the child's own facial affect. It is interesting that Dolores speaks of "the" face, not "her" face.

> Dolores: The good face doesn't want my badness though, and then—I'm all alone. Then I can't find the good face anymore. I know it's there, but I can't find it. I just can't find the good feelings in me....

Here she illustrates the dyadic organization of experience: Her own good feelings are organized in relation to the good face. If her relationship with the good face is disrupted in her own mind, then her own goodness is lost.

> Dolores: I remember a time playing with my [adoptive] mother. I looked at her face, but I remembered *another* face. I remembered it so vividly that I felt I actually saw it. When I saw this face, I felt *alive* and good. I *was* good. I felt it in my molecules, the face, and how it tells me I am. I know from the face what I can be, and what it wants from me: when to be happy, and when to be scared; when I'm good, and when I'm not. I know everything

about me from the face. It tells me what's next. I know when it will love me, and when it won't.

Her description captures the concept of "expectancies" in infant research: the idea that the infant comes to expect the moment-by-moment sequence of how the faces go and what will be next. Here, however, she frames the description more in terms of the impact of the adult's face on the child's face. Her description also evokes the visual cliff experiment (Klinnert, Campos, Sorce, Emde, & Svejda, 1983) in which a toddler is placed on a glass table, next to mother. Under the glass table, there is a "visual cliff." At the far side of the table are some very interesting toys. As the child begins to cross the table toward the toys, eventually he or she notices that there seems to be a cliff. The child looks back to mother. When the mother is instructed to show a smile face, the child proceeds without hesitation to the toys at the far end. When the mother is instructed to show a fear face, the child does not cross the "cliff." The child thus knows what to feel and what to do, whether to be scared and not cross, or to be unafraid and cross, from the face of the mother.

Dolores's use of the word *molecules* links her words to the visceral, bodily level of experience, reminiscent of Loewald's (1980) concept of "linking" of words to preverbal experience (see Mitchell, 2000). Bucci (1997) also emphasizes the link between visceral, bodily experience and emotion in language, with her concept of depth of referential imagery. Dolores's own capacity to make these links was a rich resource in the treatment.

Dolores: I don't want to be so angry at the good face; I want her to help me.
BB: You're angry at the good mother because she left you, and you're worried about being angry?
Dolores: Yes. But I'm so ashamed of what happened. I don't want the good face to know about it. The good face didn't come back to get me because she knew I was bad.

Her fear of shame and of exposure of her "badness" may have contributed to her fear of looking, of being seen as well as seeing. Perhaps the good mother would see something bad in her face.

BB: I can understand how you came to think this way, even though somewhere you know that no baby is bad. That is a 2-year-old's theory. I think you are telling me that it is so important for you to remember the love that was there for you from the good mother, even though you were later abused.

Here I have affirmed her love of the foster mother. I sensed the pivotal importance of this love. I also learned here how her shame over whatever happened in this period, and her anguish over being left, disturbed her contact with her memory of her good foster mother. Much later we were to delve into the storm of her rage at the foster mother for letting her go. Eventually I learned that the biological, abusive mother had told her that the foster mother had left her because she was a bad little girl; that the foster mother had found another, good little girl to take her place; and that is why the foster mother never came back.

Dolores: Can you help me let the good face know what happened, and see if she still thinks I'm good?

BB: Maybe you and I together can let the good face know what happened. You so long to feel the good mother's face. Without her, it seems so hard to feel that you are good yourself.

Dolores: Maybe if you know that babies aren't bad, maybe you and I could say that there still could be a good face of the mother and a good face of the baby? I don't want to leave the session. I need you to hold the two faces together.

BB: You are struggling to hold together the face of the good mother and the face of the good baby, even though you were abused.

Dolores: If the good mother knew the bad things, the baby would still be good?

BB: Yes.

Setting the frame of the therapy, I respond strongly that the child is good. By asking if I can help her let the good face know what happened, she goes right to what she needs. In this segment I join her capacity to be in the Winnicottian transitional play-space: "Maybe you and I together can let the good face know what happened." Together we have created a capacity for play, improvisation, and, at times, humor. Her capacity to be in this play-space, and to invite me in, is a rich resource in the treatment.

Her urgent request that the two faces be held together, for she cannot proceed with her development without being able to hold together her own face and that of the good mother, can be related to the "dialogic origin of mind" proposed by Meltzoff, Trevarthen, and Stern (see Beebe et al., 2003). She needs to be able to hold onto that early "face dialogue." As the three infant theorists have eloquently argued, prior to language there is a rich face (as well as vocal and touch) dialogue, nuanced and complex, as Dolores was well aware. My own background in research on face-to-face interaction led me to think of the face dialogue (as well as gaze, orientation, voice) as a complex arena for expressing and responding to emotions rather than a mimicking or manipulation of faces. The following fragment illustrates one of the major themes of the treatment: how Dolores engaged me to help her in her quest to integrate her different mothering experiences, each with a radically different set of expectancies.

Not Being Found by the Adoptive Mother's Face: Fragment From the First Weeks of Treatment

Dolores: I searched my [adoptive] mother's face, and there was no rest for me there, where faces meet and match. This is what I lost, though I know I *did* once have it. Help me wake up. I do not want to go dead. [*pause*] I know I did not look right to my [adoptive] mother. I didn't know why, I knew my face wasn't right. I couldn't look at her and find me. [*pause*] I had it once, though not for long, I know I did. And that is what is here with you.

BB: That is what you came looking for?

Dolores: You can help me find it. I have a resting place here, a coming alive, feeling recognized, someone who doesn't turn away. I won't live if I don't get it. [*pause*] My [adoptive] mother needed to stop me. She never found herself in me, so I never found myself in her. I shut down. Though once I had it, I know I did.

Dolores has described the terrible impact of a disruption in the mutual facial mirroring process between her and her adoptive mother and the disaster of not being "found" (Winnicott, 1965, 1974). I admired her striving to hold on to "the good face" and to her aliveness.

When she speaks of the powerful impact of feeling me respond to her, I am drawn closer. I am very affected by her invitation, but I also hear the panic: She will not live if she does not get it. Her plaint has made me feel worried as well.

"Where the faces meet and match" is reminiscent of the description of matching found in the body of work of Meltzoff, of Trevarthen, of Stern. "Meeting and matching" seemed to be the essence of a certain kind of aliveness for her, and without it she would "go dead." A central dilemma is that she urgently wanted this meeting and aliveness, and yet she could not accomplish it. "Going dead" is reminiscent of the infants who are later classified as disorganized attachment at 12 months (Lyons-Ruth, August 18, 1999, personal communication; Jaffe et al., 2001; Beebe, 2003). At 4 months these infants lose postural tonus and go limp, "playing possum" (see Papousek & Papousek, 1987) or "inhibiting responsivity" (see Beebe & Stern, 1977), presumably in a move toward conservation-withdrawal (Perry, 1996). Eventually a feeling of inner deadness became one of the most pressing issues of Dolores's treatment, reminiscent of deadness as a core clinical concern in Ogden's (1986, 1994) theory of intersubjectivity.

Dolores seemed to "recognize" in me someone who "recognized" her. This bedrock of the treatment was established almost immediately. Her determination to regain the feeling of being alive, to find the place where "faces meet and match," to find herself in the face of the other, continued to be a source of hope in the treatment, a counterpoint to her deadness.

"I Don't Have a Face of My Own": Fragment From the First Weeks of Treatment

Dolores: You know, there is a lot of confusion about my face. When I'm more stressed, bad things happen. Sometimes I feel very young. I have the sensation then of a thin piece of skin over my eyes, and the sensation of my face turning to stone.

BB: It seems you feel your face stopped moving and your eyes stopped seeing, in reaction to not having your good mother's face to respond to you. You must have been so terribly depressed with the abusive mother.

I am tender, warm, worried. Here she returns to a visceral experience of deadness, feeling her face turning to stone. Her face went dead after she lost the good foster mother, and sadly she did not regain the aliveness of her face with her adopted mother. The face going dead seems to be a metaphor for the self going dead after losing the good foster mother. Her state at that time, without an attachment partner, without a face-dialogue, constituted the loss of any possibility of intersubjectivity, however defined.

Dolores: [*continues*] I feel alienated from my face. My face doesn't *feel* like *me. I don't have a face of my own.* I look at *other* people's faces to see what *my* face looks like. My adoptive mother looked at me like a stranger. I didn't feel my face looked right. I couldn't look at her and find me.

BB: It seems that your adoptive mother wasn't able to be *responsive* enough to your face. Each of you couldn't really respond to the other, and then you developed the idea that there was something *wrong* with your face.

Dolores: Maybe *you* could understand [*pause*] that I might not *have* a face. Maybe something *is* wrong with my face. Maybe I *do* have a bad face. I need to see your face, to feel that I am looking at the good face, and to feel good myself.

Dolores has two traumatic ideas here: that she has a bad face or, worse, that she might not have a face at all; and that her face turns to stone, is dead. These experiences of her face are presumably coordinated with an unresponsive or an abusive partner. She again states one of the core issues of the treatment, that she needs my face to regain her own inner aliveness and goodness. Yet she cannot look at me.

> BB: A child gets her own face from the face of the mother, and the mother gets her feeling of being a mother from the face of her child. You feel that you had it, and then you lost it. Then evidently all you had was the bad face. That made you feel like your own face is bad. Now you want to see my face, to reflect back to you your own good face. But it's very hard for you to look.
>
> Dolores: I understand. I have to find you, to find your face, to find my own face. I don't like feeling like I don't have a face. You recognize me. Maybe you could understand that I might not have a face.

It is remarkable that Dolores knows that she must find my face to find her own. In some very palpable sense, it is true that Dolores does not have a "face," or facial–visual responsiveness that she can use in cocreating our engagement. She essentially defines for us one of the central goals of the treatment. Her ability to reflect on the process in this way was another essential resource. My comments emphasize that Dolores's experience of her face was developed in relation to a lack of appropriate responsivity in both the abusive, biological mother and later in the adoptive mother. I was very touched by Dolores. I responded to her longing for engagement with me.

I was moved by the horror of her early childhood. My experience of her terror was perhaps most palpable when I approached her warmly in the waiting room to greet her. She would back away from me, with the look of a frightened animal. I learned to approach her very slowly and to keep my distance at first. In the Ainsworth separation–reunion test of attachment at one year, backing away from the mother upon reunion is a behavior characteristic of infants classified as disorganized (Main & Hesse, 1992).

My Difficulty Reaching Dolores

Following a half dozen initial sessions during which she told me her story in a halting manner filled with intense emotion, and quite coherently, Dolores began to sit with her body oriented away from me, without looking, barely talking. She seemed out of contact, dissociated. At this early point in the treatment I tried many different strategies to make contact with her. I noticed that at various points, without looking, she oriented toward and then away from me. I suggested that, instead of trying to talk, perhaps we could begin by trying together to become aware of when she was able to move her body to be oriented to me and when she oriented away. Over the course of the ensuing months, Dolores began to elaborate on the metaphor. She would say, "I'm in your orient" or "I'm falling out of your orient." Dolores's ability to respond in this rather poetic way was very touching, and it helped us work on maintaining a sense of a bond.

But it continued to be difficult to make contact with her with a more usual verbal narrative, and she continued to be dissociated for long periods without speaking. Eventually I experimented with moving my chair into a more "biological" face-to-face distance, the two chairs at right angles, with a small table in between. This distance is approximately that of usual adult face-to-face interaction distance, closer than usual face-to-face psychotherapy, but not as close as that between mother and infant. This arrangement facilitated my making contact with Dolores: She seemed more aware of my presence, and the long dissociated periods became less frequent and prolonged. We have maintained this arrangement.

How was I affected by not being able to "get" Dolores's gaze or face? I experienced her muted face and voice as fear, rather than as withholding. I felt patient, as when I was interacting with the infants of my research. I tried to have no agenda but to stay with her, to try to sense what she felt and follow what she said. Dolores frequently told me how important I was to her. I am certain that, if she had not been as forthcoming in this regard, I would have had a much more difficult time, and the treatment would have taken a very different course. Her own generous and loving approach to me was a critical catalyst in the treatment.

Because after the first year of treatment Dolores's teaching position required that she live at a considerable distance from my office, much of the treatment was conducted on the telephone. The sessions in person every other week were usually long double sessions. Whereas we were usually successful in generating a genuine engagement in the sessions conducted in person, over the telephone the sessions were very difficult. Dolores was often completely quiet for long periods. And she was in agony over the long periods without seeing me in person. She explained that she could not remember me in between sessions. She had tried and tried to remember the good foster mother. Every day she had thought that today maybe she would come back. And day after day after day, the mother did not come back. Until, eventually, one day, Dolores described that her "mind snapped: It was a physical feeling of breaking." After that, something changed, something had been broken.

Introduction of Videotaping

About a year and a half into the treatment, when Dolores was having a great deal of trouble adjusting to seeing me less frequently in person, she brought up the idea of videotaping some sessions. She knew that my research involved videotaping mothers and infants. We discussed it and were both interested in the idea. I thought that, because Dolores could not look at me, the videotape might help her to sense more of my feeling for her. I believed that her ability to engage with my face was essential in reclaiming her relatedness and aliveness. Initially Dolores asked a friend to videotape us briefly, for 10 or 15 minutes at the end of a long double session. Some of the footage was of Dolores and me together, but some of it was of my face only, as I interacted with her. Later we videotaped without the friend.

At this point, Dolores was barely looking at me, except for rare fleeting glances. In her peripheral vision, however, she could certainly detect my body movement and facial changes, although not the exact facial expression. Obviously she could monitor my vocal rhythms, contours, and cadences. For my discussion here, I have selected portions of the videotape that I have permission to show to professional audiences; only my face is visible. My face reflects what I see in her, what I see her feeling, as well as my own response. Her face is omitted according to her wishes. In this portion of the videotape, her speech was nearly inaudible, requiring close attention to understand it. Her voice was muffled and childlike.

The following are based on close videotape analysis. I distinguish vocal rhythm (see Jaffe et al., 2001), vocal contour (Fernald, 1987), and pitch. I also comment on my degree of bodily activation, self comforting self-touch, hand gestures, and face (see Beebe, 2003). Although Dolores's words often are barely audible from the videotape, the rhythm of her words is usually detectable. I generally repeat what I hear her say, because I am straining to understand her words. Although I may have been aware of some of my nonverbal behavior, most of it was out of awareness. For example, I know that I was being "quiet" with my body in the first section I describe, but only after I examined the tape did I realize how completely quiet I had become, so that I could adjust to her level of fearfulness. I am aware that I also slow down and reduce my level of activity when I interact with infants. But for Dolores I did so in an even more dramatic fashion.

Moments When Dolores and I Reach Each Other: Videotape Illustration I, 1-1/2 Years Into the Treatment (2 Minutes)

As this moment opens, my face is in side-view. My body is completely still. I am careful not to make sudden movements. In contrast to my usual high-energy style, I have lowered my arousal to the very bottom of my range. I am leaning forward, with an intent, direct, sustained focus. I am paying very careful, tender attention to Dolores. I listen to every word and am clearly working hard to understand what she says. It is as if nothing else in the world exists for me except for her. Dolores does not look at me.

> Dolores: In the, in the [*pause*] good way [*pause*] that [*pause*] that I [*pause*] that I feel [*pause*] complicated about…

Dolores's speech is hesitant, dampened, stop–start, stuttering, fragmented, with a staccato rhythm. She seems to be in considerable distress and is struggling to express a complicated feeling.

> BB: In that good way? In the good way that you feel complicated about?

My tone is very soft. I repeat her phrase but bring it into a more flowing and coherent rhythm. I don't hesitate. The contour rises by the end of the sentence, with a feeling of "questioning" and "opening." The rising intonation at the end is slightly enlivening. It is as if I am sensing her longing to connect to me, despite her terror, and I am elongating the moment, as if to say, "Stay here in this moment with me." As I work hard to understand her words, my rhythm and tone render her fragmented communication more coherent, as I convey "I am getting it." As I say, "In that good way," my chin is tilted upward and my left hand holds my chin. But as I continue with, "In the good way that you feel complicated about," my hand moves upward and I hold the side of my face and forehead. My own self-soothing acknowledges her level of distress. This interaction illustrates not a "matching" but a "difference" response. My rhythm is clearly different from hers, but it facilitates the relatedness. I provide more opening, enlivening, and coherence, which she then partially joins when she reaches "good but sad" in the ensuing dialogue. This interaction illustrates one form of distress regulation: I enter the rhythm and cadence of her distress, but I also slightly transform the expression of it. This would qualify as a "difference" response, rather than a "matching."

Dolores: Uh-huh.

    BB: The good way of being connected to me that's so complicated?

Here I repeat her phrase but elaborate it, adding the phrase "of being connected to me," a symbolic elaboration. My rhythm is flowing. I emphasize her longing to connect.

Dolores: [*long pause*] Good but sad.

"Good but sad" is an important integration that Dolores achieves here. Her rhythm here is flowing, more organized. Perhaps my increased coherence through the rhythm of my speech, and my symbolic elaboration, enabled her to describe this poignant dilemma.

    BB: You feel good but *sad*? [*pause*] Good but *sad*? [*long pause*]

Here I match the rhythm of her phase but again slightly elaborate on it as well. I use a rising intonation and elongate the word *sad* with a question intonation, conveying an opening quality. By repeating her phrase twice, I tarry in the feeling of it, giving us both a moment to absorb it. My intent face conveys the intensity of my listening. Dolores's ability to endorse the positive and the negative feelings alike is extremely important, and my repetition underscores it. This interaction again illustrates a form of distress regulation, in which the matching aspect of my response constitutes entering her distress, but my elaboration on her rhythm is a form of slightly reorganizing it.

    BB: Is the complicated part about having to leave? [*pause*] Are you thinking about that right now? And whether you'll turn to concrete?

I connect her feeling to the imminent end of the session. "Turning to concrete" is a phrase she used earlier in the session to describe her feeling about leaving. With each sentence, I slightly change the pattern of the way my hand is self-soothing my face, registering my own efforts to regulate my intense feelings with Dolores. Dolores's feet are visible in the videotape at this moment, and her toes wiggle, then rub up against each other, self-soothing.

Dolores: [*inaudible*]

    BB: [*repeating what I think I hear*] But you're planting a flower before you leave?

My chin moves upward, in a greater focus of attention, and my body is completely still. This may convey to Dolores how intent I am on what she is saying and feeling.

> Dolores: [*inaudible*]
> BB: You're planting a flower that you're coming back?
> Dolores: [*inaudible*]
> BB: Before you turn to concrete?

My eyebrows go up in a concerned expression. The more hope she has, the more she dreads that she may lose me. Leaving is excruciating. On the other hand, in this vignette she integrates the opposites of her experience: good but sad, alive flower and inanimate concrete.

The next time Dolores came to a session in person, together we watched this videotape that we had made. She watched the video without taking her eyes off it. She was riveted, and tearful. This was the first prolonged period that she had been able to see my face, and she was utterly moved to see me. We talked about how she still could not look at me while we actually interacted, but how important it was to her to be able to see me on the video.

Reaching Each Other Through an Expanded Range: Videotape Illustration II, 3 Months Later (1 Minute)

In this session my body moves around slightly, with greater range, suggesting that I sense that at this moment Dolores is not as vulnerable as she was in the earlier session, when my body (although not my hands) stayed completely still. Now my body uses the three dimensions of space and shapes the space in a more open, embracing way than in the previous vignette. My chest has a concave shape, similar to that of a mother snuggling her baby into her chest. My gestures have a soft, circular, undulating quality. My head tilts and bobs at times, and overall the movements of my body are more playful.

> BB: You told me something important that will help us with why it's so hard. [*pause*] You told me that if you look at me [*my head tilts, I lean forward, and I gesture with my right hand*], maybe I'll become the mother you'll never see again. [*pause*] If you let yourself *have* my face, it will be like the mother whose face you *lost*. That if you *look* at me, you'll never *see* me again. [*pause*] So no wonder you wouldn't want to look at me [*my eyebrows go up*]. [*long pause*]

Dolores: Unh.
    BB: If you don't look at me, it won't happen. That's your idea, right? [*long pause*]
    BB: [*slight smile, with soft sadness: I see something on her face.*] You're worried about leaving aren't you? [*long pause*]
Dolores: If I don't look at you, it won't happen. [*for a split second Dolores glances at my face*]
    BB: [*big, soft smile*]

A few minutes later in the same session:

    BB: [*picking up on something she has just said*] [*smiling*] If you look at the videotape, it will put my face in front of your eyes, but not through *your* looking.

I am referring here to the fact that the first time she really looked at my face for more than a split second occurred when we both watched the first video of a session together a few months earlier. She was very moved to see my face, and tearful. She could tolerate seeing me in the videotape better than in vivo. My tone is playful, with rising contours. I am gently teasing her about not looking at me, and we are sharing some humor. Earlier in the exchange, my head-tilt, leaning forward, with a hand gesture, emphasize my verbal communication. Head tilting or slight shifts of head orientation, as well as orientational changes and hand gestures, are important markers of the exchange, accentuating the moment.

Dolores: [*inaudible*]
    BB: [*repeating what I think I have heard her say*] My face jumped into your eyes, for one little second? [*pause*] Really? [*pause*] Well, *that's* good.

My eyebrows go up, I have a big smile, and the phrase, "Well, that's good" has a "sinusoidal" contour, known in infant research as a "greeting" contour. I am greeting her playful effort at engagement.

    BB: [*Big shift: I see something on her face*] You feel sad.
Dolores: [*inaudible*]
    BB: [*repeating what I think I have heard her say*] Leaving is the worst thing that could happen?

Her positive feelings rapidly move to sadness. I match the rhythm of her words, including her emphasis on "worst." I add a slightly questioning intonation at the end. My body becomes very quiet. I briefly close my eyes, and

I let out a soft sigh. This interaction illustrates a form of distress regulation that is very close to an exact matching. I elaborate in two subtle ways: the questioning intonation, which leaves open the possibility of other feelings, and the sigh, which elaborates on the sense of loss.

> Dolores: [*inaudible*]
> BB: All the wrong faces will come back?

I repeat her sentence but add a question intonation at the end. Again, this slight elaboration of the question intonation holds open the possibility that this might or might not happen.

> Dolores: Unh.
> BB: And will you get rid of *my* face?

I want to help her to connect to my face in every possible way. I imply that she is active in keeping or losing my face. This is where I hope the treatment is going (see Kohut, 1977; Loewald, 1980), although at this point she seems to have very little ability to hold on to the image of my face.

> [*long pause*]
> Dolores: [*inaudible*]
> BB: You won't be able to take the subway to come see me.

Here I exactly match the rhythm and contour of her statement. There is no question that she will not be able to take the subway to see me during the next period, when the sessions will be held on the telephone. My face has a "woe-face" expression, giving a palpable form to the feeling in her words.

> Dolores: [*inaudible*]
> BB: Or call up down the street.

Dolores is referring to the fact that the next period of sessions will be on the telephone, and she lives so far outside the city that she will not be able just to take a subway to see me, as she could if she lived in the city. On this particular day she had called me from her cell phone down the street as she was coming to the session.

I nod my head. My face is quiet. But my head and my words exactly match the rhythm and contour of her statement without changing anything. Exact matches can constitute a very particular form of empathy; here I have no agenda but to stay exactly in her feeling. I am accepting her very coherent statement of loss, exactly as she expresses it. This interaction also illustrates a form of distress regulation that I term "joining the dampened state" (see Beebe, 2000, 2003; Cohen & Beebe, 2002). The cross-modal matching of my head and her words illustrates Stern's concept of affect attunement.

Dolores: [says something inaudible; I don't repeat it.]
    BB: [gentle laugh; body moves]

In this fragment of the session Dolores is experimenting (ever so slightly) with looking at me. After I elaborate on her own interpretation of why she does not look at me (that I might become the mother she will never see again), she glances at my face. Then I gently tease her about looking at me, and she glances at me again. My expanded nonverbal range, with more bodily movement, laughing, without marked self-comforting self-touch, parallels Dolores's own increased engagement and verbal participation. It contrasts with the session three months earlier when my own nonverbal range was more constricted, presumably in an effort not to overarouse or frighten her and to stay closer to her own range of activation. Immediately following the increased engagement and aliveness of the first portion of this vignette, Dolores goes into the sadness of the imminent end of the session, poignantly expressing her feelings. But by the end of the vignette, Dolores again introduces some gentle humor, and I softly laugh. In this approximately 1-minute vignette, Dolores shows an expanded range by integrating experimentation with looking, sadness about loss, and humor.

The Struggle to Discuss Dolores's Early History: Second Half of Second Year

These videotapes document aspects of our slow, careful work of bonding. They show how we both contributed to the possibility that Dolores might feel less distressed, more engaged, and at times comforted. A period then followed in the second half of the second year when Dolores made a concerted effort to tell me some more about her early history. It was extremely difficult for Dolores to tell me anything concrete. We might spend an entire session struggling to make it possible for Dolores to communicate one piece of information.

During this period, at the point at which she might begin to discuss any of the details, she would become agitated, her body would tighten, and eventually she would hold her breath, as if in an effort to hold everything in. She would hold her breath for long periods, unable to stop, until she would begin to panic. Eventually I began to try to get her to synchronize with my breathing. I made soft, rhythmic sounds as I breathed in and out. Dolores called it the "breathing song." Together we began to be able to anticipate when an episode of breath-holding was about to begin, and we would do the breathing song together before she became extremely agitated. Over the course of the next couple of years, the breathing symptom gradually became less frequent.

In another dramatic expression of her difficulty communicating the details of her early history, she would abruptly fall into a deep sleep after revealing something particularly painful. The sleep would last for the rest of the session, and she could not be awakened. I would sit near her head, and while she was sleeping I would softly tell her what had just happened and why I thought she had to fall into a deep sleep. Then I would stay next to her while she slept and every once in a while softly tell her that I was there while she was sleeping. Toward the end of the session, she was able to wake up and would listen while I again told her what I thought had happened. Gradually she would be able to reorganize. I would walk with her around the room until I felt she had regained her full consciousness and could leave. Very often a friend met her at the end of the session.

Going to sleep as a way of escaping these painful memories gradually yielded to a less severe form of retreat, in which Dolores's eyelids would begin to flutter and she would declare that she was "going behind her eyes." This became a way of communicating to me that she was becoming overwhelmed and needed to retreat. Our validating her need to retreat would very often make it possible to proceed.

During this period she touched the same two scarred areas on her body, over and over, in a quasi-trance-like state. She would ask me if she was bleeding. From this behavior we were able to understand that she had been beaten in childhood. She remembered that she would hide in the closet to escape the abusive (biological) mother. She whispered over and over to me, "Shhh. Don't move. Be quiet. Shhh." Her body was tight with fear.

During the periods in which she was struggling to tell me something about the sexual abuse that occurred during the period with her biological mother, she vomited on her way to the sessions. There was a tightening in her face around her mouth, and she did not want anyone to come near her mouth. These symptoms, together with other memories, associations, and drawings she brought me, were eventually linked to oral sexual abuse.

She also had an impulse to smash her glasses on the wall of my office. This smashing of glass was linked by her to memories of jumping out the window, breaking the glass in her effort to escape from the abusive mother and look for the first mother. During this period of the treatment she remembered that she had once gotten on a bus, around the age of 20, and traveled all day and all night, looking for the first, good mother. She had found a file that belonged to her father with information about the adoption. In that file she had also found the photograph of the little girl with the bruised, swollen face.

Dolores's Discovery of a Man in My Life:
Toward the End of the Second Year

Six months later Dolores discovered that I had a man in my life. This revelation reminded her of the last day she had seen the first, good mother, who had left with a man. To her, "the man" had taken her mother away. She was convinced that "the man" would take me away from her and that she would lose her "place" with me. Much later in the treatment we discovered that this traumatic theme, that the father figure would take the mother away, was repeated in various ways in all three of her family constellations.

The presence of a man in my life evoked in Dolores this core traumatic theme, which, from then on, became a central aspect of the treatment. Our "honeymoon" was over. She began to struggle with the feeling of being "kicked out," as she had felt "kicked out" by the first, good mother. For the first 6 months after discovering "the man," Dolores barely spoke to me. It was an "ice-rage." The sessions over the telephone were particularly difficult for us. It was quite a loss for me to endure such a profound withdrawal of her love. At first I felt terribly guilty, and the situation evoked a core traumatic theme from my own early childhood, my own "badness."

My reaction sent us into quite a tailspin. It became extremely difficult for me—for us—to tolerate how enraged she was. Slowly I came to terms with the idea that this theme had to emerge, that it would have happened sooner or later, and that it would be essential to her recovery. I also acknowledged to her that some of our difficulty was coming from something in me, something from my own childhood, that had been reevoked. This acknowledgment meant a lot to her, and she did not press for details. Slowly she began to talk to me again. Although we have continued to struggle with this theme throughout the entire treatment, we have increasingly been able to think together about what it means.

Dolores's Use of Viewing the Videotapes to Foster
an Internalization Process: Making My Faces on
Her Face, 2-1/2 Years Into the Treatment

These are notes taken during a session on the telephone. While she was alone, Dolores had been looking at the videotapes taken a year and a half into the treatment, described earlier.

> Dolores: I was looking at your face looking at me. I saw the way it's different when I'm with you.
> BB: You saw it watching the video?

Dolores: Yes.

BB: What did you see?

Dolores: I saw that you were seeing me. I wasn't seeing you when I was with you in person, but later, when I was watching the video and I saw you, I felt much more real.

BB: Wow.

Dolores: Yes. In a way that, when I am with my feelings alone, sometimes I don't. But when I saw my feelings on your face, I felt more, feeling my feelings. I felt kind of familiar. But I don't *feel* them, necessarily, when I'm alone.

BB: That's very interesting. "To feel them" means what, really?

Dolores: When I'm alone with them I feel more confused. When I see them on your face, I can read them better. When I'm having them all by myself, there isn't any sense to them—that's part of what feels so bad, nobody to make any meaning.

BB: Can we make the same meaning when we're talking on the phone, now, without the faces?

Dolores: I need to see, or I need to *feel*. I have the picture of you, looking at me, and I like it; you never take your eyes away from my face. But now, on the phone, your voice floats on the ear, floats away. I want your eyes looking at me.

This session shows how Dolores began to use watching the videotape as an adjunct to the internalization process. Internalization can be reconceptualized as an expectation of an interactive process in which the inner organization is based on reciprocal coordinations, joint bidirectional interactive patterns, that regulate the exchange (Loewald, 1980; Benjamin, 1988; Beebe & Lachmann, 1994). Watching the videotapes provided a format in which she could actually see and take in more information from my face. And, recall, videotaping was her idea. From my research on the facial interchange between infants and mothers, I am convinced that she needed to see my feelings for her in my face as well as hear my emotions through my voice. The videotape gave us a powerful way to do that. At this point in the treatment, she still was not looking at me, and we did not yet completely understand the dynamics behind this behavior.

The research of Dimberg et al. (2000) can help us imagine what was happening when Dolores watched my face as I watched her. Out of her own awareness or conscious intention, Dolores's expressions probably matched mine. The work of Ekman (1983; Ekman et al., 1983; Levenson et al., 1990), showing that particular facial expressions are associated with particular patterns of physiological arousal, suggests that Dolores had visceral as well as facial responses as she watched my face. This research is consistent with Gergeley and Watson's (1998) suggestion that, in the parent–infant face-to-face exchange, one function of facial mirroring is to amplify the infant's inner state. Seeing his or her own facial expression reproduced or elaborated on the face of the partner may help the infant sense and register his or her own face and associated proprioceptive feedback.

Something like this seems to have occurred between Dolores and me. She was learning more about her own feelings by watching me experience her. Her inner registration and identification of her feelings had been difficult for her. When she was able to "see" herself in my face, she was able to sense her own inner state more clearly (George Downing, 2001; July 18, 2001, personal communication). She was also better able to register her own response to me in a verbal mode: She *liked* the feeling of my face watching her so closely. The discovery of "mirror neurons" is also relevant to Dolores's watching the videotapes. Simply by her watching my actions, for example, a moment of tender response on my face, her brain may have been activated in the premotor cortex, as if she herself were performing those actions.

At the end of this portion of the video, she poignantly reminds us how difficult it is for her on the telephone. Her great difficulty remembering me in between sessions was exacerbated by the unfortunate necessity that we have so many sessions over the telephone.

Further Work on Internalization: "Those Good Face-Feelings: That Is What I Have Inside Me."

[*Continuing over the telephone 1 week later*]

Dolores: I'm thinking about how I used the video to remember you. Because I don't look at you when I'm with you. I don't have the memory of my face *interacting* with your face, because I don't *do* that. But when I was *watching* you, on the video while I was alone, I was interacting with your face. When I wanted to have certain feelings, I called up the feeling of your face. *I was making your faces on my face.*

Here her experience brings to mind the work of Meltzoff (see Beebe et al., 2003). Dolores is describing a "like me" experience. She can get back to her own experience through my face. First she senses that, as I interact with her, my face is like hers: I feel her and my face reflects what I feel. Then, as she matches my face in the video while she is watching it, her face is like mine. In this way she has gotten back to her original feeling.

BB: Like imitating?

Dolores: Yes, but not imitating exactly. More remembering the feeling of your face talking to my face—not the words. I said your "face-talk" *on my face*. I was getting the feeling for what was happening in the faces, and that's how I remembered certain feelings, certain good feelings—how I remembered feeling comforted—during watching the video and after—during the good period when I wasn't saying that your face isn't for me, anymore.

Here Dolores is referring to her reaction after she discovered the presence of a man in my life: She felt that her face was no longer for me, and my face was no longer for her—the trauma with the good foster mother. But nevertheless she is able here to talk about a profound feeling of facial connection between us.

BB: I'm so sorry that you feel that now. But I still feel that my face *is* for you.

Dolores: You have such good faces. I have those good face-feelings. That is what is *inside me*. I sometimes have bad face-feelings too. Your good faces, the "still-lake-face," the "resting-face"—I like best your "just-watching-all-the-time-face," it makes me safe.

BB: I'm so happy that you can see what my face feels for you. And how did you remember us after you watched the video?

Dolores: I wanted the feeling again. *One strange thing: afterward I made your face.*

BB: Oh! Which one?

Dolores: A certain face. A picture of my feelings. Deep. Like when you see I'm worried or sad.

BB: Then you made my "worry-sad-face"?

Dolores: Yes. I moved my face. I could just feel you.

BB: You could feel me responding to you?

Dolores: If I don't have a responder, I can't even have that feeling. It's *you*, feeling *me*, and it's *me*, seeing myself on your face. *Then I can feel more real, then I know that it is me.* On the video, when I let myself be with your face, *then I knew that your face was for me*, the second time I watched it. I could see that your face was not bad or scared or mean. The face is the beginning of a person. This faces loves me; I'm okay.

BB: I think you felt this once before, with the face of the first, good mother, and now you feel it again with me.

Dolores: I guess I took it away from you.

BB: Because you think that my face is not supposed to be for you anymore because of "the man"?

Dolores: I don't want there to be three faces. If there are three, only two go together, and my face isn't in it.

BB: You're describing to me a way of using the video to help your-self know that I sense you. But because of this terrible tragedy when you lost your first, good mother, and you think a man took her away, your ability to know that my face is for you has been disrupted. This is very difficult and sad for us.

Dolores: All the other times I looked at the video I saw your face, but I didn't let myself *be* with your face, and I didn't let your face *be with me*. This time I did. It caught me by surprise.

BB: You really let yourself have it this time? You need my face to feel my reach for you, and to feel yourself.

Dolores: Otherwise I'm like a blind baby.

She is even more articulate in this session than in the last one about how she uses the videotape as an adjunct to an internalization process. Her statement, "those good face-feelings: that is what I have inside of me" is a way of talking about how she can both viscerally and symbolically sense my appreciation of what she feels. She is active in the process of matching my faces on the video, participating, creating, rehearsing. She also uses her memory of looking at the videotapes to call up certain feel-ings, and she makes subtle differentiations among my faces. This is a big shift in her own capacity and activity. The discovery of a man in my life threatens to disrupt her emerging but still very fragile internalization of our relationship.

Being Sensed: One Year Later, Early in the Fourth Year

[*Notes taken during a telephone session*]

Dolores: When I get so sure inside that I don't have a face, and then I disappear, when I don't have a sensing—I don't know which is first, my face or the other face—then I don't have my senses, even breathing, because all my senses are in the face.

BB: In the face of the other person, in relation to your face?

Dolores: Yes—in *your* face. I don't have a face if I'm not sensed. If I'm not in your senses, then there's no way to be alive. You don't have any of your own senses or sensings without the other per-son. Then you can't talk.

BB: Is that maybe why you couldn't talk and went mute?

Dolores: I think so. I did not have any senses. I couldn't sense anyone else's senses, or anyone sensing me—even the touching
sense—touching is still in the face.

BB: That must have been so terrible.

Dolores: Yes.

BB: And do you feel that way again now?

Dolores: Yes.

In this vignette Dolores tells me how much she needs my sensing her in
order to have a sensing experience of herself. The experience of not being
sensed by me, and not sensing herself, typically occurred during a telephone session and almost never face to face. She is also very coherent and
articulate in this session, particularly in contrast to material from the middle
of the second year. Earlier in her life she had had an image of herself as
completely alone, a "little creature without a head." My association to this
session is that she "took off her head" in response to the traumatic loss of a
sensing, loving presence when she lost her first, good mother. She could not
sense herself alone, and she felt she had lost her head.

Your Face in Response to My Face: You Let
Me Affect You, Early in the Fifth Year

[*Notes taken during a session in person*]

Dolores: My whole life I have had big feelings about a lost face I was
looking for. It reminds me how I felt after I lost the relationship
with James [the long relationship that did not work out], and I
was in unbelievably deep grief and mourning. I don't have the
words for it, but I know a huge part of the loss had to do with
how I had affected him, how I saw his face respond to me.
That was a metaphor, maybe, for a total way of responding. You
know, how as a dance makes music visible, a face makes a whole
heart visible.

BB: How did his face respond to you?

Dolores: Part of what was so missing was his face—his face-in-response-
to-my-face. I learned about myself when I saw my impact on his
face. I created something—to see yourself, to see your impact
on the other person. I can make that face do a lot of different things. You know, we seek the pleasure and the desire on
someone else's face. [*long pause*] It was not just that I missed his
face, but the conversation, what I could make happen. The loss
was being able to make a difference. [*Dolores cries*] When I met
you—Sally [Dolores's previous therapist] was quite wonderful,

but she kept hiding. She was uneasy about letting me have an impact on her, except she would use her own reactions, but only in terms of what I might have evoked in her. The therapist can say, you know, I find myself feeling angry and can use that to talk about the patient's anger. But do you think a therapist ever says, you know, I found myself feeling loved?

BB: [*laughs*] I do feel that.

Dolores: That is what is different here. From the very beginning you let me affect you. That is what I've been missing my whole life.

BB: How did I do it?

Dolores: [*cries*] You accepted it, what my feelings were, or what my face was or offered—you met it. You felt affected or changed by it. Not like Sally. With Sally it was about my unconscious exerting a pressure on her to feel a certain something, and what did that say about me. It wasn't about "me and you," the way it is here.

BB: I did feel so moved by you and by your story. I remember so vividly the first day I met you.

Dolores: You shook my hand in that little waiting room, the first day.

BB: And the next time I saw you I ran into you in the street.

Dolores: You recognized me—

BB: And we were both so surprised and delighted in the moment.

Dolores: Because of the power of our first meeting.

BB: Yes. I know I did let myself be affected by you, by your story. I remember I wrote down some of the things you said about your face in those first few meetings.

Dolores: Your response to me made me more hopeful. It helped me identify what it was I needed.

BB: I'm so happy you feel this way. [*pause*] And will you remember this on Monday?

Dolores: No. I am too upset when I remember it and don't have it. Maybe I remember the loss of it.

BB: Yes. I think so. The loss of our conversation, even temporarily, becomes more salient than what we had. Like Stern's infant research example of one mother who attunes to enthusiasm when the little girl is having fun and becoming excited, on the way up the arousal curve; and another mother who attunes to "*ex*thusiasm" when her little girl is on the way down, after the blocks fell: Don't worry honey, we'll build it up again. You code "*ex*thusiasm."

Dolores: Psychoanalysis is best at entering the patient's distress, not the patient's joy. But the psychoanalyst as the person may resist entering the full despair.

> BB: And sometimes you feel I have trouble entering the full impact
> of your despair.
> Dolores: Yes.

The remarkable range of Dolores's functioning is again evident here as she describes the lost relationship with James. Her ability to value her impact on James, and on me, helps to repair the profound helplessness of her early years. Again, at the end of the vignette I am concerned about her difficulty in holding on to these feelings.

Taking Both of Us Into Account: Two Years Later, Seventh Year

[Notes after a session in person]
We uncovered her feeling that her face did not have enough to give me. It was at a moment of her deep despair, when I had been feeling that I did not have enough to give her. Her association was that she must have felt that was why the first good mother had left her, that her own face did not have enough to give, and that perhaps I experienced with her what she had felt about her first mother. Increasingly now Dolores has a remarkable ability to take both of our experiences into account.

Beginning of the Ninth Year: Together We Watch the Videotapes We Made in the Second Year

This vignette is based on a session in person. Dolores and I are watching the videotape sections from the second year, described earlier. She has given me permission to show these clips of my face to a professional audience, and she wants to review them. The following exchange is based on notes taken during the session. We are looking at the section where I am saying, "Good but *sad*? Good but *sad*?"

> Dolores: You have an energy here. You have heard something. It marks the
> moment. You have a lot of hope in me. For me it seems like I'm
> waking up, being discovered. Same as now. You bring me alive. I
> was feeling that leaving would turn me to concrete, like going into
> a coma. You are transforming things—my hope of being found.

[*Now we are looking at the section of the video where I am saying, "If you look at me, you feel I'll become the mother you'll never see again." Dolores says, "If I don't look at you, it won't happen." Then, after a long pause, she looks at me for a split second and I smile.*]

Dolores: You are so happy to see me look at you!

[*Now we are looking at the video section where we are teasing.*]

Dolores: These are the faces that I wait for. They bring me to life.
    BB: These are beautiful things to say to me. [*pause*] You are so much more able to look at me now. What do you think made the difference in shifting it?
Dolores: Your harassment and bullying. [*we both laugh*] I can see now that I could come to look at you because you gave me so much with your face. I couldn't stand, after a while, not giving you mine. Which I wouldn't know really if I weren't looking at this with you now. How could someone who is looked at the way you look at me not reciprocate? Because one of the important reasons I feel so dead is not being able to give someone my own face.
    BB: That is also a beautiful thing to say to me. I think the other thing that helped us was analyzing the fantasy that, if you looked at me, my face would turn into the monster [one of her abusers], or I would see you as a monster.
Dolores: I looked at your face. I did not see a monster, so that could tell me *I* wasn't a monster either. Your looking at my face didn't make you into a monster. You gave me a good sweet face; it must mean I'm not a monster.

The analysis of Dolores's fantasy that if she looked at me she would see the face of a monster, her abuser, or that she herself would have a monstrous face, went on over the course of at least half a decade. Only very gradually did this terror diminish until finally, at this point in the treatment, she seems to feel relatively free of it.

Dolores: I know the feeling, being on the other side of it. I wonder how *others* perceive it, how close it was to what I felt. What do *others* see about *us*?
    BB: I think the audience was very moved by my being willing to show myself to them.
Dolores: But *really* what they were seeing was your willingness to show yourself to *me*. Therapists are not usually willing to show themselves. The face of Jason [one of her former therapists] was like a stone.
    BB: I'm grateful that you felt comfortable enough to let me show the videotape.
Dolores: Now that I see it, I feel I'm totally protected.

In this vignette Dolores is able to revisit our early interaction with delight. She takes pleasure in my energy, my happiness when she can look at me even for an instant. She is very clear that my response to her has helped her come alive. She uses this moment to realize that she needed to reciprocate, to give me her own face. This is something so essential that we have been struggling to accomplish. Her capacity for spontaneous delight, for reflection, for humor in teasing me, for appreciation, all indicate a widening emotional range.

Dolores's Face in the Ninth and Tenth Years

Dolores's face has undergone quite a transformation. It is soft and hesitant, but her emotions are visible. She is slow to make eye contact but can sustain a steady gaze at times. At some point in the session, she can usually open up into a smile. At the beginning of every session in person, there is still a question of how long it will take her to take off her sunglasses. I feel very shut out when she wears them, and it is a sure sign that she is feeling distant when she does not take them off for quite a while. Usually these days she takes them off quickly. But more time will be needed before she will be able to look at me in a more ongoing and sustained way.

More Work on the Theme of Being Kicked Out by "The Man"

In the ninth and tenth years we made more progress on the theme of being "kicked out" by the presence of "the man" and her continuing anger at me that somehow, whatever I do, it is not right, or not enough, or not what she needs. This anger was usually very palpable on the telephone; it hung heavy in the long silences between us. We were able to agree that her silences on the telephone were her way of pouting and protesting without putting into words how neglected she feels. She was able to comment that she knew her feelings did not really quite make sense, even though she still felt them as strongly as ever: she felt "squeezed in, stuck on, a 'post-it.'" Eventually she was able to tell me, "If I don't hold myself back, angry and stony, I'll just be begging you not to leave, not to end the session. I'm always on the verge of doing that. If I don't let myself be with you, I won't be in a state of panic when the session ends. I feel powerless: It doesn't matter what I feel or want; I'm not going to get what I need, because of the man. Which I know isn't really true."

Dolores was now developing a new, tentative relationship with a boyfriend. Although the increased security in our relationship had made this new boyfriend possible, she felt that something more needed to shift between us if the new relationship was to be possible. The new boyfriend added a new urgency to our need to solve this problem.

In an important series of sessions, she commented that she was always in a "waiting mode," waiting for the time that she would really have me, but she never did. She felt not alive, spending her life waiting. In a very familiar vein, I commented on how painful it was to be waiting for the mother who never came. But then I suggested that perhaps she had a fantasy that someday she would really "have" me—maybe like a mother or a "primary partner"—so she didn't have to be alive now or really use what we had now. Instead, she stayed half-dead, waiting, until she got her mother back. Dolores could not in this session focus on or hold on to this idea. In the next session (in person), however, Dolores was more forthcoming:

Dolores: In between our sessions, the waiting is interminable. I'm protesting the waiting. Even though I know that it's not really *you* who made me wait. This is what I feel when we talk on the phone: angry, you've made me wait, the way I had to wait for my mother, and she never came.

BB: [*I refer back to the previous session's idea that she has a fantasy that she will eventually "get" me, so she doesn't have to use me now.*]

Dolores: What I have with you is not sufficient, so I'm not going to settle for it. I'm not going to let it count as the real thing.

BB: The "real thing"?

Dolores: Something that can never be. Something that I never had, a better past, a real mother. If I make it okay, what I have with you—though it *is* wonderful—then I would have to accept what has already happened, and what will never happen.

BB: You seem to have the idea that the loss is not irrevocable, you could get her back, you could get me back, it could be "just you and me" the way it was originally just you and your first mother.

Dolores: Probably. I know I can't go back to being a *baby*. "The man" has something I want; he has the advantage; I'm diminished.

BB: You are having difficulty mourning for the terrible, irrevocable loss. You are holding out for something else, something better, getting your mother back, getting us as a primary mother–child unit, that I could somehow be the real mother. And you had these difficulties before "the man" entered the picture.

Dolores: I want to go ahead with this new boyfriend—whatever is happening with him is so different—but I have the idea that if I do go forward, I will give up the opportunity to find something that I already lost. A grown-up relationship runs counter to the fantasy of getting my mother back.

BB: To be able to go forward with this new relationship, and to accept that I am your "real" therapist now, require facing this mourning.

Dolores: [*crying*] My only hope was to get her back. I knew it was impossible. I always knew this. But I try anyway. It keeps me from having a life. I can't think about it.

[*Later in the session*]

Dolores: The man—pushes me out—is probably connected to the idea that I can't grieve. If I keep him there, kicking me out from being with you, then I'm holding on to the idea that I *could* have you. It's because of the man that I can't have you, rather than the problem with grieving.

BB: That is such an important realization.

Sharing This Paper With Dolores and the Impact on the Treatment: Tenth Year

In the process of obtaining Dolores's permission for me to write up our treatment, I gave her a draft of this paper to read. This event became a catalyst for reviewing the treatment together. This vignette occurred over the telephone.

Dolores: In the videotapes you were sitting so quietly, so respectful, so careful. Did you know that you were honoring the potential overarousal of my longing?

BB: I did feel careful. I felt your fear. I felt your longing, your terror of loss, a huge love and a huge loss.

Dolores: I was longing for engagement, but it was intolerable to get it. I shut down interaction in the arena most important to me.

BB: Yes, you shut down facial engagement and looking, but you engaged in other ways: you really did talk to me. Even during the periods that you were so dissociated and didn't remember, you were always trying to explain what had happened and struggling to remember all the traumatic things.

Dolores: I might not have looked at you directly, but I took in enough of your face. I took it in the very first time I met you, the very first minute, in that little waiting room. I *saw* it, and I *had* it. I made it a good face. I had your face instantly. You looked right at me, and I felt totally welcome. You were totally welcoming me. Any time I did look, your face was always right there, always waiting for me. And your voice always had a face. I got glimpses of your expression, and I got enough to make a strong image of a good face in you.

I believe that something very important happened for Dolores as she saw my face for the first time. We did, however, continue to struggle in the early years of the treatment: if she looked at me, my face might look like the "monster," or her face might look like a monster as well. In addition, by avoiding gaze, Dolores was trying to keep out a face that might evoke too much painful longing, or a face that might abandon her. If she looked at me, she might lose me. It took years of testing out to see if my face might be safe to look at.

I Feel on My Face the Feeling on Your Face: Tenth Year

[*Notes taken during a telephone session*]

Dolores: I was thinking about the "good" between the faces, and how I hold on to that feeling. When I have to leave you, I feel on my face the feeling on your face, saying "good, but sad."

BB: As you see it on my face, you feel it in yours?

Dolores: Yes. I feel *you* on *my* face. I see your eyebrow furrowed, trying to see something. You're listening to me so intently. And I can *feel* it on my face, in my body-face. I use it on my own face, the good-mother face, your face. [*pause*] When you have the good-face-in-relation-to-the-good-face, you get to be the good face; you get to have the good face.

BB: You remembered this, and it became the foundation for your beautiful capacity to love.

Discussion

Dialogic Origin of Mind

One of the central ideas of the infant theorists of intersubjectivity illustrated by this case is the dialogic origin of mind. In early infancy Dolores lost her biological mother and she was given to a foster mother. At approximately age 2 years Dolores lost the dialogue—of face, voice, touch, smell, and some words—with her first (foster) mother. This loss was further compounded by the substitution of the abusive (biological) mother and sexually abusive men. The theory of mind based on presymbolic intelligence, briefly described in Paper I, posits that infants code expectancies of "how interactions go." One aspect of the trauma that Dolores suffered was a profound violation of her expectancies of "how the faces go." She expected a warm and loving face, the face of the first mother, whom she could make happy—and instead she was "faced" with the angry, hostile mother who told her she was bad, and she had to deal with sexually abusive men. One reason she did not look at me was that she anticipated that either she or I would have the "monster face" associated with the abusive men. She essentially had learned three different sets of expectancies of interactions, three different sets of implicit relational knowing: one with the good mother, one with the abusive mother and men, and one with her adopted family. We were always working with all three, trying to integrate them, while validating her very different experiences in them.

But eventually her voice and face went mute, when she was approximately 4 years old. She described this experience as "going away," "going dead," "defeated," "lost," being "in the quiet place." Perhaps Winnicott's (1958) concept of the loss of going-on-being comes close to describing this trauma. This profound disruption in the *dyadic* organization of her experience threatened the dialogic organization of her mind. It resulted in a loss of *all* forms of "intersubjectivity" during this period. This state of mind continued to threaten her as an adult.

The Role of Correspondences and Matching

Our central focus in the early stages of the treatment was to find a way into Dolores's "closed system," as she later described it. Despite her verbalized longing to "find my face," she was shut down and inaccessible for long periods. Arranging our chairs at a more "biological" face-to-face distance helped to create more "immediacy" of my presence during periods of her profound dissociation. But a great deal of the work of "finding" Dolores was based on variations in the nonverbal correspondences and matching described by Meltzoff, Trevarthen, and Stern, the three infant theorists. These correspondences provided the most basic ways I sensed and entered her experience, promoting a feeling of "being with" and "shared mind."

The matching concepts of Trevarthen and Stern provided one foundation of the treatment. Trevarthen's concept is that each partner is able to be aware of the other's feelings and purposes without words and language by matching communicative expressions through time, form, and intensity.

Stern's concept of tracking slight shifts in the partner's level of activation of face, voice, or body, and *changing with* the partner as a way of "feeling into" what the partner feels, adds further specificity to the concept of matching. I felt my way into Dolores's experience through the way her lower lip might tremble, through her rapid foot jiggle when she was anxious, through the muted quality of her face and movements, through her drastically lowered level of bodily activity—the "deadness." I matched her very reduced activity level, her pausing rhythms and long switching pauses, the rhythm and contour of her words.

For Trevarthen, rhythm is perhaps the central mechanism through which immediate sympathetic contact is created in the earliest protoconversations (see also Jaffe et al., 2001). Since Dolores initially did not make much use of the facial-visual channel of communication, the early phases of the treatment were carried through my rhythms (of voice and body) rather than my face. Matching her rhythms constituted the *process* of how I reached for her, how I tried to sense her state, and she could come to sense mine. Both Stern and Trevarthen argue that matching of communicative expressions simultaneously regulates both interpersonal contact and inner state. Dolores gradually came to sense a "comforted" inner state as she became more aware of how I matched her. Thus matching of expressions through time, form, and intensity was a powerful nonverbal mode of therapeutic action.

The video heightened Dolores's awareness of my response to her. Perhaps the same results could have been accomplished without the video, but, in any case, Dolores felt that the video helped us. I agreed. Like Winnicott's (1971) child playing the squiggle game, who becomes aware that another is aware of what the child is aware of within, by watching the video Dolores discovered that I was seeing what she herself "carried" in her face and body, or "sensed" about herself, without being able to describe it verbally. Seeing my face seeing her, and hearing my sounds responding to hers, alerted her to her own inner affective reality. After reading this chapter, she declared, "I recognized myself in your face recognizing me, for example, when you said, 'good but sad,' and I came to feel myself more and to feel more alive. I saw myself, and I saw you, recognizing me, and I felt the promise of an 'us' as a new possibility. And I came to feel an inner sense of feeling comforted."

Like Meltzoff's description of the infant's face gradually approximating that of the model by using the proprioceptive feedback from facial muscles, Dolores would find herself "putting on" my facial expressions while watching the video. By "wearing" my face, Dolores became more affectively aware of her own inner experience, presumably through the proprioceptive feedback of her face as well as the feedback from various physiological arousal systems (see Ekman, 1983). Meltzoff's concept that by imitating, the infant experiences that the other is "like me," is in play here. As Dolores matched my various faces, she experienced that she was "like" me. But since I was trying to sense my way into *her* experience, she found *herself* in my faces.

Dolores's matching also illustrates Stern's concept of "feeling-what-has-been-perceived-in-the-other." As she watched the video alone, Dolores experimented with letting herself "change with" my face and thereby to feel what I had perceived in her.

The description of mirror neurons may illuminate Dolores's experience watching the films of my face interacting with her and matching some of my faces. By simply watching my face moving in heightened affective ways, simultaneous activation of mirror neurons in her own brain might provide her with a link between my action and her neuronal "participation" in my action (Pally, 2000; December 18, 2001, personal communication). But, as Pally observed, it was not enough for Dolores simply to watch my face in the video; she had to *make the faces herself.* In this way she presumably obtained more overt sensorimotor feedback from her own body. Her own actions of matching seemed to be important in giving her back her feel of herself.

The Role of Difference

As important as these matching interactions were, matching alone did not fully characterize the nature of my interventions. "Matching" is too global a concept. Instead, in most of my responses, similarities and elaborations, as well as differences, were apparent. For example, I might repeat her phrase, which was punctuated with stops and starts, but bring it into a more coherent rhythm. I might add a rising intonation at the end of the sentence, with a feeling of questioning and opening, as if to hold open other options. I might elongate and emphasize a particular word, giving us a longer moment to absorb its impact. If I saw a shift on her face, such as a sudden sadness or a smile, I tried to put it into words. Usually my face showed the varying emotions that I sensed in her, even though her face usually did not. I might repeat her phrase but then add a "sinusoidal" greeting contour, heightening positive affect. I might elaborate a moment of humor with more rising and playful contours than hers, expanding the range of playfulness. At many points I verbally elaborated on what she said; I might link it with an earlier comment or anticipate the ending of the session.

These varieties of matching responses with subtle elaborations and differences were aspects of the regulation of positive states, but they also provided forms of distress regulation in which I both entered her experience but also slightly added something of my own. They often held open the possibility of just slightly broader ranges of experience, similar to Loewald's (1980) concept that the therapist holds an image of where the patient might be able to go. The moments when I exactly matched without altering were rare. I consider them to be very particular forms of distress regulation, consistent with Stern's concept of "share without altering," in which I had no agenda but to stay in her feeling, with exactly the range of nuances that she expressed. For example, joining a sad and dampened state without shifting it is a powerful way of sharing and accepting the distress (see Cohen & Beebe, 2002). As Schore (1994) argues, expanding the capacity of the patient as well as the analyst to stay in distress states, and to find more modulated ways of regulating them, is essential to transforming the distress. Cassidy (1994) argues that distress regulation is an essential aspect of the attachment process. On the positive side, Stern and Trevarthen note that expanding the capacity of both partners to join in positive states is essential to creating a secure attachment bond. Schore (1994) notes that expansion of positive states in the dyad will ultimately alter the opiate circuits in the brain associated with positive affect.

The Role of Self-Regulation

Various nonverbal movements of self-regulation provide powerful additional information about the inner experiences of both partners as well as about the state of relatedness. The contribution of my own self-regulation is visible in the videotapes when I rested my face in my chin and then slowly moved my hand up my face. This movement suggests a self-soothing and holding of distress. Varieties of head tilts function in many ways, including questioning, marking shifts of attention, and accenting ongoing verbalizations. Sighing is a release of one's own distress, but it also can communicate an entering of the other's distress. My own self-regulation movements not only highlight the moments in which I am experiencing particular stress but also communicate to Dolores my participation in her distress. In one session later on in the treatment, when Dolores noticed that I was rubbing my feet together (a self-soothing movement that I recognize from my childhood), she commented that I was doing it while she was refusing an interpretation that I was offering. This moment also illustrated her remarkable ability to hold both our experiences in mind.

More global forms of Dolores's self-regulation are seen in her drastically lowered level of bodily movement, her childlike, barely audible voice, her long periods of silence, her inability to look at me. Ongoing nonverbal signs of Dolores's self-regulation movements are harder to depict because she is seldom in the videotaped segments analyzed. At one moment, however, a rapid foot-jiggle is visible, expressing a moment of tension or anxiety. Another powerful form of self-regulation was her wearing sunglasses at the beginning of every session in person. This presumably provided her with a safer distance: She could see out, but I could not see in. The light was also dampened, perhaps lowering the level of stimulation and providing some soothing.

Whether and when she would take off the sunglasses was a complicated interaction for us. Earlier in the treatment I accepted long periods, perhaps half an hour, with her sunglasses on. But, as the treatment progressed, I became more impatient and gradually more insistent that she take them off after 5 or 10 minutes.

The Role of Interactive Regulation

One of the most essential aspects of what was reparative in this treatment was Dolores's sense that she could affect me and that I could affect her. She could sense, and see, and see again in the video, how her agony affected me: how it shifted my face and voice, created tenderness in me, and was comforting. She frequently told me how I affected her, both by making her feel cherished and by making her feel "kicked out," imagining that "the man" was the one that was important to me and she was not. After reading this paper, she commented on how important it was to her that I had understood "about the profound loss of feeling my impact on the other, of finding my impact on their face."

The basic concept of the mutual-regulation model—that each partner affects the other—is broader than the concept of matching. Each partner senses in herself an ongoing receptivity (or lack of receptivity) to the other, in adjusting, coordinating, and being "influenced," and each has an ongoing impact (or failure of impact) on the other. This is the bedrock of the entire treatment, the foundation of all human communication. Matching is a very specific form of this more general process of bidirectional interactive regulation.

Balance Model

When we began the treatment, Dolores could be characterized as preoccupied with self-regulation, largely sacrificing engagement (Figure 5.1). She was emotionally withdrawn, rarely looked, and frequently was silent for long periods. Essentially she refused a face-to-face exchange. When she did speak, she was hesitant, slow, and childlike. Her inner state was one of "icing over" deadness, or terror. However, she did participate in slow dialogic rhythms with me, even though in a halting, fragmented way. And she did at times try very hard to communicate verbally.

For my part, at the beginning of the treatment I could be described as being in a state of "therapeutic hypervigilance": not taking my eyes off

Initial years of treatment

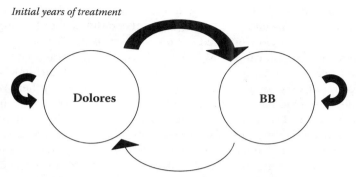

Dolores was preoccupied with self-regulation: withdrawn, muted, gaze-avoidant, regulating terror and deadness. She was intermittently verbally responsive, but childlike. Nonverbally she showed tentative tracking of BB's rhythms.

BB drastically altered her usual range of self-regulation to become slow, soft, with very low activation. BB was verbally and nonverbally a "therapeutic vigilant hyper-tracker."

9th and 10th years of treatment

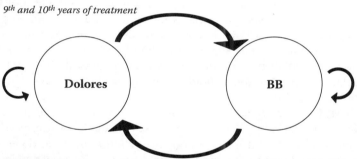

Dolores's self-regulation is less extreme with greater range. She gazes tentatively, is still frightened, but can feel "comforted." She is verbally responsive, reflective and generative, "thinking together." She is nonverbally responsive.

BB's self-regulation has returned to her usual range, with higher activation, not "careful." BB's tracking of Dolores's verbal and nonverbal behavior is more midrange, no longer hypervigilant.

Figure 5.1 Transformation of the interactive system in the treatment of Dolores.

her, tracking every shift in her body or voice, straining to catch her words, but drastically lowering my level of activation (in retrospect so as not to frighten her), and, when I was not speaking, frequently (out of awareness) keeping my body *perfectly still*. This was, however, a very "active stillness" (Gerhardt & Carnochan, November 25, 2001, personal communication). I did not intrude or "chase." While my body might be still and I listened while remaining verbally silent, my face remained open, expressive, and receptive (Kaufmann & Kaufmann, August 12, 2001, personal communication). I often leaned forward but remained contained within my own space (Tortora, June 2, 2002, personal communication). When I did speak, my vocal rhythms often matched her slow rate, and I participated in very slow, turn-taking rhythms; I tolerated very long "switching pauses," never hurrying her. My primary mode of interaction was to "go with" the shifts of tone, rhythm, activation, or face that I saw in her, as described by Stern. These adjustments, which I made largely out of awareness, moved me into her range. Much of my nonverbal behavior with her was based on what the infants had taught me. After reading this paper, Dolores declared, "You insinuated yourself into an interaction with me, into my closed system, where I had shut everything out."

Ten years into the treatment, we have both shifted our positions toward the "midrange," with a greater balance of self- and interactive regulation (Figure 5.1). We have regained face-to-face relating, in large part. Dolores is far less preoccupied with drastic forms of self-regulation, and she is much more engaged. She talks more, her voice is more audible, and her vocal rhythms are fluent. She participates in a fair amount of mutual gazing, looking and looking away in a more usual adult pattern. She reports a "comforted" inner state, at least some of the time, particularly when we are physically together rather than on the telephone. She talks about how hard it was to "relax her grip," to relax "holding on to herself," and says that she still has trouble with this.

For my part, I am no longer "hypervigilant" in my attention to her, and I am no longer dramatically altering my own self-regulation patterns in an attempt to make contact with her. I am not struggling to dampen down my arousal. My range of body movement is not inhibited, my level of activation of voice and face are more within my usual range, my speech rhythms are not as slow, and I am not as "careful" with her as I once was. I can be more relaxed and playful. The narrative is far more coherent. The treatment progresses in a more usual verbal interchange, and the nonverbal communication is generally more in the background. The verbal–nonverbal distinction is not as rigid: Verbal and nonverbal create more of a seamless process. A videotape of my face taken ten years into the treatment shows far more movement in me, particularly head movements. There are no periods where my body is perfectly still. My smiles are softer and have more of a range, my expressions are less "officially nice" (Heller, February 18, 2002, personal communication), and I even allow myself a blank face at one moment. I seem to feel less pressure to be "on," and I am not straining or trying so hard.

In this particular videotape Dolores has given me a book, and with her permission I allow myself the pleasure of reading a passage that is particularly meaningful to our relationship. There is "space" for me now, too (Heller,

February 18, 2002, personal communication). In her outside life, Dolores's relationship with her new boyfriend is progressing. She has become much more involved with professional colleagues as well as friends, so that she is less isolated. But she is still having trouble producing work on her own.

Concrete versus Constructivist Theory of Mind

At the beginning of the treatment, Dolores could be seen as partially stuck in a "concrete" theory of mind: It was difficult for her to know that how things appeared to her might not be how others saw those same things. She tended to misread her current reality, and conflate it with the experience of the abusive mother or the loss of the good mother. I addressed her difficulty in comparing old realities with her current life and her difficulty holding together different ideas from different eras of her development. Increasingly, though, Dolores had access to a constructivist theory of mind, which was a precious resource in the treatment. Increasingly she was aware of how her mental life was both similar to, and different from, that of others. For example, she could acknowledge that I might not actually be kicking her out to go to the man, even though she so strongly felt that I was.

Dolores's tremendous difficulty mourning the loss of the first, good mother derived in part from a concrete theory of mind in which she believed that she would get the first mother back. This belief became a life-saving fantasy: she felt that it was all she had to hold onto to stay alive. Two developments were necessary before we could analyze this fantasy: access to her "constructivist" theory of mind increased, and her relationship with me became sufficiently strong and "real" to her that she could tackle this immense loss (Kaufmann & Kaufmann, August 12, 2001, personal communication). The analysis of her wish to continue waiting for the first mother to return and of her difficulty using our relationship to become alive because it was not "the real thing," did not take hold until the ninth and tenth years. It was, however, essential to the treatment. It is here perhaps that the necessity for the explicit, verbal mode of psychoanalytic technique for the treatment is seen most vividly. The nonverbal and implicit relatedness created the foundation of the treatment, but it would not have been sufficient for the treatment to flower (see Bucci, 1985).

The Transformation of Implicit Relational Procedures

Dolores can be described as struggling with multiple, inconsistent, and often contradictory implicit relational models, stemming from her three primary caregiving situations, the first good mother, the abusive mother, and the adoptive family (see Lyons-Ruth, 1999). Within the model with her first good mother, Dolores had to deal with the radical inconsistency of two realities: she felt this mother really loved her, yet this mother had "left her for dead." Retaining contradictory, unintegrated images of this first mother was Dolores's way of "using" the image of the good mother, who, if Dolores could only wait long enough, would return to reclaim her rightful place as "the real thing." This coping strategy had, however, derailed Dolores's development and prevented her mourning. In the course of the treatment, she and I together developed a fourth model, in which we struggled to integrate in the same person the good mother and the abandoning mother, and we also developed our own new ways of relating.

The description of this treatment is one response to Lyons-Ruth's (1999) call for greater attention in psychoanalysis to how implicit and nonverbal modes of intimate relating are transformed, and to the analyst's specific, collaborative participation in this process as a "new kind of relational partner." She suggests that new ways of "being with" must be created at the enactive, procedural level as well as the symbolic level. The building blocks for transformations of the system occur in micromoments, small, mutually constructed sequences, over an extended period of time. Much of the detailed description of Dolores's treatment was an effort to illustrate how these transformations can occur in those ways. Lyons-Ruth suggests that these transformations of implicit ways of "being with" cannot occur through verbal instruction; instead, they are created through mutually participatory, collaborative "action" dialogues, which are constructed predominantly outside verbal awareness. Because implicit relational knowing is predominantly outside awareness, and seldom in focal attention, Lyons-Ruth argues, much of the subtlety and complexity of what the analyst knows is never put into words. It is for this reason that my examination of the videotaped interactions revealed much about my behavior that I could not have described without them and why it was difficult to find a language to describe them.

Conclusion

The variety of forms of implicit nonverbal intersubjectivity, including matching, difference, and their subtle intertwinings, patterns of self- and interactive regulation and their balance, and patterns of distress regulation, are many, difficult to catalogue, and probably unique to each psychoanalytic pair. Nevertheless we urgently need to study them. Interactions in the nonverbal and implicit modes are rapid, subtle, coconstructed, and generally out of awareness. And yet they profoundly affect moment-to-moment communication and the affective climate. They organize modes of relating, Stern's (1985) "ways of being with." Implicit, procedural, and emotional memories organize transference expectations and provide a degree of continuity and emotional functioning from childhood to adulthood (Clyman, 1991; Grigsby & Hartlaub, 1994; Sorter, 1994; Bucci, 1997; Stern et al., 1998; Lyons-Ruth, 1999; Knoblauch, 2000). Critical aspects of therapeutic action occur in this implicit mode and may never be verbalized, yet they powerfully organize the analysis. The collaborative participation of the analyst in this process is an essential, but little-explored arena. We can teach ourselves to observe these implicit and nonverbal interactions simultaneously in ourselves and in our patients and thus expand our own awareness and, where useful, that of our patients.

References

Adelmann, P., & Zajonc, R. (1989). Facial efference and the experience of emotion. *Annual Review of Psychology, 40*, 249–280.

Beebe, B. (2000). Co-constructing mother–infant distress: The micro-synchrony of maternal impingement and infant avoidance in the face-to-face encounter. *Psychoanalytic Inquiry, 30*, 421–440.

Beebe, B. (2003). Brief mother–infant treatment: Psychoanalytically informed video feedback. *Infant Mental Health Journal, 24*, 24–52.

Beebe, B., Knoblauch, S., Rustin, J., & Sorter, D. (2003). Introduction: A systems view. *Psychoanalytic Dialogues, 13*(6), 743–775.

Beebe, B., & Lachmann, F. (1994). Representation and internalization in infancy: Three principles of salience. *Psychoanalytic Psychology, 11*, 127–165.

Beebe, B., & Lachmann, F. (2002). *Infant research and adult treatment: Co-constructing interactions*. Hillsdale, NJ: The Analytic Press.

Beebe, B., Rustin, J., Sorter, D., & Knoblauch, S. (2003). An expanded view of intersubjectivity in infancy and its application to psychoanalysis. *Psychoanalytic Dialogues, 13*(6), 805–841.

Beebe, B., Sorter, D., Rustin, J., & Knoblauch, S. (2003). A comparison of Meltzoff, Trevarthen, and Stern. *Psychoanalytic Dialogues, 13*(6), 777–804.

Beebe, B., & Stern, D. (1977). Engagement-disengagement and early object experiences. In N. Freedman & S. Grand (Eds.), *Communicative structures and psychic structures* (pp. 35–55). New York: Plenum.

Benjamin, J. (1988). *The bonds of love: Psychoanalysis, feminism, and the problem of domination*. New York: Pantheon.

Bion, W. (1977). *Seven servants*. New York: Aronson.

Bower, B. (2001). Faces of perception. *Science News, 160*, 10–12.

Bucci, W. (1985). Dual coding: A cognitive model for psychoanalytic research. *Journal of the American Psychoanalytic Association, 33*, 571–608.

Bucci, W. (1997). *Psychoanalysis and cognitive science*. New York: Guilford Press.

Cassidy, J. (1994). Emotion regulation: Influences of attachment relationships. In *Monographs of the Society for Research in Child Development* (Vol. 59, pp. 2228–2249). London: Wiley-Blackwell.

Clyman, R. (1991). The procedural organization of emotions: A contribution from cognitive science to the psychoanalytic theory of therapeutic action. *Journal of the American Psychoanalytic Association, 39,* 349–381.

Cohen, P., & Beebe, B. (2002). Video feedback with a depressed mother and her infant: A collaborative individual psychoanalytic and mother–infant treatment. *Journal of Infant, Child, and Adolescent Psychotherapy, 2,* 1–55.

Davidson, R., & Fox, N. (1982). Assymetrical brain activity discriminates between positive versus negative affective stimuli in human infants. *Science, 218,* 1235–1237.

Dimberg, U., Thunberg, M., & Elmehed, K. (2000). Unconscious facial reactions to emotional facial expressions. *American Psychological Society, 11,* 86–89.

Downing, G. (2001). Changing procedural representations. Unpublished manuscript.

Eigen, M. (1993). *The electrified tightrope.* Northvale, NJ: Jason Aronson.

Ekman, P. (1983). Autonomic nervous system activity distinguishes among emotions. *Science, 221,* 1208–1210.

Ekman, P., Friesen, W., & Ancoli, S. (1980). Facial signs of emotional experience. *Journal of Personality and Social Psychology, 39,* 1125–1134.

Ekman, P., Levenson, R., & Friesen, W. (1983). Autonomic nervous system activity distinguishes among emotions. *Science, 221,* 1208–1210.

Fernald, A. (1987). Four-month-old infants prefer to listen to motherese. *Infant Behavior and Development, 8,* 181–195.

Freud, S. (1913). On the beginning of treatment. (Further recommendations on the technique of psycho-analysis.) In J. Strachey (Ed. & Trans.), *The standard edition of the complete psychological works of Sigmund Freud* (Vol. 12, pp. 133–134). London: Hogarth Press, 1958.

Gergeley, G., & Watson, J. (1998). Early social–emotional development: Contingency perception and the social-biofeedback model. In P. Rochat (Ed.), *Early social cognition* (pp. 101–136). Hillsdale, NJ: Lawrence Erlbaum.

Grigsby, J., & Hartlaub, G. (1994). Procedural learning and the development and stability of character. *Perceptual Motor Skills, 79,* 355–370.

Heller, M., & Haynal, V. (1997). A doctor's face: Mirror of his patient's suicidal projects. In J. Guimon (Ed.), *The body in psychotherapy* (pp. 46–51). Basel, Switzerland: Karger.

Izard, C. (1971). *The face of emotion.* New York: Appleton-Century-Crofts.

Jaffe, J., Beebe, B., Feldstein, S., Crown, C., & Jasnow, M. (2001). Rhythms of dialogue in early infancy. *Monographs of the Society for Research in Child Development* (Vol. 66, pp. 1–32). London: Wiley-Blackwell.

Klinnert, M., Campos, J., Sorce, J., Emde, R., & Svejda, M. (1983). The development of social referencing in infancy. In R. Plutchik & H. Kellerman (Eds.), *Emotion: Theory, research, and experience, vol. 2: Emotion in early development.* New York: Academic Press.

Knoblauch, S. (2000). *The musical edge of therapeutic dialogue.* Hillsdale, NJ: The Analytic Press.

Kohut, H. (1977). *The restoration of the self.* New York: International Universities Press.

Laird, J. (1984). The real role of facial response in the experience of emotion. *Journal of Personality and Social Psychology, 47,* 909–917.

Levenson, R., Ekman, P., & Friesen, W. (1990). Voluntary facial action generates emotion-specific autonomic nervous system activity. *Psychophysiology, 27,* 363–384.

Levinas, E. (1974). *Otherwise than being.* Pittsburgh, PA: Duquesne University Press.

Loewald, H. (1980). *Papers on psychoanalysis.* New Haven, CT: Yale University Press.

Lyons-Ruth, K. (1999). The two-person unconscious: Intersubjective dialogue, enactive relational representation, and the emergence of new forms of relational organization. *Psychoanalytic Inquiry, 19,* 576–617.

Main, M., & Hesse, E. (1992). Disorganized/disoriented infant behavior in the strange situation, lapses in the monitoring of reasoning and discourse during the parent's Adult Attachment Interview, and dissociative states. In M. Ammaniti & D. Stern (Eds.), *Attachment and psychoanalysis* (pp. 80–140). Rome: Guis, Laterza & Figli.

Mitchell, S. (2000). *Relationality: From attachment to intersubjectivity.* Hillsdale, NJ: The Analytic Press.

Ogden, T. (1986). *The matrix of the mind: Object relations and the psychoanalytic dialogue.* Northvale, NJ: Jason Aronson.

Ogden, T. (1994). *Subjects of analysis.* Northvale, NJ: Jason Aronson.

Pally, R. (2000). *The mind–brain relationship.* London: Karnac Books.

Papousek, H., & Papousek, M. (1987). Mother and the cognitive head start. In H. R. Schaffer (Ed.), *Studies in mother–infant interaction* (pp. 63–85). New York: Academic Press.

Perry, B. (1996). Childhood trauma, the neurobiology of adaptation, and "use-dependent" development of the brain: How "states" become "traits." *Infant Mental Health Journal, 16,* 271–291.

Sartre, J. (1992). *Being and nothingness.* New York: Washington Square Press.

Schore, A. (1994). *Affect regulation and the origin of the self: The neurobiology of emotional development.* Hillsdale, NJ: Lawrence Erlbaum.

Sorter, D. (1994). Therapeutic action and procedural knowledge: A case study. *International Forum of Psychoanalysis, 4,* 65–70.

Stern, D. (1985). *The interpersonal world of the infant.* New York: Basic Books.

Stern, D., Sander, L., Nahum, J., Harrison, A., Bruschweiler-Stern, N., & Tronick, E. (1998). Non-interpretative mechanisms in psychoanalytic therapy. *International Journal of Psychoanalysis, 79,* 903–921.

Tomkins, S. (1962). *The positive affects, vol. 1.* New York: Springer.

Tomkins, S. (1963). *The negative affects, vol. 2.* New York: Springer.

Tronick, E. (1989). Emotions and emotional communication in infants. *American Psychologist, 44,* 112–119.

Weil, E. (1958). The origin and vicissitudes of the self-image. *Psychoanalysis, 1,* 15–18.

Winnicott, D. W. (1958). *Collected papers: Through paediatrics to psycho-analysis.* London: Tavistock Publications.

Winnicott, D. W. (1965). *Maturational processes and the facilitating environment.* New York: International Universities Press.

Winnicott, D. W. (1971). *Therapeutic consultations in child psychiatry.* London: Hogarth Press.

Winnicott, D. W. (1974). *The mirror role of the mother and family in child development: Playing and reality.* Middlesex, UK: Penguin.

Winton, W. (1986). The role of facial response in self-reports of emotions: A critique of Laird. *Journal of Personality and Social Psychology, 50,* 808–812.

6

Impasse Recollected in Tranquility

*Love, Dissociation, and Discipline in the Analytic Process**

Stuart A. Pizer

▼ ▼ ▼ ▼ ▼

Wordsworth defined poetry as "emotion recollected in tranquility." I've titled this paper "Impasse Recollected in Tranquility," in part because I share with you here a session from late in Rebecca's analysis in which her own insightful recognitions spoke to me with the voice of poetry and in part because that very pivotal session nearly didn't happen in just the ways I want to depict for you as a particular feature of impasse.

Impasse can be, and has been, usefully formulated from a number of perspectives. Elkind (1992) described what happens when a patient's transference collides with a therapist's own primary vulnerability. She offers impasse consultations to introduce a three-dimensional resource that may help reopen a foreclosed therapeutic potential space or close down the treatment through humane and responsible support for grieving and planning. Atwood and Stolorow (1984) cogently described the intersubjective quagmire that can occur when two profoundly conjunctive or disjunctive subjectivities meet together over time, exerting unreflective reciprocal impact on each other. Benjamin (2000) elaborated her view of impasse as a particular breakdown within intersubjectivity, when the structures of mutual recognition and acceptance of difference collapse, and the therapeutic couple sinks into a pervasive monotony of doer-done-to complementarity that defies the inclinations of either party to return to a surface where self

---

* This paper originally appeared in *Psychoanalytic Dialogues, 14*(3), 2004, pp. 289–311. Reprinted with permission.

and other can once again see each other. Ogden (1994) offered a resonant concept: moments when the intersubjective third (the creative and potential space between analytic partners) shifts into a deadening and coercive subjugating third. Russell (1975) described the crunch that occurs when the repetition compulsion brings the therapeutic relationship to the brink of recapitulating an emotional catastrophe. Barbara Pizer (2003) wrote eloquently of the relational (k)not, an insidious form of crunch characterized not by moments of explosiveness but by stretches of mystifyingly tangled and double-binding nonrelatedness in which thought, affect, or engagement is snuffed out. Ringstrom (1998) has explored the double bind in his own examination of impasse (invoking Steven Stern, 1994), as a snagging of the logical levels of needed and repeated relationship. In these moments, the analyst's efforts to engage with the patient in the patient's needed relationship disqualify and are disqualified by their very reenactment, for the patient, of a malignantly repeated relationship—and neither party can attain a metalevel of perspective to comment on, and thereby break through, this fearful symmetry. McLaughlin (1991) helped us to recognize impasses as the consequence of the analyst's own "dumb spots, hard spots, and blind spots" (pp. 600–601)—that is, rigidity introduced into the treatment process by the analyst's inexperience, parochialism, or unreflective subjectivity. And, of course, we can usefully invoke a more classical view of impasse as a cousin of negative therapeutic reaction, when a patient's hate or envy is turned outward toward defeating and destroying the therapist, or inward as a spiteful destruction of possibilities for the self.

My own thinking has benefited from all of these perspectives, and I commend them to your attention. I wrote about impasse (Pizer, 1998) in terms of what I call the nonnegotiable: that is, an entrenched or recalcitrant barrier to unfolding negotiations of relatedness and meaning-making between analyst and patient. The nonnegotiable may be determined by the patient's relational history of pervasive misrecognitions, despair over the potential for a mutually adaptable relational world, and a malevolent intrapsychic pattern of repetitions that perpetuate the patient's relational paradigms of hopelessness; or the posttraumatic residue of unbridgeable dissociations within the self that renders the patient unable to straddle the challenging paradoxes of the therapeutic frame and relationship. On the analyst's part, the nonnegotiable may entail a failure to straddle the exquisitely delicate paradoxical position of remaining true to himself or herself and grounded in his or her analytic purpose and mission, while making those tacit internal adjustments of being and relating that are necessary for the analyst to be and to feel enough of what the patient requires that he or she be and feel. As I describe the nonnegotiable, potential space and reflective functioning or metalevel thought—in either analyst or patient, or both—fall casualty to the collapse of paradoxes too intolerable or unbridgeable for a particular analytic dyad at a particular moment. The peremptory, coercive, concretizing, or polarizing expectations and pressures that may follow and occupy the mind of a patient or analyst render important pathways of potential experience, affect, inquiry, curiosity, reflection, formulation, recognition, surrender, or transformation temporarily, or permanently, impassable within that analysis.

But, although any or all of these perspectives can be detected in the fabric of what I present to you here, I emphasize a particular perspective close to Donnel Stern's (1997, 2003) ideas. Stern described strong dissociation, a defensive proscription (usually the patient's) on the formulation of experience, and weak dissociation, a failure to discern features of experience embedded in the familiar, or ritual—a failure of the analyst (or patient) to notice a place for asking a question. As I see it, the analyst's weak dissociation may set up or perpetuate a subtle impasse simply by letting a patient's seemingly innocent remark—or the analyst's inkling of a question—slip from mind or comment, rather than becoming a focus for useful attention and joint inquiry. We usually think of impasse as something going dramatically wrong in a treatment. But I describe how impasse can work in the wings like a silent killer. Impasse may lie in a trail of lost opportunities for reflection. And that, I believe, is how Rebecca's creative session nearly didn't happen.

Before focusing attention on that particular session late in Rebecca's treatment, I turn now to recollections of Rebecca's entry into her therapeutic passage, to supply some background. I wrote elsewhere (Pizer, 1998, 2000) about Rebecca, and I briefly summarize from that material now.

Rebecca, one of my first patients, entered therapy with me in her early 20s. Although a creatively gifted person, she had finished her senior year of college by the skin of her teeth—having engaged in heavy drug and alcohol use, reckless driving, and similarly reckless relationships. She lived an urchin-like existence, abhorred loneliness, and frequented bars so she could "stand in the crowd between two people and feel like I exist." She wore torn denims, claimed to identify with Clint Eastwood, and announced that she was "incapable of loving." Rebecca stayed initially for eight sessions, and then she left to attend her out-of-state college graduation. Our plan was for her to return to Boston, and to her therapy, in a month. Instead, she disappeared. After 4 months of whereabouts unknown, Rebecca resurfaced at my office door. She had been on a binge of drugs and various forms of high speed. ("One night," she said, "I danced barefoot on beer bottles and ended up with a staph infection.") Seeing Rebecca's state and fearing that she might soon end up dead in a ditch, I hospitalized her that day, mobilized her extraordinarily ungiving family, and undertook a therapy that would last 9 years. In the course of this treatment, I devoted myself to offering her a sponsoring and sheltering provision in therapy. For example, during her 6-month hospitalization, I drove to the hospital to hold her sessions rather than use the hospital's policy of sending patients out to their sessions by public transportation or taxi, because I feared she'd become a runaway and because I believed in offering her an experience of containment. Rebecca became highly dependent on a sustaining relationship with me, which included phone calls between sessions, a very low fee when her family eventually washed their hands of her, and occasional hugs at the end of sessions when she reported feeling particularly fragile and ungrounded—like a kite without a string, with nothing to hold her to earth. Rebecca also withheld information, manipulated me by either exaggerating or underplaying her states of danger, and evoked in me acute feelings of worry, helplessness, and exasperation. At times, I felt like a mother whose infant would not eat; at other times, I felt ridiculed for offering love. Rebecca would only haphazardly talk about fragments of her life history, requiring us to focus on the chaotic surface of her current daily life. In those early days of clinical practice, I brought to the work my inexperience and earnest naïveté. At that time, I did not have the benefit of more recent work on the treatment of childhood abuse survivors to confirm my suspicion that her alcoholic father had sexually abused her. Although Rebecca readily reported that her father had made raunchy remarks to her and snapped her bra strap during her adolescence, she recalled no further boundary crossings. What she did recall was the progressive deterioration of her family life as she approached adolescence, with both parents sinking deeper into alcoholism and her mother submerging repeatedly into depressions for which she was hospitalized every 2 years. Looking back on the period of this treatment, I would say that Rebecca's therapy was limited then by unbridgeable paradoxes. That is, her childhood history of severe privations and violations led Rebecca to require me to be an environment mother unalloyed by father elements that may have rendered transferential access to her dissociated abuse memories.

Rebecca needed a prolonged period of shelter on an island sanctuary where I was an unquestioned environment mother, as manifested in part through her inability to use, or to indicate that she was using, the interpretations I offered her.* An aspect of this role segmentation was that it opened the place for her, at times, to enact the sadistic, attacking father while preserving her defensive dissociation. For example, in the months following her hospitalization, Rebecca would fail to show up for appointments or answer her phone,

---

* Discussants of an earlier version of this paper have expressed an interest in the flavor of my interpretations in the early phase of Rebecca's treatment. I offer one instance: Early in Rebecca's hospitalization, when she sat shivering in the room on the hall assigned to us for her therapy sessions, I asked the staff to provide more heat. But, also mindful that Rebecca's mother was arriving the next day for her first visit to the hospital (she now lived, remarried, in Europe), I said to Rebecca, "I think you're feeling very anxious anticipating your mother's visit tomorrow. Because she relates to you so much through the private language she developed with you, you feel pressured to join her in it. I think you're afraid that's the only way to connect with her when she's here."

thereby staging the illusion of having run away again. Or she would exhibit agitation and say, "I'm upset, but I can't talk with *you* about it."

I "survived" (see Winnicott, 1971). Important as this was in itself, given the psychological residue of Rebecca's unfortunate developmental experiences, she and I could not negotiate the full paradoxes of our relationship. But, although Rebecca and I neither accumulated our insights into a thoroughly coherent narrative reconstruction nor worked through the sadomasochistic features of transference–countertransference repetitions, over time she apparently ceased her drug use, stabilized practices of self-care and self-soothing, developed a solid career, and (just before abruptly quitting treatment after 9 years) married a successful professional.

So I was both startled and pleased when Rebecca phoned me 13 years after ending her treatment and asked if she could come for a visit. Both of us now middle-aged, we found ourselves again opposite each other in my office as Rebecca told me that she had come for three specific reasons—to apologize to me, to inform me, and to thank me. Her apology was succinct and astoundingly incisive. She said, "I could not bear to be so dependent on you. At the same time, I was furious that you wouldn't just fix my life for me. So I set out to destroy you. I had to make you suffer. I'm sorry." Rebecca made a second apology: She had quit therapy abruptly because she and her new husband had begun a pattern of heavy alcohol dependence, which she feared she could not continue to keep from me. At that time, her secret alcohol abuse had been nonnegotiable. The information she wanted me to have was, that during a subsequent time when she had been trying to get pregnant and had joined Alcoholics Anonymous and ceased her drinking, she recovered memories of extensive sexual abuse by her father. She had then entered another therapy to address these memories more thoroughly. Finally, she thanked me: "We couldn't address my alcoholism together. Or the abuse. I wasn't ready yet. But you did everything right. You stood by me. I felt loved and sheltered. You made it possible for me to stay alive long enough, until I was ready to face the work I had to do. You gave me the hope that I held onto even when things got worse, until I could find it in myself to make them better."

I was personally touched and grateful for what Rebecca said to me. Her visit, and her message, exemplified for me how even an incomplete therapy, one that fails to negotiate significant symptomatic or transference conditions, may still serve a vital purpose. In the course of our work together, Rebecca's abuse history and her own substance abuse remained nonnegotiable, or impassable, issues. Yet her message to me in this visit affirmed my sense that in therapy we do what we can when we can within the limits of each therapeutic duet. At the time of Rebecca's visit, I was in the midst of writing my (1998) book on paradox and negotiation and was contemplating a chapter on the nonnegotiable. Rebecca's message struck me as aptly summarizing the process of therapeutic work in the face of the nonnegotiable. So I wrote this story of Rebecca's therapy and her subsequent visit into that chapter.

By coincidence, when I finished writing a draft of the chapter and was about to contact Rebecca to ask for her permission to use her material in my book, I encountered her in town. I told her I had written about her visit to me and asked if she would read my draft and consider giving me permission to publish the account. Rebecca expressed her willingness, so I mailed her a copy, along with a cover note in which I reiterated her editorial and veto power and, out of concern for the delicacy of her story, offered to meet with her if she wanted to after reading what I had written. Soon thereafter, she phoned me. She gave her consent for me to publish the account as written, and then she said she would like to meet with me. When we met, Rebecca made a surprising request. She said, "Having read what you wrote about our work together, I'd like to know if this meeting can be a consultation on whether I may reenter therapy with you now to see if I can finally negotiate what was nonnegotiable before." I was thunderstruck. In the conversation that followed, Rebecca recognized that, in reading what I had written, she had learned something of how she had existed in my mind—as I had continued to exist in her mind all these years. She felt the hope that further growth was possible, if risky. We decided together to resume the therapeutic work set aside 14 years earlier. As that session ended, Rebecca stepped toward me to engage the kind of hug that had been, long ago, a familiar event between us. Moved by this expression of a long-standing bond yet also taken aback, I accepted and warmly returned Rebecca's hug. I then said, "This is the last time I will hug you in this way." I could see a flutter in her face. We did not speak of this moment again until the pivotal session that I describe here.

In retrospect, this hug could have been one of those passing moments that never pass—an impasse in the making. I believe that my comment represented my sense that Rebecca was asking tacitly, and concretely, whether the treatment ahead would return to a familiar regressive mode. In the earlier therapy, I had been guided by an implicit developmental model—sometimes actually a part of my explicit thinking about Rebecca—that entails a maturing cognitive hierarchy spanning, inclusively, from enactive to iconic to symbolic modes of representation. Although this was not a strategic blueprint that I had followed, I did believe that Rebecca truly needed to be grounded and welcomed into life by concretely embodied gestures of loving provision that could help her to embrace life and to piece together new iconic representations of loving maternal and benign paternal provision, with the hope that such enactive and iconic representations might hold open a space for eventual symbolic elaboration. Rebecca had needed an experience of containment and hatching. Now, in this moment of hugging, I knew—without thinking it—that Rebecca both could and had to bridge the multiple and paradoxical representational modes from the enactive to the symbolic. Hugs and holdings (see McLaughlin, 1991) would now take more differentiated form as the words that hold meanings to be held in mind. Implicitly taking Rebecca's hug as a question—or, more truly, a set of questions asked on all simultaneous levels—I responded enactively to her vulnerable gesture with a reciprocal gesture of the deep and abiding affection of kindred spirits. Then, in my statement, I told her that, in the therapeutic work that followed, we would *look* backward but *move* forward to a more differentiated mode.

Thus Rebecca and I undertook what was to become a 5-year analysis. I entered this second phase of Rebecca's treatment with hope and anxiety, wondering whether or how we might negotiate now the previously impassable ground of her sexual abuse history, her compulsive and enacting modes of personal narrative, our own history of malleable and uncertain boundaries, the primal passions inherent in the intensities of our therapeutic process, and our deeply invested mutual attachment. In retrospect, I am left with gratitude for this rare gift of a second chance, an opportunity to face together with our maturing resources the impassable terrain of our earlier therapy, which, although unquestionably life-giving for Rebecca and intensely meaningful to us both, had left so much essential analytic work unnegotiated. On one hand, Rebecca credited me with making possible her current life as a wife, mother, and creative professional. On the other hand, she conceded harboring for 14 years the fantasy that I would appear, like a rescue helicopter, and lift her from the pain, conflict, and ongoing struggles of her life. In a sense, my representation in Rebecca's mind constituted both an icon and an impasse—even as it continued to carry the hope and potential for her to move more sustainedly into the symbolic mode and live with the reality principle. Rebecca said she had returned to find out whether she could either make her fantasy come true or truly give it up. Hearing Rebecca's statement of this binary goal, I felt not only like an idealized talisman but also like a ghost that haunted her. I wondered how my unreflective devotion to her in the earlier therapy had disserved her even as it served her. I wondered how the paradoxes of our relationship could be faced together, articulated, and held now as paradox. To paraphrase Loewald, I wondered how *this* ghost could become, for Rebecca, an ancestor.

I now fast-forward to the session that, I believe, heralded Rebecca's passage into terminating her analysis. I hope my detailed rendering of that session illustrates how impasse may lurk as an everyday possibility just around the corner; how easy it is, in moments that may seem too trivial for us to particularly notice them, for potential space and process to become—or simply to remain—shut down, or else, if we are mindful in the moment, to open up with surprise and the liberating wingspread of freedom and change. This session is also a narrative pivot for looking back at our several impasses throughout the treatment, now made available for analytic recollection in our hard-won tranquility.

Rebecca arrived for this session, her last in the week, 3 minutes late, breathless from the rush of carpooling her son to school on her way. She glanced at the clock. "So," she said, "it's supposed to be 9:15 today." The clock now read 9:18. "So, do you have the 3 minutes at the end?" After a pause, in which I was feeling uncomfortable saying yes (although it was literally true that I had the 3 minutes) and uncomfortable saying no (because she seemed so upset and was asking for so little), I heard myself saying, "Probably." At this, Rebecca glanced again at the clock, and said, "So, then we'll stop at 10 [our usual ending time]. Good. Now I know. It's excellent that I asked the question." Then Rebecca fell silent, and her face seemed to reflect an active settling out of her thoughts. In this silence, my own thoughts were quite active and questioning: Do I stay with this enacted moment or allow Rebecca to move on to whatever else she'd come with in her urgent state? If I question her request for 3 minutes of extended time, would I be experienced as intrusive, controlling, interruptive, or scolding? But what if I don't question what just happened—would I be avoiding something, and would we have lost an opportunity? I felt a reluctance to nudge Rebecca's attention toward our relationship, when she seemed to have arrived with more to address already than the hour could hold. Yet something in Rebecca's tone when she said, "Good... excellent" led me to feel an uneasiness. Although I did not at the time explicitly formulate it in my mind, I can recall Rebecca's sounding pleased and self-affirming yet also seeming deflated, as if she were backing off from her request and needed these words to comfort herself as she set aside her own feelings in the face of my answer. I felt tugged inside by a responsibility to punctuate the moment, to not leave unnoticed between us what could be an enactment of Rebecca's obliging adjustment to me accompanied by her defensive recourse to a dissociative slippage in her own experience. So, if I opted to overlook what had just occurred between us, presuming to allow her the associative lead, I could well be silently signaling a collusion not to question our relationship. I could not be sure, and I could not wait to be sure. I have come to believe that it is in just this sort of moment, often seemingly innocuous, everyday, trivial—indeed, barely noticeable—that our next choice negotiates a step that will move the treatment into or out of impasse or perpetuate a subtle leitmotif of impasse that maintains its familiar (that is, undetected) grip in the relational field.

What I chose was to ask Rebecca, "Do you think your question was about anything more than specifying the time we end?" I almost didn't ask this question. But I did, and here's what followed.

Rebecca replied, "Well, it *was* about the time. It was brave of me to ask. I guess a braver question would be for me to ask you why you said probably. But, anyway, it was good that I asked for what I wanted." And then, after a pause, and with a tone of deliberateness, Rebecca asked, "Why *did* you say probably"?

In response to Rebecca's risk of asking her deliberate question, I decided to share openly with her the range of considerations and concerns that tacitly had underwritten my enacted response. I said, "Rebecca, I had a mix of thoughts and feelings. And that word, probably, is what I came up with at the moment to express the mix and my sense of ambiguity and uncertainty. In part, I am mindful of our frame and keeping the frame in mind. Also, a part of me reacts somewhat rigidly in a situation like this, as if to think, 'Hey, *you're* the one who's late. Why should *I* owe you time?' But, then again, with you I don't simply have that rigid reaction. I don't feel ill-used by you. And there's a side of me that's very much with you, rooting for your venturing to ask for what you want, and I don't want to discourage it. So that word, probably, was what I could find at the moment to express all that muddle and try to hold things open for us."

With an immediate smile and glance of recognition, Rebecca said, "I could see all of that in your face." And then Rebecca proceeded to elaborate, for herself and for me, her own reflective formulation of the meaning of her therapeutic and analytic experience with me over time. She said, "I think I said we'd end at 10 partly to take care of you—to spare you the tension and the struggle. But it's more than that—more than just taking care of *you*. It's also about my being a peer of yours and sharing the responsibility here for our relationship, and our boundaries. I think lately we've been working on maternal transference stuff. And of course I want to be totally, boundlessly loved. I want more. And probably at some time I did have more—maybe more connection with my mother, at the beginning anyway—otherwise I couldn't be doing *this*. And of course there are moments when I want to stay really little and have you be big and take care of me. But we're also peers. I've thought of you as older, even though you're not that much older. But I've needed to see you as the one who's older...and takes care of me. But now it's more like you're about 5 minutes older than me. And *I* can take some responsibility between us. I mean—yes, I need to be filled inside and surrounded on the outside by peace and comfort—it's like twinning with people. But it's a repetition—there's no growth in it. It's like turkey and stuffing and gravy—it's the same every year for 48 years. It's a comforting Thanksgiving ritual, but it never changes. Three minutes of more time would be a repetition of the same. And holding to the boundary means I can long for more but choose otherwise. And I can help *you* choose—not just leave it up to you. You're older. You're mother and father to me. But we're also peers. You're 5 minutes older than me now."

Then, reflecting further on her enacted request for those 3 minutes, Rebecca said, "In the beginning session of each week, I bring the world here. Then I settle in. In our last session, I'm negotiating our intimacy. Thursdays

I'm more regressed. So I complain about how hard life is. Thursdays *are* harder mornings. But I complain about how hard it all is so you'll take care of me. Now I don't need to be late on Thursdays anymore."

And then Rebecca turned her poetry—that is, the metaphoric power of words to recollect experience—toward these reflections on the heart of our analytic relationship. She said, "I can say what I *want*—and I'm glad that I could and did—but I can also say, 'This is what I *want,* and *this* is what I *choose.*' And also I can help you choose. This is a boundless love—a boundariless love—*in a boundaried relationship.* And that's what's precious and excellent about it. The sexual boundaries are the easiest to keep, really. I mean, it was important to me to know you could find me attractive and that I feel passionately for you. But, more important, I could ask for the 3 minutes. And I *don't* assume that *I'm* late so *you* owe me. I know *that* doesn't make sense. But I can still say, like, I can be *free to be unreasonable* and say, 'Can I still have those 3 minutes?' And what could *you* say? At one level, I want you to say, 'Sure, stay all morning.... Stay till noon, and then we'll have lunch!'" With this, Rebecca laughed, and then she said, "Now I know that I can have my longing. And my longing is not bad. It's not destructive, like I thought it was with my father, *and* my mother. I think of the dignity of your saying to me that time, 'I won't be hugging you like this anymore.' So, my question is not only about 3 minutes, but can we step outside the frame? Does it have to be? But this frame *is* real. What's real is that you and I *do* meet for 45 minutes, and that we are intensely involved *for that time.* And that's an important covenant between us. And, in the past, you've had to keep it while I challenged it. And now, I also can participate in protecting our excellent agreements. And it's a way I can love you, and a way I can be all of myself. Because I'm more than the child who wants merger. I'm a grown-up woman. And this will help me to leave."

And so Rebecca's session ended—on time at 10:00—and so the termination phase of Rebecca's analysis began. Our 5 months of termination were both a celebration and a grieving and offered us much opportunity to recollect together, in the tranquility of now, our negotiation of impasses along our way. Rebecca emphasized how nonnegotiable her alcohol abuse had been. As she now teaches others whom she visits through AA outreach at the same hospital where she once stayed, alcoholism is always an impasse. Rebecca also reflected on how long her life, and her therapy, snagged on her unreadiness to retrieve her memories of childhood sexual abuse from its defensive dissociation, its scrim of substance abuse, and its camouflage of enactive repetition—all forms of the nonnegotiable. Ultimately, Rebecca felt forgiveness toward her father, long since dead, and experienced a sadness for him because, as she put it, "In a way that he could never comprehend, he did lose his daughter."

Rebecca also had assumed that love was nonnegotiable—that all relationships of care and passion were corruptible and all human attachments would degrade to a sadomasochistic default position, what Benjamin (1988) would term the reversible complementarity of doer and done-to. Rebecca reviewed the many times she had set out to do me in emotionally. She also recalled her procession of dreads and anxieties about me after she'd courageously returned to treatment. She'd wondered, was I an alcoholic? Was I mentally disturbed? Would I exploit her? Would I die? Would I break the frame? Would I break her heart? Would she have to stay forever to reassure me that she loves me?

Rebecca recollected her statement, in her first visit with me, that she was "incapable of loving." Wistfully, she now reinterpreted that statement, long held as a given, to mean that she had known intrinsically at that time that she would never feel free to give or receive love until she became, psychologically, "an orphan"—that is, released from loyal and submissive attachment to internal bad objects (for instance, a father who sexually exploited and abandoned her; a mother who withdrew from noticing Rebecca's telltale posttraumatic states, and who called her "the meanest baby born in New York City"). "And that," she said, "was impossible. It's what I came for and, of course, I had to fight it." Now literally an orphan, Rebecca finds herself free to accept intimations of her particular identifications with each parent. She recalled a stuck point a year or so into her resumed treatment when she felt stalled, in her attachments, between guilt and shame. As she stated it then, "In relation to my parents, I feel guilty that I'm attached to you; and, in relation to you, I feel ashamed that I'm still so attached to them."

At one point, Rebecca reflected on periods of impasse strikingly in terms of intersubjectivity. She said, "Sometimes it just felt like a matter of my pride. I had to be right. You know how important it is for me to be right. So *you* couldn't be right. I couldn't accept any view other than my own. For the longest time, I couldn't even let you be different."

Rebecca and I reviewed together the history of our attachment, now spanning more than a quarter of a century. She remembered the Christmas card she had handed me long ago, 2 years into her treatment. She had taken the enormous risk of giving me a card in which she had simply written the threshold message: "Love, Rebecca." The cover of the card had an Alexander Calder drawing of animals in cages—some open and some closed—with a ringmaster standing in their midst. Rebecca reminded me of my incredibly obtuse enactment when I received her card. What I did was offer her some intellectualized Fairbairnian interpretation of the animals protected from the ringmaster and the ringmaster protected from the animals. As Rebecca now so aptly put it, "At some level, you were probably even right. But how could you! I told myself, 'I'm never giving *this* guy a card again!'" Grimacing with mortification 26 years after the fact, I could now say to Rebecca, "I remember that card and that moment so well. And the truth is, it felt so good to receive your message that I was afraid. So I figured I'd better hurry up and make some therapeutic use of it." Rebecca said, "You should have just shut up." I said, "Yes, or I should have just said 'Thank you.'"

In the spirit of inquiry, Rebecca and I talked about our hugs and their various meanings. In the course of our exploration, placing these hugs in the context of our total therapeutic mission, Rebecca said, "We were doing a high-wire act without a net. We hear about a lot of therapists and patients who hugged and eventually fell from the high wire. I think we didn't fall because throughout it all we both knew there was an essential love between us. There was something sacred about that."

On another occasion, looking back on our hugs, Rebecca said wryly, "It was the 70s." For her, hugging fit a cultural commonplace. For me, in retrospect, hugging fit an idealistic hope to bring my healing wishes to my patient—my own youthful *furor sanandi*. And now, as I juxtapose in my thoughts my hugging Rebecca and my defensively interpreting her Calder card, I can look back on the contradictory and conflictual perspectives regarding therapeutic technique and therapeutic action with which I grappled, unsupervised, in those days. Between Rebecca's departure from therapy and her return, I had gained the rewards of psychoanalytic study and supervision, and then full training. I also had given considerable thought to boundary issues in therapeutic and analytic relationships and had founded an ethics committee for the Psychoanalytic Consortium. Certainly, over the intervening years, I had changed—and I had grown and aged. Matters of the frame and love within the frame had become more conceptually, affectively, and procedurally integral with my evolving personal way of being analytic. I realize that I now most likely would not proceed clinically with another Rebecca who arrived today in just the way I did then—I most likely would not drive to the hospital for each session, or accept so many phone calls, or exchange hugs, or be so generally adoptive in my countertransference. But I must face wistfully that, although my current technical practice perhaps represents a more mature, more considered, more experienced, more articulated, and more integrated analytic self (or perhaps just a more cautious and world-weary analytic self), I thereby might well fail ever to offer so fundamental an entry into life as that which transpired, over time, between the Rebecca she was and the Stuart/therapist I was as we found our way at that time.

And perhaps our community of aging and world-weary analysts may need to reconnect—and to develop a literature of integrative concepts that reconnect us—with the embodied origins of early psychological life based in biological and physical necessities and grounded in the enactive experiencing of holding, object presenting, affect attunement, and recognition that provide for procedural patterns of being, self-regulating, and relating. Perhaps our technique needs to be more multimodal and multileveled, bridging the copresent enactive, iconic, and symbolic modes of representation, organizing psychoneurological patterns of affect and state regulation and communication through the processes of dyadic interaction (see, e.g., Beebe & Lachmann, 2002; Schore, 2003; D. N. Stern, 2003), and building along the spectrum from active to symbolic articulations and elaborations of self, other, reality, and recognition. We need at least to question whether our technical precepts, when they are limited to narrow and curtailed definitions of interpreting mental contents, may fall short of the totality and multi-leveled complexity of a process of analytic love that may yet hold the power not only to explain lives but also to aid in saving, cultivating, and transforming them.

Yet, ultimately, as I believe the session I've shared with you conveys, the most subtle elements of impasse to Rebecca's movement through and beyond her analysis may have been the familiarity of loving, caring, tending, and sponsoring in our relationship. Indeed, so many sessions over the years had ended with our enacting together, without commenting on it, a session extended for a few minutes in the face of her manifestly unsettled state and my engaged responsiveness. Perhaps what made this particular session different—or what made it possible to make this session different— was Rebecca's asking me explicitly, at the beginning, "Do you have the 3 minutes?" Perhaps Rebecca's step constituted what Bromberg (1995) might call a marker that some resistance to change was yielding to an internal accommodation of conflict, or a straddling of paradox, within Rebecca. Perhaps I could read that marker at what Mitchell (2000) called the level of affective connection between us, enabling me to make the choice that nudged this moment for Rebecca and me from the level of our relatively fixed relational configurations to a level of emergent recognitions, insights, and freedoms.

I still can shudder when I think of how that threshold moment with Rebecca might so easily have played out differently. Embedded as I was in the weak dissociations of our special and familiar kinship, I could so easily have failed to inquire into the small detail of 3 minutes. But impasse is often in the details. And, as I stated earlier, the sweetness of "kinship" between analyst and patient can be a silent killer of the treatment process. Life may stop or start with small acts of misrecognition or recognition—or, as Donnel Stern (1997) might say, freedom begins with our noticing in the seamless fabric of the familiar the place to ask a question. And, as Stephen Mitchell (2000) wisely wrote:

> There is a great delicacy in finding a constructive balance between cultivated and questioned love in the transference and the countertransference. Who makes these decisions? Of course, they are made to some extent collaboratively. But I think it is disingenuous to assign the patient equal responsibility for these judgments regarding timing. (pp. 138–139)

I want to emphasize what, for me, made Rebecca's treatment relational. It was not my trips to the hospital, the phone calls, the hugs, or the disclosures per se. Indeed, as I regard this clinical process, I think of the hugs in multiple ways: as expressions of dedication, comfort, love, naïveté, and much else. I think of the phone calls as both an occasional lifeline and a repetition of projective identifications and role-responsive enactments. I think of my travel to the hospital as expressive of responsible and caring containment as well as indicative of an idealized rescue fantasy. Many interpretations of the meanings of these enactive moments—even contradictory interpretations—are valid and relevant. However, I declare that what made this therapy and analysis relational was the overarching and ultimate commitment to a thoroughgoing, mutual, open, and explicit reflection in the treatment dialogue on the multiple conscious and unconscious meanings of our reciprocal interactions, including both their links to historical roots in Rebecca's developmental past (and their recursive residue) and my accountability for my own particular participation in that context. Rebecca and I could not complete a relational analysis without our many conversations and our shared pursuit of understanding regarding the life-enhancing and life-curtailing impact of our interactive experiences as well as the insight-promoting and insight-obscuring impact of each form of therapeutic action, whether it was a hug or an interpretation of a Christmas card.

The Paradoxical Analytic Triangle

Somewhere in the months that constituted our termination, as we reviewed the impasses and the passages along our way, Rebecca declared, "I am the product of the love between you and me." I found her statement immediately remarkable. It felt powerfully and poignantly true. It also stayed in my mind as the nucleus of a concept, taking hold and gestating. Here is how I unpack Rebecca's statement or bring forth the concept she seeded. In brief, I conjecture that any gendered combination of analyst and analysand, open to the intimacies and passions of the process—and its pre-oedipal, oedipal, and post-oedipal complexities—can form, experience, and use analytically what I call the *paradoxical analytic triangle.*

The paradoxical analytic triangle consists of the analyst, the patient, and the patient. We may visualize this triangle, through a lens that appreciates a multiply constituted self and multileveled organizations of separate centers of experience, in terms of the following dyads: the relationship between the analyst and the oedipal patient; the relationship between the analyst and the pre-oedipal patient; and a tacit relationship between oedipal and pre-oedipal centers or states within the patient. We might think of these dyads as existing throughout each treatment, potentially from the start, but shifting from potential to realization (and back), or from background to foreground (and back), either progressively over time, in an oscillating dialectic of states, or as an unfolding yet circular field of complex interrelationships. What I mean to emphasize is that patients who experience themselves as the beneficiary of their analyst's attentive care—and who feels grateful, dependent, and desiring as well as envious, unrequited, and jealous of a life they cannot share—have not been just passive in the context of pre-oedipal provision or bereft and hateful in the face of oedipal exclusion. Instead, the oedipally excluded patient retains a glimmering awareness that the analyst has not been alone in providing for the patient, that all along there has been a vital joining of something in the analyst and something in the patient that testifies to the patient's agency and essential participation in creating and developing a competent and fruitful partnership.

In a cogent exploration of oedipal and post-oedipal transference–countertransference constructions, Davies (2003) called for "a postmodern eye ... one that appreciates the potentials of multiple realities and the paradox of simultaneous yet irreconcilable contradictions" (p. 8). I believe the concept of a paradoxical analytic triangle dovetails nicely with Davies's assertion that "in the most optimal situations [the Oedipal crisis] is both won and lost" (p. 10). Davies is referring both to a healthy developmental process and to a transformative analytic process. I postulate that the potential for the patient's negotiating and assimilating complex and contradictory triangular experiences in the exquisitely paradoxical analytic relationship constitutes a powerful vehicle for the repair of failed, interrupted, or aborted oedipal integrations. Thereby, the analytic relationship can help a patient to develop "the capacities to negotiate experiences of both inclusion and [more] painful or tantalizing exclusion" (pp. 7–8). Indeed, we might assume that it is when the patient has bridged the paradoxical coexistence of an aspect of self that participates as agent, or partner, in a romantic relationship with the analyst in which he or she is *included* and another aspect of self that experiences that very relationship (between self and analyst) from the outside and feels *excluded*, that the patient arrives at the threshold of a post-oedipal relationship with the analyst—in which both partners together hold, tolerate, and straddle the multiple and paradoxical relationships coexisting between them.

I believe that our recognition of the paradoxical analytic triangle helps us to face down the question of what could possibly be analytically or therapeutically useful, or humanly decent, about our sponsoring and participating in intimate relationships of intensely dependent and tender attachment and powerfully erotic enlivenment in a transference–countertransference relationship, only to subject both partners to ultimate relinquishment and loss. Why should either partner volunteer for such heartbreak and grief? The post-oedipal child at least returns home for visits and family rituals of celebration and support, and all the intimate exchanges accompanying growth and aging in family life. The post-oedipal patient may never return—at least, may expect not to—and patient and analyst alike often face the absence of a cherished other. Many a patient has protested, "Why allow myself to become dependent; why fall in love? Why encourage me to love you if I must give you up? Do I have you or not?" In Rebecca's terms, she would either make her fantasy come true or truly give it up. What could make this painful enterprise worthwhile?

I believe that the patient and the analyst may experience in their paradoxical analytic triangle a negotiation of the binary, the concreteness of "either–or," and the heartbreak of inclusion or exclusion, winning or losing, keeping or letting go. The paradoxes of "both/and" offer the analytic couple complex challenge and potential comfort, as well as a chance for essential growth.

Here is how I elaborate the nature of the multiple coexisting relationships between patient and analyst that make up the paradoxical analytic triangle: In one interpersonal dyad, analyst and patient are partners in the analytic project and process, cocreating an intimate partnership in which, over time, passionate and exciting loves and hates, tender and cherishing attachments, romantic idealizations, admiration, vulnerable familiarity, and intense states of awareness and recognition become emergent, mutually evoked, and jointly shaped features of shared experience at deep affective levels. The other interpersonal relationship in the paradoxical analytic triangle is conceptualized commonly in the metaphor of a maternal dyad (parent–analyst and child–patient), as reflected, for example, in Loewaldian or self psychological literature. But I propose that we consider this dyad in terms of another, more paradoxical, metaphor: the child–patient basking in the nurturant context of a relationship with that other analytic dyad, *the analyst's and the patient's jointly constructed loving partnership.* Of course, moments of dependency sustained and provided for in an analysis can be thought of meaningfully in terms of the patient's being held by the environment mother, and the patient's experience in these phases is intensely dyadic because *that's just how it feels.*

Nonetheless, I wonder whether it is more common than we have recognized that the intrapsychic relationship between that part of the patient included in the oedipal analytic dyad and that (pre-oedipal?) part of the patient excluded from the oedipal analytic dyad—a function of the patient's standing in the spaces (Bromberg, 1998)—supports the patient's tacit awareness (albeit unformulated, an unthought known) of the continuously coconstructed nature of this process. Hence, the patient (participating in the enactive realization of the more developmentally dependent, more pre-oedipal, features of deep analytic work over time) remains, paradoxically, both a consumer and an agent, or co-provider.

Rebecca reported that, from the perspective of her young self, "I thought the reward of completing therapy was that I got to marry you." Here is the oedipal success fantasy of the excluded child. And when Rebecca envisioned me as her rescuer in a helicopter, I was an idealized oedipal object, out of reach, as well as a pre-oedipal *deus ex machina*, a singular omnipotent provider. When Rebecca declared, "I came back to find out if I could make my fantasy come true or truly give it up," she was expressing the win–lose binary, the either–or thought structure of oedipal desire, competition, and conflict. Either you are included or you are excluded. The loss and heart-break and, perhaps most significantly, the shame and humiliation of the patient's relinquishment of oedipal hopes surely have kept many a patient hostage to the impasse of a perpetual unrequited transference love.

Indeed, many a treatment relationship comes to grief or a tragic end. The patient may feel excruciatingly excluded and left alone with an irresolvable rage. We can never know in advance which analysis will lead to intolerable and irreparable feelings of exclusion that abort the process. And when the process falls apart in this way, the analyst is left feeling guilt and mortification, perhaps defective in loving or blind to signals of danger. In Rebecca's case, the darker side of her passionate attachment to me was manifested in her unverbalized reaction to my actual unavailability for a real marriage: the spitefulness that hastened her own problematic, albeit superficially plausible, marital choice and her abrupt departure from the first phase of therapy. It was only after many years that Rebecca could formulate for herself and communicate to me the undeniable and life-shaping costs of her tit-for-tat enactment of exclusion in reverse.

However, an appreciation of the paradoxical analytic triangle may help us understand something of how a patient may let go of the idealized analyst and move on into the potentials of his or her own life with dignity, self-possession, and power. In the paradox of "both–and," the patient has been both the included partner and the excluded child. And that child, growing up and leaving a transference "home," is leaving not only the all-powerful analyst mother, or the elevated analyst father, but also the loving couple that has consisted of the analyst and the patient. While grieving a loss, the patient joins the analyst (during the period that Davies, 2003, emphasized as post-oedipal love) in celebrating a mutual success.

In more metaphorical terms, I am suggesting that, in an analytic process that is not aborted during a patient's paroxysms of oedipal exclusion, the mutual success that patient and analyst ultimately may celebrate is aptly represented in the trope of pregnancy and birth. The analytic partners may be comforted, as they approach their termination losses, by their recognition that together they have succeeded in being an analytically fertile couple. Invoking Rebecca's evocative terms, we may say that in the paradoxical analytic triangle, the love between her analyst and Rebecca One gave birth to Rebecca Two. And indeed, there may be a second, and reciprocal, paradoxical analytic triangle. The analyst too is transformed, perhaps profoundly and forever, by the experience of a particular analytic partnership. I recognize that, in beginning to describe Rebecca's influence on the development of these ideas, my own unbidden and unselfconscious selection of terms (such as *nucleus, gestating,* or *bring forth the concept she seeded*) indicates my tacit experience of my mind's being impregnated by Rebecca's loving words. So, as my own ideas come to life, I can say that Rebecca and Stuart One gave birth to Stuart Two. Perhaps, in more generic terms, it is not uncommon for a second paradoxical analytic triangle to consist of the patient, the analyst, and the analyst. If the patient and Analyst One are the fertile partners in this analytic transitional space, Analyst Two is the real person of the analyst, forever and appropriately prohibited from the generative intimacies that have existed metaphorically in analytic space yet remaining the beneficiary of a transformative love that the analyst-person, too, both mourns and also keeps.

An essential part of the patient's growing facility for negotiating life's paradoxes is his or her experience of having and not having the analyst at the same time—just as, in the course of healthy development, children experience the flat truths of not having their oedipally fantasized romantic couplings with an adored parent while also experiencing full well the very intense and special ways in which they uniquely have their parent's adoration, affirmation, and delight. In the paradoxical analytic triangle, the patient experiences in the transference–countertransference relationship both oedipal inclusion and oedipal exclusion. Again, as Davies (2003) wrote, "In the most optimal situations [the Oedipal crisis] is *both* won *and* lost" (p. 10). In analysis, as in development, this is how the person may pass through need to desire, to love, to agency, to self-possession and freedom of choice. As Rebecca ultimately was able to say, "Now it's more like you're about 5 minutes older than me" and "*This* is what I *want* and *this* is what I *choose*." And, again, as Rebecca so creatively declared, "I am the product of the love between you and me."*

Coda

As Rebecca and I approached the final session of her analysis, I found myself wondering if she would again punctuate a leave-taking, this one her last, with a move toward a hug. With my own wishes and fears in my

---

* Another account of the paradoxical analytic triangle is narrated poignantly in Barbara Pizer's (2005) paper, "Passion, Responsibility, and 'Wild Geese': Creating a Context for 'the Absence of Conscious Intentions.'" Note particularly the poetic condensation of this concept in the patient's dream of an infant son and Pizer's statement that she (as author of the clinical narrative) and her patient, Sam (as collaborator in the process), "together named him Sam."

clear view, I felt concerned that such a surprise action at the very moment of good-bye could leave Rebecca with emotional residue that we would have no way to explore further. So I decided to raise the issue with her. I asked Rebecca if she had thought about how she wanted to say good-bye at our last meeting. Rebecca said, "I know that I don't want a hug. I mean, while it would feel good, it would not be true to who we are to each other. I'm leaving, in part, because we don't and won't have a relationship where we are free to hug each other. It's sad; it may even feel disappointing not to have a hug. But it's truer. And I want that symbolized in the way we say good-bye."

I'll end this paper on impasse recollected in tranquility with these lines from the poetry of William Wordsworth:

> Thanks to the human heart by which we live,
> Thanks to its tenderness, its joys, and fears,
> To me the meanest flower that blows can give
> Thoughts that do often lie too deep for tears.

Ode: Intimations of Immortality

References

Atwood, G. E., & Stolorow, R. D. (1984). *Structures of subjectivity: Explorations in psychoanalytic phenomenology.* Hillsdale, NJ: The Analytic Press.

Beebe, B., & Lachmann, F. (2002). *Infant research and adult treatment: Co-constructing interactions.* Hillsdale, NJ: The Analytic Press.

Benjamin, J. (1988). *The bonds of love.* New York: Pantheon Books.

Benjamin, J. (2000). Intersubjective distinctions: Subjects and persons, recognitions and breakdowns: Commentary on paper by Gerhardt, Sweetnam, and Borton. *Psychoanalytic Dialogues, 10,* 43–55.

Bromberg, P. (1995). Resistance, object-usage, and human relatedness. *Contemporary Psychoanalysis, 31,* 173–191.

Bromberg, P. (1998). *Standing in the spaces: Essays on clinical process, trauma, and dissociation.* Hillsdale, NJ: The Analytic Press.

Davies, J. M. (2003). Falling in love with love: Oedipal and postoedipal manifestations of idealization, mourning, and erotic masochism. *Psychoanalytic Dialogues, 13,* 1–27.

Elkind, S. N. (1992). *Resolving impasses in therapeutic relationships.* New York: Guilford.

McLaughlin, J. (1991). Clinical and theoretical aspects of enactment. *Journal of the American Psychoanalytic Association, 39,* 595–614.

Mitchell, S. A. (2000). *Relationality: From attachment to intersubjectivity.* Hillsdale, NJ: The Analytic Press.

Ogden, T. H. (1994). *Subjects of analysis.* Northvale, NJ: Aronson.

Pizer, B. (2003). When the crunch is a (k)not: A crimp in relational dialogue. *Psychoanalytic Dialogues, 13,* 171–192.

Pizer, B. (2005). Passion, responsibility, and "wild geese": Creating a context for "the absence of conscious intentions." *Psychoanalytic Dialogues, 15*(1), 57–84.

Pizer, S. A. (1998). *Building bridges: The negotiation of paradox in psychoanalysis.* Hillsdale, NJ: The Analytic Press.

Pizer, S. A. (2000). A gift in return: The clinical use of writing about a patient. *Psychoanalytic Dialogues, 10,* 247–259.

Ringstrom, P. (1998). Therapeutic impasses in contemporary psychoanalytic treatment: Revisiting the double bind hypothesis. *Psychoanalytic Dialogues, 8,* 297–315.

Russell, P. (1975). *The theory of the crunch.* Unpublished manuscript.

Schore, A. (2003). *Affect dysregulation and disorders of the self.* New York: Norton.

Stern, D. B. (1997). *Unformulated experience: From dissociation to imagination in psychoanalysis.* Hillsdale, NJ: The Analytic Press.

Stern, D. B. (2003). The fusion of horizons: Dissociation, enactment, and understanding. *Psychoanalytic Dialogues, 13,* 843–873.

Stern, D. N. (2003). The present moment. *Psychotherapy Networker, Nov/Dec,* 52–57.

Stern, S. (1994). Needed relationships and repeated relationships: An integrated relational perspective. *Psychoanalytic Dialogues, 4,* 317–346.

Winnicott, D. W. (1971). *Playing and reality.* New York: Basic Books.

7

Whose Bad Objects Are We Anyway? Repetition and Our Elusive Love Affair With Evil*

Jody Messler Davies

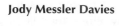

It was a Thursday afternoon, the kind of day on which the coldness simply could not be stopped. Sweaters, space heaters, and the assorted accoutrements of winter were insufficient to the task. I had a sore throat and a terrible head cold. Achy and irritable, I was unsure how I was going to make it through my four remaining sessions that afternoon. I wanted only a pillow for my head, a warm comforter for the aches and pains, and a thermos full of hot tea and honey. To make it worse, Karen was coming next. At that moment I needed someone "easy"—someone who would be willing to cut me a little slack in my present condition. But that was not to be. One could simply never hide from Karen's keen and unrelenting eye. She was never easy!

We had been working together for almost 3 years, and though much of our analytic work had been productive our relationship itself had remained tense and unpredictable, fraught with unexpected twists and turns, seemingly impossible demands, sudden disappointments, frustrations, and angry outbursts. There was little that was fluid and comfortable. As I came into the waiting room, Karen was hunched over inside an enormous down jacket. Her face was particularly stormy and brooding, even for her. My heart sank, and my spirits took a nosedive.

"You're still sick?" she asked, half complaint, half admonishment. "I can't believe you haven't shaken that thing yet." Suddenly, I felt slow and stupid, my cold a matter of immunological ineptitude. She sat in the chair facing

* This paper originally appeared in *Psychoanalytic Dialogues, 14*(6), 2004, pp. 711–732. Reprinted with permission.

me, ensconced within her ballooning jacket. We were silent. From deep within her stare I detected a gleam—a noticeable quantum leap in energy and excitement. In response, my stomach churned and my muscles stiffened. Even before words could explain, it seemed as if my body knew that *something* was coming, and my body told me it wasn't good. It must mean that we had occupied this place before—that my muscles were remembering, before my mind could catch up, that something dangerous loomed ahead of us.

"I need an earlier session on Monday," Karen proclaimed, her words piercing the air. "I have jury duty, and you know how essential a Monday session is for me." I thought I saw steamy breath surrounding those words— the heat of her disowned rage penetrating the frigid environs surrounding us. Ah, yes, here it was: the impossible demand, the necessity of the moment that I simply could not provide. Why did Karen never ask me for things that I could give her? I braced myself for the struggle that I knew was coming. "I do know how important it is for you," I responded, "and I so wish that I had a time. But you know how impossible my Monday morning schedule is, how inflexible it always is on Mondays when we need to change something. I'm afraid I can't unless I have a cancellation." I finished my sentence and clung to the arms of my chair for strength and balance. Karen pursed her lips and narrowed her eyes, but behind the hungry pursed lips an unmistakably palpable smile of satisfaction: within the sad desolate eyes, a piercing stare and the steely glint of sadistic triumph. For Karen, it was a moment of profound desolation and abandonment but also a place of safe familiarity and comforting self-recognition.

But what of me? What of my complex reactions to this evocative, provocative moment, so reminiscent of many moments with Karen? "Who needs this?" I thought. "If I'm so awful, why doesn't she just quit? So many interesting referrals I'm not free to take, and I'm not helping her one iota…uh-uh…not one little bit." In this moment, I struggled to evoke images of patients I thought that I was helping: patients who saw me as warmer, more caring, more therapeutically helpful than Karen did; patients who affirmed my own preferred vision of myself, patients who I thought saw me more "accurately." Unknowingly, I dug my heels in as firmly as Karen. From the recesses of my mind came a small and unwanted voice: "You know you could come in an hour earlier if you don't do school drop-off. You could see her. You would do that, you know, for some of your other patients; you have done it on occasion. You don't like to disappoint the children, but you've done it before. It's Karen; you don't want to do it for Karen." Now I was starting to feel really cranky. It had begun to feel as if even my own other self-states were conspiring against me. "But," I answered my annoying little voice, "I'll do it for Karen and she won't even appreciate it. I'll disappoint the kids, and for what? In two days it will disappear down the black hole of borderline entitlement, and the next time she's frustrated with me she won't even remember how hard I've tried to accommodate her." "Hmm, a diagnosis," retorted my voice, "borderline, no less? You really are angry. Who is this angry, petulant, withholding, unempathic Jody?" "Oh, shut up," I countered. "This is old stuff, an old place, not an issue for me anymore. It's her; it's Karen. She has an uncanny ability to bring all of this stuff out of me." "Sure," came the inevitable reply. "And if she gets angry enough and goes away, then that part of you can skulk back into the cave marked Old News—Need No Longer Think About, and you can be safely self-satisfied again." "That's right," I said, by now consumed by oppositional but entirely self-righteous entrenchment. "Karen and I will never witness the coming of morning together!" My heels dug holes in the carpet. Karen and I glared at each other in silent rage: both of us from places we knew, both of us from places we hated within ourselves. In the lexicon of professional jargon, it was a moment we have come to think of as a therapeutic impasse but a moment of profound mutuality and engagement as well.

What enables us to explain the repetitive cycles of self-destructive, self-defeating behavior that we all struggle to help patients overcome? What explains the malignancy that can infuse the transference–countertransference relationship, often suddenly and without warning?

Why do some treatments blow apart under the strain of such mutually repetitive, negative, and intransigent processes?

Much has been written in psychoanalysis about the so-called negative transferences, about the importance of letting ourselves become "bad objects" for our patients and, in so doing, allow for the expression of their more aggressive, hateful, and malignant thoughts. It seems intrinsic to relational thinking that these "bad object relationships" not only will but must be reenacted in the transference–countertransference experience, that indeed such reenacted aggression, rage, and envy are endemic to psychoanalytic change within the relational perspective. In my own work on treating adult survivors of childhood sexual abuse, the patient's identification with her abuser and her tendency to reenact this abusive object relationship within the transference–countertransference process forms the crux of what is regarded as essential for psychoanalytic change. I am not alone in this belief. The works of Stephen Mitchell (1997), Irwin Hoffman (1998), Jessica Benjamin (1988), Philip Bromberg (1998), Stuart Pizer (1998), Barbara Pizer (2003), Lewis Aron (1996), Stephen Cooper (2000), Margaret Black (2003), and Darlene Bregman Ehrenberg (1992), to mention only a few, are replete with vivid descriptions of working through the difficult, rageful, envy-filled transference–countertransference reactions that occupy so much of good solid psychoanalytic process.

But one question with which many of us have struggled in our writing as well as in our clinical work is exactly how we can evoke and work with the patient's more intense negative transference reactions, as well as with the countertransference states that can be evoked in response, without witnessing the collapse of potential, self-reflective space into the inexorable vortex of meaningless traumatic reenactment. To evoke the bad object relationship without concretely becoming the bad object. To invite the reemergence of traumatic histories of affective intensity and pitch without being swallowed up and destroyed by them seems to be our most complex therapeutic challenge. To dance the dance of then and now, past and present, abuser and victim, doer and done-to, we dance on the head of a pin, spinning dizzily amid these points, changing perspectives, shifting identifications, blurring boundaries, spinning a tapestry of meaning and nuance that has the potential for depth, subtlety, ambiguity, and a multiplicity of rich, self–other experience, but a dance that also holds the forbidding prospect of spinning out of control, of falling over the edge into a miasma of projective–introjective enmeshment, boundarylessness, and deadly negativity.

It is just such a space that Karen and I occupy on this frigid February afternoon. Leaning precipitously close to the edge of the head of this now claustrophobic pin, we each struggle frantically to regain some perspective on the meaning of our work together. We search desperately to remember some of the good times we have shared, to evoke positive images and more caring, nourishing self-states in which we can exist together, memories with which to halt a catastrophic fall into traumatic reenactment.

"You're such a bitch," Karen insists. "You're cold and unfeeling and ungiving. You've never been there for me—not ever. I mean, sometimes you pretend, but it's just skin deep. Down deep inside you where I can see … it's just ice. The least you could do is to admit it."

I stare at Karen in stunned silence, overwhelmed by the intense hatred in her voice. I think of the emergency sessions, the extra phone calls, the many heroic attempts to "be there for her" that seem to disappear at times like this. I try to hold onto her hateful image of me, to work with it clinically, to understand its meaning and history. But parallel to my therapeutic self, I seethe at her description of me and I struggle against it. I am ashamed of the things I feel. There is something about the notion of "working through the negative transference" or "being a bad object" that seems somehow unequal to this moment—*too* in the past, *too* in the other, *too* defined by distortion to capture what is happening. For in this moment it is not simply that Karen hates me, or that I have reached a place where I hate her. What is most significant, I believe, is that we have reached a place together in which I hate the self that I have become with her. I *am* the bitch she describes, and I am horrified and chilled by the ice that lies below the surface, hardening over the well of good intent and affection that at other times defines the more loving relationship we "also" have. As I stare into the opaque deadness of Karen's relentless gaze, I know that she is hating herself as well: hating the entitled, demanding, raging self she has become in these moments with me—hating that self, and all the time deeply ashamed and frightened by its internal tyranny.

Our session draws to an end, and it has become quiet. Then, "You hate me," says Karen—the "crunch" as Paul Russell (1973) termed it. "Mhmm," I tell her. "Sometimes we hate each other, I think. Not always, not even usually, but sometimes we can get to this place together. I guess we're going to have to see where we can get to from here. Neither of us likes it much; it just is." "Yeah," said Karen, "it sucks."

"Yeah, it does," I answer. A comment takes shape in my mind. It buzzes around, and I struggle with whether to say it. It feels right, but it has appeared suddenly and I haven't had time to think about it. I decide to hold the thought, not to share it at this moment with Karen. The thought that I consider sharing with Karen goes something like this: "You know, Karen, I might have said, it's very hard and painful to hear when you feel like you hate me, and it's very hard and painful to feel hatred for you, but what really, really bugs me—the thing I think is the hardest thing to feel—is that sometimes when you and I are in a place like this I feel as if I'm starting to hate myself as well. And that just pushes me over the top, and I feel that I simply can't move." But the moment passes. And the words are not said.

I have long been of the opinion that "becoming a bad object" for the patient, evoking the "negative transference," represents no great therapeutic challenge. It is in fact a far easier task than most of us would choose to have it be, despite our awareness of its essential therapeutic function. But simply becoming a bad object for the patient does nothing to erode the analyst's sense of sanity, boundaries, and internal therapeutic intent. Indeed, the very language suggests that we are letting ourselves be used by the patient for some therapeutic function. The bad object we are becoming is the patient's bad object, projected onto or into us; residing there temporarily; a temporary tenant or interloper. We can "hold" such bad objects without losing our self-reflective capacities, our more tempered hold on the meanings of such transference–countertransference moments. We can think about who these objects are for the patient. We can examine our own countertransference for clues to such understanding. Our boundaries remain intact. Our thinking, though altered and affected, remains clear. Even when projective identification holds sway and we are snagged by a projection that takes root and flourishes within us, we understand that the experience is part of the therapeutic process, something painful but something that emanates from the patient, something that will leave us when the hour is over. In essence we feel ourselves to be doing good, difficult, but necessary therapeutic work, filled up by some kind of badness that belongs to the patient's past—to his or her internal object world. We stay focused. We feel therapeutic. We do not lose our minds.

What is not so easy, I would suggest, and what represents, to my way of thinking, a much greater therapeutic challenge is finding a way to evoke and manage the emergence of our most secret and shame-riddled "bad selves," our own and the patient's—those needy, greedy, envious, hateful, manipulative, entitled aspects of self who have grown up in relationship with our bad objects, in relationship with our parents' own dissociated and evacuated bad self-states. It is, I believe, these selves who tyrannize us internally; who fill us with shame, self-hate, and self-loathing; who fuel relentless repetitions and internally occupy moments of intolerable therapeutic impasse. In early work that I coauthored with Mary Gail Frawley O'Dea (Davies & Frawley, 1992, 1994) on the treatment of patients traumatized in childhood, we pointed out the clinical dilemma that occurs when the analyst, much like the parental perpetrator of childhood abuse, must be both the object of the patient's transferential rage over abuse, abandonment, and betrayal as well as the one who helps the patient contain, soothe, modulate, and ultimately come to terms with such experiences. We employed Winnicott's metaphor that every baby needs both an environment mother and an object mother to suggest that each patient also requires an object and an environment analyst. And we cautioned about the particular countertransferential pitfall in which the analyst comes to feel so guilty about evoking the patient's horrendous memories of early abuse and betrayal that he or she will attempt all forms of inappropriate heroic rescue, attempts that ultimately interfere with the patient's need to mourn lost idealized objects and the analyst's need to mourn the limits of his or her therapeutic omnipotence. Bromberg (2000) struck a similar theme, considering the possibility that the analyst's shame over being the one to evoke the patient's experiences of such profound pain may precipitate a dissociated state in the analyst, in which he or she becomes unable to resonate with the patient's experience of profound hopelessness and despair. For Bromberg, this failed communication between patient and analyst fuels much of the repetition in clinical work.

In the present paper, I focus not only on the guilt and shame evoked by the analyst's therapeutic and object functions but also on the fate of the analyst's primary areas of shame, guilt, and despair (see also Elkind, 1992). In this more specific sense, I have not simply evoked a negative transference or become a bad object for my patient. Instead, it is more accurate to state that, at such heightened moments of impasse, something about my current interaction with this patient forces me to become aware of what is and always has been "bad" within myself, something that I know and have always known to reside squarely within the part of myself I choose to consistently avoid and disown. My point here is to suggest that it can become the passionate mission of such guilty, shame-riddled self-states (whether in patient or analyst) to predict, seek out, and provoke the very worst in the other, to literally extrude the badness—to locate and confirm that the badness lies comfortably outside the self. It is I believe in the countertrans-ferential push to extrude these self states of our own, to locate them in the other (in this case, the patient), that the boundary confusion and collapse of self-reflective functioning endemic to moments, of what Pizer (1998) termed nonnegotiable therapeutic impasse, may take hold.

We relational analysts have always emphasized the patient's capacity to appreciate the multiplicity of self–other configurations and organizations of experience, the capacity to exist in a heightened moment of emotional and interpersonal engagement while sustaining the capacity to exist outside that moment as well, appreciating the specific self–other dyad of the moment as only one of many self–other configurations that define the experience of the self and of the particular relationship at hand. In my own work, I termed the patient's capacity to appreciate the tension between one particularly heightened transference–countertransference experience against a back-drop of multiple other potential interactions as a *therapeutic dissociation* (Davies, 1996), and I have regarded the analyst's counterpart (i.e., the capac-ity to move fluidly from one particular transference–countertransference paradigm to another without becoming mired in the repetitive reenactment of any one configuration) as a relational redefinition of analytic neutrality. In a similar vein, Mitchell (1997) spoke of "bootstrapping," Pizer (1998) of building bridges between dissociated self–other configurations, Hoffman (1998) of constructing a dialectic of positions, Bromberg (1998) of "standing in the spaces" between these states, and Benjamin (2004) of the patient's capacity and the analyst's capacity to establish and sustain a third position. Despite subtle differences, each of us has tried to capture in these writings the importance of being in the moment and out of it at the same time, of allowing for an intensity of psychic experience while sustaining the capac-ity to reflect on that experience, to balance emotional immediacy with an appreciation of alternative possibility.

In my work with Karen and others like her, it is precisely this self-reflective space of multiple possibility and potential that feels most threat-ened. I often find myself feeling that I am engaged in some kind of life and death battle for my sanity and mental integrity. I often feel pressed into a position in which the only way to affirm a patient's sanity and experi-ence of reality is to accept a vision of myself that is so toxic and malignant that it feels threatening to my own sense of stability and identity, and I begin to feel crazy myself. The presence of a psychotic parent—of one who forced the acceptance of an insane reality as the precondition for a loving relationship onto and into a vulnerable child—hovers around the consult-ing room, exuding a malignant and sulfurous stench, fueling the game of projective–introjective hot potato from which the patient and I struggle to emerge intact. There is a desperate frenzy to our struggle, as though we are playing the children's card game "Old Maid," in which the dark and foreboding queen of spades skulks around the table—inside one hand and then another, inside me and then you, popping up here and then there: "Not me; I don't want her. Get rid of her; pass her on to someone else. I don't want to be left holding the witch/queen." Perhaps the dilemma in dyadic relationships is simply this: if it is not me, then it must be you. And how do we allow for the presence of such toxicity if the queen lives in both of us and neither of us all at the same time? The specific dynamic I am referring to is an inherent feature of a range of doer–done-to complementarities that Benjamin (1988, 2004) and Frawley and I (Davies & Frawley, 1992, 1994) have all written about.

Karen's father died suddenly when she was 9 years old, and I have often suspected that her mother struggled with bouts of depressive psychosis. Karen refers to her mother's "dark spells," times when mother would become withdrawn, despondent, and brooding, her depressions spilling over into bouts of intense jealousy, rage, and obsessive cleanliness; times when Karen was expected to "care for" her mother and to devote herself almost unceasingly to her mother's moods and whims of the moment. My most visceral sense of Karen's mother grows out of my interactions with Karen herself and with my own countertransferential states when Karen and I go through one of our own dark spells. I often feel as if something toxic and untrue, something malignant in a psychotic sense, is being forced inside me. "You are ice," Karen screams, "just admit it." Admit it, I think. Grant it admission; let it inside you. I know at such moments that if I accept the "truth" of what Karen wants me to own, she will calm down—she will be mollified; but I also know that I will feel two things. I will feel as if I have betrayed my therapeutic function by submitting to a psychotic process in Karen and allowing it to dominate our intersubjective space, untouched and unchallenged. And I also know that I will begin to feel crazy myself, as if I have surrendered my mind and my sanity for a few moments of bartered connection and relief.

What does a child do when a parent's reality is so vastly different from her own, when a parent's sense of that child's innermost core is so vastly different from the child's own felt experience? How far will a child go for love? How does she protect the integrity of her mind while sustaining, at the same time, her loving connection to the parent on whom she depends for survival? I feel with Karen as if I hold that child's questions within myself, within my experience when I am with her. To feel sane, I must recognize that this very significant other is insane. I have my mental integrity, but I am alone and unprotected in a hostile world; to feel safe and protected and cared for I must accept a psychotic reality and live within my mother's world, supporting and believing in it. In these moments with Karen, I understand that child's dilemma. I feel that I know what Karen has gone through, but I know it in my bones. To feel sane, I must forego love, and to feel loved I must render myself insane. I believe the process I am describing here to be a very special form of what Philip Ringstrom (1998), in a more general sense, termed a *psychoanalytic double bind,* or what Barbara Pizer (2003) termed a *relational knot.*

I have no doubt that we all have our "Karens." But there is also no doubt in my mind that my Karens are not necessarily your Karens. It is not any particular form of pathology in the patient, or any particularly malevolent introject in either patient or analyst that, to my way of thinking, creates impasse. It is, I believe, for patient and analyst alike, the particular quality of the individual's idiosyncratic interaction with his or her own parent that will influence both the quality and content of what I think of as a certain receptivity to projections, the capacity to temporarily accept a projection without becoming it or drowning in it. Was there something that my own parent absolutely could not metabolize and own? Was there something that I was forced to accept as being inside me in order to feel myself in some loving relation to that parent? How invasive, alien, and toxic did that something feel when I took it inside myself to be loved? How defining of my entire self did it come to be? Ultimately, the question I am posing is how might that which I felt forced on me dovetail and interact with what any particular patient felt forced on her? What happens when something intolerable in the patient's parent touches on and interacts with something that was intolerable for the analyst's own parent?

Given the developmental universality of projective–introjective processes between parents and children, we might want to consider that the kind of interaction I am describing exists on a continuum from the more "normal" and fluid attribution of qualities to the more toxic, evacuated, and entrenched forms of projection. How toxic these processes will become developmentally, for the child, depends on the intersection of two dimensions: how toxic and shame-inducing is what is evacuated by the parent into the child, and how complete, dissociated, and unremitting is the projection itself—essentially, the content and the dynamic of the projection. To what degree does the loving relation to the parent depend on the child's complete and total acceptance that she is the only one who holds these negative attributions, that such qualities are the patient's own unique, self-defining, and shame-ridden burden to bear rather than being shared with the parent and being universal in human nature? In essence, the child accepts the projection but identifies as well with the parental belief that to possess such qualities threatens survival, that these qualities must be evacuated and located in others at any cost, in precisely the way the parent has evacuated them into the child.

In both the developmental and the therapeutic endeavor, then, the capacity to maintain relatedness, albeit a compromised one, becomes dependent on a particularly intractable dissociation and oscillation of self–other configurations that sustain and protect this projected status quo. In the first of these self–other configurations, the child/patient accepts the toxic projections, accepting herself as crazy, hateful, envious, icy, or dead depending on the particular content projected, but she guarantees herself loving protection under the now benign eye of her all-good parent, who is thus preserved as a loving, sane, and reliable caregiver. This is Fairbairn's (1943) "moral defense"; as he so succinctly puts it, "better to be a sinner in a world ruled by God, than to live in a world ruled by the Devil" (pp. 66–67). But Fairbairn was a one-person theorist. What is left out of his all-important formulation is the second-person dimension: the idea that God loves sinners, not only because sinners sustain God's goodness but also because it is so easy to love those who own their own bad qualities (not to mention your own) and who also appeal to us for help in overcoming these problems. The paradox of the first self–other configuration is, therefore, that while the child or patient believes herself to be bad, crazy, evil, or hateful, she also experiences more of the parent's or analyst's love and positive regard than she would if she failed to view the parent's negative qualities as her own. The sacrifice in this self-state is that the child/patient must blind herself to many of the negative aspects of the other, thus rendering herself "crazy" in terms of her capacity to judge reality.

It is my belief, however, that the child who internalizes and identifies with parental abusiveness in such a way must also maintain simultaneously and in dissociated form an accurate capacity to read the interpersonal emotional landscape with clarity and sensitivity to nuance. Her all-important reality-testing skills, indeed her very connection to certainty and sanity, are ensconced in a self–other relationship in which the dangerousness or potential abusiveness of the other is clearly perceived and held in mind while the innocence of the self is reestablished. When parental behaviors or projections are particularly toxic and relentless, however, such a state can only be established by an equally forceful and relentless counterprojection. The second significant self–other paradigm is therefore one in which badness is projectively evacuated into the other, and the self once again feels a sense of internal goodness, innocence, and sanity. The child is able to withstand parental projection and adequately perceive that all badness does not lie within herself—as long as she perceives no badness whatsoever in herself. The therapeutic dilemma in this self-state is that, although it allows the patient to experience her own internal sense of goodness and to rely more constructively on her internal sense of sanity, she can be projectively blinded to the significant aspects of her own participation that contribute to evoking these more negative interactions. The intensity of the counterprojection required by the patient to sustain her innocence requires that such an innocence be total and complete. The paradoxical aspect is that, although she believes herself to be more lovable, in this self-state she has experientially sacrificed the important state of feeling adequately loved by the other, because the "devil," once projectively constructed, is incapable of loving the other. The analyst buffeted by relentless malignant projections finds it quite difficult, sometimes impossible, to locate analytic love for the patient. Once again, to feel loved she must render herself insane; to feel sane she must forego feeling loved.

In her work on malignant envy, Melanie Klein made it possible to understand how one can hate what is good. She taught us how to integrate a hatred for the good object into our clinical work. She clarified how when the patient stands up and screams, "I hate you," she is often saying, "I hate that I love you. I hate that I need you. I hate that you can give me what I cannot give myself." In the present paper, I am grappling with the inverse unconscious paradigm: the ways we often seek to find, engage with, and love our most malignant objects (our patients' and our own); the ways provoking, seeking, and engaging with the worst that the other has to offer unconsciously secures our own internal sense of goodness, righteousness, and innocence. It is only by acknowledging that we often hate what is good in others and love what is most evil that we bring into conscious awareness the unconscious and dissociated complementarity that can fuel such repetitions and collapse self-reflective functioning.

To the extent that we see this split in our relationship to bad objects as universal, we must of course look at the analyst's experience of these oscillating states as well. Most of us now accept that the analyst comes to the therapeutic endeavor struggling with his or her own internal demons, striving to heal others, but, in so doing, striving also to reaffirm and revitalize his or her own sense of internal goodness. Let me suggest the possibility that the analyst as child among his or her own bad objects struggled to feel sane amidst insanity; to preserve his or her sense of mental integrity by seeing more clearly the pathology of others. "To feel sane I must forego love." In later work with patients, the analyst is caught between the counterbalancing needs of continuing to locate pathology clearly in the other and not the self and also of curing the other, who is seen as sick, so that the analyst may be loved and nourished once again. Perhaps more than others, we analysts are subject to this particular vulnerability (Anthony Bass, 2001, personal communication).

However, even if the therapist can free herself from her own toxic self-states and from her need to evacuate them into the patient long enough to reflect on what is happening in the therapeutic relationship and to interpret that process; the therapeutic/interpretive dilemma remains problematic. For if I manage to offer my patient an interpretation that feels empathic and resonates with her own internal sense of our shared experience, the transference–countertransference complementarity shifts, and rather than feeling warmed and nourished by an empathic and meaningful comment that she can take in and use, the patient feels shamed and humiliated by my empathy (because it challenges and contradicts her projections). Here her own inner sense of goodness and sanity, a sense held in check by the evacuation of all that is bad into me, ricochets back against her and resurrects her own episodic and dissociated sense of internal badness. When the therapist is experienced as nurturing it fills the patient with shame and not warmth. The therapist is either bad and has nothing to give, or the therapist manages to touch and reach the patient, and in response the patient feels so hateful, shame filled, and loathsome that she feels that she deserves nothing. It seems that something in the therapeutic stalemate must shift so that both badness and goodness can be jointly held and experienced together. It is not that the patient must give up seeing the bad object in the analyst but that she must first give up seeing this badness as residing exclusively within herself. Then and only then can she believe in the analyst's actual rather than total and projected badness, and only then can she see the process of her own projection without blinding shame. Likewise, the analyst must come to see the ways in which she searches for pathology as the most acceptable derivative of badness in the patient, to accept her own projective resistances to allowing the patient to occupy both good and bad self-states simultaneously.

On Friday afternoon I am still sick, anticipating a weekend of soft blankets and hot liquids. I brace myself for Karen's entrance. She looks at me as if sizing up my physical state, my preparedness to engage in a battle worthy of our history together. But I notice, almost immediately, that something feels palpably different. The air feels warmer, her eyes look softer and more searching, and my own body seems to relax even before I can formulate the experience. The words follow. "You really do look lousy," she says, with an uncharacteristically warm and playful smile. "I feel lousy," I counter, smiling to let her know that my form of "lousy" is tolerable and manageable by me but seeing no point in attempting to deny the obvious. I am transfixed by this "other Karen," attempting to hold her there with my response, continuing to perpetuate this other form of relatedness by the words I choose and the kind of playfulness I might offer.

Karen reaches down into her book bag and pulls out a large silver thermos and mug. As she opens the thermos and begins to pour, the warm smells of honey, vanilla, and cinnamon fill my office. I am mesmerized as I watch Karen, intrigued with her swift and competent movements. "This will be good for you," she says. "My grandmother used to make it for me when I was sick. It is a combination of hot tea and hot milk with a lot of other wonderful stuff." She holds the mug out to me, an expression of intense pleasure and hopefulness suffusing her face. As I reach for the mug, our fingers touch for an instant, and I recall that my own grandmother brought a similar recipe with her from Russia, one that she would prepare for us when someone in the family was sick with a cold. There are now two more personas squeezing into our already overcrowded analytic space: Karen's grandmother and my own. The evocation of both of our alternate mothers seems not accidental.

I will myself to think, despite the feverish buzz in my head. My patient is attempting to feed me warm milk. There must be an incredible interpretation in this somewhere! Who was I at this moment in the transference? Was Karen afraid that I was going to die like her father? How did this relate to the unconscious fantasies she harbored about the reasons for her father's sudden death and about the role of her own aggressive and murderous thoughts? Should I interpret her outrage and horror at his abandonment, her sense of guilty responsibility for his death, her compulsive need to destroy and then feverishly resuscitate all that is good in her present relationships? Or was this interaction about a more loving, less ambivalently attached, more genuinely nurturing self who had somehow died along with her father? Had I unconsciously spoken in her father's voice, exhibiting his demeanor—his unique affective array—in relation to her? In so doing, had I unknowingly resuscitated a ghostly self-organization that had existed only for him? Did I need to engage this emergent, unconscious aspect of Karen's self, talk to her, accept her offerings, actually drink her warm milk? Did I need to do so long enough for this fledgling wisp of self-experience to organize itself, to shape itself around my words and emotional response, to set down roots that would sustain it through the trials and tribulations of more traditional interpretation?

But maybe this wasn't about Karen's father at all. What of her mother? How enraged would Karen be if I allowed her to nurse and take care of me as she always had to manage her mother's illnesses, if I drank her milk instead of offering her mine? How exploited might she feel? What of the omnipotent mother who lurked behind the sick one? What angry, competitive feelings existing between us would fail to get elaborated and contained in the analytic space if I was not able to interpret Karen's enactment and encourage her to reflect on her present behavior?

Ironically, all of these interpretive musings seemed important; all things that Karen should understand. Most of them were interpretations that I would have to make at some point. But the maddening dilemma of such therapeutic moments is that they allow space for only one analytic response out of myriad possibilities. The therapeutic choice is not which interpretation is right and which is wrong but rather which comment out of all possible comments is the most important one for Karen to hear—and to hear at this particular moment of time and opportunity. For me—and, I believe, for many relational analysts—a full engagement with this question involves not simply a consideration of the content of any possible interpretation but a full analysis as well of the self-states of analyst and patient that occupy this interpretive moment. As I have stated the question in previous writing, we must ask ourselves, "Who in the analyst will speak in this particular moment, and who in the patient will be listening and receiving that inter-pretation (Davies, 1999, p. 193)?

As Karen leans toward me with the cup of tea, I am suddenly awed and humbled by the remarkable, almost incomprehensible complexity of psychoanalytic process and change. It is not simply that any analysis consists of an infinite number of such moments, but also that each moment contains a multitude of different interpretive channels and modalities: words, actions, facial expressions, body language. Do I chuckle when I say something; do my eyes express warmth, concern, playfulness or frustration? "You look lousy," says Karen. "I feel lousy," say I. But I smile. It is not premeditated, it just happens—the intersubjective meeting between my self-state of the engagement and hers. The smile honors Karen's recognition and sensitivity to my condition. She is noticed and appreciated in that moment. She has dared to enter my world, and she finds herself welcome there. How different "I feel lousy" would seem if it were accompanied by emotional flatness and withdrawal or by a sense of overwhelmed desperation akin to her mother's depressions.

I take Karen's mug in my own hands, breathing in its healing, aromatic warmth. I feel a moment of guilt as the intoxicating smells and moist heat penetrate and soothe. I grow aware of an insidious little burst of shame over how much I had hated Karen on the day before and had dreaded her session this afternoon. Perhaps I have been wrong about her. Perhaps I am the one who is cold and withholding and stuck. Perhaps I am unde-serving of such kindness. I take passing note of the countertransference complementarity, as I take a long, deep, healing gulp of Karen's milk, not so much to be a good object for her as to acknowledge the hopeful plea for recognition of her goodness and generosity, a plea that is written all over her face: a plea to let her be a good self. "My milk is good and nourishing; it will heal you," says Karen's gesture. "Yes, your milk is good and nourishing and healing," responds my action. I think of Harold Searles's (1979) belief that the patient needs to feel capable of healing the analyst. I think also of Thomas Ogden's (1994) description of "interpretive action" as follows:

> ... The analyst's use of action to convey to the analysand specific aspects of the analyst's understanding of the transference–countertransference which cannot at that juncture in the analysis be conveyed by the semantic content of words alone ... It accrues its specific symbolic meaning from the experiential context of the analytic intersubjectivity in which it is generated. (p. 219)

I smile at Karen through the steam, and she smiles back. Not only do I like her again, but I like myself as well. I am also good—capable of being nourished, of accepting warmth. There is now such a warm, fragrant, milky goodness between us that it would be easy to hang on, to stay there, to let the "milkiness" of the moment drown out the opportunity rather than potentiate it. How can I sustain Karen's smile, her love of self, in this moment, while at the same time work to bring the events, experiences, and affect states of the day before, the self–other organizations of evacuated evil and envy, into conscious contact and coordination? Is there a way for each of us to hold and sustain the extruded malevolence that defined our therapeutic impasse of the day before with the loving goodness of the present moment?

"I like it better in here today," beams Karen. "Yes," I respond, taking another gulp of Karen's milk, hoping that my "interpretive drinking action" will sustain Karen's present self-state yet allow for the emergence of the other selves, hers and mine, for whom I now reach with interpretive words. "But what of those two other people who were in here yesterday?" I ask her. "They were pretty awful. What are you and I to make of them?" Will it be possible, I wonder, for word and action to move in two different directions, holding complementary self–other organizations in simultaneous awareness. Can I "drink in" our goodness while speaking of our enormous potential to hurt and shame each other?

"You hate that me," declares Karen, her eyes becoming narrow and her face darkening. "Yeah, sometimes," I acknowledge, hoping that the enactment between us will sustain Karen's good self while I make use of the moment to verbally acknowledge my hatred for the other. I flash to the night before, to the interpretation I held at bay in order to reflect on it further. "But hating you isn't even the worst of it," I counter. Karen's eyebrows are raised. The darkness is held at bay for a moment; it hovers, waiting. "The worst part of yesterday, of times like that between us, isn't that I start to hate you," I tell her. "It's that I start to hate myself. I really hated myself last night more than anything, certainly more than I hated you." The darkness dissipates for a brief moment. My patient's eyes seem to register curiosity. Karen giggles despite herself. Her giggle surprises me and catches me off guard. "Really?" Karen asks. "You really hated yourself more than me? I mean, you sometimes hate yourself?"

I think here of Emmanuel Ghent's (1992) notion of "object probing." "I often hate myself," I say, and before I become conscious of it, I find that I am laughing, too, giggling with Karen. For this very brief moment, we have become coconspirators, coconstructors of alternative selves too toxic to be owned independently but now held, sustained, even tentatively enjoyed as a moment of commonality between us. The shame that had filled our respective experiences of the night before is now rather tenuously held at bay by the strength we bring jointly to the endeavor. It begins to transform ever so slightly and to become tolerable.

"You wouldn't consider telling me what you hate about yourself, would you?" Karen asks. "I don't know; I might. Maybe we could take turns," I answer. My eyebrows go up. I smile. We are playing with each other. "You are good, Karen," say my eyebrows and my smile. "You can afford to be a bad self sometimes. You can be both." In this manner, a kind of Bionian transformation occurs in which the analyst holds the patient's toxic projections, transforming them internally, and handing them back as not quite so horrendous or deadly. Of course, in these moments with Karen, I think of none of these things explicitly. It is not that I am aware of my eyebrows, my lips, or whether I drink or don't drink at a particular moment. Such movements are part of an unconscious psychoanalytic sensibility, controlled and coordinated by the fluid mix of transference–countertransference processes. But they speak along with our words. In many cases, they determine the nuances and textures of how our words are taken in and of what our words come to signify for the patient. "Yes, I am bad like you. I have an evil self, too. And yet (unlike your parent) I can think of, even speak of, my evil self and survive. I can even smile. We can be bad together." Here, the repetitive complementarities in the transference–countertransference (which I discussed earlier) begin to break down. Karen does not have to be the only bad and crazy one to feel loved by me. Nor does she have to demonize me in order to feel sane. For me, a space has been created in which my own shameful self-states become tolerable. Aspects of my own behavior that may be touched with anger, envy, indifference, self-absorption, or self-interest can now be taken back into the self so that Karen can watch me survive the owning of them.

I tell Karen a little something about the icy, bitchy self I had to struggle with when we fought in our last session, about how painful and shameful it was to feel that part of myself in my work with her. She was amazed that I could feel shame about parts of myself and was uncharacteristically quiet and reflective. "I hate myself most of the time," she tells me almost in a whisper. "Deep inside, I'm evil. You'll say that's not true, but it is true. I'm evil. The only time I feel good is when I find the evil parts of other people … like with you. It makes me feel less alone." Something is clearly happening here to the experience of shame. I can speak with Karen about feeling vulnerable: how it feels for me to be vulnerable with her, how it feels for her to be vulnerable with me, the different ways one can respond to the vulnerability of a loved other. Some people would call the things I share with Karen as we reflect together on our more hated characteristics "self-disclosures," but I disagree. I suspect that, in those moments, I tell Karen little about myself that she has not already discerned for herself from our interactions. Rather, I like to think that the message here is in the process: that shame is tolerable, that it won't necessarily destroy, that it can be met with love and recognition and self-acceptance even though the aggression and its effect on others must be taken seriously.

As analysts, I believe that we must be able to fully occupy the counter-transference as it is constructed in the enactment with any given patient. My point has been to emphasize that particularly toxic impasses can occur when something in the patient's history of extruded self-states engages with something in the analyst's history of extruded self-states. In such instances, the boundary between self and other collapses in the mutual spit-fire projections and counterprojections that ensue. The analyst's space for self-reflective processes becomes compromised and potentially shut down when overwhelming shame contributes to his or her rejection of a patient's unconscious communication. The analyst struggles not just to hold a bad object representation for the patient but also to fend off an intolerable, shame-riddled self-representation of his or her own as part of the formidable effort to coconstruct with the patient a space in which each can feel loved and sane in the same moment.

In this context, I have come to think of certain impasses in psychoanalytic work not as enactments one can't get out of but rather as nascent enactments that one can't fully enter and get into, because occupation of the countertransference component of the enactment is blocked by the analyst's dissociated, shame-riddled self-states. If the experience of self evoked by the enactment is too shame filled and toxic to be held and experienced by the analyst, then the therapeutic couple can get caught in a state of perpetually resisting entry into the very enactment that they must enter to occupy a particular transference–countertransference state long enough to understand it from the inside and together create something different.

I conclude by relaying a dream that Karen reported to me several months after the sessions described here, during the time when she and I were actively involved in exploring her more shame-filled and loathsome self-states. Karen reports:

I am walking out on a long pier that reaches out into an enormous body of water. I'm surrounded by water on three sides and must balance on this somewhat old and rickety dock. At the end of the dock, in the water, I see something, some kind of creature … extraterrestrial or something. It is made of steel and metal, with a sticklike body and a cube for a head. It has a face and two enormous eyes. It seems to be drowning in the water, gasping for breath and going under, then coming up and gasping again. It reaches an arm out toward me, and in this unbelievably awful, inhuman, synthesized voice it sort of whistles, "Help me." It wants me to reach out and grab its hand, but I can't. I am repulsed and revolted by the very idea. The thought of touching the thing makes me feel ill. I notice that the creature has something in one of its eyes. It looks like a foreign body, like oil on water. The eye is irritated and painful, and the creature keeps blinking, to try and clear it out. But it doesn't work. It keeps repeating, "Help me, help me." And so finally I take a deep breath and reach out for its hand. As our hands touch, I feel cold metal, and I am overwhelmed by nausea and dizziness. I close my eyes, because the feel of the creature sickens me and I think I will throw up. But when that feeling passes and I open my eyes, I see that the creature is crying, from both eyes, not because it has something foreign in its eyes but because it is grieving. They are sad tears. And I notice, also, that the creature is beginning to grow skin. It is becoming human.

References

Aron, L. (1996). *A meeting of minds: Mutuality in psychoanalysis.* Hillsdale, NJ: The Analytic Press.

Benjamin, J. (1988). *The bonds of love: Psychoanalysis, feminism, and the problem of domination.* New York: Pantheon.

Benjamin, J. (2004). Beyond doer and done-to: an intersubjective view of thirdness. *Psychoanalytic Quarterly, 63,* 5–46.

Black, M. (2003). Enactment: Analytic musings on energy, language, and personal growth. *Psychoanalytic Dialogues, 13,* 633–656.

Bromberg, P. (1998). *Standing in the spaces: Essays on clinical process, trauma, and dissociation.* Hillsdale, NJ: The Analytic Press.

Bromberg, P. (2000). Potholes on the royal road: Or is it an abyss? *Contemporary Psychoanalysis, 36,* 5–28.

Cooper, S. (2000). *Objects of hope: Exploring possibility and limit in psychoanalysis.* Hillsdale, NJ: The Analytic Press.

Davies, J. M. (1996). Linking the "pre-analytic" with the postclassical: Integration, dissociation, and the multiplicity of unconscious process. *Contemporary Psychoanalysis, 32,* 553–576.

Davies, J. M. (1999). Getting cold feet, defining safe-enough borders: Dissociation, integration, and multiplicity in the analyst's experience of the transference–countertransference process. *Psychoanalytic Quarterly, 68,* 184–208.

Davies, J. M., & Frawley, M. G. (1992). Dissociative processes and transference–countertransference paradigms in the psychoanalytically oriented treatment of adult survivors of childhood sexual abuse. *Psychoanalytic Dialogues, 2,* 5–36.

Davies, J. M., & Frawley, M. G. (1994). *Treating the adult survivor of childhood sexual abuse: A psychoanalytic perspective.* New York: Basic Books.

Ehrenberg, D. (1992). *The intimate edge.* New York: Norton.

Elkind, S. (1992). *Resolving impasses in therapeutic relationships.* New York: Guilford.

Fairbairn, W. R. D. (1943). The repression and the return of bad objects. In *Psychoanalytic studies of the personality* (pp. 59–81). London: Routledge.

Ghent, E. (1992). Paradox and process. *Psychoanalytic Dialogues, 2,* 135–160.

Hoffman, I. Z. (1998). *Ritual and spontaneity in the psychoanalytic process: A dialectical-constructivist view.* Hillsdale, NJ: The Analytic Press.

Mitchell, S. (1997). *Influence and autonomy in psychoanalysis.* Hillsdale, NJ: The Analytic Press.

Ogden, T. (1994). The concept of interpretive action. *Psychoanalytic Quarterly, 63,* 219–245.

Pizer, B. (2003). When the crunch is a (k)not: A crimp in relational dialogue. *Psychoanalytic Dialogues, 13,* 171–192.

Pizer, S. (1998). *Building bridges: The negotiation of paradox in psychoanalysis.* Hillsdale, NJ: The Analytic Press.

Ringstrom, P. (1998). Therapeutic impasses in contemporary psychoanalytic treatment: Revisiting the double bind hypothesis. *Psychoanalytic Dialogues, 8,* 297–316.

Russell, P. (1973). Crises of emotional growth (a.k.a. The theory of the crunch). Unpublished manuscript.

Searles, H. (1979). The patient as therapist to the analyst. In P. Giovacchini (Ed.), *Countertransference* (pp. 95–151). Northvale, NJ: Aronson.

8

Body Rhythms and the Unconscious

Expanding Clinical Attention With the Polyrhythmic Weave*

Steven Knoblauch

> All the works in the exhibition are predicated on doubts about language. ... If the *Meridians* deal with that which cannot be expressed, with displacement in language, then the *Descriptions* deal with the futility of our attempts to describe. Description of an exhibit of works by Avis Newman (The Museum of Contemporary Art, Sydney, Australia, June–August 2003)

The focus of this paper is the dilemma captured in the opening quote concerning the limitations of symbolization because of the displacement effect of language and the futility that language meets as description of lived experience. As psychoanalysts involved in the "talking cure," how do we work with these limitations and still constitute therapeutic engagement with our patients? Using a clinical illustration to build on a perspective I have been developing based on the metaphoric value of jazz improvisation for attending to, and participating in, a psychoanalytic interaction (Knoblauch, 2000), I offer a strategy and theoretical perspective. This perspective shares with those of La Barre (2001), Gentile (2007), Orbach (2000, 2003, 2004, 2006), Reis (2009), Sletvold (in press), Sonntag (2006), and others (Aron & Anderson, 1998; Anderson, 2008) a privileging of nonverbal embodied communication in a way that has rarely been demonstrated in clinical practice (see my discussion of precursors to our perspectives in Knoblauch, 2000, pp. 51–76). The process of improvisation in jazz requires careful attention

---

* An earlier version of this chapter appeared in *Psychoanalytic Dialogues*, *15*(6), 2005, pp. 807–827. Reprinted with permission.

to nonverbal embodied dimensions of communication, particularly rhythm, tone, and gesture, for recognizing and expressing affect. A similar process is ongoing in the clinical exchange with rich potential for recognition and expression when words are not being used, a condition particular to communication of unspeakable trauma.

Attention to *process* (I use the term *process* in a particular way to refer to the micropolyrhythmic dimensions of the interactive exchange) has traditionally been given little to no descriptive significance in narratives of clinical action. Rather, attention to *structures* of experience in the subjectivities of analysand and analyst has been the preferred metaphor for representation and explanation. The approach I am describing expands analytic attention with particular focus given to process or how structured experience is "formed into." This is a dimension of meaning making concomitant with communicative experience we semantically mark with terms such as symbolization or representation, information as delineated form. Here I am additionally inviting particular attention to a sense and narration of experience *in formation*. This expanded view offers a way to navigate the challenge of the dilemma framed in the opening passage and to work with expressions of trauma about which analysands are often not able to give verbal representation. This perspective incorporates embodied experience in addition to verbal symbolization as a portal into unconscious meaning and its centrality to therapeutic action.

In his landmark contribution to understanding human development Daniel Stern (1985) makes an observation similar to the quote with which this text is initiated. He addresses the relationship between words and the experiences they are constructed to represent, explaining:

> Language is a double-edged sword. It...makes some parts of our experience less shareable with ourselves and with others. It drives a wedge between two simultaneous forms of interpersonal experience: as it is lived and as it is verbally represented. ...Language...causes a split in the experience of the self. It...moves relatedness onto the impersonal, abstract level intrinsic to language and away from the personal immediate level intrinsic to...other domains of relatedness. (pp. 162–163)*

Stern's point in 1985 was that what is lived is unable to be fully captured with its representation in words. This is a price we pay for constituting a mode whereby we can begin to both reflect on, and share experience, at least to some degree, with others.

---

* Stern recently augmented this position, incorporating a view that language can be part of a gestalt that is immediately intuitively grasped so that language can be abstract in its representational capacity but also an embodied lived experience for both speaker and listener (Boston Change Process Study Group, 2008).

Implicit to Stern's observation is the point that the operation of represent-ing experience with word symbolization "permits the child [allows the adult] to begin to construct a narrative of his own life" (p. 162). But it also becomes the form by which experience is split across different modes of relatedness. Speaking is a different register than what we feel. Lacan (1977) addressed this phenomenon with more pessimism. He claimed "...the symbol mani-fests in itself first of all as the murder of the thing, and this death constitutes in the subject the externalization of his desire" (p. 104). Stern addresses the cognitive aspect of the effect of symbolic representation. Lacan's point origi-nally made about the effect of symbolization as an abstract representation of something lived and unable to be fully represented without important loss, has implications beyond just cognitive experience. Lacan's observation also concerns the effect of symbolic representation on affective experience. For Lacan, the splitting that Stern describes devitalizes or "murders" the thing represented. It reduces it to an object, which by its abstraction and externalization can remove it from the immediacy of affective impact. Thus, representation or symbolization constitutes a gap between what has been experienced and what is *re-presented*, a form of desire for that experience which has been lost. Lacan puts it this way:

> ...The subject is not simply mastering his privation by assuming it....He is raising his desire to a second power. For his action [the symbolizing or objecti-fying of an experience with words] destroys the object that it causes to appear and disappear in the anticipating *provocation* of its absence and its presence. His action thus negatives the field of forces of desire in order to become its own object to itself. (p. 103, italics added)

Another way to think about what Lacan says is to recognize that the sym-bolizing function of language memorializes an experience so that narrative can emerge. Narrative is requisite to memory, the process of representing an experience for storage and retrieval. But this form of memorialization, this process of representation, according to Lacan, requires a delimiting and delineating of experience such that it is *frozen in time*, deadened and devital-ized as it is arbitrarily removed from the flow, process, or polyrhythmic weave of continuous interactive experience. This splitting off and categorization of experience into a discrete noncontinuous, symbolized "thing" creates two effects: loss, and desire for what one had experienced but is now lost, though capable of being "*re-membered*," and thus reexperienced affectively, through the storage and retrieval functions that representation makes possible.

This understanding of how meaning is made possible for narration is central to Freud's method, the "talking cure." For it is attention to forms of condensation, displacement, and substitution in the construction of narrated meaning that is the basis of the analytic method. Freud's evenly hovering attention emerged as the strategy for how the analyst could use herself to recognize, organize, and respond to these particular structures of subjectivity in the patient's experience and begin to help the patient become conscious of experiences of loss and desire that were "repressed" when language was not available for remembering such experience. Freud's idea of trauma is central to this view as it was the affective unbearability of a particular experience, understood as an inability to manage libidinal energy (i.e., sublimate rather than discharge), that resulted in the splitting off of that experience not into a word but into some unconscious symptom. This understanding, in itself, presents an interesting problem since symptoms were generally enacted or expressed somatically. Thus, experience could either be sublimated through symbolization or enacted symptomatically. In either case a splitting occurred, either into a "re-presentation" as word or a "re-presentation" as enacted or somatized symptom.

Freud believed the talking cure of free association was a way to heal the splits caused by symbolization or symptomization. But central to his idea of this process were two assumptions: (1) the capability of the analyst to attain a neutral and objective stance in providing interpretations; and (2) the capability of the analysand to attain an attitude where associations would be produced uncensored. When this became problematic, the analysand's difficulty was to be interpreted as defense. Recently, Hoffman (2006) offered a compelling review of this second assumption building on his previous review (Hoffman, 1983) of the first assumption. In his landmark 1983 paper, Hoffman carefully demonstrates the impossibility of neutrality and therefore objectivity for an analyst through an examination of the *subjective biases* inherent in different theoretical stances characteristic of different psychoanalytic approaches to treatment. In his 2006 paper he expands his argument to include the subjectivity of the analysand as well as analyst. He convincingly demonstrates how clinically pivotal relational influences occur as a result of critical subjective coloring of experience on the part of both analytic participants. Building on Hoffman's contribution, I would agree with Mitchell's (1997) observation that expectations for free association from the analysand or neutrality and objectivity from the analyst create unattainable ideals at best, if not, illusions that could contribute to exceedingly brutal transferential or countertransferential self-evaluations (pp. 13–14). Hoffman's perspective frees us from these persecutory expectations. Here, I want to add specificity to Hoffman's emphasis on relational dimensions of the transference–countertransference field or matrix to demonstrate how such specificity can expand analytic attention. First, let's consider the implications of his deconstruction of the free association method.

Freud's method of free association is critically built upon the assumption of an ideal of purifying observation, of making it free of biases, feelings, or other influences that could affect what comes to mind. Hoffman (2006) describes how this assumption is built on "1) the denial of the patient's agency, 2) the denial of the analyst's and the patient's interpersonal influence, and 3) the denial of the patient's share of responsibility for coconstructing the analytic relationship" (p. 43). Hoffman argues that in fact the *personal involvement of the analyst* (compare this notion to the ideal of neutrality) leads to a different emphasis in therapeutic action that "amounts to a huge difference in terms of the kinds of experiences that are promoted and the likely basis for therapeutic action" (p. 51). He does not argue for the jettisoning of insight as central to change but rather for "a climate that encourages both imaginative construction and critical reflection on the constructive process itself." He emphasizes, "Insight is embedded in a multi-faceted *relationship* the *whole* of which offers a complex kind of corrective experience" (p. 52).

But if in relational analysis we focus, as Hoffman would have us do, on the ways that what we enact with our patients can provide the material for reflection and further imaginative construction of meanings, the question remains, *how* are we doing this? If free association as a method contains the assumptions of attainability of ideal states that are not attainable and so is questionable as the central, mutative method catalyzing therapeutic action in psychoanalysis, what, then, might be?

The norm that has been emerging for a relational method has been to focus attention on what is enacted (see Aron, 1996; Bass, 2003, 2007; Black, 2003; Cooper, 2003, 2007; Davies, 1998, 2003, 2005; Hoffman, 1998; Jacobs, 1986, 1991; Ringstrom, 2001, for illustrative examples), or created, not just by the patient but by the patient and analyst in coconstructed patterns and meanings. As Hoffman illustrates in his work, reflecting on these enactments post hoc can lead to important therapeutic movement. In Hoffman's clinical illustrations as well as in those of several other relational analysts (see Bromberg, 1998; Stern, 1997; Davies, 1998; Cooper, 2003; Ringstrom, 2001; Mitchell, 1997; Harris, 1998, 2005; Dimen, 2003; Lichtenberg, Lachmann, & Fosshage, 2002, for illustrative examples), there has been a trend to develop meaning, that which, previously, has not been consciously articulated or recognized, out of attention not just to symbolic communication but to what Hoffman (1998) called noninterpretive interactions (pp. xiii–xvi, 182–183). In contrast to Hoffman's emphasis on this kind of attention and responsiveness as noninterpretive, Ogden (1994) described these kinds of interactions as interpretive. He explains, "By 'interpretive action' (or 'interpretation-in-action') I mean the analyst's communication of his understanding of an aspect of the transference–countertransference to the analysand by means of activity other than that of verbal symbolization" (p. 108). I want to try to further unfold the implications of this trend and to give it more specific conceptual clarity for sharpening and expanding possibilities for analytic focus.

Freud saw association as a kind of repair or re-membering of a broken connection caused by repression. Repression would occur because of the unbearability of the affective meaning associated with whatever experience was repressed. Revisiting Freud today, we might wonder that repression is a problematic concept for trauma. I say that because our understanding of trauma has led us to recognize a major effect of trauma is that affective meaning does not get represented in words but rather split off in bodily symptoms. The split that Lacan and Stern describe is the effect of the trauma of using the word to create symbolic representation, not the effect of trauma resulting in embodied symptoms. The split pointed to by Lacan and Stern is central to Freud's method of free association in which the goal is a repair of this split. But this method fails to address the impact of trauma when words have not been created. It is difficult to reconnect a word to a thing when no word and no thing were ever recognized and symbolized. Attempts to do so often result in retraumatization. A close reading of Kohut's description of his difficulty with offering verbal interpretations to Ms. F gives us a vivid example of how this repetitive retraumatization occurs and can develop into an impasse. So, now we are talking about a different kind of split than Freud's method addresses, the split or gap caused by dissociation, what Kohut called the vertical split. This is a splitting off of experience on an affective register where affect is communicated and registered without the availability of word symbols. This recognition has led to significant pioneering work expanding analytic praxis to understand and conceptualize affect (see Spezzano, 1993; Stein, 1999) and to account for and work with dissociative processes (see Bromberg, 1998; Davies & Frawley, 1994).

Building toward a relational "method," the innovative contributions of these clinicians and others have led to a number of revisions in understanding and approaching a patient's experience. Central to this work has been the placing of enactment in addition to verbal association at the center of analytic attention. Here, as Hoffman emphasizes, insight is not jettisoned, but part of the interactive experience that is promoted and the basis for therapeutic action. Thus, relational treatment, consistent with Kohut's intent following his insights about his work with Ms. F, shifts and expands the emphasis of analytic attention rather than replacing it. Within this expansion words are not just symbols but also forms of action and thus enactment. Similarly actions are not always, and just, "acting out" (Jacobs, 1986), but also ways patients communicate affectively and construct meaning in interaction with their analysts. So, if free association can be used to access affective meanings that are being communicated symbolically, how do we access what is being communicated through enactment but not symbolized with words?

Part of the difficulty is most of what is enacted falls under the radar of symbolization as Lacan and Stern observe. But it is clear in reading the compelling clinical descriptions of the previously mentioned authors and others that important and *different* kinds of attention is being paid to *different* experience other than just the semantic meaning of what is being communicated, and this activity is critical for analytic attention.

How can we talk about these differences? How can we describe and narrate this other form or these other forms of attention, these alternative foci to symbolizing activity? This challenge clearly contains a paradox because to describe the nonsymbolic activity to which one attends, one needs to find a way of representing or symbolizing it with words. Stern would have us talk about lived versus symbolized experience. But, of course, we would still have to find a way to symbolize this lived experience in a way that would not repeat the problem of splitting off important registers that symbolization erases. Lacan, more pessimistic than Stern, would have us recognize the devitalizing effect of the word and how it constitutes the tension of desires, a gap between experience and its representation that is impossible to communicate and fully "know."

Recent attempts by relational theorists and infant researchers have not closed this "gap" so much as to begin to attempt to explore what seems to be happening in the "gap." Bromberg has described this as *standing in the spaces*. Donnel Stern described an attitude of curiosity that focuses the analyst on what is going on between patient and analyst but *unformulated*. The infant researcher Alan Fogel (1993) distinguished between the *discrete state* and the *continuous process*. The cognitive researcher Wilma Bucci (1997) distinguished symbolic from *subsymbolic* levels of activity. She explains, "The categorical function, by which the continuous gradients of perceptual experience are chunked into discrete prototypical images, is the core of the symbolizing process" (p. 142). In comparing *subsymbolic* with symbolic levels of cognitive processing, she explains, "These [varieties of information processing] include representations and processes in which the elements are not discrete, organization is not categorical, processing occurs simultaneously in multiple parallel channels, high level units are not generated from discrete elements, and explicit processing rules cannot be identified." She then points out:

> Subsymbolic processing accommodates infinitely fine variation; this processing is not represented by standard metric systems or computational rules. We recognize changes in the emotional states of others based on perception of subtle shifts in their facial expression or posture, and recognize changes in our own states based on somatic or kinesthetic experience. (p. 194)

I would add to face and posture the subtle shifts in vocal tone, rhythm and turn-taking. Fivaz-Depeursinge and Corboz-Warnery (1999) in their empirical study of family interactive patterns find similar subsymbolic or what I call nonsymbolic levels of processing to the phenomena reported by Bucci:

> [Family members] use multiple physical modalities in playing: their pelves, torsos, heads, gazes, facial expression, voice intonations, and gestures. Whereas these modalities come in "packages" (for instance, leaning the torso forward, orienting the face "enface" and greeting (Beebe & Stern, 1977; Cohn & Tronick, 1988; Weinberg & Tronick, 1994), they also constitute distinct layers or levels (Fogel, 1992). Indeed, the partners can delineate different interactive domains with the pelves, torso, gazes and expressions. (p. 58)

The Boston Change Process Study Group calls shared discrete states, *moments of meeting,* and the activity in which such moments are embedded, a context of *implicit relational knowing.* Alexandra Harrison (2003) describes video research in child treatment illustrating a way that symbolized and nonsymbolized events can be tracked and related, at least contiguously, as a basis for making subjective judgments about the coconstructing of affective experience and its significance for therapeutic action. I and my colleagues, Beebe, Rustin, and Sorter (2005) reviewed eight models of intersubjectivity contributed in both the literatures of adult analytic treatment and infant research. We tracked differences in what was attended to as central to therapeutic change in the interactive process that is enacted. Attempting to integrate these different approaches in a treatment, Beebe described her use of videotaping to focus in on critical details of the implicit relational context and demonstrate how mutative activity occurred in treatment, at times, without symbolization. Using our own subjective and particularly affective participation in treatment interaction, Ehrenberg (1992, coming from an interpersonal perspective she calls *the intimate edge*), Ogden (1989, coming from an object relations perspective which he calls *the primitive edge*), and I (Knoblauch, 2000), coming from a relational perspective which I call *the musical edge*, each working with an intersubjective frame, have offered approaches whereby we expand our attention beyond the symbolizing process of free association to attend to other nonsymbolized levels of activity where affective communication is occurring and meaning being constructed. How can we better understand these new kinds of analytic attention and their implications for the kinds of noninterpretive interaction that Hoffman and others describe?

I believe that Bucci's observations in cognitive research, and those of Fogel and Fivaz-Depeursinge and Corboz-Warnery in infant–parent interaction, point to different registers of communicative experience. These registers of experience require new and different kinds of attentional strategies that can be useful in psychoanalytic practice. In this chapter, I offer a clinical example in which shifts in focus of attention can be tracked to illustrate how the analyst's rhythms of attention between *formed symbolic communication* and *the processes of formation on acoustic and kinesthetic registers* can enrich the texturing of meaning constructed in analytic interaction and improve descriptions of what is happening in the "gap" between experience and its various registrations and representations that can constitute affective "gaps" (dissociations) between as well as within interacting subjects. I want to say more about the relationship between attention to structures of formation or *information* and attention to a process *in-formation*. To ground these further observations with clinical illustration, consider this narrative of a particular analytic encounter between Denise and me.

Denise and Me

As Denise flopped herself into the chair in front of me, her chest rose filling with air, as much as she could take in. Then when fully engorged, she suddenly and swiftly released the gas, with a deep grunt... no growl. The trumpeter Rex Stewart would similarly punctuate the plaintive soundscape of an Ellington depression era dirge. It was a cold damp January morning, dark and lonely with cloud cover obscuring the few hours of sunlight and relative warmth that we are sometimes allowed during these short days of deep winter. Often, and particularly recently, Denise had begun sessions with a similar intake and outflow of air, but the quality of her body resonance, the complex interaction of abdominal muscles, throat constriction, and facial display had usually constructed a moan of despair. When Ornette Coleman's alto saxophone would moan similarly in the midst of his freeform jazz solos of the 1960s, I would experience a visceral resonance in the back of my head, gut, and spine, a kind of internal downward spiral toward bottomlessness. Interestingly, I had never attended to Denise's moans with analytic curiosity until this morning. But now, I was impacted noticeably by this shift to a grunt. I was startled and moved in the way that I had been by Coleman's saxophone sounds. Denise was clearly different, and her gesture cut a definite opening, a shift in my attention to her body and my body and the meanings that were being constructed kinesthetically.

My body? Well, before I could even begin to recognize the difference between now and then, or maybe, as the register in which recognition was first taking shape this morning, I found my gut swept with an indescribable sense that I can call only a soft sadness, a movement in muscles and hormones toward tears. But I did not begin to cry. Rather, I too took in a deep gutful of air. I sensed how it seemed to regulate my sadness, slow down the muscular constrictions and increasing skin temperature that accompanies the onset of tears. When I had filled to capacity, I released the breath, but with a different resonance, one of a deep quiet sound that came from the chest area and was somewhere between a moan and a sigh. Here our sound shapes briefly created an area of affective space, a space made possible (at this point out of our awarenesses) for something new to begin to emerge. We had coconstructed a pause in time, but one that immediately seemed to plummet in space as a parachutist out of a plane.

Then, just as rapidly, our eyes met. We exchanged brief nervous smiles. But, the tension in the muscles of our faces, clearly suggested this was not fun. I could feel it in my response and see it in hers. Now the space was closing, as the time shifted. The rhythms of our "eye dialogue" here were quick and nervous, starting and stopping like the twists and turns that Bartok would command in his compositions, or Cecil Taylor would explode in his piano improvisations. These syncopations, combined with our earlier sound shapes, constructed feelings of uncertainty and hypervigilance.

Denise, often depleted and hopeless in these states of uncertainty and hypervigilance, would speak of her sense of failure and inability to feel as if she were measuring up to anything in her professional growth and personal life. She could find no satisfaction, no vitality in anything, not in her relations with her colleagues, not in her accomplishments, not in her intimate life. Nothing mattered. Yet she could see how others would tell her that she was performing effectively in her job or that sex was satisfying and she and her lover were getting along well and fighting with more fairness compared with earlier in their relationship. But no, nothing was good enough.

I noted that Denise seemed hopeless as before, but now rather than depleted, as we began to speak, her tone was strengthening and her rhythmic forward pressing flow, felt full with anger, a different affective texture for our context. Was hopelessness shifting to hope on some unformulated level of experience (Stern, 1997)? I couldn't tell at this point. I wondered about her satisfaction with me and the treatment, her inability to find anything good enough in what we were doing, in how responsive or not I had been or was being to her. I noted the parallel meanings to her life descriptions and our work, our relationship. She replied, slightly shifting to sadness but then regaining the forward movement of her anger, that yes, she was unhappy with what we were doing, or maybe not doing. Then, ambivalently she began to shift again. Yes, we had been making some progress. There were those sessions in which we seemed to get very close and deep, in which she felt maybe for a brief moment or two, I was getting her, that she was *feeling* gotten. We had explored these moments when they occurred earlier and found them to be shot through with erotic and destructive feelings constructing a kind of mutual devouring, mutually engorging emotional experience of each other. As part of this experience, Denise noted that our week of sessions seemed to have a rhythm marked by a dissociated, devitalizing start that then moved toward a last session of the week climax, fraught with complex somatic and semantic encounters, stimulating, if not overstimulating, but never enough, only to be drained of feeling and meaning into some dissociated space again by the beginning of the next week.

I had wondered with her in the past about how much she was experiencing me transferentially as some version or versions of her father, to whom she had been very close and whose death had only exponentially potentiated her eating disorder and self-mutilating, which took her through a series of hospitalizations. Maybe in the weekly rhythm, we were reenacting the loss of her father resonated by the death of my affective responsiveness to her, as recreated in the unfolding affective patterning, consisting of the unbearable sense of her inability to continue to vitalize him or me for which she either punished herself as previously recreated in her starving and bleeding or dissociated.

While her previous treatments had been a path back to relative satisfaction and relatedness as she pursued a somewhat successful athletic career and then higher education for the current professional activity in which she was clearly excelling and developing status and recognition, nothing had ever been enough. She could never hold onto, in fact, even *ever feel*, a sense of fulfillment, of having enough. It was never enough. Nothing could ever be enough. We both sat in the silence of the long pause of despair that this emptiness, this absence of presence had created between and within us. Again, we were constructing, though with significant pain, a space expanding time warp, an opening for some new melody or syncopation to come forth and begin to constitute a new meaning between us.

Suddenly it occurred to me that either I had never asked about or had dissociated the time in her development when her eating disorder and self-mutilation had begun. We had always focused on the difficulty she had accepting the death of her father and never attempted to wonder about the fact that her difficulties had begun much earlier in life, as I now began to remember. My question was tentative but clear. Denise responded to my query with a shift in body, rhythm, and tone. Her face and posture, relaxed. Her tone shifted from the punishing whine of adolescent anger to a lower register of sophisticated curiosity and collaboration. She began to recall how close she had been with Dad as a child. In fact, she had almost been his little boy. They had done so much athletically together. She would do things with him like biking, swimming, mountain climbing, and running. She became her father's number one companion in these activities with which they both filled themselves as much as possible.

But now she remembered. It was when she began to grow breasts and her body shifted from that hermaphroditic phase that can be achieved in prepuberty but rarely sustained with the onset of menses that she began to despair and self-destruct. I wondered whether her enacted symptoms were not a crying out into the world by the "boy" companion she had been to her father and longed to be forever, of that young "boy's" sense of annihilation. That self-version of Denise was disappearing and would be extinguished by her awful body that refused to obey her desire. The only thing to do was to punish her body, so she did.

Her eyes widened, and her voice shifted to a rhythmic vitality that I could recognize from the past but never really see and hear as I was hearing now, the voice of that young boy, that subjective experience of being father's special companion that had been sequestered to the ghost realms by the curse of genetic physiology and against which Denise had battled with alcohol, drugs, food, and blade to no avail. Now *we* could be two close collaborating companions.

Denise spoke more of her relationship with her father, of how wonderful those days were, and of how her father withdrew from her after puberty. It was as if their *relationship* had died. My body was suddenly filled with a different set of sensations than I was used to in responding to Denise. Previously, such emotional closeness had catalyzed powerful feelings of erotic desire or strange dystonic feelings of aggressiveness or fear. We had spoken about an early childhood experience she had had with boys in which they would play a game of holding someone's head underwater until that person was almost close to drowning and then at the last minute letting him up for air. I think I had sometimes felt as if she were pushing my head underwater forcing me into confusion and self-doubt as to whether or how I could ever be good enough for her as an analyst. As we talked about this, she noted that she had similar feelings as a patient, as you would expect in line with the self-doubt and denigrating feelings with which she was constantly haunted. We had observed how much analysis could feel at times to both of us as if we are masochistically holding our heads underwater too long. Now, as I write this narrative, I can see how we constructed a sadomasochistic pattern when we found ourselves repeatedly enacting in our interaction, the dynamics of her internal struggle with her sequestered "boy" self whom she unconsciously rarely allowed up for air but whose presence kept popping up in the rhythms and tones between us until now, when I finally could recognize and name him and begin to sense what it might have felt like to be him.

This shift into vital lively rhythm and tone was suddenly perturbated again. Was Denise about to hold my head under? Her verbal stream had decelerated. The boyish enthusiasm had left her face and voice. But now there was something touchingly little girlish and sad in her expression, and her voice came from the throat constrictions that construct higher frequencies, the tonal realm of childhood discourse, again a different version of self. She looked directly into my eyes, her eyes wide with wonder and questioning. She noted that when she thinks of her father in her reveries, it is not the lively companion of her "boyhood." But rather she sees the dying father gasping for his last breath on his hospital bed. As she spoke, my body filled with feelings that were not erotic, aggressive, or fearful. Rather I found myself now unable to use breath to regulate my sadness. A deep and initially indecipherable grief flowed up from within. Then I experienced a brief internal memory fragment of my father lying in his death as I viewed him before his funeral. My eyes began to fill with tears. Sensing this palpable shift in me, Denise queried, "What's the matter?" There was a tender tone of motherly comfort in the delivery and flow of her utterance suggesting still another self-state. I wondered if her inability to hold onto feelings of satisfaction with and relatedness to her achievements, colleagues, partner, and me were not colored by the unconscious and until this moment, dissociated internal tie with her dead father. Stunned, she dropped her gaze to the floor and attempted to self-regulate. She looked up to say that she never had considered this but that it felt true. This time her voice shifted from a soft maternality to a deeper, firmer strength, should I risk saying paternality. But, no, this was a different sense of authority or agency than Lacan would attribute to the paternal. Rather, this voice seemed to combine the resonance of a child's wonder, a mother's capacity to hold and absorb, and a father's capacity for delineation. In fact, these generational and gender stereotypic distinctions fail to discretely capture what more accurately seemed to wash and blur in the unparsed continuous sense of her hermaphroditic voice and body as I sat in my chair still trying to regulate my own flow of teary awe at the depth of connection and companionship that was momentarily filling our space together. Maybe for a moment we were both vulnerable little boys. Or maybe we were just both vulnerable in a heightened momentary flowing sense of self and other and loss, unfettered by discrete categorical distinctions of gender or age.

I close this description still wondering about how this unfolding patterning of tone and rhythm on kinesthetic and affective edges of shifting self-states affected my own countertransferentially dissociated potential for multiplicity, of how much I was experiencing my mournful little boy crying with the little boy/girl whose loving father had also died and who couldn't be a little boy anymore, at the same time that I was holding a soft, safe place in time and space, at the same time that I was recognizing, reflecting, and delineating in words the significance of the internal presences of an annihilated little boy/girl and dead father, which had become black holes of emptiness in Denise's self experience. In subsequent sessions Denise has begun to talk more about how "masculine" she feels and how confusing it is as she feels good about herself in this way but also feels that others become threatened or upset if she does not hide this aspect of herself.

Discussion

In my opening comments I emphasized that relational treatment shifts, and I now would add expands, the scope of analytic attention rather than replacing it. Let's look at the different attentional foci that I employed in my narrative of the clinical sequence with Denise and how these interacted in the process of forming meaning. I will briefly review 31 points of foci for attention occurring on both symbolic and nonsymbolic registers, 3 of which marked nodal points where the registers intermingled to construct meaning. Note here that I am using the term nodal point to designate a moment in which attention to non-symbolic communication facilitates a symbolic representation of affective experience.

But first, an important cautionary note. This highly discrete, symbolic analysis constructed *post hoc* should not be taken as a model or prescription for analytic attention. Rather, it is a writing practice, an exercise in reflection that can allow us to consider previous processes that occurred often without reflection or verbal articulation. While many of the events I have selected for attention were conscious and intentional on the part of the analyst or analysand, the important point to be illustrated is the way spontaneously improvised, unconsciously enacted phenomena, at times, can be recognized and responded to for their mutative potential as they interweave with reflected upon activity in psychoanalytic interactions.

Point 1 occurs as Denise growls, a nonsymbolic registration. Point 2 occurs as I experience a soft sadness in my gut, a nonsymbolic registration. Point 3 occurs as I release breath between a moan and a sigh, a nonsymbolic registration. Point 4 occurs with the exchange of our eyes and nervous smiles, a nonsymbolic registration. Point 5 occurs as I reflect on Denise's pattern of negating her thoughts and actions, "nothing was good enough," a symbolic registration. Point 6 occurs as Denise's tone and rhythm strengthen, a nonsymbolic registration. Point 7 occurs when I articulate the parallel between her hopelessness in herself and in me, a symbolic registration in response to her nonsymbolic registration. This is the first of 3 nodal points.

Point 8 occurs as Denise reflects on her anger and our work, a symbolic registration. Point 9 occurs as we sit in the silence of despair over Denise's never feeling fulfilled, a nonsymbolic registration. Point 10 occurs when I reflect in reverie that I had never inquired about the time her eating disorder began, a symbolic registration. Point 11 occurs when I give this question verbal articulation for Denise, a symbolic registration. Point 12 occurs as Denise's tone shifts from an adolescent whine to a lower register, a nonsymbolic registration. Point 13 occurs as Denise recalls her closeness with her father, a symbolic registration. Point 14 occurs when Denise's voice shifts to the rhythmic vitality of a young boy, a nonsymbolic registration. Point 15 occurs when I reflect in reverie that *we* could be two close companions, a symbolic registration. Point 16 occurs when Denise reflects how the relationship with her father "died" at the onset of her puberty, a symbolic registration. Point 17 occurs when I feel my body respond with vitality to Denise's reflection, a nonsymbolic registration. Point 18 occurs as we revisit in words her early childhood experience of holding another's head under water, a symbolic registration. Point 19 occurs as we articulate in words the similarity between the feeling of her early childhood experience and what we do to each other in treatment, a symbolic registration. Point 20 occurs as I reflect in *post hoc* reverie on the possible transferential and countertransferential meanings of her childhood experience as the sadomasochistic dynamics of that experience are reenacted in treatment, a symbolic registration. This is the second nodal point marking the culmination of transducing the nonsymbolic registrations of Denise's impact on me and my impact on her into transferential and countertransferential symbolization.

Point 21 occurs as Denise's verbal stream decelerates and her tone shifts to childlike high frequencies, a nonsymbolic registration. Point 22 occurs as Denise articulates with words the shift in her reverie from her "boyhood companion" father to her dying father, a symbolic registration. Point 23 occurs as I find myself unable to regulate my feeling of sadness with breath, a nonsymbolic registration. Point 24 occurs as I experience a memory of viewing my father just prior to his funeral, a symbolic registration. Point 25 occurs as my eyes fill with tears, a nonsymbolic registration. Point 26 occurs as Denise inquires about my state, a symbolic registration. Point 27 occurs simultaneous to 26 in which I sense the maternal tone of Denise's utterance, a nonsymbolic registration. Point 28 occurs as I suggest that Denise's feelings of not being good enough are related to an unconscious and, until this moment, dissociated tie with her dead father, a symbolic registration. Point 29 occurs as Denise stunned, drops her gaze to the floor, clearly attempting to self-regulate, a nonsymbolic registration. Point 30 occurs as Denise confirms my interpretation, a symbolic registration. Point 31 occurs simultaneous to 30 in which I sense the tone of Denise's voice to combine a kind of hermaphroditic synthesis in voice and body, a nonsymbolic registration. This is the third nodal point marking a culmination intermingling symbolic and nonsymbolic registrations, a recognition of this polyrhythmic weave, a process forming into a structured point of interpretation and a shift in Denise's capacity to symbolize her internal experience and to regulate and express her grief.

With this analysis, I have tracked 16 points of nonsymbolic registration and 15 points of symbolic registration. It would be interesting to analyze the clinical narratives of those reporting on the impact of symbolic associations or those who include descriptions of enactments. I would guess that the first group would reveal a scarcity of attention to nonsymbolic registrations, overlooking the significant, in-process micro-moment *forming-into* of meaning occurring with those registrations. I would guess that the second group would be impacted by nonsymbolic registrations but rarely reporting the bidirectional influence of these registrations and their pivotal impact on mutative moments in treatment. I would guess this because enactments are only infrequently attended to with descriptions of *micro-moment detail* where in-process construction of meaning is being carried along affectively significant registers of voice and body movement.

At points in an analysis where the patient brings an analyst to the edge of what might be comprehended or communicated with words, indications of meaning are often being communicated on embodied registers of experience. At such points, the analyst is often affectively flooded or anesthetized, confused, if not uncertain and/or caught in a frozen moment of fright. Attempts to regain psychic equilibrium for the analyst's self regulation/organization can be facilitated by the kind of expanded focus to include nonsymbolic embodied registrations of experience/communication. But at this point in the discussion I want to use the *post hoc* perspective made possible in this writing exercise to think about how an analyst's attention comes to include any particular dimension of the clinical exchange, symbolic or otherwise. I do this with a consideration of the theory or metaphor of mind implicit to the analyst's scope of attention. How an analyst conceptualizes mind is central to how an analyst represents her own or her analysand's subjective experience. The capacity of an analyst to represent in narrative, the impact of particular dimensions of subjective experience (both *structural* and *process dimensions*), can contribute significantly to the delineation of the scope and boundary of what is cognitively recognizable or affectively bearable at any moment in a particular analysis for both analyst and analysand. What is not represented or unbearable is often dissociated. With this in mind, I have offered three ways with which mind can be conceptualized, each of which has been associated with particular clinical approaches. We can see the potential of each of these conceptualizations for creating particular openings in the clinical activity in my encounter with Denise.

First, let's consider a conceptualization of mind I have called the hydraulic model of mind (Knoblauch, 2000, p. 91), a kind of algebraic metaphor in which a finite amount of libidinal energy is distributed within a closed system of three structures. Too much energy in any place in this closed system can be experienced as unbearable, causing structural fragmentation as in the kind of ego splitting earlier described by Freud and further elaborated by Fairbairn and Kohut.

This conceptualization of internal splitting effectively captures the way that neither Denise nor I would be able to hold onto the intensity of the erotic sadomasochistic exchanges that would characterize the final sessions of our weekly meetings, when we would begin the following Monday. Rather, Denise described the initial moments of our encounter in the first weekly session as devitalized and dead. This conceptualization then helps to organize how dissociation can disorganize/reorganize both reflective and affective registrations of experience. Our encounter was once again given breath and rhythm with the emergence of a focus of attention on our embodied experiences that shaped the present moments unfolding in the new week. For both of us, in the opening moments of each set of weekly sessions, feelings of aliveness and connectedness to our own embodied experience as well as to the other's, were unavailable, and conceptualized as fragments split off from awareness.

A second conceptualization recognizes organizations of identifications and counteridentifications, complementary and concordant (Racker, 1968), volleying back and forth between patient and analyst, which can precipitate transference–countertransference enactments. This metaphor constitutes an elaboration of the hydraulic mind. With such a representation, the scope of analytic attention is expanded to recognize the interaction between two subjectivities to be the field within which mind is being constituted. (This is a view developed by the various intersubjectivity theorists writing over the past 2 decades; see our work acknowledging these contributions, Beebe et al., 2005, pp. 2–3.) This view is further augmented with the recognition that subjectivities are always constituted within cultural contexts, often multiple and complex in their impact such that the subjective experience of having a mind is always constructed within and constricted by a network of shared beliefs and practices. This contextual cultural matrix makes certain kinds of experiences visible and certain kinds of experiences invisible on the basis of a hierarchy of power gradients of value. Mind differentiates into an increasingly complex kaleidoscope (Davies, 1998) of possible patterning. I have called this the plastic model of mind, a kind of geometric metaphor in which an increasing number of systemic arrangements of representations with affective valence are emerging out of the experience of interaction with others (Knoblauch, 2000, p. 92).

This conceptualization of kaleidoscopic patterning shaped within a field of intersubjective experience captures the way that Denise and I eventually came to recognize how we constituted a particular enactment of the traumatizing loss of mutual recognition and desire as experienced with her father, in the patterning across our weekly rhythms of interaction. Once we were able to recognize this patterning we could begin to reflect further about past and present patterns as meanings were emerging and reemerging in the rhythms of our interaction.

It is just this subtle and difficult-to-represent fluidity of interaction on which meaning is in formation that constitutes a third way to conceptualize mind. This is not a model of a space or place but rather a model of movement and interactivity. We can speak of minding or giving attention to the polyrhythmic weave on embodied (acoustic and kinesthetic) dimensions of the interaction from which faintly sensed meanings are not yet emergent, but possibly beginning to gain a degree of representation, not yet fully symbolized. Minding is a lively interactive process not a structure. I have called this process a resonant model of minding, a kind of calculus metaphor, a sense of movement in attention that shapes the conceptualizing process, a movement that happens in the gaps between, and accounts for the breakdown and coalescence of the experience of discrete symbolic representations as structure (2000, p. 95).

This conceptualization of a process of minding can provide analyst and analysand with a compass for navigating the uncertain and sometimes frightening interacting currents constituting the fluidity of meaning that is still in formation and not yet structured. It is an experience of resonance, an embodied dimension of the interaction within which faintly sensed indications of meaning come as form, intensity, and timing (see Trevarthen, 1993, p. 126; Jaffe, Beebe, Feldstein, Crown, & Jasnow, 2001). Attention to these dimensions, what Bucci (1997) calls the subsymbolic and I am here calling the nonsymbolic, were the indications from which Denise and I were able to create articulation for particular self-states of varying affective bearability and give eventual symbolic meaning to our experience. For example, the emergence of the adolescent self, the childlike self, the maternal-like self and the paternal-like self, each were heralded by a shifting patterning in voice tone and rhythm, facial expression, eye focus, or body movement. Attention to these registrations opened up the opportunity for recognition and reflection, thus enriching the meaning-making exchanges occurring on a symbolic register for both of us. Note that such recognition of registration was sometimes bidirectional and sometimes self-reflective, as both Denise and I attended to different registrations in ourselves and each other.

The polyrhythmic weave of movement back and forth between symbolic and nonsymbolic registers (as well as within and across embodied modalities) allowed for the construction of more finely tuned and complexly intertwined meanings for different discrete states experienced subjectively by analyst and analysand, initially emerging, or coming into, a recognizable and representable form out of the flow of affective currents generated intersubjectively. This made possible nodal point 1 in which I was able to interpret the resonance between Denise's pattern of recurring hopelessness throughout her life experience and now within our relational patterning, nodal point 2 in which I was able to articulate our previously enacted transferential–countertransferential sadomasochistic patterning, which was the way that hopelessness was sustained in our relating for further attention and generation of meaning, and nodal point 3 in which I, and then Denise, was able to both symbolize and affectively experience the splitting off of a loving tie between father and child to protect against the pain of grief which

Denise was then able to begin to feel and express, and finally how much the meaning of that loss had to do with Denise's gender spectrum of self-experience, which, as reflected in the rhythms and meanings of the session's weave, were constricted by conflict and ambivalence over expressing certain forms of strength.

Nodal point 3 demonstrates a critical benefit that a resonant minding scope of attention can afford. Working with this particular conceptual lens can help the analyst to expect the kind of uncertainty, multiplicity, and vulnerability that can trigger self-protective moves by the analyst, experiences of victimization leading to retreat or retaliation, or, in the most unbearable moments, dissociation. Attention to embodied experience of one's own or of another, provides the analyst, not with a theoretical life preserver but rather with an expanded navigational strategy for negotiating the complexity and blind spots of the psychoanalytic interaction. Such a strategy involves attention to often subtly registered signals, enacted communications in the analytic exchange, which can help the analyst in her struggle to regain equilibrium and focus in the face of disequilibrating experience and loss of cognitive organizational capacity. Feelings in one's gut, muscular constricting or collapse, facial configurations, melodic or syncopated dimensions of speech flow or hand or foot movement (i.e., pauses), punctuations or cross modal "phrasing," in concert with other embodied cues construct intuitive bridges across the gaps within and between subjectivities. For the analyst, these intuitive bridges become important registrations of experience in the face of vulnerability, struggle and bearing the affective weight of not knowing. In my moment-to-moment struggle to bear the hopelessness that Denise frequently brought me in touch with, both concerning her experience of her life and our experiences of the analysis, attention to registrations in Denise's body from her groans and growl, to her eye movement, to her vocal tonal/rhythmic shifts, and also to registrations in my body including muscular constrictions, the rhythms of my visual and vocal activity in interaction with Denise, as well as my tearing up, helped me to navigate and work with Denise to create more nuanced meanings out of the powerful symbolic and nonsymbolic weave that we constituted.

These points of consideration contribute to an emphasis on the significance of expanded forms of analytic attention as a way to elaborate our narrations of what is happening in the "gaps" that emerge in our work. While these gaps can ultimately never be closed, the approach I am illustrating emphasizes attention to subtle embodied micro-exchanges occurring in any analytic interaction as a way to expand our participation and reflection. This expansion in analytic attention can make possible a broader and richer range of meaning and affect available for both analyst and patient to construct and inhabit.

References

Anderson, F. (Ed.) (2008). *Bodies in treatment: The unspoken dimension.* New York: The Analytic Press.

Aron L. (1996). *A meeting of minds: Mutuality in psychoanalysis.* Hillsdale, NJ: The Analytic Press.

Aron, L., & Anderson, F. (1998). *Relational perspectives on the body.* Hillsdale, NJ: The Analytic Press.

Bass, A. (2003). "E" enactments in psychoanalysis: Another medium, another message. *Psychoanalytic Dialogues, 13,* 657–675.

Bass, A. (2007). When the frame doesn't fit the picture. *Psychoanalytic Dialogues, 17,* 1–27.

Beebe, B., & Stern, D. N. (1977). Engagement–disengagement and early object experiences. In N. Freedman & S. Grand (Eds.), *Communicative structures and psychic structures: A psychoanalytic interpretation of communication.* New York: Plenum Press.

Beebe, B., Knoblauch, S., Rustin, J., & Sorter, D. (2005). *Forms on intersubjectivity in infant research and adult treatment.* New York: Other Press.

Black, M. J. (2003). Enactment: Analytic musings on energy, language, and personal growth. *Psychoanalytic Dialogues, 13,* 633–655.

Boston Change Process Study Group (2008). Forms of relational meaning: Issues in the relations between the implicit and reflective-verbal domains. *Psychoanalytic Dialogues, 18,* 125–148.

Bromberg, P. M. (1998). *Standing in the spaces: Essays on clinical process, trauma and dissociation.* Hillsdale, NJ: The Analytic Press.

Bucci, W. (1997). *Psychoanalysis and cognitive science: A multiple code theory.* New York: Guilford.

Cohn, J., & Tronick, E. (1988). Discrete versus scaling approaches to the description of mother–infant face-to-face interaction: Convergent validity and divergent applications. *Developmental Psychology, 24*(3), 396–397.

Cooper, S. H. (2003). You say oedipal, I say postoedipal: A consideration of desire and hostility in the analytic relationship. *Psychoanalytic Dialogues, 13*(1), 41–61.

Cooper, S. H. (2007). Begin the beguine: Relational theory and the pluralistic third. *Psychoanalytic Dialogues, 17,* 247–271.

Davies, J. M. (1998). Between the disclosure and foreclosure of erotic transference–countertransference: Can psychoanalysis find a place for adult sexuality? *Psychoanalytic Dialogues, 8,* 747–766.

Davies, J. M. (2003). Falling in love with love: Oedipal and postoedipal manifestations of idealization, mourning and erotic masochism. *Psychoanalytic Dialogues, 13,* 1–27.

Davies, J. M. (2005). Transformations of desire and despair: Reflections on the termination process from a relational perspective. *Psychoanalytic Dialogues, 15,* 779–805.

Davies, J. M., & Frawley, M. G. (1994). *Treating the adult survivor of childhood sexual abuse.* New York: Basic Books.

Dimen, M. (2003). *Sexuality, intimacy, power.* Hillsdale, NJ: The Analytic Press.

Ehrenberg, D. B. (1992). *The intimate edge.* New York: W. W. Norton & Co.

Fivaz-Depeursinge, E., & Corboz-Warnery, A. (1999). *The primary triangle.* New York: Basic Books.

Fogel, A. (1992). Movement and communication in human infancy: The social dynamics of development. *Human Movement Science, 11,* 387–423.

Fogel, A. (1993). Two principles of communication: Co-regulation and framing. In J. Nadel & L. Camaioni (Eds.), *New perspectives in early communicative development*. London: Routledge.

Gentile, K. (2007). *Creating bodies: Eating disorders as self-destructive survival*. Mahwah, NJ: The Analytic Press.

Harris, A. (1998). Psychic envelopes and sonorous baths: Siting the body in relational theory and clinical practice. In L. Aron & F. S. Anderson (Eds.), *Relational perspectives on the body* (pp. 39–64). Hillsdale, NJ: The Analytic Press.

Harris, A. (2005). *Gender as soft assembly*, Hillsdale, NJ: The Analytic Press.

Harrison, A. M. (2003). Change in psychoanalysis: Getting from A to B. *Journal of the American Psychological Association, 51*(1), pp. 221–256.

Hoffman, I. Z. (1983). The patient as interpreter of the analyst's experience. *Contemporary Psychoanalysis, 19*, 389–422.

Hoffman, I. Z. (1998). *Ritual and spontaneity in the psychoanalytic process: A dialectical-constructivist view*. Hillsdale, NJ: The Analytic Press.

Hoffman, I. Z. (2006). The myths of free association and the potentials of the analytic relationship. International Journal of Psychoanalysis, 87, 43–61.

Jacobs, T. J. (1986). On countertransference enactments. *Journal of the American Psychoanalytic Association, 34*, 289–307.

Jacobs, T. J. (1991). *The use of the self*. Madison, CT: International Universities Press.

Jaffe, J., Beebe, B., Feldstein, S., Crown, C., & Jasnow, M. (2001). *Rhythms of dialogue in infancy*. Monographs of the Society for Research in Child Development, No. 265, Vol. 66, No. 2.

Knoblauch S. H. (2000). *The musical edge of therapeutic dialogue*. Hillsdale, NJ: The Analytic Press.

La Barre, F. (2001). *On moving and being moved*. Hillsdale, NJ: The Analytic Press.

La Barre, F. (2005). The kinetic transference and countertransference. Contemporary Psychoanalysis, 41, 249–279.

Lacan, J. (1977). *Ecrits: A selection*. London: Norton.

Lichtenberg, J. D., Lachmann, F. M., & Fosshage, J. L. (2002). *A spirit of inquiry: Communication in psychoanalysis*. Hillsdale, NJ: The Analytic Press.

Mitchell, S. (1997). *Influence and autonomy in psychoanalysis*. Hillsdale, NJ: The Analytic Press.

Ogden, T. (1989). *The primitive edge of experience*. Northvale, NJ: Jason Aronson.

Ogden, T. (1994). *Subjects of analysis*. Northvale, NJ: Jason Aronson.

Orbach, S. (2000). *The impossibility of sex*. New York: Touchstone.

Orbach, S. (2003). The John Bowlby Memorial Lecture Part I: There is no such thing as a body. British Journal of Psychotherapy, 20, 3–26.

Orbach, S. (2004). What can we learn from the therapist's body? Attachment and Human Development, 6(2), 141–150.

Orbach, S. (2006). How can we have a body: Desire and corporeality. Studies in Gender and Sexuality, 7(1), 89–110.

Racker, H. (1968). *Transference and countertransference*. Madison, CT: International Universities Press.

Reis, B. (2009). Performative and enactive features of psychoanalytic witnessing: The transference as the scene of address. International Journal of Psychoanalysis, 90, 1359–1372.

Ringstrom, P. A. (2001). Cultivating the improvisational in psychoanalytic treatment. *Psychoanalytic Dialogues, 11*(5), 727–754.

Sletvold, J. (in press). Training analysts to work with unconscious embodied expressions: Theoretical underpinnings and practical guidelines. *Psychoanalytic Dialogues.*

Sonntag, M. E. (2006). "I have a lower class body." Psychoanalytic Dialogues, 16, 317–332.

Spezzano, C. (1993). *Affect in psychoanalysis: A clinical synthesis.* Hillsdale, NJ: The Analytic Press.

Stein, R. (1999). *Psychoanalytic theories of affect.* London: Karnac.

Stern, D. B. (1997). *Unformulated experience: From dissociation to imagination in psychoanalysis.* Hillsdale, NJ: The Analytic Press.

Stern, D. N. (1985). *The interpersonal world of the infant: A view from psychoanalysis and developmental psychology.* New York: Basic Books.

Trevarthen, C. (1993). The self born in intersubjectivity: The psychology of an infant communicating. In U. Neisser (Ed.), *The perceived self: Ecological and interpersonal sources of self-knowledge* (pp. 121–173). New York: Cambridge University Press.

Weinberg, M., & Tronick, E. (1994). Beyond the face: An empirical study of infant affective configurations of facial, vocal, gestural and regulatory behaviors. *Child Development, 65*, 1495–1507.

9

Analytic Impasse and the Third

*Clinical Implications of Intersubjectivity Theory**

Lewis Aron

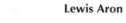

A bright, talented, and experienced supervisee, whose office is in down-town Manhattan, presented a dilemma to me in consultation soon after 9/11. She was treating a man who, following the calamity, confided in her that he actually was not very upset about the event. As a matter of fact, he said, he found the whole thing exciting and energizing. During the morning of September 11, he stood upon his Manhattan rooftop, like many New Yorkers, with binoculars and camera in hand, and in the aftermath of the attack he was glued to CNN enjoying the prospect of war. My supervisee told me that she was privately horrified by his callousness. She had long known of his narcissistic tendencies but was not sure how to approach this material. She, like so many of our colleagues in the psychoanalytic community, had been volunteering her time and was actively engaged in disaster-relief efforts. It disturbed my supervisee to think that such raw aggression and pitilessness could so dominate her patient's mind. She told me that in the midst of the session she became determined to make every effort to sustain "an empathic stance." She found this quite difficult and uncomfortable and doubted that she could maintain an empathic attitude in any way that felt genuine.

As a supervisor, I had the distinct advantage that I was not caught up in the immediacy of the transference–countertransference enactment. I was able to help my supervisee to see that there were many ways of

* This paper originally appeared in *International Journal of Psychoanalysis*, 87(2), 2006, pp. 349–368. Reprinted with permission.

understanding her patient's reactions on the basis of what we already knew about him. For one, her patient had a chaotic inner life, filled with images of violence, unconscious fantasies of bodily damage, and themes of sadomasochism. It seemed to me quite understandable that her patient felt relief in the midst of the city's catastrophe, simply because, at least momentarily, the violence and chaos, the destructiveness and the destruction, were externalized, concretely taking place, for once, not in his own mind but externally in the world of others.

I pointed out that, with the patient so directly barraging her with his aggression, it would be hard to know what it might mean to him if she responded with exaggerated or feigned empathy. Together we explored to what degree my supervisee had become fixed in her identification with the victims and the rescuers, thus locking her patient into his reciprocal identifications with the powerful and frightening terrorists. But, from the reverse perspective, how much was the patient's being locked into one set of identifications pushing the therapist into identifying with the complementary roles? As Davies (2003) wrote:

> Such cases of apparently inescapable therapeutic impasse always pose for me the dilemma that patient and analyst become prisoners of the coercive projective power of each other's vision; each becomes hopelessly defined by the other and incapable of escaping the force of the interactive pull to act in creative and fully agentic ways. (pp. 15–16)

As we will see shortly, what Davies here refers to as the coercive projective power of each other's vision, and of being defined by the position of the other, is closely related to what Benjamin (1999) called "complementarity" (p. 203).

This initial supervisory discussion, though tentative and incomplete, allowed my supervisee to begin to genuinely empathize with her patient. The therapist had tried to sustain "an empathic stance" as a technique because she could not at the moment come to any meaningful sympathetic understanding of her patient due to a temporary blockage in her free-floating responsiveness to experience shared identifications. She might have confronted his indifference and aggressiveness in an attempt to resist his assault and prevent his hijacking of the analysis. But, while an expression of her shock and disgust might have been spontaneous, it not only would have been unempathic but also would have obscured a great deal of my supervisee's authentic, although not immediately available, loving feelings for her patient.

As a supervisor, I often feel that my job is to give a nudge to the analyst's relational compass, freeing the analyst to take up more varied identifications and relational positions, which in turn, since the analytic dyad is a complex system, may encourage the patient to assume new roles. As Davies and Frawley (1994) illustrated in their groundbreaking work with adult victims of childhood sexual abuse, it is essential that the analyst remain open to take up all of the patient's multiple unconscious identifications: with victims and terrorists, rescuers and witnesses. My supervisee was caught between two perceptions, two contradictory organizations of her experience. She could be outraged at her patient's indifference and heartlessness, but then she felt unempathic and unresponsive to his therapeutic needs. She might get herself to identify with the patient's sadistic pleasures in the violence and destruction exploding around them, but this felt like a betrayal of herself and of her own experience and values. In her compensatory and exaggerated efforts to be empathic she felt obliterated, while in her phantasized expression of authenticity she risked annihilating her patient. The ostensibly contradictory options amounted to the same thing: dominate or be dominated, terrorize or be terrorized, kill or be killed; in each instance, someone is obliterated. Attempting to alternate between these two positions inevitably left her off balance and confused. She was trapped in this "complementarity" where either, empathy or authenticity, was the simple inverse of the other. The feeling that we must either submit or resist is the hallmark of the doer–done to relationship (Benjamin, 2005). Here, the supervisor, as so often happens in psychoanalytic supervision, acts as a third to the analytic dyad. My interventions opened up a third perspective, until then unavailable to the dyad. My nudging the compass needle, which had become stuck between opposing binary poles, freed it up to swing to alternative positions, creating space with potential for multiple positions where previously there had been only a simple line between two fixed points.

Once in touch with the patient's chronic fear and internal battle, with the relief provided by the external concretization of his anguish, the supervisee no longer had to choose between victim and victimizer, between a sadistic and masochistic response, between doing or being done to, between empathy and authenticity. A third option reconfigured her experiential organization. Until then, patient and analyst had been caught in an extreme moment of negation where the acceptance of one person's subjectivity meant an obliteration of the other's. In Benjamin's (1999) words, they had become "thrown onto the axis of reversible complementarity, the seesaw in which our stances mirror each other" (p. 203). There must be a move beyond this power struggle to a level of metacommunication that allows the dyad to return from complementarity to mutuality and recognition. What Benjamin and I (Aron & Benjamin, 1999) attempted to theorize was a point of thirdness that allows the analyst to restore a process of identification with the patient's position without losing her own perspective, to move beyond submission and negation, thus reopening intersubjective space.

I also found the psychoanalytic understanding of the conflicts of identification posed by the primal scene to be helpful to me in understanding the reactions of this patient and analyst. This is not in any way to reduce the horrors of 9/11 to infantile phantasy but rather to gain an understanding of the conflicting reactions that require management when bearing witness to trauma. It is as if the patient had gone from containing a chaotic, violent primal scene being fought out within his own mind to becoming a witness to such a primal scene but now as an observer struggling to maintain an identification with only one party to the scene. His therapist, in turn, had become caught up in observing the same external scene and may similarly have struggled to contain her own terror by identifying rigidly with the other actor in the scene. One aspect of experiencing unconscious resonances of the primal scene is the intense conflict concerning with whom to identify, and we often manage such conflict by rigidly identifying with one actor and disidentifying with the other. This is perhaps the central conflict with which people struggle in witnessing the primal scene.

I have previously (Aron, 1995) elaborated on Britton's (1989) suggestion that the child's management of the primal scene facilitates the creation of a "triangular space," which allows for the possibility of being a participant in a relationship and observed by a third person and of being an observer of a relationship between two other people. To clarify this, simply think of the child at one moment looking on at the two parents acting in relation to each other, leaving the child as the excluded third, and then imagine the next moment when the child is interacting with one parent while the other parent is left out or looking on. The child oscillates between moments of observation in which he or she is left out of some dyadic activity, and other moments of active participation as part of a dyad, where someone else is excluded.* Here is the way Britton (1989) described it:

> The closure of the oedipal triangle by the recognition of the link joining the parents provides a limiting boundary for the internal world. It creates what I call a "triangular space"—i.e., a space bounded by the three persons of the oedipal situation and all their potential relationships. It includes, therefore, the possibility of being a participant in a relationship and observed by a third person as well as being an observer of a relationship between two people. (p. 86)

---

* Indeed, this description of the vicissitudes of the primal scene closely corresponds to the research paradigm used by the Lausanne Group in their study of triadic intersubjectivity (Fivaz-Depeursinge, Favez, & Frascarolo, 2004); I will have more to say about this project as the paper proceeds.

The Oedipus complex entails not just the child's viewing the parental relationship from the perspective of an excluded outsider; it entails the myriad phantasies of the child in which the entire system of family relations is experimented with and internalized. The little boy or girl is at one moment the small, excluded child barred from the gratifications of adult sexuality; at another moment the same child is the phantasied rival of the father for mother's love and at the next is seeking a separate, private, and exclusive relationship with the father. The child alternates between seeing himself or herself as an outside observer of a two-person relationship consisting of the mother and father and then as inside a two-person relation while being observed by a third, the excluded parent. Thus, it is in the oedipal stage that the child first alternates between observation and participation within what is now conceived by the child as a triangle. This fact is clinically important because this oscillating function is the basis from which a person can participate in an analysis as it is through this route that we learn to alternate among a variety of perspectives or vertexes. Benjamin and I (Aron & Benjamin, 1999) argued that important varieties of triangulation take place pre-oedipally as well and that thirdness already exists within the mother–infant dyadic unit (a point I will return to soon). Nevertheless, I believe, along with Britton, that significant transformations take place at the oedipal level that contribute to our capacities for reflexive self-awareness and lead to qualitative advances in intersubjectivity. While there is a pre-oedipal history of oscillation and participation, it occurs and is experienced as a series of dyads rather than being integrated into a triangular system.

The work of the Lausanne Group requires a reconceptualization of some of these assumptions. Fivaz-Depeursinge et al. (2004) investigated threesome intersubjectivity in infancy. They differentiate "triadic" interactions between two people about a nonhuman object and "triangular" interactions between three people. But the third as elaborated by the Lausanne Group is neither necessarily another person nor an object but rather a third focus within a dyad. Fivaz-Depeursinge and her colleagues found that the triangular capacity is already evident at 3 and 4 months of age. At this early age, triangular relations are immediate and context dependent. By 9 months they exhibit the beginnings of an intentchild–patiential stance, and with the advent of symbolic thought and the moral emotions they gain self-reflexivity. It may turn out that primary triangular processes exist from very early on in life and that what is most characteristic of the oedipal stage is not triangularity per se but rather symbolic thought, narrative structure, and reflexive self-awareness (for a similar examination of the implications of this research, see Stern, 2004, pp. 98–99).

To recapitulate, dyads, couples, and systems tend to get stuck in complementary relations. This complementarity is characterized by a variety of splitting in which one side takes a position complementary to—the polar opposite of—the other side. If one is experienced as the doer, then the other becomes the done to (Benjamin, 2004a); if one is the sadist, then the other becomes the masochist; if one is the victim, then the other becomes the victimizer; if one is male, then the other becomes female; if one is active, then the other becomes passive. Polarities are split between the two members, and the more each one locks into a singular position, the more rigidly the other is locked into the opposing, complementary position, thus heightening the splitting and tightening the polarization. At any time, the split may be reversed without significantly changing the structure of the complementarity. The active member may suddenly become passive while the passive member becomes active; thus, their surface roles are switched, but the dyadic structure remains split between activity and passivity. Benjamin (1988) analyzed this manifest exchange of roles without a change in the underlying relational structure, demonstrating that it constitutes a simple reversal that maintains the old opposition (p. 223). Her initial work in this area developed in the context of her study of gender relations and especially in analyzing relations of dominance and submission and the structure of sadomasochism. In later work, she expanded and further developed these understandings, applying them to a variety of clinical and social contexts.

In the clinical example that we are discussing, the analyst experienced the patient as aggressively identified with the terrorists, now terrorizing her and hijacking the analysis. She did not want to submit to this terrorization but felt done to, locked into a victimized position rationalized by her sense that she was "supposed to" empathize with and understand her patient. She was locked into a structure she could not escape so was then tempted to attack her patient in return. She could confront him or intervene in a manner that would challenge his sadism, but in the very act of doing this she might become the active, sadistic terrorist pushing him into the role of the passive, masochistic victim, hence achieving only a simple reversal.

Let us examine the structure of complementarity and the related conceptualization of thirdness. Drawing on Britton (1989) and Benjamin (2004a), I would like to use very simple mathematical ideas (like the third) to explain the structure of this complementarity. I do not use these terms to appear scientifically precise or to quantify these conceptual ideas: rather, these simple geometric terms are useful to me clinically in that they provide a clear, elegant model of therapeutic impasses and how to transform them.

The structure of complementarity is best thought of as a straight line (remember the image of the compass needle stuck between two fixed points). A straight line has two end points opposite to each other. The line has no space; it exists in two dimensions only. You can move only forward or backward along the line, but you cannot step outside of that line since it exists in only two dimensions and there is therefore no lateral space. For a couple, a therapist and patient dyad, for example, this means that the structure of complementarity keeps them locked into a relational position-ing in regard to each other so that one member is diametrically opposite to the other in some significant respect and that there is no way to move or rearrange this structure other than to move toward each other, closer, or to move away from each other, more distant, or to implement a simple reversal and to flip the line around and reverse polarities.

A useful image here is the seesaw. Think of two people on a seesaw where one is on top and one is below. As long as they want to stay on the seesaw, the choices are either moving toward each other or further back toward the edge of the seesaw, thus slightly adjusting their relative power on the fulcrum. That is the only kind of movement possible without getting off the seesaw. Picture this. One is up high, the other is way below. They can maintain their positions or they can switch, creating a simple reversal. But the underlying structure is maintained; they are still on a straight line in which one's position on the seesaw determines the other's. It is possible that each could be in a middle position, sitting evenly or level on the see-saw. But while this seems like an improvement—a more egalitarian, level relationship—it maintains the same structure of rigidity. It remains a single line with the two participants opposite each other and one's position fully determining the position of the other. They remain locked into one pat-tern of relating. They cannot both be up or down together and one's push downward continues to pressure the other to swing upward. This is the model Benjamin (2004a) developed of complementary, doer–done to, push me–pull you relations, and it elegantly depicts what happens in therapeutic impasses and stalemates.

Another image that metaphorically captures the rigidity of complemen-tarity is the fixed pendulum. In describing chaos theory as a model for a relational developmental theory, Harris (2005) uses the fixed pendulum as a model of a rigid attractor. She contrasts the rigid, change-resistant quali-ties of the pendulum to the less predictable strange attractor that is always on the edge of chaos, a state that can be disequilibrated and then reor-ganized in unexpected ways. The image of the fixed pendulum is similar to the seesaw, and it captures the experience of therapeutic impasse and reversible complementarity described by Benjamin in that it moves only from one side to the other, back and forth, without any of the freedom, flexibility, and unpredictability needed for a relationship of two autono-mous individuals interacting in a system of mutual recognition of indepen-dent subjectivities.

So how does one move from the structure of complementary relations to a more flexible arrangement? The two participants must find a way to go from being positioned along a line toward opening up space. I am referring, of course, to psychic space, transitional space, space to think, space to breathe, to live, to move spontaneously in relation to each other interpersonally. The conceptualization of the third attempts to model this state in that a line has no space, whereas a triangle does. Britton (1989) spoke about being able to free himself to think to himself while with a patient, to take a step to the side within his own mind so as to create mental space. Picture this literally in terms of geometric space. While on a seesaw, one literally cannot take a step to the side; moving sideways is just not an option. As soon as one can take a step to the side, one has transformed a line into a triangular space with room to think and to relate. One has created options enabling the two members of the dyad to position themselves with some degree of flexibility and freedom of movement. One's position within triangular space does not completely determine the position of the other as it does on a seesaw.

One significant consequence of being stuck on a straight line in complementary twoness is that the line represents an unconscious symmetry (Benjamin, 2004a). Both partners on the seesaw mirror each other inversely; they are flip sides of each other; they inhabit reversible perspectives. This structural arrangement captures the mutual experience of their deep, generally unconscious, identification with each other. While each partner plays out one side, both of them identify with both positions. We know that the sadist identifies with the masochist, and vice versa, even if these identifications are repudiated in consciousness. Thus, when patient and analyst get stuck in complementarity, even while each feels, "You are doing this to me; you are forcing me into this position," there remains a deep connection between them because they unconsciously recognize that they are locked together in this binary relation, however polarized.

Again, let's return to my supervisee and her patient. When she could begin to think about her situation, she could see that he was not all sadistic terrorist but also terrified hostage. When she could begin to think about herself and realize that she was locked into identification with the victims, then she could begin to imagine other parts of herself, other identifications, say, with the power of the terrorists. Once she could take a step to the side, outside of the "push me–pull you" tug of war with her patent, then other relational positions became immediately available to her. Thinking and feeling within the newly created triangular space allowed her to shift from the limiting structure of a polarizing flat line to a space with possibility and depth. As long as the compass needle was stuck, there was just one line from the center of the compass toward one point on the periphery. Once unstuck, the needle could rotate freely making use of all of the points of reference within the compass. The supervisor, not locked into the established "transference–countertransference interlocks" (Wolstein, 1959, pp. 133–134), helps the analyst to develop some perspective from outside the closed system. A new configuration emerges that presents both patient and analyst with additional options for how they position themselves in relation to each other. Now they are enabled to renegotiate (Pizer, 1998) who they are to each other. Rather than following the rigid and predictable back-and-forth movement of a pendulum, transference can begin to serve as a "strange attractor" allowing the emergence of surprisingly new configurations and unpredictable interpersonal adjustments.

What is meant by "the third"? The third is a concept that has become popular across a variety of schools of psychoanalysis. It has been developed and extended by some of the leading theorists of psychoanalysis, including Ogden, Green, Benjamin, and a variety of Lacan-influenced writers, but it is often defined ambiguously and inconsistently across schools. For some, the third refers to something beyond the dyad, a context within which we emerge; for others, the third is an emergent property of dyadic interaction, yet for others the third is a dyadic achievement that creates the psychic space necessary for reflexive awareness and mentalization (Gerson, 2004; see also the entire issue of *Psychoanalytic Quarterly*, 73(1), 2004, surveying the topic of the third). Here I elucidate a variety of meanings of the third, especially as the term is used within the theoretical framework of Benjamin's intersubjectivity theory.

Benjamin has described a variety of different kinds of thirds, or perhaps different ways of thinking about the third, different aspects of thirdness. Her understanding of the third is embedded within her broader contributions to relational theory where she has elaborated the intersubjective dimension as necessary along with, *not* as replacing, the realm of the intrapsychic. Here I will clarify what she means by the third and illustrate two main types because I believe that Benjamin's contributions to intersubjectivity theory are among the most useful ideas to emerge within contemporary psychoanalysis—ideas with direct and powerful clinical implications that I hope to elaborate and extend (see also Benjamin, 1988, 1990, 1995, 1998, 2004a, 2004b).

Benjamin differentiates between what she calls the one-in-the-third and the third-in-the-one. These conceptualizations are complicated and can be confusing, and it should be noted that these two understandings of or aspects of the third are interconnected. To add to the potential for misunderstanding, Benjamin has used a variety of terms to signify various aspects and dimensions of the third. I explain these terms again and refer to them with some simplification by using prominent examples of each.

What Benjamin has in mind in speaking about the one-in-the-third (which she also called the nascent third or the energetic third) is that rhythmic or harmonic element of oneness that is essential to the experience of thirdness. It may be more easily understood by calling it a *rhythmic third*, keeping in mind Sander's (2002) term, the principle of rhythmicity, or what I suggest referring to as mutual accommodation. Benjamin very clearly describes this in terms of two people sharing a pattern, a dance, a rhythm with each other. Think of the rhythms established by the mother–infant dyad in eye gaze, reciprocal speech, gestures, movements, and mutual mirroring. In discussing Sander's work, Benjamin (2002) usefully described this as resembling musical improvisation, in which both partners follow a pattern that both of them simultaneously create and surrender to, a cocreated third. With the phrase "the-one-in-the-third," Benjamin is trying to capture that experience of oneness, mother–infant oneness or the oneness of a jazz band improvising in sync. Each member is accommodating not only to the other but also to the cocreated rhythm that the couple or group has already established. The principle of mutual accommodation thus expands what we know to be ongoing mutual influence to include the ways not only that two people influence each other but also in which they are continually influenced by the very patterns and rhythms that they have previously established with each other.

It is critical to note here that this form of thirdness may well be pre-oedipal, in that it emerges out of the mother and infant's accommodation to each other as well as to their own prior accommodations. This form of thirdness does not require an oedipal father to sever the child's connection to mother. In arguing that thirdness emerges within the pre-oedipal mother–infant dyad, Benjamin differentiates her ideas from those of Lacan who saw the father as having to symbolize the third. This is not to say, however, that mutual accommodation and rhythmicity do not acquire new meanings and become richer and further differentiated and elaborated during the oedipal and post-oedipal phases. To some degree, it may be that what seems like an argument about pre-oedipal triangularity may be an artifact of differing theoretical, cultural, historical, and linguistic traditions in psychoanalysis. For Lacan and many European analysts, as well as for others who write about the third, such as Green, the mother–infant dyad is always already triadic in the sense that the mother herself is engaged in the symbolic world, thus a third structural element is always already present even if the father himself is not concretely a figure on the scene. Ogden (1987) provided a description of the mother–infant dyad that beautifully elaborates on such a position. He wrote, "The paradox of the little girl's transitional oedipal relationship (created by mother and daughter) is that the first triadic object relationship occurs in the context of a two-person relationship" (p. 485). Nevertheless, I want to highlight some of the subtle differences among these theorists. In Ogden's example, it is the mother who contains the third element intrapsychically, while, in the rhythmic third, the thirdness is a new creation emerging within the space of the dyad rather than in the mind of one or the other participants alone.

Now let us take up the other of Benjamin's prominent thirds, the third-in-the-one, which she also called the symbolic or the moral third (2004a). Benjamin also suggested the "intentional third" (personal communication, January, 2005) to highlight that this third creates a space for differentiation in what is ordinarily called oneness. Benjamin (2004a) illustrated this principle by referring to the term "marking" or "marked response." The idea of markedness was originally developed by György Gergely and was described by Fonagy, Target, Gergely, and Jurist (2002) where they elaborate a social-biofeedback theory of affect mirroring. Recent conceptualizations of "mirroring" emphasize that, no matter how well attuned a parent is to the infant's state, her mirroring facial and vocal behaviors never perfectly match the infant's behavioral expressions. Mothers, and other adults, "mark" their affect-mirroring displays (i.e., they signify that these responses are reflections of the other's feelings rather than being expressions of their own feelings) by exaggerating some aspect of their own realistic response. The mother "marks" her mirroring response to her child to signal, so to speak, that it is *her* version of *his* response. The marking (the exaggerated affect display) is meant to differentiate the response from what would have been her own "realistic" response. It is markedness that indicates that it is not mother's affect display but her reflection (her understanding, her version) of the infant's affect. The exaggerated quality provides a personal stamp or signature, signifying that it is neither a perfect reflection of the other nor a completely natural response of the self. The infant recognizes and uses this marked quality to "decouple" or to differentiate the perceived emotion from its referent (the parent) and to "anchor" or "own" the marked mirroring stimulus as expressing his or her own self-state. An illustration will help clarify this process.

When a mother sees her young child fall and bruise his knee, she exclaims, "Ohhh," in a way that signifies her empathy with the child's pain and fear. Nevertheless, the mother is not (or should not be) responding with the same degree of disorganization as her child. She both identifies with her hurt, frightened child and marks her response (usually by some exaggerated feature) by signifying that she is not reacting exactly as the child is but that she is separate. In the infant's experience, the parent's mirroring behaviors convey a sense of "nearly like, but clearly not identical to me." Nor, however, are they viewed as real emotional expressions of the parent. Neither are they realistic authentic responses of the self, nor are they perfectly matched reflections of the other. Emotional attunement, mirroring, and empathy all have built-in elements of authenticity along with reflections of the other. Mirroring, and empathy itself, dialectically contain elements of authenticity and do not wipe out the features of either self or other. It is neither a sadistic destruction of the other nor a masochistic betrayal of the self. Therefore, mirroring, with its marked component, is a dyadic phenomenon, functioning as a differentiating third point emerging between the infant and the attuned parent. Think of the third here, once again quite literally, as constituted by three points: the child's immediate response; the mother's response identifying with her child's fear; and then that more adult, differentiated component of the mother's response in which she knows that the child is not dying and will get over it.

Thirdness thus emerges here from within the dyad without needing a literal third object to intervene and separate mother from child. This is what Benjamin and I (Aron & Benjamin, 1999), describing the origins of self-reflexivity in intersubjective space, called an incipient third. It is in this way that mirroring creates a third symbolic intersubjective space of representation between infant and parent allowing for and facilitating mentalization and affect regulation. The marked response is thus an excellent example of the third-in-the-one or intentional third in that it facilitates the differentiation of the self and other within their very connectedness. It should be clear that this understanding of mirroring is quite different from the classic Lacanian understanding in that in this view of mirroring, the mother is not at all a united image providing false imaginary unification but rather is split between two subjective positions, one aligned with the child and one distinct and marked. This will have clinical implications for the analyst as we will soon see as we turn to examine how the analyst's mirroring responses provide the patient access to their analyst's own inner conflicts and double-mindedness.

Recall that Benjamin's work is to a large extent inspired by the contributions of Winnicott. In an examination of the mirroring metaphor in the history of psychoanalysis, Reis (2004) explained that, for Winnicott, when the mother looks at her infant she identifies with her own experience of being an infant as well as what it feels like to gaze at her own child. So for Reis—and here he extended the earlier work of Ogden (1994)—what the mother reflects back to the infant is the experience of sameness within difference. Note here the structure of thirdness, the third-in-the-one. In Reis's scheme, there is the infant, the mother identified with her own experience of being an infant, and the mother experiencing what it is like to gaze as a mother at her own infant.

The one-in-the-third and the third-in-the-one are interconnected, rhythmicity and markedness go together, with the former emphasizing connectedness and the latter emphasizing difference; each is necessary to the other. Perhaps it is worth highlighting once more that both of these principles of thirdness—rhythmicity and markedness—are found in pre-oedipal mother–infant relations and that both principles become further differentiated, elaborated, and structured during the oedipal and post-oedipal phases. Nevertheless, thirdness itself arises conceptually as independent from oedipal triangulation. The empirical study of early family group relations, relations beyond the dyad that include triadic and familial relations, is itself in its infancy, and further research is bound to clarify the developmental issues surrounding dyadic and triadic social functioning in the pre-oedipal, oedipal, and post-oedipal stages (McHale & Fivaz-Depeursinge, 1999). Like

Stern (2004), I believe intersubjectivity is best conceptualized as an independent motivational system fostering group formation and group cohesion in a hypersocial species; as such, it is most likely innately present in rudimentary form very early in life. From an evolutionary perspective, it is likely that as a social species we would be born with some innate competence to deal with multipartite relationships.

I will now turn my attention to some of the clinical implications of intersubjectivity theory and the notion of the third. One way to understand why contemporary psychoanalysis has become interested in the third is that thirdness is one way to conceptualize reflection and symbolization. It is a theory of thinking that transcends the mind in isolation, a relational theory of symbolization. I want to make the case that certain forms of the analyst's self-disclosure are best understood as legitimate and at times necessary attempts to create thirdness. By disclosing aspects of their inner processes, particularly their own inner conflict or self-disagreement, analysts conduct a dialogue with themselves in the presence of their patients, thus introducing a third element into the dyad. At times these self-disclosures operate as strange attractors, breaking up the single-lined stuckness of the seesaw and introducing a third dimension, thus creating psychic space for reflexive awareness and mentalization.

Contemporary Kleinians view the third as an oedipal construct, conceiving the third as an aspect of the analyst's mind rather than a shared cocreated experience. From this perspective, Britton (1989) understood his patient as attacking the third in the analyst's mind because it represents an oedipal rival third that cannot be tolerated. However, by placing exclusive emphasis on the oedipal situation, Britton, like most analysts who have written in this area, bypassed the important forerunner of triangular space that emerges from within the mother–infant dyad.

Britton (1989) presented the case of Miss A to illustrate the patient's inability to tolerate knowledge of parental intercourse because accepting this triangular relation would entail a threat to an all too tenuous internal and external relationship to her mother. Any attempt on Britton's part to engage in a perspective outside Miss A's own was experienced as intensely threatening to her and for a long time resulted in her becoming violent. Gradually, Britton learned to allow an evolution within himself of his own experience while articulating to Miss A his understanding of her point of view, something like what we call mirroring. This progressively allowed Miss A to begin to think. Britton retained the oedipal metaphor and used this imagery creatively, stating that parental intercourse could take place only if the knowledge of it did not force itself in some intrusive way into the child's mind.

Benjamin and I (Aron & Benjamin, 1999) argued that Britton's superb clinical sensitivity is better formulated in the following way. Britton constructed a relationship with Miss A in which he reflected back her own point of view as it was inevitably filtered through his own thought processes and emotional responsiveness. He successively elaborated his thinking about her point of view in such a modulated manner that she could gradually begin to identify herself with an image of him thinking about her. He thereby created a sense of mutual identification or attunement, which allowed her to gradually feel that the other understood her experience sufficiently well so that his thinking did not replace or supersede hers. His thought became available as an object for her use, facilitating reflection, each person thinking about the other's thought. Thus, he did not intrude as a third element into their dyadic relationship, but, much like in the mother–infant dyad, a third space was jointly constructed out of the dyad. This occurred as Britton began to think *about* her point of view but inevitably *from* his point of view and as she was able to identify with his thinking about her thoughts, thus taking her thinking to a second power.

Britton concluded that, since his patient cannot tolerate the analyst's thinking, which represents the analyst's sexual relation to an oedipal third, all the analyst can do is to allow the evolution within himself of his own experience, to articulate this to himself, while communicating to the patient only the analyst's understanding of the patient's point of view. Britton therefore called for triangular space to be opened up only in the analyst's mind. But it seems to me that this account really does not explain how this internal thinking in the analyst eventually leads to any shift in the patient. Does Britton mean to suggest that articulating understanding completely from the patient's point of view will eventually allow the patient to tolerate a third perspective? Perhaps. But I would argue that Britton, and all analysts, try as they might to stick with the patient's perspective, to articulate the world as it is experienced by the patient, inevitably introduce some difference, some marking of their reactions as different from the patient's. I would certainly agree with Britton that the analyst's own perspective may have to be offered with great subtlety, marking the response only slightly; nevertheless, at least conceptually, this markedness conveys some degree of thirdness and differentiation and thus gradually creates analytic space (Aron & Benjamin, 1999).

Let us again think in very simple concrete terms about what it is that the analyst is doing. If the analyst is really thinking only silently about the patient in a differentiated way, without conveying any of that to the patient, then how does this create space between them? Sooner or later, at least in some small measure, does not the analyst have to be able to demonstrate to the patient that the analyst can think about his or her own reactions? Does not the analyst have to have some kind of dialogue with himself or herself, something in the form of, "I am of two minds about this idea; I can hold onto two ideas, two points of view, some conflict or disagreement with myself"? It is the analyst's reflexive self-awareness, a dialogue with oneself, that creates a third point within what was a simple dyad, a triangular space where there was only a line.

A superb account of this clinical process is "the dialectics of difference" described by Bollas (1989). Bollas encouraged the analyst to differ with himself or herself, to express some conflict, for example, about making a particular interpretation, or to explain to a patient something of the internal process that led to arriving at an interpretation. Bollas might disagree with himself, for example, saying to a patient that he feels his last interpretation was not quite right and here is why. Bollas advocated this form of self-disclosure with the intention of helping the patient to gradually accept and articulate conflict of his or her own.

Similarly, Hoffman (1998) advocated that analysts may at times reveal various conflicts about their analytic functioning. He offered numerous examples along the lines that he would like to say X but he is worried about Y. For example, he told one patient that he would like to offer her support about a particular activity but he worried that offering such support would encourage her dependency. Numerous analytic authors have argued for some increased acceptance of the analyst's self-disclosure, emphasizing a variety of rationales for this hitherto discouraged technical option (see my review of Bollas, Hoffman, and the topic of self-disclosure in Aron, 1996).

Yet another clinical theorist who articulates a rationale for some increased sharing of the analyst's inner workings is Bach (2003). In the following passage, note how Bach, just like Bollas and Hoffman, not only advocated analysts sharing with patients the inner workings of their minds but also very specifically emphasized the importance of analysts disclosing certain aspects of their own double-mindedness, ambivalence, or inner conflict:

> I try, whenever possible, to explain the reasoning behind my comments and interpretations and, better yet, I allow the patient to witness my mind at work in the process of free-associating or making formulations, so that the interpretation becomes a mutual endeavor and is thereby much improved. It is especially useful for such patients to experience the analyst as he tries to deal with doubt and ambiguity, or as he tries to hold two ideas or two roles in mind at the same time, for it opens up the possibility of their doing the same. Most importantly, since I am implicitly asking my patients to trust me with their minds, I struggle to attain a position where I can trust them with my own mind and feel that I have nothing to hide from them. (pp. 403–404)

Here is one further clinical illustration from the work of McLaughlin (2005). McLaughlin, a seasoned analyst, was working with Mr. F, who was engaging in high-risk sexual encounters during the early years of the AIDS epidemic. McLaughlin tells the story of how closely he came to being pushed beyond his personal and analytic tolerance. In spite of his best efforts to remain neutral and nonintrusive and to refrain from imposing moralistic or overly protective restraints in regard to Mr. F's anonymous homosexual encounters and cruising, McLaughlin could not conceal from his patient his own aversion and his wishes to restrain his patient. McLaughlin beautifully described the resulting impasse between him and Mr. F as well as his personal struggles to see the situation from Mr. F's perspective and his own deep self-analytic efforts. Ultimately, for Mr. F the difficulty was not McLaughlin's concerns but rather his "dissembling," his lack of directness about his feelings. Having arrived at this understanding, McLaughlin was able to directly disclose his own conflict to Mr. F. "I was able then to speak about the quandary of my wish to urge him to do the sensible thing, countered by my concern for his need for autonomy" (p. 220). It was this collaborative work and direct acknowledgment of the analyst's conflict that led to the resolution of the dangerous cruising behaviors and the associated analytic impasse.

In my view, the understanding of thirdness as central to intersubjectivity provides the single best explanation for the clinical importance of certain types of self-disclosure as well as for understanding its limits and boundaries. The technical interventions described by Bollas, Hoffman, Bach, and McLaughlin may be creatively explained using Benjamin's and my own elaboration of the notion of the third. Bollas's description of the dialectics of difference; Hoffman's clinical examples of revealing some aspect of his own conflict to a patient; Bach's argument for allowing a patient to witness his own mind at work especially in regard to keeping two ideas in mind; and McLaughlin's sharing with Mr. F his own quandary in conducting his treatment may each be seen as various ways to begin to create analytic space by bringing in a third point of view. By disclosing their own difference with themselves or conflict or double-mindedness, what they are doing is saying, "I am of two minds about this intervention." They are saying, "Okay, there are at least three of us here. There is you, and then there is the I who wants to support you, and the I who is afraid of encouraging your dependency." Or they are saying, "There is the you who heard my last interpretation and felt whatever you felt, then there is the I who said it, and the I who now disagrees and feels somewhat differently." In the examples provided by Bollas, Hoffman, Bach, and McLaughlin, it is the analyst who goes first, in the sense that the analyst feels free to own his or her own conflict or inner difference before the patient is expected to do so. Similarly, Benjamin (2004a) argued that, in an impasse that is structured along the lines of complementary twoness, of doer–done to relations, analysts may have to go first revealing their own vulnerability before expecting this of the patient. It is not simply a matter of going first in the sense of sequence, rather, it is a matter of the analyst taking responsibility for participating in the push–pull by having said or done something that contributed to it. This relates to the all-important recognition that enactment and co-participation are essential and facilitative aspects of the analytic process. This does not mean that just any self-disclosure is clinically productive or that the analyst should just speak his or her mind or that anything goes—obviously not. The analyst's response must be marked, it must in some small way differentiate itself from the patient's response (the differentiating or intentional third or markedness), yet it also must reflect the analyst's accommodation to the needs and perspective of the patient as well as to the various accommodations, rhythms, previously established between them (the rhythmic third as mutual accommodation and negotiation).

To return to my initial clinical example, suppose the analyst could find a way to say something to the patient about her understanding of how his excitement about the attacks was understandable because it could feel so exhilarating to see the violence out there in the world, outside of himself, to identify with the excitement of having that much impact and control of the whole world. This could be said in a genuine way, by which I mean that the analyst could genuinely identify with the power and the excitement of the power, without losing her own sense of the horror of the destructiveness. I think, however, that to say this would not simply be a mirroring of the patient's affective state, but rather would include inevitably some markedness, some difference between the reaction of the patient himself and what is captured by the analyst's interpretation. This very point of difference leaves open an invitation to the patient to correct the analyst, to dialogue with her about the difference between his lived experience and what is captured by her remark, as well as to negotiate the meaning of these experiences between them. Clearly, neither empathy nor negotiation is a steady process; rather, intersubjectivity is constructed and lost, ruptured and repaired (Beebe & Lachmann, 1994). This very process of rupture and repair may be well understood as drawing on the power of the third, the dialectic, or, put another way, the negotiation of difference.

But consider another intervention. I could also see the analyst saying to the patient something along these lines: "Oh I see, I was missing something. I was so appalled by the violence and so saddened by the loss of life that I didn't want to let myself see that I also felt some excitement by the very power involved in the horror." Would it really be so surprising if following an intervention like this the patient could begin to notice that he also had more than one set of feelings about the disaster? Might not the patient react with something like: "Oh, you mean you can actually find the aggression exciting too? Can you at times really feel pleasure at innocent people's death the way I can?" The answer to this question, whether articulated to the patient or not, would be: "Yes, I can feel such excitement, and it is so appalling to me, so frightening to let myself feel such sadism that I'd rather be repulsed by it in you than recognize and acknowledge it in myself." The analyst here is taking a step to the side; she is beside herself, dialoguing with herself, thinking out loud. Where until now there has been a simple line with patient and therapist at opposite ends, there is now triangular space with some increased room to move. As Benjamin (2004b) wrote in commenting on the work of Davies, "In order to speak about the coercive, hateful, or destructive aspects of the relationship, there must be a shift from destructive, table-turning tit for tat into the mode of feeling free to tell it like it is, to own up to feelings" (p. 744). As this illustration makes clear, I do not think of the third as describing a kind of analytic space that exists free of enactment. As Davies (2004) very usefully clarified, the third does not reestablish a form of objectivity free of distortion and coparticipation. Rather, it is one step in an always shifting dynamic process, an effort to create a psychic space within which to think together about ways in which patient and analyst are similar and different, merged and separate, identified and differentiated from one another. We should not expect the third to be a stable or static achievement. The nature of thirdness is that it is an ever-shifting, dynamic process. Intersubjectivity consists of a dialectic process of mutual recognition and breakdown into complementarity.

The conceptualization of thirdness presented here clearly rests upon the assumption that transference and countertransference constitute an intersubjective dyadic system in which both continually influence each other and must be resolved in relation to each other. Exploring the nature of therapeutic impasses and treatment plateaus, as long ago as 1959, Wolstein defined what he referred to as "transference–countertransference interlocks" (pp. 133–134). Wolstein, whose writing was dense and abstract, was a leading clinician and theoretician within the interpersonal tradition, and his work is therefore hardly known among analysts of other schools or for that matter outside of New York where he taught and practiced. Wolstein's early portrayal of analytic impasses is remarkably similar to what Benjamin and I described in our work on the third. Wolstein argued that, in these situations of interlock, transference and countertransference automatically emerge in correlation to each other's development. In situations of interlock, in that area or dimension where the two coparticipants are stuck, "neither participant is capable of free and independent movement" (p. 135). Indeed, Wolstein used the same figures of speech that Benjamin and I have been using, speaking of the "reactive kind of push-and-pull cooperation" (p. 137) and of transference and countertransference as "interpenetrating" (p. 141). Over and over again Wolstein points out that the end result of these interlocks is either that the patient finds a way to leave, or the analyst gives up, either by coming to the conclusion that the patient is too disturbed or unanalyzable or by literally ending the analysis. The alternatives to this bleak ending involve either the analyst getting supervisory help by going to a third party, a consultant or analyst, or, preferably, the analyst turns to the one person who is in the best position to make observations about the countertransference, namely, the patient.

In opening himself or herself up to exploring the countertransference by attending to the observations of the patient, the analyst can transcend the dualism that structures the interlock. While not literally using the language of the third, Wolstein anticipated and influenced much of the contemporary interpersonal and relational focus on the interplay of transference and countertransference, mutual enactments, mutual influence, and the intersubjective third. Just as Benjamin and I placed special importance on the need for analysts to acknowledge their role in creating the impasse, and just as contemporary analysts have emphasized many mutual processes in psychoanalysis (see Aron, 1996), so too Wolstein (1959) wrote:

> Once an interlocking of transference and countertransference sets in, the analyst may be said to need his patient's recovery because, in a sense, his own is actually involved. It is not simply a matter of invested time and energy; instead, a real opportunity for personal growth is at stake. This is the crucial dynamism in the experiential field that works toward a therapeutic outcome: both the analyst and his patient have now to find a way to a level of relatedness and integration that will be richer and more meaningful than the one they are capable of at this point. (p. 169)

Before ending with another everyday clinical example that illustrates the practical usefulness of thinking in terms of the third, first I want to introduce Gentile's (2001) penetrating discussion of the origins of intersubjectivity. Gentile reexamined Winnicott's theory of transitional space by elaborating on several contemporary psychoanalytic theories of the third. She demonstrated that Winnicott never fully developed his conception of intersubjectivity or integrated it with his ideas about transitional space. Symbolic space exists as a third to the dyad, and intersubjectivity is predicated upon transitionality, a space that lies at the crossroads of subjective and material life. Gentile highlighted how the creation of the transitional object involves the paradox of surrendering to the unyielding aspects of materiality while simultaneously transcending it through imagination and omnipotent subjectivity. Interpretive space is opened between the symbol and the symbolized, between brute reality and subjectivity. Brute reality and materiality is given meaning and is thus transformed.

If materiality is one, and omnipotent fantasy is second, then meaning and symbolic space are the third. Consider the following everyday clinical illustration. A patient arrives some minutes late to a session and explains that the

New York City subways were once again late. She had given herself plenty of time had the trains only been reasonably on time. The patient, however, may go on to blame herself. Of course it was her fault. She should have anticipated the delayed train schedule and left even earlier; it must have been her own resistance. She's not motivated enough, not a good enough patient. Now, of course, the analyst too can become caught up in one of, or alternate between, these two positions—blaming or excusing the patient. The analyst may alternate between wanting to interpret the patient's resistances to the treatment and wanting to interpret the patient's omnipotence in thinking that she can be and should be in such total control of all contingencies. Too often these polarities are enacted between patient and analyst on the seesaw of the transference–countertransference where one party embodies the accuser and the other the defender, one championing omnipotence and one surrendering to forces beyond one's control, or, in traditional terms, one interprets and one expresses resistance. This back and forth, mutual projection of accusation and defense, interpretation and resistance, resembles the rigid attractor of the fixed pendulum. Here patient and analyst can so easily become locked into a stalemate or impasse.

But consider now what happens when the patient and analyst can play with the fantasy that the patient could control the timing of the trains, when the patient can joke about how she so wanted to come late that she wished the trains were delayed or calculated arriving just after the last train left the station. The patient needs to be able to do this lightly, not sarcastically or cynically or masochistically, moving beyond surrender to the objective facts or omnipotent control of reality to play in transitional symbolic space. Only with this third possibility, when the patient can entertain the fantasy that she purposefully made the trains late, without getting caught up in exonerating herself by pointing to the concrete unavoidable realities and also without becoming trapped in omnipotent, masochistic self-blame, guilt and shame—only then can she use her free-associative skills that permit the growth of mentalization and symbolization. This is the structure of analytic symbolization.

Let me elaborate several extensions of this illustration. Instead of a late train, consider a patient's playing with getting a cold that keeps him from attending a session, or a young single woman exploring why she never meets eligible men, or a man wondering why he repeatedly ends up working for demanding and authoritarian bosses, or another patient wondering why he always seems to find therapists who get bored and sleepy with him. In each of these instances, both the patient and the analyst can easily fall into the following two positions: In position one, they each may hold the patient responsible, highlighting the patient's agency but perhaps reinforcing omnipotence and masochism; in position two, they each may exonerate the patient of all responsibility, emphasizing material reality and the patient's acceptance of what is beyond their control. Or, as is so commonly the case, the patient and analyst may alternate between these two polarities in a series of simple reversals. Only when they are both able to achieve a third position, transcending the first two, have they moved beyond sadomasochism, beyond a transference–countertransference interlock, and beyond binary thinking into the transitional, symbolic space of thirdness and intersubjectivity.

Psychoanalysis has been plagued by its preoccupation with binaries, polarized between theorists and schools that emphasize drive or culture, self or object, attachment or separation, autonomy or relations, the individual or the social, the intrapsychic or the interpersonal. In our own dialogue and development, we as psychoanalysts become stuck in impasses and stalemates, locked in heated battles between representatives of these polarized positions. Each theorist or school stares across the divide into its mirror image, locked in complementarity. Conceptualizing the third is one attempt to move beyond such oppositions and to create triangular space within which psychoanalysis too can think more freely, open dialogue, grow, and develop.

References

Aron, L. (1995). The internalized primal scene. *Psychoanalytic Dialogues, 5*, 195–237.

Aron, L. (1996). *A meeting of minds: Mutuality in psychoanalysis.* Hillsdale, NJ: The Analytic Press.

Aron, L., & Benjamin, J. (1999, April). *The development of intersubjectivity and the struggle to think.* Paper presented at the Spring Meeting, Division of Psychoanalysis (39), American Psychological Association, New York.

Bach, S. (2003). A mind of one's own: Some observations on disorders of thinking. In R.Lasky (Ed.), *Symbolization and desymbolization: Essays in honor of Norbert Freedman* (pp. 387–406). New York: Other Press.

Beebe, B., & Lachmann, F. M. (1994). Representation and internalization in infancy: Three principles of salience. *Psychoanalytic Psychology, 11*, 127–165.

Benjamin, J. (1988). *The bonds of love: Psychoanalysis, feminism and the problem of domination.* New York: Pantheon.

Benjamin, J. (1990). An outline of intersubjectivity: The development of recognition. *Psychoanalytic Psychology, 7*, 33–46.

Benjamin, J. (1995). *Like subjects, love objects: Recognition and sexual difference.* New Haven, CT: Yale University Press.

Benjamin, J. (1998). *Shadow of the other: Intersubjectivity and gender in psychoanalysis.* New York: Routledge.

Benjamin, J. (1999). Afterword. In S. Mitchell & L. Aron (Eds.), *Relational psychoanalysis: The emergence of a tradition* (pp. 201–210). Hillsdale, NJ: The Analytic Press.

Benjamin, J. (2002). The rhythm of recognition: Comments on the work of Louis Sander. *Psychoanalytic Dialogues, 12*, 43–53.

Benjamin, J. (2004a). Beyond doer and done to: An intersubjective view of thirdness. *Psychoanalytic Quarterly*, *73*, 5–46.

Benjamin, J. (2004b). Escape from the hall of mirrors: Commentary on paper by Jody Messler Davies. *Psychoanalytic Dialogues*, *14*, 743–753.

Benjamin, J. (2005, April). *Our appointment in Thebes: The fear of doing harm, and the need for mutual acknowledgement.* Paper presented at the annual meeting of the Division of Psychoanalysis (39), American Psychological Association, New York.

Bollas, C. (1989). *Forces of destiny: Psychoanalysis and human idiom.* London: Free Association Books.

Britton, R. (1989). The missing link: Parental sexuality in the Oedipus complex. In J. Steiner (Ed.), *The Oedipus complex today: Clinical implications* (pp. 83–102). London: Karnac.

Davies, J. M. (2003). Falling in love with love: Oedipal and postoedipal manifestations of idealization, mourning and erotic masochism. *Psychoanalytic Dialogues*, *13*, 1–27.

Davies, J. M. (2004). Reply to commentaries. *Psychoanalytic Dialogues*, *14*, 755–767.

Davies, J. M., & Frawley, M. G. (1994). *Treating the adult survivor of childhood sexual abuse: A psychoanalytic perspective.* New York: Basic Books.

Fivaz-Depeursinge, E., Favez, N., & Frascarolo, F. (2004). Threesome intersubjectivity in infancy. In D. Zahavi, T. Grünbaum, & J. Parnas (Eds.), *The structure and development of self-consciousness: Interdisciplinary perspectives* (pp. 21–34). Amsterdam: John Benjamins.

Fonagy, P., Target, M., Gergely, G., & Jurist, E. L. (2002). *Affect regulation, mentalization, and the development of the self.* New York: Other Press.

Gentile, J. (2001, November). *Beyond privacy: Transitional intersubjectivity and the transitional subject.* Paper presented at the 24th Annual International Conference on the Psychology of the Self, San Francisco, CA.

Gerson, S. (2004). The relational unconscious: A core element of intersubjectivity, thirdness, and clinical process. *Psychoanalytic Quarterly*, *73*, 63–98.

Harris, A. (2005). *Gender as soft assembly.* Hillsdale, NJ: The Analytic Press.

Hoffman, I. Z. (1998). *Ritual and spontaneity in the psychoanalytic process: A dialectical-constructivist view.* Hillsdale, NJ: The Analytic Press.

McHale, J. P., & Fivaz-Depeursinge, E. (1999). Understanding triadic and family group interactions during infancy and toddlerhood. *Clinical Child and Family Psychology Review*, *2*, 107–127.

McLaughlin, J. T. (2005). *The healer's bent: Solitude and dialogue in the clinical encounter.* Hillsdale, NJ: The Analytic Press.

Ogden, T. H. (1987). The transitional oedipal relationship in female development. *International Journal of Psychoanalysis*, *68*, 485–498.

Ogden, T. H. (1994). *Subjects of analysis.* Northvale, NJ: Jason Aronson.

Pizer, S. A. (1998). *Building bridges: The negotiation of paradox in psychoanalysis.* Hillsdale, NJ: The Analytic Press.

Reis, B. E. (2004). You are requested to close the eyes. *Psychoanalytic Dialogues*, *14*, 349–371.

Sander, L. (2002). Thinking differently: Principles of process in living systems and the specificity of being known. *Psychoanalytic Dialogues*, *12*, 11–42.

Stern, D. N. (2004). *The present moment in psychotherapy and everyday life.* New York: Norton.

Wolstein, B. (1959). *Countertransference.* New York: Grune & Stratton.

AFTERWORD: GHOSTS, MONSTERS, MULATTOES, QUEERS, UNDECIDABLES, AND OTHER THIRDS

In the years since writing this paper, I have focused on the concept of thirdness along very specific lines by applying the notion to the deconstruction of the psychotherapy/psychoanalysis divide.* I have been extending the idea of the third, which was formulated in regard to clinical concerns, to apply it to psychoanalysis as a professional institution and theoretical enterprise. Having done so, I return to a reexamination of its clinical implications. Here I provide a highly condensed version of my argument.

Freud was a brilliant interdisciplinary thinker, synthesizing knowledge from a wide range of the sciences and humanities of his era (Makari, 2008). Eager to differentiate psychoanalysis from what he considered the more primitive treatments of his day, which were based on suggestion, Freud repeatedly proclaimed that he could eliminate suggestion from his treatment of patients. His concerns were the following: If suggestion was at play, then how could one be sure that the findings of psychoanalysis were objective? If suggestion was operating, then couldn't psychoanalysis be considered a projection of Freud's own complexes? If suggestion was behind his findings, then psychoanalysis could be considered nothing but an idiosyncratic "Jewish science." Having witnessed his teacher and hero, Charcot, fall from his position of eminence precisely because Bernheim and others had demonstrated that his findings were contaminated by suggestion, Freud had learned his lesson.

As psychoanalysis became the dominant form of treatment in American psychiatry following World War II, the psychoanalytic establishment went to great lengths to differentiate psychoanalysis from other psychotherapies. Intent on aligning psychoanalysis with the growing prestige of medicine and its increasing specialization (and the associated economic benefits), the psychoanalytic establishment was determined that psychoanalysis be considered a form of medical treatment. In the context of American medicine of that era, *treatment* was sharply differentiated from *care*: treatment was active intervention that led to cure, whereas care (as in nursing) was palliative or supportive.

In the American context of the 1950s, when these differentiations were first established and institutionalized, independence and autonomy were culturally designated masculine values, whereas dependence

---

* This work was done in collaboration with Dr. Karen Starr, and I thank her for her help with this afterword. Our forthcoming book, *Defining Psychoanalysis: The Surprising Relevance of Racism, Anti-Semitism, Misogyny, and Homophobia*, will elaborate in detail on this short précis.

and relationality were marked as feminine. Defining itself on one side of a cultural binary, psychoanalysis—at that time an overwhelmingly male, medical profession—saw itself as promoting independence, autonomy, depth, and intrapsychic change through insight and rationality, whereas psychotherapy was viewed as promoting dependence, support, reliance on the other, superficial adjustment, and emotional catharsis. Psychoanalysis was scientific, rational, and only suitable for patients who had sufficient ego strength to tolerate such a process, whereas psychotherapy was for those who were less "structured." Psychoanalysis embodied the masculine and civilized values of the time, especially autonomy, and projected onto psychotherapy all that was relational and marked as feminine or primitive. Psychoanalysis was therefore depicted as "pure" in contrast to "applied," medical (read "masculine') treatment, rather than nursing (read "feminine") care, from which it had to be kept separate so as not to be "contaminated." This ideology supported the economic and socially elitist aspirations of a high status and growing profession seeking to limit and restrain competition.

This study of "the third," and especially my long-standing collaboration with Jessica Benjamin, whose work I tried to illustrate, elaborate, and develop in this paper, led me to focus on impasses and stalemates in analytic therapy by recognizing the ways patient and analyst became polarized around certain issues and for one reason or another could not negotiate those polarities: hence, "doer–done to," "push me–pull you," "seesaw" or "one up–one down," "my way or the highway," sadomasochistic relations. In examining these dynamics, I recognized not only that analysts get caught up in these clinical interactions with patients but also that something about psychoanalysis itself, its history, its institutionalization, and its social and economic structure, actually contributed to enacting these configurations socially and professionally. Psychoanalysis had defined itself in opposition to, and hierarchically elevated above, suggestion and psychotherapy along the lines of a set of binaries in which psychoanalysis was always on top (Aron, 2009; Safran, 2009). Furthermore, the very structuring of the analytic process lent itself to the analyst and the analytic functions being viewed as hierarchically elevated relative to the patient. Hence, only a search for some form of "the third" could free us from the various clinical and cultural impasses in which psychoanalysis has been trapped.

According to Derrida (1976), Western thought, especially metaphysics, is based on dualistic oppositions that are often value laden and ethnocentric and that create a hierarchy that inevitably privileges one term of each pole. The deconstructive strategy does not rest with reversing dichotomies but rather aims to undermine the dichotomies themselves and to show that there are "undecidables," items that do not belong on either side of a dichotomy. These "undecidables" are "third" terms. Deconstruction contends that in any text, there are inevitably points of "undecidability" that betray any stable meaning an author might seek to impose upon his or her text. According to Derrida, the dominance of reason, the logos, is allied with the archetypically male will to dominate society, which he described as "phallogocentrism."

One can easily see how feminists such as Helene Cixous (2004) could use Derrida's concepts to develop a deconstructive approach to the usual binaries by which men and women, as well as stereotypical male and female characteristics, were polarized, and where the male term was always hierarchically superior to the female term, dominating it, with the entire scheme used to dominate women. Cixous argued that masculine sexuality and masculine language are phallocentric and logocentric, fixing meaning through such binary oppositions as father–mother, intelligible–sensitive, logos–pathos, which rely for their meaning on the primary binary opposition between male and female, phallic–castrated, all reproducing patriarchy and the domination of women. The hierarchization of meaning serves to subordinate the feminine to the masculine. Benjamin (1988) demonstrated that gender was socially constructed by repudiating and splitting off of all that was weak and dependent to create femininity. Applying deconstructive principles to relational psychoanalysis, Muriel Dimen (2003) wrote, "Dualism's separate-but-equal masks a hierarchy: the one behind the two is always on top. In the table of opposites that have been around since the pre-Socratics—for example, male–female, light–dark, reason–emotion, mind–body, nature–culture—one term is always implicitly better or higher than the other. Hence the usual deconstructive reading: a binary always conceals a hierarchy" (p. 7).

For an overview of feminist poststructuralism, see Weedon (1987); for the application of these ideas to the splitting of autonomy and relationality by gender, see Layton (1998). Modern anthropology and postcolonial studies have also benefited from Derrida's poststructural critique of binary oppositions (Brickman, 2003). Nineteenth-century evolutionary theorists such as Spencer contrasted primitive savages and civilized Europeans, sorting all of the world's population into one or the other of these two categories. The civilized side of the binary was elevated over the primitive so that evolutionary theory provided the ideological rationalization used to justify colonialism and other forms of exploitation.

Derrida's approach (itself significantly influenced by Freud) attempted to deconstruct binary oppositions by examining the "undecidables," the cases that fell in between (for a clear exposition of Derrida's life and work see Mikics, 2009). By focusing on undecidables, Derrida tried to show how the binary opposition broke down. But Derrida made mistakes and slipped into a form of relativism (i.e., his failure to take a stand against the Nazi past of his friend Paul de Man). An understanding of these dichotomies and how they have structured psychoanalysis is a radically liberating insight. Once we see how these dualities undergird psychoanalytic thought, we are in a much better position to recognize and correct trouble spots in the theory and practice of psychoanalysis. The process involves finding "undecidables" or "thirds" and using them to break down polarized thinking. The psychotherapy–psychoanalysis binary is just one example of this approach but one that is central and has ongoing practical implications. One must be careful to clearly keep in mind that deconstructing a polarity does not mean eliminating difference. As you think through my deconstruction of the psychotherapy–psychoanalysis binary, keep in mind that the point is to critique the polarization and hierarchization rather than to eliminate all difference. For example, I am not contending that seeing a patient once a week and seeing him or her four times a week are equivalent. Rather, the issue is whether to think of psychotherapy and psychoanalysis as dichotomous.

The argument I am making is that psychoanalysis has always defined itself in opposition to something else. At first, in Freud's work, that something else was suggestion. Later, in America, it was psychotherapy. From its inception, psychoanalysis identified itself and the analyst with what was masculine, autonomous, rational, scientific, and objective as opposed to what it viewed as feminine, relational, irrational, unscientific, and subjective—all characteristics that were later attributed to psychotherapy, which was then devalued. In an era in which Jewish men were debased as effeminate, immoral, and concrete, Freud projected these debased characteristics onto women (Gilman, 1993; Boyarin, 1997). Likewise, in America in the 1950s, psychoanalysis projected the devalued qualities of dependency and relationality onto psychotherapy, keeping itself at a distance from these contaminating effeminate and primitive qualities. (Most American psychoanalytic institutes would not even teach psychotherapy, as it might contaminate the purity of analytic training.)

Genius that Freud was, he was nevertheless caught in a matrix of binaries that permeated his culture and his very existence. As a Jewish man in Austria, he was regarded by his anti-Semitic countrymen as effeminate, perverse, homosexual, and circumcised. In this virulently anti-Semitic milieu, Jews were viewed as immoral, degenerate, and neurotic, tied to the concrete and the body, and incapable of rationality and science. Like all colonized and oppressed people, Freud, to some degree, internalized these attributes (Gilman, 1993; Boyarin, 1997).

Larry Friedman (2006) celebrated psychoanalysis as being freakish, weird, bizarre, and unnatural—a monster. The salient characteristic of a monster is precisely that it does not fit neatly into natural categories. As a monster, psychoanalysis is neither art nor science—not quite a method of research nor a medical treatment. To insist that psychoanalysis is one thing or another is to tame the beast. Similarly, ghosts are not quite alive but not thoroughly dead. Psychoanalysis is haunted—*heimlich* and *unheimlich*, home and not home—and, as Freud proclaimed, could have been invented only by "a Godless Jew" (vii); that is, someone who never fit neatly into standard categories.

According to Philip Reiff (1966), "A tolerance of ambiguity is the key to what Freud considered the most difficult of all personal accomplishments" (p. 57). Fortunately for psychoanalysis, Freud's thinking was always more complex and nuanced than the binaries in which he was culturally caught. Freud's very place on the boundaries, as both insider and outsider and as neither insider nor outsider, is precisely what allowed him to appreciate ambiguities. Freud was neither Austrian nor German nor Jew; neither White nor Black, as Jews were regarded as mulattoes. He was a doctor, but not a real university doctor, as Jews could not obtain those positions. While in some ways conventionally straight and even patriarchical, from the point of view of his anti-Semitic surround, Freud was not a phallic man, since he was circumcised and therefore castrated and effeminate. Nor was he a woman, onto whom he would project all dependency, shame, and inferiority. Rather, according to the anti-Semitic trope, Freud, like all Jewish men, was effeminate and perverse; in some ways Jewish men were a third sex. Boyarin (1997) wrote, "Gilman has provided a vitally important piece of information by observing how thoroughly Jewishness was constructed as queer in fin de siècle Europe" (p. 214). He continued, "The Jew was queer and hysterical—and therefore, not a man" (p. 215).* Freud had been in love with a male friend, Fliess, with whom he championed bisexuality, had regular "congresses," and compared menstrual cycles. In short, Freud was a monster: a ghost, queer, undecidable, mulatto, circumcised, *unheimlich*, a third. Who else could discover such a monster as psychoanalysis? Janus-like in his doubledness (Boyarin, 1997, p. 244), always on the boundary's edge, quoting Freud can always serve as a basis for drawing diametrically opposed conclusions. His work is the basis for both conservative and radical projects. Freud longed to be culturally German, civilized, cultured, but was always vulnerable to prejudice, to castration.

---

* Johnson (1998) challenged the myth of Jewish male menses as Medieval but affirmed that it was a belief in the modern era.

In my view, the central binary relevant to psychoanalysis and psychotherapy is vulnerability and invulnerability.* Celia Brickman suggested (personal communication, 2010) that what analysts mean by "primitivity" is essentially "vulnerability." For Freud, this was expressed in terms of penetrating and being penetrated. To penetrate was to be phallic, whole, and firm, whereas to be penetrated was to be castrated, permeable, and vulnerable. Nussbaum (2010) demonstrated that misogyny is rooted in "projective disgust" (p. 15). Males distance themselves from bodily, animal vulnerability by associating women with bodily fluids, and dissociating themselves from their own corporeality. Homophobia is structured along the same lines as misogyny. "What inspires disgust is typically the male thought of the male homosexual, imagined as anally penetrable. The idea of semen and feces mixing together inside the body of a male is one of the most disgusting ideas imaginable—to males, for whom the idea of nonpenetrability is a sacred boundary against stickiness, ooze, and death" (p. 18). As a 19th-century European man, Freud believed the height of civilization was the achievement of individual autonomy, later theorized as "ego autonomy." Having clear and firm boundaries meant that you were independent and whole, phallic and impenetrable. To be merged with another, to experience the "oceanic feeling," fluidity, was to be penetrable, vulnerable to the influence of the other, susceptible to infection. This was primitivity (Brickman, 2003), and, as Nussbaum argued, it signified vulnerability and mortality. It was the primitive who was suggestible—the hysteric, the woman, the African, Asian, or Jew, the poor and uneducated. For the Western Jew, it was the Eastern Jew. Primitivity was vulnerability to penetration, contamination, and death. In Freud's day, Jews were regarded as smelly, contaminated, and contagious. This ideology culminated with Hitler, for whom Jews were "maggots inside a rotting body" (quoted by Nussbaum, 2010, p. 23). As circumcision was the embodied mark of the Jew as feminine and castrated, castration anxiety took on a central role in Freudian clinical theory and practice. This explains why Freud (1937) believed that the bedrock of psychoanalysis was "the repudiation of femininity" (p. 403). This was not just a slip or passing sentiment—it was at the core of his values. Phallic–castrated and masculine–feminine were binaries running in parallel with Aryan–Jew, White–Black, heterosexu-

---

* See Judith Butler's *Precarious Life* (2004) as well as Martha Nussbaum's *From Disgust to Humanity* (2010). Schofer (2010) argued that vulnerability is the bedrock of Jewish, that is, Rabbinic, ethics. It is striking that Freud similarly attributed ethics to condition of human vulnerability. He wrote, "The initial helplessness of human beings is the primal source of all moral motives" (1895, p. 318). Elsewhere, building on my earlier study of mutuality and asymmetry in *A Meeting of Minds* (Aron, 1996), I elaborate on the concept of "mutual vulenerability" in further detail.

al–homosexual, civilized–primitive, health–illness, and life–death. From this perspective, to help a patient get better by using suggestion could only reinforce the patient's primitivity, even if it helped them in other ways (so-called transference cures), or was necessary due to practical circumstances, such as limited resources. Psychoanalysis proper had to eliminate suggestion. Certainly it did not eliminate "influence," for how else could you help someone? Freud distinguished between two types of influence. He objected to the kind of influence based on interpersonal effect—the force of one's personality or subjectivity. Rather, as an enlightenment science, analysis influenced the patient through rational means. To be influenced by accepting a rational argument means you have used your own reason to evaluate the influence, so you remain independent and autonomous—that is why in its later formulation, psychoanalysis was supposed to work by interpretation alone (Gill, 1954, p. 775). In contrast, in hypnotic influence, you are subject to the direct interpersonal influence of the other person. Hypnotic suggestion relies on dependence and merging with the will of the other—penetration and passivity—homosexual submission to the father, and hence is thought to reinforce dependence and "primitive" lack of differentiation.

Celia Brickman (2003), in her brilliant book *Aboriginal Populations in the Mind*, demonstrated that the origins of psychoanalysis coincided with European colonialism. She made use of postcolonial studies to show the influence of evolutionary anthropology on Freud's thinking. The racialized "primitive, savage, and barbarian," together with the religious "heathen, infidel, pagan," were the outsiders, the "not-us." Much to Freud's credit, he demonstrated that primitivity is universal: Each of us has a "primitive" part of our minds. We each carry primitivity within us. That was quite an achievement at a time when those around him saw themselves as civilized. Freud showed that we each have an ego and an id, an ego and a "Yid," a German and a Jew. The id, the unconscious, is primitive, unstructured, timeless, unbound, incapable of reason or delay, dark and feminine. This is consistent with Freud's championing of bisexuality—we each have male and female parts. We all have unconscious perversion and unconscious homosexual inclinations. This was a revolutionary idea. However, by arguing that we all have a "primitive" mind, with "primitive" drives, Freud reinforced the duality of civilized–primitive. While that duality might be universal, it remains a duality and a hierarchy.

In the Middle Ages, religion was dominant and the duality was Christian–heathen. With the advent of the Enlightenment, the human mind "matured" into "rationality" and there was a "simple reversal," in which now in "civilized" circles, to be religious was to be primitive, superstitious, or magical. In the operation of any binary, one can flip

the power relations but maintain and even reinforce the binary structure. Hence, while Christian–heathen was originally lined up with right–
wrong, heaven–hell, and mature–immature, the hierarchy was then
reversed, such that the binary became secular–Christian, lined up with
rational–irrational, and mature–immature. With increasing industrializa-
tion, the value of delayed gratification, considered by evolutionary theorists to be the mark of the civilized man, became more prominent. To
be "civilized" and adult was to be disciplined, while "primitives" were
thought to be impulsive, seeking immediate gratification. Adult–child
lined up with civilized–primitive, conscious–unconscious, White–Black,
responsible–irresponsible, and culture–nature. To be civilized was to
have a history, to live in time. To be primitive was to be prehistoric, out
of time. The unconscious, being primitive, does not know time.

All of these polarities were mapped onto male–female. Men were
considered civilized and adult, whereas women were regarded as more
like children—irrational, concrete, immoral, and impulsive. If psychoanalysis was about replacing the (Y)id with the ego (and by extension,
the superego), then it was also about dealing with our femininity. The
"bedrock" answer for both sexes was to "repudiate femininity"; for men,
the fear of castration, and for women "penis envy." For Freud, masculin-
ity was active, while femininity was passive. To be a woman (or male
homosexual) is to be passively penetrated. The masochistic wish is to be
penetrated, just as it is the wish of the "primitive" to be dominated. To
be phallic is to be the active one who does the penetrating/dominating.
To be phallic and not penetrable is to be solid, bounded, invulnerable,
and autonomous. To be female is to be penetrated, porous, vulnerable,
submissive, masochistic, and dependent. To be female is to be embodied, while to be masculine is to be cerebral, abstract, disembodied, and
therefore invulnerable, not subject to decay, castration, or death.

Ultimately, to be primitive is to be subject to domination and penetration—embodied and hence vulnerable. In analysis, this dichotomy positions the patient as primitive and the analyst as civilized. The analyst, of
course, was to be "opaque," impenetrable, and courageous. The patient
is childish, pathological, out of time and history. The dark, feminine,
unconscious is penetrated by the analyst's interpretations—the "analytic instrument." The analyst in this binary scheme is phallic, abstract,
rational, autonomous, disembodied, a blank screen, a surgeon—and
therefore not vulnerable, primitive, feminine, dark, Jewish, embodied,
or castrated.

With this background set of binaries clarified, let's return to contemporary relational theory, which is an attempt to move beyond these binary
oppositions both intrapsychically and interpersonally, itself a binary that
requires ongoing deconstruction, finding a third. Jessica Benjamin (see the

afterword to her paper in Volume 4) now speaks of three kinds of thirds. The language she has recently been using is that of the "moral" third, the "rhythmic" third, and the "symbolic" third. The rhythmic third is what she referred to previously as the "one-in-the-third," the early oneness of mother–infant as mediated by the rhythm established between them and to which they both are regulated. The symbolic third is more about the recognition of difference between the two, and the moral third—perhaps the most misunderstood, is about the sense of lawfulness and trust in reestablishing connection after disruption. Patient and therapist establish a rhythm, a steady state. At some point it inevitably breaks down and the difference between the two is highlighted. Then come repair and reestablishment of connection. This is "the law" of intersubjective life; it is about the cocreation and breakdown of patterns of mutual regulation and mutual recognition. Analysis is a study of these configurations as they are relived, reenacted, and reworked while being examined and articulated. Benjamin credits Ed Tronick and Beebe and Lachmann, who described this cycle of rupture and repair. Benjamin and I traced the origins of this approach directly to Ferenczi (see especially his *Clinical Diary*, Dupont, 1988; Aron & Harris, 1993). Ferenczi was explicit in arguing that the analyst would inevitably repeat (we would say "enact") with the patient the traumatic experiences of childhood, but unlike the earlier objects who denied their participation in the crime analysts had to take responsibility and acknowledge their participation and guilt.

Benjamin said that the analyst acknowledges the rupture and, through this nondefensive validation, reestablishes the steady state, leaving the patient with a feeling of having been recognized. The analyst's acknowledgment shows that the injury is perceived as a violation of an expectable pattern, "the law," and thus it relieves the felt emotional abandonment. Both patient and therapist "surrender" to the trust that exists between them, trust in the process, trust in love, in faith, some call it God, in something beyond them, to which they both surrender. Thus, they are not submitting to the other so much as surrendering to thirdness, to a moral law, to lawfulness itself—the law that all relationships inevitably are constituted by rupture and repair and can then go on being or be resurrected into new life. By the way, if this sounds suspiciously religious, it is. Benjamin absorbed German idealism, particularly Hegel. It reverberates with Christian theology about the Trinity but also can be traced very clearly to prominent themes in the Hebrew Bible. Karen Starr addresses these themes in her book *Repair of the Soul: Metaphors of Transformation in Jewish Mysticism and Psychoanalysis* (2008), and Marie Hoffman (2011) examines this theme in *Toward Mutual Recognition: Relational Psychoanalysis and the Christian Narrative*.

When patient and therapist are in an enactment or impasse, it often takes the form of a clash, a tug of war, a push me–pull you, doer–done to, or sadomasochistic enactment. This is precisely where Benjamin (1988) began in *The Bonds of Love*, looking at gender relations in terms of sado-masochism. When in these states, we are often dealing with binaries. Either I am guilty or I am a victim, either you started it or I did, either it's your fault or mine, either you really are withholding from me or I am too demanding, either you really let me down or I expect too much, either you are the best therapist in the world or you suck, either you are crazy or I am. Each of these is a binary and we are talking about splitting, but we are talking about two people who both get caught in splitting. This is why we call it complementarity—it is complementary splitting. Benjamin argued that the therapist needs to acknowledge the way they have hurt the patient, broken the trust or the rhythm, acknowledge how they were unattuned. Benjamin's perspective is developmental rather than technically prescriptive. She is predominantly focusing on analysts acknowledging to themselves their own participation in enactments, and also their validating the patient's sense of having been injured by them. What I have emphasized in this article is that the therapist needs to open space within herself to reflect on how she is conflicted or torn, how she can think or feel more than one way about something, and how she can open up to differences within herself; "stand in the spaces" (Bromberg, 1996) or "build bridges" (Pizer, 1998) to her own multiple self-states. For example, the therapist may be both angry with the patient and blaming himself for something. In creating some room for difference within the self, one creates triangular space or thirdness, perhaps something like what Bion (1962) meant by "binocular vision" (p. 86). Rather than being stuck in a polarization, there is some room within which to think or feel. When stuck in impasse or deadlock the analyst's search for third-ness within himself may pave the way for a shared third. In sum, what Benjamin and I are both calling for is a change in analytic sensibility from analytic opaqueness and impenetrability toward greater interpen-etrability and mutual recognition of shared vulnerability. Stated in the more contemporary language that has become associated with relational psychoanalysis and especially with the contributions of Jody Davies, Philip Bromberg, and Donnel Stern, the analyst's acknowledgment of their participation in enactments involves a form of mentalization that creates room for multiplicity and dialog among multiple self-states, within the analyst, the patient, and intersubjectively, in cocreated shared space between patient and analyst.

In her afterword, Benjamin clarifies that she never intended intersub-jectivity to be thought of as something imposed on the patient; indeed, any such attempted imposition proscribes the attainment of mutual accommodation. Similarly, let me be clear that I am not calling for self-disclosure as a prescribed technique under some simplistic rationale that it leads to thirdness or intersubjectivity. The analyst's disclosure of conflict or of multiple perspectives can, under some circumstances, be one factor in creating shared analytic space, but if a patient does not yet experience the therapist as having depth, a three-dimensional inner world, if they view themselves and others as flat, and are not yet capable of mentalization and the symbolization of difference, then such self-disclosures can just as well lead to a breakdown of containment or holding or premature disruption of bonding (Slochower, 1996). Like any other clinical intervention, these technical choices need to be considered on an individual basis. But at times it may be the analyst who opens some bit of psychic space, by giving himself or herself, and perhaps the patient as well, access to his or her own conflict and multiplicity. The dialectics of difference require permeability; the therapist implicitly or explicitly reveals something about being moved by the patient. The therapist is not masochistic or without boundaries but is penetrable, movable, reachable. Neither patient nor therapist need be phallic or castrated, civilized, or primitive. Meanings and interpretations are not given and received as much as negotiated and cocreated. Empathy and even acknowledgment are not given by the therapist but are mutual and bidirectional, even if the therapist tries to lead in some areas of conflict. Thirdness means moving beyond binary oppositions and the inevitable hierarchy that accompanies splitting, thus opening up space to think or feel.

The very opposition of binary thinking to moving beyond binaries is itself a binary; contrasting split complementarity with the third may be read as yet another binary even when it is intended to be dialectical. If it seems that while deconstructing various binaries that I have myself become stuck in binary thinking or created yet new oppositions, that is inevitable. It is the law, the law of rupture and repair, of deconstruction as an ongoing and always unstable activity, of the third not as some final resolution but as a fleeting moment.

In *A Meeting of Minds* (1996), I presented relational psychoanalysis as characterized by a variety of forms of mutuality, including mutual influence, mutual recognition, mutual resistances, mutual empathy, the mutual generation of data, and many other dimensions of mutuality, even if it was also characterized by some aspects of asymmetry in role, function, and responsibility. Here I want to add an explicit emphasis on mutual vulnerability. In acknowledging one's own permeability and vulnerability—one's embodiment, mortality, and humanity—one does not need to project all of the conflict, splitting, shame, disgust, animalistic embodiment, penetrability, and vulnerability onto the patient. Davies (2010) described relational practice as characterized by "mutual interpenetrability" and "the acceptance of vulnerability" by both patient and analyst and by the analyst's "acknowledgment of penetrability" (p. 91)—not only in the clinical interaction but also as a profession and discipline, by owning our vulnerability, attachment, and dependency, by not refuting femininity, psychoanalysis need not split itself off from psychotherapy as its inferior, shameful other. Hence, intersubjective methodology might help analysts not only with clinical impasses and stalemates but also with professional, theoretical, sexual, cultural, and historical deadlocks.

References

Aron, L. (1996). *A meeting of minds: Mutuality in psychoanalysis*. Hillsdale, NJ: The Analytic Press.

Aron, L. (2009). Day, night, or dawn: Commentary on paper by Steven Stern. *Psychoanalytic Dialogues, 19*, 656–668.

Aron, L., & Harris, A. (1993). Sandor Ferenczi: Discovery and rediscovery. In *The legacy of Sándor Ferenczi* (pp. 1–35). Hillsdale, NJ: The Analytic Press.

Benjamin, J. (1988). *The bonds of love*. New York: Pantheon.

Bion, W. R. (1962). *Learning from experience*. London: Tavistock.

Boyarin, D. (1997). *Unheroic conduct*. Berkeley: University of California Press.

Brickman, C. (2003). *Aboriginal populations in the mind*. New York: Columbia University Press.

Bromberg, P. M. (1996). Standing in the spaces: The multiplicity of self and the psychoanalytic relationship. *Contemporary Psychoanalysis, 32*, 509–535.

Butler, J. (2004). *Precarious life*. London: Verso.

Cixous, H. (2004). *Portrait of Jacques Derrida as a young Jewish saint* (B. Brahic, Trans.). New York: Columbia University Press.

Davies, J. M. (2010). Transformations of desire and despair. In J. Salberg (Ed.), *Good enough endings: Breaks, interruptions, and terminations from contemporary relational perspectives* (pp. 83–106). New York: Routledge.

Derrida, J. (1976). *Of grammatology* (G.C. Spivak, Trans.). Baltimore, MD: Johns Hopkins University Press.

Dimen, M. (2003). *Sexuality, intimacy, power*. Hillsdale, NJ: The Analytic Press.

Dupont, J. (Ed.) (1988). *The clinical diary of Sándor Ferenczi* (M. Balint & N. Z. Jackson, Trans.). Cambridge, MA: Harvard University Press.

Freud, S. (1895). Project for a scientific psychology. In J. Strachey (Ed. & Trans.), *The standard edition of the complete psychological works of Sigmund Freud* (Vol. I, pp. 281–391). London: Hogarth Press, 1950.

Freud, S. (1937). Analysis terminable and interminable. *International Journal of Psychoanalysis, 18*, 373–405.

Friedman, L. (2006). What is psychoanalysis? *Psychoanalytic Quarterly, 75*, 689–713.

Gay, P. (1987). *A Godless Jew: Freud, atheism, and the making of psychoanalysis*. New Haven, CT: Yale University Press.

Gill, M. M. (1954). Psychoanalysis and exploratory psychotherapy. *Journal of the American Psychoanalytic Association, 2*, 771–797.

Gilman, S. (1993). *Freud, race, and gender*. Princeton, NJ: Princeton University Press.

Hoffman, M. (2011). *Toward mutual recognition: Relational psychoanalysis and the Christian narrative*. New York: Routledge.

Johnson, W. (1998). The myth of Jewish male menses. *Journal of Medieval History, 24*, 273–295.

Layton, L. (1998). *Who's that girl? Who's that boy? Clinical practice meets postmodern gender theory*. Northvale, NJ: Jason Aronson.

Makari, G. (2008). *Revolution in mind*. New York: HarperCollins.

Mikics, D. (2009). *Who was Jacques Derrida?* New Haven: Yale University Press.

Nussbaum, M. C. (2010). *From disgust to humanity*. New York: Oxford University Press.

Pizer, S. (1998). *Building bridges: The negotiation of paradox in psychoanalysis*. Hillsdale, NJ: The Analytic Press.

Reiff, P. (1966). *The triumph of the therapeutic*. New York: Harper & Row.

Safran, J. D. (2009). Interview with Lewis Aron. *Psychoanalytic Psychology, 26*, 99–116.

Schofer, J. W. (2010). *Confronting vulnerability: The body and the divine in Rabbinic ethics*. Chicago, IL: University of Chicago Press.

Slochower, J. A. (1996). *Holding and psychoanalysis*. Hillsdale, NJ: The Analytic Press.

Starr, K. E. (2008). *Repair of the soul: Metaphors of transformation in Jewish mysticism and psychoanalysis*. New York: Routledge.

Wallerstein, R. S. (1995). *The talking cures*. New Haven, CT: Yale University Press.

Weedon, C. (1987). *Feminist practice and poststructuralist theory*. Cambridge, MA: Blackwell.

10

When the Frame Doesn't Fit the Picture*

Anthony Bass

▼ ▼ ▼ ▼ ▼

Consideration of the "psychoanalytic frame" typically refers to the "rules of the game," most particularly those that initiate, define the boundaries of, and provide a structure for the analytic process.

A patient, Helena, came to see me for consultation and let me know right away that she was flat broke. Atypically, she raised concerns about the way we would handle some of the arrangements that analysts consider to be part of the "frame" of the work even before she began to tell me why she wanted my help. Usually such discussions take place after I have spent at least a couple of sessions listening carefully to the prospective patient, trying to grasp something about what has brought her to see me. By then, the patient and I have started getting to know each other and have some beginning sense of how it might be to work together. Indeed, the work is already under way.

But for Helena, the troubles for which she was seeking help and the ways we could approach the work were inextricably intertwined, making it important to consider some of the ground rules right away. A recovering addict, she could commit to only one session at a time. She proposed paying at the end of each session, in cash. In her view there could be no question of paying for missed sessions, which, in response to her question, I had told her was my general and preferred practice, because between any missed session and the next one she attended she would owe me the fee for the session.

To be in debt to me would constitute a slippery slope, which she had reason to fear could send her sliding back into serious trouble, the kind that

---

* This paper originally appeared in *Psychoanalytic Dialogues*, *17*(1), 2007, pp. 1–27. Reprinted with permission.

she cautiously, somewhat skeptically hoped analysis might help her to transcend. With a history of extreme debt that went along with poly-drug abuse, her view, based on agonizing experience, was that to owe me money would be akin to using cocaine. She had been over her head in debt and variously addicted and knew all too well the seductively compelling sirens that had repeatedly lured her to self-destruction. To allow her to owe me money would also implicate me in a codependent relationship with her, which would threaten to bring us both to our knees. She told me that in debtors anonymous meetings that she attended, therapist/addicts regularly spoke about how their patients owed them thousands of dollars, enacting collusive codependent relationships in which the therapists themselves would incur great debt while waiting impotently, pathetically, for their patients' everelusive, tantalizing payment. For these therapists, each session was a roll of the dice, a chance to hope once again that their ship was about to come in and finally get them out of the debt, both literal and symbolic of the morass in which they lived with their patient, that they had themselves incurred. Professional therapists who couldn't collect fees from their patients would sit together with patients who owed their therapists money at these meetings, telling their stories, helping each other with the shared problem that they had often found themselves helpless to conquer in their own personal therapy. She wondered if I had trouble collecting money from my patients, having come to believe that such forms of codependence were a difficulty shared by many therapists. She could not afford to risk enacting that type of emotional choreography with me. I paused, thought about that for a few moments. She waited.

I inquired as to whether she had picked up something about me that worried her that way, wondering to myself whether her psychic radar had already homed in on a disavowed part of me that would be receptive to engaging in the very enactment that she both dreaded and unconsciously sought. I wouldn't have necessarily wanted to reassure her about how I would be able to handle our financial affairs in any case, preferring to first explore her apprehensions and her fantasies, but there was something about her and her question that had me feeling insecure on the point right away, imagining that in certain states of mind quite likely to emerge with her I would become part of the problem before, and hopefully on the way to, contributing to some solutions.

Her vivid descriptions of the meetings led me to sense that perhaps she had put her finger on an occupational vulnerability suffered by many who had gone down the path of becoming professional therapists. My thoughts turned to recent threads on my institute list serve, in which distressed, frustrated, angry therapists shared experiences about trying to collect fees from runaway patients. "Were small claims court and collection agencies advisable measures to take?" they queried one another on the list.

Discouragement, anger, guilt, and fear emerged in these conversations, as some advised against taking such measures lest they stir up a hornet's nest of trouble in the form of dreaded malpractice suits. "Better just leave well enough alone and write it off," some advised. These conversational threads were generally of a concrete, practice management sort, reflecting anxiety and did not engage the unconscious enactments and personal vulnerabilities on both sides that had led to a breakdown of the therapeutic process symbolized by the stemming of the flow of money for the unique and complex set of experiences that psychoanalysts offer.

Though I had not regarded collecting fees from my patients as a chronic problem, as Helena spoke, several situations began to come to mind in which a patient seemingly "suddenly" owed me several months worth of fees, enacting a problem in the transference–countertransference field that remained dissociated from my awareness until it became large enough to threaten the analytic work itself. I recalled one patient, like the cartoon character Wimpy, who would famously say, "I'd be glad to pay you Tuesday for a hamburger today." She uttered the constant refrain, "Well, you know I'll pay you eventually, don't you?" shaking her head in considerable umbrage, rolling her eyes in long-suffering, irritated impatience as she read my concern about her mounting bill as a sign that I actually distrusted her. She was mystified at the source of my distrust that kept me from relying on her evident integrity. I didn't distrust her in the way that she assumed, knowing that ultimately she would pay her fees, but I felt thwarted nevertheless, wanting her to pay her fee today so that I could pay for my hamburgers today. It took years of analysis before my point of view about payment became of interest or concern to her.

On at least one of the occasions of mounting debt that Helena's description was bringing into focus for me, the therapy ended when the patient and I belatedly realized that she could simply not pay my fee as a result of some career change choices and the related, not consciously anticipated termination of a generous insurance policy. A large debt has yet to be paid off, though once or twice a year a $100 check still floats in, folded into a flowery, perfumed greeting card with a brief note that she intends to resume therapy one day, a sign that she hasn't forgotten me and doesn't want me to forget her either.

In Helena's view, even paying me by check would constitute too great a risk to take, because a check can bounce, falsely symbolizing money that isn't actually there. Technically, then, paying me by check would be tantamount to owing me money, pending the check clearing existing until then in a potential space of bad faith. Even paying my bill at the end of the month, my usual practice, represented a form of debt, because Helena would always be in the position of owing me money for services provided until the end of any given month when payment was due.

We faced a paradox from the opening moments of the first session. We couldn't really begin our work until we reached an agreement on essential ground rules, because the ground rules themselves threatened to become implicated in an immediate collusion and enactment of threatening symptoms. Our negotiation, including our joint reflection on the establishment of these ground rules, had to be our point of entry into the work. We learned a lot about each other in the first few sessions.

An atypical set of ground rules began to emerge. If she had money that day for a session, we would work. If not, she would let me know that she was tapped out, and we would forego sessions until she could pay for one. Missed sessions would not be charged, but she would not miss any session that she could afford to pay for. We would both have to understand and bear the knowledge that any session could be our last. She would do her best to make enough money that week for a session or two (she was talented and savvy, having a track record of making a very good income when she was not spiraling out of control), but she had come to recognize that her life was best lived as a one-day-at-a-time proposition, and if I were going to be able to help her, I would have to live with that as well. Her analysis would happen one day at a time or it wouldn't happen at all, a useful life lesson that Helena began to teach me beginning with our first encounter, more than 3,000 days ago.

But the plan that was beginning to take shape in those first exploratory meetings was leaving me feeling uneasy. How would I feel having her terminate the sessions on the spot if she found that she could not pay for sessions? I worried, based in part on past experiences that she described to me, that Helena would sabotage herself and our work at a difficult or a promising moment by seeing to it that she couldn't pay. A dysfunctional week in which she wasn't earning money would immediately translate into the suspension of sessions, which could intensify her sense of failure and shame, leading to even greater paralysis and a potential spiraling into destructive self-states that had been part of the fabric of her experience.

The prospect of beginning to work together under these circumstances didn't feel altogether responsible, yet I could sense a bind. She wanted to work with me, and I felt both game and apprehensive. I imagined finding myself having to choose between leaving a patient in trouble in the lurch because of what amounted to a temporary cash flow problem and playing a role in an analysis whereby my patient and I found ourselves in the grip of a mutually destructive enactment in which her seeing me for sessions she couldn't afford led us down the road to perdition. We spoke about many of these concerns in those first few days of sessions.

I had never worked with a patient under such circumstances, and indeed, when it came to my own financial needs, I preferred a more predictable approach to structuring my practice and planning my income. Yet if I wished to work with this patient I would have to change my way of doing business. And I would have to bear the anxiety of working in a new way. So I did, and these arrangements (about payment and missed sessions) were made in a quite concrete way initially, without a great deal of attention to the meanings and symbolism held in our choices. Once we agreed on the basic ground rules for the therapy, there was a lot Helena needed to tell me about what brought her to this point in her life.

As is often the case in situations in which idiosyncratic frame arrangements take hold, aspects of the way Helena's therapy was structured helped illuminate aspects of her emergent history as well as elements of the shifting transference–countertransference field. In our work together over time, particular features of the cocreated frame and the meanings associated with them furthered exploration of analytic material as it evolved, material that illuminated features of her history as well as features of our relationship as it developed.

For example, 3 years into the therapy, the choreography of payment became once again a subject of discussion. For a woman who had difficulty with closeness to men and whose sexual history had included considerable trauma, the exchange of cash at the end of each session was a subtle maneuver. The daily handoff of money brought us but an inch or two from each other, carefully, never actually touching, a complex physical and emotional balancing act, which eventually became of interest to both of us, providing access to fantasy material that never before had been discussed and that took us to unanticipated depths.

Our awareness of the delicacy of such moments, apparently mutually dissociated until this juncture, and our newfound capacity to think about them together in the context of emerging aspects of her history and the evolving state of our relationship had not been accessible to us until much had been accomplished. Two years further into the therapy, Helena found that she preferred that I bill her at the end of the month and began paying her bill with a check, which impressed both of us as a meaningful marker of change.

The "frame" remains an essential reference point throughout any analysis. Although in one sense it is meant to create and stand for, both practically and symbolically, a therapeutic structure with clear and safe boundaries in which the process of therapy unfolds, the establishment of a frame is, at the same time, paradoxically an integral part of the process itself. That is, the establishment of the frame serves both as a relatively fixed, clearly defined container for the therapeutic work and as a point of departure for the negotiation of transference–countertransference elements, and enactments, and the working through of such enactments in an intersubjective field. Aspects of the patient's and analyst's psychic lives, and the way their relationship is taking shape, are expressed and negotiated through the establishment of a frame for their work together.

The essential shape of any given psychoanalytic process, given definition by the frame, is often set forth by the analyst as "rules" or "policies," typically most explicitly delineated at the beginning of an analysis in the first few sessions. The frame is constituted of the various arrangements that define the unique shapes, functions, and boundaries of an analysis, differentiating it from other sorts of interpersonal relationships. Although Freud never used the concept of the frame per se, and study of his published cases and reports from his patients reveal a more flexible approach to technique in his own clinical practice than his theorizing suggests, the frame of traditional psychoanalysis includes many of the elements set forth by Freud in his technical papers.

Freud recognized the necessity for establishing the frame early on in the treatment in his oft-cited metaphor of clinical psychoanalysis as a chess game, in which rules for the opening moves are more systematically formulated and easily mastered than approaches to the far more complex middle game, where play becomes increasingly subtle and the successful player relies increasingly on experience, intuition, and creative breakthroughs rather than preconceived rules to move the play forward.

The experienced psychoanalyst, like the chess master, knows the "book moves" well, and in the asymmetrical roles that analyst and patient typically assume, the analyst bears the lion's share of responsibility for managing the proceedings with these rules in mind. (It should be noted, too, that the book moves, whether in chess or in psychoanalysis, do change over time. Creative breakthroughs in technique lead to innovations in theory, which open up new possibilities for technique, eventually leading to alterations in what is regarded as standard procedure.)

Equally important, though, as Hoffman (1998) pointed out, is the option to toss out the book from time to time, to respond with spontaneity and creativity to unique features of any given patient, to feel one's way in the immediacy of experience, and to free up what may have become the constraints and rigidities of "policy." Such "acts of freedom" (see also Symington, 1983), crucial to the analyst's repertoire, are highly personal, expressive of the analyst's personality as well as his understanding of the patient, and integral to the analyst's art. Indeed I believe these rogue interpretive moments lie at the heart of therapeutic action.

Although Freud did note that subjective factors guide each analyst's preferences regarding technique and the structure of the psychoanalytic situation, starting with his own, there has been a tendency—at least among traditional American analysts who have taken up the question of the frame explicitly—to favor a relatively fixed and definitive structure for psychoanalysis. Perhaps the most prolific theoretician on the subject of the frame as an explicit reference point is Robert Langs, from whose perspective an unvarying frame must be set and maintained actively by the analyst, holding the shape and structure of the analysis and carefully interpreting any threat of compromise.

For Langs (1982), modifications of the frame, departure from classical technique (e.g., making noninterpretive interventions or indulging in extraneous or social remarks, or any form of self-disclosure), are likely to generate what he called a "misalliance" with the patient and always reflect disturbances in the analyst (countertransference difficulties) that the patient takes note of consciously or unconsciously and responds to by trying to cure, virtually always to the detriment of the process and the patient's own best interests. In such a model, self-disclosure, noninterpretive forms of participation, or varying kinds of participation in transference–countertransference enactments are regarded as destructive because they compromise traditional framing principles of anonymity, neutrality, and nongratification—all key shibboleths of Freudian analysis.

The use of the metaphor of the frame was probably introduced into psychoanalytic discourse in 1952 by the artist/analyst Marion Milner, evoking the image of a picture frame:

> The frame marks off the different kind of reality that is within it from that which is outside it, but a temporal spatial frame also marks off the special kind of reality of a psychoanalytic session. In psychoanalysis it is the existence of this frame that makes possible the full development of that creative illusion that analysts call transference. (p. 182)

So in Milner's usage, the creation of a frame represents the analyst's activity in marking off a special kind of space in which certain unusual, quintessentially "psychoanalytic" kinds of experience may occur—potential space, to use Winnicott's term. Loewald (1980), in elaborating his view of psychoanalysis as an art, and the fantasy character of the psychoanalytic situation, compared psychoanalysis to a dramatic art, in which the analyst and patient conspire in the creation of an illusion, a play (p. 355). Patient and analyst are, in a sense, coauthors of the production. If analytic work is conceived as an artistic creation fashioned by analyst and patient together, the frame, or the set design in the theatrical metaphor, also lends itself to collaborative creative effort, patient and analyst working on and with each other to achieve the right blend of materials to achieve their joint vision. As Loewald felicitously put it:

> In the mutual interaction of the good analytic hour, patient and analyst—each in his own way and on his own mental level—become both artist and medium for each other. For the analyst as artist his medium is the patient in his psychic life; for the patient as artist the analyst becomes his medium. But as the living human media they have their own creative capabilities, so they are both creators themselves. (p. 369)

Whether visual or dramatic, the artistic metaphor suggests that "function," the actualization of the shared creative effort, is paramount, whereas specific, concrete elements of frame or set are secondary, playing a supportive role to the unique therapeutic vision created by the therapeutic dyad. What are the rules, elements, shapes, and structures of the psychoanalytic situation that make for the most powerful and effective therapeutic transformations in any given collaborative process? To a great extent, the answer to the question lies at the heart of the work of any given psychoanalytic couple. Indeed, the negotiation of framing activity may, itself, be a medium carrying potential therapeutic action, in the patient's discovery of a negotiable relational world, or the development of competence in negotiation, both of which carry interpersonal and object relational implications for change (S. Pizer, personal communication).

The interpersonal and intrapsychic negotiation of how we find ways to be ourselves with one another and accept others on their own terms is a developmental achievement that psychoanalysis may be uniquely situated to facilitate through attention to the vicissitudes of the ongoing negotiation and analysis of that negotiation in the analytic situation. In the living, unfolding quintessentially generative relationship with each patient, different structures or different ways of negotiating the rules that sustain an analytic setting and process may be more or less suited to the task in any given dyad. Milner's use of the concept of "marking off" areas in which different kinds of reality operate presaged extensive theorizing in other fields about the nature and function of frames.

Gregory Bateson's influential anthropological and ethological studies on frames as containers for divergent realities led him to conceptualize psychotherapy as a kind of frame-repairing enterprise (Bateson, 1972; Bromberg, 1982). By comparing the rules of psychotherapy to that of more formally structured games, Bateson suggested the following:

> [The] process of psychotherapy is a framed interaction between two persons, in which the rules are implicit but subject to change. Such change can only be proposed by experimental action, but every such experimental action, in which a proposal to change the rules is implicit, is itself a part of the ongoing game. It is this combination of logical types within the single meaningful act that gives to therapy the character not of a rigid game like canasta but, instead, that of an evolving system of interaction. The play of kittens or otters has this character. (pp. 191–192)

In other words, in Bateson's view, the rules of psychotherapy, like that of other forms of structured but free play, cannot be clearly distinguished from the process itself. The rules are themselves in play.

Goffman's (1986) sociological study *Frame Analysis: An Essay on the Organization of Experience*, in which frames are defined as containing the rules and practices that create the context in which everyday experience is understood, introduced ways of thinking about frames well suited to considering the forms and functions of psychoanalysis. Goffman's work provides us with more flexible paradigms capable of holding and engaging the complex intrapsychic and interpersonal experiences we regularly encounter in analytic work.

Frames generate what Goffman referred to as "guided doings"; in his model, any act or behavior can really be understood only within the context of the particular frame in which it takes place, and confusion is inevitable when we try to understand experience without reference to its framing context. For example, in observing one man pointing a gun at another, Goffman observed that it would be crucial to recognize that the context of the act is a movie set rather than an actual bank robbery. Any observer's response to the scene will necessarily be different given that important piece of framing information.

Similarly, psychoanalytic moments, interactions, and choices can be understood only in the context of the particular psychoanalytic frame in which they take place Failure to take such variables into account has frequently led to the unfortunate fruitless but familiar form of psychoanalytic discourse and dissing that typically takes the form of suggesting that what the other person is doing is "not psychoanalysis." We know that many innovations in psychoanalytic technique were originally dismissed as not psychoanalytic. That is, they could not be understood without reference to the newly developing paradigm that framed them.

For example, the analyst's self-disclosure was regarded as problematic because it transgressed fundamental traditional psychoanalytic principles of anonymity and neutrality. But contemporary psychoanalytic frames of reference reconsider that prescription and replace it with a principle that suggests that self-disclosure can be helpful to the patient in psychoanalysis or problematic, depending on the specific context in which the moment is framed (Bass, 2001, p. 721). There are times when self-disclosure—especially but not exclusively of one's experience or state of mind in relation to the patient—is useful, opening up new possibilities, enriching and shaping new forms of experience of self and others while further elucidating established forms. And there are times when self-disclosure simply reenacts and reinforces entrenched ways of being, nipping change in the bud. The art of psychoanalysis resides in how well we go about trying to tell the difference and how resourcefully we are able to manage to move forward with the work when we are unsure.

When Freud (1913) set forth his own recommendations for technique, he wrote that whereas his suggestions might seem like mere details, their justification was that they were the rules of the game, acquiring importance through their connection to the whole game plan (p. 342). His rules—captured in rich metaphor of the analyst as mirror, surgeon, and interpreter of patients' dreams and unconscious life—served his plan exceptionally well, generating a unique and powerful psychoanalytic reality designed to highlight the unfolding of transference experience as drive derivatives from deep inside the patient, with minimal "contamination" by the analyst.

A century later, we are in a position to observe that psychoanalysis does not take place in a vacuum but rather evolves in particular cultural milieus, social, and intellectual contexts (J. Davies, personal communication). New frames of reference that apply to physical reality (by way of contemporary physics and field theories) and psychic reality (reflected a variety of two-person relational and interpersonal perspectives) have changed our vantage point for considering a number of psychoanalytic assumptions. Freud developed his approach in a time and place in which the analyst's authority enjoyed a different, perhaps less ambivalent standing. Parents were themselves seen as absolute authorities, and the ideal "child/patient" was expected to follow the parent's/analyst's rules as prescribed. The capacity to negotiate rules in appropriate ways, emphasizing an intersubjective field of experience, was not yet understood or valued as it is today.

From another perspective, the movement from omnipotence to an appropriate form of self-regard, for analyst and patient alike, in which both triumphs and disappointments were not only possible but also necessary, was not yet theorized. Social, cultural, and intellectual trends during the past century have contributed to the creation of new norms and therefore different analytic goals and expectations. We would expect that the rules and frames of analysis would shift to reflect such changing mores.

We have observed that different values, sensibilities, and ways of understanding the psychoanalytic project generate different psychoanalytic realities, alternate frames, other "doings." In Mitchell's (1998) terms, "Each analytic tradition has its own notion of what it is that the analyst should try to do and be: neutral, empathic, holding, containing, authentic" (p. 170). Analytic rules are relative to analytic goals. Each analyst must define and refine the relationship between the particular qualities of the frame that he creates with his patient and the goals and values that guide his psychoanalytic vision. And each analyst will construct a personal map in accordance with the particular vision that guides the doings. Each analyst's work is guided by a particular, personally constructed set of intentions.

In describing his own analytic intentions in relation to his management of the frame, Mitchell (1993) suggested:

> What is most important is not what the analyst does, as long as he struggles to do what seems, at the moment, to be the right thing; what is most important is the way in which analyst and analysand come to understand what has happened. What is most crucial is that, whatever the analyst does, whether acting flexibly or standing firm, he does it with considerable self-reflection, and

openness to question and reconsider, and most important, with the patient's best interests at heart. If the patient and analyst together find a way to construe the event constructively, as an opportunity, the process opens up and is enriched. If both end up experiencing the event as the defeat of either the patient or analyst, the process closes off and an opportunity is lost.... In short, the process itself is more important than the decision arrived at. And the process does not end at the point at which the analyst makes a decision with regard to the analysand's request.... A critical dimension of making constructive use of these situations is an openness to a continual reevaluation of their meanings over time. (p. 196)

Similarly, Coltart (1992) noted that although attention to general principles of technique is essential:

We must recognize the ever-present phenomenon that every patient is unique, and any generalized statement about how to do what, when, where and why, must always be subject to modifications in the light of the patient's uniqueness and our unique developing relationship to him and our personality.... The atmosphere of the analysis is the joint creation of the patient and analyst, and between this unique pair it grows and happens. In fact, if I were to settle for which of the pair in the therapeutic dyad has more influence than the other on the whole way of being of an analysis, I would say it is the patient. (p. 99)

From the latter vantage point, I find it helpful to recognize that I will most likely participate in the cocreation of and be guided by quite different frames of analysis in a day's work, each frame containing, reflecting, and blending aspects of the two separate and unique subjectivities engaged in an analytic process. My unconscious life with any given patient is implicated, and the unique construction of any given frame for analysis is likely to carry with it enactments of aspects of our experience that will be unlike that with any other patient. This process is itself likely become the subject of joint analytic consideration and is often highlighted when aspects of the way a frame is constructed change over time in the course of an analysis.

Because analysts work within different frames over the course of a day's work, and because different analysts work with different intentions in mind, a notion of the analytic frame is misleading and may work to the detriment of the process. Rather, analytic frames come in many different shapes and seem to be constructed out of a variety of materials, varying in intent as well as the technical details that express that intent. The notion that "one size fits all" doesn't quite fit anyone, and enacting and eventually understanding and articulating the particular ways the frame doesn't fit inevitably becomes an integral aspect of an evolving therapeutic process. A patient with whom I recently began to work commented in the midst of some negotiation of the fee that his grandfather, a wise and successful entrepreneur, used to say that a good negotiation is one in which no one is entirely happy. In our case, meeting his grandfather's criterion for good-enough negotiating, we were both sufficiently satisfied with the outcome of our negotiation, neither of us getting exactly what we wanted.

Just as physicists came to understand that light has properties of both particle and wave, psychoanalysts began to see that a frame for analysis has properties of both process and structure (Bass, 2001, p. 718). Technical issues related to the management of the frame are therefore always contextual and can never effectively operate according to "received" doctrine or prescription. Elements of process and structure move from foreground to background as the analysis unfolds.

The patient's conscious and unconscious observational and interpretive work on the analyst is an ongoing dimension of the psychoanalytic experience, whether the analyst recognizes it or not. Presumptions of a patient's naïveté regarding his analyst's psychology notwithstanding, the analyst's relation to the setting and rules of engagement with any particular patient provide a rich source of data for the patient about aspects of the analyst's personality and character as well as about the analyst's unconscious life as it shapes the contours of his relationship both to his preferred theory and to the patient.

Sometimes the process of frame construction occurs in a relatively seamless way, only faintly observed, whereas in other analyses or at other points in the same analysis, the shaping of a frame becomes a more central, consciously negotiated, or contentious aspect of the process. A frame functions to define where attention is to be directed. In the case of the picture frame, it is what is inside the frame that is worth considering. Sometimes strong differences of opinion between analyst and patient regarding what is inside the frame and what is outside become the source of impasses, stalled or failed analyses, or mutually mystifying enactments in the transference–countertransference. Sometimes they lead to fruitful working through of differences, moments of mutual analysis of transference–countertransference processes or enactments.

In one such moment in my analysis, as I anxiously pressed my analyst about his contribution to what I regarded as a disturbing enactment in our work, Benjamin Wolstein encouraged me to press on with my analysis of his unconscious countertransference by recounting a story from his own analysis with Clara Thompson. He reported that he has raised a pointed question about the meaning of something she had done in a session. She told him that its meaning was something that didn't belong there, that it was for her to sort out privately, in her own self-analysis. He quoted himself as having said to her, "Well, if it doesn't belong in my analysis, what is it doing in here?"

Impasses in analysis often represent the emergence of an incompatibility of frames; bringing such incompatibilities into joint awareness is frequently the first step toward inquiring into the possibility of a negotiation of the frame activity that can become an important part of the psychic work for both participants. Such phases of analytic work often generate considerable anxiety in both participants, as mutual blind spots and dissociative processes may begin to come into awareness in ways that can be quite disorienting at first while holding considerable potential for mutual growth.

In such situations, it can seem as though the patient and analyst have come to be living in different analyses altogether. This may have something of the feeling of a couple in a long marriage recognizing that they need to work on their marriage following the recognition that they have grown in different directions or that they no longer want the same things in the relationship as they had in the early years of their marriage. With many psychoanalyses today lasting longer than average marriages (it is not unusual for analytic relationships to outlast the marriage of both analyst and patient), changes in the relationship over time are often reflected in the need to reconsider aspects of the way the relationship is structured. Sometimes such junctures lead the therapist to seek consultation or the patient to confer with another analyst on the state of his therapy. "Can my therapeutic relationship be saved, or is it time to cut my losses and move on?" is a common theme in analytic consultation. I have heard of cases in which a patient and therapist go together to a consultant in a kind of therapeutic "couples" session. Either participant in the analytic couple may initiate a change in the frame, as either patient or analyst may be the first to feel the need to break out of a frame that no longer fits (see Symington, 1983, for some examples of this). Over the course of any long analysis, both patient and analyst will inevitably grow and change, and most likely they will have contributed in no small way to the changes each have been able to make. The relationship must grow to encompass these changing needs or it can be at risk.

Fixed and rigid frame constructions can become impediments to necessary changes in the relationship. Indeed, they are frequently implicated in the failure of an analysis to get off the ground in the first place. Too rigid a sense of the necessity of a particular kind of frame has all too often taken the form of an assessment that the patient is "not analyzable." I have seen in my practice a surprising number of patients (frequently psychoanalysts) who carry with them the scars of having been told while applying for analysis at classical institutes in New York that they were unsuitable for analysis, a diagnostic prediction that almost invariably turns out to be premature and incorrect, more a statement about disclaimed incompatible frames of reference than a genuinely psychoanalytic assessment.

My own approach to participating in the establishment of a frame in which psychoanalytic work can be initiated and has the opportunity to flourish has become increasingly elastic over these past 20 years of practice. Over time I have come to recognize that any frame for an ever-deepening analysis benefits from allowing more play to stretch and fit the unforeseen.

As the patient and analyst change, learn, and grow, the frame for analysis is likely to prove unwieldy unless it is built to accommodate surprises. Too fixed a frame may take on a Procrustean rigidity, constraining, even perverting the process, which may require struggling to cast off one carapace so that another more suitable might grow in its stead. On the other hand, too loose a frame or one too quickly abandoned might fail to provide proper engagement and traction in the process, producing a flaccid, deadened experience ill-suited to helping the patient negotiate the inner obstacles to further self-differentiation, individuation, and self-awareness.

The process of negotiating such transformations is an essential part of an approach to analysis that regards "enactments" not as pathological junctures to be avoided but as a necessary part of the creation of a therapeutic environment through which heretofore unformulated aspects of inner life and experience come into being in new ways in the immediate shared experience of patient and analyst. In other words, each unique frame construction will inevitably reflect enactments in the transference–countertransference field. But in putting too fine a point on the external characteristics that constitute an analytic frame, we threaten to turn the frame into a kind of fetish, limiting the scope, flexibility, and full potential of the intrinsic process, thereby thwarting the possibility of a living, changing, mutually engaging, and mutually transforming relationship.

In his 1928 paper on technique, Ferenczi introduced a phrase coined by his patient, "elasticity of technique." "A patient of mine once spoke of the elasticity of technique," he wrote. "The analyst, like an elastic band, must yield to the patient's pull, but without ceasing to pull in his own direction, so long as one position or the other has not been conclusively demonstrated to be untenable." (p. 95)

The yielding and pulling in Ferenczi's metaphor captures something of my experience of how a frame, or more aptly a series of transformations of framing elements, is cocreated in any given analytic process. The shape of the frame that my patients and I create both performs its function in defining the work's boundaries, and its establishment also becomes at the same time an essential part of our experience together and of each other, and so part of the data of analysis. In other words, the frame embodies the paradox of being both structure and process simultaneously.

I generally prefer to see a patient at least three times a week, with payment expected for missed sessions. I sometimes prefer that a patient use the couch (though this is less of a preference now than it was several years ago) and begin sessions telling me what is coming to mind, following with associations. Yet I find that each preference that I hold evokes recollections of multiple exceptions to any given "rule." In one case with a patient who became frozen at the beginning of sessions shortly after we began, we agreed that I would begin sessions for a period of time. A few weeks later, she resumed her initiating position, and we were able to gain some understanding of the context and meaning of her temporary paralysis. Different arrangements concerning the payment of fees, physical positions on the couch, in the chair, standing, in one case lying on the floor; arrangements about phone contacts and phone sessions, phone analyses, most recently e-mail contacts, arrangements about payment, vacations, missed sessions are all variables rather than constants.

As Pizer (1998) averred, the nonnegotiable realm in psychoanalysis is quite limited, except when a history of trauma complicates the field with the detritus of dread, hopelessness, and exploitation, creating a sclerotic condition that can be enacted at the heart of the analysis itself. Appropriate nonnegotiability is easily defined. We don't have sex with our patients or go into business together, although we all know of too many unfortunate and mutually destructive exceptions to these rules. We commit ourselves to work with our patients' best interests in mind and at heart. As best we can, we pay attention to whatever evidence we can find of our patients' and our own unconscious experience with one another, using it, ourselves, and the evolving relationship we offer in the service of deepening and enriching the process and bringing about growth and healing change.

A man came to see me following a long classical analysis in connection with a long-standing symptom that was once again plaguing him after some years of control. The context of his concern currently, however, was that he was living with cancer that had metastasized to the lung, and so his life was at a particularly vulnerable and uncertain juncture. He was seeing another therapist, a cancer specialist, for help coping with his illness, and she had concurred that he might find someone to help him with this other symptom, as they had agreed that it was important to keep on living and working out his life issues as long as he could.

He very quickly plunged into what impressed me as a remarkably deep analysis, in which some of these ground rule arrangements became the subject of a good deal of attention. Talk of an eating disorder (the presenting symptom) led to talk of sexual practices and problems, to mother, to incestuous feelings and behaviors, to mother's controlling personality, to his difficulty separating from her, a dawning recognition that he had only ever seen his father through his mother's eyes so that he never could really have his own relationship to him, and so on. The transference–countertransference field was rich and intense from the get-go. He was angry with me about my fee (higher than his psychiatrist's, a younger woman toward whom he felt a great deal of rather paternal affection) and about my stopping sessions more or less on time (which she did not and which he felt expressed her love for him, but at the same time he somewhat patronized her about it). He had a great deal to talk about and an awareness of the limits of time, and he was put out when I would stop a session before another patient had rung my bell. "Your next patient isn't here yet," he would protest.

He was drawn to and envied my relative youth, apparent health, and presumed virility, a quality he believed he lacked and about which he harbored enormous shame. Despite his protestations and his annoyance and hurt feelings with me, and perhaps because of them as well, he became deeply engaged in our sessions, deciding to stop seeing his cancer therapist so that he could devote his full energies to our work. He pushed and I pulled. Exploring his response to my fee, time arrangements, and other manifestations of boundaries to which I felt it important to hold firm for my sake, as well as for his, the frame became an important aspect of our conversations, and little by little he began to see changes in himself in relation to his own boundaries. We both came to believe that these changes, his increasing sense of self-differentiation and individuation, had something to do with confronting our differences, our unique ways of being, forged under the pressure of time constraints.

He began to respond to friends differently. He took enormous pleasure from the way in which old acquaintances were now becoming real friends, showing up at his house for visits that really meant something to him and, he knew, to them. He told me with a sense of wonder that he had many more real friendships than he had ever had before, and he knew and took pride in his sense that these changes started with the changes in himself that he was beginning to feel from the inside out. He was able to be clearer with his wife about his own needs, and his relationship to food began to change. He was developing a new (his own) relationship to his father and separating from his mother, both long dead. He was becoming more open with his wife and friends, finding bittersweet richness in his life and in our psychoanalytic explorations.

After awhile, his illness progressed further. The cancer metastasized to the bone, breaking some of them so that he was in great pain, and he couldn't get around anymore. He wouldn't be able to come to sessions. Would I consider coming to his house to continue the analysis, he wondered. Now questions pertaining to the ground rules for analysis existed in a different context, as a new set of meanings took central stage. Intimacy, love, and loss became central themes, and my presence at his bedside as he approached death became an enormously important symbol of where he and we had come to.

He recognized that he had become important to me and that my coming to his house for sessions was now a necessity that we both felt. Our relationship no longer seemed defined by the particular asymmetries that defined some of our earlier discussions of ground rules. Sensing that I was struggling with feelings about losing him, he asked me if I had someone to talk to about all this, my own therapist or supervisor.

I felt grateful for his recognition and sensitivity to my feelings for him, and I said that I would have access to that sort of help when I needed it but that it was also helpful for us to be able to talk about what we were feeling and going through together in our sessions. He came to feel that I had changed as much in our time together as he had and that the changes that our sessions along with his life circumstances had brought about in him had had a complementary and positive effect on me. He could see that I had changed too. My flexibility and responsiveness to his needs regarding how we could conduct our sessions were only part of what he had observed in me that he felt reflected my own growth with him. And, of course, I knew that he was right.

Each psychoanalytic relationship carries with it the potential to engage and promote newly evolving aspects of both patient and analyst, which may be reflected in transformations of an evolving analytic frame. This may be particularly the case in long analyses in which the extended deep and intimate engagement of two personalities at conscious and unconscious levels brings about mutual personality change that is felt at the heart of the process and that reverberates at the very core of the structure of the work itself.

The following vignette is intended to capture something of the complex and evolving shaping and reshaping of a custom-made frame meant to provide a full-enough context for an analysis that spanned many years of change. A striking young woman, Nicole, started treatment some years ago. Recently relocated to New York City, she let me know in the initial phone conversation, as she (accurately) heard in my voice some uncertainty as to whether I could begin with a new patient, that she could be quite flexible about time and that my fee would not be a problem either. She was anxious to work with me because of a strong recommendation that had come from a trusted friend who also told her that I tended to be busy and might not have time available, so she wanted me to know that it would be worth my while to work with her.

Several elements of the frame of Nicole's analysis became of interest early in the consultation and quickly came into play in enacting various aspects of our psychic life together in what would become an extensive exploration of the role of money, boundaries, exploitation, control, need, and power. She reported an erotic dream in the second consultation hour in which I appeared undisguised as a workman in her apartment whom she paid for sex. She made it clear that she was quite prone to "acting out" and that traditional therapeutic frames had failed to hold her in the past. She had an affair with a former therapist, initiated by her as she reported it, one that she reported as having been in no way disturbing, let alone traumatic. Surprisingly, she appeared to regard the experience as quite positive, with no hard feelings or any sense of betrayal, though it later emerged that she herself had used sex on a number of occasions to betray her partners. In fact, she grew impatient and frustrated with my apparently uptight attitudes about such arrangements and my tiresome, irritating need to clarify with her that my approach to analytic work excluded them.

Her frame and mine often seemed distinctly at odds, leading to conflict in early sessions, at times to disturbing effect. One day I was blinded at her arrival, seeing nothing but spots as I opened the door, stunned, disoriented, and upset as I took a moment to realize that she had taken my picture with a flash camera as she entered the room. She told me she intended to use the photo so that she could look at it and soothe herself at night in bed when she was feeling stressed and lonely. She could use it to help her go to sleep. She felt that my presence in this quite concrete form would provide necessary relief, better than taking a Valium. She was perplexed and more than a little wounded by my less than enthusiastic response to her snapping my picture, a unilateral act, neither negotiated nor discussed. She wasn't sure if my difficulty with it stemmed from some personal difference between us, or something about my view of analysis, or maybe I felt that she was just "acting out." Like my original ambivalence on the phone, my response suggested to her that she loved me more than I loved her, wanted me more, something that she often felt in her relationships.

We had agreed to begin analysis three times a week, and though she could easily afford my fee she did have some concerns about spending that much money on herself. She had access to considerable financial resources, having inherited a substantial amount of money, and lived a lifestyle that included expensive apartments and vacation homes, but she had presented among her initial self-reflections the paradox that despite great resources and expenses she would have enormous difficulty spending a few hundred dollars on a handbag that she liked. Although enormously wealthy, she didn't believe she deserved to spend money on herself, because not having earned the money she didn't really think it was hers to spend. Nevertheless, she agreed to pay my fee.

A complication arose, however, as we tried to work out arrangements about missed sessions. She had houses in a number of vacation spots around the world and liked to use them for a couple of weeks at a time. When I told her that I generally charged for missed sessions, she let me know that arrangement would be impossible for her. It was not that she couldn't "afford it," but psychologically, to pay for a session that she was already missing would be adding insult to injury, somehow like missing a session twice. It was bad enough to be missing it once. This concern became an occasion for some exploration of her somewhat dissociated sense of agency, as it was difficult for her to fully identify with the fact that she could choose to stay in New York for sessions if she preferred. Her traveling schedule was a given, organized by a part of her that had quite different needs from the part of her that would have a terrible feeling of loss about missing sessions.

Efforts to explore her experience of this and to grasp the distressing meanings associated with "choosing" to travel and yet acknowledging the missed sessions (and my missed income and my economic needs) in the form of payment to me didn't take us very far, other than to highlight some aspects of a kind of dissociative quality to her experience. In Bromberg's (1998) terms, she was having some trouble standing in the spaces between her loss of the session and her need to be away, and perhaps the reality and impingement of her analyst's economic needs. As we considered our options, I felt that we were facing a possible impasse. I did not relish the idea of holding hours open for her for a couple of weeks at a time to accommodate her traveling schedule, and she could not bear to pay for sessions that she had already "paid" for by "having to miss."

I felt stumped, holding my ground for the moment but wondering whether I would feel impelled to draw a line in the sand about my typical preference that patients pay for missed sessions, which could threaten to terminate the work before it had begun and before either of us were in a position to understand what is was that we might be enacting. Out of an extended silence, uncomfortable (at least for me) she proffered a novel suggestion, one I had never encountered in the first 15 years of practice. Could she "make up" sessions in advance? If she knew she would be away, could she put in extra sessions in the weeks prior to her leaving?

As we explored the concrete practicalities as well as the more nuanced meanings to her of this arrangement, the following proposal began to take shape. Because she would often be away a couple of weeks at a time, it wouldn't be practical to make up that many sessions in the week or two prior to her trip. So, she suggested, what about the idea that we could meet four times a week rather than three, with the fourth session each week being banked as a makeup session against future misses. She would, under that arrangement, technically still be in a three-times-a-week analysis but stockpiling makeup sessions against future absences.

Having some hours open, I agreed to this arrangement, though not without considerable reflection, with her, both prior to and following the change, on some meanings and feelings associated with our new approach. Did her making up the sessions in advance provide a magical solution to the problem of loss or the terrible sense that she was missing out on something? Did our arrangement mean that she didn't have to feel those feelings, that she wouldn't have to take responsibility for her choice to travel and miss sessions, or that she could avoid feeling angry with me for my greed and stubbornness? Did it take me off the hook of feeling that I was exploiting her by charging her for so many unused sessions, enforcing a unilateral paid vacation policy for me that I secretly relished? Did it mean that I could avoid feeling guilty about charging her for many sessions that she would not use or that I could elude being the object of her anger and disappointment, depriving her of the opportunity to express such feelings? Were we colluding in dissociating feelings that might have arisen about missing sessions on the weeks that she was away by treating the "extra" sessions as substitutes rather than fully facing and acknowledging the reality that we were doing analysis four times a week? Much ground was covered in these explorations, while I sensed that other soil remained untilled.

Nevertheless, it wasn't evident to me at the time that her suggestion was any less tenable, to use Ferenczi's guideline, than my preferred approach, and I could find no compelling reason not to arrange things as she required. She seemed pleased and surprised that I took her experience of the matter and her suggestion seriously, and analytic work continued, including, of course, some ongoing exploration of the experience of our way of negotiating and working out what had seemed to be a difficult problem. She was moved to feel that I was taking her needs seriously and that I could modify my approach in response to her creative solution, about which she felt considerable pride and gratitude. She was pleased that she was able to provide a solution that both of us could accept. It brought to mind and into the analysis other successful solutions that she had found in the past and became an occasion for her filling me in on forms her creativity had taken in successful business ventures as well as exploring how it was that her creative assertiveness had gone missing in recent years. Her pleasure gave way to intense sadness as she came into contact with what an unusual experience it was for her to get what she needed and to participate actively in negotiating a solution that could potentially work out well for her.

After a couple of years, the work had deepened. Nicole began to feel that the arrangement no longer felt right to her. After all, it was now clear to her that a four-time-a-week analysis is what she needed and counted on. It didn't really hold water any longer to operate under what now seemed clearly an illusion of a three-time-a-week format, with makeup sessions. Fewer than four sessions a week no longer felt that it met her needs, so now the fourth session no longer felt valid as a makeup session. It was not fair to me then to regard it as such. She wondered whether the solution might be to start coming five times a week, the fifth session playing the role of the extra makeup one, but that didn't feel quite right or necessary to either of us. By now she was opting to be in New York more so as not to miss sessions, and our relationship had evolved to the point that missed sessions no longer evoked the same anxiety that they had earlier, so we agreed that she would now pay for missed sessions, as was my usual custom.

That worked well for a while, but then we entered a period in which she would miss sessions with some frequency for one reason or another, and I could rarely make them up due to a very busy clinical schedule; I never had an hour available on the only day that she did not have an appointment. When she realized that I was thinking in terms of making up sessions on days that we had not already met, she questioned another fixed aspect of frame: once-a-day meetings. It had never occurred to me to meet with a patient twice on the same day, with the occasional exception of double sessions when conditions warranted it, unless he or she was in special need or crisis and a second session seemed crucial. But in response to her suggestion that two sessions in a day could be just as useful to her as two on contiguous days, we did try that on several occasions when an hour became available. It generally turned out to be extremely fruitful, an alternative that never would have occurred to me without her direct intervention and one that I have subsequently integrated into my repertoire of clinical options.

But because even that solution was most often impossible to arrange, she was again feeling disturbed by my inability to offer makeup sessions. By now it was becoming increasingly clear that the issue was not really about money at all. She realized that she felt tantalized by my policy that I would make up sessions when able. We discovered this by way of her associations to an older sister (and later to her father as well), who had always promised to be there for her in a variety of ways but who, when push came to shove, would invariably let her down.

This issue was further elaborated in yet another transference–countertransference enactment. Nicole expressed interest in taking a painting class that would interfere with one of her sessions, about once a month or so. She wished to change the hour on a regular basis to make it possible to take the class, but no alternative hours were open. As we explored the situation, her distress mounted about having a regular hour that she would once again face missing on a regular basis. Perhaps she would just drop the class (which I hoped she wouldn't do) or drop the session altogether (for what seemed like complicated and overdetermined reasons). After several sessions of exploration of the problem and its meanings, seizing on one of the several obstacles that had come up in our exploration of the matter, I was finally moved to say "OK, how would it feel if when it comes to that particular event I won't charge you for those sessions you miss to attend it?"

To my surprise (obviously a countertransference blind spot in its own right, as retrospectively, it is surprising that I was surprised), this was far from a satisfying solution, as she realized immediately that every month or so she would have to choose between the class and our session and go through the anguish of giving up one or the other. Either way it was spoiled. If she chose the seminar she wouldn't get as much out of it because of the feelings of loss regarding the session and vice versa. In either case, she would be tantalized, frustrated, and ultimately saddened by the sacrifice. What I consciously intended as a flexible solution that would meet both of our needs (I was happy to have an occasional open hour) turned out to be a much more complicated matter that brought into focus unattended aspects of the transference–countertransference and the fact of loss and the inevitability of her mourning.

She found my proposed solution to be quite tantalizing and frustrating to her and expressed a preference that I simply stop attempting to make up sessions altogether, the most galling part of my "policy," and that rather than charging for them I should simply raise my fee to the point that the economics of it would not be burdensome. Her suggesting that I raise my fee brought into focus another complicated issue that I had avoided up to this point. I became aware on her suggestion that I had indeed not raised her fee in quite some time, as fees for new patients and other ongoing patients had in fact gone up. It wasn't clear to me exactly why I had hesitated to raise hers, but I did reveal to her as we explored our experience of this situation that I would actually like to raise her fee but that that would not resolve the issue of how we should handle missed sessions.

The disclosure that I had delayed raising her fee led into what seemed like a most revealing exploration of the ways she recognized that subtle suggestions on her part might have contributed to discouraging me from raising her fee. She also hypothesized that I might have held back because my full fee at four sessions a week would mean that she would be paying me a really substantial amount of money every month and that I might have hesitated to create a situation in which I would feel so dependent for income on a single patient. This impressed me as an intriguing and quite plausible bit of analysis. But she also viewed my semiconscious responsiveness to her pressure not to raise her fee as a reflection of my concern about her, and the outcome of our mutual analysis at this juncture was that she agreed to the fee change and was able to separate its meaning from the question of how missed sessions would be managed. But as the work proceeded, other dimensions of this enactment came into focus, and more work on the various forms of mutual care, control, suggestion, tantalization, dependency, and loss followed. Explorations of all of these themes weaved back and forth between her life with me in the transference–countertransference field of our experience and many places in her relationships outside of analysis.

During this same period, while these changes and the work that was taking place around them were leading me to think more about how we might gain access to the meanings of complex enactments and the potential for therapeutic gains in the context of fluid and changeable frames in the analytic situation, what appeared to be an uncanny moment transpired, which suggested to me the title for this essay. As my patient lay on the couch, gazing at the painting on the wall in front of her—a painting showing several different doors off a hallway, some slightly ajar, some closed, others ambiguous—she suddenly said, "Is that a new frame for that picture?

The frame seems different." How do you mean? I asked. "It seems somehow lighter. Has it always been that light wood? I have never noticed this before. I know I have seen that picture and frame a thousand times, but somehow, now it doesn't seem to fit that picture."

Indeed, this interaction took place at a moment in our work in which the particular arrangement about missed sessions and how they were being handled felt to her that it was not quite right anymore. It just didn't seem to fit, and her projection of that feeling onto the literal frame that had been hanging on the wall in front of us both since we had started our work together several years earlier became a point of entry into the question of what sort of frame fit our picture best at this particular juncture. As I recognized that there was something about our arrangement that perhaps we had both outgrown and no longer seemed to fit either of us, Nicole felt extremely relieved and felt that I had understood something about her that had not been recognized before. A few days later, she looked at the picture again and couldn't remember what had felt wrong about the frame such a short time before.

The lack of fit between the frame and the picture could then be explored, not simply as a concrete illusion perhaps attributable to the change of light and shadow in the autumn afternoon of her session but as a symbolic representation of our work that seemed to have something to do with changes that had taken place in her, that allowed greater freedom and flexibility. She was also convinced that changes in me as a result of my work with her were also being reflected, and she spent some time enumerating the ways that she had seen me change and grow and what she had contributed to these changes. In one of several notes that she wrote to me for the first couple of years after ending her analysis, she told me that her life was going well, that she had married, was happy, and looked upon our work as having helped her in many different ways. But she also observed that one of the things that had been especially helpful was her sense that I had changed too and that there had been ways that her insights into my personality had helped me as well.

Each analysis bears innumerable roads not taken, and it is of course one of the existential realities of our work that it is impossible to know how any analytic relationship would have evolved given different choices along the way. In every analysis worth its salt, both participants change along the way for having encountered one another. Nicole expressed a sense that her analysis with me, with all the shifting arrangements of frame that marked different phases of the work, had made possible deeper and more transformative experiences than many of her past therapeutic efforts had yielded. In accordance with what I have discovered about myself with my patients over the course of these extended relationships in analysis, analyses guided by principles of elasticity and flexibility of a frame intended to facilitate ongoing development and negotiation of a relationship seem to offer the greatest opportunity for mutual personal transformation. I believe that, within the surface negotiation of the frame, deep consolidation of a wide variety of intrapsychic and intersubjective elements are being created, worked through, and recreated, to the ultimate benefit of both participants.

References

Bass, A. (2001). Mental structure, psychic process, and analytic relations: How people change in analysis. *Psychoanalytic Dialogues, 11*, 717–725.

Bateson, G. (1972). *Steps to an ecology of mind.* New York: Ballantine.

Bromberg, P. M. (1982). The supervisory process and parallel process in psychoanalysis. *Contemporary Psychoanalysis, 18*, 92–110.

Bromberg, P. M. (1998). *Standing in the spaces: Essays on clinical process, trauma, and dissociation* (pp. 95–110). Hillsdale, NJ: The Analytic Press.

Coltart, N. (1992). On the tightrope: Therapeutic and non-therapeutic factors in psychoanalysis. In *Slouching towards Bethlehem* (p. 99). New York: Guilford.

Ferenczi, S. (1928). The elasticity of psycho-analytic technique. In M. Balint (Ed.), *Final contributions to the problems and methods of psychoanalysis.* New York: Bruner/Mazel.

Freud, S. (1913). Further recommendations in the technique of psychoanalysis. In *Collected papers* (Vol. 2, No. 8). New York: Basic Books, 1959.

Goffman, I. (1986). *Frame analysis: An essay on the organization of experience.* New York: Harper & Row.

Hoffman, I. Z. (1998). *Ritual and spontaneity in the psychoanalytic process: A dialectical-constructivist view.* Hillsdale, NJ: The Analytic Press.

Langs, R. (1982). *Psychotherapy: A basic text.* New York: Aronson.

Loewald, H. W. (1980). Psychoanalysis as art. In *Papers on psychoanalysis.* New Haven, CT: Yale University Press.

Milner, M. (1952). Aspects of symbolism in comprehension of the not self. *International Journal of Psychoanalysis, 33*, 181–194.

Mitchell, S. A. (1993). *Hope and dread in psychoanalysis.* New York: Basic Books.

Mitchell, S. A. (1998). *Influence and autonomy in psychoanalysis.* Hillsdale, NJ: The Analytic Press.

Pizer, S. A. (1998). *Building bridges: The negotiation of paradox in psychoanalysis.* Hillsdale, NJ: The Analytic Press.

Symington, N. (1983). The analyst's act of freedom as agent of therapeutic change. *International Review of Psychoanalysis, 10*, 283–291.

11

The Black Man and the Mermaid

*Desire and Disruption in the Analytic Relationship**

Dianne Elise

This paper considers the impact of desexualization of the maternal on the development of female sexuality. A "chance encounter" revealing a desire in the female analyst, previously unsuspected, disrupts a female patient's prior sense of homoerotic immersion with the analyst. I argue that a girl's would-be oedipal competition is encased within a patriarchal structuring of sexuality where the mother is rendered solely reproductive and preoedipal, not erotically sexual. I examine the meanings for a patient of internalizing a female figure, her analyst, who is viewed as both maternal *and* sexual. I suggest that a female sense of genital inadequacy and inferiority may have a component of not being able to link the mother's (and in the transference, the analyst's) use of her genitals with her use of her mind/maternal function. I unfold a thesis regarding maternal desexualization that I believe, given mother–infant symbiosis, has rather extensive applicability, and that can lead to viewing any third party as a "dark" interloper.

***

My patient tells me, "In my mind, I talk with you all the time, while I'm brushing my teeth, eating lunch with a friend, making love with my husband, when I wake in the middle of the night—*then* I really have to stop myself because I could go on all night talking to you and never get any sleep. I have to tell myself over and over, like a mantra: you can talk to Dr. Elise tomorrow, you can talk

---

* This chapter originally appeared in *Psychoanalytic Dialogues, 17*(6), 2007, pp. 791–809. Reprinted with permission.

with her tomorrow. I have this intense desire to be speaking to you, almost incessantly. You've become my constant companion. Is this weird, is this what's supposed to happen? Am I abnormal?"

So began a Monday session with my favorite patient. Yes, I confess—my favorite patient. I hesitate to say "favorite." I imagine readers thinking, "She's not supposed to have a favorite patient; something's wrong with that."* But, if truth be told, I almost always have a favorite patient (or two). It makes my professional life feel especially alive, adds excitement and spice to my workday. I am reminded of the crush I had on Scott Courtney all through eighth grade. The academic year was much more fun; every day I looked forward to my encounters with Scott as compensation for the grind of geometry. So yes, I do have favorite patients. Is this weird, not supposed to happen? Am I abnormal?

This particular patient's focus on me has become especially intense and passionate, and it represents, I believe, an unleashing of her creative energies by the analysis—energies previously held in check but now bursting forth. In addition to my belief that this intensity is a positive development for the patient (and later in the paper I detail developmental theory, and her own history, in support of this claim), I also just enjoy this energy. I like intense people. I am intense, and this passion for passion is something that this patient and I share. But we are both questioning whether we are allowed to let this amount of desire into our relationship. She is a clinician herself, so she can easily match me in pathologizing our enthusiastic preoccupation with one another. The difference is that she does not know, at least consciously, about my desire for her desire, for her engagement with me.

The Mermaid

The initial year of the analysis had involved a slipping into themes of mutual immersion in a watery world. She recounted a girlhood game of swimming underwater for as long as possible, imagining herself to be a mermaid, twisting and turning with legs and feet held together in a flutter kick. This memory developed into a transference fantasy that she and I were mermaids, and, similar to dolphins with wet slippery skin, we glided around each other and together swayed in ocean waves and swells. Although we also encountered

---

* The topic of favorite patients, raising many interesting issues, merits a paper in itself. The professional persona of generalized care and concern for each patient seems to lead to the belief that having favorites is inappropriate. Yet given the immense variability in connection between any two people, how could it be otherwise? In my clinical example here, I am highlighting the parallel (not equity) in the transference and countertransference in intensity of focus, with the sense of abnormality and confession that often attends such passion. See Elise (2002) regarding the transgressive element in passion.

stormy seas and our share of rocky shores, I viewed this transference fantasy as a productive regression to early, preoedipal engagement—a womb-like, oceanic bliss.* We swam in the unconscious and in a sea of sensuality and erotic attachment—a primary maternal preoccupation, the preoccupation the baby has with the mother as well as vice versa.

In Winnicott's (1956) version of primary maternal preoccupation, the erotic connection between mother and infant is not the focus. However, as Wrye and Welles (1994) have written, a preoedipal erotic environment exists between mother and baby (see also Laplanche, 1970; Stein, 1998; Bollas, 2000). I have described the nursing couple as engaged in the first, primitive act of intercourse, with breast-feeding sexually stimulating for infants of both sexes as well as for the mother (Elise, 1998b; see also Kohout, 2004). With mother and daughter, we encounter various levels of female homoeroticism: the early sensuous contact of the nursing couple, elements of which develop throughout the preoedipal period and eventually extend into a more focused genital and romantic desire for the mother, traditionally labeled the negative oedipal complex. I prefer to think of this complex as the primary maternal oedipal situation—given maternal caretaking, first both temporally and in archaic intensity for the girl (as well as for the boy; Elise, 2000)†

In clinical work, we see that mother–daughter eros unfolds into multiple and shifting expressions of erotic transference at each level. As the work with my patient progressed, I experienced preoedipal erotic transference as oscillating, like seaweed in the waves, with a more genital, oedipal-level erotic transference. Reminiscent of descriptions in Irigaray's (1990) work, we were wet, pressing up against one another in an ebb and flow of excitements in our moist realm. Of course, as in development, this mother–daughter mermaid silkiness was to be disrupted, but neither my patient nor myself was prepared for the particular form this rupture would take.

The Black Man

In an agitated manner, my patient rushed to the couch and began speaking before her head hit the pillow: "I was coming out of a movie theater last night with my husband and two kids. You were walking along holding hands with a tall black man!" After a slight pause, as if waiting for me to account for myself, she continued

---

* It is interesting to note that, in French, *mer* (sea) and *mère* (mother) are indistinguishable in sound (Tseelon, 1995). (Also that in English, without the accent, the meaning is reduced to "mere"—a minimalization that dovetails with my thesis regarding maternal sexuality.)

† Klein (1928) introduced the concept of oedipal "situations," a formulation that allows for the multiplicity actually present in development.

her astonished accusations: "You were wearing a short black skirt, a low-cut top in wild colors and 'come fuck me shoes'! He moved his hand around your waist, almost on your butt. I just about screamed to my husband, Is *that my analyst?!* And who is that black man? I heard that man say something to you; I don't think he's from this country; he had an accent; he's a foreigner."

After another very brief pause when I again said nothing, she began exploring her reactions to this event: "I'm astounded; I'd been thinking you might be gay. This experience sure squelches that idea.... Maybe it wasn't really you. I don't suppose you'll tell me. Could I have been mistaken? Analysts aren't supposed to dress like that. I've never seen you looking like that. You always wear long, flowing things, like the outfit you have on now. Your body is always covered up. I've never been real clear about the outline of your figure. Well that's sure changed! You left nothing to the imagination last night! That *was* you, right? *Unbelievable!* Here I'm leaving a family-oriented animation film while you're strutting your stuff into some divey blues bar."

I noted to myself, beneath the overt astonishment and possible condemnation, muffled tones of both envy and jealousy. She went on to recount what she imagined me doing the rest of the evening and night— my having a wild and sexy time. Becoming more subdued, she posed another question:

> P: So what *is* your orientation? I don't know anymore if you're homosexual, heterosexual, or bisexual.
> A: Just that I'm sexual. And something about *that* is disturbing to you.

Although I sounded calm in this, my first, comment of the session, I was extremely relieved that my patient was on the couch and could not see my face or expression and that I had almost 40 minutes to figure out what my expression would/should be by the time she looked at me as she left the session. As I listened to this material, I did not know whether I was being positioned to feel defiant or shamed, self-assured or caught out in some "slutty" behavior that for complex reasons is felt to be completely at odds with my identity as an analyst. Later, in writing this paper, and upon considerable reflection, I decided that I would say nothing here (as with the patient) about whether it was actually *me* who she saw—a parallel ambiguity with which you as the reader might play. In what follows I take up the material, as I did in the treatment, as real in the world that counts—the patient's internal world.

With the arrival of the foreign black man, so arrived my sexuality— equally foreign—into the treatment and the patient's awareness. She had been thinking I "might be gay." I understood this conjecture as not solely her musing on my lifestyle but as significantly influenced by the transference–countertransference dynamic of mother–daughter erotic merger where my sexuality was an implicit and muted response to her(s). Now my explicit, adult heterosexuality had intruded to challenge her transference fantasy of our homoerotic coupling.

For my patient, *my* desire had come into the room—my desire for this man and my dressing to be desired by him, our sexuality evident, in "public view." A desire in the female analyst previously unsuspected by this female patient was now quite apparent and was disrupting her sense of our prior "gay" immersion in one another. The analyst's desire for someone other than the patient was a passion unforeseen, and most definitely unwelcome. The mermaids were knocked out of the water. I seemed no longer to be one molded piece from the waist down; while I was swishing my tail walking down the street, it seemed clear I would soon have my legs *apart*. My outfit had announced me to my patient, and no doubt more generally, as a woman who has a sexuality. My patient had thought homosexual, sees heterosexual, concludes in favor of bisexual, but undoubtedly I had now become sexual, and that was clearly the most disturbing "orientation." Referring to her wild fantasies regarding the remainder of my evening, she acknowledged, "I was awake all night wondering what you were doing!"

It is not uncommon for patients to come into a session saying they have just had sex. What about the analyst; have you or I just had sex? And what difference might it make? The question rarely seems to enter anyone's mind. Why? My patient regularly recounted to me her sexual experiences with her husband as well as fantasies about other men. A subtle assumption prevailed of her having all the men and of me having none. She had once remarked, "The world is divided into two kinds of people—those who are having sex and those who aren't." "Which group am I in?" I inquired. Taken aback, my patient stammered, "Uhh ... I hadn't thought about *you*. I *guess* you have sex, but I can't quite imagine it. It doesn't seem to fit in with my experience of you. But I can't see why you wouldn't be having sex; I definitely think of you as in a relationship. It's weird; I don't know; it doesn't seem to compute somehow."

What does it mean for psychoanalysis and sexuality that the practitioners, especially the women, I believe, are too often seemingly celibate— that the analyst's sexuality is so back-pedaled?* What would happen, not happen, if female analyst and sexy were not, in some general sense, an oxymoron? A group of close women colleagues "let their hair down" and acknowledged (admitted?) previous and/or other "lives": The collected "résumé" included various sexy roles in theater productions, belly dance and flamenco, nude modeling in art school, and the occasional cocktail waitressing in French maid outfits and the like. There was a sense of perverse glee at the astonished looks. But why are

---

* Of course, how various female analysts experience themselves and are perceived will differ depending on individual dynamics in themselves and in particular patients. I am trying to identify a generalized lacuna, or selective inattention, on the part of both patients and analysts.

these activities *so* astounding if not for their dystonic relation to the professional ego ideal? What is the meaning to the work we do that there tends to be an underlying attitude in patients and colleagues alike that analysts are not sexy people and that is how it *should* be—a superego prohibition buttressed by some mutually agreed-upon "analytic identity." We tend to play our analytic identity as asexual. "Neutrality" can devolve into neutered.

When considering the (a)sexual persona of the analyst, we get into issues regarding the Freudian "surgical" model versus the object relational shift in theory and technique to a maternal holding environment, analyst as containing function versus penetrating/stimulating interpreter. Also relevant are variations due to geographic, historical, and cultural differences. But basically I focus here on gendered differences in generalized expectations for analysts. For the female analyst, sexy is often seen as disempowered (the familiar film representation where the woman analyst falls out of her professional role into the patient's arms), whereas male analysts can be viewed as phallically powerful, both directly sexually and metaphorically. Of interest, if perceived as phallically powerful, a female analyst is likely deemed not sexy (with Dr. Melfi of *The Sopranos* a rare exception). Like women more generally, female analysts are vulnerable to the "dumb blonde" caricature where sex and thinking are split. We think of sexy and thoughtful or intelligent as opposed *in women* but not in men. A *key* subset of the general lack of subjectivity accorded to the mother (Benjamin, 1988), sexy and maternal just do not go together in many minds. A difficulty exists in making this charged affective link, placing as it does so much power in one place. What is the impact of this desexualization of the maternal on the development of female sexuality in successive generations of daughters?

The daughter is in a double bind; she wants to compete sexually with mother for the desire of the oedipal father, yet, as Benjamin (1988) emphasized, she also needs to be able to internalize a sexually empowered mother. Many have noted the absence of positive maternal figures in myths and fairy tales; the "good" mother is often dead or has disappeared, replaced by a witch or wicked stepmother (see Dinnerstein, 1967). Rarer still is the active presence of a "sexy mom." In the myth of Persephone and Demeter (see Holtzman and Kulish, 2003) a good mother exists, for half the year, but she is not in a sexual relationship, and Hades, a paternal figure, is having sex with the daughter, Persephone.

The Phantom Father Figure

In pursuing the theme of the Black Man, my patient and I uncovered her sense that my sexuality was foreign and located in this man from some far-away country. (I now capitalize Black Man to indicate a fantasy theme in the material.) In the analysis I was certainly going to take up and work with the patient's material as it unfolded for her. In writing this paper, I want to address directly, versus further entrench, the racism in the familiar sexual stereotype of black men. My patient is white, as am I. Our presumed encounter on the street would likely have taken on a number of different symbolic meanings if either one or both of us were black ourselves.

A long history exists of projecting sex, deemed as bad, onto "lesser," devalued others. Typically sex has been designated female, dark, and foreign by the white, male paterfamilias. (From this vantage point, women of all colors and black men have often been in the same "slutty" boat.) Thus it is especially worth noting that when sex transforms and becomes something good to have—sexual subjectivity and agency—it changes gender and is attributed to men.* Central to my argument here, is a need shared by people in many cultures to project sex away from the "pure white" Madonna-like mother onto *anyone* else. A man of whatever race is "foreign" and "dark" to the familiar glow of preoedipal symbiotic experience. Clearly, the issue of racial stereotyping is incredibly nuanced and deserves much further articulation in the analytic literature (see Altman, 2000; Leary, 2000; Josephs & Miller, submitted). My intent here is to analyze the patient's fantasies and associations and to unfold a thesis regarding maternal desexualization that I believe, given mother–baby symbiosis, has rather extensive applicability and that may lead to viewing any third party as a "dark" interloper.

For my patient, my companion's unfamiliar accent, language, and dark good looks evoked associations to Zorro, Dracula, and Phantom (of the Opera), each a man of the night. Erotic, scary, enticing, exciting, a sexually powerful male arrives and then departs in the dark (the "Midnight Marauder" as one patient put it; Holtzman and Kulish, 2003). But he may never let you go. My patient recalled being captivated with the film versions *Bram Stoker's Dracula* and *The Phantom of the Opera*. In exploring these two stories, we noticed intriguing parallels in the plots. The title figure (entitled patriarch) is a threatening but sexually exciting, dark man who is not quite human—who "seems a beast, but secretly dreams of beauty" (*Phantom;* Hart and Webber, 2004a). He prowls only at night, fearful to all but also erotically enthralling to the ingenue. She is caught between the sensible love of a young, paler fiancé, promising marriage and stability, and this mysterious erotic stranger who appears from some underworld that she might disappear to forever, an eternal Bride (of Dracula). Themes of sexuality and death are intertwined; the heroine will give up normal, daily life for dark eroticism in a ghostly world of the undead.

---

* I must leave off here with the racial variations of meanings among men, where typically white men purport to have the phallus (omnipotence) contrasting with black men who are devalued as being a phallus (part object).

Notably, there is no mother figure in either of these stories; she has evaporated before the story begins. We find only our heroine torn between two lovers. She must choose between a "tall, dark, and handsome" phantom of a father, promising an eternal honeymoon of lust and sensuality but for which she will be damned to hell, or a more tempered love with the "boy next door," with marriage and children the imminent outcome. As seductive lyrics of *Phantom* proclaim, equally applicable in *Dracula,* she is almost "past the point of no return ... [2004b] where senses abandon defenses ... [She must] turn away from light of day, surrender to dark dreams. Turn away from the life you knew before, live as you never lived before, a strange new world where you long to be, only then can you belong to me; let your darker side begin" (Hart and Webber, 2004c). Is this not the oedipal father bidding her say farewell to preoedipal life? But in spite of the trance-like induction, fears abound in the heroine about the wisdom of this course. Is this the Angel of the Night or a devil in disguise— an erotic union that seems heavenly but that may lead to death and decay? How differently toned these themes are from the innocence of Hans Christian Anderson's (1837) "The Little Mermaid."*

The Black Man, both in these films and in my clinical vignette, is scripted to represent the oedipal father who intrudes on the mother–daughter dyad, beckoning the daughter forward in her (hetero) sexual development. We are familiar with this positioning of the paternal penetrating role (see Elise, 2001). But why is it not the oedipal mother who furthers the daughter's sexual development by introducing maternal genital sexuality, her relationship to the father (or female partner), such that an erotic couple is presented to the daughter *by the mother* (see Benjamin, 1988). This introduction would present a triangular relationship to the girl and an image of maternal sexuality available for identification, as well as continuing to offer the mother, in addition to a father, as an erotic object for the girl. Recognizing the mother's desire for the "black man" allows the daughter to identify with a desiring mother, a point central to Benjamin's work. However, recognition of such a desire is also what shocked and dismayed my patient. Unlike in the films, the Black Man had not come for the daughter, but instead, was *with me.* My sexuality and erotic power had to be reckoned with. This confrontation with maternal sexuality is an affront to the daughter's narcissism but, if left unrepresented, is even more costly in undermining female sexual agency that needs to be based on the internalization of a sexually agentic maternal figure.

---

* It is interesting to note that the Little Mermaid is faced with giving up (pre-oedipal) watery immortality (as is my "mermaid" patient) for a man, sex, (and death) in another world (like the ingénue in the films discussed; see Dinnerstein, 1967; Tseelon, 1995).

The Vanquished and Vanished Erotic Mother

In the films previously mentioned, fear, sexuality, consummation, and death are all explicitly linked and illustrate a girl's likely approach to sexuality when the sexual mother is not present as a third and as a figure for internalization and identification. We usually theorize the father as the third intervening in the symbiotic orbit and introducing time, sex, and generational boundaries to the child. I suggest, following Benjamin (1988), that it is the lack of the oedipal mother—a sexual contender in her own right, functioning as a third—that distorts the daughter's oedipal story. The daughter is left to be forever an eroticized "Daddy's girl," never fully growing up, never fully taking ownership of her own sexuality by internalizing a maternal figure who can do likewise. Instead of mother as a goddess—in both its sexual and powerful connotations—as the daughter's inheritance, female sexuality can still fall under the sway of patriarchal dominance (God, our Father) and suffer from inhibition, so-called frigidity.* Sex then becomes positioned for women as bad and dirty, pathologized as "bestial," a devalued, foreign experience, enticing but eternally tabooed, something the woman can never "master." She will remain a "mistress," the object, not the subject, of desire.

Such devaluation can attend any representation of a mother who *does* embody her sexuality. When evident, a mother's sexuality may be viewed with suspicion; too often, such a woman loses her status as a "good" mother. For example, a female patient expressed a very negative reaction to a television character who was both a new mother and sexy. The patient reported feeling repelled and critical: "She should be thinking about the baby!" As soon as sexuality is introduced, it can become a challenge to maintain a respectful view of maternality. This particular patient struggled to access a positive image of a woman who is both maternal and sexual: "I come up with a blank."

If there is no positive representation of a maternal figure with erotic subjectivity, if a good mother has no desire of her own, a daughter is forever locked in the underworld of incestuous, eroticized union with the father. Hades, Phantom, Dracula, suck her into "death" rather than her being free to have her sexuality in the light of day and not at the price of life, relationships, children, home. Here the movie themes link up exactly with Persephone's plight; she can only have sexuality in Hell with Daddy, sacrificing all else, or be reunited with a preoedipal Mommy where neither mother nor daughter have a love life beyond one another and where sexuality remains muted in a mermaid sensuality.

Unlike the portrayal of Demeter, a mother does not just want "springtime" with her daughter, nor is she just a mermaid swimming in oceanic oneness with her daughter. These scenarios deny the reality of the mother's sexuality

---

* See Elise (1998a) for a critique of the psychoanalytic conceptualization of frigidity.

and of her relationship with the father. Those breasts, exposed in the mermaid guise, are not solely to feed and provide sensuous delight to the child— the Good (or Bad) singular, psychoanalytic Breast (see also Stein, 1998; Kohout, 2004). Breasts, twin emblems of desire, form an erotic pair—the mother flaunting her stuff—and, along with legs that are not molded shut but part to engage genital stimulation and incorporative pleasures, encompass the mother's adult sexuality with her lover.

We might keep in mind both Meltzer's work on the aesthetic position (Meltzer & Harris Williams, 1988)—the infant's encounter with the unparalleled beauty of the mother—and Chasseguet-Smirgel's (1976) theorizing regarding the omnipotent maternal imago. Both theories speak to the awe of, as well as defenses against, the mother's beauty and power. Originally, it is the *mother* who is Beauty with her "Beast," the mother who is sexual *and* powerful, and whose choice it is to have a relationship with the father in addition to that with the child. The father can not be recycled to the daughter; *this* union would constitute the denial of generational boundaries,* of the reality of aging and mortality, the passage of time, and would indeed shroud the daughter's sexuality in themes of death, removal from life. It is notable that, at the end of both *Dracula* and *Phantom,* the heroine releases the dark beast from his tortured longing for her by kissing him good-bye and going on her way with her generational peer.

I propose that an oedipal fantasy where mother and father figure compete for the daughter, as do Demeter and Hades in the Persephone myth, is not truly triangular for the daughter but two dyads split apart. Likewise, the familiar drama of father and fiancé/boyfriend vying for the ingenue daughter is also not triangular for the daughter but represents competing dyads. Both scenarios lack a sexual mother in erotic union with her mate. This theme perseverates because it merges patriarchal assignment of powerful, adult sexuality to the father (incestuously relating to the daughter figure rather than to the mother) with a daughter's oedipal wish that she be the only sexually desired female. These oedipal scenarios represent *a failure of triangularity,* both involving parallel dyads rather than the daughter being confronted with *another dyad external to herself—a couple that, in relation to, she stands as a third.* Each scenario obliterates the mother as an erotically powerful figure in consort with her male companion (quite unlike mythic Goddess figures). The primal scene, primal *couple,* is erased from (the daughter's) view. The girl's would-be oedipal competition is encased within a patriarchal structuring of sexuality where the mother is solely reproductive and

---

* Whereas in Lacanian-influenced thinking (i.e., Chasseguet-Smirgel, 1991, among many others) it is the "law of the father" versus any law of the mother (see Mitchell, 2000) that is viewed as essential to establishing generational boundaries unrecognized in maternal–infant symbiosis.

preoedipal, not erotically sexual—a womb but no genitals. As Benjamin (1988) stated, "Though the image of the woman is associated with motherhood and fertility, the mother is not articulated as a sexual subject, one who actively desires something for herself—quite the contrary. The mother is a profoundly desexualized figure" (p. 88).

Boys learn to compete with a sexually powerful father and to identify with the father's phallicism as a powerful aid to their own sexual self-esteem and agency. The boy's oedipal story does not begin with missing, castrated fathers—quite the opposite; Oedipus has to kill his father, the King, in hand-to-hand combat before he can even get to the mother. Thus we cannot take for granted, based solely on the competitive factor, that a child erases in advance the same-sex parent from the narrative. Only girls eliminate the mother without any direct competitive encounter, matching fathers who tend as well to erase the maternal consort, to lose track of the generational boundary, in leaping down to the daughter as sexual complement.

The Sexy Mind

Through chance encounter (whether imagined or real, *vivid* in the patient's emotional reality), my patient was pressed to contend with me as a sexually agentic being, but she thus also expanded her own sexuality. Over the next many months, we explored the meanings for the patient of internalizing a female figure, her analyst, who is viewed as both maternal *and* sexual. This led to an opening up for the patient of her own sexuality in relation to her sense of self, to her husband, and to me.

When the patient began her analysis, she had presented with conflicts related to self-expression in many areas, including sexuality. She tended to doubt her own perceptions as well as the value of her thinking when it departed from those around her. These inhibitions undermined her authority in relation to many people. Although she had access to sexual fantasy and an active sex life, being sexually active in reality and in her mind is one thing, but it does not tell us the quality or nature of the "activity." She saw herself as the sexually provocative Daddy's girl to be wisked off by various powerful men with their dangerous "dark" sex. Sexual agency was projected onto the male other (definitely not the (m)other) just as she initially did in relation to me in the transference and in our "encounter." She viewed her own mother as a sexually attractive but essentially passive woman in relation to her father, "a real powerhouse." The mother seemed to have unfulfilled potential and talent in a number of areas, as did my patient. In being unable to internalize a sexually agentic maternal figure, she could not integrate ownership of sexual desire into her albeit very sexy self. She fell back from fully inhabiting her capacity for creative expression and passionate engagement.

As the treatment progressed, especially around these issues of maternal sexual agency in the transference, my patient's own sense of agency developed, authorizing her sexuality, but also more generally her mind, her creativity. Like many women, she suffered from a perceived split regarding intelligence and sexuality, mind and genital. She struggled with the idea that, as a woman, you've either got one or the other—not both.

> P: Any acknowledgment of my genitals, of my being turned on— "hot"—seems to equate to being stupid. This makes my genitals, what's between my legs, seem dumb.

This is a line of thinking that she and I came to refer to as the "mermaid tail defense." The sexiness of the female sense of self seems dumb, degraded, and the use of the mind seems to desexualize the female self.

It is evident to patients that the analyst uses her mind in an intelligent way; is the analyst's sexuality also evident? A female sense of genital inadequacy, inferiority, may have a component of not being able to link the mother's (and in the transference, the analyst's) use of her genitals with her use of her mind/ maternal function. The mind is de-sexed; the genital is stupid. This is not a conclusion to which early psychoanalytic theory should lead us. Freud (1905) identified that the "sexual researches of children" are intimately linked with the development of the mind, with curiosity, learning, and creativity. Klein's (1928) concept of the epistemophillic instinct/ impulse rests on a passionate foundation. Bion (1959) conceptualized "attacks on linking" as blocks in the patient's mind about productively bringing two or more thoughts together in a mental "intercourse" that produces new thoughts and actually constitutes the ability to think. Meltzer (1973) extended this model of linking to describe creative capacities as based in identifications with a parental couple engaged in mutually rewarding sexual intercourse. I am emphasizing, in accord with both Chasseguet-Smirgel (1976) and Benjamin (1988), that the love affair with the phallus (overly idealized paternal figure) serves to defensively distract from envy of the generative primal couple and from the unmistakable (super)power of female sexuality.

We are all well aware that too many women can feel that if they are sexy, they will not be respected and will lose something in terms of a (professional) reputation. The assumption is that one cannot have both versus the possibility that each might inform the other. Quoting my patient,

> P: I hesitate to admit this, but I often get my most creative ideas while masturbating. My mind seems to get "turned on" as my genitals are. I get excited by the flow of ideas, and the building of my thoughts, at the same time as my body is getting more excited and building to orgasm. I'd never tell anyone this, but I got my last

work idea in consulting to a school program while masturbating. Is this what the term "mental masturbation" means? No, I don't think so. That's pejorative and *not* sexy—de-sexed. What I'm talking about is positive—everything's flowing together, body and mind.

The patient was able to integrate her sexuality into her image of herself as a therapist and as a thinker. More generally, with her mind and her sexuality no longer split off from one another, she could use her mind to choose what she desired rather than her previous tendency to submit to the desire of the other (see Slavin, 2003, regarding the interplay of agency and sexuality).

This development in the patient occurred in response to a chance encounter outside the consulting room that "forced" the issue of maternal sexuality. It is quite complicated to consider how a productive disruption of this nature can occur *within the symbolic encounter* of an unfolding treatment. How does a female analyst embody her sexual agency within the normal boundaries of the analytic relationship? Many complex questions arise, only some aspects of which can I begin to tease out here.

How does a female analyst choose to present her sexual self? What "choices" are involved, are possible? Choices regarding attire and various adornments (see Roth, 2006) are only the most concrete surface manifestations of a quality that would be more deeply internalized. But as Roth has written, surface matters, and matters deeply. As Butler (1995) emphasized, we perform our gender. It must also be the case that we perform (or not) our sexuality.

Unlike men, women have an immense number of decisions regarding personal appearance to make on any given day as to how they will present their sexual selves. This is true for women analysts as well. What outfit, hairstyle, shoes to don—all of which, as women well know, run a sexual gamut from "neutral" to not (or should I say "hot"). One might deem this issue of attire to be trivial, a mere personal choice that any individual woman analyst is free, and should be capable, to make. However, as Muriel Dimen (personal communication, April 2006) noted,

> psychoanalysis has been slow to take in the idea of woman as mind and body, and that practices and behaviors are socially contextualized, not only personal choices. These are challenging ideas for many individuals and for the entire body of thought; one way to dismiss them is to personalize them.

Attire calls attention to the body and often, especially for women, to the sexual body. Encompassed within clothing suitable for work is a range of choices for women that, although often subtle, have significant effect on a felt or perceived sense of sexuality. These choices reflect underlying feelings and then further influence self-concept at a deeper level. It is difficult for these choices to be a non-issue, as almost any decision about attire will say *something*. When it comes to sexuality, a neutral stance will be quite a statement, one that I propose fits in with a transference–countertransference stance that is most comfortably unnoticed, unremarked upon by both parties in the female clinical dyad, and that is reflective of a deeply recessed wish by most everyone to see a maternal figure as a Virgin Mary.

A thin, uncertain line wavers between one's sexuality being covered up/over, and obscured, versus being provocative or seductive. Where is that line? A too-often exceedingly narrow space exists where female sexuality can be evident without being considered pejoratively to be provocative. (We have only to think of the familiar "defense" of rape: "She asked for it" *often* refers to how the woman/girl was dressed "revealingly.") If the female body is visible, it is considered inherently "provocative." I am approaching this issue of outer apparel and appearance as the "tip of the iceberg" of female embodiment of sexuality—a microcosm of conflicts in underlying intrapsychic layers.

My patient continued to pursue this relationship between my attire and my self. Months after the encounter on the street, she reiterated these thoughts:

> P: You weren't dressed like you are at your office. *Here* you dress *like* your office: neutral, not especially colorful or lively. There's something more to you than I've seen. It makes me feel that your real life is somewhere else, not here [with me]. Funny, I never thought of myself as not liking this office before, but now it seems too pale. I used to like that. I once saw a therapist who had all this colorful art in her office that was very distracting, including a big picture over her chair of a knife slicing through a piece of fruit—scary! But I think now that your blander colors have allowed me to feel merged with you versus having a sense of difference. I feel some sadness that it is not like that now that I see your more colorful, sexy side.... I feel like going to sleep.... Didn't I feel this way yesterday too? I can't remember.

We see progression and then, in the face of loss, regression that, for this patient, was only temporary in an overall momentum forward into a depressive position recognition of both loss and gain.

Analysts tend to develop fine-tuned sensitivity to when our dress, décor, or some less tangible expression of self might "slice through a piece of fruit" and be unnecessarily distracting and unproductively disruptive to a vulnerable patient. We are necessarily cautious out of concern to not harm. We may, however, err in this direction and miss seeing the limitations (for our patients and ourselves) of our various self-effacements. My patient had now alerted me to this other side.

The incident made me aware that my professional persona and dress were possibly *too* "professional" and lacked certain human aspects—like sexuality. I was intrigued by my attention (and that of my patient) repeatedly returning to the issue of color, both racially, as in people of color, and in the symbolic meanings of the color palette. I considered that not only did the patient see my (and her) female sexuality as located in the Black Man (and that I needed more palpably to embody ownership of my sexuality) but that the color of my style of dress, and personality, also played some role.

I came to feel that I had indeed been somewhat bland, expressed in a tendency to wear muted colors (reflective of a muted identity), and that this "mutation" constituted an analytic costume—shared by most of my colleagues, I might add. Our professional wardrobe tends to be more subdued than that of many other jobs. One is more likely to find black and gray, "spiced" with sage or copper rather than a juicy profusion of tangerine, lime, red, or "hot" pink. I needed not only to "take back" sex from my black man but to take color itself back into my work wardrobe and colorfulness into my professional identity.*

This ongoing reflection and self-inquiry on sexual agency and the colorfulness of my psyche effected a subtle shift in the self I am in my consulting room. I needed to allow more of the full palette of my psyche a place within the clinical venture versus my being restricted to some pale version of myself. At the same time, I also had to work to not *expel* the patient's various ideas of me and my sexuality (see Carpy, 1989, on holding the countertransference rather than jettisoning the patient's projections). Interpretations can function as subtle corrections.

As I hope I have in this paper, I attempted to live out as fully as possible my role assigned to me by my patient, and in interacting with that role, I changed my idea of the self I can bring to my office. That internal journey in my countertransference allowed for travel in the patient's transference fantasies regarding maternal/female sexuality. We both changed. I became a more sexy mom, and she grew up to be one as well. This is what I can say here about the "progress of treatment" rather than detailing further any particular dialogue. In hearing the conference presentation (2006) of this paper, colleagues have asked, "Can you say what *actually happened* in the subsequent response to this accidental encounter?" No, I can not. The issue was too subtly threaded throughout our sessions over many months, and even years, for me now to recreate it further here. Like a small fiber inextricably woven throughout a tapestry, it is an element that I can no longer isolate.

The clinical challenge that this "chance encounter" poses to us all is the following question: If not forced on the dyad by external circumstances, in what

---

* People of color are often very colorful in dress, and here we also get into issues of class as well as race.

other ways are the positive benefits described in this treatment to be integrated into an analysis between a female patient and analyst? My aim in this paper is to stimulate collective consideration of this question. I do not expect, or even desire, to "answer" it, as that would foreclose the topic.

Discussion: Oedipal Eruption/Disruption

We have arrived at a conception of the thinking genital and the "turned-on" mind, both joined in a productive intercourse and leading to further conceptions (see Bion, 1959), on and on. We see the significance of using one's mind to foster one's sexuality and one's sexuality to foster one's mind and creativity. My patient's awareness/recognition of my sexuality had been ushered in by the encounter with the Black Man—an encounter that was disruptive but productive. Such an encounter, usually symbolic, is necessary and will always be inherently disruptive. In my interpreting along lines theorized in this paper, I managed slowly to convey to my patient my ownership of my sexuality—a sexuality that belonged to me, no longer located in a foreign man, and no longer seemingly estranged from my intellect. In the face of her reiterated musings about *her* being "the one" to be on the arm of the dark stranger, *I became the one to disrupt* my patient: With the marriage of my intellect and my sexuality, I eventually interrupted, "Ah, but the 'Black Man' belongs to me!"

Because exclusion from the parents' sexual relationship represents such a fundamental aspect of reality for the child, as Rusbridger emphasizes, (2004) "analysis of the patient's responses to the oedipal situation constitutes the central task of analysis" (p. 731). Given that analysts of various persuasions debate whether analyzing the oedipal crisis is the central task of an analysis, it is important to understand the Kleinian emphasis on the oedipal complex as a fundamental dynamic of the mind, that then structures the mind. "This turns on the subject's response to witnessing a relationship … from which he is excluded" (Rusbridger, p. 733).

The child's reaction to reality, as represented by the oedipal situation, is what determines his ability to use his mind. Intertwining themes of my paper concern exclusion from the parental sexual couple and the challenge this experience poses to the perception of reality: "That was you, right? Unbelievable! Maybe it wasn't really you. Could I have been mistaken?" As the patient gradually absorbed the emotional truth of her perceptions, she enlivened her capacity for creative linking on many levels. The clinical material demonstrates how coming to terms with oedipal reality does develop the capacity to use one's mind in a productive, fruitful manner, where thinking is clear and creative, an "intercourse" with one's thoughts (see Britton, 1989).

My particular aim in this paper is to highlight unconscious fantasy material regarding oedipal exclusion in its gender specific, mother–daughter form. Too often in analytic theorizing, the daughter has been viewed solely as competing with the mother for the father. I have elaborated the element of competition with the father for the mother, where desire for, and sense of betrayal by, the mother complicates the female oedipal drama. I hope the reader, female or male, has been drawn into a reencounter with the emotional impact of the oedipal situation. For it is the case that each sex is confronted by the oedipal crisis with an assault on dyadic relating and omnipotence. I have tried to recreate in as vivid a manner as I can, the startling sense of shock and disruption that ensues.

Ogden (2005) wrote that

> When we read an analyst's written account of an experience with a patient, what we are reading is not the experience itself, but the writer's creation of a new (literary) experience while (seemingly) writing the experience he had with the analysand.... At the same time, the "fiction" that is created in words must reflect the reality of what occurred. (p. 16)

This intriguing play on the concepts of reality and fiction captures a core dilemma of the oedipal situation: What is real? Did I make this up? Did I find this or create it?

The emotional experience of oedipal disruption does center on the startling sense of challenge to preoedipal (dyadic) "reality," leading to initial denial, a period of confusion, having to think things through, and, eventually, coming to some sort of personal conviction regarding oedipal (triadic) reality that then becomes foundational for going forward. As Rusbridger (2004) underscored, these dynamics are fundamental aspects of the mind coping with an experience of disruption, assaulted by a "new" reality. My patient's encounter, although extra-analytic, brings to life—"to the streets"—what is there to be discovered (or not) in the mind.

I analyzed the material as I would a dream to retain the ambiguity ("did this happen/was this real/was that you?") that *is exactly the dilemma the oedipal child is faced with* in the unconscious regarding the relation *between* the mother and the father. My intent was to fully engage with the patient's fantasy without collapsing into a concrete relation to "events" that should be understood as psychic. In not identifying to the patient or to the reader whether it was actually her analyst that she encountered on the street, my aim was to keep open the symbolic space for the emotional reality of fantasy. I believe that there are good clinical reasons for this approach. An analyst needs to accept a patient's projections in a deep way, and over time (Carpy, 1989), in order to have an experience of living the transference, and the countertransference, with the patient. If a clinician were to give a concrete answer to such a question directly posed by a patient, one would have to be equally ready to say "yes, that was me," or "no, that was not me," depending on the actual circumstances. In the case I have presented, affirming would be the more favorable clinical route, though disruptive and challenging, as it would more align with the oedipal task. Yet such an affirmation would eliminate the confrontation with the question, "Did this really happen?" that is central to the oedipal task, and that needs to be worked through over time.

And what if I were able to "comfortably" disconfirm? Both analyst and patient would most likely use concrete reality to shore up defenses against contending with oedipal threats: "Oh, good, (sigh of relief) we're still 'safe' here in this mother–daughter cocoon; 'real' sex with (foreign) men—(no one *we* know)—is out there somewhere in a distant, shadowy land." In spite of the best efforts of the most clinically committed analytic couple, it would be an uphill battle to keep the emotional reality immediate and the conflicts alive. I think this is the difficulty to keep in mind regarding these types of potential disclosures on the part of a clinician; concrete answers do not present an equal opportunity for the clinical trajectory. One side (confirmation) leads to collapse into a singular concrete event that is then likely ejected from the patient's psychic contents and attributed to "idiosyncrasies" of that particular analyst; the other (disconfirming) provides an escape hatch (for both parties) from the confrontation altogether.

In unfolding the clinical sequence, I am inviting the reader to step into the dream world that is psychic reality—the patient's unconscious fantasy regarding the oedipal situation, made accessible by the "encounter" just as it would have been by a dream of such an encounter. In not commenting to the patient on the concrete level (and she did not ask me to do so, being more engrossed in what had been stimulated in her internal world), I hoped to keep her "dream" alive for her and for me to fully inhabit. I believe that I owned my sexual subjectivity much more deeply, than would be the case in a simple disclosure, by staying in the symbolic realm. A living (transference) dream remains affectively intense over time and, ripe with continued feeling, demands ongoing analysis, not premature conclusions that foreclose experience and thinking. When asleep and dreaming, we all feel/believe that what is happening is real. Whereas upon awakening, psychic reality dims and becomes confused; memory is interfered with: "Did I dream that?" We soon distance as well from the emotional impact that becomes increasingly remote over time. So what does my patient's "waking dream" tell us about the oedipal situation?

Rusbridger (2004) identified two links, separate in nature, between the three figures of mother, father, and child: the sexual link between the parents, and the link of dependency from the child to each parent. Although the parental sexual link has created the (dependent) child, from the child's perspective the chronology is reversed. First there is (after "oneness") the dependent dyadic link to the mother and then to the father. The erotic link to each parent starts to form as the child moves from preoedipal into oedipal experience. It is only then that the child discovers a sexual link between the parents—a traumatic discovery, hoped for some time to be a fiction, only imagined, not true.

Specifying a crucial gender difference, Green (1992, p. 141) described the Oedipus complex as an

> open triangular structure in which *the mother occupies the place of the central link,* for she is the only one who has a double bodily relation with both the father and the child…. What is essential seems to be *situated in the moment* of transition when the fusional relation of the dyad—doubled or complimented by the thought of the father in the mother's mind—is followed by *the moment when he effectively appears in reality.* (as cited and translated by Van Haute, 2005, p. 1675; italics added)

The mother's desire for, and bodily relation with, both partner and child places her, not the phallus, as the central link. The unwelcome reality to the child of not being the sole object of the mother's desire is at first denied. Rupture of mother–child dyadic union is blamed on the "moment" of the father, a moment that takes bodily shape in the image of a powerfully aggressive phallus.

Rusbridger (2004), as well, in discussing oedipal dynamics, speaks of "reactions to moments of meaningfulness" (p. 731). Although we know that meaning is built up over time, recognition of a new, fundamentally important and reconfiguring idea takes place like lightning striking. Momentous change often occurs in a moment, not typically in external reality but in that the feeling of surprise and shock creates a sensation of a traumatic encounter.

Even when well integrated in any given woman, the mother's heterosexuality is an affront to the dyadic omnipotence of the child.* Here, "heterosexual" translates in the child's mind to "other(than-with-me)sexuality." The mother's sexual partner being of a gender other than hers is not critical; her partner being other than her child is key. The child is not developmentally ready to perceive this "other-sexual" reality for some time, and to do so is rarely a smooth ride. Moving fully into the oedipal situation, and negotiating its challenges toward optimal resolution, requires realization of the sexual independence of the mother's desire, something neither sex is eager to do.

---

* I want to underscore that the attribution of "slutty" to the "street-walking" analyst is the oedipal child's view of mother's sexual desire going elsewhere—"not the sex I want to see." In a similar situation, some people view gay couples as "flagrant" and "flaunting" their sexuality when seen holding hands or kissing in public. The particular image of this "sexed up" woman on the street is not suggested as (or excluded from) a model of female sexuality.

Epilogue: Subjects of Beauty

At a gathering of analysts after a presentation of my paper, conversation among the women quickly shifted to surreptitious, almost confessional, tones regarding professional wardrobe dilemmas. Shoes, how heeled, how "strappy," length of skirts, dip of blouses, earring styles/length, how "bold" the color of toenail polish, and so on—all debated as to where these items fell on the "too" sexy/not sexy ("professionally appropriate") continuum. The conversational atmosphere conveyed that this subject was to be kept quiet between women, a private concern, as if even the attention to these items would be disruptive if voiced more loudly or would be dismissed as trivial "women's issues." The fact that in a profession now "female dominated" so few analytic papers, or even conversations, take up this topic is, I think, indicative of repression at the level of group dynamics as well as of the intrapsychic.

In many cultures, female sexuality is felt to excite and distort the sensibilities of the male; it then becomes the responsibility of each individual woman to titrate this effect, with attire a critical variable. "Choices" are made in accord with what is considered normative within a given context. Consciously and unconsciously, women take on the project of wardrobe as a regulator of sexual excitement (their own, as well as that of the other).

Requirements regarding the expression or suppression of female sexuality come in many forms and from many directions. The "politically correct" aspect of the women's movement often functioned as a restrictive series of "do not"s regarding attire and appearance. A double bind still exists: If one wears nail polish, lipstick, form-fitting clothes, and so on, is this a male or a female aesthetic at play?

Women are viewed as objects of beauty, their beauty "objectified" by the gaze of the other. Are women *subjects of beauty?* Can women be the subject of their own sexual, sensual aesthetic of beauty? Where is the space for the subjective experience and expression of one's beauty (including the erotic) as a woman? How is this engagement with self expressed, embodied, inhabited?

Familiar possibilities include the sensuousness of swaying strands of hair, playful painting of face and nails, colorful materials, flowing scarves, sparkling jewelry (all of which, in some cultures, men choose as well to express themselves; Elise, 2006). Certainly women most everywhere experience beauty as a pleasure for themselves. Even when presented for men, does this display of female beauty necessarily signal oppression? Is it not a form of sexual signaling, a communication to a desired other? My question is this: Do various female mating "calls" necessarily preclude a communication with oneself as a woman and with other women?

I suggest that female (erotic) beauty is a communication not solely to men, but between women, within any given woman, and at core (Meltzer and

Harris Williams, 1988) between mother and infant (see Elise, 2006). An aesthetic of beauty, although changing in every society, seems to be an eternal element of human culture given its centrality in the mother–infant relation. The ability to experience, and subsequently express, maternal beauty and sexuality is, one hopes, handed down to and inherited by successive generations of daughters as their birthright. Nor can we as women clinicians expect to foster the development of healthy agentic passions in our female patients without these aspects of self palpably alive and embodied in *our* presence in the clinical encounter. Each woman in the clinical dyad must participate in this primal mother/daughter interplay in order that either, and hopefully both, can develop and grow.

References

Altman, N. (2000). Black and White thinking. A psychoanalyst reconsiders race. *Psychoanalytic Dialogues, 10,* 589–605.

Anderson, H. C. (1846). The little mermaid. In *80 fairy-tales* (pp. 46–63). Odense, Denmark: Hans Reitzels, 1976.

Benjamin, J. (1988). *The bonds of love.* New York: Pantheon.

Bion, W. R. (1959). Attacks on linking. *International Journal of Psychoanalysis, 40,* 308–315.

Bollas, C. (2000). *Hysteria.* London: Routledge.

Butler, J. (1995). Melancholy gender: Refused identification. *Psychoanalytic Dialogues, 5,* 165–180.

Carpy, D. (1989). Tolerating the countertransference: A mutative process. *International Journal of Psychoanalysis, 70,* 287–294.

Chasseguet-Smirgel, J. (1976). Freud and female sexuality: The consideration of some blind spots in the exploration of the "Dark Continent." *International Journal of Psychoanalysis, 57,* 275–286.

Chasseguet-Smirgel, J. (1991). Sadomasochism in the perversions: Some thoughts on the destruction of reality. *Journal of the American Psychoanalytic Association, 39,* 399–415.

Dinnerstein, D. (1967). "The little mermaid" and the situation of the girl. *Contemporary Psychoanalysis, 3,* 104–112.

Elise, D. (1998a). The absence of the paternal penis. *Journal of the American Psychoanalytic Association, 46,* 413–442.

Elise, D. (1998b). Gender repertoire: Body, mind and bisexuality. *Psychoanalytic Dialogues, 8,* 353–371.

Elise, D. (2000). Woman and desire: Why women may *not* want to want. *Studies in Gender and Sexuality, 1,* 125–145.

Elise, D. (2001). Unlawful entry: Male fears of psychic penetration. *Psychoanalytic Dialogues, 11,* 495–531.

Elise, D. (2002). Blocked creativity and inhibited erotic transference. *Studies in Gender and Sexuality, 3,* 161–195.

Freud, S. (1905). *Three essays on the theory of sexuality.* In J. Strachey (Ed. & Trans.), *The standard edition of the complete psychological works of Sigmund Freud* (Vol. 7, pp. 125–243). London: Hogarth Press, 1953.

Hart, C., & Webber, A. L. (2004a). I remember/Stranger than you dreamt it [Recorded by Peter Manning and Sylvia Addison]. On *The Phantom of the Opera* [CD]. New York: Sony.

Hart, C., & Webber, A. L. (2004b). The point of no return [Recorded by Peter Manning and Sylvia Addison]. On *The Phantom of the Opera* [CD]. New York: Sony.

Hart, C., & Webber, A. L. (2004c). The music of the night [Recorded by Peter Manning]. On *The Phantom of the Opera* [CD]. New York: Sony.

Holtzman, D., & Kulish, N. (2003). The feminization of the female oedipal complex, Part II: Aggression reconsidered. *Journal of the American Psychoanalytic Association, 51,* 1127–1151.

Irigaray, L. (1990). This sex which is not one. In C. Zanardi (Ed.), *Essential papers on the psychology of women* (pp. 437–443). New York: New York University Press.

Josephs, L., & Miller, A. (submitted). White identity, racialized oedipal splitting, and pathological narcissism.

Klein, M. (1928). Early stages of the Oedipus conflict. *International Journal of Psychoanalysis, 9,* 167–180.

Kohout, E. (2004). The breast in female sexuality. *International Journal of Psychoanalysis, 85,* 1235–1238.

Laplanche, J. (1970). *Life and death in psychoanalysis* (J. Mehlman, Trans.). Baltimore, MD: Johns Hopkins University Press.

Leary, K. (2000). Racial enactments in dynamic treatment. *Psychoanalytic Dialogues, 10,* 639–653.

Meltzer, D. (1973). *Sexual states of mind.* Perthshire, Scotland: Clunie.

Meltzer, D., & Harris Williams, M. (1988). *The apprehension of beauty.* Strath Tay, Scotland: Clunie.

Mitchell, J. (2000). *Mad men and medusas.* New York: Basic Books.

Ogden, T. (2005). *This art of psychoanalysis.* New York: Routledge.

Roth, D. (2006). Adornment as a method of interior design. *Studies in Gender and Sexuality, 7,* 179–194.

Rusbridger, R. (2004). Elements of the Oedipus complex: A Kleinian account. *The International Journal of Psychoanalysis, 85,* 3, 731–748.

Slavin, J. (2003, June). *I have been trying to get them to respond to me.* Presented at 92nd annual meeting, American Psychoanalytic Association, Boston, MA.

Stein, R. (1998). The enigmatic dimension of sexual experience: The "otherness" of sexuality and primal seduction. *Psychoanalytic Quarterly, 67,* 594–625.

Tseelon, E. (1995). The little mermaid: An icon of woman's condition in patriarchy, and the human condition of castration. *International Journal of Psychoanalysis, 76,* 1017–1030.

Van Haute, P. (2005). Infantile sexuality, primary object-love and the anthropological significance of the Oedipus complex: Re-reading Freud's *Female Sexuality. The International Journal of Psychoanalysis, 86,* 6, 1661–1678.

Winnicott, D. W. (1956). Primary maternal preoccupation. In *Through pediatrics to psychoanalysis* (pp. 300–305). London: Hogarth Press, 1978.

Wrye, H., & Welles, J. (1994). *The narration of desire.* Hillsdale, NJ: The Analytic Press.

12

Privacy, Reverie, and the Analyst's Ethical Imagination*

Steven H. Cooper

▼　▼　▼　▼　▼

There are a variety of registers from which the analyst can illuminate points of transference–countertransference enactment and our reverie is often quite useful in this process. The modality by which the analyst communicates these formulations of unconsciously held object relations and defenses also varies and includes verbal interpretation through symbolic speech, interpretive action (Ogden, 1994), and, at times, interpretations that involve "analyst disclosure"—a construction of the analyst's subjectivity put forward to enhance the patient's understanding of enactments of the transference-countertransference (Cooper, 1998a, 1998b). In this paper I describe varying ways of using and thinking about forms of analytic reverie and the analyst's privacy.

Clinical papers illustrating aspects of expressive use of countertransference have often addressed points of impasse and stalemate in analytic work. Generally speaking, however, analysts interested in more active use of countertransference have not paid equal attention to "quieter" moments in analytic work. The work of Ogden is a major exception to this observation.

My thinking about the analyst's privacy and reverie in clinical analysis is substantially influenced by Ogden's many contributions (Ogden, 1994, 1997, 2004). Ogden has become one of the frontier cartographers of the psychoanalyst's privacy and reverie, particularly the understanding of the "specific unconscious, intersubjective relationship" with each patient (Ogden,

---

* Portions of this chapter appeared in *Psychoanalytic Quarterly,* 77(4), 2008, pp. 1045–1073. Reprinted with permission.

1997, p. 588). Like Ogden, I formulate reverie as a road to the unconscious, intersubjective objects in the mind of the patient and analyst. However in my view, the interpersonal is interfused with those of the "unconscious, intersubjective" internalized object relation described by Ogden. I will try to demonstrate how I expressively make use of reverie, particularly the register from which I sometimes speak to a patient about the bearing of my own experience of intersubjective objects in the mind of the patient. The analyst's receptivity to the patient's mind and his own involves an "ethic of hospitability" (Civitarese, 2008) which, in turn, includes an ethic of responsibility about both his attunement to the patient's unconscious life and his or her participation in that life within the analytic process.

Theoretical Background

Freud's (1912) suggestion that the analyst "should simply listen and not bother about whether he is keeping anything in mind" (p. 112) is a common marker for most analysts who are interested in the reverie process. For Ogden (1996, 1997), like Freud, the analyst's privacy and reverie afford him a psychic space and actual time to make associational linkages and largely unconscious contextualization for listening to the patient. Ogden's (1996) helpful translation of Freud underscores the importance of the analyst creating conditions in which the analyst can maximize his capacity for a receptivity and play of the mind.

It is interesting and a bit paradoxical that in many ways most psychoanalytic models have more procedural transparency regarding maintaining the analyst's privacy than is so for the relational model. For most models, the injunction to be anonymous is quite clear and unambiguous to the patient regardless of how much the patient might protest that anonymity or seek to change, affect, or even destroy the anonymity of the analyst. For Freud the analyst's privacy ensures an ideal canvas for the patient's freedom of association and securing the maximal opportunity for the analyst's associational drift. In contrast, in the relational model, there are instances when the analyst might make use of and even reveal aspects his experience. Moreover, while many models of analytic work agree with Hoffman's (1983) observation that the patient is often reading us in many ways, the relational model emphasizes the analyst's technical proclivity to follow up on the patient's perceptions as a mode of bringing the transference into more conscious experience (e.g., Gill, 1983; Aron, 1991).

Ogden (1996) draws connections between Bion's (1962) characterization of reverie as the absence of "memory and desire" and Freud's notion of "simply listening." In both states the analyst doesn't try too hard to remember or even understand too much, instead using his own capacities or states to "catch the drift" of the patient's mostly unconscious experience. In part, Bion's (1962) magnificent poetic of the analytic space—"we're both in this alone"—was his way of describing his own requirements for having access to the patient in ways other than those permitted in conventional forms of interpersonal exchange.

Ogden's efforts are to place into focus the dialectical interplay of states of reverie of analysand and analyst, resulting in the creation of a third analytic subject. The asymmetrical experiences of the analytic third by patient and analyst promote understanding, verbal expression and symbolization of the "drift" of the analysand's unconscious internal object world. Reverie is the state of mind that allows for experiencing and expanding the analytic third.

Like Ogden, I find that many experiences of my reverie are not immediately translatable in a one to one fashion about what is going on in the analytic relationship. In my experience many of the images and associations that come up in response to the patient are just as likely to be defensive as clarifying and a judicious process of filtering and considering these experiences over time seems well justified. Reverie, like much countertransference data, can be enticing as an invitation to more quickly elaborate confusing and contradictory information or problematic affective states in the analyst and analysand. Ogden is correct to emphasize that these experiences need to accrue to discover whether and how they are meaningful and that we do need to let ourselves be adrift without forcing our forms of reverie into interpretations.

I also like Ogden's commitment to not automatically dismiss our reverie as somehow idiosyncratically personal. While we may have experiences during reverie that suggest a failure to be receptive or understanding of the patient, we usually can't know that without obtaining more data. At first glance, there are many instances when my thoughts go in directions that seem pressed by my own needs and are not immediately useful to understanding the patient or are actively obstructions to understanding the patient (e.g., Schwaber, 1992). Sometimes, however, closer examination might suggest useful connections to points of unconsciously held transference–countertransference phenomena. Thus I do not subscribe to the notion that countertransference is always best understood as an obstruction to the listening to the patient's experience. Time and repeated experience afforded by the intensity and continuity of analytic work are a great help in the process of deciphering what might be an impediment or an aid in elaborating points of the unconsciously held transference–countertransference experiences.

Obviously the experiences of privacy afforded to patient and analyst are a part of what allows for the analyst's experience of reverie. Bion (1959) noted that the analyst's abstinence produces what he called, "the sense of isolation within an intimate relationship" (p. 73). Reverie within the analyst is intimately, intersubjectively related to the privacy and solitude afforded for the analyst.

It is to preserve the place of privacy for both patient and analyst that Ogden (1996) has criticized the fundamental rule of association—that the patient to try to say everything that comes to mind. Ogden questions the rule because it minimizes the dialectical interplay of the capacities of both analyst and patient for reverie. He fears that it can pose the danger of becoming a kind of "frozen injunction" for any analytic dyad. Ogden is concerned that a longstanding appreciation of the place of solitude and privacy, particularly as espoused by the Independent tradition of psychoanalysis (e.g., Winnicott, 1958) can be overlooked or even violated in the invitation to say everything that comes to mind. Ogden adds to this invitation his statement or reminder to the patient who begins analysis that each of the two participants needs to also have a place for privacy.

I have always had a rather complex reaction to this recommendation to the patient. I have concerns that telling a patient that "we must both have a place for privacy" may run the risk of unnecessarily conveying something about my own wishes for distance or emphasizing my attunement to the patient's needs for distance. In my experience patients are quite adept at maintaining privacy and editing their thoughts despite the issuing of an invitation to tell me what's on their mind. I can or at least try to manage my own needs for privacy. While there may be instances when I tell a patient about my wish to maintain levels of personal privacy, I prefer to talk about that in a particular clinical context with a particular patient rather than as a general statement at the beginning of my work with patients.

Moreover, I am concerned that I might be construed as issuing a kind of nonimpingement promise—that is that I will try not to invade their privacy. While I think that respect for the patient's privacy is paramount to analytic work, even a precondition for analytic exploration, I can't promise to not impinge or invade their privacy. I have referred to forms of "good enough impingement" (Cooper, 1998, 2000) as an inevitable part of analytic work involving various forms of misattunement, countertransference enactment, or what Balint (1968) termed "the poverty of interpretation." I have little doubt that, in reminding the patient of his and the patient's need for privacy, Ogden is not promising that he will not impinge. I do wonder, however, whether for some patients this reminder might unconsciously or consciously resonate with either a fear of invading the privacy of the analyst or a fear of the analyst's process of getting to know him.

My use of reverie is usually associated with an interspersing of images, fantasies, and recollections, which alternate with a very conscious form of thought and formulation. My mind is rarely adrift for an extended period of time. Instead, I somewhat reflexively move from types of reverie into much more formulated private interpretations and often imagined dialogue with a patient about my formulations.

Put another way, it's my sense that in comparison to Ogden's descriptions, my reverie is more fleeting, imperfect, and a more porous vessel. My reverie often leads immediately to private, imagined interpretations of what has been and perhaps is being enacted. These imagined interpretations are I suppose a kind of associational linkage but they are often tried on and often discarded. Sometimes this "postreverie" thinking leads me quite productively to anticipate how these formulations might also involve particular kinds of enactments such as truncating various kinds of elaboration of meaning or repeating various patterns of object relating in the patient's life. But often my reverie and postreverie thinking are what allow me to productively explore how I'm enacting patterns of the transference–countertransference as well as the potential meanings and enactment that might accompany an interpretive transition with a patient.

These forms of postreverie thinking all comprise what I call the analyst's *ethical imagination*. The term ethical imagination refers to the analyst's modes of thinking about various forms of enactment of the unconscious transference–countertransference or psychical entanglement between patient and analyst. The analyst's thinking that sometimes follows associational drift is often a precondition for clarifying the unconscious intrapsychic-interpersonal implications of an interpretive shift or transition in our understanding with the patient.

The analyst's ethical imagination covers territory that lies partially outside the kind of maternal reverie described by Bion. However within this imaginative form of contemplating or formulating reverie, the analyst is adrift in a different kind of way, allowing himself to imagine the usefulness of a form of understanding or the potential impact of such an intervention. The impact might include particular fantasies of helping a patient to understand something new. The impact might also include fantasies of hurting or impinging upon a patient—a kind of collateral damage of sorts. Since it is an unconscious aspect of transference–countertransference enactment that I'm pondering, it is never entirely possible to know in advance either its usefulness or accuracy about what we are intending to illuminate. It is because of this uncertainty that I find it useful to think of our imagination, our ability to formulate something as related to an ethic of responsibility or accountability. What characterizes the analyst's ethical imagination is the attempt to think about what we are doing and what we are about to do in our participation with the patient.

Since my imagination is often directed toward the ubiquity of enactment as a feature of analytic process, it is of course a construction of what I imagine I'm enacting; it is never entirely possible to know this in advance. This privacy, reverie, and the subsequent formulations I refer to as the analyst's ethical imagination might seem like a kind of injunction that he tries to think about what he's doing and what he's about to do in his participation with the patient. I don't view it as a form of technical advice or a conscious attempt to leave no clinical stone unturned, instead believing that to a large extent it is what most analysts do as they use forms of reverie and associational linkage, absorption of affect, transference attributions, and the like. We think about the various kinds of impact that have and will result from the choices we make either through acts of extending or constricting interpretive range, through shifts in interpretive focus or sometimes in the holding off an interpretation.

Ogden's (1994) fascinating discussion of his use of "interpretive action" within the analytic third is an example of moments I refer to as the analyst's ethical imagination. Ogden describes a series of patient's with whom he conveys his understanding of the transference–countertransference through what he calls interpretive action. The latter might include self-conscious forms of silence at times when he would usually make an interpretation or refusal to engage in invited activities elicited by the patient that he had previously enacted. These are self-conscious efforts to stand outside particular forms of repetitive transference–countertransference enactments and are accompanied by the analyst's silently formulated interpretations. These examples are very close to what I have in mind in describing the analyst's ethical imagination, though I'm not referring to "actions" in Ogden's use of the term. Instead, my formulations and interpretations are primarily verbally based understandings about new formulations or interpretations.

One of the most important ways that I differ from Ogden's use of reverie in making interpretation is that I sometimes say something about a construction of my own experience or how I'm implicated within points of transference–countertransference enactment. Ogden's use of reverie does not include instances when the analyst uses conscious or deliberate attempts to reveal a construction of the analyst's experience to illuminate the unconscious transference–countertransference.

My intention at these moments of more direct statement of countertransference experience is not to provide gratuitous, exhibitionistic, or diversionary statements of personal feeling. Instead, on those occasions my intention is to express something from the register of my countertransference experience as it relates to particular points of unconscious transference–countertransference. In fact I don't consider these moments of speaking from this register as best described as "self-disclosure" at all, instead preferring to term them "analyst-disclosure" (Cooper, 1998a, 1998b). This register relates very little to the analyst's person or self and instead, when used judiciously, is the result of highly formulated experience (Stern, 1983). I have suggested the distinctions between analyst and self-disclosure because the subjectivity of the analyst is central to all kinds of interpretive processes in analytic work. I view the register from which the analyst speaks of countertransference experience as embedded within particular aspects of the transference–countertransference and is no more expressive of the analyst's "self" than is any other kind of analytic intervention or interpretation. Like all interpretations it is partially motivated by unconscious experience. To be sure there are varieties of countertransference disclosure, which emanate more from "unformulated experience" (e.g., Stern, 1983), but these are not the variety of interpretations I am focusing on in this examination of the analyst's use of reverie.

I view "analyst disclosure" as quite similar to Ogden's formulation of the paradox at the heart of our personal and private reveries in clinical work. Ogden (1997) highlights that as personal as our reveries feel to us, they are not best understood as personal creations because reverie is at the same time an "aspect of a jointly (but asymmetrically) created unconscious intersubjective construction." Ogden (1994, 1996) refers to these constructions as the intersubjective third. Similarly, Symington (1983) refers to these phenomena as "corporate entities"—points of shared transference–countertransference that are jointly but asymmetrically held by patient and analyst. These phenomena both illuminate points of unconsciously held transference and can serve as obstructions to better understanding points of transference–countertransference impasse.

Through a series of brief clinical vignettes I will try to focus on the analyst's use of reverie in the area I refer to as his ethical imagination. I will present vignettes, which vary in whether or how the analyst makes use of his own countertransference and expressive countertransference.

The Analyst's Privacy in the Patient's Mind

The following vignettes are from the third month of a four-times-a-week analysis. Sam lies down on the couch and begins the hour: "Your haircut makes you look younger this week. I think it's your haircut. You look younger than your stated age." Sam starts laughing, and behind the couch I'm smiling too. He has immediately come to the awareness that I've never stated my age. We start looking into what the notion of "my stated age" means to him.

Sam, a man in his mid-20s, often comes into analytic sessions looking at me intently with a probing survey of my mood and dress. He is prone to comment on my appearance, particularly on whether I'm wearing a tie or a suit jacket. Sometimes I'm dressed more formally and sometimes more informally. Sam believes that he is gay though confused about the fact that he is emotionally drawn to women for his closest relationships. He feels that he is not and has never been sexually turned on by women. His best friend is a woman, and they feel that they love each other. She wants to be with him—to live with him and potentially get married and have children despite her knowledge that when they have tried to have sex he has found it unstimulating. Sam has been honest with her about his sexual liaisons with men, though he has never had a male boyfriend, instead preferring the companionship of this woman friend and, earlier, other women. When Sam masturbates he thinks exclusively of men. Sam and his woman friend agree that their seldom lovemaking is not occasioned by his sense of passion and excitement. He has never fallen in love with a man, nor has he longed to have a man as a life companion as he has with this woman, despite his lack of sexual excitement.

As we start to look into Sam's beginning statement—"You look younger than your stated age"—what emerges in the session is how much he idealizes many around him and me. He says that he always wants to think the best of his friends and professors at graduate school. I'm aware of having some new hostile feelings toward Sam as he explores "my stated age." I realize that his attempts to idealize others and me never quite feel positive to me. Instead they have a competitive and somewhat aggressive feel to them. I realize that, in fact, I sometimes find it patronizing and more hostile than I've previously realized. Then I ask myself: Is it a competitive feeling from Sam, or is it the way he imagines and experiences me (creating a conversation with me as one who reveals something), is a private, autoerotic process that leaves me out?

Sam continues in his associations and says that he is fascinated and humored by his creation of my private self. I privately associate to a business involving a hostile takeover. He keeps laughing and says that in his mind I've stated my age, and it's almost as though he's laughing at someone in his head that is me with whom he's conversing. My thoughts go to how he has privately, psychically, invaded my privacy and taken over a reality that is unpleasant for him—that I haven't revealed many things about myself. He has always been angry about my not sharing more about my life. He wants us to be friends and to spend time together socially. He's told me that I'm too old for him sexually but that he wants me to be an older friend. He enjoys when we have briefly conversed together more naturally a few times. We have some areas of overlapping intellectual interest, and I imagine that I would enjoy talking to him more about our shared interests than the sense I have of Sam's anger about my not stating things (my "stated age") and his attempt to take that matter into his own hands and mind.

As the hour continues, some of my private thoughts seem to become clearer. My private life, my vital statistics, and maybe my private parts too— age, marital status, religion, my private thoughts—all exist in his mind as a "stated something." He speaks more of how much he wants to have access to things he doesn't have control over. He associates to his tendency to find a way around feeling the lack or deficit and how looking on the bright side makes many of his relationships more superficial. I imagine that he co-opts my privacy into a defense against hostility. He knows that he finds it hard to bear my privacy as something out of his control and that we are bringing it into the open—his piracy is something he is willing to give over to the court of therapeutic exploration and interpretation. Sam associates to his girlfriend's anger at him about not making up his mind about women or men as well as a developing successful professional career, which could lead him in two very different directions in the future. He needs to decide at some point soon about each of these different directions, the choices available to him romantically and professionally.

At some level the hour is productive and interesting in that we come upon this interesting part of Sam's mind or internalized object relation—"your stated age." The patient's in conflict about the parts of him that he knows make for superficiality in glossing over what he knows and doesn't know and that he has to find a way to bring himself more fully to those with whom he is intimate. He has to work with the conflict he feels and anxiety he feels about his anger toward me about not stating my age or not knowing me in the way he wishes to know himself and me. It seems implied that we may eventually be able to explore more about why he may be anxious about asking.

While I'm very fond of Sam, I end the session aware that I'm no less annoyed now than during the hour. What is it about Sam that caused me to feel annoyed? Over many sessions prior and subsequent to this one with Sam, I visualized Sam at home organizing his surroundings, folding clothes, and cleaning up the house. I fell upon these kinds of visual images of Sam despite the fact that they didn't come from him. It is not uncommon for me to find that as I listen to patients I locate them in various places, and this reverie can be very useful. Sometimes the location of a place is related to a point of transference–countertransference that helps me locate a sense of unconscious fantasy or an object relation that I've not previously noticed. At other times I'm aware that I'm engaging in a form of defensive distancing, a kind of isolation of affect that allows me to locate the patient outside the consulting room or somewhere other than with me.

Sam's self-sufficiency and organization were adaptations to a family life in which he felt his parents were largely laissez-faire, from his point of view, to a fault. They wanted him to feel that "on his own" he would come to his own sense of values, beliefs, and interests. He was an only child, and, although highly valued, he never felt as though he was treated as a child. Conversations with his parents seemed always pitched at an adult level with what he regarded as expectations that he be mature before his time—in fact, pseudo-mature. He envied his closest friend in grade school and high school whose parents were directive, opinionated, and sometimes dictatorial. During one session early on in his analysis, he associated to his friend's father as dictatorial. In association to "dictatorial," Sam said that he wished his father had had more of a dick. He wanted his father to be stronger with his mother, and he often deferred to her judgment with self-effacing, cheery cooperation. He recognized some of these character traits in himself, often glossing over differences and sometimes disappointment in others and him.

Over the course of a number of sessions as I began to make use of these images and my continued mild irritation toward Sam's use of the analyst in his mind, "my stated age," I became aware of how I felt myself to be continually "folded into," as it were, an internalized scenario that Sam held. When I made interpretations they often seemed too immediately or easily incorporated by Sam. In turn, his understanding would sometimes seem a bit too superficial. I realized more than I ever had that Sam often seemed quite pleased with whatever I'd have to say and that his affective range was quite focused on being cheery and cooperative. At one point during one of our sessions my mind turned toward a fantasy of making a mess of Sam's apartment, overturning things that had been neatly stacked and throwing things out of the closet. In association to the "closet" at this point in the analysis I imagined that Sam's persistent masturbatory fantasies about men and only men might be a clue that he would prefer to be with men and that his girlfriend might partially protect him from seeking more intimacy with men—thus, the fantasy of throwing things out of the closet. This series of thoughts marked a movement away from a particular form of uncertainty I'd held in my mind up to this point in the analysis about whether Sam used men as a defense against intimacy with women or vice versa. While I was still quite uncertain about whether Sam would decide ultimately to be with a man or a woman, I began to believe that his confusion served his purposes to not get too close to anyone in an intimate relationship.

These associations began a slight shift in my mode of formulation and interpretation with Sam. I realized that I'd been quite content to have Sam work with "my stated age" in his head, the internalized representation of me because it would help us elaborate aspects of his unconscious fantasy life. His idealizations of me and senior colleagues seemed too easy to accept and that I could easily slide into his proscribed roles for others and me. He also seemed so consistently unassailable with his girlfriend. He would say to her that he "just couldn't figure this out yet"—whether he wanted to be with her or with men. He felt guilty that he was making her wait, yet he needed to know what he wanted to do. It was clear to me that he was waiting for her to decide what they would do or perhaps for me to tell him what to do about her, men, or his career choices or even to volunteer my age (though he continued to never ask). He would create a private, "unstated/stated" age or stated position of uncertainty about object choice until pushed to do otherwise. I had been enacting a form of compliance with his unconscious, quiet, but tyrannical hold on my asserting something about my independence from the analyst in his mind. Indeed, in my continued passivity to take this up I was enacting something about being a laissez-faire parent, allowing him to feel, fraudulently, at the helm of his family. When I arrive at an understanding about something related to what Ogden refers to as the unconscious transference–countertransference or unconscious object relation, interpretations begin to form more clearly in my mind. I also arrive with more clarity at what I may have been enacting with the patient. It is at this point when I'm struck with a variety of clinical choices and this is what I refer to as the analyst's ethical imagination.

The phrase, "You look younger than your stated age," now seems more obvious as a complaint cloaked within a compliment—a complaint that he didn't know me more intimately and perhaps even that I didn't confront him about his wish to know me more intimately. He wants to avoid expressing his own wishes and needs to know. His language has demonstrated how I'd enacted some process of allowing him to a pseudo-mature boy, a boy who thinks he knows the facts and who doesn't know the facts. I began challenging Sam more actively. I told him, "I think that you're waiting for me and others in your life to give you advice and act like parents who are engaged and want to give of themselves to you. Parents should know the facts like what to do with your penis or your career." Sam seemed relieved to be able to speak more freely about these wishes as we began to get more deeply into how insistent he was about wanting this advice. He joked, "That's the idea. So now can we proceed to the advice."

In essence I take up what was in some ways obvious all along—Sam's wish to know my stated age without having to ask or to have to show his desire to know. This is what he had been warding off, a warding off of many feelings of sadness and anger camouflaged in some ways by autoerotic and self-sufficient fantasy processes.

My imagination regarding these various kinds of reverie also require me to consider the sobering prospect that as I become more actively confrontational about these processes, I may very well be enacting his wishes for me or someone in his life to be forceful, parental, and guiding and to tell him what to do—a dick, as it were. I consider it the work of the analyst to ponder the inevitable continuing aspects of enactment intrinsic to whatever direction our interpretive focus takes us.

This particular set of clinical observations also raises complex aspects of the analyst's ethical imagination. I have to challenge more actively Sam's autistic attempt to experience me as stating my age when I haven't while making no promises to actually ever state my age. This is a familiar place for many analysts who run the risk of needing to make interpretations that may stoke the fire of the patient's curiosity about us as "real" objects while not promising to provide any more information about us as real objects. Naturally this can become another form of enactment including the possibility of enacting a retaliatory teasing object as a response to Sam's self-sufficient antidote and private way of not wanting to be in the position of feeling needs or desire to know me more.

Note that in this clinical example I've taken up matters quite similar to Ogden's (1997) use of reverie as "simultaneously a personal/private event and an intersubjective one" (p. 568). I haven't spoken directly with the analysand directly about my own experiences and instead attempt to speak to the analysand "from" what I'm thinking and feeling.

The Chicken and the Egg

In this clinical example I try to illustrate how my own needs for reverie and privacy help me when I express more direct parts of my experience during the interpretation of points of transference–countertransference entanglement.

Josh is a man in his early 50s who often gets himself into masochistic relationships with others. Josh felt that he couldn't get his mother's attention as a young boy. From his point of view she was unavailable largely because of her ambitious career and outside romantic interests. His father was more available to him but not very easy to admire. Josh's father wore his neediness and sexuality on his sleeve. He was damaged in Josh's view, unproductive in a career in which he never lived up to his potential. Josh's father seemed to "hang on" his mother in ways that seemed pathetic to Josh, particularly since she rebuffed his attempts to hold and touch her. She seemed annoyed and turned off by her husband's attempts to be affectionate. Later in his 20s, Josh learned that his mother had been involved in one serious extramarital relationship during his adolescence and that she had at least a few affairs during his childhood. Josh's parents split up when he went to college, and he now feels as though their marriage was held together quite precariously throughout his childhood.

Josh's transference involved feeling unimportant to me, not wanting to risk whether he mattered. He treated his sessions like they were unimportant to me because they involved him and that I would be more interested in patients who mattered more to them and to me. He was often late to sessions, sometimes recounting ways in which he felt unworthy of the attention he wanted from me and from others. I regarded our relationship as something akin to what he felt with his mother—that for Josh I was largely unaware of him, finding him unappealing in his view, and not really registering any need or desire of my own to get to know him. He would sometimes laugh (with sadness) about this as something that he knew not to be true but that nevertheless, he felt "in his bones." From the beginning I'd wondered if Josh's mother was as inattentive as he'd experienced or was his identification with his father as someone rejected by mother important in some ways to hold to either assuage his guilt or to remain close to his father.

Josh arrives at his session at the beginning of his second year of analysis and starts talking about his law partners, two females and one male, whom he feels devalue his work relative to their own. He feels he sometimes doesn't exist in the room with them. I hear this as an allusion to a way he feels he doesn't exist for me. I find myself getting distracted, thinking about what I'll be doing that night and later that day, work I have to do, and some creative writing I've been experimenting with lately.

I hear Josh say to me through the distraction of my reverie: "I want to know what you think about this." He is referring to the ways he doesn't exist in the room for his colleagues and how devalued he feels with them. Of course I'm thinking about the ways I just made him not exist by thinking about some of my own ideas separate from Josh. I was struck by his very unusual inquiry about what I was thinking about this frequent complaint of being unimportant to his colleagues. I'm thinking to myself that I want to comment on the more proximate inquiry related to how I understand his experience of not existing with his partners. I'm aware that by doing so I get myself out of the very uncomfortable position of knowing that I was enacting something in the room with him that he describes feeling all the time with others in his life. I'm not sure I want to talk more directly about that yet, if ever.

I say, "I'm struck that you've asked me about the partners ignoring you in a way that is unusual. By asking, you've done something that's hard for you to do—to legitimize your own need to feel that you matter and that you have the authority to ask. In asking me what I think about that, you'd like to feel that I think you matter or that they should pay more attention to you."

His thoughts go in a direction that is somewhat typical for Josh: "I'm thinking that a part of me is glad that you'll be away soon [on vacation]. I usually think that at least you need my money even though I don't think you need or want anything else from me. Then when you go away I get sad because I think, 'He doesn't even need my money.'"

"You feel expendable."

"Yes, you need nothing from me like my mother needed nothing from me."

"But you just disappeared again with me. You asked me directly what I thought about your partners ignoring you, and then you went away and said that you're forgettable to me by dint of my willingness to go on vacation."

"I was forgettable to her, but I can't help but want to be significant to her. I can't stop trying."

"And you feel like if you ask to matter to me or her the less likely it is that she will be there for you or that I will be. She doesn't need you, and I don't need you. So then you disappear again."

In the moment of reverie that I've described, the moment in which I'm privately disappearing from him, I'm likely enacting the role of his mother. Josh is talking about that experience with his colleagues and perhaps symbolically with his mother and me. He may also be attuned to my actual disappearance with him. I believe that I'm enacting this not because it has happened for the first time but because it is the first time that I became aware of it when he is alluding to it in displacement. This way of knowing for me is private at this point, but he may feel it. I'm not ready to tell him because I fear that by telling him that it is so, I might be enacting something even harder for him to deal with which is that I am pulling away. I worry that he will conclude that it is because he is not worthy of being memorable or loved. I know that this will have to be discussed, or do I? My thought at this point is that I may very well tell him about this interaction if it is happening repeatedly, but I'm not ready to yet. I need my privacy to think about this and see whether it keeps happening. But I suspect that he and I are in a chicken–egg process, a mode of reciprocal influence in which he may feel me disappearing so he disappears. But he may also be reacting to an internalized maternal object whom he experienced as neglectful. I feel him disappearing, and when he does sometimes instead of pointing that out to him at times I go off somewhere else. Where it all begins is, of course, hard to say.

In these moments, I ask, "Why do I need some privacy?" I'm aware that I'm afraid of hurting him. By underscoring my moments of distractibility, I might be requiring of him a capacity for reflection that exceeds his ability to regulate his self-esteem. Is the fear of hurting him real or imagined by me? Another side of my ethical imagination is to think about whether I'm protecting myself from conveying to him in vivid, more observable terms how I was leaving him and relegating him to the realm of the unimportant? Might it let him see more about the impact of his own self-imposed disappearance on others? Would showing him this allow him to consider more the plausibility reality and substance of his inner life and cognitive process in contrast to how he often reflexively dismisses this level of experience? Will showing him the analyst's correlate experience allow him to feel something about how I'm assailable and culpable in this way, or is it a way to unload my own sense of guilt and culpability? He has a right to be angry with his mother and me. More importantly, he has a right to trust himself and his own authority. Like any dilemma involving complexity I need to be able to sit with the affective implications or fallout, which comes from anything, I decide.

Outside the hours with Josh my thoughts sometimes go in a more theoretical direction to papers by Steiner (1993) from a Kleinian perspective and Slochower (1996) from a relational perspective in which each describes patients for whom interpretation which implies aspects of the analyst's subjectivity can be destructive for periods of time during analysis. Steiner describes how sometimes "patient-based" interpretations feel to blaming or intrusive to some patients. Similarly, Slochower describes patients for whom the act of revealing aspects of the analyst's experience can repeat the patient's earlier experiences with parents who were overinvolved with their own experiences and neglectful of their children. Then I think of a contrasting view of Bass (1996), who suggests that if we make this assumption about the destructive use of the analyst's subjectivity we may be more likely to find it. In my view this to me is not a debate that is possible to be resolved except in the privacy of the analyst's imagination and through discovery with a particular patient. It is a kind of ethical imagination of the analyst in which his reverie and need for privacy can play and work. This debate doesn't resolve itself in any way other than that these are matters to consider with each patient–analyst dyad.

I use my privacy and reverie engaged in these clinical imaginings and I try to think about it also from various theoretical perspectives, which matter to me, what I call the pluralistic third. My use of this privacy and reverie, in contrast to Ogden's wonderful illustrations of the use of reverie, may result in direct statements of affect, ideas, or behavior, which the patient wouldn't have a way of knowing without what I refer to as *analyst disclosure*. I refer to it as analyst disclosure rather than self-disclosure (Cooper, 1998a, 1998b) because it relates to the use of my privacy. I retain a strong sense of a private self when I disclose affects, ideas, and behaviors that are part of the interpretive work. Privacy and reverie are what allow my private self to bring forward parts of me that I try to help the patient to understand about himself in relation to me.

On occasion, the pattern of my own distractability matched Josh's description of important others (e.g., mother, me, and colleagues) who did not seem to register his presence. Eventually, I did in fact talk to Josh about this pattern of my inattention that accompanied his experience of other's inattention during a session when I was *not* distracted. He seemed increasingly present, telling me more directly that he didn't feel memorable to me and important. I told him, "I notice myself being most likely to be distracted with you when I experience you as giving up on yourself, particularly when you're withdrawing from alive, sexual, funny, and hostile parts of yourself." He said, "Maybe when I need you most." I said, "Yes, I imagine that it is when you need me most to show you what you're doing or encourage you to do otherwise." At the point that I chose to talk to him from this register, I could do so particularly because I was not in the middle of feeling overwhelmed by my own feelings of guilt about my withdrawal from him. Josh was becoming much stronger, trusting himself more, and willing to talk to me more directly about what he wished for from me.

I don't want to suggest that this is a necessary technical prescription for anyone else. While it was my guess that Josh would have had a hard time with a more direct disclosure at the moment when I initially became aware of this confluence of intersubjective events that I've described, it is quite difficult for me to know. Instead, I made my clinical decisions based on my own sense of what I was able to convey about how his tendency to feel forgettable might sometimes engender or augment that experience in others. In fact, we discussed how much his growing awareness of feeling unimportant to others and recognizing these feelings in others, while not always correct, were probably part of his own process of growing trust in his own mind and experience. This clinical moment began a process by which Josh became more aware of trusting some of his own experiences of neglect and his own agency in seeing how unconsciously he disappeared from others before they could withdraw from him.

Some Paradoxical Aspects of Being Oneself as Patient and Analyst

In this brief example I aim to illustrate a register close to what I have previously referred to as analyst disclosure in the analyst's use of privacy and reverie. While it is a different register than that used and elaborated by Ogden (1994, 1997), I think it shares in common his appreciation of the paradoxical interplay of private yet deeply personal reveries and how these reveries help us create unconscious intersubjective constructions, which illuminate points of transference–countertransference engagement.

Susan is a very effective and in many ways satisfied mother and attorney in her early 40s. Her main complaint is an inability to stop feeling a relentless pressure about making everyone in her life happy. She is hypersensitive to disappointing her husband, her two children, an 11-year-old girl and 7-year-old boy, her colleagues, fellow partners at her firm, and, now in our analytic work, particularly me. During the third year of her analysis we've come to a point in which she feels, very problematically, that I don't smile at her enough when she is entering and leaving my office.

She has some potent and durable theories about this. In fact, at the time of this vignette she is worried that her concern about whether she pleases me is privately off-putting. In Susan's mind, I'm drawn to a very secure and strong woman who is beyond the need for affirmation.

I admire and think of Susan as smart, funny, and physically attractive. In my view and Susan's she is partly experiencing me as her father who withdrew from her when she was 14. She felt that he was critical of her as she diverged from him in terms of becoming somewhat iconoclastic in her intellectual and artistic interests. She felt that her mother silently approved of her choices but would never speak on Susan's behalf or her own. Her two older sisters worked in the family business during high school and after college. In particular her oldest sister was regarded by Susan and her parents as almost being the same person as their father. As Susan's adolescence continued, both sisters became critical of her, and she felt that she lost their interest and pleasure in her as the youngest, cute little sister. They saw her interests as constituting a betrayal of the family's ideals, particularly regarding her growing interest in art and left wing politics. She married a man who was from a different religious background than hers (Susan is Catholic and her husband Jewish), which seemed to cement her status as an outsider.

During the first year or so into this analysis, I often felt a kind of ease with what I regarded as an "empathic" attunement about her longings to have her father's approval despite her being different than he. She had struggled throughout her with a conflict of wanting to show herself and not show herself, often trying to camouflage those interests that diverged from those of her family. She seemed to feel relieved that she could show herself to me in the analysis. I had been taking it up in terms of how this expressed a longing for affirmation and a set of needs from her father that she was feeling and letting me know about in her analysis.

At the time of this vignette, during her third year, Susan became more vigilant to whether I was smiling but not particularly curious about why this was so. I wasn't aware, initially, that this was the case and instead thought that she was moving into a deeper set of wishes to be able to express how much more she wanted. She disagreed, instead insisting that she had reached some tipping point with me and that I didn't really like who she was. Over many months I, indeed, began to feel that empathy for Susan's sadness and anxiety was tempered with another feeling more controlled by Susan. In fact, I was aware that, at times, I even felt burdened by her sense that if I didn't smile at her warmly when I greeted her or said good-bye (often something that I was not aware of) she felt rejected. I was reminded of the feedback she received at the beginning of our work when she made partner: that the partners wanted her to work more independently and to ask for reassurance less frequently.

At this point in our work, during one session I was thinking about how diminutive Susan is in relation to me. She is very petite, rather small in stature, and has a beautiful but soft voice that I can barely hear behind the couch at times. At this moment I felt a bit like a bull in a china shop in comparison with her. Sometimes I visualize this. But in this session my mind moved to Gulliver with the Lilliputians and then to Dr. Frankenstein's son, Frankenstein, who come to mind from time to time in my work. But I began to think less of the impact of Frankenstein or Gulliver on those around them and more about them each as misunderstood giants. Frankenstein didn't ask to be created. He was the victim of his father's Promethean ideas and fantasies. Was I thinking about how Susan was asked to be her father's creation and how she didn't know how to be herself and still loved by him? Then I went back to my sense of how much power I had over Susan from her point of view and how now I felt controlled by her from mine.

This reverie began a process of thinking more fully about my negative feelings about being this transference object for Susan. I *imagined* something like the following verbose formulation: "I'm feeling controlled by your insistence that my not smiling enough at you means something negative or that I don't like you. Maybe I'm actually not smiling at you in the same way when I greet you. You want me not to have a private life in which I might be thinking and feeling any one of a number of things about you or other matters that you won't know or can't know. I want to have that privacy, just like I think that you wanted to feel like you were loved by your father while having yours, individuality, privacy and separateness. You're afraid to have your privacy and risk being unloved and letting me have mine. You're trying to make this better by (unconsciously) being like him rather than seeing if you can feel safe being different than him or me and us each having our freedom to feel what we feel." I felicitously call this *rougherie,* a variation on reverie.

In my imagination, I'm aware that by putting Susan's identification with her father front and center, I'm at a great deal of remove from Susan's anxiety about what my not smiling in the way that she wishes might mean. My mind goes to feeling constrained by this set of feelings and choices or lack thereof. I feel as if I can't be "myself" as Susan's analyst, an ironically held conflict if ever there was one. I can hear the irony of an analyst who is in some ways never "himself," yet the words seem meaningful. I imagine that this lack of choice, this conflict may also be something like what Susan feels, and I try to talk to her about my dilemma rather than choosing a particular side of this set of experiences and conflicts. The next time that Susan brings up her anxiety about my failure to smile at her in the way she wished as she left the previous session, I say, "It's so tough for you to be yourself at work, with your father and me, and still feel our approval, our smile. It's tough for me to find a way to be myself with you as your analyst without making you feel betrayed, hurt, and worried about how I feel about you. It may even be making for less of a smile. You don't like your choices, why should you and maybe in a way that's similar to the way I don't like mine."

Susan had many reactions to this shift in my interpretive position. She was initially relieved that I could voice this to her, and she recognized the similarity in our position. She also felt degraded and inadequate that she wasn't being a good patient because she feared that she had succeeded in creating a form of analytic impasse. We looked at how some of these feelings of inadequacy and badness were a familiar way for her to resolve differences and standstills with her frustrated love in relation to her father. I suggested that by blaming herself she was able to preserve her relationship with her father and me. The complexity and layering of even this brief part of the analytic process is far beyond the scope of this paper but it is important to say that the density of these points of transference–countertransference experience and enactment were the stuff of our work together and allowed her to get much more into some of the erotic and aggressive aspects of the wanted smile. Much later, in a moving moment of parapraxis, Susan was speaking of why it was difficult to get started in her sessions. She wished to say, "I wonder why I can't get started." Instead she said, "I wonderful." She burst into tears as she knew quite well what this was all about.

Conclusion

There is some overlap with what I call the analyst's ethical imagination and what Benjamin (2004) refers to as "the moral third." Benjamin the part of the analyst's mind and experience that considers how to reach a patient and aspects of moral responsibility in doing so. I do not, however, conceptualize this activity with developmental metaphors in mind. It also overlaps with the notion of the "future of interpretation" (Cooper, 1997), and it borrows from Loewald's (1960) model of how interpretation takes a patient simultaneously one step into regression and one step into an unknown and new psychic future. Sometimes the analyst's anticipation of this psychic future is helpful in challenging a patient to examine new dimensions of conflict or self-state experiences, while at other times it may enact too far a psychic reach, unanticipated or underappreciated by the analyst.

These moments of repetitive transference–countertransference enactment sometimes also invite the opportunity to think outside the boundaries of our own theoretical preferences. When I have this kind of privilege in my analytic work, I also use what I've called the *pluralistic third* (Cooper, 2007), which includes the opportunity to think about these choices from several differing perspectives including theoretical choices which are different from the one that I believe I've used. This pluralistic third includes the analyst's attempt to think about the transference–countertransference especially by trying to step outside what might be my "overvalued ideas" and "selected facts" (Bion, 1963; Britton & Steiner, 1994) to build on my understandings. In other words, the analyst's dyadic relation to his own theory creates its own blind spots in integrating forms of reverie or any other form of clinical data. The pluralistic third, like the analyst's ethical imagination, is a way of thinking about spontaneously occurring events within the analyst's mind. It is a way that we sometimes reach outside our usual modes of thinking to draw on our body of ideas and cumulative knowledge in clinical psychoanalysis (e.g., Pine, 2006). It helps develop what Britton (2003) termed *vulnerable knowledge* of our patient rather than fixed belief.

I have tried to illustrate some examples of varying ways I try to make use of forms of analytic reverie and my privacy. I have also tried to illustrate a few different registers from which the analyst can illuminate these points of unconscious transference–countertransference enactment. The goal of using such reverie in the course of analytic work is to help show the patient specific and hopefully rather immediate dimensions of the analyst's understanding of the transference–countertransference enactments, which have and continue to exert influence within the work. It is likely that the analyst's use of reverie is vitally related to therapeutic action in ways that relate not only to the analyst's "uncovering" of unconscious phenomena but also to the analyst's curiosity about his own mind. The patient has an opportunity to see the analyst's mind at work, using his experience and the imagery that emerges to know his (the analyst's) own mind to know better his patient.

References

Aron, L. (1991). The patient's experience of the analyst's subjectivity. *Psychoanalytic Dialogues*, *1*, 29–51.

Balint, M. (1968). *The basic fault*. London: Tavistock.

Bass, A. (1996). Holding, holding back, and holding on. *Psychoanalytic Dialogues*, *6*, 361–378.

Benjamin, J. (2004). Beyond doer and done to: An intersubjective view of thirdness. *Psychoanalytic Quarterly*, *73*, 5–46.

Bion, W. R. (1959). Attacks on linking. *International Journal of Psychoanalysis*, *40*, 308–315.

Bion, W. R. (1962). *Learning from experience*. London: Heinemann, 1984.

Bion, W. R. (1963). *Elements of psychoanalysis*. London: Heinemann, 1984.

Boesky, D. (1990). The psychoanalytic process and its components. *Psychoanalytic Quarterly*, *64*, 282–305.

Britton, R. (2003). *Belief and imagination*. London: Routledge.

Britton, R., & Steiner, J. (1994). Interpretation: Selected fact or overvalued idea? *International Journal of Psychoanalysis*, *75*, 1069–1078.

Busch, F. (1993). "In the neighborhood": Aspects of a good interpretation and a "developmental lag" in ego psychology. *Journal of the American Psychoanalytic Association*, *41*, 151–177.

Civateresse, G. (2009). *The intimate room: Theory and technique of the analytic field (the new library of psychoanalysis)*. London: Routledge Press.

Cooper, S. (1997). The future of interpretation. *International Journal of Psychoanalysis*, *78*, 667–681.

Cooper, S. (1998a). Countertransference disclosure and the conceptualization of technique. *Psychoanalytic Quarterly*, *67*, 128–154.

Cooper, S. (1998b). Analyst-subjectivity, analyst-disclosure, and the aims of psychoanalysis. *Psychoanalytic Quarterly*, *67*, 379–406.

Cooper, S. (2000). *Objects of hope: Exploring possibility and limit in psychoanalysis.* Hillsdale: The Analytic Press.

Cooper, S. (2007). Begin the beguine: Psychoanalysis and the pluralistic third. *Psychoanalytic Dialogues, 17*(2), 247–272.

Freud, S. (1912). Recommendations to physicians practising psychoanalysis. In J. Strachey (Ed. & Trans.), *The standard edition of the complete psychological works of Sigmund Freud* (Vol. 12, pp. 109–120). London: The Hogarth Press.

Gill, M. (1983). The interpersonal paradigm and the degree of the therapist's involvement. *Contemporary Psychoanalysis, 19*, 200–237.

Gray, P. (1973). Psychoanalytic technique: The ego's capacity to view intrapsychic activity. *Journal of the American Psychoanalytic Association, 21*, 474–492.

Gray, P. (1990). The nature of therapeutic action in psychoanalysis. *Journal of the American Psychoanalytic Association, 38*, 1083–1099.

Hoffman, I. Z. (1983). The patient as interpreter of the analyst's experience. *Contemporary Psychoanalysis, 19*, 389–422.

Kris, A. (1990). Helping patients by analyzing self-criticism. *Journal of the American Psychoanalytic Association, 38*, 605–636.

Loewald, H. (1960). The therapeutic action of psychoanalysis. *International Journal of Psychoanalysis, 41*, 16–33.

Ogden, T. (1994). The analytic third: Working with intersubjective clinical facts. *International Journal of Psychoanalysis, 75*, 3–20.

Ogden, T. (1996). Reconsidering three aspects of psychoanalytic technique. *International Journal of Psychoanalysis, 77*, 883–899.

Ogden, T. (1997). Reverie and metaphor. *International Journal of Psychoanalysis, 78*, 719–732.

Ogden, T. (2004). The analytic third: Implications for psychoanalytic theory and technique. *Psychoanalytic Quarterly, 73*, 167–196.

Pine, F. (2006). The psychoanalytic dictionary. *Journal of the American Psychoanalytic Association, 54*, 463–492.

Racker, H. (1968). *Transference and countertransference.* New York: International Universities Press.

Schwaber, E. (1992). The analyst's retreat from the patient's vantage point. *International Journal of Psychoanalysis, 73*, 349–361.

Slochower, J. (1996). The holding environment and the fate of the analyst's subjectivity. *Psychoanalytic Dialogues, 13*, 451–470.

Smith, H. (2000). Countertransference, conflictual listening, and the analytic object relationship. *Journal of the America Psychoanalytic Association, 49*, 781–812.

Smith, H. (2003). Can we integrate the diverse theories and practices of psychoanalysis? *Journal of the American Psychoanalytic Association, 51*(Suppl.), 145–161.

Steiner, J. (1993). *Psychic retreats.* London: Routledge.

Stern, D. (1983). Unformulated experience. *Contemporary Psychoanalysis, 19*, 71–99.

Symington, N. (1983). The analyst's act of freedom as an agent of therapeutic change. *International Review of Psychoanalysis, 10*, 283–292.

Winnicott, D. W. (1958). The capacity to be alone. In *The maturational processes and the facilitating environment.* New York: International Universities Press.

13

"Grown-Up" Words

*An Interpersonal-Relational Perspective on Unconscious Fantasy**

Philip M. Bromberg

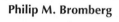

A group of kindergartners were trying very hard to become accustomed to the first grade. The biggest hurdle they faced was that the teacher insisted on no baby-talk. "You need to use 'Big People' words," she was always reminding them. She started by asking Chris, "What did you do over the weekend?" "I went to visit my Nana." "No, you went to visit your grandmother. Use 'Big People' words!" She then asked William what he had done. "I took a ride on a choo-choo." She said "No, you took a ride on a train. You must remember to use 'Big People' words." She then asked little Alex what he had done. "I read a book," he replied. "That's wonderful!" the teacher said. "What book did you read?" Alex thought really hard about it, then puffed out his chest with great pride, and said, "Winnie the shit."

I, too, thought really hard about how to write this chapter. Like Alex, I tried to corral my mind into using "Big People" words, but I fear that some readers might discern a similarity in our developmental level of *unconscious fantasy*. In the absence of negotiation, we each seem reluctant to substitute the language of what is observable with the more grownup conceptual language learned through familial training. I'll be satisfied if my effort to negotiate the two is even half as successful as Alex's was.

The notion of unconscious fantasy is an idea first proposed by Freud (1897) in a letter to Fliess. The formulation was intended to account for the

---

* This paper originally appeared in *Psychoanalytic Inquiry*, 28, 2008, pp. 131–150. Reprinted with permission.

fact that every human being appears to be possessed by an unconscious scenario that is played out repetitively and leads to certain life choices that seem to have a life of their own. For some individuals, these repetitive choices take the form of a drama that shapes the course of their lives in a way that overrides both judgment and memory of past experience. As Langan (1997) wryly put it, "What is one to do with the fractionating discovery that, as the poet Allen Ginsberg remarked, 'My mind's got a mind of its own'?" (p. 820). The importance of unconscious fantasy as a foundational element in both Freudian and Kleinian psychoanalytic theory is long-standing. It has offered clinicians a way of viewing the complex nature of consciousness that has allowed them to make sense of mental phenomena that are otherwise difficult to comprehend. Despite this, the concept has never appealed to me either conceptually or clinically, and in the remainder of this paper I will to address the question of whether the term *unconscious fantasy* continues to be central (or useful) to the theory and practice of psychoanalysis.

I begin by looking at two recent papers, Grotstein (2004) and Bromberg (2003), published about 1 year apart. In these articles each of us addressed the phenomenon of unconscious experience in the same way that Albert Goldbarth (2003) spoke about the ineffable subjective experience that takes place in the "incomprehensible lacunae" when "reality blinks." Becoming aware of the gaps in our subjectivity, Goldbarth wrote, is to become aware that "we don't know *what* takes place in those betweens" (p. 133). Because we are unable to stare at these gaps too long, "any more than at sunspots" (p. 133), as Goldbarth put it, I suggest that we have found a term—*unconscious fantasy*—that lets us believe we know more than we do. As Levenson (1983) noted, citing Count Alfred Korzybski (1954), "the illusion of clarity increases with the level of abstraction" (p. 122).

The ineffable experience to which I refer is the "ghostly" intrusion into an analyst's subjectivity of a *not-me* presence so difficult to capture in language, that Grotstein and I each used poetry to introduce our papers in hope of evoking its essence through metaphor before we attempted to conceptualize it. It is an experience too easily lost in translation if we try to make it submit to psychoanalytic explanation. In my own selection of poetry, I favored the lyricism of Emily Dickinson (1863/1960, p. 333), and Grotstein drew upon the more classical imagery of Alexander Pope (1714/1939, pp. 354–364), but we each recognized that the metaphor of hauntedness would best communicate the affective presence that led Dickinson to speak of "ourself behind ourself, concealed"—what analysts have called unconscious fantasy (spelled *phantasy* by Kleinians). In Pope's words, "Unnumbered spirits around thee fly...though unseen, are ever on the wing," and in Dickinson's, "One need not be a chamber to be haunted—One need not be a house." Freud saw these ghosts as pathological epiphenomena of unconscious fantasy, whereas Klein saw these unconscious phantasies as developmental necessities that are potentially transformative. "Freud and Klein emphasized contrasting aspects of the everyday usage of the word *phantasy*.... Freud's usage emphasizes the fictitious, wish-fulfilling aspect of the everyday usage, whereas Klein tended to focus on the imaginative aspect" (Spillius, 2001, p. 362). Spelling the word *fantasy* with a *ph* rather than an *f* has helped analysts to build a bridge between Freudian and Kleinian theory and also between pathology and creativity. But notwithstanding Bion's seminal contribution to constructing this bridge, the relational heart of the matter doesn't seem yet to have been addressed: Is the concept of unconscious fantasy, no matter how one spells it, a help or a hindrance to comprehending that clinical process is a relational act of meaning construction? Grotstein (2004), from a Kleinian–Bionian vantage point, put his finger on this dilemma by pointing out that no matter what we choose to tell ourselves all that an analyst can ever truly address with his or her patient is conscious fantasy.

> Traditionally, when psychoanalysts interpret unconscious fantasies to analysands, the predominating point of view has always been that of external factual reality, for instance, "When you were in the waiting room and heard me on the phone you thought that I was talking with my mistress" (in fantasy)—implying that, factually, I was not. In other words, phantasies have been understood as the prime cause of pathology, and debunking the phantasy by a safe restoration of reality has been thought to constitute the cure. (pp. 115–116)

The irony in this example is that it is not, in fact, an interpretation of unconscious fantasy but of *conscious* fantasy (acknowledged by Grotstein's spelling fantasy with an *f*) simply because it is already at the level of thought when the interpretation is made. An unsymbolized affective experience can reach consciousness only through symbolization, and this requires an experiential relational context to organize the meaning of an interpretation. In this regard, consider what R. D. Laing (1967) had to say about fantasy:

> Fantasy is a particular way of relating to the world. It is part of, sometimes the essential part of, the meaning or sense implicit in action. As relationship we may be dissociated from it ... [and] we may ... refuse to admit that our behavior implies an experiential relationship or a relational experience that gives it a meaning. Fantasy ... is always experiential and meaningful; and if the person is not dissociated from it, relational in a valid way. (pp. 31–32)

If Laing is accurate, then the concept of unconscious fantasy, which unfortunately implies buried thought rather than particular ways of relating to the world—or as we now refer to it, *procedural memory*—can be a hindrance. Thus, my reluctance to embrace the concept of unconscious fantasy involves scruples more clinical than conceptual, although the latter are, indeed, present. I have made a suggestion (Bromberg, 1989) similar to that made by Laing with regard to unconscious fantasy: "In a psychoanalysis, patients do not reveal their unconscious fantasies to the analyst. They *are* their unconscious fantasies and live them with the analyst through the *act* of psychoanalysis" (p. 153, emphasis in original). This is a way of saying that unconscious fantasy comes to exist while it is being constructed through the interaction of the various and shifting self-states of both patient and analyst. It could, therefore, be argued that the reason the same dynamic is enacted again and again during the course of an analysis is that, within a given analytic relationship, what seems to be a patient's *repetition compulsion* isn't in fact a real repetition. Each so-called repetition changes the relationship, and in the same sense that Heraclitus said, "One cannot step into the same river twice," it can be similarly said, "One cannot step into the same enactment twice." The point at which the analyst becomes aware that the enactment is a different "river" is the point at which he or she wakes up and recognizes that something is going on between them and that he or she is a partner in its creation. This recognition undermines the analyst's need to believe that what is taking place is simply a return of material from the patient's past and can be understood solely in terms of the patient's contribution. The necessary conditions are now present to permit a process of interpersonal comparison and interpersonal negotiation between the respective self-states of analyst and patient that were dissociatively engaged with each another in ways that shaped the enactment. Through this interpersonal negotiation between self-states, a similar process of *intrapsychic* negotiation is facilitated in the patient, whereby self-states that formerly had not been able to coexist, much less communicate, become increasingly able to participate as aspects of a coherent sense of "me" that is now available to the experience of internal conflict.

Lyons-Ruth and the Boston Change Process Study Group (2001) focused particular attention on this view of therapeutic action and argued that it may be the next major step in the growth of psychoanalysis. I refer to what they call "a nonlinear enactive theory of psychotherapeutic change" whereby "the process of psychodynamic therapy can usefully be thought of as the pursuit of more collaborative, inclusive, and coherent forms of dialogue between the two therapeutic partners."

> If clinical process is affect-guided rather than cognition-guided, [then] therapeutic change is a process that leads to the emergence of new forms of relational organization. New experiences emerge but they are not created by the therapist for the benefit of the patient. Instead, *they emerge somewhat unpredictably from the mutual searching of patient and therapist for new forms of recognition, or new forms of fitting together of initiatives in the interaction between them.* (p. 17, italics added)

Specifically, these researchers argued that enlarging the domain and fluency of the dialogue is primary to enduring personality growth in treatment; it is this that leads to increasingly integrated and complex content. This does not mean that content is unimportant; rather, it is in the relational process of exploring content that the change takes place, not in the discovery of new content per se. The content is embedded in relational experience that embodies what they call *implicit relational knowing*—an ongoing process that is, itself, part of the content. Rather (2001), writing from a contemporary Kleinian perspective, has recently brought this argument directly into the domain of analytic technique by challenging, in self-state language, the time-honored conceptualization of "resistance" (cf. Bromberg, 1995). Rather wrote that "resistance occurs not only to the specific *contents* of the unconscious, but also to the very existence of the 'other' from which unconscious phenomena are felt to emanate. The aim of psychoanalysis may be [in one way] conceptualized as the formation of a collaborative internal relation with an aspect of the psyche I have termed the 'unconscious other'" (p. 529). It is this issue that I believe creates the strongest argument against retaining the concept of unconscious fantasy. Why? Because if the self is multiple as well as integral, reality is nonlinear and cannot be distinguished from fantasy in absolute terms. The ability of different parts of the self to recognize other parts as *me* is always relative. Consequently, reality (me) for one part of the self will be fantasy (not-me) to another part. What we call "unconscious" will depend on which part of self has access to consciousness at that moment.

Fantasy and Reality

Webster's Unabridged Dictionary (1983) gives three definitions of the word *fantasy* (spelled also *phantasy*) that pertain to its meaning as a psychological event. All three definitions imply a conscious mental phenomenon that is either illusory or odd: (1) imagination; (2) an unreal mental image or illusion; (3) in psychology, a mental image as in a daydream, with some continuity. The concept of *unconscious* fantasy does not actually extend the meaning of the term *fantasy*; it changes its essential nature, and I suggest that this is the primary issue that led Arlow (1969) to lament that "it would seem that a concept so well founded clinically and so much a part of the body of our theory would long since have ceased to be a problem for psychoanalysis" (p. 3). I'm not as bewildered by this as Arlow was. The psychoanalytic theory of mind has, in general, tended to conflate supporting evidence with observations based on the theory that it is designed to support simply because its data source has been largely subjective. Thus, the concept of unconscious fantasy, not to mention other fundamental principles that are "so much a part of the body of our theory," is less "well founded clinically" than Arlow chose to believe. As an example of what I mean by conflation of evidence with observations based on the theory that the evidence is designed to support, Moore and Fine (1990), in their dictionary of psychoanalytic terms and concepts, stated, "There is a vast amount of evidence that most mental activity is unconscious. This is especially true of fantasy" (p. 75). Quite a statement if you look at it closely. The first part of the definition offered in these two sentences, that "most mental activity is unconscious," is indeed supported by objective evidence; the second part (sort of slipped under the door), which claims that "this is especially true of fantasy," not only lacks objective support but also totally changes the meaning of the term *fantasy*. What concerns me most, however, is not conceptual, but clinical. If the term *unconscious fantasy* permits an analyst to believe that something exists in the patients mind that is an unconscious replica of what we all know subjectively as fantasy experience, I would wish to retain my view that the term does us more harm than good and should be eliminated from the psychoanalytic vocabulary. But in light of the relational shift taking place in our field from metatheory to clinical theory, I think that a "let's wait and see" attitude might better support the evolution already occurring in analytic thinking at this point in time.

Enactment and Multiplicity of the Self

Lyons-Ruth (2003) emphasized the major contribution of relational theory to this new understanding of the source of therapeutic action. She urged that work should continue toward developing "a language and structure that moves beyond a narrow focus on interpretation to encompass the broader domain of relational interchanges that contribute to change in psychoanalytic treatment" (pp. 905–906). I believe that the interpersonal-relational emphasis on working with enactment and not-me experience is a major step toward providing "the language and structure" of which she speaks, because it encompasses the essence of the interpersonal and intersubjective matrix without losing the focus on the intrapsychic. The issue of whether the concept of unconscious fantasy is central to the theory and practice of psychoanalysis is also brought into high relief.

As an experiential process, enactment considers both partners as an interpenetrating unit. It is a dyadic event in which therapist and patient are linked through a dissociated mode of relating, each in a not-me state of his own that is affectively responsive to that of the other. This shared dissociative cocoon has its own imperative; it enmeshes and (at least for a time) traps the two partners within a not-me (Sullivan, 1953) communication field that is mediated by dissociation. In short, enactment is an intrapsychic phenomenon that is played out interpersonally, and it is through this interpersonal engagement that not-me—the otherness of what has been termed *unconscious fantasy*—comes to be symbolically processed as me, a relational aspect of selfhood. I believe it to be nothing less than a sea-change paradigm shift from content to process, which prompted Mitchell (1991), in developing his now seminal view of the mind as relationally organized, to write the following:

> The key transition to postclassical psychoanalytic views of the self occurred when theorists began thinking … of the repressed not as disorganized, impulsive fragments but as constellations of meanings organized around relationships … versions of the person [that] embody active patterns of experience and behavior, organized around a particular point of view, a sense of self, a way of being, which underlie the ordinary phenomenological sense we have of ourselves as integral…. The result is a plural or manifold organization of self, patterned around different self and object images or representations, derived from different relational contexts. *We are all composites of overlapping, multiple organizations and perspectives, and our experience is smoothed out by an illusory sense of continuity.* (pp. 127–128, emphasis added)

Similarly, LeDoux (2002) proposed, in neurobiological terms, that the enigma of brain processes is related to the enigma underlying multiplicity of self:

> Though [the self] is a unit, it is not unitary…. The fact that all aspects of the self are not usually manifest simultaneously, and that their different aspects can even be contradictory, may seem to present a complex problem. However, this simply means that different components of the self reflect the operation of different brain systems, which can be but are not always in sync. While explicit memory is mediated by a single system, there are a variety of different brain systems that store memory implicitly, allowing for many aspects of the self to coexist…. As the painter Paul Klee (1957) expressed it, the self is a "dramatic ensemble." (p. 31)

Fantasy, Affect, and Meaning Construction

Recall Fingarette's (1963) oft-quoted observation that "insight is not like discovering an animal which has been hiding in the bushes. Insight does not reveal a hidden, past reality; it is a reorganization of the meaning of present experience, a present reorientation toward both future and past" (p. 20). I offer the view that what is taken to be evidence of buried unconscious fantasy is an illusion that is inherent to the ongoing development of meaning construction made possible by the interpersonal-relational nature of the analytic process. It is what the patient does with the therapist that allows the unsymbolized affect (not fantasy) of each participant to engage in a cocreated process through which the patient's self-narrative is expanded. I would describe this process as brought about by greater and greater ability to hold opposing parts of the self in a single state of consciousness without dissociating, which, in turn, increases the patient's capacity for self-reflection that is affectively safe.

What looks like the uncovering of a *hidden fantasy* (i.e., unconscious cognition) is the inch-by-inch development of self-reflectiveness in areas of experience that previously foreclosed reflection and permitted only affective, subsymbolic enactment (Bucci, 1997a, 1997b, 2001, 2002, 2003). Self-reflection, as it gradually replaces dissociation as the automatic process safeguarding stability, also underwrites self-continuity (cf. Mitchell, 1991, p. 139) through fostering the illusion of something "emerging" that has been "always known but warded-off." It had indeed been known but not thought (cf. Bollas, 1987)—an affective imperative that did not belong to what is symbolized as me. It thus seems to me that to call this unsymbolized affect a *fantasy*, it is essential to accept that it is not a fantasy held by the person but vice versa; the person is possessed by the fantasy—a not-me experience that is dissociated from self-narrative and from narrative memory.

In a review of Steiner's (2003) edited book *Unconscious Fantasy*, Rizzuto (2004) cited Solms's chapter, "Do Unconscious Phantasies Really Exist?" as underscoring the point that there is a real danger in speaking about unconscious fantasy as though it were a perceivable event rather than a theoretical construct. In Rizzuto's words, "Solms examines the role of *perception* in the grasping of internal and external reality…. As a psychic phenomenon, unconscious fantasy is solely the result of inference" (p. 1289, emphasis added). Belief in an unconscious cognitive text that is operating on its own perpetuates the myth of uncovering a buried fantasy that was too dangerous to be held in consciousness—a kind of daydream that was repressed and is being allowed to emerge to the surface. This myth, by continuing to influence an analyst's clinical stance, stands in the way of allowing the relational nature of analytic growth to be fully used on the behalf of patients.

In this light, the next question one needs to address is whether unconscious fantasy can be said to exist in the absence of dissociation. Donnel Stern (2003) argued that "the absence of dissociation is not defined by the presence of some particular experience that has been prevented from existing. That way of thinking would be a simple-minded dualism" (p. 867). I believe that this is especially true with regard to the notion of unconscious fantasy as an experience already existing as a text somewhere in the psyche. It is not true, however, of experience organized by unsymbolized affect. With regard to the latter, the absence of dissociation is, indeed, defined by the presence of some particular experience that had been prevented from existing—actually, prevented from coexisting with other self-states in a single state of consciousness as part of a coherent self-configuration amenable to reflexive functioning. Its coexistence would have been destabilizing enough to coherent selfhood that any attempt to hold these incompatible states as an experience of conflict would have threatened to evoke uncontrolled hyperarousal of affect and the potential disruption of self-continuity. In other words, whether dissociation is present or absent, if the concept of unconscious fantasy is to be retained it needs serious reexamination and, I submit, recontextualization within a view of the mind that includes dissociation as a central aspect of function and structure.

I have suggested (Bromberg, 1984, 1989, 1993, 2000, 2003) that retaining the notion of unconscious fantasy interferes with full acknowledgment that clinical process, as well as mental functioning, is inherently relational. Traditionally, thinking in terms of unconscious fantasy demands from an analyst at least implicit loyalty to the belief that the therapeutic action of psychoanalysis is tied to the process of interpretation, and that a patient must be analyzable as a prerequisite. Fifteen years ago (Bromberg, 1993), I offered a challenge to this perspective in my view that "the shadow and substance of unconscious fantasy are captured and reconstructed in a new domain of reality; a chaotic intersubjective field where the collision between narrative memory and immediate perception contains the simultaneous existence of multiple realities and disjunctive self-other representations" (p. 180).

What do I mean by the shadow and substance of unconscious fantasy? I was here trying to wrestle with the issue of how to understand the mental processes underlying the transition between dissociation and conflict so that self and otherness can coexist intersubjectively. To the degree that the capacity for internal conflict begins to develop in those areas where it had been foreclosed or limited, dissociations begin to find a negotiable interface with the capacity to use interpretation (otherness). I see the phenomenon of enactment (subsymbolic communication of not-me) and the phenomenon of intersubjectivity (symbolic communication of a relational me) as discrete domains of mental process, not a continuum. The transition from dissociation to a capacity for intersubjectivity allows the development of a relational state of mind that is different from either enactment or interpersonal relatedness; this transitional state of mind contextualizes the development of intersubjectivity in those areas of the personality in which dissociated self-experience can only be enacted. It is a unique, cocreated state with characteristics inherently its own. I've written about it (Bromberg, 1996) as "a space uniquely relational and still uniquely individual; a space belonging to neither person alone, and yet, belonging to both and to each; a twilight space in which incompatible selves, each awake to its own 'truth,' can 'dream' the reality of the other without risk to its own integrity" (p. 278).

Bonovitz (2004) described this as a "transformation of fantasy through play, which in turn shifts psychic structure" (p. 553). He believed, as do I, that this transformation rests upon the fact that "fantasy is elastic in that it serves to generate multiple realities and multiple versions of oneself, versions that one may inhabit and may use to make meaning from experience and work through conflicts" (p. 561). I've offered the view that the very nature of this cocreated playground is that it doesn't stay experientially stable but changes in the act of symbolizing it, expressing it in words. In this twilight space, the generative elasticity of fantasy makes room for the multiple realities and multiple self-states of both patient and analyst, creating and simultaneously symbolizing in the process of creation, what analysts have called *unconscious fantasy.* Through this ever-shifting interface of perception and self-narrative, analysts come to experience the shadow and substance of clinical process and its inseparability from dissociation and enactment. This being said, then why retain the concept of unconscious fantasy? In point of fact, I acknowledge the heuristic power that is held by the concept, providing it is accepted as coconstructed dissociated experience rather than as symbolized thought (a daydream) that is repressed in the mind of one person. In a 1998 paper I wrote the following:

> Each of the three patients, despite dramatic differences in personality, history, and the language they used, seemed to be possessed by the powerful presence of *the same unconscious fantasy*—largely unsymbolized by language—that permeated and organized their use of imagery, and as it emerged subsequently, informed the enactments played out with their respective analysts. In this *dissociated fantasy*, some central but unknown aspect of what each felt to be his or her "true" self was being held captive inside of the mind of an other—an other who refuses to know it—and the patient was prevented from attaining his right to the experience of self-wholeness that depends upon the mutual interrelation of psychic and somatic experience as the felt unity that Winnicott (1949) called psyche-soma. (pp. 311–312, emphasis added)

In other words, I prefer a more impressionistic view of transitional process than is offered by the hard-edged concept of unconscious fantasy, whether Freudian or Kleinian. I suspect that the burgeoning work in neuroscience and cognitive research will inch us closer to an understanding that will bridge classical and postclassical thinking and, as this takes place, I predict that the concept of unconscious fantasy will be among those that are either revised or replaced. Bucci (2002), similarly, put it that "the goal of psychoanalytic treatment is integration of dissociated schemas" (p. 766) and that Freud's repression-based conception of the therapeutic action of psychoanalysis is in need of serious reconsideration, requiring that "concepts such as regression and resistance need to be revised as well" (p. 788).

One of the most persuasive and intriguing lines of thinking about this is the work of Fonagy, Moran, and Target (1993), who made the distinction between developmental and conflictual psychopathology. What they call *developmental pathology* I call *dissociative pathology*, but the distinction we each make is between structural (noninterpretable) pathology and dynamic (interpretable) pathology. They speak to this distinction (Fonagy, Moran, & Target, 1993) in their elaboration of "two aspects of the self: a *'pre-reflective or physical self,'* which is the immediate experiencer of life, and a *'reflective or psychological self,'* the internal observer of mental life" (p. 472, italics added).

Enhancing the functioning of the patient's reflective self, state these authors, is not simply the accurate mirroring of mental states but has to move beyond it, offering a different yet experientially appropriate rerepresentation that reflects the analyst's subjectivity as well as the patient's. In other words, the analyst must show his representation of the patient's representation, and to do this *the analyst must be himself while being a usable object.* In their words, "A transactional relationship exists between the child's own mental experience of himself and that of his object. His perception of the other is conditioned by his experience of his own mental state, which has in turn been conditioned developmentally by his perception of how his object conceived of his mental world" (Target & Fonagy, 1996, p. 460). "Unconsciously and pervasively, the caregiver ascribes a mental state to the child with her behavior, this is gradually internalized by the child, and lays the foundations of a core sense of mental selfhood" (p. 461). The role of the analyst, then, is to enhance a patient's ability to symbolize not only his emotional experience of events but also his capacity to symbolize his experience of his own mental states—"a representation of a mental representation" (p. 469). This is the underpinning of the so-called *observing ego* that analysts rely upon for interpretations to be a viable mode of communication with a given patient.

Whether working with children or with adults, "the greater the unevenness in development," Fonagy (1991) argued, "the less effective will be a technique which relies solely upon interpretations of conflict, and the greater will be the need to devise strategies of analytic intervention aimed to support and strengthen the ... capacity to tolerate conflict" (p. 16). Similarly, and even more to the point (Fonagy & Target, 1995), "Interpretations may remain helpful but their function is certainly no longer limited to the lifting of repression and the addressing of distorted perceptions and beliefs. ... *Their goal is the reactivation of the patient's concern with mental states, in himself and in his object*" (pp. 498–499, emphasis added).

When an analyst wishes to help a patient deepen his emotional experience of an event he is describing, the intervention that is most typically offered is some variation of the question "What did you feel?" or "What was the upset-feeling like?" This question itself will often evoke a switch to a different self-state or lead to a symptom, either of which can then become an object of attention if it seems potentially useful. It is a moment such as this that most closely links my clinical vantage point with Fonagy's through our shared recognition that "psychic reality is sensed not only through belief, but also, through *perception*" (Target & Fonagy, 1996, p. 471, emphasis added). In the typical question, a patient tries to remember what he felt as a past event in linear time. I am proposing a clinical process in which a patient is requested to simultaneously perceive the moment, not as a narrative to be told but as a space to be reentered—a nonlinear reality. The term *unconscious fantasy* is, in this regard, misleading.

Perception, Fantasy, and Self-States

What I call the structural shift from dissociation to conflict is clinically represented by the increasing capacity of the patient to adopt a self-reflective posture in which one aspect of the self observes and reflects (often with distaste) upon others that were formerly dissociated. This differs from what classical conflict theory would call the development of an observing ego in that the goal is more than the pragmatic treatment outcome of a greater tolerance for internal conflict. In healthy human discourse, there are always self-states that are not symbolized cognitively as me in the here-and-now of any given moment because they would interfere with routine, normal adaptation. For the most part, this creates no problem. It is where certain self-states are *hypnoidally isolated* from other modes of defining self and reality as a protection against affect dysregulation, that they become not-me, and limit personality functioning. For all patients, to different degrees, not-me self-states will make themselves known through enactment, signaling the presence of what Fonagy called *developmental pathology* and I call *noninterpretable pathology*.

I thus believe that an intrinsic part of every analytic treatment is the analyst's ability to accept, as a valid aspect of therapeutic action, a process in which his patient observes and reflects upon the existence of other selves that he or she hates and would like to disown, but can't. This process requires the analyst's willingness to do likewise with his own not-me experience. In some patients, their initial shift in perceptual experience is dramatic, and becomes the foundation of a major personality reorganization. In its most extreme form, it is paradigmatic for the successful treatment of severe dissociative disorders, but the basic perceptual transition is one that I have encountered in every analysis during all phases. Helped immeasurably by the analyst's own affective honesty (Bromberg, 2006b; Levenkron,

2006), an opportunity is provided for an internal linking process to take place between a patient's dissociated self-states by broadening his perceptual range of reality in the transference–countertransference field. In the linking process, fantasy, perception, thought, and language each play their part, providing the patient is not pressured to choose between which reality is more *objective* (Winnicott, 1951) and which self is more *true* (Winnicott, 1960, 1971).

If we think of a person as speaking from different self-states rather than from a single center of self, then the analyst will inevitably listen to the multiple voices of himself and his patient. It demands an overarching attunement to the speaker, an attunement that addresses the same issue described by Schafer's (1983) "action language" mode of listening and interpreting, in which "the analyst focuses on the action of telling itself ... [and] telling is treated as an object of description rather than ... an indifferent or transparent medium for imparting information or thematic content" (p. 228). From a nonlinear perspective, this means a special attunement not only to the impact that the speaker is having on you at any given moment but even more so to the shifts in that impact as close to the time they occur as possible. I look at these shifts as representing shifts in states of self that are to be held by the analyst as an ongoing focus of attention.

It is a way of listening different from that of hearing the person feel differently at different moments. The latter takes the switches in states of consciousness as more or less normal background music, unless they are particularly dramatic. The former takes them as the primary data that organize everything else you are hearing and doing; as an analyst it organizes how you approach the issue of unconscious fantasy and the reconstruction of personal narrative.

The patient's ability to move from dissociation to conflict depends on the analyst's ability to relate simultaneously to "me" and "not-me" self-states in himself and his patient. It is through this process that relational bridges are built between self-experiences that could not formerly be contained in a single state of mind without leading to dissociation, a principle so central to clinical psychoanalytic work that it led me to title my most recent book, *Awakening the Dreamer* (Bromberg, 2006a). An analyst, to use the frame of reference discussed here, does not have to abandon his or her own school of thought and work in some new way that is incompatible with his present clinical attitude. Historically, the stance of any given analyst has tended to slant toward one of three postures partly organized by individual differences in metapsychology: interpretation of conflict, detailed inquiry, or empathic attunement. It is striking to observe, however, that, regardless of differences in metatheory, built into each stance is an acceptance of the fact that the transference–countertransference field is where the action takes place. In other words, any analysis from any theoretical context that has as its goal enduring and far-reaching characterological growth is grounded in this understanding, based on its own clinical logic. Why?

Clinically, the transference–countertransference field is characterized by its vividness and its immediacy. But why is this fact so important that it is able to transcend conceptual differences among analysts as to how to best use this field? My own answer is that, regardless of a given analyst's metapsychology of therapeutic action, we are all either explicitly or implicitly attempting to clinically facilitate a patient's access to the broadest possible range of consciousness through enhancing *perception*. Josef Breuer, in his theoretical chapter in *Studies on Hysteria* (Breuer & Freud, 1893–1895), remarked that in response to trauma, "*perception too*—the psychical interpretation of sense impressions—is impaired" (p. 201, emphasis added). Echoing this, Enid Balint (1987) wrote, "If the ability to perceive is lacking because it is too traumatic or too alien, can one think of an individual as being truly conscious?" (p. 480).

When psychoanalysis is successful as a method of psychotherapy, the reason is that the process is a dialectic between seeing and being seen, rather than simply being seen into. That is, analysis simultaneously frees our patients to do unto us, with equivalent perceptiveness, what we are doing unto them, to see us as part of the act of listening to us. I argued (Bromberg, 1994) that in every technical approach the use of transference creates its analytic impact to the extent that the patient is freed to see the analyst while the analyst is seeing him. Dissociated domains of self achieve symbolization primarily through enactment in a transference–countertransference context because experience becomes symbolized not by words themselves but by the new perceptual context that the words come to represent. Speak!—that your patient might *see* you, that his dissociated states of mind may find access to the here and now of the analytic relationship and be lived within it. The power of self-truth will remain unchanged unless unchallenged by perception. A relational context, an act of meaning, must be constructed so that it includes the realities of both self and other. Unless this takes place, the immediate perceptual context will be only an enactment of the patient's fixed, affective memory system that includes some other trying helpfully and logically to extract the person's own reality and replace it with theirs (albeit a "better" one).

The Human Mind as a Relationally Configured, Self-Organizing System

In earlier work I referred to unconscious fantasy as an obsolete concept that I felt had its day. Harry Smith, more than any other analyst committed to a Freudian perspective, took my challenge seriously. He was influenced by my clinical argument, but not by my suggestion that Freud's theory of mind needed major overhaul (Smith, 2000, 2001, 2003). For example, Smith (2003), in an excellent paper on "Conceptions of Conflict," discussed my work as follows: "Bromberg says that thinking of the dissociative organization of the mind helps him to stay with the patient's current state—not to overlook one self-state or another, nor to value one at the expense of another.... *It is not clear why Bromberg's technical recommendations need to be buttressed by a new theory of mind*" (p. 82, emphasis added). Smith may be right that it is not clear, but I believe his point would appeal largely to those analysts who believe that I am offering "technical recommendations." However, such was never my purpose, and the idea makes me cringe a bit. From the point of view of conflict theory, however, he has good reason to object to my insistence that a new theory of mind needs to replace the old in order to accept the inclusion of dissociation into the mix. Surely I am asking for too much. Harry Smith has accepted the validity of my argument as a clinical position. That is already a lot. If I am right, then that itself should gradually influence the theory of mind upon which praxis is based. I sometimes forget that old theories, like old soldiers, never die; they just fade away. Sorry for that, Harry. Eventually, we may both be proven right, but in the meantime I can enjoy support from another neo-Kleinian, Jorge Canestri (2005), who challenges Harry Smith's attempt to formulate the phenomenon of dissociation as simply a form of conflict that can be assimilated into contemporary conflict theory. Canestri writes:

> Smith (2003) proposes that the activity of dissociation, when it appears in clinical work, is a compromise formation and can be analyzed as such.... Smith's solution is to bring conflict back to the interaction between various areas—to which I have already objected, since, to me, this is always an ad hoc hypothesis intended to salvage the theory of conflict as an organizing principle omnipresent in the mind. (p. 308)

My broadest aim as a psychoanalytic author has been to explore the clinical and conceptual implications of viewing the human mind as a relationally configured, self-organizing system. I've argued that personality functioning, normal and pathological, is best understood as an ongoing, nonlinear repatterning of self-state configurations, and that this process is mediated at the brain level by a continuing dialectic between dissociation and conflict. Normal dissociation, a hypnoid brain mechanism that is intrinsic to everyday mental functioning, assures that the mind functions as creatively as possible, selecting whichever self-state configuration is most adaptive to the moment. Johnson (2004) compared this to Edelman's (1989, 1992, 2004) view that the internal mechanisms of both the brain and the immune system run mini-versions of natural selection:

> Think of those modules in your brain as species competing for precious resources—in some cases they're competing for control of the entire organism;

in others, they're competing for your attention. Instead of struggling to pass their genes on to the next generation, they're struggling to pass their message on to other groups of neurons, including groups that shape your conscious sense of self. Picture yourself walking down a crowded urban street. As you walk, your brain is filled with internal voices all competing for your attention. At any given moment, a few of them are selected, while most go unheeded. (p. 199)

When dissociation is enlisted as a defense against trauma, the brain uses its hypnoid function to limit self-state communication, thereby insulating the mental stability of each separate state. Self-continuity is thus preserved within each state, but self-coherence between states is sacrificed and replaced by a dissociative mental structure that forecloses the possibility of conflictual experience. Clinically, the phenomenon of dissociation, although observable at many points in every treatment, comes into highest relief during enactments, requiring an analyst's close attunement to unacknowledged affective shifts in his own and his patient's self-states. Through the joint cognitive processing of enactments played out interpersonally and intersubjectively between the not-me experiences of patient and analyst, a patient's sequestered self-states come alive as a "remembered present" (Edelman, 1989) that can affectively and cognitively reconstruct a remembered past. Because the ability to safely experience conflict is increased, the potential for resolution of conflict is, in turn, increased for all patients. It allows one's work with so-called good analytic patients to become more powerful because it provides a more experience-near perspective from which to engage clinical phenomena that are immune to interpretation, such as *intractable resistance* and *therapeutic stalemate*. Further, it puts to rest the notion of *analyzability* and allows analysts to use their expertise with a wide spectrum of personality disorders often considered difficult or unanalyzable, such as individuals diagnosed as borderline, schizoid, narcissistic, and dissociative.

According to Kihlstrom (1987, quoted from LeDoux, 1989), "in order for unprocessed subjective experience to become symbolized in conscious awareness, a link must be made between the mental representation of the event and a mental representation of the self as the agent or experiencer. These episodic representations ... reside in short-term or working memory" (p. 281). The more intense the unsymbolized affect, the more powerful the dissociative forces that prevent isolated islands of selfhood from becoming linked within working memory. High levels of stimulation from the amygdala interfere with hippocampal functioning. When this occurs in treatment (and it occurs inevitably), the sensory imprints of experience that are stored in affective memory, continue to remain isolated images and body sensations that feel cut off from the rest of self (unconscious fantasy?). The dissociative process that keeps the affect unconscious is, above all else, a process that has a life of its own—a relational life that is interpersonal as well as intrapsychic and is played out between patient and analyst in the dyadic dissociative phenomenon that is termed *enactment.* Bucci (2002), in a similar vein, conceptualized this process as pivoting around whether changes take place in what she termed emotion schemas—specific types of memory schemas dominated by subsymbolic sensory and somatic representations. She presented an argument much like my own:

> Emotion schemas can be changed only to the extent that experiences in the present and memories of the past are held in working memory simultaneously with the pulses of core consciousness that depend on activation of the bodily components of the schema.... *The activation of the dissociated painful experience in the session itself is central to the therapeutic process. This is a very different perspective from the metapsychological principle that structure depends on the inhibition of drive or desire.* (p. 787, emphasis added)

In brief, psychoanalysis must provide an experience that is perceivably (not just conceptually) different from the patient's narrative memory. Sullivan (1954), recognizing that self-discordant, perceptual data must have an opportunity to structurally reorganize internal narrative for psychoanalysis to be a genuine "talking cure," emphasized the powerful relation between personality change and what he called "the detailed inquiry" by the analyst. This latter phrase referred to the clinical reconstruction of perceptual detail, the recall of affects, areas of perception, and interpersonal data that are excluded from the narrative memory of the event as reported to the analyst. A central aspect of this process is that the patient–analyst relationship itself is inevitably drawn into the telling of the narrative and enacted by both parties as a living entity that must be continually renegotiated as the analysis proceeds. The core of the negotiation is that the meaning of the relationship is intersubjectively, although asymmetrically, constructed out of the patient's self-narrative and the perceptual differences from it. It is in this sense that psychoanalysis breaks down the old narrative frame (the patient's story) by evoking, through a process of negotiation, perceptual experience that doesn't fit it; enactment is the primary perceptual medium that allows narrative change to take place. Alternative, consensually validated narratives that contain events and experience of self-other configurations formerly excluded begin to be constructed because these events, as I said earlier, become symbolized not by words themselves but by the new perceptual context that the words come to represent.

Coming full circle back to ghosts and spirits, I am going to end my discussion of unconscious fantasy on a biblical note. The Book of Daniel (5:28, *Oxford Annotated Bible,* 1991, p. 1136) described how the son of King Nebuchadnezzar of Babylon became terrified when he read the "handwriting on the wall" written in flame. Especially frightening were the words: "Your kingdom is divided, and given to the Medes and Persians." It has been said that this line is now appearing on the walls of psychoanalytic institutes and that some people are fearful. Others, however, are said to believe that perhaps it is all to the good because the Medes and Persians should be given a chance. The problem is that Medes and Persians are, in one respect, not so different from Babylonians. Once holding the "reigns," any kingdom is susceptible to interpreting its own belief system as though it came straight from the "horse's mouth." Perhaps the truth, simply, is that one man's Mede is always another man's Persian.

References

Arlow, J. A. (1969). Unconscious fantasy and disturbances of conscious experience. *Psychoanalytic Quarterly, 38,* 1–27.

Balint, E. (1987). Memory and consciousness. *International Journal of Psychoanalysis, 68,* 475–483.

Bion, W. R. (1962). Learning from experience. In *Seven servants.* New York: Aronson, 1977.

Bion, W. R. (1963). *Elements of psychoanalysis.* London: Heinemann.

Bion, W. R. (1965). *Transformations.* London: Heinemann.

Bion, W. R. (1970). *Attention and interpretation.* London: Maresfield.

Bollas, C. (1987). *The shadow of the object: Psychoanalysis of the unthought known.* London: Free Association Books.

Bonovitz, C. (2004). The cocreation of fantasy and the transformation of psychic structure. *Psychoanalytic Dialogues, 14,* 553–580.

Breuer, J., & S. Freud. (1893–1895). Studies on hysteria. In J. Strachey (Ed. & Trans.), *The standard edition of the complete psychological works of Sigmund Freud* (Vol. 2). London: Hogarth Press, 1955.

Bromberg, P. M. (1984). Getting into oneself and out of one's self: On schizoid processes. In *Standing in the spaces: Essays on clinical process, trauma and dissociation* (pp. 53–61). Hillsdale, NJ: The Analytic Press, 1998.

Bromberg, P. M. (1989). Interpersonal psychoanalysis and self psychology: A clinical comparison. In *Standing in the spaces: Essays on clinical process, trauma and dissociation* (pp. 147–162). Hillsdale, NJ: The Analytic Press, 1998.

Bromberg, P. M. (1993), Shadow and substance: A relational perspective on clinical process. In: *Standing in the spaces: Essays on clinical process, trauma and dissociation* (pp. 165–187). Hillsdale, NJ: The Analytic Press, 1998.

Bromberg, P. M. (1994). "Speak! That I may see you": Some reflections on dissociation, reality, and psychoanalytic listening. In *Standing in the spaces: Essays on clinical process, trauma and dissociation* (pp. 241–266). Hillsdale, NJ: The Analytic Press, 1998.

Bromberg, P. M. (1995). Resistance, object-usage, and human relatedness. In *Standing in the spaces: Essays on clinical process, trauma and dissociation* (pp. 205–222). Hillsdale, NJ: The Analytic Press, 1998.

Bromberg, P. M. (1996). Standing in the spaces: The multiplicity of self and the psychoanalytic relationship. In *Standing in the spaces: Essays on clinical process, trauma and dissociation* (pp. 267–290). Hillsdale, NJ: The Analytic Press, 1998.

Bromberg, P. M. (1998). "Help! I'm going out of your mind." In *Standing in the spaces: Essays on clinical process, trauma and dissociation* (pp. 309–328). Hillsdale, NJ: The Analytic Press, 1998.

Bromberg, P. M. (2000). Reply to reviews by Cavell, Sorenson, and Smith. *Psychoanalytic Dialogues, 10*, 551–568.

Bromberg, P. M. (2003). One need not be a house to be haunted. *Psychoanalytic Dialogues, 13*, 689–709.

Bromberg, P. M. (2006a). *Awakening the dreamer: Clinical journeys*. Mahwah, NJ: The Analytic Press.

Bromberg, P. M. (2006b). Ev'ry time we say goodbye, I die a little...: Commentary on Holly Levenkron's "Love (and hate) with the proper stranger." *Psychoanalytic Inquiry, 26*, 182–201.

Bucci, W. (1997a). Patterns of discourse in "good" and troubled hours: A multiple code interpretation. *Journal of the American Psychoanalytic Association, 45*, 155–187.

Bucci, W. (1997b). *Psychoanalysis and cognitive science: A multiple code theory*. New York: Guilford.

Bucci, W. (2001). Pathways of emotional communication. *Psychoanalytic Inquiry, 21*, 40–70.

Bucci, W. (2002). The referential process, consciousness, and sense of self. *Psychoanalytic Inquiry, 22*, 766–793.

Bucci, W. (2003). Varieties of dissociative experience: A multiple code account and a discussion of Bromberg's case of "William." *Psychoanalytic Psychology, 20*, 542–557.

Canestri, J. (2005). Some reflections on the use and meaning of conflict in contemporary psychoanalysis. *Psychoanalytic Quarterly, 74*, 295–326.

Dickinson, E. (1863). Poem 670. In T. H. Johnson (Ed.), *The complete poems of Emily Dickinson* (p. 333). Little, Brown and Co., 1960.

Edelman, G. M. (1989). *The remembered present: A biological theory of consciousness*. New York: Basic Books.

Edelman, G. M. (1992). *Bright air, brilliant fire*. New York: Basic Books.

Edelman, G. M. (2004). *Wider than the sky: The phenomenal gift of consciousness*. New Haven, CT: Yale University Press.

Fingarette, H. (1963). *The self in transformation: Psychoanalysis, philosophy, and the life of the spirit*. New York: Basic Books.

Fonagy, P. (1991). Thinking about thinking: Some clinical and theoretical considerations in the treatment of a borderline patient. *International Journal of Psychoanalysis, 72*, 639–656.

Fonagy, P., & Target, M. (1995). Understanding the violent patient: The use of the body and the role of the father. *International Journal of Psychoanalysis, 76*, 487–501.

Fonagy, P., Moran, G. S., & Target, M. (1993). Aggression and the psychological self. *International Journal of Psychoanalysis, 74*, 471–485.

Freud, S. (1897). Letter 69 (September 21, 1897): Extracts from the Fliess papers (1950 [1892–1899]). In J. Strachey (Ed. & Trans.), *The standard edition of the complete psychological works of Sigmund Freud* (Vol. 1, pp. 259–260). London: Hogarth Press, 1966.

Goldbarth, A. (2003). *Pieces of Payne*. Saint Paul, MN: Graywolf Press.

Grotstein, J. S. (2004). "The light militia of the lower sky": The deeper nature of dreaming and phantasying. *Psychoanalytic Dialogues, 14*, 99–118.

Johnson, S. (2004). *Mind wide open: Your brain and the neuroscience of everyday life*. New York: Scribner.

Kihlstrom, J. (1987). The cognitive unconscious. *Science, 237*, 1445–1452.

Klee, P. (1957). *The diaries of Paul Klee, 1898–1918*. Berkeley: University of California Press.

Korzybski, A. (1954). *Time-binding: The general theory*. Lakeville, CT: Institute of General Semantics.

Laing, R. D. (1967). *The politics of experience*. New York: Pantheon Books.

Langan, R. (1997). On free-floating attention. *Psychoanalytic Dialogues, 7*, 819–839.

LeDoux, J. E. (1989). Cognitive-emotional interactions in the brain. *Cognition and Emotion, 3*, 267–289.

LeDoux, J. E. (2002). *The synaptic self*. New York: Viking.

Levenkron, H. (2006). Love (and hate) with the proper stranger: Affective honesty and enactment. *Psychoanalytic Inquiry, 26*, 157–181.

Lyons-Ruth, K. (2003). Dissociation and the parent–infant dialogue: A longitudinal perspective from attachment research. *Journal of the American Psychoanalytic Association, 51*, 883–911.

Lyons-Ruth, K., & Boston Change Process Study Group. (2001). The emergence of new experiences: Relational improvisation, recognition process, and nonlinear change in psychoanalytic therapy. *Psychologist-Psychoanalyst, 21*, 13–17.

Mitchell, S. A. (1991). Contemporary perspectives on self: Toward an integration. *Psychoanalytic Dialogues, 1*, 121–147.

Moore, B. E., & Fine, B. D. (Eds.) (1990). *Psychoanalytic terms and concepts* (3rd ed.). New Haven, CT: American Psychoanalytic Association and Yale University Press.

Oxford Annotated Bible: New Standard Version (1991). New York: Oxford University Press.

Pope, A. (1714). The rape of the lock. In L. I. Bredvold, A. D. McKillop, & L. Whitney (Eds.), *Eighteenth century poetry and prose* (pp. 354–364). New York: Ronald Press, 1939.

Rather, L. (2001). Collaborating with the unconscious other. The analyst's capacity for creative thinking. *International Journal of Psychoanalysis, 82*, 515–532.

Rizzuto, A.-M. (2004). Book review of R. Steiner (Ed.), *Unconscious fantasy*. *Journal of the American Psychoanalytic Association, 52*, 1285–1290.

Schafer, R. (1983). *The analytic attitude*. New York: Basic Books.

Smith, H. F. (2000). Review essay: Conflict: *See under* dissociation. *Psychoanalytic Dialogues, 10*, 539–550.

Smith, H. F. (2001). Obstacles to integration: Another look at why we talk past each other. *Psychoanalytic Psychology, 18*, 485–514.

Smith, H. F. (2003). Conceptions of conflict in psychoanalytic theory and practice. *Psychoanalytic Quarterly, 72*, 49–96.

Solms, M. (2003). Do unconscious phantasies really exist? In R. Steiner (Ed.), *Unconscious fantasy*. London: Karnac, 2003.

Spillius, E. B. (2001). Freud and Klein on the concept of phantasy. *International Journal of Psychoanalysis, 82*, 361–373.

Steiner, R. (Ed.) (2003). *Unconscious fantasy*. London: Karnac.

Stern, D. B. (2003). The fusion of horizons: Dissociation, enactment, and understanding. *Psychoanalytic Dialogues, 13*, 843–873.

Sullivan, H. S. (1953). *The interpersonal theory of psychiatry*. New York: Norton.

Sullivan, H. S. (1954). *The psychiatric interview*. New York: Norton.

Target, M., & Fonagy, P. (1996). Playing with reality II: The development of psychic reality from a theoretical perspective. *International Journal of Psychoanalysis, 77*, 459–479.

Webster's New Universal Unabridged Dictionary (2nd ed.) (1983). New York: Simon & Schuster.

Winnicott, D. W. (1949). Mind and its relation to the psyche-soma. In *Collected papers: Through paediatrics to psycho-analysis* (pp. 243–254). London: Tavistock, 1958.

Winnicott, D. W. (1951). Transitional objects and transitional phenomena. In *Playing and reality* (pp. 1–25). New York: Basic Books, 1971.

Winnicott, D. W. (1960). Ego distortion in terms of true and false self. In *The maturational processes and the facilitating environment* (pp. 140–152). New York: International Universities Press, 1965.

Winnicott, D. W. (1971). The place where we live. In *Playing and reality* (pp. 104–110). New York: Basic Books.

14

Leaning Into Termination

*Finding a Good-Enough Ending**

Jill Salberg

▼   ▼   ▼   ▼   ▼

It is never easy to say good-bye, to end a relationship or to leave someone you care about and feel connected to. We start treatment with patients, knowing that at some point it will come to an end. Despite this knowledge, both parties become engaged and, if things go well, deeply attached. What we ask of patients and of ourselves is not easy. The kind of attachment that is needed for the analytic work to be most effective is a thick, saturated one. How do we, patients and analysts, take leave of one another when we have developed such unprecedented closeness and richness of experience? Bergmann (1997) argues, "For many analysands, transference love is the best love relationship that life has offered" (p. 163).

As a consequence patients may fear ever replacing this closeness with others in their lives and so the loss feels too great. As analysts we too may resist losing the closeness with our patients but additionally we may wonder, did we do enough, have things sufficiently changed for our patients to enable them to now carry on the work without us? Therefore, I believe ending treatment can create for many patients and for us a kind of crisis— the crisis of having to end and say good-bye. At that moment we and the patient may wish for time to stand still, for things to not change while they are changing (Bromberg, 1998).

Although Freud (1914) had written some early papers on technique, the question of termination was first raised in a monograph by Ferenczi

---

* This paper is a revised version of the original paper from *Psychoanalytic Dialogues*, *19*(6), 2009, pp. 704–722, and also includes material from *Good Enough Endings: Breaks, Interruptions and Terminations from Contemporary Relational Perspectives*, Chapters 1 and 7 (Routledge, 2010).

and Rank (1924), *The Development of Psychoanalysis*. They proposed that when a full transference neurosis had developed in the patient then the analyst "sets a definite period of time completing the last part of the treatment" (p. 13). Rank's *The Trauma of Birth* instigated a heated debate about the shortening of treatment. Rank and Ferenczi experimented with setting a time limit, finding that this stirred up separation anxiety and maternal transference. For Rank, separation carried the meaning of separation from mother as well as the final separation of death, so the time limit of therapy evoked both maternal separation anxiety and existential death anxieties. Unfortunately the controversy surrounding Rank, who became known for short, time-limited treatments, ultimately became a problem for Ferenczi who wished to remain loyal to Freud.

The earliest paper to fully consider termination was written by Ferenczi (1927) after having broken away from Rank and may have partly been his attempt to differentiate himself from his prior work with Rank. Ferenczi now argued against the shortening of treatment and emphasized working for as long as the patient wanted to continue. It is a paper filled with idealism along with high standards for the analyst. He believed that the analyst "must know and be in control of even the most recondite weaknesses of his own character and this is impossible without a fully completed analysis" (p. 84). What standard of a "fully completed analysis" was Ferenczi thinking of? Clearly it couldn't have been his analysis with Freud, an analysis that had been three brief, interrupted sets of meetings which overall totaled 7–8 weeks. Further, Ferenczi felt that Freud, by not continuing the analysis, abandoned the process too soon before a negative transference could be elaborated and worked through (see Aron & Harris, 1993). In fact, later in his paper he says, "The proper ending of an analysis is when neither the physician nor the patient puts an end to it, but when it dies of exhaustion.... A truly cured patient frees himself from analysis slowly but surely; so long as he wishes to come to analysis, he should continue to do so" (p. 85). For Ferenczi, termination involved a gradual and spontaneous mourning of childhood longings, something he had not been able to fully do with Freud. One can imagine only that Ferenczi was chiding Freud.

Freud did not articulate his own views on ending analysis until quite late in his life, 1937. He writes, "The discussion of the technical problem of how to accelerate the slow progress of an analysis leads us to another, more deeply interesting question: Is there such a thing as a natural end to an analysis—is there any possibility at all of bringing an analysis to such an end?" (p. 219). Ferenczi's and Freud's papers, while written 10 years apart and late in their respective lives and careers, feel very much in dialogue with each other (see Reich, 1950; Bergmann, 1997). Ernest Jones* reports that one of the cases Freud discusses is of a discontented analysand, already an analyst in the field (who Jones believes is Ferenczi). After ending his analysis, this man became a teacher in the field who ends up berating his analyst for not having "finished the analysis," something Ferenczi rebuked Freud for. We need to remember that at this point many analyses were quite brief, sometimes 3–6 months, and that was considered typical and complete. The psychoanalytic method was still in its infancy, and, unlike today, training analyses were not only brief but also less formally organized. Sounding disheartened, Freud comes to the conclusion that even a successful analysis is *not* a prophylactic against future illness, perhaps suggesting some awareness of the limitations of his technique.

Freud, more pessimistic in tone than Ferenczi, raises three points of view regarding termination. He refers to them as the skeptical, the optimistic and the ambitious. Freud (1927), who reminds us that our ideals are often illusions and that the road to reality is lined with disappointments, holds the skeptical and, I might add, somewhat ambivalent view. The optimistic stance, held by Ferenczi, reveals his deep belief in the possibility of a fully curative analysis, perhaps exposing his longing for a deeper, more fully elaborated analysis with Freud. This very well may have been Ferenczi's ambition toward which his experiments with "active" technique and mutual analysis were directed (see Ferenczi, 1988). His experimental work provoked condemnation from Freud, who felt that Ferenczi was departing from the techniques of psychoanalysis as Freud had conceived of them.† What has become known as the "relational turn" hinged in many ways on the rediscovery and consideration of these alterations in technique.

Freud (1937) acknowledged that many of the cases he was treating (as opposed to the early days of psychoanalysis) were "training analyses," a relatively new concept for the first generation of analysts and not a requirement as it is today. In this next part of his paper Freud, no longer skeptical or ambivalent, writes, "There was no question of shortening the treatment;

---

* See Freud (1937, p. 221).

† A footnote from Ferenczi's letter to Freud (#1236, August 29, 1932): "When I visited the Professor ... I told him of my latest technical ideas...The Professor listened to my exposition with increasing impatience and finally warned me that I was treading on dangerous ground and was departing fundamentally from the traditional customs and techniques of psychoanalysis. Such yielding to the patient's longings and desires—no matter how genuine—would increase his dependence on the analyst. Such dependence can only be destroyed by the emotional withdrawal of the analyst...This warning ended the interview. I held out my hand in affectionate adieu. The Professor turned his back on me and walked out of the room" (p. 443).

the purpose was radically to exhaust the possibilities of illness in them and to bring about a deep-going alteration of their personality" (p. 224).

Here is ambition laid bare—we as analyst–patient need a radical transformation of ourselves to effectively cure our patients. Is there any way to hear this but as a kind of grandiosity entwined with idealization? What would such an alteration look like and doesn't this then become an impossible standard for an impossible profession?

I believe the ambitious point of view, one that was held simultaneously by both Freud and Ferenczi, reveals the ongoing problematic relationship the field has inherited regarding termination. There is an unspoken but nonetheless prevalent idealization of what a fully complete analysis might look like. Certainly the bar is set high for analysts, but have we really given termination the same reconsideration as other theoretical and technical reformulations? I think not.

Freud died when the world was thrust for the second time into the violent chaos of World War. Many of the first generation analysts had already fled Europe, mostly for England and America with some going to South America and Palestine. The psychoanalytic world had endured multiple and compounding losses. Freud had died—a loss whose impact on psychoanalysis would be nearly impossible to comprehend. Concurrent with Freud's death was the personal dislocation of so many analysts fleeing war-torn Europe and the dangers of the Holocaust that were no longer a threat but a reality. The devastation to families, homes, countries, and the world as they knew it was incalculable.

The war ended and the British Psycho-Analytic Society held in 1949, what I believe was the first symposium on the topic of termination titled "Criteria for the Termination of an Analysis" (later published in *International Journal of Psychoanalysis, 31*, 1950).* It is not surprising that loss, mourning and endings began to preoccupy this generation of analysts; it would take years, generations even, to fully process those losses and integrate them into our understanding of how things end. The papers ranged from discussing actual technique of terminating to the formulation of termination criteria, and some experiential case material. Marion Milner (1950) argued that as analysts we have effectively bypassed true termination, having become analysts ourselves and therefore living out our identifications with our analysts.

Writing in 1950 and 1957, Melanie Klein compared termination to a nursing and weaning experience in which mourning, associated with depressive position anxieties and loss, is the crucial experience to be tolerated. But she also tempers this position by pointing out the limitations of the

---

* For a more extensive review of the literature see Salberg (2010), Chapter 1, "Historical Overview."

psychoanalytic method. She states, "When the loss represented by the end of the analysis has occurred, the patient still has to carry out by himself part of the work of mourning. This explains the fact that often after the termination of an analysis further progress is achieved" (1950, p. 80). Although similar in tone to Freud's ideas regarding loss, mourning and the internalization of the object, I want to highlight that Klein's notion suggests the limitations of what transpires during an analysis, specifically that some meaningful work continues to happen posttermination.

Although the American literature for many years was slight regarding termination, many analysts agreed with the ego psychological emphasis of that time and considered a checklist of criteria as a way of evaluating when a patient was ready to terminate. These included making the unconscious conscious, lessening of defensive structure, enlarging of ego functioning, ameliorating a harsh superego, thorough analyzing of the transference and coming to a realistic appraisal of the analyst, and so on (see Firestein, 1974; Blum, 1989; Bergmann, 1997). Loewald (1988) questioned whether we can analyze termination at all: "There remains the irreducible fact that precisely this form of experiencing and understanding itself is about to end, is itself about to become part of the historical past.... During therapy, we say, everything is grist for the mill; but what if the mill itself is to be dismantled?" (p. 156). Ultimately Loewald, agreeing with Klein, believed that mourning is the central problem and task of termination.*

In 1993, at the Annual Spring Meeting of Division 39, a panel was given titled "Go the Distance: Thoughts on Termination."† From this panel, Bergmann (1997) stands out, along with the earlier work of Blum (1989), as one of the few people willing to criticize the field for not having developed a paradigm for termination. Bergmann believes that a necessary criterion for termination rests on the analysand's ability to replace the analyst with an internal capacity for self-analysis. Novick also was on the Division 39 panel and has written extensively on the topic of termination from a traditional framework. As part of the later journal compilation, Novick (1997) raised a new angle from which to view the problems of termination, suggesting it is our own reactions as the therapist–analyst to the concept of termination that have prevented us from both formulating a theory of termination and teaching it. He argues that this approach has made termination an "inconceivable" idea, which he traces back to Freud. The early forced terminations by Freud with analysands who later became analysts

---

* Britton (2010) and Schafer (2002) also agree with the Kleinian view of termination as a mourning process.
† The panel's papers were later compiled, along with other invited writers, for a Special Section on Termination with guest editors Lane and Hyman, *Psychoanalytic Psychology*, 1997.

have instilled a kind of transgenerational transmission of traumatic end-ings embedded within the field. He further believes that "we" analysts effectively bypass true termination by the fact that, like it or not, we see and interact with our former analysts and patients within our institutes and at professional gatherings.

Novick, to my view, struck an important chord by both looking back to the early foreparents of psychoanalysis and then tracing the trauma across generations in our work and theories. What we bypass in the field is the necessary process of true mourning and loss, for both analyst and patient, inevitably limiting our conceptions of termination. I would consider this as the realm of the subjectivity of the analyst, which must be part of the mix when working with patients. A relational perspective conceives of the ana-lytic relationship as being cocreated and, to my mind, also gives rise to the idea that termination would be conceived of through the mutual and differ-ing experiences of a particular dyad.

Many of the concepts that relational authors have written about in general can apply equally to and be useful as constructs regarding termi-nation, although there have been only a few writers who look at termina-tion from a particularly relational perspective. Stephen Mitchell (1993), in *Hope and Dread in Psychoanalysis*, believed that the ending of an analysis is unnatural but nonetheless necessary. Mitchell maintained that "ending is necessary, if the analytic work is not to become a static alterna-tive to a fully lived life." Further, Mitchell also believed that, "this subtle dialectical process [is] central to all analyses—the capacity to hear, hold, and play with an interpretation, neither surrendering to it as powerful magic nor rejecting it as dangerous poison—not as a criterion of analyz-ability but as a criterion of readiness to terminate" (p. 83). What Mitchell is reminding us to remain cognizant of is that within ending some of the very necessary integrative work of analysis occurs, and only then can someone fully incorporate and put to use the gains they have made within the analysis.

Hoffman (1998) sees ending as "a matter of reaching a point where it seems desirable to end, to absorb the pain of real loss, in order to get that much better, in order to take what is mutually understood to be that further developmental step" (p. 257). He also argues the importance of the existen-tial aspect of our own mortality and that avoidance of termination issues is a kind of grandiose maneuver to evade the issue of death—the analyst's or the patient's.

Davies (2005) wrote that termination can be viewed as an iteration of the concept of multiplicity; it is not one good-bye but numerous ones from each of the multiple self-states of both the patient and the analyst. She believes that the complex intersubjective matrix of loving and hating feelings, of vulnerabilities and anxieties, as well as the analyst's and the patient's defensive positions reemerge during this phase, along with the transformations that the analytic work has fostered.

The termination phase thus becomes much more difficult for both participants to traverse, perhaps explaining why many analyses become either inextricably long or end by a forced situation, such as relocation due to work or new life situations such as marriage, divorce, or death. Bromberg (2006) absolutely believes not only that termination is not such a "benign" phase but also is one that often will be drawn into yet another round of enactments crucial to ending. He writes, "In this final stage of treatment, a relational context of new shared meaning could be created (or more accurately, co-created) from what was being enacted around the termination itself" (p. 19).

Consider the ways we, throughout the treatment, paradoxically limit and suspend time with patients. We give patients set times for their appointments and limit the length of the hour and despite all of that, we invite them into an ongoing dialogue, perhaps even an endless kind of conversation. Then at some point we say, time is up, the hour ends, and then further down the road we say that our talking has come to an end. Additionally, think about how time can seem both relevant and irrelevant. We keenly observe the use of time: if a patient arrives on time, early or late; if they are living within "current time" versus in the past or wishfully in the future; and if they make good "use" of our time and of us. Time feels necessarily relevant. Now think of how the unconscious fractures time: Past and present can be conceived of as coexisting simultaneously and within dreams we know that time often becomes irrelevant. In treatment both parties suspend time while we all too well know time is moving ahead, perhaps ever closer toward our ending.

Although there is a last session, a final meeting between patient and analyst, I have found that the processing of the ending and consequently of the treatment experience will often continue posttermination. In this way time becomes quite subjective, endings can become beginnings for some patients and one treatment can illuminate another for some analysts. As a consequence, terminations become complex affective transactions between both people that cannot be simplified or codified. I believe that terminations can be understood as cocreated enactments of complex unconscious processes between patient and analyst and will directly reflect the dyad and the relational dynamics at play during the treatment. Terminations are filled with processes often primed for enactment for both the analyst and the patient. I discovered as much during an extended process of writing about ending with a patient who proposed "staying in therapy forever," a kind of interminability that ultimately led to my decision to terminate her treatment.* Even so, it was a case that continued to occupy a place in my ongoing thoughts and memory; it haunted me. In this paper I track my own evolving ideas regarding termination across three treatment endings—my own first analysis and my work with two patients—while being mindful of the theme of time: its presence, its slippage, and then its passage. This journey reflects my own continual processing and reworking internally of overlapping endings. The story begins with ending my own analysis.

First Endings

After 13 years in analysis I raised my wish to terminate to my analyst and was met with skepticism. Was I resisting further work? I listened to his concerns and stayed 2 years longer, wondering if there were things I had not gotten to, hadn't wanted to open up or know more about? It was perplexing: I felt ready; my analyst saw me as unfinished. Although I continued, another feeling persisted—that I felt ready to try life on my own, with the tools I had acquired. Two years later I raised again that I felt I wanted to end. Again my analyst raised his concerns about my overlooking some unfinished business, and it was suggested I needed to finish my work, not terminate. I did not believe I could open up what now felt like a stalemate and further discussion felt as if I'd be talked out of leaving. I terminated a 15-year analysis in what felt like a less than satisfactory manner. I was saddened to leave, in this way, what had been a transformative experience. I later wondered what had been unconsciously enacted and in play for both my analyst and myself?

My own experience, not surprisingly, has profoundly affected my work with patients around ending treatment. I present the following case, not as a model case but as a problematic treatment, which raises important questions for us to reflect on. Is it possible to consider that certain dyads can only go so far? Are there obdurate feelings that create impasses that cannot be worked through and remain impasses? Guntrip (1975), in writing about the differences and benefits in his two analyses with Fairbairn and Winnicott, suggested, "Perhaps no single analyst can do all that an analysand needs, and we must be content to let patients make as much use of us as they can. We dare not pose as omniscient and omnipotent because we have a theory" (p. 155). Guntrip was helped by both analysts but in very disparate ways. In suggesting the limits of our theory, he is also warning us about the false empowerment that our theories can stir within us. If we "lean" into termination, can we surrender our wish for an idealized ending and see more

---

* See Salberg (2009) for the extended case write-up.

clearly that it is quite a complicated dilemma, staying or going, for both the patient and for the analyst?

Growing Old Together: A Case of Termination as Enactment

When Ellen first came to see me she was an attractive and deeply sad 32-year-old woman, single, unemployed, and living at home with her widowed mother. She told me about the losses in her life: her father's death from a brain tumor and her older brother's long history of drug and alcohol abuse and early death at age 32. Ellen had retreated from life, and her pain was palpable. She talked about her wishes yet profound fears to move out of her mother's house into an apartment of her own. She fantasized about becoming a paraplegic, which captured her feeling of paralysis and deep wish to be taken care of. She feared that leaving her mother was tantamount to killing her. I felt sympathetic toward Ellen, who was caught in such a life and death loyalty battle. Her guilt was heroic, she was ready to sacrifice her life, and in fact she had sacrificed "real" living.

Ellen told me how hard her life had been growing up in a family where her brother's problems were little understood and hugely overshadowed her life. Ellen became the target of much of her troubled and acting-out brother's hostility and contempt. Whenever she walked past him he would spit at her. They shared a bathroom, and he would spray urine all over the walls. She would feel disgust and then impotent rage since her parents seemed unable to effectively control him or help her. Her brother had always felt like a constant crisis, and since she was quiet, did well in school, and behaved well she had felt completely forgotten about. She had felt very guilty while also relieved over his death.

Her brother, married with two children, had never worked steadily or been able to manage his life. He was often in and out of drug and alcohol rehabs, never staying sober for long. Finally his wife had asked him to leave. Ellen recounted the following scene to me many times during our work. Ellen had moved back home to help her mother with caring for her father during his terminal phase of battling cancer. Soon after the father died, her brother arrived at the family home with a paper bag of his things, hoping to move back in. Ellen answered the door, opening it only a crack. He asked to come in saying he needed a place to stay. Ellen flatly refused to let him "come home," and 2 years later he was found dead in a motel room in a neighboring state, probably from a drug overdose. Could Ellen forgive herself for her own wish to have a life even if it included a wish for her brother's death?

In this punishing and pervasive way, Ellen kept her brother alive, albeit as a fixed image that resisted any change, as if time stood still. Her constant belief that she caused his death was painstakingly chipped away at, but in some way this would haunt our work in terms of what use Ellen could make of me, my words, my feelings, my thoughts, even my presence. Ellen envied her brother, deeply wanting the attention and place he held in her family but she was unable to see that he might have envied her as well. Neither one felt powerful.

Ellen had spent her life waiting to take her brother's place, the coveted throne of infant tyrant. Now our sessions began to take on a predictable routine quality of Ellen crying, appearing to feel understood, but nothing would appreciably change in her life. This cycle of her unyielding dependency and need for some kind of loving, sympathetic response that, when given, was then ignored or diminished left me in a state of helplessness. If I could help her she would feel inadequate; if I held the sense of inadequacy she couldn't be helped and was left with abject need. Ellen did eventually move out of her home into an apartment but one that her mother helped her to buy. Ellen found a job but one that was a much lower level than her training and was arranged by an ex-boyfriend. How could she feel empowered when others were the source of agency?

Further, I didn't see that Ellen was also spitting at me, spraying my office with her contempt. I missed her refusal to take in, swallow, and make use of anything I said. Ellen was locked in this drama of dependency and power struggles, and it clearly played out with me in similar dimensions. This was brought into focus by Ellen's anger when I moved my office and she saw the decorative style of painting I had done on my walls, something she had secretly wanted to do in her apartment. She had complained about being unable to fix up her apartment, and my own independent action had unwittingly invited envy fully into our relationship. A recurring enactment had been set in motion and one that I had been unable to see. Ellen was often crying and feeling envious longing for what she perceived others had, and I was often feeling inadequate and ineffective as her analyst. Neither of us felt effective or powerful, nor did we seem to have access to a way to transform the enacted memories into usable forms.

In the seventh year of treatment Ellen had been raising the idea of ending, not in a deeply serious way—partly out of despair and partly as a threat. In one session she said, "To acknowledge that this isn't working, my immediate conclusion is that I have to stop. I come and do my part but you're really supposed to be doing all the work, [*tearily*] you are to fix up my life." I was struck by the complex conflict Ellen was beginning to express that she and I had been in. Ellen could not allow anything I said to really affect her, thereby revealing me to be weak and helpless to help her. She could then remain in control, feeling superior to me but at the cost of her own suffering. Ellen further explained how fearful she was of being disappointed if I couldn't help her, but she also resented whatever I said. She says, "It's not fair to come in and out of my life. I guess by acting incompetent and not knowing what to do it's asking someone to come and take over. Maybe that's why I resent you. You want to come and tell me what to do sometimes, but then you say it's your life, you can do whatever you want to do. It doesn't change my life and it's not fair." I asked, "What would be fair?" She said, "You have to be there *all the time*. I have the image of you teaching me how to ride a bicycle and you disappear, disappear too soon."

Ellen wanted a kind of presence that she could control but that felt as if it came wholly from me. She continued, "I guess if it was up to me I would stay in therapy forever, we'll grow old together. But I also feel I'm going to show you, you're so good, why do I have to do all the work? Can't I just show up?" This sounded promising in that Ellen was verbalizing the conflict I had felt so embroiled in with her, but I also felt her undertow. She deeply wanted to just "show up" and have it happen for her.

A year later, very little had changed, Ellen kept coming, crying, and talking. She reported this dream: "I was in the bathroom going to take a shower. My mother was there in the house and I turned the water on. I started taking my clothes off and the water stopped. I opened the door and asked my mother about that, thinking I really need a shower to get ready for work. I started to step into the shower, clothes all over the floor but I still had more clothes on. Every time I took off a t-shirt I still had another. Maybe it has to do with therapy. No matter how many layers of clothes, I couldn't get everything off and I couldn't get clean. [*Teary*] No matter how much I come here and I think I'm sincere, I don't think I can manipulate you very well, I never seem to get down to bare skin." I agreed silently to myself.

I began to accept that I had gone as far as I could go with Ellen and that she and I seemed to share some idea of a miraculous change. Berry (1987) wrote:

> The decision to terminate is always a compromise between the demands of reality, and in particular of the passage of time, and those of the analyst's ego ideal, of the ideal of perfectability.... The patient's expectations of undergoing a metamorphosis prove to have been illusory; the analyst's desire to change the other proves to have been over-ambitious. (p. 102)

I returned to supervision to discuss Ellen, and that process helped me to acknowledge the ways I knew I had helped Ellen and begin to accept the limits of my help. In some way, it gave me a space to think, something that had been shutting down within the transference–countertransference power battles. Once I had access to more of my own thoughts I realized that I had gone as far as I could go with Ellen and that ending treatment might be necessary.

It was October of what would become her ninth year in treatment when I decided to suggest ending to Ellen. She was furious, feeling that I was "kicking her out." I said, "I think I have said everything to you I can say. It is really up to you now if you want to make changes in your life or not. Sometimes the changes can be better seen or risks more easily taken when you are no longer in treatment." She said, "So you are finally pushing me off that bus, abandoning me." I said, "I know you are angry about this idea. But I do feel that it's about doing things in your life now outside of here. I propose we spend the year working on this. If at the end of the year before we break for vacation we feel that something has shifted and there is something else to continue to work on, then we can reconsider. If not, then we will end." We spent that year in what felt like a stalemate, mostly with Ellen feeling justified in raging at me for "kicking her out of therapy." We ended that summer at the end of July.

A Few Years Later

I had written up this case and knew that I would have to call Ellen for her permission to present our work together. That is what made her call to me feel so uncanny. She wanted to come in for a session, something had happened and she wanted to "check in." Ellen arrived and was somewhat nervous and chatty. When I asked what had made her call, she told me that something had happened at her apartment's co-op board meeting that had left her agitated, and upon arriving back home she fell off a step ladder. She worried that she might be hurting herself due to guilt. She told me that she was now the president of the co-op that she lived in, and that night had helped the board reach a difficult decision for the building, refusing a request that the prior president had made. When I asked her what had left her agitated about this decision she said, "It's just like when I locked my brother out of the house, didn't let him back home and he killed himself." I said, "Do you really still believe that you killed him?" She said she did.

Suddenly I had a new picture of our work together and what had felt to me as my unilateral decision to terminate. I now realized that the termination had been an enactment in two ways. First, just as she had closed the door on her brother, I had closed the door on Ellen. I believe that, unconsciously, I had understood that something had to be repeated and relived for her to be able to metabolize and fully process the experience of her brother's death. Ellen and I had to reexperience that moment when I fully insisted that she had to leave, and she had to accept those terms. However, unlike with her brother, this time no one died; rather, both of us maintained the capacity to have independent lives. Only then could Ellen be freed from the shutting down of her life, a self-erected prison of memory and guilt. I too had become a prisoner, held captive by her and my own memories. Additionally, I realized that my wish that my analyst had supported my ending treatment was revitalized and enacted in my insisting on Ellen's ending. Aron (2009) posits, "We mistakenly polarize memory and enactment, inner experience and outer behavior" (p. 14). I understand Aron to mean that enactments are a form of memory, and I would add that they are a form of working through. I am suggesting that my ending the treatment with Ellen, albeit an enactment, had been reparative around the original trauma of her brother's death.

When I could, I told Ellen that I had suddenly realized that my insistence to end our work created a reliving of what had occurred with her brother. "In some way I had to close the door on you and say, 'You can't come back,' but in a way in which no one died, no one was killed." I felt that Ellen understood what I was saying and began telling me the ways her life had improved. We spent the rest of the session discussing what had been enacted between us. I ended the session by suggesting that she think about what we discussed and by inviting her to call to continue processing it with me. At the same time, I assured her that it would be alright not to call. I didn't hear from Ellen, which felt like a good thing.

After It's Over: Frozenness

How do we really *know* when to say good-bye? Some patients come to see us and are wary of attaching, keeping us at arm's length, while others eagerly connect sharing the intimate details of their lives. I have found that some patients haunt us during the work, while others haunt us after we end. Ellen did both for me. I now believe that she and I were engaged in a forestalled mourning process. Clearly Ellen had real reasons to be in mourning, and that is how she first came to me; however, less clear were the ways that she and I would become entangled and enmeshed in parallel and intersecting mourning struggles. Separation issues—which, in some cases, involve a sorrow for what never was—dotted Ellen's life and resonated with aspects of my own.

What I was less aware of was the impact of my own unfinished mourning process around ending analysis and how it would implicate me in my work. What obscured this was the fact that Ellen and I were in reversed positions; I had wanted to leave analysis and had wanted my analyst to support my doing this—while she wanted to stay forever and be welcomed in doing so. Clearly our situation was primed for an enactment. I have come to believe that many, if not all, terminations, are primed for enactment. The mutual processes of attaching and detaching, of growing close and then saying good-bye, elicit powerful feelings and equally powerful dissociative processes.

I can no longer think of my treatment and termination with Ellen without conjuring up the ending of my own first analysis. While finishing the earlier sections of this paper for presentation I received in the mail two articles written by my former analyst with a brief note: "Dear Jill, I hope you and your family are very well. Enclosed reprints 1-old and 1-new. Best wishes." I was quite surprised, shocked even, to say the least, but I was equally puzzled. We had not seen or spoken for many years, and I could not figure out the reason for this contact. Additionally, while brevity had been his long-standing style this note felt positively cryptic. Why was he contacting me in this manner? He is probably in his 80s, having retired from private practice a number of years ago. I felt a mixture of fear and curiosity. Why contact me *now*?

I wrote back to him, "I was surprised to receive your two papers without much of a note letting me know why the contact after so many years." I also filled him in on my life and my family and sent him two pieces of my own published work as well—one a memoir essay in which I felt he would recognize many of my family stories from our work together. I received back a letter from him in which he was noticeably conversational about life in retirement, and he responded quite positively to the pieces I had sent him. But also, embedded in the letter, was a paragraph in which once again I could distinctly hear the voice of my former analyst, "I wish you would not be so harsh with yourself or with me and could ease up and enjoy more fully the present without marring it with grievances and disappointments of the past and being too critical. No one likes to be admonished or made to feel guilty."

I was stunned. I read this part over and over again. I had not been in treatment with him for 20 years; he *still* sounded as if he thought of me as his patient, and I *still* heard him as my analyst. Had I been admonishing? How was it, that in an instant I was back in time, back on the couch and filled with recrimination with his feeling the necessity to enlighten me? Did we both still hold each other in mind in some unchanged form from the time that we had ended?

I no longer believe in some idealized termination whereby the transference–countertransference relationship, now fully analyzed loses its affective gravitational pull and the analytic dyad, diluted of its intensity, becomes normalized. The kind of interaction that occurred between my former analyst and me suggests that in some way we may remain for each other, as if, frozen in time within our memory. Despite long discussions prior to ending, I now can see that my terminating my analysis with him and his ending with me, in essence "our ending," had been incomplete on deeper levels. Our "frozenness" was a signifier of a loss not fully acknowledged and thereby incompletely mourned.

Before I say more about this I want to turn to my most recent contact with Ellen that occurred a few months after I received my former analyst's letter. Although she had given me permission a long time ago to write and present our work, I knew I needed to speak with her about the possibility of publishing it. I called and explained this to her, suggesting that I would mail her the write-up and then we could meet to discuss it. When she came in I could sense how anxious we both seemed to be feeling. She quickly said she was upset by the write-up* and that I hadn't portrayed her in an attractive light. Obviously, I didn't like her. She repeated this again, and I responded by saying that I did like her and cared very much about her but that I hadn't liked what she had stirred up in me, how I had ended up feeling so stuck, and that no matter what I tried I felt unhelpful and worse, inadequate. After our meeting, I remembered that I had liked her a great deal earlier in the treatment but that it had gotten lost in the struggles we had been continuously enacting with each other. I could see how the focus of my writing on those difficult feelings might have left her seeing only the most challenging and worst of my feelings.

Interestingly, she also didn't remember, or fully believe, what I had written about her intense and angry reaction to my new office and the way the walls had been painted. She remembered a dream that she now spontaneously reported: "I dreamed that the walls in your new office were white and that you had brown bookcases. When I actually saw your office I felt relieved that it wasn't what I had dreamed." She then said, "I did wonder if we had been too close in age and that I had envied you, your life." I agreed that we were close in age and wondered as well if that had been a problem. I then suggested that my recollection of her reaction to my new office decor had brought her envy into the room and into our relationship while her dream, which was unfamiliar and I don't think she had ever told me, kept envy at bay. She now said she didn't like me very much at times during our work.

I began to feel like I used to feel in sessions with her. Things felt slippery, moving quickly from what she felt was inside of me (you don't like me) to now it's inside her (I don't like you), like a hot potato that got tossed back and forth. This rapidly shifting landscape where I never quite knew where I stood or what I was feeling felt very familiar.† Was she right? Did I not like her and paint her in a poor light to make my own case regarding ending her treatment? At the time we were ending I had hoped I was doing what would be best for her and the treatment. Now I no longer was so sure.

The hour was almost over, and I raised with Ellen that if there were particular things she wanted me to change in the paper I would consider doing that or if she wanted to write something herself I would consider including it. I also clearly stated that I would not publish this if she didn't want me to. It felt important to me that this meeting be reparative, not injurious to her. She left saying she would think about it and get back to me.

---

* Ellen read the more extensive case write-up that was published in the paper "Leaning into Termination," *Psychoanalytic Dialogues, 19*(6), 2009, pp. 704–722.
† For a further exploration of hateful and enacted countertransferential feelings, see Davies (2004) and Grand (2003).

During this waiting time, I thought how reminiscent it felt to be with Ellen and the uncanny parallels with what had simultaneously transpired with my former analyst. Once again I wondered, how is it that we had become frozen, locked in our memories of each other? Frozenness has multiple aspects; it preserves something from the ravages of time while preventing anything from changing. However, in this kind of dormancy, some memories slumber while others are awake and active. Ellen and I reentered a part of our past transference–countertransference struggle, remembering each other by enacting our prior relational positions in the most intense and alive way—*as if* we had not terminated.

At the end of 2 weeks, Ellen did call and come in for another session. She said she had realized after we met that she hadn't told me how much she felt I had helped her. She said, "I have so much to be grateful for, my mother is in her 90s and is in good health, I am also in good health." While she was telling me this, I remembered how many deaths had occurred in her family—good health was something not to be taken lightly. I thanked her for telling me, feeling the wish to repair our ruptured ending and the role I had played in it. I said I wanted her to know that when I ended our work I had worried that I hadn't helped her enough to change jobs or in her desire for a long-term relationship. Perhaps that was part of my need to end the work but that I had really cared about her. She said she thought that we both had become too stuck on her changing jobs or meeting someone. Ellen then said she wanted to give me full permission to publish. I thanked her for this and for the opportunity to truly work something through with each other, to say good-bye in a new, more mutual way that freed us both from the old ways in which we had been stuck. In this reliving of memory and action a deeply reparative moment was allowed to occur, and I believe we could now free each other to make greater use of the past.

A few months later I wrote back to my former analyst. In realizing that I had been keeping the termination of that analysis somewhat on ice, I hadn't let myself continue a certain process, which I now entered. I realized that subtly in my response I had indeed scolded my analyst for the manner in which he contacted me. I was still harboring an injury over what felt like his nonrecognition of my need to terminate. By coming to this awareness I further realized that I also had withheld a deep gratitude for the work we had done together. I wrote to him explaining my complicated responses and telling him how much our work had given me and done for me. He wrote back saying how much he appreciated hearing my warm feelings about our work. I cried reading his letter, both glad that I had extended to him my deep gratitude and truly feeling this loss because we had now fully ended.

In writing about termination, Novick (1982) believes that to enter a terminal phase of treatment, a necessary milestone needs to have been achieved: "This is the necessity for disillusionment, the necessity to experience the analyst and the analysis as a failure" (p. 350). He is referring to a deideal-ization of the analyst and the work, but this could easily be extended to the field and our theories. There are always limits to what any analysis can accomplish. On the other hand, a great deal can be done, and we all know the deep benefits an analysis can provide. This side-by-side combination of disappointment and gratitude seems to be in the mix when terminating, but how do we decide when it is "good enough"? And can we suspend our ana-lytic ambition and begin to formulate what good enough looks like?

I return to Freud's German words in the translated title "Analysis termi-nable and interminable," *endliche* and *unendliche*, perhaps better translated as finite and infinite (Leupold-Löwenthal, 1987, p. 62). I'd like to speculate that Freud was trying to hold in tension what can be accomplished during the finite time of an analysis and the infinite work one does beyond the analysis. Each time I revisit my work with Ellen, in the writing of this paper, in discussion with colleagues, or even when ending with another patient, a new piece of my mourning and processing of the work takes place. It has compelled me to work through my own unfinished mourning of my first analysis. As a consequence, I can see the ways I might have done things differently with Ellen but also the ways in which I feel I did help her. In this way, ending is not really a termination meant as a complete cessation of something but more a continuation of a process in some new form. It is the closing of one door to open another, albeit unsure of where it might lead.

Ending on Her Terms

Many of these ideas were already part of my internal lexicon when it was time to terminate with my patient Shelley,* someone I had worked with for close to 20 years. She was the youngest in the family of four, born 10 years later than her next oldest sibling. Shelley's mother had had polio as a young girl, which left her legs badly weakened and necessitated leg braces and a cane for her to walk. Her father was an electrician and was chronically depressed. She often described him as if he were ghost-like, barely regis-tering a presence because of his withdrawn, silent states. Shelley's earliest memory is of being in her crib, alone, with no one to pick her up. She spoke of feeling invisible in her family and of playing alone on the floor, never able to sit in her "crippled" mother's lap. Aloneness and loneliness were perva-sive in her early life. I had for some time thought that given all of this, end-ing might be nearly impossible. Despite the great deal of work we had done and many improvements in her life, Shelley still felt to me to be very alone.

---

* For a fuller case write-up see Salberg (2010), Chapter 7, "How We End: Taking Leave."

She had a few close friends, and I feared I was her only intimate attachment and as a consequence could never detach from me.

Shelley surprised me and brought up ending. We set a date for our last session and then nothing much seemed to happen. Shelley would come into sessions without thoughts or feelings. When I would ask what she felt regarding our ending, without much affect in her voice she would say fine. As we got closer to our ending date Shelley felt panicked about a downturn in her business and went into a tailspin. I felt it unreasonable to ask her to now face relinquishing her tie to me, one that had taken many years of difficult work for us to establish. This is exactly the sort of crisis that termination can pose for many patients and for us. I had already seen how holding a firm line with my other patient Ellen around a termination date had prevented both of us from fully accessing the dissociated feelings that suffused that enactment. I knew that telling patients whether I thought they were ready to leave felt disempowering and so I decided to try something different and see if I could be more flexible, follow Shelley's lead and stay curious about what was being enacted between us. Therefore, I agreed to cancel the ending; Shelley calmed down, and things in her life seemed to improve.

We went through this scenario several times over the better part of a year before I fully realized that, despite real work crises, both Shelley and I were enacting our reluctance to terminate our work. These enactments held for her the dissociated feelings of the collapse of her internal world as well as her disbelief that she could calm herself down and function in her life. In response to our ending she inhabited the helpless child self-state. My part in the enactment was a kind of complementary panic response feeling. I began to feel guilty that I was somehow pushing her into leaving—it had been a long treatment, and somehow she couldn't leave. My "guiltiness" led me to believe, in the face of her panic, that I couldn't abandon her, necessitating my agreeing to call off our ending. As I began to better understand my own part of the enactment I realized that in the agreeing to set an end date I now had, unwittingly, become a rejecting, bad object. Despite it having been her request, I began to realize that not all of Shelley had wanted me to concur.

Often this deep ambivalence, stemming from the multiple self-states and the competing wishes those selves may have, dominates treatment endings (see Davies, 2005). I propose that this is an aspect of the destabilization during termination that analysts get caught in as much as patients do. I've come to understand that we enter a sort of liminal state: a place in between the shank of the treatment when both of us are engaged in the work and that future place of posttermination. Perhaps we both panic because in not knowing what the future will be like we fear that there is no future.

In my believing I was helping Shelley to end when and how she wanted to I saw an opportunity for her to successfully regulate and negotiate a complex part of our relationship. Nonetheless, I was inexorably pulled into the drama of how hard it is to detach after years of working with someone whose attachment issues are complicated. Additionally, it is hard to give up feeling needed in the ways we feel needed by our patients and to relinquish the pleasure we derive in reparative work. I began to realize that each time I agreed to a new termination date, I became for Shelley the mother who was too willing to let her go and who was not fully engaged with her. Each canceled ending became a triumph for her child self-state, no longer invisible and now having an impact on her environment. I addressed this with Shelley, saying that these crises were what life is like now and that I felt her panic had more to do with some terror over our ending. For me to begin these interpretative discussions I had to be willing to accept that I would be disappointing one part of Shelley. I had to believe in a future that I could not know while assuring Shelley that she could continue "going-on-being" without me.

Despite my concerns about incompleteness, I decided we could do more work through the process of terminating. I began to realize that it was most important for Shelley to take control of our ending not without input from me but not planned by me. Shaping how and when we ended began to feel a necessary component of our work, a means to transform the past while the present became a new experience. We were now able, after more than a year of end dates, cancellations, and renegotiations, to truly complete an ending process. Nonetheless, I do believe we needed all of that time and it was very much part of *our* ending process, how Shelley and I needed to construct it and find our way.

The tenor of this ending process was possible directly because of what I had gone through with Ellen years earlier. This is the way time, not in its concrete linearity but more in its linking capacity (Loewald, 1972), is actively involved in our psychic lives. Now with Shelley, I was "linked" in my mind and in time with Ellen, our reworked endings and my own complicated ending of analysis along with the prior and current enactments with Shelley. What I have come to see is that the working through, particularly when ending the treatment, contains and is composed of enactments and dissociated self-states. It is important to understand that it is not regression that is occurring; rather, it is a deep resonant response to the possible rupture of the profound attachment between analyst and patient. We need to appreciate that this attachment is one we have spent the entire treatment developing and understanding in terms of the patient's history and internalized relational world as well as our own. Even with a great deal of time preparing for ending it is nonetheless a rupture, an experience in many ways without precedent. Ending treatment for the analytic pair foreshadows an unknown future that can arouse not only past endings, ruptures, and losses but is a rupture, occurring even as it is being considered and discussed as a possibility.

The nature of my termination with Ellen, years earlier, was not so much in the foreground of my mind, but clearly I had been deeply affected and changed by it. It felt more important to empower Shelley to walk away, for her to be the one to leave me. With this in mind we set a new ending date. Soon after, she requested an extra week, which I agreed to. The second to last session arrived and Shelley walked in calm, relaxed, and announced, "Today is our last session; I really don't need another session next week." Although I was surprised, nonetheless it felt right to me; Shelley was ending on her terms. At the end of the hour she asked if she could hug me good-bye. I said yes and found myself being not just hugged, but squeezed so tight that it hurt, and I spontaneously said, "Ow." Shelley let go of me and laughed, saying she didn't realize how strong she was.

References

Aron, L. (1996). *A meeting of minds: Mutuality in psychoanalysis.* Hillsdale, NJ: The Analytic Press.

Aron, L., & Harris, A. (1993). *The legacy of Sándor Ferenczi.* Hillsdale, NJ: The Analytic Press.

Bergmann, M. (1997). Termination: The Achilles heel of psychoanalytic technique. *Psychoanalytic Psychology, 14*, 163–174.

Berry, N. (1987). The end of the analysis (D. Macey, Trans.). In J. Klauber (Ed.), *Illusion and spontaneity in psychoanalysis.* London: Free Association Books.

Blum, H. P. (1989). The concept of termination and the evolution of psychoanalytic thought. *Journal of the American Psychoanalytic Association, 37*, 275–295.

Britton, R. (2010). There is no end of the line: Terminating the interminable. In J. Salberg (Ed), *Good enough endings: Breaks, interruptions and terminations from contemporary relational perspectives* (pp. 39–50). New York: Routledge.

Bromberg, P. (1998). Staying the same while changing: Reflections on clinical judgment. *Psychoanalytic Dialogues, 8*, 225–236.

Bromberg, P. (2006). *Awakening the dreamer: Clinical journeys.* Mahwah, NJ: The Analytic Press.

Davies, J. M. (2004). Whose bad objects are we anyway? Repetition and our elusive love affair with evil. *Psychoanalytic Dialogues, 14*, 711–732.

Davies, J. M. (2005). Transformations of desire and despair: Reflections on the termination process. *Psychoanalytic Dialogues, 15*(6), 779–805.

Falzeder, E., Brabant, E., & Giampieri-Deutsch, P. (2000). *The Correspondence of Sigmund Freud and Sándor Ferenczi, volume 3: 1920–1933* (P. Hoffer, Trans.). London: The Belknap Press.

Ferenczi, S. (1927). The problem of termination of the analysis. In M. Balint (Ed.) & E. Mosbacher (Trans.), *Final contributions to the problems and methods of psychoanalysis* (pp. 77–86). London: Hogarth Press, 1955.

Ferenczi, S. (1988). *The clinical diary of Sándor Ferenczi* (J. Dupont, Ed.). Cambridge, MA: Harvard University Press.

Ferenczi, S., & Rank, O. (1925). *The development of psychoanalysis.* Washington, DC: Nervous and Mental Disease Monograph Series, No. 40.

Firestein, S. (1974). Termination of psychoanalysis of adults: A review of the literature. *Journal of the American Psychoanalytic Association, 22*, 873–894.

Freud, S. (1914). Remembering, repeating and working-through. In J. Strachey (Ed. & Trans.), *The standard edition of the complete psychological works of Sigmund Freud* (Vol. 12, pp. 145–156). London: Hogarth Press.

Freud, S. (1927). *The future of an illusion.* In J. Strachey (Ed. & Trans.), *The standard edition of the complete psychological works of Sigmund Freud* (Vol. 21, pp. 1–56). London: Hogarth Press.

Freud, S. (1937). Analysis terminable and interminable. In J. Strachey (Ed. & Trans.), *The standard edition of the complete psychological works of Sigmund Freud* (Vol. 23, pp. 211–253). London: Hogarth Press.

Grand, S. (2003). Lies and body cruelties in the analytic hour. *Psychoanalytic Dialogues, 13*, 471–500.

Guntrip, H. (1975). My experience of analysis with Fairbairn and Winnicott. *Review of Psychoanalysis, 2*, 145–156.

Hoffer, W. (1950). Three psychological criteria for the termination of treatment. *International Journal of Psychoanalysis, 31*, 194–195.

Hoffman, I. Z. (1998). *Ritual and spontaneity in the psychoanalytic process: A dialectical-constructivist view.* Hillsdale, NJ: The Analytic Press.

Klein, M. (1950). On the criteria for the termination of a psycho-analysis. *International Journal of Psychoanalysis, 31*, 78–80.

Klein, M. (1957). Envy and gratitude. In *The writings of Melanie Klein, vol. III: Envy and gratitude and other works* (pp. 247–263). London: Hogarth Press, 1975.

Leupold-Löwenthal, H. (1987). Notes on Sigmund Freud's "Analysis Terminable and Interminable." In J. Sandler (Ed.), *On Freud's "Analysis terminable and interminable."* International Psychoanalytical Association Educational Monographs, No. 1.

Loewald, H. W. (1960). On the therapeutic action of psycho-analysis. *International Journal of Psychoanalysis, 41*, 16–33.

Loewald, H. W. (1972). The experience of time. *Psychoanalytic Study of the Child, 27*, 401–410.

Loewald, H. W. (1988). Termination analyzable and unanalyzable. *Psychoanalytic Study of the Child, 43*, 155–166.

Milner, M. (1950). A note on the ending of an analysis. *International Journal of Psychoanalysis, 31*, 191–193.

Mitchell, S. A. (1993). *Hope and dread in psychoanalysis.* New York: Basic Books.

Mitchell, S. A. (1997). *Influence and autonomy in psychoanalysis.* Hillsdale, NJ: The Analytic Press.

Novick, J. (1982). Termination: Themes and issues. *Psychoanalytic Inquiry, 2*, 329–365.

Novick, J. (1997). Termination conceivable and inconceivable. *Psychoanalytic Psychology, 14*(2), 145–162.

Reich, A. (1950). On the termination of analysis. *International Journal of Psychoanalysis, 31*, 179–183.

Rank, O. (1924). *Das trauma der Geburt and seine Bedeutung für die Psychoanalyse.* Leipzig/Vienna/Zurich: Verlag.

Salberg, J. (2010). *Good enough endings: Breaks, interruptions and terminations from contemporary relational perspectives.* New York: Routledge.

Schafer, R. (2002). Experiencing termination: Authentic and false depressive positions. *Psychoanalytic Psychology, 19*, 235–253.

15

"You Must Remember This"*

Adrienne Harris

▼　▼　▼　▼　▼

This chapter was first given as a keynote address at the Division 39 Spring Meeting in Toronto in 2007, held at the Royal York Hotel, a massive stone pile, a dramatic icon of old Toronto. The setting was a crucial provocation for the paper. Toronto is the city I grew up in, a city, therefore, for me, both imaginary and material. Toronto, perhaps like everyone's home, is a location nostalgically misremembered and fiercely reacted against. The topic of the conference was change and momentum, but I began, in odd determination, with a story that looked backward. It's a Toronto story, a story about memory and about time stopped. A year before the talk, my 92-year-old mother announced that there was something she wished to discuss with me. Something long-stalled and frozen was now working through her memory, for over 60 years, as it turned out. The story was, at first glance, utterly simple. My father was returning from a 5-year absence at the end of the Second World War. His train was due in at Union Station—just about 400 yards from the conference headquarters and the ballroom where I was giving the keynote—and my mother went to meet him. They embrace, but at the car she says to him, "Shall I drive?" and he says, flashing with anger, "How could you say such a thing?" They will drive home, suddenly, unexpectedly, two strangers, to find their 4 1/2-year-old—me—who is waiting to meet her father for the first time and who will (now one sees) spend the next decades parceling out that encounter, repairing and caretaking.

My mother had saddled the memory with all the difficulties that had followed. How to unpack *Nachträglichkeit*—Freud's great insight into the backward action of present upon past—to a 92-year-old. In my mother's narrative, that moment foreshadowed, predicted, and determined all that

* This paper originally appeared in *Psychoanalytic Dialogues, 19*(1), 2009, pp. 2–21. Reprinted with permission.

followed. It was a scene that picked up traumatic momentum as the years rolled by. We did have a useful conversation about the war, its toll on couples. I was mindful of the repetition. I was still caretaking, interpreting, making sense of difficult psychic matters—my job in the family and, as it turns out, not by accident, my job in life.

Each of my parents had arrived at that moment expecting happiness. They were privileged young people. My mother's father was one of the architects of Union Station, and her uncle had his own railway car. She was an adolescent before it dawned on her that the railway was a public transportation system. The conjunction of entitlement and dashed hopes at that train station is acute. And, as she said, by way of explaining her distress after the reunion, "I wore my best French dress."

Months earlier my father had written a letter to her at the end of one of the fiercest battles of the war. Brief understated accounts of fighting are woven into lyrical descriptions. "We began to climb on a narrow road that hung off the mountain like a necklace.... We could look back down to the green valley with the river winding past." He conjures up a scene. Shells land, mules bray, an isolated Italian stationmaster sits alone in a ruined station wearing his official cap. My father reports on the fighting, on troops moving in the dangerous, dark, mountain night. At the end he closes so hopefully with, "Our day is coming very soon." But in this story of return and reunion, we know already that their time did not come, that, sadly, their time had already passed. Like all people who have weathered traumatic loss or rupture in whatever way they could, there is the imaginary freedom, the feeling that survival itself has separated you from suffering, only to discover years, perhaps decades later, that you are at the beginning, you must begin again. We know this with and for our patients. We try to help them bear up under this knowledge, not be intimidated by the stark significance of the idea of irrevocable loss. We need to consider this truth for ourselves, as well.

I am going to continue to approach the topic of clinical momentum and change this way, by turning backward. I gave my keynote in a large glittery ballroom, a room I had last been in 50 years ago. Winter holidays in Toronto, in the late 1950s, entailed coming to the Royal York to attend an endless and enervating series of formal dances in which nice young persons were groomed and prepped for Toronto society or, more accurately, for faux-adult social life. In my memory, I stand sulkily on the sidelines, convinced that I have been badly dressed by my mother in some frothy evening gown, waiting for some equally anxious young man to fill a spot on my dance card. It's the 1950s, but curiously the band plays the ballads of our parents' generation, gauzy melancholy wartime tunes of the 1940s. "Sentimental Journey." "I'll See You Again." Time seems to be standing still, the evocative slowed-down nostalgia of the 1940s cast across our youth as well, holding us in its pained and nostalgic grip.

A decade later, I am proud to say, I had given away all those dresses to my newly-out gay housemates John and Jeffrey, and I plunged with probably too much abandon into the intensely charged 1960s. A hyperspeed time of civil rights, antiwar work, the woman's movement, gay liberation. My children's views of this dive into history are divided. My son remembers his childhood with fondness and feels trouble began with the Reagan administration, specifically Nancy Reagan. I take this as a transference comment. My daughter prayed nightly to the gods of sitcom that she could be teleported into the TV series *The Brady Brunch* and thus be saved from her mother's communal household and the perturbations (social and familial) of that time. Once in the second grade in Ann Arbor, she tells me (and she has presumably told this story in rather many therapy sessions) that a prized boy approached her on the school playground. "I know something about you," he said menacingly. She quaked in her boots. "Your father threw a brick at the police on University Avenue" (a site of some antiwar demonstration). She had a moment of discordant wild feeling, "That wouldn't be my father. That would be my mother," but knew gloomily that her status in the second grade had gone irretrievably south.

We came back to Toronto for my first grown-up job at York University and to live in proximity to my family and to enjoy the unexpected pleasures of normalcy and extended family. But that sojourn in Toronto, that time in the 1970s, was one of significant losses for me, the kind of adult experience that made me first a therapist and then a psychoanalyst. I circled back out of Toronto for the adventures of New York, and a reprise of radical politics, this time in the world of mental health. In New York, a group that included many close friends, many of them comrades to this day, formed a group: The Group for a Radical Human Science. We had a radio show, a writing forum, and we tried to weather the thousand contradictions and conflicts that stood in the way of a low-cost analytic clinic. We organized a streak of sit-ins and political actions, and, inevitably, we foundered on an all too familiar set of internal dissensions, the bane of progressive life through the 20th century. It was an experience and a time configured by our youth, mostly manifest in our ability to stay out late and take time for politics. Yet this nostalgic look back at radical youth masks the real losses, the missteps, the endless rewriting of personal and larger history. At this moment, my regrets, shared I suspect very widely among my generation, are most acutely for the loss of a political culture.

Given this history, I think that I am certainly a person to talk about change and momentum. Yet there I was standing in the same room of my adolescent introduction into faux adulthood. I was still carefully dressed, though with much better sartorial advice. Most women in our profession craft their paper-giving outfits with the care and performative savvy that only careful reading of Joan Riviere's (1929) "Womanliness as a Masquerade" could possibly explain. A woman looked up from her breakfast as I made my way through the dining room and said in alarm, "Your slip is showing." Indeed, I had to tell her, yes it was. It was part of the look.

In this way, I suggest that return and repetition are always elements of change, that change is, above all, nonlinear, that, in change, time moves in manifold directions and that our experiences, collective, dyadic, or solitary, are always multiply configured. Actually, I have tried to sneak into this introduction many of my themes on the topic of change. There is, in efforts to change, an impulse for freedom, always lived with a mixture of exhilaration and destructiveness. There is melancholy and a sense of loss and sadness that weaves through change. Grieving, I will argue, is one necessary and irreducible element for clinical momentum for all the participants.

There is also, in my story, evidence that the force of history can galvanize personal change. The swoosh as you enter history and history enters you. In clinical work, this experience is what Janine Puget, an Argentinean analyst writing about analysis in terrible political and social conditions, has called the "radioactive" identifications and transferences in which social forces invade and envelope clinical work, to say nothing of personal life (Puget & Sanville, 2000). This encounter, this mix-up, this tussle of history, practice, and theory, has been very acute in the elaborations and transformation in our understanding of gender and sexuality and, more recently, our excavations of race (Altman, 1996, 2006; Corbett, 1993, 2001; Dimen, 2003; Goldner, 1991, 2003; Leary, 2000; Suchet, 2007).

Clinical Impasse

I am going to approach the problem of change and momentum along a melancholy and paradoxical pathway: I start by looking at moments when change appears blocked and momentum comes to a halt. Looking at our psychoanalytic literature on impasse or deadlock, I was struck by how rarely, in the past, the analyst's contribution to impasse is noted. There are several notable exceptions, but really until the mid-1990s countertransference serves mostly as a kind of sentinel, an early warning system as to the brakes and constrictions and impasses in the internal world of the patient. There is a subtle and intricate account of impasse, but it is centered in the *transference*. A great deal of our clinical work leans on, indeed depends on, these insights, centering on the power of the analyst, understood primarily as a feature in the patient's mind. Impasse is an outcome of the patients' murderous inner attacks, externalized and often evacuated through intolerable levels of shame and envy in the analysand and lived in the transference through many subtle and gross acts of undoing and sabotage.

In the aftermath of some collapse or impasse, patients describe feelings of uncanny spooky oddness, a feeling of being in the midst of a clanging terrible internal and external battle that simultaneously seems to be taking place in a ghost town. Time is uncannily moving and still. Our clinical inquiry has mostly centered on whom it is, in these patients' internal worlds, that arises with such peremptory and unstoppable charge to say "no" to momentum and movement? What compels me, now, in thinking about impasse, is whether we can ask the same question in regard to the analyst.

Although until the mid-1990s this question went mostly unasked, I found two notable exceptions. McLaughlin, wonderfully helped to his 2006 book by William Cornell and Lewis Aron, wrote in 1988 that impasse in treatment has always something to do with an impasse in the analyst. In his case, his own *wood shedding*—a term he gave his own self analysis— led him to recognize a core, intense, dynamic of shame, which he linked, in his own history, to maternal abandonment, an abandonment in the form of a bereavement. McLaughlin believed he carried with him always the ghost of an idealized doctor father, dying through selfless heroism in caring for patients in the 1919 influenza epidemic. He was aware also that he lived always in an intense internal relation to a mother, overworked and mournful, who was caught up in a bereavement that turned her gaze away from her children. And he makes this curious and important connection between abandonment and shame, a link we might find explanations for in the work of Alan Schore (1994), who describes shame as an outcome of the exuberance of the young child met with silent mismatch by the parent, a mismatch that leads to a wildly disregulated affective crash in the child.

The other discovery for me was Sasha Nacht (1962, 1969), an analyst in Paris, a Rumanian exile, who, in the 1960s, writes of the centrality of the analyst's presence: "It is not so much what the analyst says as what he is. It is precisely what he is in the depths of himself—his real availability, his receptivity and his authentic acceptance of what the other is—which gives value, pungency and effectiveness to what he says" (1969, p. 597). There are Ferenczian echoes here as well.

The relational contribution to thinking about impasse has been to take all the insights about the dangerous and damaged internal figures in the analysand's internal world and weave an intersubjective story in which two people, asymmetrical but mutually implicated, cocreate an experience in which, through illusion and resonance, each has become the other's worst nightmare. Beyond the now conventional idea about countertransference as a kind of situational illness, we need to see the inevitable presence in the analyst of wounds that must serve as tools, aspects of the analyst's capacities that are simultaneously brakes on and potentials for change. In this way, relational theorists are, I would argue, absolutely faithful to the deepest idea in psychoanalysis, namely, the irreducible presence of unconscious phenomena. This faith and the discipline, which must support faith, are expressed through a commitment to the inevitable immersion in enactment and the living with one's own toxicity as well as the patient's.

This vision of the clinical dyad does not center on symmetry or equivalence or some exclusive narcissistic focus on analytic subjectivity. Rather, in looking at clinical interaction, I am asking us to pay attention to the analyst's internal world as participatory in analytic process, in particular to impasse and then to change and momentum. Two-personness can seem to indicate equivalence, a democracy of action and reaction. But really, two-personness means that you cannot afford the luxury of believing you know fully the boundary of self and other. You cannot ever fully have the precise coordinates of interiority and exteriority. The relational canon on enactment outlines the powerful impact of disavowed badness, sadism, excitement, and desire in the analyst all working their effects on stalled and deadlocked treatments. The analyst becomes transfixed or enthralled (Davies, 2003a, 2003b), enters a complementarity of doer and done-to (Benjamin, 1995), colludes and collides with the affective processes and fantasies of omnipotence, simultaneously in analyst and in patient (Slochower, 1996). Slochower (2006) makes us mindful of the porousness of illusions, the density of defensive omnipotent illusions, and the paradox of hope and hopelessness that therapeutic dyads must traverse and retraverse. The analyst's contribution is thus inevitably multileveled, both intentional and unconscious, both fantasy driven and deliberate (Aron, 1996; Bass, 2007; Bromberg, 1998; Cooper, 2003; and others). Clinical momentum and impasse are both provisional states.

I have not invoked ideas about thirdness in regard to the negotiating of impasse in a relational treatment. There are two reasons. First, I want to stress the dimensions of temporality not structure. Second, I want us to see even in the most profound places of impasse blocked identifications and symmetries, that sameness and differences always coexist. Fantasies of fully exhaustive identification are fantasies. It is a hallmark of the nonlinear dynamic systems theory that small differences are sufficient for movement. Slight shifts in experience can give rise to change and great complexity and difference within very short time frames. In many ongoing dynamic processes there is a tipping point, a point of. Optimal turbulence has a profound effect on systems' equilibriums, whether the system is dyadic or more multiply configured (see Galatzer-Levy, 2004; Harris, 2005; Olds, 2000;

Piers, 2000; Pizer, 1998; Seligman, 2005, for elaborations of this theoretical perspective). Therapeutic action and the breaking up of impasse can occur through very minute shifts in the dyad or the individuals.

To take up a metaphor Jody Davies developed in the online colloquium on Thirdness, we might think of impasse or the potential for contact and recognition embodied as two compasses with arrows pointed toward each other. But, as natural objects, two compasses pointed together would be active not static, the points moving, jumping, oscillating, disjunctively and in pattern with each other. Movement occurs in the wake of discrete and small distinctions. The internal worlds of analyst and analysand can be mutually evocative and resonant, but intersubjective space is always also filled with distinction, difference, and otherness. For that reason, the shared intermingling of two sensibilities will always have the potential to be a site of movement. In circumstances of impasse, then, there is always a paradox. Deadness and stasis can seem locked in and the dyad trapped into polarized complementarities. But within impasse there is always the potential for the use of an object, for a weathering of destructiveness, or a slight shift in the psychic equilibrium of one or both participants. Deadness and a point of optimal turbulence are actually closer than one might imagine. Here I am asking us to pay attention to the small shifts that might open in the analyst around omnipotence. Enactment and surprise are surprisingly adjacent and closely intertwined as so many of Bromberg's clinical examples reveal (Bromberg, 2006).

The Analyst's Contribution to Impasse

My contribution to these theoretical innovations is to suggest that when we consider the analyst's constitutive contribution to the distinct and yet interdependent experiences in clinical we also consider the developmental history of the analyst's contribution to these impasses, a history that must hold some continuous residual potency, if we do in fact take seriously the notion of an unconscious. This history, I am going to argue, is linked to early loss and rupture of many different kinds, losses that so often seem to bring shame, bound inexorably into omnipotence, like an unwelcome but closely hovering fellow traveler. It is these very primary and difficult affects, very wound into intersubjective as well as intrapsychic experience for the analyst, that contribute to difficulties in clinical impasse.

I am concerned with two affects in particular: shame and sadness. Shame and grief are interesting to consider in tandem. They are linked and at odds with each other, as McLaughlin suggests. Shame is a curious shadow state, attendant on grieving. Loss somehow often signals badness in the loser, leading to the self-beratement so often noticed in mourning. Omnipotence can be a powerful defense against both sadness and shame. Shame is itself a crucial affect to unpack and analyze. Schore's (1994) account is illuminating: a dramatic mismatch between affective states leads to a sharp and experientially catastrophic dysregulation. Michael Lewis (1992), in conceptualizing the impact of shame on early psychic life, notes the totality of the collapse in moments of shame. It is the whole self that implodes and shatters. Shame is perhaps the signal affect to consider for its two-personness, an idea that can be traced to Sylvan Tomkins (1962, 1963). As many people have noted, shame is a particularly powerful transpersonal affect. It has the performative effect of doubling itself. Shame of being ashamed can derail even the most subtle empathic comments and interpretive work. And as many people have noted, shame and rage can cycle in a lethal and unsettling combination. I want us to pay attention to the intermingling of all these aspects of shame in the analyst's own process of grieving and metabolizing loss.

Jody Davies did a memorable discussion of a paper by Sharon Zalusky, on a "failed" case (Davies, 2004). For Davies, this patient, named (perhaps poignantly) Freda, was the emblematic patient we all treasure and dread. Tragic, haunted, damaged beyond imagination, this is the patient, often of our early years in training and practice, the one we go beyond all limits for, whose impasses and stalemates break our hearts. Davies notes that this patient is almost always a stand-in for some crucial figure or figures in our internal world. Freda is the reason we became analysts. Whether originally a parent, a sibling, or an ancestor, the project of saving our Fredas haunts our vocation, our ambition, and our sense of self-worth. And to be sure, internal objects are complex, not always so distinctly mapped to single, external characters. Amalgams, part objects, ghosts, and monsters in many forms, remnants of our early experiences, return transformed, translated, reconfigured but haunting.

Davies's analysis of the failed case links to some ideas I have been exploring on the analyst's vulnerability (Harris, 2005; Harris & Sinsheimer, 2008). I have argued that the evolution of relational thinking places increased demands on the analyst. Always we produce and are exposed to more than we can master, know, or manage. However you use your countertransference, it is both crucial and only ever imperfectly masterable. That mix of powerlessness, shame, and insistent demand is actually a terrible combination, a prescription for dissociation and trauma. I think this may be one of the indissoluble, irreducible conditions of analytic work. Alan Wheelis (1987), quoted in an essay on boundary violations by Foehl (2005):

> It can happen, having foolishly been playing at the edge of a precipice, a mile high face of merciless granite ... having stumbled and fallen ... even so, that

for a few crucial moments one will bounce and tumble and scrape against the topmost rocks and projections, one's falling being slowed just enough to catch a branch.... (Wheelis, 1987, pp. 71–72)

This is some job description.

I am going to link thoughts about the analyst's vulnerability to some speculations on outcomes of our early caretaking and attachment histories. However well worked in analysis, and in development, and however much sublimation and integration of early history has occurred, some unconscious presence of these damaged or damaging internal objects, these Fredas, must persist, carrying with them residues of difficult affects: sadness, shame, fear, rage. The implications of this idea for the analyst's working ego is that the need to have open access to unbearable affects in ourselves is one of the challenges that makes psychoanalytic work so difficult. The relational turn invites us to enter deep process with patients that inevitably encompasses material well beyond our mastery or theirs; sadness and desires beyond reason. This may be one reason that discussions of relational technique can be frustrating and frightening. A certain degree of indeterminacy in affective life itself is part of the ordeal of the work and that must include unmetabolized elements in the analyst as well as the analysand.

Analysis is daily work, and perhaps because of its repetitive habitual nature, analysts may underestimate the conceptual problems the idea of an unconscious entails (whether repression or dissociation is involved). The radical otherness in our very core, whether that otherness is indigenous or transpersonally constituted, must keep us permanently unsettled. Unconscious forms or processes generate unpredictable effects that we know mostly retrospectively through traces, fantasies, and enactments. It is simply a daunting problem to build a theory of technique without leaning too heavily on the comforts of the Enlightenment.

I draw on the attachment literature, hopefully with a care not to be reductionistic a caution that Seligman (2003) argues for. We need to be thinking of multiple positions within one parent. There are multiple developmental narratives, a complex cast of characters in most families. Often, broad areas of competence exist in a primary caretaker who nonetheless may live with particular "sinkholes" around experiences of trauma and intense affect. Attachment styles and the child adaptations are both variegated and particular. I have been strongly influenced by Karlin Lyons-Ruth's review of longitudinal data on disorganized attachment. Lyons-Ruth's primary work has been to outline what arises when a crucial securing figure is a dangerous, frightening, or frightened and damaged figure (1999, 2003).

Attachment, she points out, is a part of the fear system; it is particular to circumstances of arousal in conditions of fearfulness and is an appeal for security. So the sinkhole in the parental figures devastates the potential for containment and safety, most precisely, at the moment secure containment is most needed. Most interesting, for my purposes, is Lyons-Ruth's account of child adaptation. In the wake of an established pattern in early infancy of disorganized attachment experiences, by toddlerhood and preschool, a child will have worked out a robust stable adaptation. I use these terms not particularly to indicate a healthy system but a trenchant and often rigid one, designed to make predictability where the system has none. This adaptation could be control (via entertainment or enactment and wildness). But most fascinatingly, adaptation could also involve caretaking and parental behaviors toward the parent. So, Lyons-Ruth (2003) says, "Tend/befriend as a mode of child adaptation can emerge along with the more obvious flight and fight responses" (p. 886). Lyons-Ruth is drawing on research data that harkens back to a seminal idea of Bowlby (1960). Early on, he had the insight that role reversal—in this case, parentification of the child—is one of the most destructive aspects of flawed attachments.

This is very startling to me, raising the question of where and how such adaptive parenting behavior might arise in circumstances where disorganization or maternal hostility or depression is prominent. It, of course, opens us to the complexity of the internal world, the multiplicity of relational matrices, arising very early in life. Reading this I found myself thinking that the conduct disorders and wild ones end up in the patient chair and the tend/befrienders end up more usually in our chairs. But, of course, in a model of mind stressing variation and multiplicity, we know that we retain the capacity for both modes of response. In clinical work and in impasses, we may have the evidence both of our painful history as parentified objects and as well the residues of the frightening and fearful creatures bristling with shame and rage in great profusion, which are often so disavowed in our characters. These residues are most usually erased or evacuated, often through the covering capacities developed through precocious self-regulation, which inevitably has elements of omnipotence. Take this abstract general description I have just given you back to the story at Union Station. The task of managing the waves of anguish and confusion emanating from that reunion are part of the shaping experiences that made me the wary little caretaker I was becoming. Now I tell my story in hopes that you will map these ideas to yours. This intergenerational transmission is contained and expressed in our many variegated individual narratives.

Looked at balefully, we could think of being an analyst as a form of repetition compulsion. Looked at more hopefully, we can see that the heart of our unconscious and relational history makes us inspired in our work *and* leaves us vulnerable. We know a lot about the strengths and vulnerability of children who have had to form their own containers. Ego precocity is the questionable talent of certain children to be able to parent self and other before there is really sufficient internal structure. But as in Bowlby's

(1960) accounts of children who "tend/befriend" there is still some mystery: Where, in the deserts and depletions of early attachments gone awry, does any capacity to care emerge?

However it is formed or constituted, omnipotence and tend/befriender adaptation have always mixed and incomplete results. The drowned, deadening, or deadly objects are never fully repaired. Omnipotence, one might say, is a brilliant and always partially doomed strategy, leaving much unmetabolized and therefore, I am arguing, much that is ungrieved. In a paper on mourning and melancholia, Jeanne Bernstein (unpublished manuscript) points out that, in Freud's essay, he links the melancholic's state to fragile ego structures, to disrupted early object relations, and to extreme difficulties with separation and fragmentation.

What I draw from all these sources is that a certain degree of omnipotence and some form of ego precocity will reside in the working state of most analysts, even as these early demands, these early melancholic or disrupted relational adaptations, may be transformed brilliantly into professional identities and solutions. Being an analyst draws on ambition, aggression, and discipline (what McLaughlin, 2006, called *aim-inhibited love*) as well as early precocity. Winnicott speaks of sacrifice and suffering, Bion (1992) talks of the analyst living with fear. Because analysts are vulnerable not only to patients' projections but also to our own histories, the task of distinguishing clinical responsibility from omnipotence is endless and exacting and always, to some degree, indeterminate. It is never solely the problem of sorting the origins of affect but also bearing the personal affective states, with all their personal historical force, in us.

Clearly, omnipotence is only part of the story. There may be, alongside clear-eyed capacity for caretaking, many bouts of dissociation, the particular hallmark of intense dyadic life with a traumatized parental figure. Lyons-Ruth (2003) makes the argument that the most powerful transmission in disorganized attachment patterns is not frank abuse but dissociation and unmetabolized terror in the caretaker.

McLaughlin (2006) frankly states his view, regarding his own contributions to impasse, that "as I now assess the power and ubiquity of the chilling shame that rejection brings into the lives of each of us, I think of it as the bond that binds us all, the low chord that causes dissonance that strikes more deeply at any age" (p. 23). And then there is the matter of envy, and here I mean the analyst's envy of the freedom in the patient to be wild and rageful and beastly. Anywhere there is shame, I would suggest, there is some remnant of pleasure and desire, pleasures particularly likely to be compromised for a tend/befriender child who has had precociously to act parental or for some reason to inhibit exuberance and vitality and rage.

I want us to hold this model of the analyst's vulnerability as a consequence of the particular demands of omnipotence. The analyst's omnipotence, organized in the service of managing shame and envy, is a crucial block to grieving because in the omnipotent stance, there is no loss, no absence. Need itself seems to have been vanquished. In clinical instances of impasse, then, it is the potential for or barrier to grieving that lives alongside, in parallel, and also distinct from these potentials in the patient. Since omnipotence blocks both grieving and the reexperience of shame and since there is pragmatic and real-life potential use of omnipotence in professional identities, the *analyst's* defensive stance in which omnipotence is prominent can be highly tenacious and resistant to movement.

Clinical Story

I have a patient who has made a home of impasse, of liminality. Jeremy made it through college, both brilliantly and in pieces, and came back home after graduation to a strange liminal existence, until he finally signed himself into a hospital. The third time in his life he had made such a choice. Described as a difficult child from toddlerhood, Jeremy lived in fantasy and his own head as a way to escape crushing and humiliating experiences with peers, difficulties in school and learning, and oscillating periods of violence and shame-riddled abjection. In mid-adolescence he chose a hospital because he was afraid to hurt others. Not through active violence. He would say only that his death would hurt his family. He was ground down and terrified.

"*Time Bandits* is one of my favorite movies." Jeremy is smiling. He would have been 15 and at the nadir of his difficulties, when the film was released. Nearly two decades later, he and I are 4 years into an intense and complex treatment and his smile is in the context of a session that gives me a rare moment of hope. The film is the story of a boy who disappears into a time hole in his bedroom to join with a band of dwarfs who surf time zones. A Peter Pan story for the sci-fi crowd.

Jeremy titrates hope for both of us carefully. He is a long-term expert time bandit. One line of reflection is explored and then we turn and undo and trace the opposite. It is a strange but energetic *fort/da* organized around Jeremy's ardent wish to stop time, stop his own growth, and remain in a melancholic container, an isolated container ringed with anxiety and fiendish levels of self-beratement. Jeremy's terror at attachment is lived in tandem with terror at loss and loneliness. I think of Jeremy's modes of being and talking and living as foreclosures on mourning. Jeremy's mourning poses particular challenges, as it must entail acceptance of decades of suffering, lost possibilities for growth and development, lost relationships. The huge weight of loss for patients with these kinds of lifelong histories of difficulty can make bearing up under the demands of mourning extremely difficult.

Jeremy fights for change and fights against the terrible feeling of loneliness that inevitably arises in change. This is a paradox, an enigma at the heart of both impasse and change, how to bear up under the sadness of movement and change. Change is loss; we say this to patients all the time. It must hit home as well. How do we bear loss without the internal structure to support grief? So we complicate the already complex sense of the problem of impasse, not just the no's in the internal object world but the sad fearfulness in any act of growth, the lonely demands of solitude and separation in creativity and change itself.

In the course of treatment, several themes have emerged. Jeremy and his family had, since his very early childhood, been caught in a familial, therapeutic, and institutional discourse. The question for everyone always seemed to boil down to "was he sick or was he bad." Only very recently have we been able to make any space for a third question: what did this or that event mean? For 25 years, solutions were moral or medical. Parental guilt, along with Jeremy's anxieties about injury and loss of control, kept at bay any sphere of ambiguity.

Trauma and repetition are represented in Jeremy's mental state, in agitated incoherence, in being unreadable, unfindable. He arrives already wrong and unfindable, unmentalizable by any other. The parental environment was characterized by depression, dissociation, and, in both parents, a history of dissociated trauma that made for key sites of absence and incomprehension in relation to Jeremy. Too often, his mother could make no sense of him, she could not make him an object of her reverie. He relives this with me. One feature of our impasse in this regard has been my inability to think in sessions, my dissociation into a kind of mindless geniality, an affectionate regard that came to strike me as very much like that of his mother. His father was too frightened to take him in and take him up as an object of identification. The father's fear of a repetition of the vicious trauma of his own early childhood left Jeremy adrift yet infused with the threat of violence, hypervigilant to a threat he had no name for until he was nearly 30. Impasse in the sense of incomprehensibility haunts us.

One of Lyons-Ruth's (2003) most trenchant ideas in regard to attachment history is the powerful, often defining impact of parental unmetabolized trauma on child mind. To consider the approach of Fonagy (2001), it is the quality and history of mentalization and being held in mind that shape an individual's capacities for self-regulation.

Here is a small but, I came to feel, deadly enactment. Jeremy was talking about dogs, including his family dog, which he did not like. He has alluded to having abused an earlier family pet. Talking about dogs in the city he spoke of wanting to see dogs stuffed, like taxidermy. About 30 seconds later I realized that I had made some comment and probably a flinched face and the topic had changed. I was aware that the flinch and the comment had shut Jeremy down. Certainly my fear had leaked out. But disgust was also disavowed. I wanted him to carry abjection. Repeatedly, fears of the contents of Jeremy's mind keep both of us inhibited. The impasse configures the transference: I am an unmentalizing even if also a fond maternal object. One lynchpin to this impasse is deeply in me in some place of refusal to know destructiveness and cruelty. The term *mentalizing* can sound too cerebral or abstract. But mentalizing describes a capacity to hold another's experience, metabolize it, and reflect it in a way that can be reabsorbed. There is a flow of experience transforming gradually between and within each person. These experiences have a sensory, a linguistic, a motoric, an affective as well as a cognitive aspect. Mentalizing and being mentalized are full body–mind experiences.

That packed but ruptured interaction between us around the stuffed dog is intensely charged. The stuffed dog, the dog without its insides, invites all kinds of links to me and to Jeremy. The assault on creatureliness is one hallmark of omnipotence and parentification of a child, so the stuffed dog carries my shame about body and substance and babyishness, and certainly the shame and anxiety about destructiveness. My constriction in working with Jeremy certainly has the earmarks of dissociation, a split in me in the face of destructiveness or destruction moving in multiple directions. When I look at my compromised capacities to think and feel with Jeremy, I see how I ward off a fall into a terrifying bottomless pit of despair (his, mine, ours) and that this inhibition in me is linked to my history. Let's think of the puppy child waiting at home for the father's return from the war. I am suggesting that, for all of us, the capacity to encompass all these experiences of vitality and exuberance that get transformed into badness and shame or destructive rage are related in some way to our capacity or incapacity to mourn the injuries linked to our earliest and most archaic object ties.

"So we beat, boats against the current, borne back ceaselessly into the past" (p. 182)—thus the beautiful novel of Fitzgerald, *The Great Gatsby*, ends, in the voice of the empathic but dispassionate narrator.

Clinical Momentum: Three Notes

From this discussion of impasse, I am going to shift now into considering change and momentum. I am going to focus on the mutative action of psychoanalysis by drawing on two sources—one very old idea in psychoanalytic theory and one more newly minted theory of development—and linking them to the process of mourning. I also explore the concept of mutative action as a process embedded in a strange geography of speech and action, time and space. As befits the early stages of my thinking on this topic I have organized the material as a series of three brief notes.

Afterwardsness

The concept *Nachträglichkeit*, termed *après coup* in French, is Freud at his most nonlinear (Freud, letter to Karl Abraham, July 7, 1907). I am going to use Laplanche's (1989, 1997) inventive term *afterwardsness*, a term I like because it evokes the paradox in temporal experience, the sense of being in more than one time zone, in being haunted and often at the same, living in the strange near future zone that Loewald reserved by transference. That subjective experience, the sense of being on the edge of something about to occur, is also very powerfully the experience in trauma. Traumatic states are lived in double time—it is as if the bad thing is about to happen, something ominous is pending, yet the past dominates everything. The trauma is simultaneously in the past and about to happen.

Afterwardsness is also an aspect of the movement, and dynamic reconfiguring and retranslating that are inevitable aspects of mourning. Psychic movement and mourning are codeterminants in the experience of afterwardsness. There is a resetting of genealogies and orders that comes from some loosening in patient *and* analyst. Though we usually track this process in the patient's material, I am also suggesting that the flourishing of psychic change in the wake of an experience of afterwardsness also occurs when the analyst can shake free of some of the powerful (and often necessary) elements of omnipotence.

Afterwardsness allows us to see time moving forwards and backwards. This process can move in two directions. There are complex dialectics here. Structural change alters our experience of temporalities, of time lines or, in the reverse, a change in the experience of being in time (whether past, present, near future, or horizon): alters identity, object history, and internal worlds. The story of my parents' reunion at Union Station, the discovery of my father's letters, set experiences of reordering and renarratizing in motion. An experience of volatility, uncertainty, and surprise sets the context for change. Afterwardsness is a crucial element in mutative action because the experience constitutes moments carried in doubled and tripled time. It summarizes the losses that preceded it, alters the meaning of those losses and changes the unraveling that follows. Psychic reality becomes constructed by its own future. The dynamism of afterwardsness arises in its complex construction and reordering of time. In the course of analysis, we renarratize these constructed time lines, and this puts us in profound, often conflicting ways of organizing experiences. The reorganizing of temporality can jumpstart mourning, or, in the opening of psychic space that arises in mourning, temporality and history are reordered.

How does the analyst's omnipotence figure in this process? I am hoping that in deconstructing that term, we can see omnipotence as our Achilles' heel, our gift, our internal site of wound and of creativity, our experience always potentiating closure and movement. The state of mind in which omnipotence is being destabilized is a strange attractor, in chaos theory terms, a place where change is potentiated. Afterwardsness, implicated in the process of mourning in analyst and analysand, in interwoven but discrete processes, makes the developmental lines within the microcosm of a treatment profoundly nonlinear, emergent, unpredictable, and manifoldly temporal. This calls, I believe, for a different model of development, sufficiently supple to encompass and describe multiple, complex experiences, some of which at least emerge in, to use Faimberg's (2004) phrase for the analyst's experience of afterwardsness, *unimaginable surprise*.

We are learning as well to consider the long shadow of historical trauma as impacting on contemporary psychic life (Caruth, 1996; Faimberg, 2004). Abraham and Torok (1994) coined the term *encrypted identities* to describe the incorporation of secrets passed unconsciously from one generation to another and often remaining secret and unknown to the receiver. Francoise Davoine (2008) offers a powerful example of this in a case report on early work with an analysand, similar in age to Davoine. Both participants were caught in powerful enactment involving the war and the Holocaust, during which time they had both been small children in France. In a first session, the analyst says, "It is your resistance that is driving you mad," feeling eerily that she is as much the vehicle of the sentence as its author. Davoine goes on to unpack the meanings nested in this sentence, a process replete with afterwardsnesses and reworking of history and trauma and psychic process. The word *resistance* has the uncanny reverberating effect of signaling both historic-political scenes and intrapsychic life.

Even as our histories differed, Jeremy and I could be and often were caught in our deployment of a stop-time triumph over growth. Uncertainty and the pressure of terrifying affects could stall the treatment. And to my regret, it is sometimes Jeremy who is more able to articulate this experience. In a terrible moment of despair Jeremy had asked accusingly, "You think it's in the depression game or else you think it's in the rage and aggression game, but really what if something has actually died, what if that is so?" For that, I had no answer and, much worse, no capacity to join him in that moment of awe and loss. My work in this treatment has been to open myself to the task of mourning, to face the unbearable to make a space to hold that for Jeremy as well. One thinks of Searles's (1961) ideas of the work of therapy being the patient's healing of the analyst. Too melodramatic a statement, perhaps, but with enough accuracy to make it important for all of us to see that being an analyst includes the endless experience of self-analysis. We need to see that in many treatments, our countertransference is aided by the freeing up of movement and nonlinearity, the willingness to accept the new/old news from the past.

Time and Development

Temporality and development are related and yet distinguishable. Clinical momentum, I am suggesting, is a complex process in which temporality is reconfigured by experience, and history, and recognitions. In turn, temporality reorganizes lines of development. These concepts beg for a theory of development of sufficient complexity and, abstract and daunting as it may be, I firmly believe complexity theory; nonlinear dynamic systems (NDS) is the ticket—a marriage made in heaven with the prenup to be yet worked out (Harris, 2005).

The shift in our thinking that NDS can offer and underwrite is that memory is not reified perception, a tiny museum of the past. Perception is not passive or solely receptive. Chaos theory is a theory of coevolution of entraining subjectivities. None of this reduces or eradicates the responsibilities or rights of the analysand, but it is a model for intersubjective engagement of subtle distinctions and overlaps that produce dramatic change and disequilibration. This theory commits to emergence and unpredictability, not deterministic inevitable unfolding of past into present. We hear the echoes of afterwardsness in the idea of nonlinearity, the development that endlessly reorganizes and reconfigures experiences such that emergence is the dominant principle of growth.

I am drawn to chaos theory because such theories bring a big shift in our thinking about process, structure, and time. Walter Freeman (2000) encourages us to think of the creation of meaning. Brains, bodies, persons have highly selective sensitivities organized as intentional goal-directed schemes. "Chaotic dynamics both selects and destroys information. What we call memory is an ever-changing refining plan to do something" (p. 133). There is an ongoing creative reshaping of brain and body in endlessly evolving ways of being and being with others. When one is remembering, this is a form of action, not a structure. Speech acts are and carry relational schemes. A speech act inhabits and expresses procedural knowing, and so memory is carried as living patterns of potential action. So any simple relational interchange, any intervention or interpretation, carries nested within it complex and multiple temporalities. Hence, the potential for movement.

In NDS theory, minds and psyches and body–minds are best thought of as transpersonal. I want us to see, even in dyadic knots in treatments, that sameness and differences always coexist. In any intersubjective engagement, subtle distinctions can produce dramatic change and disequilibration. It is a hallmark of chaos theory that small differences are sufficient for dramatic and transformative movement. Therefore, the internal worlds of analyst and analysand even when they are evocative, and resonant, are always also filled with distinction. Difference here is as crucial as resonance. Fantasies of fully exhaustive identifications and fusions are just that—fantasies. Otherness can never be fully banished even from the most fused and mirroring dyads. The shared intermingling of two sensibilities will therefore always have the potential to operate as a site for movement.

A key process in chaos theory is the emergence in some process of what are termed *strange attractors*: relational and intrapsychic knots that have the potential to give way to moments of motility and unpredictability. When such processes emerge there is an unsettled possibility: things can close down or open, revert to frozen impasse, or open into an experience in which time, narrative, process is reconfigured, retranslated. Mourning in such moments is possible but not predetermined. The melancholic foreclosure, the omnipotence stance, always beckons, because the move into deep loss and then into terror, is very frightening—for analyst or analysand.

Chaos theory is above all else a theory of interlocking systems and in our current models of intentionality, what Gallese (2009) terms *embodied simulation* we now have increasingly powerful models for intersubjective entrainment at levels of brain and neurophysiology. Our sociality (Trevarthan, 1979, 1993), our deeply rhythmic and resonant ways of being together, imagining another and slowly accommodating the irreducible differences and commonalities between subjects is one powerful primate trait, raised to new levels of coordination and distinction among ourselves. Relational brains, chaotic brains, mutative brains, deeply known through embodied cognition, the place where action, intention, and registration are closely coordinated. It is precisely this very mobile, volatile, intersubjective model of mind that makes psychoanalysis both possible and impossible and makes the relational challenge to work with analytic subjectivity very necessary and very difficult.

Mutative Action in the Space Between Speech and Action

Within psychoanalytic history the question of change and momentum has often been approached in terms of dichotomies. Does mutative action arise through the vehicle or speech or of action? Is an interpretation the agent of structural change or do we conduct Ferenczian cures by love? Do we track structural change or affective shifts and entrainments? Is movement conveyed through symbolic process or "now" moments? What might characterize the relational turn is the attempt to find a way to go from either/or to both/and.

Lewis Aron and I (Harris & Aron, 1997) wrote about Ferenczi's semiotic theory as a way to see how early in our psychoanalytic history the line between speech and action had become blurred and shaky. Embodied cognition, the interdependence of emotion and cognition, the materiality of words and sentences, the transpersonality of mind and subjectivities, the study of intentionality and theory of mind as an outcome of early dyadic life—all these new domains of work and research move us far beyond the old dichotomies. The focus on speech as action, on the embodiment and intersubjectivity of speaking and listening, is at the heart of relational ideas (see Harris, 2005, Chapter 9, for an extended discussion of the interweaving of speech and action and of meaning making as set both in culture and in bodies).

I found a very prescient account of this intermingling of persons and affect states in Nacht's (1962) essay on curative factors in psychoanalysis:

> The essence of this relationship lies, therefore, *beyond the verbal level.* The spoken word is, at least at the beginning of treatment, an element which confirms and increases the *separation* between them—and separation, as we have said, engenders fear. Only this other form of relationship, the non-verbal, can be felt as reassuring, provided the object is felt as "good." I am not unaware that these ideas imply an extreme intersubjectivity that is, on the face of it, contrary to the scientific spirit, for which pure objectivity is essential. But surely, no science would deny that true objectivity lies in admitting the real nature of something and its correct solution, whatever may be the path which has led there. (p. 211)

Actions and interpretations carry meaning and are sites of psychic movement. Enactments may be the place where speech and action meet and mingle. I think it is a central feature of the relational approach that we are never outside transference but that transferences are always in multiple and shifting forms. We never operate outside relational matrices of many interlocking types. The idea that interpretation is always a site of action raises lots of questions about the nature of language and speech. What makes an interpretation "work"? In my own approach, speech is more usefully thought of as pragmatic than purely symbolic. This is the tradition of Bakhtin (1981) and of the American language philosophers Lakoff and Johnson (1980, 1999), who cite the capacities for meaning making as embodied and intersubjective. I think there is always an addressee in speech. Speech is always dialogic. Many object relations, hidden and visible, are nested in any sentence. And to add the analytic aspect, one is spoken often as well as one is speaking. There are multiple speakers in any sentence and in any analytic conversation, not all under our management. Davoine's (2008) unconscious use of the word *resistance*, in the example cited earlier, registers the presence of complex ghosts in the speech acts of analyst and analysand.

So here is my attempt to make an end run around the split of speech versus action. I am going to talk about mutative action as action built on reveries, as action that colors and stains speech and dialogue. Mutative action is potentiated by virtue of an analytic stance or, rather, by shifts in the internal world of the analyst. These internal shifts in the analyst will be reflected in complex but distinct speech actions, often not fully intelligible to speaker or listener. One is spoken and one speaks.

You have to follow me now out of relational theory and clinical experience into a realm of metaphor and fantasy. I am going to draw you into the cultural and literary and postmodern world of Homi Bhabha, a thinker whose project is often the complexity of identity, its hybridic nature in terms of place, and time. In *The Location of Culture* (2000) he worked out two: Let's call them metaphoric spaces or temporalities. Tangiers and Casablanca, he named them, and I want us to think about the action of analysis, the idiom of analysis, to use Judith Butler's (2005) terms, our place of work and speech as occurring always in and between and around these two sites— Tangiers and Casablanca. Both sites are carriers of melancholy and loss. In conjuring them up for you now, I also set a place for certain kinds of reverie in the analyst.

"Tangiers" refers to a wonderful passage from Roland Barthes (1975) in which he remembers sitting, sleepy, in a bar in Tangiers. In reverie and in retrospect he remembers the sounds: "the stereophonic music, conversations, chairs, glasses, Arabic, French" (p. 75). The kind of music and musicality Steve Knoblauch (2000) evokes for us in considering the improvisational rhythms of clinical work, its polyrhythms:

> Through me passed words, syntagms, bits of formulae and no sentence formed, as though that were the law of such a language. This speech was at once very cultural and very savage, was above all lexical, sporadic: It set up in me, though its apparent flow, a definitive discontinuity. It was what was outside the sentence. (p. 75)

This is a way of thinking about an analytic idiom, a stance, a form of clinical speech and clinical listening, a way of living in reverie, where the boundaries inside and outside the self are less firm, where there is doubling and splitting, a dreamscape, a bodyscape. Barthes termed his method *writing aloud* and in this he speaks to the way we, as analysts, speak and are spoken. Our activities and modes of being carry and convey experiences that require, use, and go beyond and outside the structure of language.

Tangiers stands for our receptivity to this aspect of transference and countertransference, with the inevitable misreadings and miscomprehensions as well as spot-on links and resonance (blind spots and bright spots). Analytic action—listening, speaking, doing, and waiting—is always very cultural and very savage. What is mutative there is on the edge of power and freedom but laced with the most archaic states of being and receptivity to others, always perfumed with loss, nostalgia, and many fictions and many truths.

The other geographic/temporal location for Homi Bhabha is *Casablanca*, and here I mean the film not the city, so we are in cultural and psychic space/time. Homi Bhabha (2000) says, "'Play it Sam'" is perhaps the Western world's most celebrated demand for repetition" (p. 261). Fascinatingly, the title is often misremembered as "Play it again Sam." Repetition sticks to this material like glue.

> You must remember this:
> A kiss is still a kiss
> A sigh is still a sigh
> The fundamental rules apply
> As time goes by.

We are in the world of causation, of temporal order, of structure and of repeating. The song evokes the world of dialogue and two-ness, of speaker and addressee, of narrative and storytelling alongside bondage, both internal and interpersonal. And we should note that it is about manifold time lines. Time is moving and time is forever reverberating.

What I love about "Tangiers" is that it pulls for surrender, for a passivity, an openness to surprise and new connections, made of linkage and destruction. What I love about *Casablanca* is its commitment to precision, to orderliness, to the power of the symbolic to carry and summarize. In this lyric and in the film, there is a demand, a push for action and also a demand for remembering. Loss is recorded, done and undone. There is an illusion of the good future that the story of the reunion at Union Station acts as counterpoint to. Perhaps now also we can hear the injunction in the first line of that song. "You *must* remember this."

Imagining the analytic stance as constituted somewhere between and within "Tangiers" and *Casablanca* would mean that interpretation is always a site of action, set within a complex set of entrained bound and separated others. We are never outside transference, never outside relational matrices of many interlocking types. But our work may also happen outside the sentence. An interpretation could be an act of melodrama, a moment where something breaks the surface of consciousness, like a fish jumping. Interpretation could be a signal of action elsewhere or a sign that finally the analyst has understood something. Interpretation could also be quite simply and classically a moment potent raw impact upon the analysand. Or all of the above. One practices then in a strange state of tension between active and passive, one's idiom or way of being and speaking in analysis is both a vehicle for unconscious force and a crafting of containment of those forces. One speaks and is spoken. There are always multiple interlocutors in any speech act, so even in my tense constricted encounter with Jeremy over the dog, we each speak to and past each other, addressing parts of our selves, our internal worlds and each other. The dog is destructive and destroyed parts of each of us. It is a moment, as Barthes might say, very cultural and very savage.

Clinical Story (Continued)

I return to Jeremy, the patient with whom I am often engaged in impasse and deadlock and whose treatment I drew on earlier in this paper to think about the stalling of clinical momentum. Two years into treatment something began to open in Jeremy. Two signs. He began to work, to teach troubled adolescents, and he began to be able to share with me more of his internal world, he began to inquire about the space between us. It was electrifying to me. Now he wonders how he and I, across so much difference, might be connected. Differences of gender, age, religion, and, most crucially, baseball loyalties: how are we to find some common ground? Could I be of use to him? Jeremy surprises me with the intensity of his attachment to me. My surprise is another kind of enactment, a sign of some impasse and refusal to think and feel. The surprise indicates as well the way I settled into an accommodation to Jeremy's oscillations and endless returns to stasis and defeat. Subtly titrating medicine and effort, moving back and forth in relation to deep internal terrors and exhaustions, Jeremy moves endlessly between open and closed. Recently he could establish with me another split, public and private. Privately with me, he feels safe and embedded. Publicly, he feels pinned down, indicted by looks and glances that see deep into him, to his lewdness, his degradation, his badness. I find a window into my impasse in relation to the experience with stuffed dogs.

In a new but uneven mood of hopefulness, he reports more memory from session to session. He begins to address his deep conflict between living only as subsistence, in prison, and another state he and I then try to name. Agency he says. Contact with another I say. We are linked together as we speak this way. He reviews an old debate in his mind. "I say here I am afraid that even if I wrote, there would be nothing. I fear there is only deficit. But I also believe deep down in the other side, that there is something I can say." He remembers a dream: In his dream, asleep (this is how he tells me), "I can play the guitar; I have written a song and am singing it." Initially he is angry and cynical. Only in my dreams can I be alive and creative. Then he adds a remembered detail. I am in prison, but I had escaped. With buddies. I ask about prison. And later take the risk of saying that one source of guilt is how frequently he dashes all our hopes—his, parents, mine, family, and friends. He nods. But again, I have asked him to carry the responsibility for impasse.

Jeremy, as he feels better, tells me the following reverie. "You know those kinds of mind transference thoughts. You imagine if you knew then what you know now. Go back—relearn the guitar, try harder, persevere, get help. But you can't and it wouldn't work anyway." Mourning must involve a tolerance of mystery and despair.

In this new and renewed space of exploring our relationship, I found a way back to the enactment around the dog and told him how it had stayed with me, how it had haunted me as a moment of failing him. He was tearful, shaken. And slowly, not at once, we began to unpack that moment between us and that history of his destructive wishes and actions in relation to the dog. What I could not bear to hear and so he could not bear to say has felt like the epicenter of his prison, holding Jeremy's conviction of his own dangerousness and badness, his fear of what he is capable of. Small slivers of mourning open in each of us.

But Jeremy's treatment is a daily reminder to me of the thesis of this talk, a thesis I am always remembering and forgetting. Time moves backward and forward. Each moment of contact for Jeremy, each potential for change and movement sets in motion a complex disequilibrium, a terror that change means death, loss, alteration, and dangerous acting. Each of us must do battle with our omnipotent fantasies, our longing expressed in one of Jeremy's signature images: to be the motorcycle without gravity.

But finding and losing my way does not yet (or perhaps ever) have a happy ending. I come again and again to the difficulties with my omnipotence, to the bedeviling question of whether hopes (Jeremy's and mine) are necessary or illusory. In the aftermath of our work on the dog and cruelty and destructiveness Jeremy began to make new plans for work and for more social engagement. He connected this mostly to new medication. But with the potential for change, everything got sluggish and exhausting. Energy leaked out of Jeremy in a terrifying way.

I had a dream about Jeremy and his family. We are in some structure traveling. There is lots of activity. Then the structure turns into a boat, and we are somewhere in the Middle East and I hear Jeremy saying, "The British warships pull all the material off the bottom of the ocean." To my growing horror, the boat we are in, Jeremy, his family, and me, sinks slowly through the water and I feel the boat settle on the ocean bottom and stop. I realize we will drown or suffocate. The dream comes at a fulcrum moment with Jeremy when I fear again for his fragile insides, his devastating history of loss and loneliness. Somehow as I work on the dream, I think of British warships, of the Middle East, and associate to both world wars and to losses for both my parents' and grandparents' generations. Drowned hopes. His or mine or the drowned hopes of my internal objects? In my difficulty in helping Jeremy bear loss and dashed hopes, I can feel the conflict in my own process, the ways that Jeremy's abyss—his ocean-deep fall to despair and mine—are linked and different. In my associations to my dream, I hear the residues of wartime, including the First War, which I realize on reflection was the signal event in my nanny's life. The loss of young men between 1914 and 1918 sent poor Scottish and English girls like her to Canada for work and some kind of reduced future. Now Jeremy has his own preoccupations with historic losses, evoked by the idea of British warships in the Middle East. My dream is a kind of supervision, a key to linked and distinct projects of mourning in Jeremy and in me. Reading the dream catches me up in multiple experiences of afterwardsness.

In this delicate and uncertain project of treating Jeremy, I go back and forth in my own impasses: hope and despair, courage and fear, action and collapse. Jeremy says to me. "I need to be in assisted living," speaking both from "Tangiers" and *Casablanca*, a sentence I recognize as requesting and refusing hope. Mindful of much I am identifying with and grieving, feeling often afraid for Jeremy and particularly afraid (transference and identification) of his rage and destructiveness. The story of the dog appears and reappears. His feelings of badness, of lewdness, of being an object of scorn and hatred emerge, go away, and reemerge. We work also on his difficulties in holding anything good inside. In one session he says to me that he is aware that he does not really know anything about love, that perhaps he does not or cannot love. And later in the same session he speaks for the first time of his need to be prepared for the loss of his parents. How will he live after their death? This has murder and hope completely entangled. What might separateness and capacity to live and work look like? Lonely, yes. Time has opened a little.

The past, its representations, internal and interpersonal, is not a museum but a living program for action and being with self and others, a program that may be deeply traumatic or filled with growth and potential. An experience of presentness in Jeremy is being built out of both of our experiences of limit. For Jeremy the future has been captured in the image of the motorcycle defying gravity. Now it is lonelier and grittier. I think of Winnicott's (1974) wonderful sentence: "Fear is just memory in the future tense" (p. 104). Fear is just memory in the future sense. And insights from Steven Cooper (2003) on the imagining of analysand's future as a necessary ingredient in the analyst in order to enable new freer object for the analysand. In this way of thinking—about brains, about clinical cases, about human minds in states of trouble—time moves in manifold directions, unspooling the past to create particular imagined futures.

I have rather deliberately not tried to prescribe what I think the analyst does with and about these internal reconfigurations. I would reprise Nacht (1962) and say that the shift in treatment, the opening of momentum, must come from authentic change in the analyst. Clinical momentum is possible when a space/time matrix opens in the analyst and when the tumble into the abyss is genuinely possible. I am hoping to have persuaded you that the idea that death and mobility are so intimately connected seems very much the essential working paradox and the engine of psychoanalytic work.

References

Abraham, N., & Torok, M. (1994). *The shell and the kernel.* Chicago: University of Chicago Press.

Altman, N. (1996). Psychoanalysis among the urban poor. *Psychoanalytic Dialogues, 3,* 29–49.

Altman, N. (2006). Whiteness. *Psychoanalytic Quarterly, 75,* 45–72.

Aron, L. (1996). *A meeting of minds: Mutuality in psychoanalysis.* Hillsdale, NJ: The Analytic Press.

Bakhtin, M. M. (1981). *The dialogic imagination: Four essays* (M. Holquist, Ed. & Trans.). Austin, TX: University of Texas Press.

Barthes, R. (1975). *The pleasure of the text.* New York: Hill.

Bass, A. (2007). When the frame doesn't fit the picture. *Psychoanalytic Dialogues, 17,* 1–27.

Benjamin, J. (1995). *Like subjects, love objects.* New Haven, CT: Yale University Press.

Bernstein, J. W. (unpublished). Mourning and melancholia revisited.

Bhabha, H. (2000). *The location of culture.* London: Routledge.

Bion, W. (1992). *Cogitations.* London: Karnac.

Bowlby, J. (1960). Grief and mourning in infancy and early childhood. *Psychoanalytic Study of the Child, 15,* 9–52.

Bromberg, P. (1998). *Standing in the spaces: Essays on clinical process, trauma, and dissociation.* Hillsdale, NJ: The Analytic Press.

Bromberg, P. (2006). *Awakening the dreamer: Clinical journeys.* Hillsdale, NJ: The Analytic Press.

Butler, J. (2005). *Giving an account of oneself.* New York: Fordham University Press.

Caruth, C. (1996). *Unclaimed experience: Trauma, narrative and history.* Baltimore, MD: Johns Hopkins Press.

Cooper, S. (2003). You say oedipal, I say postoedipal: A consideration of desire and hostility in the analytic relationship. *Psychoanalytic Dialogues, 13*(1), 41–63.

Corbett, K. (1993). The mystery of homosexuality. *Psychoanalytic Psychology, 10,* 345–357.

Corbett, K. (2001). Faggot = loser. *Studies in Gender and Sexuality, 2,* 3–28.

Davies, J. M. (2003a). Falling in love with love: Oedipal and postoedipal manifestations of idealization, mourning, and erotic masochism. *Psychoanalytic Dialogues, 13,* 1–2.

Davies, J. M. (2003b). Reflections on Oedipus, post-Oedipus and termination. *Psychoanalytic Dialogues, 13*(1), 65–75.

Davies, J. M. (2004). Analysis of a "failed" case: Discussion of Zulusky. Paper presented at the American Psychoanalytic Association annual conference, New York, NY.

Davoine, F. (2008). The characters of madness in the talking cure. *Psychoanalytic Dialogues, 17,* 627–638.

Dimen, M. (2003). *Sexuality, intimacy, power.* Hillsdale, NJ: The Analytic Press.

Faimberg, H. (2004). *The telescoping of generations.* London: Karnac.

Fitzgerald, S. (1925). *The great Gatsby.* New York: Charles Scribner and Sons.

Foehl, J. (2005). How could this happen to me: Sexual transgressions. *Journal of the American Psychoanalytic Association, 53,* 957–969.

Fonagy, P. (2001). *Attachment theory and psychoanalysis.* New York: Other Press.

Freeman, W. (2000). *How brains make up their minds.* New York: Columbia University Press.

Galatzer-Levy, R. M. (2004). Chaotic possibilities: Toward a new model of development. *International Journal of Psychoanalysis, 85,* 419–441.

Gallese, V. (2009). Mirror neurons, embodied simulation, and the neural basis of social identification. *Psychoanalytic Dialogues, 19,* 519–536.

Goldner, V. (1991). Toward a critical relational theory of gender. *Psychoanalytic Dialogues, 1,* 249–272.

Goldner, V. (2003). Ironic gender/authentic sex. *Studies in Gender and Sexuality, 4,* 113–139.

Harris, A. (2005). *Gender as soft assembly.* Hillsdale, NJ: The Analytic Press.

Harris, A., & Aron, L. (1997). Ferenczi's semiotic theory: Previews of postmodernism. *Psychoanalytic Inquiry, 17,* 522–534.

Harris, A., & Sinsheimer, K. (2008). The analyst's vulnerability: Preserving and fine-tuning analytic bodies. In F. Anderson (Ed.), *Bodies in treatment* (pp. 255–274). New York: Routledge.

Knoblauch, S. (2000). *The musical edge of therapeutic dialogue.* Hillsdale, NJ: The Analytic Press.

Lakoff, G. (1987). *Women, fire and dangerous things.* Chicago: University of Chicago Press.

Lakoff, G., & Johnson, M. (1980). *Metaphors we live by.* Chicago: University of Chicago Press.

Lakoff, G., & Johnson, M. (1999). *Philosophy in the flesh.* New York: Basic Books.

Laplanche, J. (1989). *New foundations for psychoanalysis.* London: Blackwell.

Laplanche, J. (1997). The theory of seduction and the problem of the other. *International Journal of Psychoanalysis, 78,* 653–666.

Leary, K. (2000). Racial enactments in dynamic treatment. *Psychoanalytic Dialogues, 10,* 639–653.

Lewis, M. (1992). *Shame, the exposed self.* New York: Free Press.

Lyons-Ruth, K. (1999). The two-person unconscious: Intersubjective dialogue, enactive relational representation and the emergence of new forms of relational organization. *Psychoanalytic Inquiry, 19,* 576–617.

Lyons-Ruth, K. (2003). Dissociation and the parent–infant dialogue: A longitudinal perspective. *Journal of the American Psychoanalytic Association, 51,* 883–911.

McLaughlin, J. (1987). The play of transference: Some reflections on enactment in the psychoanalytic situation. *Journal of the American Psychoanalytic Association, 35,* 557–582.

McLaughlin, J. (2006). *The healer's bent.* Hillsdale, NJ: The Analytic Press.

Nacht, S. (1962). The curative factors in psycho-analysis. *International Journal of Psychoanalysis, 43,* 206–211.

Nacht, S. (1969). Reflections on the evolution of scientific knowledge. *International Journal of Psychoanalysis, 50,* 597.

Olds, D. (2000). A semiotic model of mind. *Journal of the American Psychoanalytic Association, 48,* 497–529.

Piers, C. (2000). Character as self-organizing complexity. *Psychoanalysis and Contemporary Thought, 23,* 3–34.

Pizer, S. (1998). *Building bridges: The negotiation of paradox in psychoanalysis.* Hillsdale, NJ: The Analytic Press.

Puget, J., & Sanville, J. (2000). Social reality. *International Journal of Psychoanalysis, 81,* 998–1000.

Riviere, J. (1929). Womanliness as a masquerade. *International Journal of Psychoanalysis, 9,* 303–313.

Schore, A. N. (1994). *Affect regulation and the origin of the self: The neurobiology of emotional development.* Hillsdale, NJ: Lawrence Erlbaum.

Searles, H. (1961). *Collected papers on schizophrenia and related subjects.* New York: International Universities Press.

Seligman, S. (2003). The developmental perspective in relational psychoanalysis. *Contemporary Psychoanalysis, 39,* 477–508.

Seligman, S. (2005). Dynamic systems theories as a metaframework for psychoanalysis. *Psychoanalytic Dialogues, 15,* 285–319.

Slochower, J. (1996). *Holding and psychoanalysis: A relational perspective.* Hillsdale, NJ: The Analytic Press.

Slochower, J. (2006). *Psychoanalytic collisions.* Hillsdale, NJ: The Analytic Press.

Suchet, M. (2007). Unravelling whiteness. *Psychoanalytic Dialogues, 1,* 867–886.

Tompkins, S. (1962). *Affect, imagery, consciousness, Vol. 1.* New York: Springer.

Tompkins, S. (1963). *Affect, imagery, consciousness, Vol. 2.* New York: Springer.

Trevarthen, C. (1979). Communication and cooperation in early infancy: A description of primary intersubjectivity. In M. Bullowa (Ed.), *Before speech: The beginning of interpersonal communication* (pp. 321–347). New York: Cambridge University Press.

Trevarthen, C. (1993). The self born in intersubjectivity: An infant communicating. In U. Neisser (Ed.), *The perceived self* (pp. 121–173). New York: Cambridge University Press.

Wheelis, A. (1987). *The doctor of desire.* New York: Norton.

Winnicott, D. W. (1974). Fear of breakdown. *International Review of Psychoanalysis, 1,* 103–107.

16

Partners in Thought

*A Clinical Process Theory of Narrative**

Donnel B. Stern

▼   ▼   ▼   ▼   ▼

The Diary of a Castaway

I had been thinking about the problem of narrative in psychoanalysis for some time when I ran across a TV screening of *The Incredible Shrinking Man*, a B movie scripted by the science fiction writer Richard Matheson and released in 1957. I had not seen the film for almost 40 years, but I remembered it fondly enough to see if it held up. I imagined that immersing myself again in the atmosphere of one of those awful, innocent 1950s science fiction movies would be nostalgic. Unexpectedly, it was a good deal more than that, and not only because the movie was better than I understood when I first saw it. I had long felt that new narrative in psychoanalysis is not simply the outcome of the analyst's objective interpretation, as Schafer (1983, 1992) and Spence (1982, 1987) portrayed it, but is instead the unbidden outcome of unconscious aspects of clinical process. Oddly enough, by helping to direct and cohere my thoughts on this point, *The Incredible Shrinking Man* jumpstarted the interpersonal-relational psychoanalytic understanding of narrative construction that I offer in this essay. The understanding I present, though, is based not only in a certain kind of theory; it is also rooted in a personal sense of clinical process. So the tone I have adopted is personal as well. This paper should probably be read as a statement of convictions, but I maintain the hope that my convictions will resonate with the reader's own.

* This paper originally appeared *Psychoanalytic Quarterly*, 78(3), 2009, pp. 701–731. Reprinted with permission.

The plot of *The Incredible Shrinking Man* rests on an absurd 10-second encounter between a man on his boat and a small radioactive cloud that just happens to be drifting aimlessly around the ocean. During the moments it takes the cloud to approach the boat, envelop it, and pass beyond, the man's wife is inside the cabin, fetching bottles of beer. She returns to find that her husband's chest is speckled with some kind of glitter. In the crazily concrete way of these films, the wife, having been inside, is spared the glitter, along with the later effects the glitter will have on her husband. The man brushes off the sparkly stuff and mumbles something to his wife about some strange fog. There is no further discussion of the matter, but the typically weird music accompanying this inexplicable moment certifies that something mysterious and sinister has come to pass.

That is the setup for the rest of the movie, in which our hero learns that he is shrinking. Wrenching losses ensue, one after another, until finally, when he has become so small that he lives in a dollhouse, his wife, still dutiful and a gargantuan in his newly proportioned world, bids him good-bye one day, goes out of the house, and accidentally lets in the cat. In a terrifying scene, the cat wrecks the dollhouse trying to get at the tiny man, who, in escaping, manages to shoulder open the door to the basement but then falls off the side of the steps a full floor down into a basket of laundry. No one knows he is there. In fact, his wife and the rest of the world, to all of whom he has become famous as the incredible shrinking man, believe that the cat got him.

It is only then that the movie hits its stride. It turns out that its improbable beginnings have been nothing more than a means of entry for Matheson, the scriptwriter, who really wants to tell a Robinson Crusoe story. And a great story it is. It is the story of a tiny, abandoned man, thought to be dead, marooned in his own basement with no chance of rescue, horribly alone, living in a matchbox, climbing ordinary stairs, each one now turned into a towering cliff, with equipment fashioned from the materials he finds, feeding on cheese left to catch mice, having to invent ways to cross chasms that are nothing more than the mouths of empty cardboard boxes, prey to a monstrous spider he fights with a needle he has found in a discarded pincushion, and threatened by a flash flood from a leaky boiler. In the end, after these compelling and strangely moving adventures, intricately imagined, and filmed with a notable attention to detail and special effects surprisingly good for the era, the man becomes so small that he can finally escape into his own backyard through the screen mesh covering the basement window. He is now too small for us to see, but we know he is there. We imagine him standing in a forest of towering grass blades, shrinking to nothing, as he offers us the final lines of his tale. At the very end, in the moments before he winks out altogether, the camera pans upward, and the tiny hero, gazing at the star-filled heavens, thinks that the infinitesimal and the infinite are much closer to one another than he has imagined before. Surprisingly enough, it is a moment of serenity, acceptance, and dignity. After the trauma, humiliations, and cynicism he has suffered in the first months of his disease, he has not only returned to himself but also transcended what has befallen him. It is hardly routine for survivors of trauma to find their suffering a provocation to grow, even if they manage to accept and live with their experiences, and of course the story of the shrinking man is a fiction, and a fantastical one at that. But this fictional little man has grown.

For the most part, the hero tells his own story. Yet during the first part of the film we have no explanation for why we are privy to the tale. We eventually find out that the tale is actually a diary of the events it depicts, written by the hero himself. In the course of his adventures, just prior to the episode with the cat and the dollhouse, the hero, cynical and miserable to the point of desperation, begins to write. This is the line in the movie that made me sit up and take notice: "I was telling the world about my life," the shrinking man reads to us from his diary, "and with the telling it became easier."

It does not require specialized training or experience to recognize the truth in this simple statement. If there is mystery here, it is mystery we are so used to living with that it does not surprise us. The fact that narrative plays a natural role in creating a meaningful life in even a B science fiction movie puts us on firm ground in agreeing with those many writers and scholars* who tell us that we shape personal meaning by organizing our experience into meaningful, sequential episodes.

But the intuitively obvious is not enough. What does the diary actually *do* for the shrinking man? Why does it help him to tell his story? *How* does it help him?

The narrative of the strange events of the shrinking man's life supplies him with a coherent and felt experiential order that he has lost in the rush of bizarre happenings. Prior to constructing his tale in the explicit terms of his diary, he has become an object in his own life, a figure suffering chaotic, incomprehensible events for no apparent reason and with little feeling. The emergence of meaning from what has felt to him like senselessness, helplessness, and despair confers agency and therefore dignity. He is once again a subject. After his fall into the laundry basket, the tiny man creates his experiential world, his story of the obstacles he faces and either accepts or overcomes, in such a way that his end has authentic pathos. After months of a growing sense of chaos and nihilism, he ends his life a deeply thoughtful and affectively alive human being.

---

* See Ricoeur (1977, 1981); Spence (1982); Schafer (1983, 1992); Bruner (1986, 1990, 2002); Sarbin (1986); Polkinghorne (1988); Ferro (1999, 2002, 2005, 2006).

In creating his diary, the shrinking man also creates a relationship with imaginary others who then serve as witnesses of what he "tells" them. The movie grips us, despite its flaws, partly because we recognize at some level the help that this witnessing offers him: we ourselves become his witnesses. I turn now to a perspective on what it means to have and to be a witness. I will return to the case of the shrinking man once these ideas are in place.

Witnessing

We first learned about the significance of witnessing from studies of trauma, in which witnessing of some sort is usually considered an essential prerequisite to the capacity to narrate one's own experience. I believe that the need for witnessing became visible first in this context because it was in the impact of trauma that some of the most damaging effects of the *absence* of the witness were first observed: Without a witness, trauma must be dissociated, and once the isolated trauma sufferer gains a witness the experience of the trauma becomes more possible to know, feel, and think about (e.g., Brison, 2002; Laub, 1992a, 1992b, 2005; Laub & Auerhahn, 1989; Richman, 2006; Boulanger, 2007). I will be discussing witnessing here as a routine part of everyday, nontraumatic experience that I believe begins in the earliest stages of development.

In fact, although Fonagy, Gergely, Jurist, and Target (2002) do not use the language I am using here, what they tell us about the beginnings of the self can be read as the proposition that the witness precedes us. As they put it, "we fathom ourselves through others" (p. 2). Caretakers identify certain feelings and desires in the infant and treat the infant accordingly. This treatment begins to organize the infant's relatively inchoate world in the terms of narrative, and self-states begin to cohere in and around these earliest stories. In one sense, then, we are called into being by acts of recognition by the other. We learn we are hungry because the other feeds us at a moment when we are having a certain uncomfortable feeling, so we then have a story that goes with that feeling: "I am hungry." We learn we are sad because the other comforts us at a moment when we are having a different distressing feeling; and so we then begin to have a story that goes with *that* feeling: "I am sad." This is one way we begin to tell and live stories; there are other ways. All the various tributaries to narrative sum to the creation of experience: Hungry is what you are when you need to be fed; sad is what you are when you need to be comforted. As Harry Stack Sullivan (e.g., 1940, 1953) writes over and over again, we know ourselves via reflected appraisals. Fonagy and his cowriters describe the same thing: "At the core of our selves is the representation of how we were seen" (p. 348), and,

"At the core of the mature child's self is the other at the moment of reflection" (p. 380).*

As development proceeds, we eventually gain the ability to formulate our experience for ourselves, internalizing the capacity that first belonged primarily to our caretakers. But we do not outgrow the need, paraphrasing Winnicott, to see our reflections in our mothers' eyes; the need becomes only more sophisticated. We may no longer need the other actually to show us the meaning of our experience, as we did when we were infants, but if we are to know our own experience in reflective terms, if we are to be able not only to construct narratives but also to be aware of the narratives we construct, we do need to believe that we are known by the other. We need to feel that we exist in the other's mind and that our existence has a kind of continuity in that mind, and we need to feel that the other in whose mind we exist is emotionally responsive to us, that he or she cares about what we experience and how we feel about it (Bach, 2006). This is what it is, I believe, to have a witness. Without a witness, even an imaginary witness, events either fail to fall into the meaningful pattern of episode that is narrative, or we merely enact our stories blindly, unable to think about them or know what they feel like. Our witness is our partner in thought.†

The witness, while it may feel like a single presence, may nevertheless be composed of parts of one's own mind or of the other's or of both

---

* Fonagy and his collaborators and Sullivan are among the contributors to what has become an extensive literature describing the structuring of the infant's and young child's world by the relationship with the mother. Some of this literature falls under the rubric of mentalization (Chasseguet-Smirgel, 1990; Fain & David, 1963; Fain, David, & Marty, 1964; Green, 1975; Lecours & Bouchard, 1997; Luquet, 1987; Marty, 1990, 1991; McDougall, 1985). Other work grows from an interest in the recognition of otherness (Benjamin, 1988, 1990; Bion, 1962, 1963; Eigen, 1981; Lacan, 1977; Modell, 1984; Segal, 1957; Winnicott, 1971a). A third relevant line of thought is rooted in the study of mother–infant interaction and the growth of the interpersonal field (Beebe & Lachmann, 1988, 1994; Sander, 1962, 1988; Stern, 1977, 1985; Sullivan, 1940, 1953). All of these branches of the literature are part of the context from which grows my interest in witnessing and its place at the roots of personality. Last in this list of citations, but certainly not least, is Poland's (2000) lovely and innovative paper on witnessing in psychoanalysis, in which witnessing is contrasted with interpretation and is characterized as the activity by which otherness is recognized. The influence of Poland's paper is ubiquitous in the present paper.

† It has been conclusively demonstrated (if the point actually needed to be demonstrated) that thought and rationality should not be equated. Thought is creative and effective only when thoroughly imbued with feeling (e.g., Damasio, 1994). Although thought and feeling are inseparable in this way, we do not have a single word that allows reference to both. Whenever I refer to "partners in thought," I mean to refer to both thought and feeling. The partnering I am describing is at least as much an affective phenomenon as it is a cognitive one.

simultaneously. The witness is the states of self or other who one imagines is best suited to fulfill the partnering purpose at the particular moment in which the need arises. It is not a simple internalization of the historical mothering one. An internalization of a loving parent who has grasped and known one's continuity is probably a necessary condition for the development of the capacity to witness oneself, but it is not sufficient. The witness begins as that kind of internalization but becomes a changing amalgam of history, fantasy, and current reality. It is not a structure of the mind but a function, or better, a way of being. Its composition is limited by one's experience, of course, but within those limits the witness changes as continuously as the events witnessed; the particular selection of parts of oneself or the other recruited to witness on any one occasion depends on that occasion's context. It is not only the witness who is in flux, however; the one who is witnessed is, as well, since the state of self in need of witnessing also changes with context. However complex it may be to describe the phenomenon in the third person, though, in phenomenological terms the matter is simpler: The witness is the one imagined, consciously or *sub rosa*, to be listening.

To have the ongoing sense that our story exists in someone else's mind (even if that someone else exists within our own mind), we must first (and very often in imagination) continuously "tell" that other person what we are experiencing. We construct what we know of ourselves by identifying with the other and "listening" through his ears to the story we are telling. We know our stories by telling them to ourselves, in other words, but we can do that only by listening to ourselves through the other's ears. Psychoanalysts work in just this way: They listen to patients in the way that allows patients to listen to themselves.* To convince yourself of this point, just think about how often, during and after your own analysis, you found yourself at odd times during your day imagining that you were telling your

---

* Some form of this point is widely recognized, probably by dozens of writers. Eshel (2004) describes "I-dentification" as "the analyst's thoroughgoing identificatory experiencing of the patient's most painful and terrifying experiences…," which "…renders them tolerable, liveable, enables them 'the possibility of being'…" (p. 331). Farber (1956) writes, "…In listening we speak the other's words. Or, to put it another way, the analyst is able to hear only what he, potentially at least, is able to say" (p. 145). Laub (1992a) says, "The listener has to feel the victim's victories, defeats and silences, know them from within, so that they can assume the form of testimony" (p. 58). And finally, or rather first, there are many passages of this sort from the work of Winnicott. This one is representative: "An example of unintegration phenomena is provided by the very common experience of the patient who proceeds to give every detail of the weekend and feels contented at the end if everything has been said, though the analyst feels that no analytic work has been done. Sometimes we must interpret this as the patient's need to be known in all his bits and pieces by one person, the analyst. To be known means to feel integrated at least in the person of the analyst" (1945, p. 150).

analyst something. I remember when I first noticed it happen. Sometime after that I realized how frequent these tellings were and how often they went unattended.

This kind of telling and listening, though, arises much earlier in life than the age at which people typically go into psychotherapy and psychoanalysis. If you have children you remember overhearing them talk to themselves in their cribs, often quite animatedly, after you put them to bed. They are organizing their experience of the day, giving it sense. But to whom are they talking? Not to "themselves," at least not exactly in the sense in which "self" will be a meaningful idea later in life. At this early age self and other are not yet conscious and coherent parts of experience; neither self nor other, for instance, can be explicitly reflected on. Besides, why speak out loud if the only audience is oneself? It is plausible to imagine that babies in their cribs are talking to their first witnesses: their parents. But these are their internalized parents, or some of their first internalized objects. These children are imaginatively listening to themselves through their parents' ears and thereby lending their experience a credence, coherence, and depth of feeling it otherwise could not have (Nelson, 1989). As a matter of fact, what we are hearing when we listen to babies creating coherence in those minutes before sleep may very well be part of the process of self-formation.

The diary of the shrinking man, like what patients say to their analysts, is an explicit kind of telling, with the difference, of course, that the shrinking man's audience, like the audience listening to the little child in his crib, is imaginary. Like the child, the shrinking man is writing to some figure in his inner world. Imaginary audiences are very common. But explicit telling is not. Most telling of the sort I am describing here, the kind of telling that allows one to listen to one's own thoughts, is implicit. It goes on hazily, not very specifically, seldom noticed except, in a leftover from our crib days, in the states that take place just before sleep in adult life or at other times when we are alone, when we sometimes notice that we are formulating our thoughts by addressing some ill-defined other. Most of the time, though, it is *as if* we were telling, and *as if* we were being listened to and then listening to ourselves. But the activity is no less crucial for being hazy and imagined. For this process to come about in the first place, probably we must be fortunate enough to have had parents who left us able to believe, in at least some states, that there exist others, especially certain imaginary others, who are continuous presences interested in knowing our experience (Bach, 2006).

When life feels arbitrary, senselessly cruel, or meaningless, as it did for the shrinking man before he began his diary, one is liable to be aware of no story at all. Events seem arbitrary and do not fall into narrative order. Affect is flattened or diminished; one may consciously feel only a kind of numbness or deadness. The living, hurt places in one's mind—actually, the injured parts of the *self,* the parts we most need to protect—despite their influence on day-to-day life, go undiscovered until *something happens in ongoing relatedness* that allows us to see that someone else recognizes the pain we ourselves have been unable to know and feel. Our grasp of our own previously dissociated experience through what we imagine to be the eyes and ears of the other is synonymous with the creation of new meaning. As a coherent narrative of the experience falls into place, there is an awakening, including an awakening of pain. In fortunate cases, there is also relief. Both pain and relief illuminate the absence of feeling in what came before.

That was the fate of the shrinking man. Until he began to tell his story, he was losing courage by the day and becoming increasingly angry and cynical. But once he began writing his diary, his imagined readers, who "listened" to him "tell" his tale, seemed to help him contact his dissociated vitality and make it once again part of the mind he felt as "me." That change was enough to bring back his determination to face whatever was in store for him. For now I merely note the following point: Imagined witnesses can be as effective as real ones.*

All right, I thought, the diary allowed the shrinking man to know his own story. But so what? Why did the character even want to go on living? Why didn't the shrinking man kill himself, or at least think about it? Wouldn't I have thought about it if I were he? Was that omission a failing of the script? The man may as well have been the last human being: he was permanently, completely, hopelessly alone. Wouldn't absolute, inescapable aloneness inevitably lead to despair?

Or did the screenwriter know something? Should we consider the hero's perseverance to be a consequence of the value that telling someone his story of isolation brought back to his life?

For another take on the question, I turned to my copy of *Robinson Crusoe* (Defoe, 1957), a story that gripped me as a boy, gripped me earlier and even more deeply than the story of the shrinking man. The entire book is the journal of Crusoe's 35 years of living alone on an island, the sole survivor of a shipwreck. In the usual manner of diaries, the entire document is written as if Crusoe were addressing someone, and you soon fall under the spell: It is as if it is *you* to whom Crusoe is telling what happened to him. I remember feeling an intimacy with Crusoe when I read the book the first time; I felt I was there on that island, just as I felt I was there in that basement

---

* I must defer to the future an exploration of the significant differences between imagined witnesses and real ones and between the process of witnessing under these two sets of circumstances.

with the shrinking man. It was one of the most thrilling reading adventures of my childhood. I remember marveling that Crusoe could live so fully by himself, and now, with the reminder supplied by my recent experience with the shrinking man, I also remember feeling, even as a boy, that the diary must have made Crusoe feel less alone.

By writing their diaries and being able to believe in the interest in their experience held by those imaginary others to whom they wrote, Crusoe and the shrinking man created partners in thought, imaginary others with whom to share life. We all create partners in thought, all the time. In most of life, though, real, flesh-and-blood others are so ubiquitous, and the stories of our lives fall together in such an unnoticed way that it is much harder to appreciate both the significance of narrative and the role of witnesses in its creation. The ongoing reciprocal process by which we quite implicitly offer one another the reassurance that we understand well enough to continue to serve as witnesses, generally goes unnoticed, just keeps on keeping on, like the Boston Change Process Study Group's (2002, 2005, 2007, 2008; D. N. Stern et al., 1998) "implicit relational knowing," unless or until misattunement interrupts the flow and forces us to attend to the break in our confidence in the other's responsive emotional presence. The very isolation of Crusoe and the shrinking man offers us the opportunity to grasp the role of their narrative creations in giving their lives meaning, and the conception of the witness allows us to understand why writing their diaries helped them as it did.

Although witnessing is mentioned often in the trauma literature, Sophia Richman's (2006) work on "transforming trauma into autobiographical narrative" contributes observations with more pinpoint relevance to what I am trying to say than others I have read. Remember what the shrinking man said about his diary ("I was telling the world about my life, and with the telling it became easier") and compare it to Richman, who tells us this about autobiography and trauma: "By sharing the creation with the world, there is an opportunity to come out of hiding, to find witnesses to what had been suffered alone, and to begin to overcome the sense of alienation and isolation that are the legacy of trauma survivors" (p. 644). Richman also quotes Joan Didion's observation that writing can make experience coherent and real. Didion made the remark during a TV interview with Charlie Rose in which she was talking about the memoir she wrote about the death of her husband: "What helped me to survive was writing this book, because otherwise I wouldn't have been able to understand what I was going through" (p. 648). And finally, Richman agrees that the witness may be imaginary. Here is what she writes about her father's memoir of life in a concentration camp: "…I believe that in order to write what he did, he had to conjure up a reader who had an interest in his story and could function as his witness" (p. 646).

Narrative Freedom and Continuous Productive Unfolding

It is as true in the clinical situation as it is anywhere else that, by the time our best stories are spoken, they just seem right, convincing generations of psychoanalysts that it was the content of what they said to their patients— that is, clinical interpretation—that was mutative. I share the view of those who see the matter otherwise: the real work has already been done by the time a new story falls into place (e.g., Boston Change Process Study Group, 2002, 2005, 2007, 2008; Bromberg, 1998, 2006; Ghent, 1995; Pizer, 1998; Russell, 1991; D.B. Stern, 2003, 2004, 2008, 2009b, 2009c; D.N. Stern, 2004; D.N. Stern et al., 1998). Because they and I are tackling the same problem, I appreciate the work of the many writers who understand the therapeutic action of interpretations as relational. Mitchell (1997), for example, writes, "...Interpretations work, when they do ... [because] the patient experiences them as something new and different, something not encountered before" (p. 52). But that is not the position I am taking here. I am arguing that the appearance in the treatment of mutually accepted new content or newly organized content, which is generally narrative in form, is not the instrument of change at all; it is rather the sign that change has taken place. It is true that a new understanding is the fulfillment of possibility, but it is to *the creation of that possibility, not the shape of its fulfillment*, that we must look for the source of change. The important thing about a new understanding— and this applies no matter whether it is the analyst or the patient who offers it—is less its novel content than the new freedom revealed by its appearance in the analytic space, a freedom to feel, relate, see, and say differently than before. This is the likely explanation for the widely recognized observation that former analysands, even those who credit their treatments with saving or renewing their lives, remember few of the interpretations their analysts made. It was not the interpretations per se that helped, but the freedom that made the interpretations possible in the first place. What *is* remembered from a successful treatment, as a matter of fact, is much less the analyst's words or ideas than something about the appearance of that freedom, something about what particular important moments *felt* like, something sensory, perceptual, and affective. The new story, then, is not the engine of change but the mark change leaves behind. Or perhaps this is better: The new story does not create change but shapes the way we represent it to ourselves.

But as much as I agree with that statement, it is also a bit of an overstatement. In the attempt to acknowledge that claims for the mutative effects of narrative interpretations have been overstated, we could find ourselves throwing out the baby with the bathwater. We must admit that each new story along the way is not only the mark of change but also helps to provoke the next round of curiosity and thus to open new narrative freedom and the stories that follow. Each new story is simultaneously what change leaves behind and part of what brings about the next generation of clinical events. In fact, we can say this in a stronger form: Each new story *belongs to* the next generation of clinical events.*

So when we observe that patients may not remember the events of their treatments primarily in narrative terms, we must also acknowledge that memory for narrative is not necessarily the best index of narrative's influence. The affective changes that take place in treatment, and that are memorialized in the new narratives that fall into place there, are reflected in our ways of remembering the past, creating the present, and imagining the future. It is in these effects that we see the most profound influence of new stories. Narratives are the architecture of experience, the ever-changing structure that gives it form. Without narrative, affect would be chaotic and rudderless, as shapeless as a collapsed tent, and, without affect, narrative would be dry and meaningless.

We see in new narrative freedom a deepened capacity of the patient and the analyst to dwell in one another's minds, to collaborate in the analytic task, to serve as one another's partners in thought. Any new understanding in the clinical situation is testimony that these two people have become better able to "tell" one another their stories and to "listen" to their own tellings through the ears of the other. I mean "tell" and "listen" in the special way that goes on in imagination and that depends both on being able to believe that you have an unshakeable existence for the other and on recognizing yourself in your imagination of the other's picture of you.

The freedom to create a new narrative in the clinical situation, or to find value in a new narrative that has been created by the other, is a specific instance of the general case of narrative freedom. Most of this new grasp of things emerges without conscious effort, unbidden, like implicit relational knowing, from the ongoing relatedness between patient and analyst. As long as there is no obstruction of the capacity of each person to serve as witness to the other, narrative freedom is the expectable state of affairs, and the capacity of analyst and patient to reveal new experience through an ever-renewed curiosity deepens over time, as their intimacy grows. There is

---

* This emphasis on the creation of new narrative freedom is not meant to suggest that either character or any of the other kinds of continuity in the personality are unimportant. But looking at character in relational terms does require us to conceive it as multiple, not singular. That is, character must be defined in context: Under thus-and-such circumstances, a particular person's conduct and experience is liable to be defined in a particular way that is at least partly predictable. But we cannot guess what anyone will do or experience if we do not know something about the nature of the interpersonal field in which that person is participating.

a sense of continuous productive unfolding. Under these conditions, there is a more or less uninterrupted flow of new affective experience and understanding for both patient and analyst. Old stories hove into view, are destabilized, and dissolve; new stories fall into place. The process is often smooth and pleasurable. This kind of clinical work goes on much of the time with many patients, more often with some patients than others. Although the process may be punctuated with minor difficulties—hesitations, bumps, and snags—the overall nature of the work is an ever richer and more thorough exploration and experience of the tolerable part of both the patient's experience and the analyst's. The analyst generally feels (and is) valued, skilled, and useful, and the patient feels helped. The analyst's unconscious involvement with the patient is present but seldom problematic. It serves as a contribution, not an obstacle, allowing the analyst to offer a different take on the patient's experience than the one the patient started with, a novel view that is generally experienced as helpful by the patient. There is the satisfying sense of a job well done. Continuous productive unfolding is, in the analyst's mind, what Hoffman (1998) would refer to as the unconstricted interplay of ritual and spontaneity, what Knoblauch (2000) and Ringstrom (2001, 2007) call improvisation in therapeutic relatedness and what Winnicott (1971b), the font of such thinking, calls play.

Not-Me

This relatively smooth and productive clinical process lasts as long as experience feels tolerable. But a very different, more troubling, and sometimes even destructive kind of relatedness takes place when the experience evoked in the mind of either patient or analyst, or of both, is *not* tolerable—that is, when the state that threatens to emerge into the foreground and shape consciousness is not recognizable as oneself. Such a state of being is *not-me* (Sullivan, 1940, 1953; Bromberg, 1998, 2006; D. B. Stern, 2003, 2004, 2009c), and in ordinary life it exists only in dissociation, apart from what feels like *me*.* Not-me has never had access to consciousness, and in its dissociated

---

* "Me" and "not-me" are ideas more substantial than their colloquial names might suggest to those unfamiliar with their long history in the literature of interpersonal psychoanalysis. The terms were devised by Harry Stack Sullivan (1940, 1953) as a means of representing the parts of the personality that exist within the boundaries of what is accepted as self ("me") and what is dissociated from self ("not-me"). The contemporary literature of dissociation, primarily the last 20 years of work by Philip Bromberg (collected in volumes published in 1998 and 2006; see also Chefetz & Bromberg, 2004), has lent the ideas new life. Recently they have also played a central role in my own thinking (D. B. Stern, 1997, 2003, 2004, 2008, 2009b, 2009c).

state it has never been symbolized: it is unformulated (Stern, 1997), a vaguely defined organization of experience, a primitive, global, nonideational affective state. It does not exist within the self, because it has never been allowed to congeal into one of self's states. We can say it this way: Not-me *would be* a self-state if it were to move into the foreground of experience. But if that were to happen, not-me would not *feel* like me. The experience would be intolerable, so not-me remains dissociated. I *must* not, *cannot* be not-me. The threatened eruption of not-me into awareness jeopardizes my sense of being the person I am. In both my own work on dissociation and the work of Philip Bromberg (1998, 2006), not-me has never been formulated; dissociated experience has that quality in common with conceptions such as Bion's (1962, 1963) beta functioning and beta elements and Green's (e.g., 2000) nonrepresentation.*

Not-me originates as a response to unbearable fear or humiliation, the experience of having been the object of a powerful other's sadism. It is the sense that one is once again that stricken person: terrorized and terrified, sometimes to the point of immobility or helpless, destructive rage; contemptible, sometimes to the point of a self-loathing that yearns for the destruction of self or other; shamed and horrified, sometimes to the point of losing the desire to live or creating the desire to kill; weak, sometimes to the point of a shameful and utterly helpless surrender that feels as if it can be prevented only by suicide or held at bay only by committing mayhem. One *will* not, *can*not be this person, because when one was, life was not bearable; yet, if not-me enters consciousness, one *is* that person.

Every personality harbors not-me, although of course the degree of trauma that has been suffered by different people varies enormously. The impact it would have for not-me to emerge into awareness and become "real" depends on the severity of trauma and the consequent degree to which not-me is vicious, loathsome, terrifying, terrified, or abject and the degree to which the whole personality is unstable and vulnerable. For those who have suffered severe trauma, and whose vulnerability is therefore unmanageable, the eruption of not-me can be catastrophic, provoking massive affective dysregulation or psychotic decompensation. For those who are less troubled, the consequence is nevertheless awful enough to be avoided.

---

* As in the case of beta elements and nonrepresentation, dissociated material cannot be addressed by traditional defensive operations, because the dissociated has not attained symbolic form: "Unformulated material is experience which has never been articulated clearly enough to allow application of the traditional defensive operations. One can forget or distort only those experiences which are formed with a certain degree of clarity in the first place. The unformulated has not yet reached the level of differentiation at which terms like memory and distortion are meaningful" (Stern, 1983, p. 73).

Enactment: An Illustration

When not-me is evoked by the events of clinical process, continuous unfolding is replaced by some variety of enactment. In the following example, for heuristic purposes I describe more about both my own experience and the patient's than I knew as the interaction was taking place.

My patient was late, and I was taking advantage of the extra minutes to have a snack. When the patient arrived, I was enjoying what I was eating and wanted to finish it, and it therefore took me a few seconds longer to get to the waiting room than it would have if I had simply been waiting in my chair. The patient was standing there, waiting for me, when I got to the waiting room. He had not sat down, which I took as a sign that he was eager to come in. Perhaps I should not have allowed myself my little delay. I was faced with a small incident of my selfishness. In a defensive attempt to avoid self-criticism (an insight available only in retrospect), I said implicitly to myself, without words, "Well, for heaven's sake, the patient was late. What's wrong with using the time as I see fit?" But I was aware of greeting the patient without my customary warmth.

The patient, because of his relationship with his demanding and easily disappointed father, has an intense vulnerability to humiliation. The experience of being snubbed (my lackluster reception) made him worry (*sub rosa*) that he was a burden or a disappointment to me, thereby threatening the eruption into awareness of not-me. In the patient's mind, my greeting confirmed what he feared: My contempt was leaking; I had tolerated him up to now only because he paid me. The secret was out. He had always had to contend with the danger of being a loathsome, contemptible boy, and he must not, could not be that boy.

What happens at such a juncture? My patient had to do whatever was possible to avoid the eruption of contemptible not-me in awareness. His usual defensive maneuvers were of no use now; the danger was upon him. In our prior work, I had been quite careful to respect his vulnerabilities, but I had momentarily failed in that respect in greeting him as I had. In the past, the patient had also defended himself by (unconsciously) influencing the relatedness with me, making sure never to disappoint or provoke me, and thereby avoiding any possibility of facing this kind of stark "evidence" of my contempt for him. But his usual ways could not help him now.

The last-ditch defense, when not-me is imminent, is the interpersonalization of the dissociation, or enactment: "*I* am not contemptible, *you* are contemptible." The patient now claimed that most of the time, when I seemed authentically interested, I had been merely pretending. I hadn't really cared—that was now clear for the first time. Other therapists didn't pretend as I had; they really did get to know and care about their patients.

My patient began to cite moments from the past that he now believed lent credence to the interpretation that I just was not very good at my job, that I should have chosen a field in which my limitations would not have hurt those I served.

I struggled with my affective response to being the object of contempt, feeling unhappy, hurt, and on the verge of anger. I was feeling the very shame that the patient was so eager to avoid. But I was nowhere near such understanding at this moment, and I said something (I don't remember exactly what it was) that protested my innocence. I knew that I sounded defensive.

This situation could have moved in either of two directions at this point. In one scenario, I come to terms with my own affective reaction to the patient and tolerate it. Under those circumstances, following my defensive reaction, I would grope toward a therapeutically facilitative response to the patient, although such a response probably would not occur immediately after the patient's provocation, because anyone's initial response to an accusation is likely to be defensive. This is actually what happened in this case, and I will tell that part of the story just below. But it is also common in this kind of situation, when the analyst is seriously threatened, for the patient's enactment of a dissociated state to call out a dissociated, or not-me, state *in the analyst*. A *mutual* enactment ensues. With my patient, such a scenario might have looked like this: In the same way the patient has begun to feel that it is not *he* who is contemptible but *I*, I now succumb (even if I "know better," which of course I usually do) to the strongly felt sense that *I* am not doing anything problematic—it's just that *the patient* is impossibly sadistic. I will almost undoubtedly feel uncomfortable in this position, probably guilty about being a bad analyst, but I will see no way out of it for the time being. Mutual enactments, which are not as uncommon as the traditional psychoanalytic literature might be read to suggest, may go on over significant periods and often pose a genuine threat to the treatment (D. B. Stern, 2003, 2004, 2008, 2009b, 2009c).

Enactment, Witnessing, and Narrative

Thinking in narrative terms reveals that enactment of either kind—that is, either with or without the dissociative participation of the analyst—is even more than the unconsciously motivated inability of patient or analyst to see one another clearly and fully. As enactment rigidifies the clinical relatedness, it also interrupts each person's capacity to serve as witness for the other. Even if the analyst does not respond with a reciprocal dissociation, in other words, the patient loses, at least temporarily, the capacity to allow the analyst to be his partner in thought. The patient also temporarily loses the desire, and probably the capacity, to be the analyst's partner. When the analyst *does* respond with a reciprocal dissociation, of course, the situation is both more troubled and more difficult to remedy. In either case, the effortless, unbidden creation of narrative that went on during continuous productive unfolding now grinds to a halt.

One way to define states of self is as narratives: Each state is an ever-changing story. Or rather, as I have already suggested, because self-states are not simply experiences or memories but are also aspects of identity, each state is an aspect of self defined by the stories that can be told from within it. Our freedom to tell many self-stories at once—in other words, our freedom to inhabit multiple states of being simultaneously—is what gives to the stories that express the ways we know ourselves and others the plasticity to change with circumstances. The many states that compose "me" not only participate in shaping the circumstances of life, but are, in the process, themselves reshaped. This continuous interchange and renewal is the hallmark of the self-states that make up "me."

But not-me cannot be told. Not-me remains insistently, stubbornly, defensively unformulated (D. B. Stern, 1997, 2002, 2009a), not yet shaped or storied at all, isolated, existing in dissociation and thereby rendered mute. This is the situation within enactments, both solitary and mutual: Neither analyst nor patient knows how to narrate the significance of what is transpiring; neither knows the meaning of the transaction nor the feelings and perceptions that make it up. So those events remain coded only in procedural terms, in action. If not-me is to come within our capacity to tell, then me, the self of the dissociator, must somehow expand to accommodate or contact it.

I continue now with the events that actually took place with my patient. I felt defensive and ashamed in reaction to the patient's accusations. My defensiveness was apparent to me and, I told myself, probably to my patient, but I did not respond with a reciprocal dissociation of my own. I pulled myself together and said something on this order: "I was taken by surprise by what you said [the patient's accusations against me]—I didn't know where that was coming from. But now I'm asking myself if the way you felt might have to do with something you sensed during the last session, or when you came in today. Did you notice something I said or did? Because I did. This may not be the important thing, but I did notice that I didn't greet you as I usually do." Despite my reaction to the patient's accusations, in other words, I was able to consider the possibility that I might have played a role in setting the patient's complaints in motion. In this context, at least, I was able to conduct an inquiry without succumbing to an answering dissociation and enactment. I did not shut down the narrative possibilities, in other words, as the patient had no choice but to do from within his own dissociative process but instead returned to being curious, relatively open to whatever emerged in my mind.

Neither the patient's dissociation nor his enactment was particularly rigid as these things go, although they certainly might have moved in that direction if I had failed to gain a perspective on my own reaction and remained defensive. But I was fortunate in this case, because, sensing that I was no longer threatened, the patient showed some interest in my foray. But he was still suspicious, and he said, "Well, but then why did you get defensive?" referring to what I said in response to his accusations. I answered, again from within my relocated stability, that I did believe that I had been defensive, and that it is often hard for anyone not to be defensive in the face of strong criticism.

The patient softened, and (to my surprise, to tell the truth) seemed to begin to search himself for something that might be responsive to what I had said. He eventually was able to say that my greeting had indeed stung him. The atmosphere cooled further. The patient had little difficulty now in seeing that my defensiveness could be understood, from within my perspective, as a response to his own critical remarks. More important, the patient had now lived through an episode in which his brief certainty that he was a burden to me and that my caring was inauthentic, was disconfirmed. This was not primarily a cognitive signification for him. The patient could *feel* or *sense* what it was like for me to be with him through the course of his accusations. That was important, but more important yet was that the patient felt for one of the first times the confidence that I had felt hurt or angry with him without losing track of my warm feelings about him (or losing track of them only very temporarily). In a small but crucial way, the patient was now someone else than he had been. Over the following months, other new experiences of this kind opened in front of him, because his growing confidence in my openness to his experience and my own made it possible for him to begin to listen imaginatively through my ears to his own feelings of being a burden. In the process those experiences gained substance and reality for him on one hand and became less shameful and more bearable on the other. Stories about these things emerged in his mind with increasing frequency, some of them articulate and others implicit. Over time, not-me became me. For my part, through my experience of my reaction to his stinging criticism, I also became more able to witness the patient, and beyond that I came to depend in a new way on the patient's capacity to witness me—the way, for example, he eventually accepted my reactions to his criticisms.

Dissociations are not breached by insight, nor are enactments dissolved through verbal understanding. Interpretation is not the analyst's key intervention. Enactments end as a result of a change in affect and relatedness, which provokes a change in each participant's perceptions (and stories) of the other and himself (D. B. Stern, 2003, 2004, 2008, 2009b, 2009c). Insight into this changed state of affairs, when it plays a role, comes later. Historical reconstruction often does take place after the appearance of the new story, and it can be quite helpful. But therapeutic action lies in becoming a different person, usually in a small way, in the here and now. The expansion of the self takes place in the present, in small increments. As enactment recedes, the treatment moves back into continuous productive unfolding, and new narratives once again begin to appear unbidden in the analytic space. The new stories my patient and I have told as the treatment has moved on have been more and more often about the contemptible little boy.

Returning to the Castaways

But if the analyst is so crucial to the patient, how do we understand Robinson Crusoe and the shrinking man? They had no analytic relationship, no relationships of any kind. (Crusoe did eventually have Friday, but that was years into his saga.) Now it may be clearer why I claimed earlier that enforced isolation makes these characters such good illustrations of my thesis. Their creators' suggestion that the characters grew and changed despite their circumstances is not mistaken, nor is it by any means a refutation of the point that we are profoundly social beings. On the contrary, such stories could not demonstrate the necessity of witnessing more clearly than they do. It seems likely, actually, that some kind of imaginary witness is invoked in all tales of enforced isolation, real and imaginary.

In the movie *Cast Away*, the character played by Tom Hanks, alone and shipwrecked on an island, finds a soccer ball floating in the surf, paints a face on it, and begins to talk to it, using the conversation as a kind of ironic commentary to himself on the matter of his own loneliness. He calls the ball "Wilson," after the name of the sporting goods company that made it. But as the years pass, irony turns delusionally earnest, and Wilson eventually becomes the castaway's dear friend, continuous companion, and confidant. Years after that, the shipwrecked man escapes from the island on board a raft he has made himself. In the calm that comes after a storm at sea, and dying of thirst and exposure, he sees that Wilson, whom he had tethered to the mast for protection, has fallen off and is drifting away from him across the swells. The movie's one truly devastating moment comes when the castaway sees that in his weakened state he cannot rescue his "friend" without losing the raft and drowning, and he calls out piteously after the swiftly disappearing Wilson, pleading for forgiveness.

Let me offer one last example, just to put it on the record that factuality reflects castaways' need for a witness just as well as fiction does. I recently read a dreadful story in the *New York Times* (Onishi, 2007) about a man in Tokyo so poor that he had not eaten in weeks and so alone that no one either knew or cared. In his last days he kept a diary. Among the last entries before his death from starvation was his expression of the wish for a rice ball, a snack sold in convenience stores across Japan for about a dollar: "3 a.m. This human being hasn't eaten in 10 days but is still alive. I want to eat rice. I want to eat a rice ball." The very fact that the diarist wrote at all testifies to his imagination of an audience. But note also that he speaks of himself in the third person. Is it credible that he would have done that if he really imagined that he was addressing only himself? Could there be a more eloquent expression of the need to listen through the ears of the other? It was preserved even as this man was dying.

To know what our experience is, to think and feel, we need to tell the stories of our lives, and we need to tell them to someone to whom they matter, listening to ourselves as we do the telling. If we have to make up our audience, so be it. Our need for a witness goes so deep that imaginary witnesses must sometimes suffice.

Witnessing One's Self

We are familiar with the idea of internal conversation between parts of ourselves. If we can hold an internal conversation, can one part of ourselves serve as a witness for another? We have seen that Richman (2006) believes so. Laub (1992a, 1992b, 2005; Laub & Auerhahn, 1989) does, too. He suggests that massive psychic trauma, because it damages the processes of association, symbolization, and narrative formation, also leads to an absence of inner dialogue, curiosity, reflection, and self-reflection. And what does Laub believe is responsible for this inner devastation? The annihilation of the internal good object, the "internal empathic other" (Laub & Auerhahn, 1989), partner in inner dialogue and narrative construction. Laub (1992b) tells the story of Menachem S., a castaway of sorts, a little boy placed in a labor camp who somehow managed to survive the Holocaust and, miraculously, to find his parents afterward. He had spent the war talking and praying to a photograph of his mother that he kept with him. "Mother indeed had promised to come and take him back after the war, and not for a moment did he doubt that promise" (p. 87). But the mother and father he refound, "haggard and emaciated, in striped uniforms, with teeth hanging loose in their gums" (p. 88), were not the parents he had maintained in his memory. Mother was "different, disfigured, not identical to herself" (p. 91). Having survived the war, the boy now fell apart. Laub writes, "I read this story to mean that in regaining his real mother, he inevitably loses the internal witness he had found in her image" (p. 88).

Richman's (2006) experience is once again germane. Here she describes the inner presence to whom she wrote during the time she was working on her own memoir (2002) of her childhood as a hidden child during the Holocaust:

> The internalized other (the projected reader) was an amorphous presence without distinguishing characteristics, but seemed to be an interested observer, a witness, someone who wanted to know more about me and my life. Perhaps the amorphous presence represented my mother, my first reader-listener, who lived to hear my school papers and received my writing with unwavering admiration. (p. 645)

Something on this order is what happened for the castaways I have cited, for the toddlers in their cribs, for all of us, much of the time, day to day. And so we see that the experience of the castaways is hardly unique; it is what we all do routinely. It is the castaways' enforced isolation, as a matter of fact, that throws the process of witnessing into high relief.

But just as Laub's internal empathic other can be destroyed by trauma, we cease to be able to invoke the imaginary internal witness as soon as the experience we must witness touches on parts of us that hurt or scare us too badly to acknowledge or that are injured in a way so central to our makeup that awareness of them threatens the remainder of the personality. The imaginary internal witness becomes unavailable, in other words, when the one who must be witnessed is not-me. Yet this is precisely the part of us that, if we are to grow, we must somehow learn to bear and to know. In such cases it is crucial to have a witness outside our own minds. In such cases we not only profit from seeing a psychoanalyst; we also need one.

Final Thoughts

The psychoanalytic accounts of narrative with which we are most familiar (Schafer, 1983, 1992; Spence, 1982) are written as if the stories themselves are what matter. Problems in living are portrayed as the outcome of telling defensively motivated stories of our lives that deaden or distort experience, or of skewing experience by rigidly selecting one particular account. Therapeutic action revolves around the creation, through objective interpretation based on the analyst's preferred theory, of new and better stories— more inclusive, more coherent, more suited to their purpose. In the accounts of narrative by Schafer and Spence, while there is room for a good deal of flexibility in the way the analyst works, clinical psychoanalysis is defined by its technique, and its technique, in one way or another, is defined by the way interpretation is employed.

Schafer (1992) believes that psychoanalytic clinical work is very much like text interpretation. This "text" is both "interpenetrated" and "cohabited" by patient and analyst. But it remains a text. Consider what the analyst does with the patient who "talks back," in other words, the patient who tells the analyst what he thinks of the analyst's interpretive offerings:

> The analyst treats the analysand in the same manner that many literary critics treat authors—with interest in what the analysand says about the aims of his or her utterances and choices, but with an overall attitude of autonomous critical command rather than submission or conventional politeness, and with a readiness to view these explanatory comments as just so much more prose to be both heard as such *and* interpreted. (p. 176)

It is hardly controversial for a psychoanalyst to claim that what the patient says often has meanings that the patient does not know. But there now exists a substantial body of literature that does take issue with the claim that an analyst can *ever* adopt "an overall attitude of autonomous critical command" (e.g., Mitchell, 1993, 1997; Renik, 1993; Hoffman, 1998; Bromberg, 1998, 2006; Stern, 1997; Pizer, 1998). This large group of writers, most of whom identify themselves as relational or interpersonal analysts, takes the position that the relationship of patient and analyst is one of continuous, mutual unconscious influence. Neither the patient nor the analyst has privileged access to the meanings of their own experience.

This is the broad perspective within which the view developed in this essay belongs. While it remains undeniable that refashioned narratives change lives, the source of this change is the patient's newfound freedom to experience, an expansion of the self, created through events of the clinical interaction that are only partially under our conscious control. It is not so much that we learn the truth, but that we become more than we were. Our greatest clinical accomplishments are neither interpretations nor the stories they convey but are the broadening of the range within which analyst and patient become able to serve as one another's witnesses. This new recognition of each by the other is a product of the resolution of enactments and the dissociations that underlie them and the resulting capacity of analyst and patient to inhabit more fully one another's experience, to listen more frequently through one another's ears. As dissociation and enactment recede, patient and analyst once again become partners in thought, and now the breadth of their partnering has grown.

Instead of thinking of narrative as a consciously purposeful construction, we should recast it as something on the order of a self-organizing system, in which outcomes are unpredictable and nonlinear (e.g., Thelen & Smith, 1994; Galatzer-Levy, 2004). Clinical process is the medium—or to use the language of nonlinear systems theory, the event space—within which narrative stagnates, grows, and changes: The destabilization of old narratives and the emergence of new ones are the outcomes of unpredictable relational events. I hope I have explained my perspective well enough by now to substantiate the claim I made at the beginning: New narratives in psychoanalysis are the emergent, coconstructed, and unbidden products of clinical process.

Without denying for an instant the necessity for careful conceptualization or clinical discipline, I intend what I have said to serve as an argument against the claim that clinical psychoanalysis can be defined by any specification of technique. Psychoanalysis is, rather, a very particular way that one person can be of use to another, a way that depends on our possession of common practices but also on our awareness that those practices are often inadequate to the experience that makes up our immersion in clinical process. For the analyst who believes that the recognition and resolution of enactments is central to clinical psychoanalysis, the personal is unavoidably linked with the professional, a point that reinforces something we have known at least since the work of Racker (1968): If the patient is to change, the analyst must change as well. In the end we find, as is so often the case, that when the mind is locked relationship is the key.

References

Bach, S. (2006). *Getting from here to there: Analytic love, analytic process.* Hillsdale, NJ: The Analytic Press.

Beebe, B., & Lachmann, F. (1988). The contribution of mother–infant mutual influence to the origins of self and object representations. *Psychoanalytic Psychology, 5,* 305–337.

Beebe, B., & Lachmann, F. (1994). Representation and internalization in infancy: Three principles of salience. *Psychoanalytic Psychology, 11,* 127–165.

Benjamin, J. (1988). *The bonds of love.* New York: Pantheon.

Benjamin, J. (1990). Recognition and destruction: An outline of intersubjectivity. In S. A. Mitchell & L. Aron (Eds.), *Relational psychoanalysis: The emergence of a tradition* (pp. 183–200). Hillsdale, NJ: The Analytic Press, 1999.

Benjamin, J. (1995). *Like subjects, love objects.* New Haven, CT: Yale University Press.

Bion, W. R. (1962). *Learning from experience.* London: Heinemann.

Bion, W. R. (1963). *Elements of psycho-analysis.* London: Heinemann.

Boston Change Process Study Group (2002). Explicating the implicit: The local level and the microprocesses of change in the analytic situation. *International Journal of Psychoanalysis, 83,* 1051–1062.

Boston Change Process Study Group (2005). The "something more" than interpretation revisited: Sloppiness and co-creativity in the psychoanalytic encounter. *Journal of the American Psychoanalytic Association, 53,* 693–729.

Boston Change Process Study Group (2007). Implicit process in relation to conflict, defense and the dynamic unconscious. *International Journal of Psychoanalysis, 88,* 843–860.

Boston Change Process Study Group (2008). Forms of relational meaning: Issues in the relations between the implicit and reflective-verbal domains. *Psychoanalytic Dialogues, 18,* 125–148.

Boulanger, G. (2007). *Wounded by reality: Understanding and treating adult-onset trauma.* Mahwah, NJ: The Analytic Press.

Brison, S. (2002). *Aftermath: Violence and the remaking of a self.* Princeton, NJ: Princeton University Press.

Bromberg, P. M. (1998). *Standing in the spaces: Essays on clinical process, trauma, and dissociation.* Hillsdale, NJ: The Analytic Press.

Bromberg, P. M. (2006). *Awakening the dreamer: Clinical journeys.* Hillsdale, NJ: The Analytic Press.

Bruner, J. (1986). *Actual minds, possible worlds.* Cambridge, MA: Harvard University Press.

Bruner, J. (1990). *Acts of meaning.* Cambridge, MA: Harvard University Press.

Bruner, J. (2002). *Making stories: Law, literature, life.* Cambridge, MA: Harvard University Press.

Chasseguet-Smirgel, J. (1990). On acting out. *International Journal of Psychoanalysis, 71,* 77–86.

Chefetz, R. A., & Bromberg, P. M. (2004). Talking with "me" and "not-me." *Contemporary Psychoanalysis, 40,* 409–464.

Damasio, A. (1994). *Descartes's error: Emotion, reason and the human brain.* New York: G. P. Putnam's Sons.

Defoe, D. (1719). *Robinson Crusoe.* New York: Charles Scribner's Sons, 1957.

Eigen, M. (1981). The area of faith in Winnicott, Lacan and Bion. *International Journal of Psychoanalysis, 62,* 413–433.

Eshel, O. (2004). Let it be and become me: Notes on containing, identification, and the possibility of being. *Contemporary Psychoanalysis, 40,* 323–351.

Fain, M., & David, C. (1963). Aspects fonctionnels de la vie onirique. *Revue Française Psychanalyse, 27,* 241–343.

Fain, M., David, C., & Marty, P. (1964). Perspective psychosomatique sur la function des fantasmes. *Revue Française Psychanalyse, 28,* 609–622.

Farber, L. (1956). Martin Buber and psychoanalysis. In *The ways of the will: Essays toward a psychology and psychopathology of will* (pp. 131–154). New York: Basic Books, 1966.

Ferro, A. (2002). *In the analyst's consulting room.* London: Routledge.

Ferro, A. (2005). *Seeds of illness, seeds of recovery: The genesis of suffering and the role of psychoanalysis.* London: Routledge.

Ferro, A. (2006). *Psychoanalysis as therapy and storytelling.* London: Routledge.

Fonagy, P., Gergely, G., Jurist, L., & Target, M. (2002). *Affect regulation, mentalization, and the development of the self.* New York: Other Press.

Galatzer-Levy, R. M. (2004). Chaotic possibilities: Toward a new model of development. *International Journal of Psychoanalysis, 85,* 419–442.

Ghent, E. (1995). Interaction in the psychoanalytic situation. *Psychoanalytic Dialogues, 5,* 479–491.

Green, A. (1975). The analyst, symbolization, and absence in the analytic setting. *International Journal of Psychoanalysis, 56,* 1–22.

Green, A. (2000). The central phobic position: A new formulation of the free association method. *International Journal of Psychoanalysis, 81,* 429–451.

Hoffman, I. Z. (1998). *Ritual and spontaneity in the psychoanalytic process: A dialectical-constructivist view.* Hillsdale, NJ: The Analytic Press.

Knoblauch, S. H. (2000). *The musical edge of therapeutic relatedness.* Hillsdale, NJ: The Analytic Press.

Lacan, J. (1977). *Écrits: A selection*. New York: Norton.

Laub, D. (1992a). Bearing witness or the vicissitudes of witnessing. In S. Felman & D. Laub (Eds.), *Testimony: Crises of witnessing in literature, psychoanalysis, and history* (pp. 57–74). London: Routledge.

Laub, D. (1992b). An event without a witness: Truth, testimony, and survival. In S. Felman & D. Laub (Eds.), *Testimony: Crises of witnessing in literature, psychoanalysis, and history* (pp. 75–92). London: Routledge.

Laub, D. (2005). Traumatic shutdown of symbolization and narrative: A death instinct derivative? *Contemporary Psychoanalysis, 41*, 307–326.

Laub, D., & Auerhahn, N. (1989). Failed empathy: A central theme in the survivor's Holocaust experience. *Psychoanalytic Psychology, 6*, 377–400.

Lecours, S., & Bouchard, M. (1997). Dimensions of mentalization: Outlining levels of psychic transformation. *International Journal of Psychoanalysis, 78*, 855–875.

Luquet, P. (1987). *Penser-parler: Un apport psychanalytique la thorie du langage*. In R. Christie, M. M. Christie-Luterbaucher, & P. Luquet (Eds.), *La parole trouble* (pp. 161–300). Paris: Presses Universitaires de France.

Marty, P. (1990). *La psychosomatique de l'adulte*. Paris: Presses Universitaires de France.

Marty, P. (1991). *Mentalisation et psychosomatique*. Paris: Laboratoire Delagrange.

McDougall, J. (1985). *Theaters of the mind*. New York: Basic Books.

Mitchell, S. A. (1993). *Hope and dread in psychoanalysis*. New York: Basic Books.

Mitchell, S. A. (1997). *Influence and autonomy in psychoanalysis*. Hillsdale, NJ: The Analytic Press.

Modell, A. (1984). *Psychoanalysis in a new context*. New York: International Universities Press.

Nelson, K. (Ed.) (1989). *Narratives from the crib*. Cambridge, MA: Harvard University Press.

Onishi, N. (2007, 12 October). Death reveals harsh side of a "model" in Japan. *New York Times*.

Pizer, S. A. (1998). *Building bridges: The negotiation of paradox in psychoanalysis*. Hillsdale, NJ: The Analytic Press.

Poland, W. S. (2000). The analyst's witnessing and otherness. *Journal of the American Psychoanalytic Association, 48*, 17–34.

Polkinghorne, D. E. (1988). *Narrative knowing in the human sciences*. Albany, NY: State University of New York Press.

Racker, H. (1968). *Transference and countertransference*. New York: International Universities Press.

Renik, O. (1993). Analytic interaction: Conceptualizing technique in light of the analyst's irreducible subjectivity. *Psychoanalytic Quarterly, 62*, 553–571.

Richman, S. (2002). *A wolf in the attic: The legacy of a hidden child of the Holocaust*. New York: Haworth Press.

Richman, S. (2006). Finding one's voice: Transforming trauma into autobiographical narrative. *Contemporary Psychoanalysis, 42*, 639–650.

Ricoeur, P. (1977). The question of proof in Freud's psychoanalytic writings. *Journal of the American Psychoanalytic Association, 25*, 835–871.

Ricoeur, P (1981). *Hermeneutics and the human sciences*. Cambridge, UK: Cambridge University Press.

Ringstrom, P. (2001). Cultivating the improvisational in psychoanalytic treatment. *Psychoanalytic Dialogues, 11*, 727–754.

Ringstrom, P. (2007). Scenes that write themselves: Improvisational moments in relational psychoanalysis. *Psychoanalytic Dialogues, 17,* 69–100.

Russell, P. L. (1991). Trauma, repetition, and affect. Paper presented at the First Symposium, Massachusetts Institute for Psychoanalysis. *Contemporary Psychoanalysis, 42,* 601–620, 2007.

Sander, L. W. (1962). Issues in early mother–child interaction. *Journal of the American Academy of Child Psychiatry, 1,* 141–166.

Sander, L. W. (1988). The event-structure of regulation in the neonate-caregiver system as a biological background for early organization of psychic structure. *Progress in Self Psychology, 3,* 64–77.

Sarbin, T. (1986). *Narrative psychology: The storied nature of human conduct.* New York: Praeger.

Schafer, R. (1983). *The analytic attitude.* New York: Basic Books.

Schafer, R. (1992). *Retelling a life: Narration and dialogue in psychoanalysis.* New York: Basic Books.

Segal, H. (1957). Notes on symbol formation. *International Journal of Psychoanalysis, 38,* 391–397.

Spence, D. P. (1982). *Narrative truth and historical truth: Meaning and interpretation in psychoanalysis.* New York: Norton.

Spence, D. P. (1987). *The Freudian metaphor: Toward paradigm change in psychoanalysis.* New York: Norton.

Stern, D. B. (1983). Unformulated experience: From familiar chaos to creative disorder. *Contemporary Psychoanalysis, 19,* 71–99.

Stern, D. B. (1997). *Unformulated experience: From dissociation to imagination in psychoanalysis.* Hillsdale, NJ: The Analytic Press.

Stern, D. B. (2002). Words and wordlessness in the psychoanalytic situation. *Journal of the American Psychoanalytic Association, 50,* 221–247.

Stern, D. B. (2003). The fusion of horizons: dissociation, enactment, and understanding. *Psychoanalytic Dialogues, 13,* 843–873.

Stern, D. B. (2004). The eye sees itself: Dissociation, enactment, and the achievement of conflict. *Contemporary Psychoanalysis, 40,* 197–237.

Stern, D. B. (2008). On having to find what you don't know how to look for. In A. Slade, S. Bergner & E. L. Jurist (Eds.), *Mind to mind: Infant research, neuroscience, and psychoanalysis* (pp. 398–413). New York: Other Press.

Stern, D. B. (2009a). Dissociation and unformulated experience: A psychoanalytic model of mind. In P. F. Dell, J. O'Neil, & E. Somer (Eds.), *Dissociation and the dissociative disorders: DSM-V and beyond* (pp. 653–663). New York: Routledge.

Stern, D. B. (2009b). Shall the twain meet? Metaphor, dissociation, and co-occurrence. *Psychoanalytic Inquiry, 29,* 79–90.

Stern, D. B. (2009c). *Partners in thought: Working with unformulated experience, dissociation, and enactment.* New York: Routledge.

Stern, D. N. (1977). *The first relationship.* Cambridge, MA: Harvard University Press.

Stern, D. N. (1985). *The interpersonal world of the infant: A view from psychoanalysis and developmental psychology.* New York: Basic Books.

Stern, D. N. (2004). *The present moment in psychotherapy and everyday life.* New York: Norton.

Stern, D. N., Sander, L. W., Nahum, J. P., Harrison, A. M., Lyons-Ruth, K., Morgan, A. C., et al. (1998). Noninterpretive mechanisms in psychoanalytic therapy: the "something more" than interpretation. *International Journal of Psychoanalysis, 79*, 903–921.

Sullivan, H. S. (1940). *Conceptions of modern psychiatry*. New York: Norton, 1953.

Sullivan, H. S. (1953). *The interpersonal theory of psychiatry* (H. S. Perry & M. L. Gawel, Eds.). New York: Norton.

Thelen, E., & Smith, L. B. (1994). *A dynamic systems approach to the development of cognition and action*. Cambridge, MA: MIT Press.

Winnicott, D. W. (1945). Primitive emotional development. In *Through paediatrics to psychoanalysis* (pp. 145–156). New York: Basic Books, 1975.

Winnicott, D. W. (1971a). The use of an object and relating through identifications. In *Playing and reality*. London: Tavistock.

Winnicott, D. W. (1971b). *Playing and reality*. London: Tavistock.

17

On Becoming a Psychoanalyst*

Glen Gabbard and Thomas Ogden

▼   ▼   ▼   ▼   ▼

Few of us feel that we really know what we are doing when we complete our formal psychoanalytic training. We flounder. We strive to find our "voice," our own "style," a feeling that we are engaging in the practice of psychoanalysis in a way that bears our own watermark:

> It is only after you have qualified [as an analyst] that you have a chance of becoming an analyst. The analyst you become is you and you alone; you have to respect the uniqueness of your own personality—that is what you use, not all these interpretations (these theories that you use to combat the feeling that you are not really an analyst and do not know how to become one). (Bion, 1987, p. 15)

In this paper we discuss a variety of maturational experiences that have been important to us in our own efforts to become analysts following our analytic training. Of course, the types of experience that were of particular value to each of us were different, but they also overlapped in important ways. We try to convey both the commonality of, and the differences between, the sorts of experience that have been most significant to us in our efforts to become (to mature as) analysts. In addition, we discuss several defensive measures that analysts in general, and we in particular, have made use of in the face of the anxiety that is inherent to the process of genuinely becoming an analyst in one's own terms.

---

* This paper originally appeared in *International Journal of Psychoanalysis*, *90*(2), 2009, pp. 311–327. Reprinted with permission.

A Theoretical Context

A variety of experiences throughout one's development as an analyst are fundamental to one's maturation as both an analyst and an individual. The maturation of the analyst has much in common with psychic development in general. We have identified four aspects of psychic growth that are essential to our view of the process of becoming an analyst.

The first is the idea that thinking/dreaming one's lived experience in the world constitutes a principal means, perhaps the principal means, by which one learns from experience and achieves psychological growth (Bion, 1962a). Moreover, one's lived experience often is so disturbing as to exceed the individual's capacity to do anything with it psychically (i.e., to think or dream it). Under such circumstances, it requires two people to think or dream the experience. The psychoanalysis of each of our patients inevitably places us in situations that we have never before experienced and, as a result, requires of us a larger personality than that which we have brought to the analysis. We view this as true of every analysis: There is no such thing as an "easy" or "straightforward" analysis. The reconceptualization of projective identification as an intrapsychic/interpersonal process in the writings of Bion (1962a, 1962b) and Rosenfeld (1987) recognizes that in these novel, disturbing analytic situations the analyst requires another person to help make the unthinkable thinkable. That other person is most often the patient but may be a supervisor, colleague, mentor, consultation group, and so on. Inherent in this notion of intersubjective thinking is the idea that, throughout the life of the individual, "it takes [at least] two people to make one" (Bion, 1987, p. 222). It requires a mother-and-infant capable of helping the infant to achieve "unit status" (Winnicott, 1958a, p. 44). It takes three people—mother, father, and child—to create a healthy oedipal child; it takes three people—mother, father, and adolescent—to create a young adult; it takes two young adults to create a psychological space in which to create a couple that is, in turn, capable of creating a psychological space in which a baby can be conceived (literally and metaphorically); it takes a combination of a young family and an old one (a grandmother, grandfather, mother, father, and child) to create conditions that contribute to, or facilitate the acceptance and creative use of, the experience of aging and death in the grandparents (Loewald, 1979).

However, this intersubjective conception of the development of the analyst is incomplete in the absence of its intrapsychic counterpart. This brings us to the second aspect of the theoretical context for this discussion: To think/dream our own experience, we need periods of personal isolation no less than we need the participation of the minds of others. Winnicott (1963) recognized this essential developmental requirement when he noted: "There is an intermediate stage in healthy development in which the patient's most important experience in relation to the good or potentially satisfying object is the refusal of it" (p. 182). In the analytic setting, the psychological work that is done between the sessions is no less important than the work done with the analyst in the sessions. Indeed, analyst and patient need to "sleep on" the session (i.e., they need to dream it on their own before they are able to do further work as an analytic pair). Similarly, in the sessions, the psychological work that the patient does in isolation from the analyst (and that the analyst does in his isolated space behind the couch) is as important as the thinking/dreaming that the two do with one another. These dimensions—the interpersonal and the solitary—are fully interdependent and stand in dialectical tension with one another. (When we speak of personal isolation, we are referring to a psychological state different from the state of being alone in the presence of another person, i.e., Winnicott's (1958b) "capacity to be alone." Rather, what we have in mind is a state that is much less dependent on external, or even internalized, object relations; see Ogden, 1991, for a discussion of this healthy state of "personal isolation.")

The third aspect of psychic growth that is essential to our conception of maturation in the analyst is the idea that becoming an analyst involves a process of "dreaming oneself more fully into existence" (Ogden, 2004a, p. 858) in progressively more complex and inclusive ways. In the tradition of Bion (1962a), we are using the term "dreaming" to refer to the most profound form of thinking. It is a type of thinking in which the individual is able to transcend the limits of secondary process logic without loss of access to that form of logic. Dreaming occurs continuously, both during sleep and during waking life. Just as the stars persist even when their light is obscured by the light of the sun, so, too, dreaming is a continuous function of the mind that continues during waking life even though obscured from consciousness by the glare of waking life. (Waking dreaming in the analytic setting takes the form of the analyst's reverie experience; see Bion, 1962a; Ogden, 1997.) The timelessness of dreams allows one to simultaneously elaborate a multiplicity of perspectives on an emotional experience in a way that is not possible in the context of linear time and cause and effect logic that characterize waking, secondary process thinking. (The simultaneity of multiple perspectives that was captured in the cubist art of Pablo Picasso and Georges Braque has had an influence on 20th-century art of every genre—the poetry of T. S. Eliot and Ezra Pound, the novels of William Faulkner and the late novels of Henry James, the plays of Harold Pinter and Ionesco, and the films of Krzysztof Kieslowski and David Lynch, as well as the art of psychoanalysis.)

The work of dreaming is the psychological work through which we create personal, symbolic meaning, thereby becoming ourselves. It is in this sense that we dream ourselves into existence as analysts, analysands, supervisors, parents, friends, and so on. In the absence of dreaming, we cannot learn from our lived experience and consequently remain trapped in an endless, unchanging present.

The fourth aspect of psychic growth that we believe to be fundamental to the way we think about the process of becoming an analyst is Bion's (1962a, 1970) concept of the container–contained. The "container" is not a thing, but a process of doing psychological work with our disturbing thoughts. The term "doing psychological work" is roughly equivalent to such ideas/feelings as the experience of "coming to terms with" an aspect of one's life that has been difficult to acknowledge or "making one's peace with" important, deeply disturbing events in one's life such as the death of a parent, a child, or a spouse, or one's own approaching death. The "contained" is the psychological representation of what one is coming to terms with or making one's peace with. The breakdown of a mutually generative relationship between thoughts derived from disturbing experience (the contained) and the capacity to think/dream those thoughts (the container) may take a number of forms that manifest themselves in a variety of types of failure to mature as an analyst (Ogden, 2004b). The disturbing lived experiences—"the contained" (e.g., boundary violations on the part of the analyst's personal analyst)—may destroy the analyst's capacity for thinking as an analyst ("the container"), particularly under certain emotional circumstances (Gabbard & Lester, 1995).

With these ideas in mind, we will now consider a set of maturational experiences that are common to analysts in the course of their development. When one completes psychoanalytic training, one often has the vague sense of feeling a bit fraudulent. One is authorized to "fly solo" without the help of a supervisor, yet one feels a degree of turbulence that can be disconcerting. At times, analysts welcome the opportunity to learn from (and mature in) the sorts of analytic situations that we are about to describe. At other times, under other circumstances, analysts suddenly and inadvertently find themselves immersed in these disturbing analytic situations and achieve psychological growth by means of "flying by the seat of their pants."

Maturational Experiences of the Analyst

In the sections of the paper that follow, we discuss a number of types of maturational experience that have played an important role in the development of our analytic identities. These experiences include the gradual process of developing one's own way of speaking with patients; developing one's sense of oneself as an analyst in the course of presenting clinical work to a consultant; making self-analytic use of experiences with patients; and creating/discovering oneself as an analyst in the process of writing analytic papers.

Developing a Voice of One's Own

In listening to oneself speak (e.g., to one's patients, supervisees, colleagues, and seminar members), one asks oneself: "What do I sound like when I speak like that?" "Do I really want to sound like that?" "Like whom do I sound?" "In what ways do I sound foreign to the person I have become and am becoming?" "If I were to speak differently, what might that sound like?" "How would it feel to speak in a way that is different from anyone other than me?" There is a paradox in the fact that speaking naturally, as oneself, is both easy (in the sense of not having to pretend to be someone other than oneself) and very difficult (in the sense of finding/inventing a voice that emerges from the totality of who one is at a given moment). When paying close attention, one discovers that there are unmistakable residues of one's analyst's voice in the words spoken to one's patients. These ways of speaking are "in our bones," internalized long ago and made part of us without our being aware of the assimilation process.

While this mode of maturational experience largely occurs in the context of speaking to others, there is also an intrapsychic aspect, a conscious and unconscious battle with oneself in the effort to find/create oneself as an analyst. The voices one hears are largely in one's head (Smith, 2001) and belong to our "ghosts" and "ancestors" (Loewald, 1960, p. 249). The ghosts inhabit us in a way that is not fully integrated into our sense of self; our ancestors provide us with a sense of continuity with the past. In the process of becoming an analyst, we must "dream up" for ourselves an authentic way of speaking that involves disentangling ourselves from our own analyst(s) as well as past supervisors, teachers, and writers we admire while also drawing on what we have learned from them. A dialectical tension exists between inventing oneself freshly on the one hand and creatively using one's emotional ancestry on the other.

No one has described better than Loewald the psychological dilemmas that are involved in the passage of authority from one generation to the next. In "The Waning of the Oedipus Complex," Loewald (1979) describes the ways growing up (becoming a mature individual in one's own right) requires that one simultaneously kill one's parents (in more than a metaphoric way) and immortalize them. The parricide is an act of claiming one's own place as a person responsible for oneself and to oneself; the immortalizing of one's parents (an act of atonement ["at-one-ment"] for the parricide) involves a metamorphic internalization of the parents. This internalization is "metamorphic" in that the parents are not simply transformed into an aspect of oneself (a simple identification). Rather it is an internalization of a far richer sort: that of incorporating into one's own identity a version of the parents that includes a conception of who they might have become, but were unable to become, as a consequence of the limitations of their own personalities and the circumstances in which they lived. What better atonement can one make to the parents one kills (Ogden, 2006)?

In the process of becoming an analyst, one must be able to commit acts of parricide in relation to one's own analytic parents while atoning for the parricide in the act of internalizing a transformed version of them. That metamorphic internalization recognizes their strengths and weaknesses and involves an incorporation into one's identity of a sense not only of who they were but also of who they might have become had external and internal circumstances allowed.

In the following clinical vignette, one of us (Ogden) describes an experience in which patient and analyst together lived and dreamed an experience that facilitated maturation on both their parts.

For a significant period of time, the analyst found himself using the word *well* to introduce virtually every question and comment that he addressed to his patients. It felt so natural that it took him a long time to recognize the fact that he had adopted this pattern of speech. He also noticed that he spoke in this way only while talking with patients and not while speaking with supervisees, conversing in seminars, talking with colleagues, and so on. On becoming aware that he was speaking in this way, it was immediately apparent to him that he had adopted a mannerism of his first analyst. He felt no need to "correct it" since, he told himself, he experienced it as an emotional connection with a man he liked and admired. What he did not realize was that he also saw no need to look into it (i.e., to think about why this identification had evidenced itself in that form at that juncture in his life and at that juncture in his work with these particular patients).

One of the patients with whom he was working in analysis during this period was Mr. A, a man who had chosen a career in the same field in which his father was a prominent figure. It was in the sessions with this patient—though there were related experiences with other patients—that he began to feel differently about what had seemed to him a harmless quirk in his manner of speech. This shift in perspective came over a period of weeks as he listened to Mr. A minimize the effect on him of having entered the same field as his father while at the same time repeatedly using the phrase "his field" instead of "my field" or "our field." During this period of the analysis Mr. A mentioned an instance in which it seemed to the analyst that the patient was very uncharacteristically teasing one of his children for "trying to act like a grown-up." Even though the analyst did not comment on the behavior, it had a disturbing effect on him.

At the beginning of a session during this period of work, the patient complained that the analyst was making too much of the effects of his choice to go into "my father's field." The analyst believed that he had been careful not to take sides on the matter, so he chose to remain silent in response to his patient's accusation. Later in the session, Mr. A told the following dream:

> An earthquake had begun with just a few short bursts, but I knew that this was just the beginning of an enormous earthquake in which I could very well be killed. I tried to gather a few things that I would like to take with me before getting out of the house that I was in. It was kind of like my house. I reached for a family photograph—one that I actually have on a table in my living room. It's a photo I took in Florida of my parents, Karen [his wife] and the kids. I felt an enormous pressure of time—it felt as if I was suffocating and that it was crazy to spend the last breath of air I had on saving the photograph. Suffocation isn't the way an earthquake gets you, but that was how I felt. I woke up frightened with my heart pounding.

(For reasons that were not at all apparent to the analyst, he, too, felt intensely anxious as the patient told the dream.)

In the course of talking about the dream, Mr. A was struck by the fact that "because I took the photograph, I wasn't in the picture. I was in it as an observer, not as a member of the cast." The analyst said, "You were initially frightened by the feeling of the beginnings of an earthquake that might increase in force to the point that it might well kill you and everything that is dear to you; later in the dream, you felt you were one breath away from dying by suffocation. I think that you were talking with yourself and with me in the dream about your feeling that you are being squeezed out of your own life—you were only an observer in the family picture, yet you were willing to use your last breath of air to preserve for yourself even that marginal place. That seemed crazy to you even in the dream."

As the analyst was saying this, it occurred to him that Mr. A, in his telling of the dream, may have been making an observation about the analyst. The patient's saying that he knew that he "could very well be killed" by the earthquake involved a phrasing that not only used the same word on which the analyst was focused but also linked it directly to the idea of being killed. This led the analyst to suspect that Mr. A was responding to something happening in the analyst that was reflected in the change in his manner of speech. It seemed to him that the patient was afraid that the analyst had developed a form of verbal tic that reflected a craziness in the analyst that would prevent him from being the analyst that he needed. If the analyst, too, were being squeezed out of his own life as an analyst and his own way of speaking (with which the patient had become familiar over the years), how could the analyst be of help to him with a very similar problem?

The analyst thought that it was highly unlikely that the telling of this dream was Mr. A's first unconscious comment on something he perceived to be significantly different in the analyst's way of speaking. The patient's dream was critical to the analytic work, not because it was addressing feelings so very different from those being addressed in other dreams, but because it was the first time that the analyst was able to hear and respond to what he believed to be the patient's unconscious effort to talk to him about his fear that he perceived an ominous change in the analyst. In retrospect, the source of the symptom (as the analyst came to understand it) had affected his ability to mature as a person and as an analyst. Also in hindsight, the analyst recognized that the patient's cruelly pointing out his child's "trying to act like a grown-up" represented a communication to the analyst regarding the patient's self-hatred for the ways he felt like a child. (We view the dream as a dream that cannot be ascribed to the patient alone, but to an unconscious subject that is coconstructed by patient and analyst—"the analytic third" (Ogden, 1994). It is this third subject that dreams the problems in the analytic relationship—in addition to the patient and analyst as individual dreamers.)

The patient's unconscious observation that he was an observer in the family photo, in conjunction with the analyst's awareness of his own anxiety while listening to the dream, led the analyst to begin a line of thought, a conversation with himself, about the meanings of his imitation of his first analyst. What was most powerful about the new awareness of the speech pattern that he had adopted was its persistence and invariability across the full range of emotional situations and across very different kinds of conversations with very different sorts of patients. It seemed to him that the impersonal quality of this generic way of speaking reflected a subliminal feeling that he had harbored for a very long time but had not previously put into words for himself: It had seemed to him during his first analysis (and subsequently) that his analyst had in some important ways perceived him in generic ways that were neither personal to him nor to the analyst. There was a way he felt that his first analyst's perception of him was unwavering and missing something important. Both of these feelings were reflected in the photograph in the dream in that the photograph, too, was unchanging and did not include the photographer. The analyst felt some disappointment in his first analyst but primarily felt ashamed that he had not had the courage to consciously recognize the impersonal quality of the way he felt he was being perceived and to register a protest. In the dream, there was a choice between the dreamer's saving the photograph and saving his own life. The analyst realized that he had metaphorically chosen to save the photograph— his fixed image of his own analyst—and, as a consequence, had given up something of his own vitality.

On the basis of these thoughts and others that followed, in the succeeding weeks and months, the analyst was eventually able to speak with Mr. A about Mr. A's feelings of shame (the shame of having betrayed himself) in having chosen to pursue a career in "his father's field" and not a career in his own field (even if it was the field in which his father also worked). (We will return to this clinical example later in the paper.)

Presenting Clinical Material to a Consultant

When struggling with a clinical situation in one's practice, analysts frequently turn to a trusted colleague. Listening to oneself in this context is significantly different from those instances in which one speaks to patients, students, or supervisees. Analysts, in speaking with a consultant, are not attempting to understand the other person as they would in their work with a patient. The gradient of maturity (Loewald, 1960) tilts in the other direction in an analyst's work with a consultant. The analyst's insecurities and anxieties are center stage given the fact that he has explicitly requested the help of the consultant. The emphasis is on what the analyst does not know. The analyst's lack of understanding—his self-doubt, anxiety, dread, shame, guilt, boredom, blind spots, lust, envy, hate, and terror—are all exposed to a colleague in an act of faith. The experience of one's own limits (as an analyst and as a person), and the acceptance of those limits by the consultant, help shape the analyst's identity in the direction of humility, curiosity about himself, and the awareness that his own analysis is a lifelong task. A portion of the analyst's identity involves conflict, ambivalence, longings and fears from childhood, and an attempt to come to terms with the fact that the analyst's personal analysis has not allowed him to transcend the internal torment that drew him to analytic work in the first place. Moreover, the fact that the consultant does not recoil in response to the analyst's struggles provides confirmation that being "good enough," in Winnicott's (1951, p. 237) terms, is acceptable to others and that the analyst will inevitably fall short of the comprehensive understanding and therapeutic results for which he may strive.

Aspects of the analyst's lived experience exceed his capacity to do psychological work with them and often emerge in the context of his encounters with his patients. Seeking out consultation may provide a much needed container when an analyst finds it impossible to process what he is confronting both in himself and in his patients. One of us (Gabbard) worked for years with a relentlessly suicidal patient who continued to plan her suicide despite the analyst's best efforts to understand, contain, and interpret the multiple motives and meanings involved in the wish to die.

After the analyst presented this dilemma to a consultant, the consultant noted that the analyst was attempting to ward off the idea that all his well-intentioned efforts were likely to come to naught, and the patient would probably end her life in spite of the treatment. The consultant stressed that the analyst was exasperated with the patient's interpersonally enacted fantasy of having omnipotent control over him and with his own inability to accept his powerlessness to prevent the patient from committing suicide. Ultimately, suicide would be the patient's choice without regard to the analyst's desires or needs. Hearing the consultant's comments allowed the analyst to work with these frightening thoughts and provided a way of detoxifying them so they could actually be thought by the analyst, accepted as inherent to the treatment situation, and heard as a communication of the patient's own feeling of not having a say about her own life or death.

The analyst's mind had been colonized by the patient's internal world and, as that colonization diminished, the analyst became aware of how his own aspirations for the analytic enterprise were being thwarted by the patient's unwavering death wish (Gabbard, 2003). Like many analysts, he harbored a powerful unconscious fantasy regarding the analytic relationship—one in which a specific form of object relationship would be generated. He would be the devoted, selfless healer, and the patient would progressively improve and ultimately express gratitude to the analyst for his help (Gabbard, 2000). His suicidal patient had not agreed to this unconscious contract, and her march toward self-destruction continued on in spite of—or perhaps oblivious to—the analyst's wish to help. With further reflection, the analyst recognized that he had been relegated to a transference position that would later be described by Steiner (2008) as the excluded observer who resents the fact that he is not the primary object for the patient.

The consultation also freed up the analyst to reflect on resonances from earlier developmental experiences where he realized his powerlessness in the face of the inevitable decline and death of others and himself, an important unconscious determinant of his career choice. Looking squarely at his magical wishes and recognizing the impossibility of determining what another human being (or himself) ultimately will do constituted pivotal elements of the maturation of the analyst. Part of knowing who one is as an analyst is knowing the limits of one's power to influence a patient and using that knowledge to be able to listen and respond to a patient who confronts her own limits (as well as those of the analyst).

One's Analytic Work as a Principal Medium for Self-Analysis

Every analysis is incomplete. As Freud (1937) stressed, termination is ordinarily a practical matter rather than a definitively determined endpoint marked by conflict resolution. It is widely accepted now that we do not "terminate" an analysis (with a belief that we have helped the patient achieve a "complete" analysis); rather the patient and analyst end an experience in analysis at a point at which they feel that a significant piece of psychological work has been achieved and that they are at a juncture at which the principal work at hand feels to them to be that of their separation. Put still differently: Transference is interminable, countertransference is interminable, conflict is interminable. A generative experience in analysis sets a process in motion that will continue throughout the analyst's life.

The analyst's self-analysis serves a contrapuntal function to the dialogue one has with a trusted consultant. The interpersonal experience of working with the consultant is punctuated by periods of isolation in which one thinks one's own thoughts in the quiet of one's car, in the wee hours of the morning when one is staring at the ceiling, or in the privacy of one's consulting room while waiting for a patient who does not appear. Psychoanalytic treatment initiates an exploration—often tentative and ambivalent—of the inner life of both patient and analyst. Self-analysis contributes to that process, but in this variation one works alone, determined to look unflinchingly at what one finds but always falling short of the mark. From this perspective, the ending of an analysis, the "end" of a piece of self-analytic work or of analytic work with a consultant is the point not at which unconscious conflict is resolved but at which the subject of the analytic work is able to think/dream his experience (to a large degree) for himself.

Discovering/Creating What One Thinks and Who One Is in the Experience of Writing

Writing is a form of thinking. Very often, in writing, one does not write what one thinks; one thinks what one writes. There is something of the feeling that ideas come out of one's pen, of watching ideas develop in unplanned ways (Ogden, 2005). Writing, however, is not necessarily a solitary activity. In psychoanalytic writing there is often a reader in mind as one proceeds. The fantasy of how the reader will react to a turn of phrase or a radical new perspective on theory or technique shapes and influences what appears on the page. Yet much of the creative process develops in isolation as one thinks about the kernel of an idea over and over in different settings. This contemplative period may take days, weeks, or even years. Most writing involves some oscillation between on one hand quiet reflection on what one has to say and on imagined responses by potential readers on the other. An imaginary audience is a fixture in Freud's writing. Time and again, he invents an imaginary skeptical audience and masterfully anticipates the objections of the audience/reader to his argument and offers a compelling rebuttal.

When the text is coauthored, further complexity is introduced into the process. In addition to the solitary contemplation and the imagined interaction with a reader, a collaboration with another writer requires a special sensitivity to one's coauthor—after all, each sentence must represent two authors, not one.

One such example of collaboration emerged in the course of writing this paper. We began with a shared idea—namely, an updating of Freud's idea that what was definitive of analysis as a treatment for psychological problems is the grounding of the work in the understanding of transference and resistance (Freud, 1914). We planned to describe how our own definition of analysis has evolved from and/or is discontinuous with Freud's ideas. We began our work on this collaborative project with enthusiasm. However, we found that the words did not flow as freely as we had hoped from either of us.

Feeling stuck in our efforts to get things moving, we reread and studied Freud's (1914) text. We were singularly disappointed as we came to recognize that much of Freud's paper was a rather vitriolic polemic against Jung's departures from Freud's theoretical premises and a fierce insistence that he and he alone was the founder of psychoanalysis. Hence we came to understand that the defensiveness in Freud's tone was a reflection of his insecurities regarding competing claims of authorship of his idea (i.e., of psychoanalysis as a discipline) and a fear that Jung would subvert what he had invented and continue to call it psychoanalysis. We had picked a quotation that caught Freud at an inauspicious moment in the history of his own psychological maturation.

As our enthusiasm waned, we had to rethink the theme of our paper.

We traded revisions back and forth until we began to clarify that what was most pressing to us was not the task of proposing a contemporary definition of psychoanalysis. Rather the collaboration itself had served to clarify for each of us how we had evolved as analysts over 30 years of practice. We talked at length with one another about how each of us had come to his current, evolving sense of himself as a psychoanalyst. Our developmental experiences in the course of analytic training and in the early years afterwards were markedly different in some respects, yet we found that there was great overlap in how we conceived of the way we work and who we are as psychoanalysts. Although we have known one another for more than 20 years, we found that we came to know one another in a new way in the course of these discussions. But with regard to the task of deciding what we hoped to achieve in coauthoring a paper, talking alone was not sufficient. Only by our repeated efforts to write our thoughts (or, more accurately, to allow ourselves to see what we thought in the very act of writing), we were eventually able to discern what it was that we wanted to attempt. Putting words to the page forced us (and freed us) to transform inchoate thoughts and feelings into concepts and an idea of what it was that we wanted to communicate in the form of a coauthored analytic paper.

In thinking about how readers might respond to our perspective, we recognized that our maturational experiences might not be shared by other analysts. We certainly did not want to be prescriptive in our tone. We thus made a concerted effort to present our ideas as simply a description of our own experiences rather than suggesting that they are universal. We became clearer with ourselves that among the qualities of an analyst that we view as most important is the way an analyst makes use of what is unique and idiosyncratic to his or her personality.

Working with a coauthor also involves an experience of having a built-in editor or consultant (whether or not one wants one) who can offer an "outside" perspective on the other author's clinical material. In the course of our collaboration on this chapter, one of us (Ogden) sent a draft to his coauthor containing the clinical vignette involving the earthquake dream. The coauthor (Gabbard) responded (in written form) with the following thoughts about the case in general, and the dream in particular:

> I very much agree with your point that the dream cannot be ascribed to the patient alone, but to a co-constructed subject. I felt that the dream was as much yours as his. My fantasy about the dream is this: that even though you had perceived your analyst as treating you in a generic manner, you felt some sort of protection—a safe harbor, if you will—in resorting to his style of speaking. In doing so, you had not separated from him and thus did not have to bear the pain associated with the loss of him. I am reminded of Freud's famous comment that the only way the ego can give up an object is to take it within. The earthquake, then, could be seen as a growing awareness in the patient that you were about to be ripped from your internally created house (i.e., the safe harbor of your analyst's office or internalized presence) and cast into a world where you must speak in your own voice. At some level, the patient felt that way about being ripped from his father's "house." What was going on in you had a great deal of resonance with what was going on in him. I did not add this to the chapter because it is purely my own conjecture and may not fit with your experience.

As this quotation indicates, a coauthor's perspective on clinical material must then be filtered through the thoughts of the author providing the clinical data to see if it is "a good fit" with the actual analytic moment described.

Ogden, who was not used to such "interference" with his writing process, found himself feeling unsettled by Gabbard's unexpected comments. He required more than 2 months of "sleeping on" (dreaming) what had been elicited in him by Gabbard's note before he was able to offer a considered response (also in written form):

> On rereading my account of my work with Mr. A, I find it telling that I saw in the invariability of the photograph in the patient's dream only stasis, as opposed to reliability; and that I saw in the absence of the photographer in the photograph only the absence of a thinking/feeling person, as opposed to unobtrusiveness. Your comments on the vignette helped me to see what had been there all along in my writing of the account: my deep appreciation of what I feel to be two of my first analyst's best qualities—his willingness to remain emotionally present during trying times in the analysis and during very difficult times in his life; and his ability to "stay out of the way" (and not reflexively make transference interpretations) when I was doing psychological work on my own in the sessions.

The coauthors view the emotional experience that Ogden describes as a current response both to his memory of his work with Mr. A and to Gabbard's comments on his written account of that experience. This exchange between the coauthors constitutes a type of maturational experience that was of value to both authors.

Daring to Improvise

With each patient, we have the responsibility to become an analyst whom we have never been before. This requires that we drop the script and enter into a conversation, a conversation of a type we have never before experienced (Hoffman, 1998; Ringstrom, 2001). This may take the form of responding to a patient's mention of a film by saying, "There's hardly a word spoken in the entire film, at least that's how it left me feeling." With another patient, improvising may mean remaining silent—not complying with implicit coercive demands for reassurance or even for the sound of our voice. Improvisation is, of course, a theatrical metaphor. The great Russian acting teacher Constantin Stanislavski (1936) noted, "The very best that can happen is to have the actor completely carried away by the play. Then regardless of his own will he lives the part, not noticing how he feels, not thinking about what he does, and it all moves of its own accord subconsciously and intuitively" (p. 13).

In an analogous way, maturation as an analyst involves increasingly allowing ourselves to be caught up in the moment (in the unconscious of the analysis) and carried by the music of the session. Analysis is not an experience that can be mapped out and planned. Events happen between two people in a room together, and the meaning of those events are discussed and understood. Analysts learn more about who they are by participating in the "dance" of the moment. The extent to which the analysis is "alive" may depend on the analyst's willingness and ability to improvise, and to be improvised by, the unconscious of the analytic relationship.

Noticing the Aspects of Ourselves That, as if of Their Own Accord, Protest Against Our Being the Analyst Whom We Have Been for So Long

What at one time might have been called being reliable, stable and trustworthy, may gradually become too easy and more than a little stale and predictable. We, at times, become aware during a session with a patient that we have become too comfortable with ourselves as analysts. "Errors," in these sessions, can often be seen as expressions of the healthiest parts of ourselves and are invaluable to our maturation if we can make use of these alerts. Such errors include the analyst's arriving late for a session, ending a session early, falling asleep during a session, and expecting a different patient when one meets the analysand in the waiting room. (Not included in this type of error are boundary violations such as having sex with patients, breaches of confidentiality, and entering into a business relationship with a patient; see Gabbard & Lester, 1995.) The errors that do not involve boundary violations very often represent the analyst's unconscious efforts to disturb his own psychic equilibrium, to force himself to take notice of the ways he has become stagnant in his role as analyst.

We believe that there is a self-imposed need to be original—not in the sense of a narcissistic display but in the sense of a need to quietly, steadily, unselfconsciously enter into conversation with the patient or supervisee in a way that could happen between no other two people in the world (Ogden, 2004a). If this is forced, it quickly reveals itself to be an empty contrivance. The development of an "analytic style" (Ogden, 2007, p. 1185) that is experienced as fully authentic is part of an ongoing effort on the part of every analyst to become an analyst in his or her own right. One can achieve this sense of having become "original" only through a painstaking effort to shed, over time, the shackles of orthodoxy, tradition and one's own unconscious irrational prohibitions (Gabbard, 2007). The analyst's struggle with theory as master or servant may be an integral part of this effort. We share the view of Sandler (1983) that each analyst develops a private amalgam or mixed model borrowing from certain aspects of various theories that are consistent with one's own subjectivity and one's own approach to analysis. At the same time we concur with Bion's notion that the analyst must endeavor to forget what he thinks he knows or knows too well to be able to learn from his current experience with the patient. Bion (1987) said to a presenter,

"I would [rely on theory only] … if I were tired and had no idea what was going on…" (p. 58).

Keeping One's Eyes Open to the Way One Is Maturing and Growing Old

As one ages, one is able to speak from experience in a way that one could not previously have done. Often one becomes aware, after the fact, that one has changed, for example, through listening to oneself speak to one's patient. Optimally, the analyst engages in a mourning process in which the loss of youth and the inevitability of old age and death are recognized, accepted and even embraced as a new form of coming into being as a person leading an examined life. The analyst may, in this way, achieve a greater appreciation for the patient's experiences of loss and the ways he has handled or evaded them.

This maturational process occurs both within and outside the analytic setting. The analyst who shows up each day in the consulting room is (ideally) never entirely the same analyst who showed up the previous day. An analyst's capacity to fully grasp a patient's grief may be limited until the analyst himself has navigated his own grief associated with the loss of loved ones and the endings of important periods of his life, for example, the era in which his children are living at home or the era in which his parents are alive.

Difficulties in Becoming an Analyst

The reasons why an analyst may fear "growing up" as an analyst, and the ways he may defend himself against such fears, are legion. In this brief paper, we cannot list, much less explore, these fears and defenses. In the following paragraph, we will offer a few examples of the analyst's flight from potential maturational experiences and forms of defense against such experiences.

The analyst may be afraid that he is so insubstantial as a person that it is not possible for him to develop a voice of his own; or be frightened of the isolation that he imagines will come with his becoming an analyst in his own terms; or fear that with a mature recognition of uncertainty will come unbearable confusion. An analyst may defend himself against these fears and others by engaging in adolescent rebellion against "the analytic establishment" in an effort to avoid defining himself in his own terms; or by speaking early on with a contrived voice of experience when he, in fact, feels painfully lacking as a consequence of his inexperience; or by embracing false certainty in the form of an intense identification with a given school of psychoanalysis, with his own analyst, with an idealized analytic writer and so on. Finally, we must remember that, as much as we love analysis, a part of us hates it as well (Steiner, 2000). Dedication to ongoing analytic work (on ourselves and with patients) consigns us not only to uncertainty, but also to face what we least like about ourselves and others.

Concluding Comments

In this paper, we have discussed some of our maturational experiences and viewed them from several theoretical perspectives. Some readers will recognize something of their own experiences of maturing as analysts in what we have described, while others will not. Indeed, a recurring theme in our essay has been that speaking in generic terms to patients, colleagues and students is antianalytic (in the sense of representing a failure to think and speak for oneself). As Bion (1987) noted in the comment cited at the beginning of this paper, part of becoming an analyst is to evolve in a direction that is neither bound by theory nor driven exclusively by identification with others: "The analyst you become is you and you alone—that is what you use..." (p. 15). Analytic discourse involves what is unique, idiosyncratic and alive in the particular experience of a given individual. Becoming an analyst necessarily involves creating a highly personal identity that is unlike that of any other analyst.

We cannot overstate the difficulty of attempting to live by this ideal. The conscious and unconscious ties that we have to what we think we know are powerful. But the struggle to overcome these ties (at least to a significant degree) is what we ask of ourselves in each session. It has been our experience that when the analyst is off-balance he does his best analytic work.

References

Bion, W. R. (1962a). Learning from experience. In *Seven servants*. New York: Aronson, 1975.

Bion, W. R. (1962b). A theory of thinking. In *Second thoughts* (pp. 110–119). New York: Aronson, 1967.

Bion, W. R. (1970). Attention and interpretation. In *Seven servants*. New York: Aronson, 1975.

Bion, W. R. (1987). Clinical seminars. In *Clinical seminars and other works* (pp. 1–240). London: Karnac.

Freud, S. (1914). On the history of the psychoanalytic movement. In J. Strachey (Ed. & Trans.), *The standard edition of the complete psychological works of Sigmund Freud* (Vol. 14, 1–66). London: Hogarth Press.

Freud, S. (1937). Analysis terminable and interminable. In J. Strachey (Ed. & Trans.), *The standard edition of the complete psychological works of Sigmund Freud* (Vol. 23, 209–253). London: Hogarth Press.

Gabbard, G.O. (2000). On gratitude and gratification. *Journal of the American Psychoanalytic Association, 48,* 697–716.

Gabbard, G. O. (2003). Miscarriages of psychoanalytic treatment with the suicidal patient. *International Journal of Psychoanalysis, 84,* 249–261.

Gabbard, G. O. (2007). "Bound in a nutshell": Thoughts on complexity, reductionism and "infinite space." *International Journal of Psychoanalysis, 88,* 559–574.

Gabbard, G. O., & Lester, E. P. (1995). *Boundaries and boundary violations in psychoanalysis.* Washington, DC: American Psychiatric Association.

Hoffman, I. Z. (1998). *Ritual and spontaneity in the psychoanalytic process: A dialectical-constructivist view.* Hillsdale, NJ: The Analytic Press.

Loewald, H. (1960). On the therapeutic action of psychoanalysis. In *Papers on psychoanalysis* (pp. 221–256). New Haven, CT: Yale University Press, 1980.

Loewald, H. (1979). The waning of the Oedipus complex. In *Papers on psychoanalysis* (pp. 384–404). New Haven, CT: Yale University Press, 1980.

Ogden, T. H. (1991). Some theoretical comments on personal isolation. *Psychoanalytic Dialogues, 1,* 377–390.

Ogden, T. H. (1994). The analytic third: Working with intersubjective clinical facts. *International Journal of Psychoanalysis, 75,* 3–20.

Ogden, T. H. (1997). Reverie and interpretation. *Psychoanalytic Quarterly, 66,* 567–595.

Ogden, T. H. (2004a). This art of psychoanalysis: Dreaming undreamt dreams and interrupted cries. *International Journal of Psychoanalysis, 85,* 857–878.

Ogden, T. H. (2004b). On holding and containing, being and dreaming. *International Journal of Psychoanalysis, 85,* 1349–1364.

Ogden, T. H. (2005). On psychoanalytic writing. *International Journal of Psychoanalysis, 86,* 5–29.

Ogden, T. H. (2006). Reading Loewald: Oedipus reconceived. *International Journal of Psychoanalysis, 87,* 651–666.

Ogden, T. H. (2007). Elements of analytic style: Bion's clinical seminars. *International Journal of Psychoanalysis, 88,* 1185–1200.

Ringstrom, P. (2001). Cultivating the improvisational in psychoanalytic treatment. *Psychoanalytic Dialogues, 11,* 727–754.

Rosenfeld, H. (1987). *Impasse and interpretation: Therapeutic and anti-therapeutic factors in the psychoanalytic treatment of psychotic, borderline and neurotic patients.* London: Tavistock.

Sandler, J. (1983). Reflections on some relations between psychoanalytic concepts and psychoanalytic practice. *International Journal of Psychoanalysis, 64,* 35–45.

Smith, H. F. (2001). Hearing voices. *Journal of the American Psychoanalytic Association, 49,* 781–812.

Stanislavski, C. (1936). *An actor prepares* (E. R. Hapgood, Trans.). New York: Theatre Arts Books.

Steiner, J. (2000). Book review of "A mind of one's own" by R. Caper. *Journal of the American Psychoanalytic Association, 48,* 637–643.

Steiner, J. (2008). Transference to the analyst as an excluded observer. *International Journal of Psychoanalysis, 89,* 39–54.

Winnicott, D. W. (1951). Transitional objects and transitional phenomena. In *Through paediatrics to psycho-analysis* (pp. 229–242). New York Basic Books, 1958.

Winnicott, D. W. (1958a). The theory of the parent–infant relationship. In *The maturational processes and the facilitating environment* (pp. 37–55). New York: International Universities Press, 1965.

Winnicott, D. W. (1958b). The capacity to be alone. In *The maturational processes and the facilitating environment* (pp. 29–36). New York: International Universities Press, 1965.

Winnicott, D. W. (1963). Communicating and not communicating leading to a study of certain opposites. In *The maturational processes and the facilitating environment* (pp. 179–192). New York: International Universities Press, 1965.

18

Knowing Oneself From the Inside Out, Knowing Oneself From the Outside In

The "Inner" and "Outer" Worlds and Their Link Through Action*

Paul Wachtel

▼　▼　▼　▼　▼

INTRODUCTION

The conception of vicious and virtuous circles that is at the heart of the cyclical psychodynamic point of view originated in my efforts to integrate psychoanalytic ideas and methods with those of behavior therapy (later cognitive-behavioral therapy) and then, further, with systemic and experiential points of view (see Wachtel, 1997). It was a crucial conceptual tool in linking the traditional psychoanalytic focus on the "internal" world and the emphasis of behavior therapists (and, often, of systemic therapists as well) on what is often called the "external," the influence of the environmental context and of the actual events that transpire in people's lives.

In attending simultaneously to the observations that were the focus of analysts and those that were at the center of interest for therapists of other persuasions, I was guided by the assumption that each sectarian

---

* An earlier version of this paper appeared in *Psychoanalytic Psychology, 26*(2), 2009, pp. 158–170. Reprinted with permission.

perspective was afflicted to some degree by tunnel vision or by an overly enamored attachment to the observations its paradigm directed the therapist or researcher to attend to. Once one's methods are devised to notice certain things (and, inevitably, to ignore or marginalize other things), the process becomes self-perpetuating. What one notices, the phenomena and causal relationships one's methods enable one to see, becomes what seems of paramount importance, and, hence, one continues to embrace the methods that enable one to see those things in particular (and consequently continues to *see* those things in particular and to have further reason to continue in the same mode of looking). This is the case whether it is the phenomena revealed by free association that shape one's views or the phenomena revealed by controlled laboratory experiments. It is only by "looking across the picket fence" (or massive border fortifications) that divide the various paradigms, and considering how one might fashion a theoretical structure that incorporates what *each* has observed, that one can begin the process of overcoming that tunnel vision.

More recently, I have linked my earlier integrative efforts to the evolving framework of relational psychoanalysis. The cyclical psychodynamic point of view preceded the emergence of an explicitly relational conceptualization of the psychoanalytic paradigm (cf. Wachtel, 1977; Greenberg & Mitchell, 1983; Mitchell, 1988). But as the relational turn in psychoanalysis began to take form and to achieve increasing influence in the psychoanalytic world, I devoted increasing attention to its literature and developed a strong interest in exploring its relationship to the cyclical psychodynamic point of view. In doing so, it became clear that cyclical psychodynamics and relational psychoanalysis were buds from the same tree and that the nature of the cyclical psychodynamic conceptualization could be made clearer and could be further developed, by explicitly exploring its relationship to the variety of theoretical perspectives that constituted the broad umbrella of relational psychoanalysis. The most detailed and elaborated examination of these matters appears in my book *Relational Theory and the Practice of Psychotherapy* (Wachtel, 2008), but the paper reprinted here provides a concise introduction to the issues.

Relational psychoanalysis is itself an integrative point of view, at least within the spectrum of psychoanalytic ideas. It brings together the concepts and clinical perspectives of interpersonal theory, object relations theory, and self psychology, as well as important elements of feminist thought, constructivism, and research on mother–infant interaction (Aron, 1996). Cyclical psychodynamic theory embraces this integrative thrust, but unites it with an interest in still further integrations—with cognitive-behavioral, systemic, and experiential approaches to therapy and with psychologically oriented social criticism (e.g., Wachtel, 1983, 1997, 1999, 2003). In all of these integrative aspects of the cyclical psychodynamic point of view, the central element is attention to how the "inner" world of motives, thoughts, fantasies, expectations, and idiosyncratic perceptions and interpretations of events *both shapes and is shaped by* the "outer" world of actual transactions between people and of larger social, economic, and cultural forces. Thus, the present examination of the relation between "inner" and "outer"—including its implicit conclusion that the very distinction between these two thoroughly intertwined perspectives on human experience is faulty and misleading—represents an excellent introduction to the cyclical psychodynamic version of relational thought, and I am delighted that it is included in this volume.

References

Aron, L. (1996). *A meeting of minds: Mutuality in psychoanalysis.* Hillsdale, NJ: The Analytic Press.

Greenberg, J. R., & Mitchell, S. A. (1983). *Object relations in psychoanalytic theory.* Cambridge, MA: Harvard University Press.

Mitchell, S. A. (1988). *Relational concepts in psychoanalysis.* Cambridge, MA: Harvard University Press.

Wachtel, P. L. (1983). *The poverty of affluence: A psychological portrait of the American way of life.* New York: Free Press.

Wachtel, P. L. (1997). *Psychoanalysis, behavior therapy, and the relational world.* Washington, DC: American Psychological Association.

Wachtel, P. L. (1999). *Race in the mind of America: Breaking the vicious circle between Blacks and Whites.* New York: Routledge.

Wachtel, P. L. (2003). Full pockets, empty lives: A psychoanalytic exploration of the contemporary culture of greed. *American Journal of Psychoanalysis, 63,* 101–120.

Wachtel, P. L. (2008). *Relational theory and the practice of psychotherapy.* New York: Guilford.

Traditionally, it has been the patient's inner life that the analyst has tried to illuminate— thoughts, feelings, affectively charged images of self and other, unacknowledged wishes, fears, and fantasies. The patient's behavior, the actual actions he or she takes in the world and the impact of those actions on others in the patient's relational world, has tended to be a secondary concern. Manifest behavior has been viewed as a surface phenomenon, something more suited to the focus of social psychology than to the deeper concerns of psychoanalysis about what underlies that behavior (see Wachtel, 2003). Thus, self-knowledge is typically pursued from the inside out (Boston Change Process Study Group, 2007).

In this paper, I want to look at the role of understanding oneself "from the outside in"—looking at how one's actions in the world lead to consequences that in turn maintain or reshape the very nature of the inner world. Such a perspective regards the inner world not merely as a residue of early relational experiences that, once they are "internalized," reside in the psyche as more or less fixed or enduring features of the personality, sealed off from the influence of later "external" events. Rather it views the inner world as genuinely dynamic, fluctuating and continually reconstituting itself in response to the ongoing experiences of daily life, even as it simultaneously shapes those daily experiences in a repeated pattern of bidirectional reciprocal causality.

As I hope will be clear as I proceed, what I mean by understanding from the outside in is not a replacement for understanding from the inside out. Rather, each perspective expands, illuminates, and deepens the understanding of the other. Just as the shaping and maintenance of the inner world by daily experience is complemented by the simultaneous shaping of daily experience by the expectancies and schemas of the inner world, so too are the dynamics of the psyche and the dynamics of overt behavior bidirectional, reciprocal, and mutually contextually embedded. The two perspectives are inseparable in the lived experience of self and in coming to know oneself more deeply and thoroughly. We cannot adequately know ourselves from the inside out without knowing ourselves from the outside in, and we cannot adequately know ourselves from the outside in without knowing ourselves from the inside out.

Stating the matter somewhat differently, and anticipating a point I will develop further as I proceed, understanding one's impact on others is utterly central to understanding oneself—and this not just because how we are experienced by others affects what our lives are like but because the very nature of the inner world is constructed from the ongoing dialectic between our already existing proclivities, desires, fears, and representations (our preexisting psychological "structures") and the life experiences that these structures and inclinations both bring about and are continually either maintained or changed by. Here again, the influences are simultaneous and bidirectional, not a matter of one perspective replacing the other. We do not know ourselves in any deep or meaningful way unless we know and understand our impact on others, nor do we understand very well our impact on others without understanding the affective and motivational wellsprings of the behavior that overtly expresses itself in our daily living. Especially is this the case because the impact of our behavior on others resides not simply in the acts per se but in the subtle qualities of affect and meaning that inevitably accompany them.

Much of the time, especially in cases of relatively severe pathology, it may look like the inner world is more or less autonomous, that it is sealed off from the influence of daily life, that it persists in "infantile" modes of thought and fantasy that are quite divorced from the mental activity that is more familiar to us from daily experience. Viewed through the lenses that have been traditional in psychoanalytic thought, the causal priority of the inner world is so obvious and compelling that the reciprocal feedback loops, the ways the inner world is shaped by the experiences of daily life as much as it is the source of those experiences, are hardly visible or, at best, recede into the background. That these equal and opposite force fields jointly maintain the consistency of personality patterns and self-experience, that the inner world is as much a product of current daily living as it is of the early experiences that originally gave rise to the images and affective predispositions that constitute it, has clearly not been the mainstream view in the psychoanalytic tradition. I argue here that it should be.

It is certainly true that the inner world has a powerful impact on what we do and how we feel about and make sense of the events of our lives. Our behavior and the emotions that accompany it powerfully reflect who we are. To deny that half of the complex pattern of feedback that is characteristic of living personalities is as foolish as denying the other half of the sequence—the ways the continuing experiences of daily living shape the inner world, maintaining some proclivities and modifying others. We fail to understand the inner world itself when we focus too exclusively on the inside-out sequences, as psychoanalytic accounts so often have. For the inner world is not some autonomous realm, sealed off from daily experience; what we call the inner world is the subjective nexus of the experience of living itself. Without understanding how responsive to the continuing events of our lives are the fantasies, images, representations, desires, and affects that constitute the inner world, we problematically restrict our understanding of the inner world's dynamics. Daily life and enduring psyche are not two separate realms. They are part and parcel of each other and of the experience of living.

A Clinical Example: Karl

Let me offer some examples of what I have in mind when I state that the inner world must be understood from the outside in as much as from the inside out. Karl was a handsome, charming man from a family of high achieving financiers and philanthropists. He was married to a woman, Eleanor, who was attractive, intelligent, and very nice. If that trio of adjectives sounds both positive and bland, it is intended to. The relationship between Karl and Eleanor had been marked more by stability than vitality. By all external appearances, Karl's family life and marriage were successful and unproblematic. They lived on Park Avenue and had two sons who were both excellent students and budding tennis stars. Indeed, the marriage was not at all the focus of the concerns that brought Karl into therapy, which centered more on certain inhibitions and conflicts in his work life. However over time, the focus of the therapy shifted, as Karl began to be more and more unhappy about the lack of passion in the marriage. This lack of vitality and passion was evident not only in their infrequent and lackluster sexual experiences together but also in the general tenor of the relationship. Karl felt hurt by Eleanor's lack of passion for him, but he also felt guilty about his own lack of passion for her. These nagging concerns had been in and out of his awareness for a long time, but they became an experienced "problem" only in the safe confines of the therapy. Previously, Karl had been too hampered by his guilt and self-disparagement to permit himself to dwell much on his dissatisfactions in the marriage; indeed, even to believe he had a right to be dissatisfied. However, when the therapy began to make room for the more vital, confident, and expansive side of Karl, which he had previously—for reasons I will elaborate on shortly—viewed as excessive and "narcissistic," he began to want more from the marriage and—very important—to feel less guilty about wanting more.

In understanding how the inside-out and outside-in directions simultaneously shaped Karl's life and subjective experience, it is important to note—and equally important not to overemphasize—that, in the fashion we have come to expect, Eleanor evoked in Karl many affective responses and self- and object representations originally associated with and evolving out of Karl's relationship to his mother. Karl's mother was a very moralistic and critical figure in his life, an overseer of standards virtually impossible to meet, because to please her Karl had to be both the high achiever/master of the universe that his father was and, at the same time, to be irreproachably modest, not too big for his breeches, free of any taint of unseemly self-regard. Karl was always both too much and not enough in her eyes, and he experienced himself as that in Eleanor's eyes as well. On both a conscious and unconscious level, this experience of Eleanor as the inheritor or carrier of his mother's affect-laden representations evoked a painful set of feelings and self-reproaches for Karl, as well as images of the potentially disastrous consequences of his being fully himself, whether as a high achiever on the one hand or as someone hurting and longing to gratify unmet needs on the other.

In the work Karl and I did together, many hours were spent exploring, in a fashion intimately familiar to a psychoanalytic readership, the unconscious desires, fantasies, and self and object representations that were associated with Karl's conflicted relationship with Eleanor. To understand Karl in the most clinically useful way, however, something else was needed as well. For every feature of this "internal" configuration was intimately related to the ways that Karl behaved in his daily life and to the ways it led Eleanor and others to behave toward him. The mix of expectations inherited from his relationship with his mother—but also constituting Karl's longstanding and still ongoing schemas of intimate relationships—led him to be deeply conflicted. He felt humiliated by the perception that he was insufficiently successful in the world (measured, that is, against the almost mythic figure of his father in his mother's eyes) and by what felt almost like a motivated refusal by his wife to be turned on by him sexually. At the same time, he felt guilty about (and humiliated in a different way by) the anger this circumstance evoked in him and even by his very desire to be admired and responded to. The result was that he often became sullen and withdrawn at home.

Karl could not find a way to actually talk to his wife about his wishes for more vitality in their relationship or to approach her in a way that might actually lead to that happening. Indeed, until he had worked through some other issues in the therapy, he could not even permit himself to appreciate very clearly that he was dissatisfied in the marriage. Instead, he simply felt vaguely unhappy, grumpy, and withdrawn—a way of experiencing himself (and of presenting himself) that fed on itself, further increasing his unhappiness and sense of unworthiness, and making it even harder to feel he had the right to ask more of Eleanor. Hence, it led him still again into impotent, silent withdrawal and the next repetition of the cycle. He experienced Eleanor as dissatisfied with him, and much of his behavior at home was designed to ward off her criticisms. However, because his most frequent way of shielding himself from those criticisms was to withdraw from her, he ended up perpetuating and exacerbating the very circumstance he was trying to evade, because Eleanor's greatest dissatisfaction was with the withdrawal itself.

Those of you familiar with the literature of family therapy will recognize here a version of the pattern that family therapists refer to as pursuer and distancer (e.g., Betchen, 2005; Napier, 1978), with Eleanor in the role of pursuer and Karl in the role of distancer. The situation was further complicated, however, by Eleanor's also having a strong element of withdrawal and distancing as her own way of warding off the painful experience of rejection. Even more ironic, both of them also engaged in such withdrawal as a means of warding off another painful feeling—emptiness. Of course, that withdrawal only added to that feeling.

In his subjective experience of this pattern of behavior on his own part and this pattern between them, Karl experienced himself as, on one hand, deadened and dull and, on the other, as unjustifiably expecting what it was unreasonable and childish to expect. He literally ran past mirrors, fearful he would catch himself being narcissistic if he looked at himself and thought himself handsome—a sort of forbidden truth about himself that he both feared acknowledging and yearned to acknowledge. This latter conflict was further exacerbated by one additional—and not surprising—response by Karl to this complex of feelings and attitudes. When he was at parties and other social gatherings, and especially when he had had a couple of drinks, he was far more seductive than he dared let himself realize, and women responded to his behavior very obviously and enthusiastically. He thus further had to cope with guilt over experiences that he both sensed and could not bear to sense he had contributed to bringing about as well as with the further pain of the contrast between the responsiveness of women who were not really part of his life and the lack of response shown by his wife.

Further adding to the ways in which the patterns of both behavior and subjective experience between Karl and Eleanor dovetailed with—and perpetuated—the internal representations that his relationship with Eleanor had inherited from his relationship with his mother. Eleanor, like his mother, derided him for the very expressions of vitality and expansiveness that Karl was struggling to accept and liberate in himself. Indeed, she, like his mother, was palpably and conspicuously hurt by Karl's popularity and ease with people, which contrasted sharply with her own unease with people. Part of her hurt and unease derived from the very obvious interest that other women showed in Karl, but it went well beyond that. It might arise just as readily after a gathering of family or friends, and be about the response of other men, who enjoyed Karl's wit and social ease, or of her own parents, who she felt liked and enjoyed Karl more than they did her. When Eleanor referred to how much everyone loved Karl, how funny and charming they found him, as she did frequently, the tone of her observations was more reproachful than complimentary. Just as was the case with Karl's mother, Eleanor's depressive experience of herself became an implicit criticism of Karl for the very qualities that he was struggling to own, qualities that he had painfully submerged to preserve whatever tie he did have to mother, and then to Eleanor. These were, of course, also the qualities that it was one of the therapy's aims to liberate in Karl.

However the pattern began—and much of what transpired between Karl and Eleanor had to do with the ways that the preexisting inner worlds of each of them intersected— once it got going, as it did rather early in their relationship, it became largely self-perpetuating. The response of each kept the response of the other the same, and hence kept his and her own response (and his or her own subjective experience) the same, over and over. The internal configuration of affectively charged images and perceptual inclinations that shaped Karl's experience of Eleanor and of what was happening between them left him feeling unable to reach out to Eleanor *or* to complain to her, at least in an explicit and manifest way. And both his experience of his own behavior with her (which made him feel ashamed both of his passivity and of his silent hostility) and his experience of her response to his behavior (which left him experiencing her as the repetition of the implacably unresponsive and critical mother of his inner world) kept the images and representations that dominated his inner world firmly fixed in place—and ready to generate anew the very pattern of mutual relational behavior that maintained them.

Put differently, the resemblances and continuities between Karl's inner state as an adult and his inner state as a child did not just persist because his internal world was sealed off, buried, like an archaeological shard, beneath covering layers (of defenses and countercathexes). His inner state was, rather, a living (though largely unconscious) response to the dynamically generated but largely unchanging conditions of Karl's life. His inner world was both cause and effect of that life, as his life was both effect and cause of his inner world.*

A Second Illustration: The Case of Arlene

A similar dynamic interplay between the patient's long-standing inclinations and representations and the actions and reactions of everyday life could be seen in the very different case of Arlene (as, I think it is important to note, it may be seen in just about every case at which one looks sufficiently closely). Arlene had grown up in a family that was rather stressed and preoccupied, with little time or psychic energy for the ins and outs of their children's experience. The family was an intact one and even a loving one (accounting for Arlene's many strengths), but it was not an attentive one. Arlene's parents were, one might say, overly "efficient." As soon as they "got" what Arlene wanted or was saying, they took action. Often the actions were reasonably close to the mark, but they missed the subtleties of her experience and gave her little sense that she had the space to elaborate on her experience or to think out loud in the presence of a supportive and attentive parental figure. As she described her current experiences with her boyfriend, her parents, or with friends or acquaintances, it seemed clear that, like Karl but with a different set of specifics, Arlene was caught in a vicious circle in which inner and outer events continuously prompted and maintained each other.

---

* It should be clear that I am not contending that Karl's subjective experience was a simple product of what was "objectively" transpiring. The idiosyncratic construction of experience out of the materials of one's lived life, the ways prior experiences shape our expectations and perceptions, the role of both wishful and defensive thinking on what we make of experiences, even the simple sheer impossibility of seeing social reality free of our situated perspective, is at the heart of contemporary psychoanalytic thought, and at the heart of my own thinking as well (see, e.g., Wachtel, 2008). However, it is essential not to confuse these insights with the idea that we simply "distort," or to fail to acknowledge how powerfully what is actually going on does shape the subjective world, how much it is responsive, not sealed off (cf. Aron, 1996; Gill, 1982, 1983, 1984; Hoffman, 1998; Mitchell, 1988).

In Arlene's case, it became apparent that from rather early in her life Arlene's response to the often perfunctory parental attention to what she was saying was to repeat herself in a fashion that could feel rather obsessional to others. Elaborating here imaginatively on the bare bones of an incident she once described in the therapy, one might imagine her, at age 12, trying to decide whether to sleep over at a friend's house the night before an exam for which they were studying together. Discussing the pros and cons with her parents, she might indicate that on one hand she did not want to hurt her friend's feelings by saying no and also that there was a possibility they might actually get more studying done if she spent the night there but that on the other hand she felt that she would do better on the exam if she had a good night's sleep in her own bed. After discussing it for a while, with her clear (if conflicted) preference being to come home after studying, her parents would, with a touch of impatience (because the discussion had gone on so long) indicate that it seemed that Arlene preferred to come home and they thought that was a good idea. Then, after agreeing that this was the best course, but not having really having had the sense that she had been carefully listened to, Arlene might say, repeating in essence what she had just said a moment ago, "So I think I'll call Sally and tell her that I don't want to stay over at her house after we study together, that I'd prefer to come home and be rested at home before the test." Having just gone over this with Arlene, and having already affirmed this thought of Arlene's more than once, her parents, this time around, would perhaps just give a perfunctory nod or "uh huh," while hardly looking up from their newspaper. This in turn would leave Arlene still feeling unsure she had been heard and had had an attentive sounding board to check out the logic of her decision. So she would again say some variant of the same thing. "Because I think I will do better on the exam if I sleep in my own bed and can go to sleep early in familiar surroundings." Here again, her parents—who were basically good-natured and did not wish to be rejecting but were also preoccupied and inpatient (and, as the pattern had evolved and repeated itself frequently, were in essence confident there was no new content in what Arlene was saying)—would give some perfunctory response to what was, for them, a rather tiresome feature of their otherwise loved daughter. However, the perfunctoriness of their response would elicit still another repetitive variation of the same response from Arlene in a sequence that could go on for a surprisingly long number of repetitions.

In her adult life, this pattern had been extended to her boyfriend and close female friends, and even to teachers and colleagues, who similarly seemed to genuinely care about Arlene and, even, to listen with real interest to her "initial" presentations of her thoughts (Arlene was very smart and often had an interesting take on things). However, they also, it seemed, began to feel a little crazy and frustrated at the repetitive and obsessional nature of Arlene's reassurance seeking and going over things again and again. And thus with them too, over time Arlene's response to their response to Arlene's response fueled the perpetuation of the pattern.

Arlene's expectancies and representations of the attitudes of others were, from one vantage point, distortions; most people in her life were not almost automatically predisposed to listen perfunctorily and with minimal attention, as her parents were. Had Arlene approached them in the fashion that most people approach thinking something through with a friend or loved one, they would probably have been attentive and responsive. And had that happened, Arlene's own tendency to repeat herself in seemingly interminable fashion would have gradually diminished, creating a positive dynamic or virtuous circle, in which each move toward greater cogency or succinctness made it easier for others to pay attention, which made it easier for her to be more concise, which made it easier for others to listen, and so forth, and so forth. However, because the relational schemas that guide us from within do not change on a dime, Arlene would continue to relate to others as if they were going to need a dozen repetitions to be wrestled into paying attention. And before her schemas could begin to accommodate to the differences between the way people were actually responding to her and the way she expected them to, her conversational partners would begin to respond to her repetitiveness and—without having had an initial inclination or tendency to be inattentive—they would begin to unintentionally "confirm" her expectations.*

Much of this would go on without awareness, either on Arlene's part or on the part of the other people in her life who served as "accomplices" (Wachtel, 1991) in maintaining the pattern. Arlene was largely unaware of the inner expectations that drove her, or of the behavior itself; that is, she was not really aware of how repetitive she actually was. She had, to be sure, been told this at times, and could be aware of it momentarily. However, in the midst of being driven to try to get the full attention of the other, she was aware only of what she was saying, of what she was thinking out loud about, not of the glazed look in the other's eyes or the relentless repetition in her own chewing over of the issue. In the fashion that is familiar to psychoanalytic clinicians, although she in some way registered both the other's response and the way it affected her own contribution to the conversation, she defensively

---

* I have elsewhere (Wachtel, 1981, 2008) depicted this process as a kind of "race" in which the question is which happens first: Do Person One's perceptual schemas change in response to the differences between Person Two's behavior and Person One's expectations? Or does Person One's behavior, based on her long-standing expectations, lead Person Two to change his own behavior before Person One has had a chance to see that her expectations were inaccurate? When the latter happens, as is often the case, we have a process of "pseudo-confirmation" (Wachtel, 1999), in which the person maintains the old expectations on the basis of what appears to be simply a matter of experience but in which the self-fulfilling nature of those expectations is never understood.

warded off focal awareness of this, effective awareness that can lead to new behavior (Allen, Fonagy, & Bateman, 2008; Fonagy, 1991; Wallin, 2007). In similar fashion, the "accomplices" too were registering what was going on; that was why their attention was beginning to flag. However, they too were largely doing this on automatic pilot rather than with focal awareness.

Not surprisingly, the pattern was evident in the therapy sessions too, and indeed, it was in part my own response to Arlene's obsessional repetitiveness—at first in the more automatic fashion that characterizes an enactment, and later with reflective awareness—that enabled me to discern the pattern more clearly and to understand its pervasiveness in her life. Such attention to the two-person processes occurring in the patient–therapist relationship is, of course, the stock in trade of contemporary psychoanalytic clinicians. It is probably evident, however, from what I have said thus far that I do not focus on that relationship as exclusively as do most other relational thinkers. Much of what I have been arguing in this paper points to a version of relational thinking in which very considerable attention is also paid to the consequential reciprocal dynamics between the patient and the *other* key people in his life (see Wachtel, 2008, especially Chapter 12). It is in the countless interactions with other people, which constitute the texture and substance of one's life, that the dynamics of personality are perpetuated or changed. Without attention to those interactions—not just as "reflections" of the dynamics of the internal world but also as the engine that maintains the images, affects, and motivational states that constitute it—the process of therapeutic change is seriously impeded.

A Potential Terminological Confusion and an Opportunity to Further Refine the Formulation Offered

In distinguishing between knowing oneself from the inside out and knowing oneself from the outside in, I am using a terminology that might readily be confused with that used by Bromberg (1991) in an important paper on "knowing one's patient inside out." Examining where Bromberg's formulation and mine overlap and where they differ may help to further clarify the implications of the point of view I am presenting here and to highlight where it represents a departure from some of the common assumptions and predilections that have guided psychoanalytic thought and practice. In this regard, it is important to notice that where Bromberg refers to knowing the patient inside out, I refer to knowing the patient "from" the inside out and "from" the outside in. What I am emphasizing is a conceptualization that addresses the *direction* of the reciprocal, interweaving casual sequences in psychic life.

Bromberg's (1991) term, knowing someone "inside out," in contrast, corresponds to the common English phrase that designates knowing someone well. We know someone inside out when we know him or her very thoroughly and deeply. The distinction is important to note here because it is precisely my point that to know someone inside out, one must know him or her both *from* inside out and *from* outside in.

Is the distinction between knowing someone inside out and knowing someone "from" the inside out just semantics, equivalent to asking what "is" is? I do not think so. Bromberg (1991) did not use a different terminology from mine simply because he did not like prepositions. What his terminology represents is a joining of the idea of knowing someone deeply and the images of depth and interiority that have long dominated psychoanalytic thought.* In elaborating his formulation, Bromberg at once affirmed that emphasis on interiority and challenged it, or at least usefully complicated it. In the history of our field, he stated, "There have been relatively few major figures who have been able to bridge the domains of experiential and observable reality as clinicians and were also able to translate the analytic process into written language that itself has one foot "inside" and the other "outside" (p. 411).

In this respect, then, Bromberg (1991) too was trying to bridge these domains, rather than to privilege inside over outside. He offered a two-person perspective on understanding the patient that is particularly rooted in the concept of enactment. We do not understand the patient simply by looking "inside" him, as an outside observer examining the properties of a separate system. We know the patient very largely through our own experience of being with him. This constitutes one important point of overlap between Bromberg's conception of "knowing the patient inside out" and my own emphasis on knowing the patient from both inside out and outside in. There are other points of convergence between his views and mine as well—for example, in his focus on "finding a voice for what may drive the self mad if it speaks" (p. 408), which seems to me to overlap with my own focus on *making room for* the experiences that the patient has fearfully cast aside rather than merely "interpreting" them and confronting the patient with their existence (Wachtel, 2008). However, there are also some important differences in what Bromberg and I view as relevant to enabling us to know the patient "inside out" and in a way that is optimally useful therapeutically.

At one point in his paper, Bromberg (1991) noted that,

> To someone more traditionally interpersonal, it might seem preferable had I described knowing one's patient "outside in" and thereby emphasized the relational field as the medium through which internalization occurs. Because

---

* See Wachtel (2003) and Boston Change Process Study Group (2007); see also Schafer's (1976) critique of spatial metaphors in psychoanalytic thought.

I choose otherwise, my terminology may make the concept of participant observation appear to be overbalanced on the side of observation...Obviously, there is always action on the analyst's part, and that includes his state of receptivity; the analyst cannot choose not to be active as a participating center of subjectivity. (pp. 415–416)

Here is where, despite the important similarities in Bromberg's (1991) conceptualization and mine, the "interiority bias" in Bromberg's formulation leads him to gloss over the role of mutual actions that I have been highlighting in this paper. Although Bromberg referred to "action" on the therapist's part, that action seems very largely limited to being an active receiver, and his emphasis on knowing the patient inside out is here framed by him as an *alternative* to knowing him "outside in." In contrast, the present formulation, while in no way less interested in subjectivity than is Bromberg or other psychoanalytic thinkers, does not privilege understanding the patient (or the analyst) as a center of subjectivity over understanding them as centers of action in the world. What I am advocating is a dialectical conception, in which the seeming contradiction between viewing patient and analyst as centers of subjectivity and viewing them as centers of action is resolved through an understanding of the ways that action and subjectivity constantly and continuously shape and determine each other. We do not understand the patient inside out if we do not understand the way his inner world and his actual behavior and its consequences continually recreate each other. In previous writing I referred to this central psychological dynamic as cyclical psychodynamics (e.g., Wachtel, 1993, 2008).

Far from distracting from or abandoning concern with the inner world, attention to the details of the person's daily life—including not just how the patient sees things or feels about things (as important as those are) but also what he *does*—is the only way to adequately understand the inner world, both theoretically and clinically. The inner world is not set in stone in the pre-oedipal years but is an alive, continually responsive attribute of a *person* who is *living-in-the-world*. There are ways, to be sure, in which the inner world can seem to be rigidly adherent to old images and old programs, can seem to be unresponsive to what is presently going on. It is these ways that lead numerous clinicians and theorists to depict the patient's desires or expectations as infantile, primitive, or archaic, and to refer to those expectations as fantasies. However, the image of a fixed inner world, unresponsive to the play of actual events and constituting instead a world of "fantasy" (or, in the Kleinian tradition, "phantasy") is a reflection of the traditional lack of attention to daily life experiences that has been a part of the psychoanalytic point of view for a long time.

In a number of conversations I have had recently with respected people in our field, they have conveyed that one of the most helpful features of my book on the clinical implications of a thoroughgoing relational perspective

(Wachtel, 2008) is that it enabled them to feel less guilty about spending a significant amount of session time discussing the patient's daily life. They were aware that they were probably not at all exceptional in paying such attention to the events of the patient's life—in truth almost everyone does—but they had a nagging sense that they were not being "psychoanalytic" while doing so and that this material was more "superficial" (cf. Boston Change Process Study Group, 2007; Wachtel, 2003).

In the history of psychoanalysis, this attitude derived at first from the prominence of free association and the interpretation of transference as central to the clinical method of psychoanalysis and from the archaeological model of depth as a key theoretical metaphor (Spence, 1982; Stolorow & Atwood, 1997; Stolorow, Orange, & Atwood, 2001; Wachtel, 2003, 2008). More recently, it has derived particularly from the advances in our understanding of enactments (e.g., Aron, 2003; Bass, 2003; Bromberg, 1996; Hirsch, 1998; Jacobs, 1986; Maroda, 1998; McLaughlin, 1991; Stern, 2003, 2004) and the move from viewing countertransference as a therapeutic error or sign of personal flaws in the analyst to the appreciation that countertransference is not only pervasive and inevitable but is also an invaluable source of therapeutic understanding. These have been enormous advances, and they have enabled our clinical interventions to be more powerful, sophisticated, and grounded in the clinical process. However it is also essential to recognize that in certain ways we have made one of our great advances simultaneously into one of our most significant constraints and blinders. There has evolved a tendency to be what we might call "session-centric"—that is, to focus on the therapeutic relationship and the experiences of the two parties in the room almost to the exclusion of everything else.

As I have just noted, this has probably not kept analysts from hearing a good deal about the patient's daily life; most patients, after all, would not tolerate this being ignored. However the tendency to view clinical work directed to the patient's daily life as superficial or not "really psychoanalytic" has hampered the development of a well-thought-through theory of everyday life or, put differently, a well-thought-through theory of the relation between the inner world and the world of daily transactions. As a result, guidelines for exploring the everyday life of the patient, sophisticated methods of inquiry that can reveal or uncover as powerfully in this realm as free association does in the realm of the patient's conflicted desires and associative networks, have been slow to evolve.* In turn, the failure to

---

* One exception to this general trend is psychoanalytic work that has been inspired by the ideas of Harry Stack Sullivan. Outside the psychoanalytic realm, important contributions can be found in the systemic inquiries of family therapists, which reveal sequences and patterns that are not at first readily apparent.

inquire in sufficient detail in this realm, and thereby to gather the data that would *justify* inquiring more carefully, has fed back to seemingly give further credence to the theories that placed everyday life in a secondary position to begin with. We thus encounter an epistemological vicious circle that, in a sense, parallels the vicious circles that I have been emphasizing thus far: The absence of attention to and of methods for effectively investigating the fine-grained reciprocal feedback processes of daily life outside the consulting room—in contrast, say, to the ways that contemporary infant researchers study such feedback processes so masterfully—has led to the bolstering of theories that privilege the past and the "internal" and manifest a relative lack of interest in everyday life and hence to still further impediments to developing the methods of inquiry that would *make* everyday life more interesting to analysts.

From another vantage point, the theoretical lacuna to which I am referring reflects a failure to notice that in large measure the evolution of the two-person point of view has been largely restricted to two domains, the transactions between patient and analyst in the session and the transactions between mother and infant. In these two realms, a thoroughgoing two-person model, emphasizing the mutual coconstruction of experience by the two parties, is strongly evident. In the realm of infancy, from Winnicott's (1975) early observation that "there is no such thing as a baby" but only a "nursing couple," (p. 99) to the groundbreaking studies of psychoanalytically oriented infant researchers such as Stern (1985), Beebe (2000; Beebe & Lachmann, 1998, 2002), and Tronick (Cohn & Tronick, 1988), there has been an increasing emphasis on the way that the early evolution of personality is coconstructed, mutual, and reciprocal. Similarly, in the understanding of the patient's experience in the session and the way that the phenomena observed in the session emerge, it is increasingly apparent that they do not simply "bubble up" from the unconscious but reflect an intricate back-and-forth in which both parties are both observers and observed (cf. Aron, 1991; Hoffman, 1983), bringing forth responses from the other even as they simultaneously respond to the other. However the rest of the patient's life, the huge swath of living between the nursery and the consulting room, has been very largely addressed, even by relational writers, in essentially one-person terms (see Wachtel, 2008). The painstaking analysis of mutual, bidirectional coconstruction of experience that is evident in the two "anchor areas" (the nursery and the consulting room) is not nearly as evident in the discussions of why the patient is having difficulty in his life. There the patient's difficulties are more often described as a reflection of the world of internalized objects, rather than as a consequence of fully two-person dynamics in which the internal world is understood as a product as well as a cause of what is transpiring, not only in the consulting room but throughout the person's life.*

The keen attention to intersubjective or two-person processes at the two anchor points has, in a sense, served to obscure the relative *absence* of a thoroughgoing two-person perspective in addressing the rest of the patient's life (Wachtel, 2008). The aim of this chapter, and of the clinical examples presented, is to call our attention to this gap and to offer a theoretical perspective, uniting traditional psychoanalytic ideas with an emphasis on consequential action that has been largely absent from psychoanalytic discourse. When such a theoretical view is employed, it is no longer necessary to supplement the two-person perspective with a dash of one-person thinking (see, e.g., Ghent, 1989; Modell, 1984) to capture the deeply unconscious, stubbornly persistent subjective roots of our behavior and experience. The latter, it turns out, is not additional to or separate from our responsiveness to the behavior and characteristics of the person with whom we are interacting but is *part and parcel* of that responsiveness (and of the responsiveness of the other, in similar fashion, to our own behavior, affective tone, and enduring characteristics).

The case material I have offered is intended to illustrate not only how the two-person and reciprocal nature of psychological causality extends well beyond the consulting room but also how the reciprocal *actions* of the patient and those he or she interacts with are a crucial part of the "glue" that holds together and maintains each party's persisting personality and individuality. In emphasizing action, I am not downgrading the importance of affect, motivation, or representations of self and other. Rather, I am suggesting that it is only when we also take into account the effects of the mutual actions that occur in patterned ways millions of times in every person's life that we adequately understand those more traditional foci of psychoanalytic thought and inquiry.

References

Allen, J. G., Fonagy, P., & Bateman, A. (2008). *Mentalizing in clinical practice.* Washington, DC: American Psychiatric.

Aron, L. (1991). The patient's experience of the analyst's subjectivity. *Psychoanalytic Dialogues, 1,* 29–51.

---

* It might be objected that concepts such as projective identification fill this theoretical gap. See Wachtel (2008) for an extended discussion of how the conceptualization offered here differs from projective identification and some of the limitations of the latter concept.

Aron, L. (1996). *A meeting of minds: Mutuality in psychoanalysis.* Hillsdale, NJ: The Analytic Press.

Aron, L. (2003). The paradoxical place of enactment in psychoanalysis: Introduction. *Psychoanalysis Dialogues, 13,* 623–631.

Bass, A. (2003). "E" enactments in psychoanalysis: Another medium, another message. *Psychoanalytic Dialogues, 13,* 657–676.

Beebe, B. (2000). Coconstructing mother–infant distress: The microsynchrony of maternal impingement and infant avoidance in the face-to-face encounter. *Psychoanalytic Inquiry, 20,* 421–440.

Beebe, B., & Lachmann, F. M. (1998). Co-constructing inner and relational processes: Self- and mutual regulation in infant research and adult treatment. *Psychoanalytic Psychology, 15,* 480–516.

Beebe, B., & Lachmann, F. M. (2002). *Infant research and adult treatment: Co-constructing interactions.* Hillsdale, NJ: The Analytic Press.

Betchen, S. (2005). *Intrusive partners-elusive mates: The pursuer-distancer dynamic in couples.* New York: Routledge.

Boston Change Process Study Group (2007). The foundational level of psychodynamic meaning: Implicit process in relation to conflict, defense, and the dynamic unconscious. *International Journal of Psychoanalysis, 88,* 843–860.

Bromberg, P. M. (1991). On knowing one's patient inside out: The aesthetics of unconscious communication. *Psychoanalytic Dialogues, 1,* 399–422.

Bromberg, P. M. (1996). *Standing in the spaces.* Hillsdale, NJ: The Analytic Press.

Cohn, J., & Tronick, E. (1988). Mother–infant face-to-face interaction: Influence is bidirectional and unrelated to periodic cycles in either partner's behavior. *Developmental Psychology, 24,* 386–392.

Fonagy, P. (1991). Thinking about thinking: Some clinical and theoretical considerations in the treatment of a borderline patient. *International Journal of Psychoanalysis, 72,* 639–656.

Ghent, E. (1989). Credo: The dialectics of one-person and two-person psychologies. *Contemporary Psychoanalysis, 25,* 169–211.

Gill, M. M. (1982). *Analysis of transference.* New York: International Universities Press.

Gill, M. M. (1983). The interpersonal paradigm and the degree of the therapist's involvement. *Contemporary Psychoanalysis, 19,* 200–237.

Gill, M. M. (1984). Psychoanalysis and psychotherapy: A revision. *International Review of Psychoanalysis, 11,* 161–179.

Hirsch, I. (1998). The concept of enactment and theoretical convergence. *Psychoanalytic Quarterly, 67,* 78–101.

Hoffman, I. Z. (1983). The patient as interpreter of the analyst's experience. *Contemporary Psychoanalysis, 19,* 389–422.

Hoffman, I. Z. (1998). *Ritual and spontaneity in psychoanalytic process: A dialectical-constructivist view.* Hillsdale, NJ: The Analytic Press.

Jacobs, T. J. (1986). On countertransference enactments. *Journal of the American Psychoanalytic Association, 34,* 289–307.

Maroda, K. J. (1998). Enactment: When the patient's and analyst's pasts converge. *Psychoanalytic Psychology, 15,* 517–535.

McLaughlin, J. T. (1991). Clinical and theoretical aspects of enactment. *Journal of the American Psychoanalytic Association, 39,* 595–614.

Mitchell, S. A. (1988). *Relational concepts in psychoanalysis.* Cambridge, MA: Harvard University Press.

Modell, A. H. (1984). *Psychoanalysis in a new context.* New York: International Universities Press.

Napier, A. Y. (1978). The rejection–intrusion pattern: A central family dynamic. *Journal of Marriage and Family Counseling, 4,* 5–12.

Schafer, R. (1976). *A new language for psychoanalysis.* New Haven, CT: Yale University Press.

Spence, D. P. (1982). *Narrative truth and historical truth.* New York: Norton.

Stern, D. B. (2003). The fusion of horizons: Dissociation, enactment, and understanding. *Psychoanalytic Dialogues, 13,* 843–873.

Stern, D. B. (2004). The eye sees itself: Dissociation, enactment, and the achievement of conflict. *Contemporary Psychoanalysis, 40,* 197–237.

Stern, D. N. (1985). *The interpersonal world of the infant.* New York: Basic Books.

Stolorow, R. D., & Atwood, G. E. (1997). Deconstructing the myth of the neutral analyst: An alternative from intersubjective systems theory. *Psychoanalytic Quarterly, 66,* 431–449.

Stolorow, R. D., Orange, D. M., & Atwood, G. E. (2001). World horizons: A post-Cartesian alternative to the Freudian unconscious. *Contemporary Psychoanalysis, 37,* 43–61.

Sullivan, H. S. (1954). *The psychiatric interview.* New York: Norton.

Wachtel, P. L. (1977). *Psychoanalysis and behavior therapy: Toward an integration.* New York: Basic Books.

Wachtel, P. L. (1981). Transference, schema, and assimilation: The relevance of Piaget to the psychoanalytic theory of transference. In *The annual of psychoanalysis* (Vol. 8, pp. 59–76). New York: International Universities Press.

Wachtel, P. L. (1991). The role of accomplices in preventing and facilitating change. In R. Curtis & G. Stricker (Eds.), *How people change: Inside and outside therapy* (pp. 21–28). New York: Plenum.

Wachtel, P. L. (1993). *Therapeutic communication.* New York: Guilford.

Wachtel, P. L. (1999). *Race in the mind of America: Breaking the vicious circle between Blacks and Whites.* New York: Routledge.

Wachtel, P. L. (2003). The surface and the depths: The metaphor of depth in psychoanalysis and the ways in which it can mislead. *Contemporary Psychoanalysis, 39,* 5–26.

Wachtel, P. L. (2008). *Relational theory and the practice of psychotherapy.* New York: Guilford.

Wallin, D. J. (2007). *Attachment in psychotherapy.* New York: Guilford.

Winnicott, D. W. (1975). *Through paediatrics to psycho-analysis. The International Psycho-Analytical Library, 100,* 1–325.

19

Principles of Improvisation

A Model of Therapeutic Play in Relational Psychoanalysis

Philip Ringstrom

▼ ▼ ▼ ▼ ▼

What does it mean to be improvisational, and what does it mean to not be? An episode of the highly acclaimed NBC television series "The Office" gives us a hint. In it, the notoriously narcissistic boss, Michael Scott (actor Steve Carell) attends an after-office-hours improvisational acting class. Throughout the show's first two seasons, fans of "The Office" became eminently familiar with Michael—recurrently being the buffoon—especially, through his grandiosely inflated self-perceptions. These include, among other things, that he is at heart a really great actor. It is in his improvisation class, however, that they see most clearly why Michael recurrently fails in work, in love, and finally, even in play.

Eager to act, Michael boorishly insists upon being in every scene, and when his teacher yields to his pressure Michael jumps "on stage" adopting the same character over and over. That is, he immediately becomes some version of a pistol brandishing law enforcement officer (e.g., cop, detective, or FBI agent), who within a matter of seconds responds to whatever his scene partner initiates by pointing his two-hand-clasped feigned finger gun while screaming, "Freeze! Detective Michael Scott!" And, no matter how his scene partners reply, he immediately shoots them, they compliantly collapsing to the floor, hand over "lethal chest wound." Sometimes, Michael would really get carried away and begin shooting other classmates who are not even in the scene. Responding to his instructor's withering plea for him to listen to his partner and be open to other dramatic choices, Michael argues

447

that the introduction of a gun in every scene is always dramatically commanding. "Far better," he mutters, than the "boring scenes" his classmates introduce.

Then something truly improvisational happens. His instructor commandingly steps onto the stage and says, "Michael! No more guns! Gimme your guns! All of them!" Caught off guard, Michael begrudgingly starts to mime pulling out a huge array of imaginary pistols from imaginary shoulder, belt, pocket, and ankle holsters, handing them over one after another as his instructor correspondingly mimes taking each and every one, placing them aside on an imaginary table. In that rare instance, Michael, caught off guard from his more typical (invariantly narcissistic) character, is thrust into a moment of playing with rather than compulsively dominating the other.

This brief exchange captures a moment of improvisation in which the *complementarity* of the dominance and submission of the "doer and done to" (Benjamin, 2004) is broken. In other words, there is a shift from *subject-to-object* relating to *subject-to-subject* relating (Benjamin, 2004), or from "I-it" relating to "I-thou" (Buber, 1970). Furthermore, their scene involves a cocreated "third" element to which neither Michael nor his teacher could claim exclusive authorship (Ogden, 1994; Benjamin, 2002; Aron, 2006).

This truly improvised scene requires both actors' creativity, replacing the previous scene's "negative thirdness" (Ringstrom, 2007a, 2007b; Frankel, 2003), a quality that stifles both parties by virtue of one's subjective world view *having* to dominate the other's. All of these terms, along with many others, will be elaborated momentarily, but for now they are suggestive of the role of liberation that improvisation can hold for an analytic dyad floundering in stalemates, deadlocks, and impasses. Meanwhile, this brief vignette also captures something quintessential about how play can fail miserably as well as what needs to happen to restore its improvisational nature.

Being improvisational in analytic treatment is both a synonym for cultivating the play that Winnicott (1971) admonished us to create in psychoanalytic treatment as well as a system of guidelines for how to conceptualize and practice playfully. Improvisation is the mode of play that Winnicott failed to articulate—especially in adult treatment—though surely it is evident in his brilliantly improvisational "squiggle technique" for child psychotherapy. What Winnicott did not have in his conceptual toolbox is that improvisation is the type of play that translates "declarative knowledge into procedural knowledge" (Allen, Fonagy, & Bateman, 2008, p. 182).

In contrast to improvisation, the constraint of play in psychoanalysis will be seen as involving something of a different process, one that will be described in further detail as a process of "mutual inductive identification."

This idea, to be elaborated upon in greater length shortly, corresponds largely with the relational construct of enactments, as well as bidirectional modes of projective identification. The comparison of improvisation with "mutual inductive identification" takes up the rich and largely unsettled question in relational psychoanalysis of the relationship of "enactments, projective identification, and interaction" (Aron, 1996, 2003). At the root of these ideas is the question: When, where, and how can the analytic dyad play with thoughts, feelings, and interactions that arise both within and between them?

Cultivating improvisational play in analytic treatment involves an implicitly radical if not even—some might argue—"subversive" paradigm for therapeutic action. That is because it is in contradistinction to the history of efforts in psychoanalytic treatment to mitigate the influence (e.g., contamination) of the analyst's mind upon the analysand's. Historically, these were understood as the three pillars of technique *abstinence, neutrality, and anonymity* (Mitchell, 1997; Hoffman, 1998). Improvisation takes up the mutual, ineluctable influence that both the analysand's transference has in contextualizing the analyst's countertransference* and vice versa in what can become an inevitable "Mobius loop" of interactivity (Mitchell, 2000; Ringstrom, 1994). Improvisation grasps how both implicitly and explicitly the minds of the analytic participants meet and coauthor a quality of "relational unconscious."

The idea of the relational unconscious (Zeddies, 2000; Gerson, 1995; Harris, 2004) is by now canonical to relational psychoanalysis, exemplified in many ways such as "the psychoanalytic third" (Aron, 2006; Benjamin, 2004; Ogden, 1994; Ringstrom, 2001c). But what has been missing thus far from relational psychoanalysis is a model of therapeutic action that informs and legitimizes the complex process of cultivating the relational unconscious. This is a process whereby the analytic dyad struggles as it teeter-totters back and forth between the radical implications of either instantiating or negating "thirdness." And this is always occurring in relation to the composition or organization of each individual's personality (e.g., will, agency, organizing principles, schemas). In short, improvisation is the melding or interface of the characters of each player while reflecting how each participant's character influences the other's either in ways that playfully open their analytic exploration or constrictively shut it down.

The radical evolutionary position improvisation entails for psychoanalysis and psychotherapy is noted by D. N. Stern (2007):

---

* Countertransference is seen merely as a way of discussing the organization of analyst's transference as it is stimulated in the context of working with the analysand, much as the analysand's is stimulated in working with the analyst.

An improvisational view is a logical next step in the field. In the last decades we have seen the application of chaos and complexity theory, along with dynamic systems theory open up our clinical eyes to various features of the therapeutic situation, such as: the emphasis on process; the approximate equality of the contribution of patient and therapist, i.e., the notion of co-creativity; the unpredictability of what happens in a session from moment to moment, including the expectance of emergent properties; a focus on the present moment of interaction; and the need for spontaneity and authenticity in such a process. (p. 101)

It is the ambition of this project to put the "flesh" of a clinical treatment model on the sterile bones of complexity, chaos, and nonlinear dynamic systems theory.

Elements for Cultivating Improvisation in Psychoanalytic Treatment

There are a multitude of elements involved in cultivating improvisation in psychoanalytic treatment. Improvisation entails states of mutual playfulness and curiosity between analyst and analysand. It constitutes a process that is both mutually regulatory while allowing for both implicit (nonverbal, often unrecognized) and explicit (verbal) elements of mutual recognition* to arise. Improvisation reflects a kind of mutual attunement that rather then necessarily being directed upon one or the other instead produces "emergent relational moments" of the "heretofore unimagined or even imaginable" (Ringstrom, 2007a). Such states are present in an analysis when there is openness within and between the two parties to play with what arises in terms of their respective feelings, thoughts, impressions, associations, reverie, and so on.

To optimize this open and mutually influential process, the customary role of attunement in improvisation is not restricted to the empathic-introspective tradition. Improvisation does not adhere to any particular analytic tradition of inquiry but is focused more upon the playful emergence of a "relational unconscious" between the two parties. In this sense, improvisation is truly a two-way version of intersubjectivity in contrast to the empathic/introspective tradition which is reflective more of a one-way or unidirectional mode. Thus, improvisation occurs around the players capacity to engage in a quality of *yes/and* communication (Nachmanovich, 2001; Ringstrom, 2001b), wherein each takes something of what is spoken or gestured and mirrors

---

* As Aron (1996) notes, that while mutual regulation and influence are inevitable, mutual recognition is lost and found while never being taken for granted in human relations including the analytic dyad. The point of improvisation is that it so facilitates the lost and foundedness of analytic treatment.

recognition of it adding something to it. Back and forth the players are both mirroring one another while also marking their differences. Hence there is both matching and a little mismatching—the latter, according to Coates (1998), lends to the emergence of a creative spark. This process is captured in the following case illustration

"I think that I am angry with you over last week's session," my typically nonconfrontational 45-year-old Eastern European engineer patient, Sami, tells me. In his mannered style, compensating for his self-consciously thick accent, he continues, "I think that I am angry that you were suggesting that I should have more feeling about my mother being hospitalized after her heart attack. I am wondering," he continues, "Who do you think you are to tell me how I should feel? Or, that I should feel anything when I don't!"

"Who am I indeed?" I ponder aloud.

Sami ignores my question and continues, "And, besides, what good is it for me to feel?! How is that supposed to solve my problems—the problem I came to you for, like my procrastination?"

"I am not sure," I venture, "but tell me more about my telling you how you should feel?"*

"It's not very good psychoanalysis, you know. It's not 'exploring my core issues.'"

"So, it looks like I am being more Dr. Phil† than Dr. Phil."

"Or maybe it's because I am not as important to you as some of your other patients."

"Why?" I inquire.

"Because they are more successful than me, you care about them more. They are more important to you."

"You mean like my rich Hollywood celebrities?"

"Yea, like 'George.'"

"You mean George Clooney?" I ask wryly.

"No, more like George Hamilton. You would only see B actors whose careers are mostly over." We're now smiling at one another as if engaged in a wicked game of ping pong.

"Now is that because I practice in the Valley instead of Beverly Hills?"

---

* So far as I recall I never told Sami anything about how he should feel. This raises an interesting question, one Mitchell often introduced, which is what might I have been unwittingly revealing nonverbally about a range of feelings I was wondering that Sami might have, or could have, or might have difficulty experiencing, and how might that be insinuated in my facial expression as an implied directive?

† Dr. Phil is a television celebrity psychotherapist who, after minimal exploration of his guest patient's *issue de jour*, instantaneously dispenses the pabulum of daily advice sandwiched between commercial breaks and the show's end credits.

"Maybe," he retorts. "Just the 'has-beens' live in the Valley." Then he stops abruptly and questions aloud, "Where is all of this coming from?!" as if he is channeling a demon heretofore never given voice.

"Let's not worry about that now; just keep going," I encourage.

Sami says, "Yeah, so no truly successful actor would come to see you! Actually, they wouldn't come to see anyone in L.A."

"Why?" I wonder.

"It's too nice here, the weather is too good, it's too sunny. You'd have to go to New York for a good psychoanalysis, where it's cold, and rainy, and dark, and gloomy, and depressing, where the analysts would all be depressed and understand you." Then Sami's expression shifts markedly to one of sadness. "I feel like crying. I won't, not here, but for the first time, I feel like maybe I could, maybe someday, maybe here too." Six months later, Sami was able to finally cry freely.

One of the first most important points that this illustration captures is that *improvisation is more than just being spontaneous.* One can spontaneously cry out "Yahoo!" without anyone else playing-off-of-and-with this gesture. It is in the ensemble work of improvisation, the playing-off-of-and-with what is being spontaneously generated by both parties, that improvisation is quintessentially relational. This underscores that the mentalizing process of analysis occurs only in the interactive processes of the "here and now" (Allen, Fonagy, & Bateman, 2008). What emerges in the participants' play is surely about the unconscious mind of each, though not seen in isolation from one another. Instead, such moments, such "beginning, middle, and end" episodes (Stern, 2004) constitute configurations of the cocreative, relational unconscious, the kind of "thirdness," in which both parties are paradoxically both distinctive authors while also inextricably coauthors. Hence, neither one may lay claim to being the sole author of their improvised moment. It is from such moments, that blossom things heretofore unimagined or unarticulated.

Thus, in our improvisational moment, Sami and I faced a challenge, though one that was knowable only in retrospect. To access Sami's complicated grief over a mother for whom he has had a very tormented and bitter relationship, a grief that remained unformulated (Stern, 1997) and unarticulated—an "unthought known" (Bollas, 1989)—Sami and I had to first engage in a kind of sadomasochistic play, That is, we had to engage in a kind of playing with his aggressive defensives, the ones keeping us from recognizing his more obscure thoughts and feelings. In doing so, however, we discovered ourselves engaging in a "scene" in which we both had to be able to encounter themes of our respective feelings of inadequacy. Sami had to be free to spontaneously enunciate his need to see me as profoundly lacking, and I had to be able to sincerely play along with his challenge. To do so we had to both accept the stereotypical charges of our respective second-class citizenships. He had to face feeling like an "eminently ignorable immigrant" and I a "comparatively inferior psychoanalyst." And for this play to be experienced as real there had to be some part of each of us that could feel our second-class status without it destroying either of us. What enables the analyst and analysand to engage in such a manner that inoculates their respective narcissistic injuries? I submit that it is the cultivation of a play space, similar to the one that children naturally convene, and that it is one in which "Bang, bang, you're dead" can be taken deadly seriously without anyone really dying.

Now, several points follow from all of this. Improvisational moments arise when the "characters" draw from something real within themselves along with who they are "casting" each other to be. This form of engagement, of course, must also be prereflectively spontaneous, indicative of the subjective unconscious minds of both participants. So, while there were undoubtedly many ways to illuminate Sami's psychic reality, playing improvisationally facilitated this illumination in a very enlivened and relational way. It gave access not only to his unknown grief but also to a pattern of aggressive defenses that he might otherwise have had to disavow to avoid shameful self recrimination. Meanwhile, the cultivation of play in improvisation puts to rest the myth of the perfectly analyzed analyst not only as impossible but also as both unnecessary and undesirable—a point seminal to the entire relational canon (Mitchell, 1993). In short, something of the analyst's own subjective issues necessarily becomes creative fodder for the analytic couples' play. Thus, becoming improvisational isn't about perfecting performances on either side of the couch. It is about playing, though taking play deadly serious.

Working improvisationally carries forth some other relationalist assumptions. First among these is that each of us experiences ourselves as "feeling like one person, while being many" (Bromberg, 1998; Davies, 1998; Harris, 1991). In improvisation, we prospectively have much greater access to our multiplicity of self-states, allowing each to come onto the "stage" of our discourse. Bass (2003) provides an exquisite example of how multiple self-states can be played with improvisationally. In his discussion of Black's (2003) work with her patient Lisa, Bass writes, "The tumbling kaleidoscope of self- and other states rush back and forth between them as though Black and Lisa were characters in a comic farce in which the performers each play multiple roles rush offstage to make lightning-fast costume changes to appear magically a second later in a different role" (p. 671). When, we can play with the multiple parts of our character, we are also much better equipped to play with the multiplicity of parts in others. We are also far more creative as well as resilient in terms of adapting to the vicissitudes of human existence.

Improvisation also relies upon our engagement in states of "implicit relational knowing" (Stern, 2004). In other words, improvisation relies heavily upon moving beyond the explicit realm of language, long valued in Freud's history of "the talking cure." Improvisation takes up, much as the interpersonalist tradition has for decades, that our psyche is as much "worn on our sleeve" as it is reflected in our verbal discourse (Ehrenberg, 1992). Indeed, it is in the schism between the meaning that language conveys and that which actions confer, that elements of everyday intrapsychic conflicts become ripe for the picking. Often, these reveal themselves in what is "implicitly relationally known" (Stern, 2004) to each partner.

"Implicit relational knowing," as evident in an improvisational exchange, involves sets of unarticulated assumptions about human nature that begin to structure a story mutually told. It is a story about something with which both are grappling analytically, though neither is necessarily aware of what the other is grappling with so much as playing non-self-consciously with it. Supportive of this idea, I often encourage patients to join me in "flummoxing" that is, in playing around with what is emergent between us without concern over its immediate correctness or fit. That "fittedness," when ready, will come. This sense of "fit" corresponds to cocreated, heightened states of affectivity, a resonating sense of mutuality, a deepening of understanding, and a promulgation of further associations. This is illustrated in the case of Sami. Thus, in improvisation, we can be more spontaneously ourselves, as we unconsciously inform and direct one another by virtue of what we each implicitly "believes" to be true in human relationships.

Improvising on a basis of this "implicit relational knowing" cultivates a field in which the subsymbolic can get played with in a manner lending to it becoming mentalized. As such, improvised scenes can become "model scenes" (Lichtenberg, Lachmann, & Fosshage, 1992, 1996) later explored or referred to as the analysis moves along. Meanwhile, all of this occurs so non-self-consciously that it can be experienced as vitalizing, and refreshingly authentic. In a sense, each party's implicit relational knowing is the transitional overlap of play that Winnicott (1971) averred.

Moments of improvisation ultimately involve moments of mutual *surrender* (Ghent, 1990; Benjamin, 2004) to the creation of "thirdness" (e.g., the "improvised script") versus submitting to the other's domination (see later discussions of "split complementarity" and "dominance and submission"). Nevertheless, this mutual surrender becomes "interaffective" (Gendlin, nd).

It is out of all of such moments that improvisation "courts surprise" (D. B. Stern, 1997) and gives rise to the heretofore unimaginable, or unarticulated (Ringstrom, 2007a), while involving experience that as Gendlin writes, "comes from underneath" (i.e., revealing the implicit of each parties' unconscious). This form of subject-to-subject relating creates moments of mutual recognition (Benjamin, 2004) that, even when not necessarily explicated, get implicitly played with, laying down a foundation of trust and relationality instrumental for secure therapist–patient attachment that lends itself to greater mentalization (Wallin, 2007).

Equally noteworthy, however, is that improvisation often entails ruthlessly playing with the other as "object" (i.e., as a functionary to one's play). In other words, the play, at times robust and aggressive, does not necessarily evidence mutual recognition, though it sets an implicit stage for it. This is because when the two parties can play with one another as "objects" they intrinsically reveal something about themselves as subjects, hence, intersubjective mutual recognition implicitly follows. We reveal ourselves in play.

Because of this mutual instantiation of spontaneous engagement, improvisation tends to be fresh and most authentic, that is, not rehearsed or "scripted." It necessarily compels us to "lean into" our experience (Ringstrom, 2006) and not away from it. Indeed, this is part of why it is so initially "scary" for both analysts and analysands, because it does not allow the defensiveness of "secondary process" reflection, or intellectualization. As Hoffman (1994) intones, there are "no timeouts" in psychoanalysis. Consider this vignette of Sara.

"So at any dinner party, no one wants to sit next to me, since I am in the weak seat," lamented Sara, a 37-year-old woman with whom I have worked multiple times a week on the couch for several years. Following a meaningful termination, marriage, and the birth of two lovely children, she intermittently returned to see me over the years regarding subsequent crises with miscarriages, infertility, and developmental issues regarding one of her offspring. The following illustrated session occurred approximately a half year into her return to once-a-week psychotherapy.

"What does the 'weak seat' mean?" I asked.

Sara elaborated, "It's the one that no one would want to sit next to, that others would avoid," followed with the same explanation she had shared many times before that its because she is less funny, less smart, less entertaining, and less interesting than the rest of her family members. This contradicted a strong impression I held about Sara, because in my mind, she could be very witty, smart, playful, and fun to engage—all qualities I deeply value and for which I have my own aesthetic sensibility. Still, equally noteworthy is that Sara also engaged in what I had come to refer to as her "behind the curtains" peek, a disconnection from the immediacy of the moment wherein she "peeks out" to evaluate how she is being received.

"Well, I trust that that is how you feel and clearly what you believe," I remarked, "but I think that if I were at a dinner party with you, I would want to sit next to you, and in fact, I believe that Marcia (my wife) would too." Sara had met Marcia at a social occasion and Marcia had also treated a family member of hers a decade earlier. Reflecting on my comment now, I believe that I spontaneously added Marcia, because I wanted to add some weight to my point.

Sara said, "So you want to know what I think about that?" To which I playfully said, "No!" and then nodded of course, which sent Sara reeling. Instantly recomposed, she said, "I think that you say that only because you want me to feel better, because you're just trying to be nice."

I said, "Seems you annihilate both of us with that."

"What do you mean?" she asked.

"Well, you wipe out my gesture, my point of view about you, while wiping yourself out too." To which she hastened, "Don't think that I am going to let you get away with being all Pollyanna on me!" I fired back, "Okay, now you're being a *bitch*, and I don't want to sit next to you." We both burst out laughing.

"But seriously," I added, suddenly flooded with a poignant but familiar sense of sadness, "this reminds me of our conversations about your foster child identity." Sara noted my sad expression. This moment, I believe, entailed one in which through play I was able to gain access to a dissociated affect. My playing involved a spontaneous association of my own to some of our past discussions—something of an intuitive grasp of something obscured in our increasingly aggressive banter. The introduction of my association also captures the bidirectional nature of the creative process in improvisation. Like being part of a jazz duet the association that emerged from within me, was like an old tune, much like one that might be introduced as a new rife in a jazz musician's performance.

In that moment, I became flooded with a sudden recollection of past insights that had culminated from our exploration of a number of befuddling dynamics in Sara's character. One such dynamic was her pattern of furtive eating, which she referred to as her own uniquely stubborn "eating disorder." Sara never binged and purged and never starved herself, but she did feel compelled to consume most of her calories through sneak eating.

In an earlier improvisational moment in the course of our work, I had shared with her that she reminded me of a foster child, always hungry for nutrition and love, stealing food, ever anxious that she might get caught and removed yet again from another foster placement. To both of our amazement, Sara informed me that her mother had in fact been a foster child moved through multiple placements, a point that had never been introduced in our years of much more traditional analytic work. This revelation culminated in my interpretation that Sara had somehow introjected her mother's disavowed childhood, one that led to a history of interaction with her mother from which Sara lived the life of an "as if" child. She was her mother's doll, one to be dressed up, posed to the world, ostensibly deeply loved, but in fact never truly known. All of this fortified her feelings that she lacked what it took to truly be worth being seen, heard, and enjoyed in her own right.

Sara exclaimed to my sad reverie, "I am thinking now of something that happened when I was about 8," as she commenced describing a "model scene" (Lichtenberg et al., 1992, 1996) that had never before arisen in our work. "My mother and I were at a T-shirt shop," she continued, "and my mother burst out laughing and said, 'We have to get this T-shirt for you!'" The inscription read, CHILD FOR RENT: CHEAP!

I felt stricken at Sara's remembrance, as she added, "Of course, I told her that I loved it too, and we got it, but it really wasn't the one I wanted." She elaborated, "The one that I wanted had a big eye with a rainbow tear coming out of it." Again, I was swept away in sadness, as is frequently the case; I feel initially more than Sara does, who, in her identification with her mother's disavowed foster child persona, often adaptively dissociates from her affect about such insights, even though she agrees that they undeniably fit. Stumped by what the T-shirt she longed for meant, I offered that it captured the eye that vigilantly scanned both her mother's and her own social surrounding hungering for a sense of belonging while privately grief stricken over never feeling truly known. The point of all this is that when analyst and analysand can playfully banter back and forth instead of currying resistance, they can open horizons of heretofore unexamined territory.

Such a brief snippet of treatment is meant to reflect that there is nothing all that unique about being improvisational in psychoanalytic treatment—it's more that we have not had a language for capturing this aspect of what occurs quite naturally in our work. This is likely the case, because it has been forbidden by a history of theory and technique. What such moments do capture, however, is what can emerge without deliberation, often out of an intensely playful but curious manner of engagement. Meanwhile, being improvisational is not meant to replace the rest of the work of analysis, such as empathic exploration, affect attunement, cognitive insightfulness, or dream work, but becomes something of a delivery medium whereby all these dimensions of psychoanalytic work are more deeply realized in a more enlivened manner. By humanizing the dyad's engagement, improvisational moments facilitate the dyad's connection amid its necessary faltering when confusion, uncertainty, deadness, detachment, avoidance, or frightening combat must hold sway.

While at times perhaps seeming chaotic, improvisation is never random.* Episodes of improvisation reflect, retrospectively, patterns between

---

* Randomness means that patterns of organization are neither predictable nor even discernable retrospectively. In effect, randomness applies to the degradation of organization in any system as in the principle of entropy. By contrast, although chaos is not predictable, it does evidence emergent patterns that are discernable retrospectively. Chaos involves enduring unpredictably developing patterns, not system degradation. So for example, though we cannot necessarily predict how the analytic couples work will unfold, we can retrospectively examines the contributions of each one's organizing principles and the influence they played in either opening or closing the analytic exploration.

the two participants that include the very process by which the analytic work is opened and deepened versus when it becomes shallow, constrained, and dead. Thus, improvisation can be further cultivated through the maintenance of a *relational ethic*, which involves the following questions being held in an implicit nonconscious "evenly hovering attention." That is, is what we are experiencing in this moment opening or closing, vitalizing or deadening, connecting or avoiding, focusing or confusing, liberating or constraining, playfully exploring or just fooling around, affirming or annihilating, recognizing or misconstruing, fencing or going for the jugular? The answer to these questions is not meant to value any particular state of experiencing over others (e.g., vitalizing over deadening, connecting over avoiding, focusing over confusing; Ehrenberg, 2005), but to see how they are taking shape in the characters in the present moment scene such that the intersubjective space of thirdness opens versus closes.

Modes of Improvisational Engagement

Another way of conceptualizing improvisation comes from Preston (2007), in what she refers to as two different tempos or what I refer to as two different modes of therapeutic action. Preston refers to them as "little *i*" improvisation versus "big *I*" Improvisation. Little *i* improvisation captures the slower, more usual, more leisurely paced exchanges that reflect a normal, "good-enough" analytic process. In this vein, ideas, thoughts, and feelings can be tossed back and forth with time to reflect upon and consider our play even as we engage in it, that is, "checking out" one another's reactions ala the implicit relational ethic questions. Here there can be something of a blending of the spontaneous with the reflective.

Little *i* improvisation corresponds to Bass's (2003) notion of "little *e*" enactments, of which he writes: "Ordinary quotidian enactments ... form the daily ebb and flow of ordinary analytic process" (p. 657). The value of redefining Bass's definition of *e*nactment in terms of improvisation, however, is that it more specifically addresses the universe of play so critical to capturing the formation of the "relational unconscious." As Aron (2003) notes, Bass's small *e*nactments merely recognize "that interaction is ubiquitous and continual" (p. 626). Improvisation takes up the ineluctability of interaction—seminal to relational psychoanalysis—and qualifies it in terms of the critical process of play-in-interaction, a point moving improvisation beyond the mere ubiquity of interaction.

Before moving to *I*mprovisation, it is important to note that Bass (2003) coined his term *e*nactment to contrast with what he refers to as "big *E*" enactments. These, he avers, "are highly condensed precipitates of unconscious psychic elements in patient and in analyst that mobilize our full attention and define, and take hold of, analytic activity for periods of time" (p. 657). This definition comes much closer to what I refer to as "mutual inductive identification" (see below) and as a precursor state to big *I* Improvisational moments.

Big *I* Improvisation captures more the spirit of what I have referred to as "improvisational moments" (Ringstrom, 2007a) when responses are far more impromptu, necessitating more of an intuitive, nonreflective, unmediated responsiveness. They entail "breaking the grip of the field" (Stern, 1997). Big *I* Improvisation is almost always in the implicit realm, whereas small *i* entails some of the explicit. Big *I* embodies more of a *high-risk, high-gain* quality (Gabbard, personal communication; Knoblauch, 2001) but is seasoned with a sense of *yes/and* mutual empathic attunement (a playing off of and with what is arising implicitly between the two partners), which provides a lively, contact-filled, spontaneously expressive alternative to more confrontational modes of engagement (Preston, 2007). *I*mprovisation, therefore, takes up what can become the fortuitous outcomes of *E*nactments or what I refer to as "mutual inductive identification."

Whether *i* or *I* improvisation, there are some "cardinal guidelines" that facilitate either modes occurrence. They involve the following:

1. Listening (and observing) intently, not only for your patient's implicit and explicit communications but also for what spontaneously emerges within yourself.
2. Don't be afraid to introduce the latter, that is, to play with that emergence.*
3. Especially, if you are also following the next cardinal guideline, which is do not negate the other's reality.
4. Instead, play off it and with it. This is the *yes/and* technique described in greater detail by Nachmanovich (2001) and Ringstrom (2001b), in which you build on whatever the other says.

Mutual Inductive Identification: When Improvisational Play Becomes Constrained and We Revert to the World of Static, Defensive "Scripts"

When the dyad is unable to be improvisational, it usually means one of the self-states within one party takes over. It dominates not only the other

---

* Emergence within the analyst may be handled by privately engaging in one's reverie or playing within oneself (Ogden, 1994) or by playing with what is emerging with the other in a more actively intersubjective, interpersonal manner.

multiple self-states but also the intersubjective field. Such domination arises from processes of dissociation, which then manifests into processes of inductive identification. In so doing, it compromises the field of nonconscious play so necessary for improvising.

Without access to one's other self-states the predominant self-state behaves as the "spokesperson" for all the rest (e.g., the "chair" of the "committee of the mind"). Such experience is suggestive of a state of mind in which self-states are incommunicado, beyond the reach of play both from within and from without. These states represent subsymbolic experience that cannot be "mentalized" (Fonagy, 2003; Fonagy & Target, 1997)—that is, connected to symbolic meaning making of one's affective experience. Absent the capacity for such self-state formulation and, therefore, absent the capacity for symbolic articulation, the prevailing sense or version of "reality" that is dominating the mind of one *must* be enacted. And it must be done in a manner that involves both parties participation (Bromberg, 2006). Indeed, when mentalization is impaired, the very capacity to generate new and vitalizing narratives is equivalently impaired. Thus, impaired mentalization connotes a "hostage-taking" of the mind—often embodying the shackles of old identifications with caregivers (Grotstein, 1997; Brandchaft, Stolorow, & Atwood, 1994) in which only old scripts rule.

Thus, Enactments (Bass, 2003; Chused, 2003), or as I prefer episodes of "mutual inductive identification" in contrast to improvisation, involve the collapse of playfulness—and are discernable by this very experience—"I/ we can no longer play with our ideas and feelings within ourselves or between us." The "scene work" that ensues from such episodes is more in the realm of what each party is inducing the other to identify with. This means that episodes of "mutual inductive identification" contrast to episodes of improvisation, insofar as they involve enacting entrenched, scripted aspects of personality. By contrast, improvisation involves playing off of and with that which exists in the service of cultivating new possibilities, new narratives. In this latter way, improvisation involves taking remnants of scriptedness and cocreating new possibility (i.e., new meaning about what just happened). This facilitates greater moments of reflectiveness.

Still, evidence of Enactments or episodes of "mutual inductive identification" is no reason to despair. On the contrary, both paradoxically cultivate a kind of "second chance" engagement with the implicit world of "scriptedness" and therefore represent an essential aspect of analytic work. The valuing of enactments highlights one of the most prominent differences between the relational canon and more traditional theories of psychoanalysis. Enactments, according to Bromberg (2006), are attempts to renegotiate "unfinished business in those areas of selfhood where, because of one degree of another of traumatic experience, affect regulation was not successful enough to allow further self-development at the level of symbolic processing by thought and language" (p. 181).

Such unfinished business, such subsymbolic experience, must become enacted through inducing the other to take on a role, that is, to become a party in the individual's inner unrecognized drama. Even when unformulated, such self-states always link some organization of self-affect-other (Davies, 2005) needing to be fully articulated, through becoming identified with, by the other. This process typically has to first pass through the other's own subsymbolic history of experience.

In this inductive manner, we see projective identification as an essential precursor to enactments (Bromberg, 1998). It is for this reason that I have coined "mutual inductive identification" because it links the relationality of the two parties' mutual projections and identifications and does so in an enacted form, which later can retrospectively be seen as an essential episode of engagement that furthers mentalization and development.

Indeed, in "mutual inductive identification" the state of mind of both the patient and the analyst must be receptive to being induced into becoming a character in the other's constricted scene. In short, it is critical that each person is "fertile" for taking on and enacting some identificatory experience of the other. Paradoxically, it is this very vulnerability that can be critical to a promising therapeutic match.

A not insignificant point, however, is that when these sub-self-state enactments go unarticulated they are at risk of devolving into states of dominance and submission. And when these are not addressed, they devolve into therapeutic breakdowns, if not impasses. This often happens in a stepwise progression. First, intrapsychically, it involves a "member" (self-state) of the "committee of the mind" running rough shod over the rest. Second, this internal version of dominance and submission gives rise to the interpersonal version of it, since axiomatically "that which cannot be negotiated within, cannot be negotiated without" (Ringstrom, in press). This dominance and submission is captured in Benjamin's concept of "split complementarity" where a person's mode of mentalization (meaning-making) comes to dominate the others. This process is also prone in most relationships to become highly reversible, as in each party reversing the positions of dominance and submission in relationship to one another. A good example of this involves the characters of George and Martha in *Who's Afraid of Virginia Woolf?*

Nevertheless, part and parcel of the relational canon is that both patient and analyst are vulnerable to participating in "mutual inductive identifications." That's because both are vulnerable to dissociating what they have at

stake in a given situation and therefore what they need from one another.*,†
Patients who have been traumatized are especially likely to do this, since
the "traumatized self-state" tends to dominate other self-states (Bromberg,
2006; Davies, 1998, 2004). This is evolutionarily encoded, since the function
of trauma is not so much about the recollection of what happened as it is
about preventing its reoccurrence. Trauma states are less about what happened than what's going to happen next! All of this is managed by adaptively recognizing any and all circumstances remotely resembling something
about the original trauma. Such recognizing becomes the trigger for a host
of autonomic, subsymbolic, prereflective reactions that treat the present
moment as if it too will be traumatic.‡

In short, "mutual inductive identification" is the process whereby we
induce the other to become a player in our unarticulated (often dissociatively disconnected) drama. Whereas patients may well need to induce their
analyst to experience something that remains outside the range of symbolization and therefore reflection and articulation (the essential principles of
talk therapy), analysts may also unwittingly induce their patients to become
the kind of patient that the analysts likes, prefers, and is most comfortable
working with. This propensity, however, is especially likely to arise when a
particular patient makes the therapist feel uncomfortable in being inducted
(Chused, 2003).

Defensively, therapists then "script" the patient back into more formulaic
styles of engagement of their own. That is, the analyst attempts to induce
the patient to do the analysis in the manner that the analyst needs to feel
comfortable. This latter state is especially vulnerable to being dissociated by
the analyst because the analyst's needs are sequestered in relation to historical psychoanalytic values of *abstinence, neutrality,* and *anonymity.* Analysts

---

* An illustration of the problem in negating the other is captured in this dreadful scene:
  Actor A says to Actor B, "What kind of cab driver are you, you're driving slower than my
  grandmother?!" Actor B kills the improvisation when he retorts, "I'm not a cab driver;
  I'm a farmer 'driving' a tractor!" Actor B is unwilling to build upon Actor A's perspective.
  Instead, he negates it replacing it with his own, thereby dominating his scene partner.
  Actor A may try to salvage the scene by acting crazy such as saying, "Oh silly me, I must
  have forgotten my meds this morning and I am hallucinating; we're in a taxi!"
† In sum, "mutual inductive identification" is often a measure of what is at stake for each
  party. It is in this manner that we recognize how the psychoanalytic process is ineluc-
  tably intertwined in both the inner and outer experiential worlds of both patient and
  therapist, each one's experience forever contextualizing the others. However, this does
  not mean that every moment is constituted by a parity of influence, since the weight of
  what might be occurring is almost always conditioned by what each party has at stake
  in it.
‡ Our predecessors who ignored the rustling leaves as the possible threat of a saber-tooth
  tiger were not the ones who became our genetic ancestors—biological evolution favors
  at least some functions of a trauma model of the mind.

are also especially vulnerable to inducing their patients to become the kind they are comfortable to work with when the patient's traumatized state of mind begins to traumatize the analyst's. This circumstance is especially ripe for a kind of mutual coercion as to how the analysis will be conducted.

Restoring Improvisation

It is in these moments, that restoring improvisation can be most helpful, but this entails a number of implicit steps. Often the first step is through engaging in a kind of "passive" improvisation, that is, in a state of private reverie (Ogden, 1994; Ringstrom, 2001a) about the emerging enactment. This may require the analyst to ask, "What is it that is getting induced within me that speaks to some dissociated aspect of the patient's experience and how is this giving rise to my dissociation?" That is, what character am I becoming in the patient's drama. Such reverie must then include, "And how am I unwittingly (dissociatively) inducing the patient to become a 'cooperative' agent in my drama—that is the kind of patient I would be more comfortable working with?" On the other hand (as in the case of Timothy that follows), playing with the mutually emerging inductions can become a source of releasing the dyad from its stranglehold as well as opening possibilities that it is rapidly foreclosing.

Yet another step to restoring improvisation may entail a kind of "meta-communication" (Pizer, 2003; Ringstrom, 2003) about the dyad's process, noting that the way the analyst is trying to be helpful is exacerbating the patient's experience of being harmed. Often such a metacommunication begins by noting that both parties seem to have lost their sense of play. Commenting on their mutuality of loss helps mitigate shaming or blaming the patient for the analytic quagmire. This leads to inviting the patient to jointly imagine how the analysis might proceed differently as well as illuminating how the manner in which both parties are feeling constrained.* In short, all of these steps entail playing with different ways of relating. Some of them are illustrated in the following case material.

An episode reflective of a big *I* improvisational moment arose in my work with 16-year-old Timothy. Entering my office for the first time one rainy Thursday afternoon, Timothy's life according to him was over. His demise

---

* It would be naïve to not acknowledge that introducing playing with new options for relating may jettison the dyad into another enactment. As just one example, a patient constrained by the strangling constraint of needing to idealize his analyst may experience the analyst's introduction of play as profoundly deidealizing. This then becomes further grist for the analytic mill, eventually leading to the possibility of playing with the patient's deidealization of the analyst, much like what happened with Sami.

came from his not getting the lead part in his high school play that he was certain should have been his. I was soon to learn that this rejection was the "last straw" in what had reportedly been "a year, no two years, no a life time" of unbearable disappointments and rejections. Timothy's outpouring competed soundly with the cloudburst outside. To my grave disappointment and frankly worry, I found myself feeling unusually judgmental in my reaction to him, weary already of his stormy narcissistic reaction to a breach of his entitlement. In the face of his outpouring, I experienced a profound sense of coercion to perform a certain role, one with a "deadening" history of scriptedness and that was to be the all embracing empathic other, devoid of an alternative perspective.

Experientially, I became frozen, especially disheartened, in fact, in relation to my more positive anticipation of his arrival. That's because, Timothy attended the same pressure-cooker college prep high school as one of my favorite patients a 16-year-old girl who I adored. Like the color red never appears redder than when placed next to the color green and vice versa, the sweetness of Stella's Nietzschean-existential anguish made Timothy's rejection-sensitive hysterics initially taste like a bunch of sour grapes.

So, while there were undoubtedly plenty of my own limitations insinuated in my having been so judgmental about Timothy, I also experienced him as the kind of patient who quickly saturates the intersubjective field with much of the coercive pressure residing within himself. Such pressure obviously affects different analysts differently. In my case it resulted in my clinical intuition (which I note now reflectively, though it was not so elaborated in my mind then) that he was not going to be able to tolerate my going into a moment of private reverie—at least not long enough for me to figure out my countertransference reaction. I felt fairly certain that in the interim we'd lose our precarious balance. I suspect that this would be the case, because I imagine Timothy becoming distressed with my own momentary discomfort in pondering what was going on with me. Furthermore, having perhaps the world's worst poker face, a point that I believe may have been true of Freud as well, I have had to respect that I am likely to readily "give away my hand."* Of course, I am not saying that I was objectively correct about what Timothy's experience would have been—which is impossible to know—but that, given my participation in this relational mix, I believe I was intersubjectively accurate.

---

* I think that Freud suffered the same problem, hence his introduction of using the couch. My suspicion about Freud is born out of witnessing the black-and-white silent home movies of him in the traveling Freudian Archives Exhibit, in which I was completely thrown by the highly energetic and animated man on the screen. His entire manner stood in stark contrast to the stolid figure so evident in his history of posed photographs. Furthermore, anecdotes from Freud's own patients suggest that he was far more interactive, far more relational than has been recognized (Mills, 2005).

So although I swiftly mirrored Timothy's sentiment that his life "surely did 'feel over' and that, understandably sucked (!)," I began inquiring about the historical "factual" basis for his conclusion. I also queried him about his assumptions about his future and what made it seem so bleak right now. In so doing, I allowed the emerging of my judgmentally tainted character into this dramatic scene to let in a little alterity, to introduce a little bit of a different point of view, a different frame of reference, even a bit of personal history into what I hoped would become a cocreated play space. I also did not fear mentioning the unmentionable. This meant that when Timothy went into greater and greater elaborations about how unfair his life was, how hard he tried, how robbed he was of the higher grades that many of his classmates receive ("who don't work nearly as hard as 'he' does") not to mention the parts in plays and chorus that he didn't get, I did not respond in the expected fashion to his anguished laments, "Why me?! Why do others get more than I do?!" Instead, I replied, "Well, maybe some of them are smarter than you…. Maybe some of them are more talented than you."

Notwithstanding my initial disquieting judgmental feelings, I did not say this to be cruel, but to speak about what Timothy wasn't saying. In fact, this comment was emergent within our intersubjective field of engagement (Coburn, 2002, 2006; Shane, 2006), that was taking shape around the constraints of both of our personalities as they each emerged into the characters we were becoming in this present moment scene. In effect, our scene work was moving into what Stern (2004) and his collaborators at the Boston Change Process Study Group (2002) refer to as "now moment" because I was saying something that Timothy seemed like he probably hadn't heard, as well as my being someone that he did not expect, at least as he would have automatically "scripted" this moment. What followed was what the authors call a "moment of meeting." Stern (2004) defines "now moments" as ones in which there is an immediate sense of threat to the intersubjective field hence they are fraught with dramatic intensity. The resolution of such moments involves the "moment of meeting" wherein there is an authentic well fitted response from therapist to patient that resolves the threat to their intersubjective engagement.

Timothy said, "Wow! That's hard to swallow!" To which I asked, "Why?" Suddenly, he seemed more relaxed, his anguish momentarily remitted, and he said with self-generated perspective, "Well, I guess there always is someone smarter than you, right?" To which I said, "Seems to be the case; I'm pretty damn good at what I do, but I believe that there are folks who are better. And I am a pretty smart guy, but I know quite a few who are smarter." Our session proceeded somewhat like this to its end, and later that night I got a call from his mother saying, "I don't know what you did, Dr. Ringstrom, but you are the first therapist Timothy has ever seen who he said he wants to come back to."

As our work progressed, more developmental obstacles from Timothy's life emerged. His parents divorced when he was 2, he lived alone with his mother, and his father was a multimillionaire playboy. When life's let-downs buckled Timothy's knees, and his mother wrung her hands and avowed how he had once again gotten a raw deal but that he should just keep plugging away since he was so unique and special. Meanwhile, his father remained ineffectually tongue-tied, instead trying to amend woes from a distance by throwing money at them, such as large donations that might grease Timothy's admission to programs that might otherwise have eluded him. So I said to Timothy, "It's sad. You come home crushed, and Mom 'pours you a warm bath,' while Dad has nothing to say. I can see that that no one has helped you develop broad enough shoulders to bear the weight of rejection and disappointment, the kind an ambitious guy like you is inevitably heir to."

Now as I said this I did not assume that I was right in my venturing so much as I was exploring how we might attempt to play together. Since playing improvisationally involves not negating one another* but playing with what each one is putting into the relational mix, when something "hits" it's pretty obvious. For example, Timothy would run with an assertion of mine—even the initially provocative one that he had trouble "swallowing" as I would run with his. We were not necessarily identifying with parts of one another, as in "mutual inductive identification," or affirming or mirroring one another's assertions as in a self psychological empathic approach so much as we were taking each other's assertions to the next plausible level of possibility. In so doing we were finding out what did and did not "fit" (Stern, 1997).

This approach argues that in the moment of play, the patient (as well as the therapist), are the arbiters of what "fits" for each in any given moment. It's an approach, adaptive of the epistemological position of "perspectival realism" that presumes neither to be the authority on reality. This is not a stance, however, that adheres to relativism, as in all perspectives are relative and therefore one is as good as another. Rather, perspectival realism asserts that what each is spontaneously averring is propositionally true to them in that moment, which then, through the further course of play and exploration, will make better sense for each or perhaps yield in part or in

---

* Illustrative of this point is the improvisational game "yes-and," wherein the participants greet one another's assertion with the affirmation of "yes-and" from which they then make their own assertion, taking what has been presented to them and taking it further. In this vein each player continues in this additive pattern until the scene reaches its own natural, readily known to both players conclusion, but by its end, it is also clear that it was a byproduct of either one exclusively, none of their imaginative coauthorship, the place of this sensibility in relational psychoanalysis has been discussed in detail by Nachmanovich (2001) and Ringstrom (2001b).

toto the other's point of view.* As Mitchell (1997) averred, it is often best to allow the patient's assumptions to play out rather than challenge them, such that in playing them out both analyst and patient can see what works or what does not.

Returning to my earliest intervention with Timothy, I suspect that why my saying, "Maybe you aren't as smart or as talented as the other kids," was so transforming in that *improvisational moment* was because I was merely hitting upon an unmentionable, unspeakable, deeply private, almost terrifying truth that Timothy had been concealing in an unarticulated fashion his entire life. What made this moment transformative was that I related to it in a manner that was heretofore unimaginable while maintaining a tone and manner that conveyed that the unspeakable could be readily discussed and embraced by both of us. This tone and manner served two purposes: one, to mitigate shame; and, two, to disabuse Timothy of his "psychic equivalence" mode of mentalization, that is, that if he thought something, it must be objectively true. As Allen et al. (2008) wrote, "Rather and converting the patient to a different way of thinking, you should aspire to help the patient to appreciate that there are different ways of thinking about the same outer reality" (p. 180).

When this happens I believe that we are engaging in what I have referred to (Ringstrom, 2007a, 2007b) as a "posi-traum" that is an improvisational moment in which something unimaginably positive happens. Just as the key element in trauma is the assault of something horrendously unimaginable (van der Kolk, 2007; Grotstein, 1997; Ringstrom, 1999), like a sudden unexpected loss for which one could have no preparation, in the case of a posi-traum, the patient is unable to imagine that the analyst (or anyone for that matter) could think or feel about something.

D. N. Stern (2007) questioned whether the term posi-traum is apt, especially when compared with trauma. First, it differs from trauma insofar as trauma is more likely to have some somatic elements, as in van der Kolk's (1996) comment, "The body keeps score." Second, no matter how impactful the posi-traum moment may be, it is new and does not have the history of repeated recollection, both implicitly and explicitly recalled over conceivably much if not most of a patient's life. Nevertheless, without knowledge of my work on this idea, Barbara Pizer (2005) and Stuart Pizer (2005) coined a comparable idea that they called "positive traumas." What the Pizers and I were independently conceiving is that an event can occur, almost always in an unpremeditated fashion that has the effect of dramatically altering an entrenched emotional conviction of a patient's.

---

* Though the analyst is not coming from a position as the arbiter of what is objectively true, at the same time, however, nor does she abdicate her position as one with some authoritative know-how about the practice of psychoanalysis.

When this occurs, something unpredictably, unimaginably positive happens. Put in terms of mentalization (Allen et al., 2008) a new narrative structure emerges. Like the unimaginable of trauma, this positive event cannot be assimilated within the patient's intransigently negative belief system. Hence the positive event forces an accommodation of a new organizing principle (i.e., a new emotional conviction). So, while it may be questionable to compare the enduring effect of the posi-traum moment with trauma—given the latter's more somatizing and repetitive impact—the invocation of the unimaginable upon salient organizing principles, is also undeniable. This, I am positing, is what Timothy's reaction entailed.

A point germane to improvisational moments is that such posi-traums cannot be deliberate, lest they risk being appropriated and nullified by the patient's subjective sense of reality. This means that they must exceed the scope of the patient's invariant organizing principles. Incapable of being assimilated the new experience forces accommodation of new organizing principles for the patient to make sense of what occurred. Hence, posi-traums typically must arise from improvisational moments that involve doing something new and surprising* (Shane 2006). Since the moment of improvisation involves something unpremeditated, it necessarily emerges from the nonconsciousness of both parties and therefore does not bear the stamp of having been scripted and rehearsed. Patients' experiences in such moments bear a quality of recognition something like, "I can't believe that you got that about me, because I hadn't gotten it about myself until you did, and only by your undoing what I hadn't quite recognized had been done to me by others and by myself—both in fact and in fantasy—am I now able to recognize new possibilities heretofore unimaginable in my theory of mind."

In this manner, Timothy and I proceeded along for several sessions, moving to and fro, sometimes losing our balance of open inquiry, dropping us below the surface of the emergence of our relational unconscious. When this happened, I would once again encourage us to play with how we were thinking about things, to be open to being tenaciously curious.

In the context of this improvisational engagement, Timothy shared another lament, saying that he hadn't been happy in years. In fact, he anguished,

---

* In a similar vein, Shane (2006) writes, "Change in analysis frequently appears to depend on a state shift in the patient provoked by an unanticipated incident, spontaneous action, or experience of surprise, as these moments are seen to emerge unexpectedly in the complex dyadic system constitutive of the psychoanalytic situation (Galatzer-Levy, 1995).... [Such] emergence describes how new unexpected, and qualitatively distinct configurations suddenly appear in complex systems, in this case the analytic dyad; and it addresses the sense of surprise human beings experience in these difficult-to-anticipate developments" (p. 36).

he "just wanted to be happy." In this context, I asked when he'd last been and to which he replied, "around age 12 or 13." I asked him what happened then, but as I did I had a correspondingly strong sense of what he then replied to almost uncannily. He exclaimed, "Well, puberty happened!" In the throes of my own preconscious experience, I proffered, "Damn, I was just wondering about that myself. What about it, the advent of puberty? I mean that's a time where you can get a lot more interested in sex, you know with girls ... maybe with guys ... I don't know...."

He fired back, "Well, I'm *not* gay!" He paused, "I mean, I don't think I'm gay." Pausing further, he continued, "I mean, I've never been turned on by a guy, I've never been turned on by a girl either." So I said to him, "Wow, the whole sex thing can really be confusing can't it ... especially, when you haven't had anyone to talk about it with. Seems to me, we ought to hang loose with this one and see over time what seems truest for you. This is a time of life when all sorts of identity issues can feel up for grabs, you know?"*

Germane to working improvisationally is that it involves ensemble work, wherein the spontaneous gestures of either party play off of and with one another's. Indeed, as Nachmanovich (2001) argued, improvisation entails working with *bricolage*—that is, working with the materials at hand. It results from one or the other party setting something in motion, with the other taking what is given and moving it one step further. Correspondingly, each one acts in kind, until they both have reached a satisfying ending, as in an improvisational scene or as in jazz. As such, improvisation cultivates a kind of mutually enhanced "free-associational" process that instantiates "unintentional" moments, laying bare the structures of the two parties subjective unconscious' revealed through their play.

Working improvisationally can also involve reintroducing background material in a manner similar to a jazz musician reintroducing an earlier though now long past rhythm in his current riff. This point relates to my response to Timothy in terms of his revelation about his confused sexuality. Undoubtedly, part of the background of my response to him was shaped by my awareness that Timothy's lack of friends was because he was so moralistic about drugs, alcohol, and especially sex, certainly a turnoff to peers who are highly inquisitive about such matters at this phase of their life. Thus, somewhere in my own background thoughts, I was undoubtedly discerning that Timothy's attitudes about sex reflected a dire sense of threat.

---

* Of special note is that by working improvisationally, I came to relish working with Timothy given the freedom of expression that it created for both of us. He still often presented in a bemoaning victimized manner, but, because we could play with it, our work was refreshing versus stagnating, uplifting versus depressing and expanding versus compressing.

Conclusion

I believe that an improvisational sensibility in relational psychoanalysis is a major vehicle for directly instantiating and playing with new possibilities in the "history and memory of coconstructed meanings between the analyst and patient." It is through the improvisational metaphors of scripts, assigned roles, dramatic arches, and sequences that the otherwise lifeless theories such as those of chaos, complexity, and dynamic systems come alive and become meaningful. The very idea of scripts, for example, embodies the semifixed and illusory ways we imbue our own character—in other words, our own sense of self as well as how we expect (and direct) the other to be in each present moment drama of psychoanalysis. Such improvised relational sequences embody beginnings, middles, and endings that become mini-narratives, and these narratives can serve thereafter as model scenes for further elaboration of the analysis. These live metaphors capture how an analytic process can proceed along an amazing sequence of improvised moments of cocreativity.

However, it must also be humbly noted that the impact of improvisational moments is also about slow accretions, tiny moments of chipping away at seemingly invariant organization—a notable example being Michael Scott's resistance exemplified at the beginning of this presentation. The writers of "The Office" clearly understood this when they made it clear that Michael's character was only minimally impacted by his instructor and their improvised scene. In a later scene in the same episode playing with an Asian classmate actor, we witness Michael quickly lean over and whisper into his scene partner's ear, to which the partner bolts his hands over his head in the position of someone about to be arrested. The flabbergasted class instructor abruptly yells, "Stop!" and asks the actor, "What are you doing?" to which the helpless actor replies, "Michael whispered that he still has a hidden gun!"

References

Allen, J. G., Fonagy, P., & Bateman, A. W. (2008). *Mentalizing in clinical practice*. Arlington, VA: American Psychiatric Press.

Aron, L. (1996). *A meeting of minds: Mutuality in psychoanalysis*. Hillsdale, NJ: The Analytic Press.

Aron, L. (2003). The paradoxical place of enactment in psychoanalysis: Introduction. *Psychoanalytic Dialogues, 13*(5), 623–632.

Aron, L. (2006). Analytic impasse and the third: Clinical implications of intersubjectivity theory. *International Journal of Psychoanalysis, 87*, 349–368.

Bass, A. (2003). "E" enactments in psychoanalysis: Another medium, another message. *Psychoanalytic Dialogues, 13*(5), 657–676.

Beebe, B., & Lachmann, F. (1994). Representation and internalization in infancy: Three principles of salience. *Psychoanalytic Psychology, 11*, 127–166.

Beebe, B., & Lachmann, F. (2002). *Infant research and adult treatment: Co-constructing interactions*. Hillsdale, NJ: The Analytic Press.

Benjamin, J. (1988). *The bonds of love*. New York: Pantheon Books.

Benjamin, J. (1992). Recognition and destruction: An outline of intersubjectivity. In N. Skolnick & S. Warshaw (Eds.), *Relational perspectives in psychoanalysis*. (pp. 43–60). Hillsdale, NJ: The Analytic Press.

Benjamin, J. (2004). Beyond doer and done to: Recognition and the intersubjective third. *Psychoanalytic Quarterly, 73*, 5–46.

Black, M. (2003). Enactment: Analytic musings on energy, language, and personal growth. *Psychoanalytic Dialogues, 13*(5), 633–656.

Bollas, C. (1989). *The forces of destiny*. Northvale, NJ: Jason Aronson.

Boston Change Process Study Group (2002). Explicating the implicit: The local level and the microprocess of change in the analytic situation. *International Journal of Psychoanalysis, 83*, 1051–1062.

Brandchaft, B., Stolorow, R., & Atwood, G. (1994). *The intersubjective perspective*. Northvale, NJ: Aronson.

Bromberg, P. (1998). *Standing in spaces: Essays on dissociation, trauma and clinical process*. Hillsdale NJ: The Analytic Press.

Bromberg, P. (2006). *Awakening the dreamer: Clinical journeys*. Hillsdale NJ: The Analytic Press.

Buber, M. (1970). *I and thou: A new translation with a prologue "I and you" and notes*. (W. Kaufman, Trans.) New York: Simon & Schuster.

Chused, J. (2003). The role of enactments. *Psychoanalytic Dialogues, 13*(5), 677–688.

Coates, S. (1998). Having a mind of one's own and holding the mind of the other: Commentary on paper by Peter Fonagy and Mary Target. *Psychoanalytic Dialogues, 8*, 115–148.

Coburn, W. (2002). A world of systems: The role of systemic patterns of experience in the therapeutic process. *Psychoanalytic Inquiry, 22*(5), 655–677.

Coburn, W. (2006). Terminations, self-states and complexity in psychoanalysis: Commentary on paper by Jody Davies. *Psychoanalytic Dialogues, 16*(5), 603–610.

Davies, J. M. (1998). Multiple perspectives on multiplicity. *Psychoanalytic Dialogues, 8*(2), 195–206.

Davies, J. M. (2004). Whose bad objects are these anyway? Repetition and our elusive love affair with evil. *Psychoanalytic Dialogues, 14*(6), 711–732.

Davies, J. M. (2005). Transformations of desire and despair: Reflections on the termination process from a relational perspective. *Psychoanalytic Dialogues, 15*, 779–805.

Ehrenberg, D. (1992). *The intimate edge*. New York: Norton.

Ehrenberg, D. (2005, February 5). *Discussion of Stuart and Barbara Pizer's papers*. Paper presented at the 16th Annual Conference for the Psychotherapies Training Institute, New York.

Fonagy, P. (2003). Some complexities in the relationship of psychoanalytic theory to technique. *Psychoanalytic Quarterly, 72*(1), 13–48.

Fonagy, P., & Target, M. (1997). Attachment and reflective function: Their role in self-organization. *Development and Psychopathology, 9*, 679–700.

Frankel, J. (2003).Our relationship to analytic ideals: Commentary on papers by Joyce Slochower and Sue Grand. *Psychoanalytic Dialogues, 13*(4), 513–520.

Galatzer-Levy, R. (1995). Psychoanalysis and dynamic systems theory: Prediction. *Journal of the American Psychoanalytic Association, 44*, 981–986.

Gendlin, E. (nd). *Improvisation provides.* Unpublished manuscript.

Gerson, S. (1995). *The analyst's subjectivity and the relational unconscious.* Paper presented at the Spring Meeting of the Division of Psychoanalysis, American Psychological Association, Santa Monica, CA.

Ghent, M. (1990). Masochism, submission and surrender. *Contemporary Psychoanalysis, 26*(1), 108–135.

Grotstein, J. (1997). Autochthony and alterity: Psychic reality in counterpoint. *Psychoanalytic Quarterly, 66*, 403–430.

Harris, A. (1991). The conceptual power of multiplicity. *Contemporary Psychoanalysis, 27*(1), 197–224.

Harris, A. (2004). The relational unconscious: Commentary on papers by Michael Eigen and James Grotstein. *Psychoanalytic Dialogues, 14*(1), 131–138.

Hoffman, I. Z. (1994). Dialectical thinking and therapeutic action in the psychoanalytic process. *Psychoanalytic Quarterly, 63*, 187–218.

Hoffman, I. Z. (1998). *Ritual and spontaneity in the psychoanalytic process: A dialectical-constructivist view.* Hillsdale, NJ: The Analytic Press.

Knoblauch, S. (2001). High risk, high gain: Commentary on paper by Philip A. Ringstrom. *Psychoanalytic Dialogues, 11*(5), 785–795.

Levenson, E. (1972). *The fallacy of understanding.* New York: Basic Books.

Lichtenberg, J. D., Lachmann, F. L., & Fosshage, J. L. (1992). *Self and motivational systems: Towards a theory of psychoanalytic technique.* Hillsdale, NJ: The Analytic Press.

Lichtenberg, J. D., Lachmann, F. L., & Fosshage, J. L. (1996). *The clinical exchange: Techniques derived from self and motivational systems.* Hillsdale, NJ: The Analytic Press.

Mills, J. A critique of relational psychoanalysis. *Psychoanalytic Psychology, 22*, 2, 155–188.

Mitchell, S. (1993). *Hope and dread in psychoanalysis.* New York: Basic Books.

Mitchell, S. (1997). *Influence and autonomy in psychoanalysis.* Hillsdale, NJ: The Analytic Press.

Mitchell, S. (2000). *Can love last? The fate of romance over time.* New York: W. W. Norton.

Nachmanovich, S. (2001). Freedom: Commentary on paper by Philip A. Ringstrom. *Psychoanalytic Dialogues, 11*(5), 771–784.

Ogden, T. (1994). *Subjects of analysis.* Northvale NJ: Jason Aronson.

Pizer, S. (1998). *Building bridges: The negotiation of paradox in psychoanalysis.* Hillsdale, NJ: The Analytic Press.

Pizer, B. (2003). When the crunch is a (k)not: A crimp in relational dialogue. *Psychoanalytic Dialogues, 13*(2), 193–204.

Pizer, B. (2005, February 5). *The heart of the matter in matters of the heart: Power and intimacy in analytic and couples relationships.* Paper presented at the 16th Annual Conference for the Psychotherapies Training Institute, New York.

Pizer, S. (2005, February 5). *The shock of recognition: What my grandfather taught me about psychoanalytic process.* Paper presented at the 16th Annual Conference for the Psychotherapies Training Institute, New York.

Preston, L. (2007, October). *Improvisation provides a window into implicit processes: Thoughts on Philip Ringstrom's work in dialogue with Eugene Gendlin.* Paper presented at the Annual Conference for the Psychology of the Self, Los Angeles, CA.

Ringstrom, P. (1994). An intersubjective approach to conjoint therapy. In A. Goldberg (Ed.), *A decade of progress: Progress in self psychology*, Volume 10 (pp. 159–182). Hillsdale, NJ: The Analytic Press.

Ringstrom, P. (1999). *Discussion of Robert Stolorow's paper "The phenomenology of trauma."* Paper presented at the 22nd Annual Conference on the Psychology of the Self in Toronto, Canada.

Ringstrom, P. (2001a). Cultivating the improvisational in psychoanalytic treatment. *Psychoanalytic Dialogues, 11*(5), 727–754.

Ringstrom, P. (2001b). "Yes, and…"—How improvisation is the essence of good psychoanalytic dialogue: Reply to commentaries. *Psychoanalytic Dialogues, 11*(5), 797–806.

Ringstrom, P. (2001c). *The noxious third: The crimes and misdemeanors in the treatment of Tony Soprano and Dr. Jennifer Melfi.* Paper presented at the 21st Annual Spring Meeting of the Division of Psychoanalysis (39), Sante Fe, NM.

Ringstrom, P. (2003). "Crunches," "(k)nots," and double binds—When what isn't happening is the most important thing: Commentary on paper by Barbara Pizer. *Psychoanalytic Dialogues, 13*(2), 193–204.

Ringstrom, P. (2004). *Body rhythms and improvisation: Playing with the music behind the lyrics in psychoanalysis.* Paper presented at the 27th Annual International Conference on the Psychology of the Self.

Ringstrom, P. (2005, June 26). *Improvisational moments: A relational perspective on therapeutic change.* Paper presented at the IARPP Conference in Rome, Italy.

Ringstrom, P. (2006). Moments of an analysis: My view from John Lindon's couch. *International Journal of Psychoanalytic Self Psychology, 1*(1), 79–102.

Ringstrom, P. (2007a). Scenes that write themselves: Improvisational moments in relational psychoanalysis. *Psychoanalytic Dialogues, 17*(1), 69–99.

Ringstrom, P. (2007b). Reply to Stern's comments on "Scenes that write themselves: Improvisational moments in relational psychoanalysis." *Psychoanalytic Dialogues, 17*(1), 105–113.

Ringstrom, P. (2007c). Inductive identification and improvisation in psychoanalytic practice: Some comments on Joye Weisel Barth's article on complexity theory. *International Journal of Psychoanalytic Self Psychology, 4,* 288–312.

Ringstrom, P. (2008a). Improvisational moments in self-psychological relational psychoanalysis. In P. Buirski & A. Kottler (Eds.), *New developments in self psychology practice.* Lanham, MS: Jason Aronson.

Ringstrom, P. (2008b). Improvisation and mutual inductive identification in couples therapy: A discussion of Susan Shimmerlick's article "Moments in relational psychoanalysis." *Psychoanalytic Dialogues, 18*(3), 390–402.

Ringstrom, P. (2010). 'Yes Alan!' and a few more thoughts about improvisation: A discussion of Alan Kindler's chapter "Spontaneity and improvisation in psychoanalysis." *Psychoanalytic Inquiry, 30*(3), 235–242.

Ringstrom, P. (in press). *A relational approach to couples therapy.* New York: Routledge.

Shane, E. (2006). A developmental systems self psychology approach. *International Journal of Psychoanalytic Self Psychology, 1,* 23–45.

Stern, D. N., Sander, L., Nahum, J., Harrison, A., Lyons-Ruth, K., Morgan, A., et al. (1998). Non-interpretive mechanisms in psychoanalytic therapy: The "something more" than interpretation. *International Journal of Psychoanalysis, 79,* 903–921.

Stern, D. B. (1997). *Unformulated experience: From dissociation to imagination in psychoanalysis.* Hillsdale, NJ: The Analytic Press.

Stern, D. N. (2004). *The present moment in psychotherapy and everyday life.* New York: W. W. Norton.

Stern, D. N. (2007). Commentary on paper by Philip A. Ringstrom. *Psychoanalytic Dialogues, 17*(1), 105–113.

Stern, D. B. (2007). *The eye sees itself: Dissociation, enactment, and the achievement of conflict.* Paper presented at the IARPP Online Colloquium, Fall.

van der Kolk, B. (1996). The body keeps score: Approaches to the psychobiology of post-traumatic stress disorder. In B. van der Kolk, A. C. McFarlane, & L. Weisaeth (Eds.), *Traumatic stress: The effects of overwhelming experience on mind, body, and society* (pp. 214–241). New York: Guilford.

van der Kolk, B. (2007, October). Annual Conference of the Los Angeles County Psychological Association.

Wallin, D. (2007). *Attachment in psychotherapy.* New York: Guilford.

Winnicott, D. W. (1971). *Playing and reality.* London: Tavistock.

Zeddies, T. (2000). Within, outside, and in between: The relational unconscious. *Psychoanalytic Psychology, 17*, 467–487.

Afterword*

From its beginning, psychoanalysis has arguably been a profession rooted in improvisation. Unfortunately, promoting this idea did not bode well for the creation of a professional mode of practice that required both ethical standards and accountability. Perhaps because of these latter concerns, the place of importance of improvisation in psychoanalysis remained a "dirty little secret," ironically lost upon many of its practitioners, though not, however, Adam Phillips, who notes that Freud was an improviser *par excellence*; Phillips (1993) writes:

> Psychoanalysis, in its inception, had no texts, no institutions, and no rhetoric; all it had to see itself with were analogies with other forms of practice. The first practitioners of psychoanalysis were making it up as they went along.... Psychoanalysis, that is to say, was improvised; but improvised... out of a peculiarly indefinable set of conventions. Freud had to improvise between available analogies and he took them, sometimes despite himself, from the sciences and the arts...Psychoanalysis began, then, as a kind of virtuoso improvisation within the science of medicine; and free association—the heart of psychoanalytic treatment—is itself ritualized improvisation. But Freud was determined to keep psychoanalysis officially in the realm of scientific rigor, partly, I think, because improvisation is difficult to

---

* Many of the ideas formulated in this Afterword are a result of discussions that took place on the IARPP Online Colloquium in May 2010, which featured my paper on improvisation in this volume. I am indebted to all the invited discussants (as well as the participants in the colloquium who regrettably involve too many to acknowledge here) for their improvisational contribution to my thinking. In countless ways, the ideas in this Afterword reflect the thinking of Tony Bass, Gil Cole, Glen Gabbard, Steven Knoblauch, Steven Rosenbaum, Donnell Stern, and Steven Stern.

legitimate—and to sell—outside of a cult of genius. With the invention of psychoanalysis—or rather, with the discovery of what he called the unconscious—Freud glimpsed a daunting prospect: a profession of improvisers. And in the ethos of Freud and his followers, improvisation was closer to the inspiration of artists than to the discipline of scientists. (pp. 2–3)

Given psychoanalysis' ambiguous relationship to improvisation, there are some questions to which my chapter did not sufficiently attend. I will cover each under its respective heading.

Might being improvisational risk preemptory comments that could interfere with the patient's capacity to "free associate" or, even worse, potentially contaminate the patient's unconscious with that of the analyst's while also concretizing the patient's defenses?

This is a perfectly reasonable not to mention expectable concern given classical psychoanalysis' history of favoring *abstinence, neutrality and anonymity* in part to frustrate drives (i.e., to "flush out" the unconscious from the shadow of "self-deception") but also to create an atmosphere of safety in which the unconscious mind of the patient could optimally engage in unfettered "play" through "free association." Given this ethic, an emphasis was placed upon sparing the patient the intrusion and contamination of the analyst's mind. Schafer (1983), for example, argued that such conditions were foundational for "preparation for interpretation," that is, of the least contaminating variety.

Coburn (1999) notes that the kind of argument Schafer makes falls into what Coburn refers to as the "objectivist" position of classical psychoanalysis in which the analyst is more or less in a position of *transcendence*, that is capable of being sufficiently removed from the patient so as not have his subjectivity be much of an influence in the patient's associations. Coburn contrasts this to more of a "subjectivist" position, in which the analyst it inescapably in a state of *embedment* in contrast to *transcendence*. This latter position suits much more the ideas of relational psychoanalysis and its understanding of the inescapable nature of each analysis coconstructing an intersubjective world of interpretation. Indeed, this is a world constituted not by the "cause-and-effect" "objectivist" epistemology wherein the patient speaks and eventually the analyst interprets his "text" but rather an ineffably, mutually influential world of coconstruction and cointerpretation.

Improvisation clearly belongs in the "subjectivist" mode of *embedment*; as such the impact of the analyst's subjectivity has been seen, within the relational tradition, as "irreducible" (Renik, 1993). The contrast of the "objectivist" and "subjectivist" traditions manifests in a dialectic that takes up what can be thought of as the "sins of omission" versus the "sins of commission" (Irwin Hoffman, personal communication, 2010). The former involves the error of too much abstinence; the latter involves the error of too much engagement. The virtue of an improvisational sensibility, however, is that the feedback regarding which error one has committed is pretty instantaneous, insofar as it manifests in the form of "shutting down" the atmosphere of analyst and analysand being able to play with their thoughts, feelings, and one another. Instead, they are thrust into an "Enactment" (Aron, 2003; Bass, 2003; Black, 2003) or what I referred earlier to as "mutual inductive identification." Neither of these conditions necessarily involves errors. Indeed, they represent different ways of getting at what is implicitly embedded in the dyad that was heretofore inaccessible to explication, until, that is, it reveals itself in the analysis of the "Enactment" or "mutual inductive identification."

Is improvisation a theory of psychoanalytic practice per se, or does it involve something of an attitudinal stance that potentially informs all modes of psychoanalysis?

Although psychoanalytic improvisation represents a system of ideas that might suggest it is a theory, I think of improvisation as more of a "stance," that is, an attitude of "listening and responding (including remaining silent)" that seeks openings and possibilities where heretofore constrictions and foreclosures commonly rule. While it is quintessentially a relational mode of treatment to the extent that relational psychoanalysis is a "big tent" housing practitioners originating out of Freudian, object relational, Kohutian, Sullivanian, Kleinian, Jungian backgrounds and more, the assumption of an improvisational stance enables the relational psychoanalyst to play-off-of-and-with any and all of these persuasions (including other modalities as well).

Furthermore, while improvisation is a stance, it is not a body of techniques. Indeed, improvisational techniques would be almost oxymoronic. There are, however, some simple listening and engagement stances such as "trying to not negate" as well as to attempting to engage in an additive and opening manner like "yes/and" (e.g., recognizing what that other has said and then adding something to it that moves it in unpredictably creative directions, which when determined by the two participants' unconscious minds lends to a unique collaboration and cocreation of the heretofore unimaginable). Though some may mistakenly think of improvisation as a kind of performance art intruding on an analysis, it is important to note that fundamental to improvisation is the "cardinal rule of listening." This is what moves improvisation beyond the narcissism of each participant. It puts them in the position of "playing-off-of-and-with" what each other is contributing.

Along these lines, it is a mistake to idealize improvisation, as in what is improvisational is "good" and what isn't is "bad." While it is true that improvisation is about playing with and cocreating openness to possibility, life is also rule bound, constrained in the ultimate by our mortality. Moreover, in the course of play, we inevitably bump up against what we cannot play with, which as mentioned earlier generates "Enactments" and "mutual inductive identifications," which become analytic fodder from which much can be learned.

What distinguishes analytic improvisational play, which certainly involves the participants "casting one another" in a variety of largely unconscious role assignments from its seeming counterpart (i.e., Enactments), or what I refer to as processes of "mutual inductive identification," in which the two parties also cast one another in roles?

From a phenomenological perspective of improvisation, Enactments (as well as mutually inductive identifications) involve each participant "casting" another in some role(s). In contrast to improvisation, however, Enactments and mutual inductive identification project roles largely determined by "static" transference–countertransference "structures." As such, they contrast with the openness that improvisation creates since being improvisational results in playing-off-of-and-with how the analyst and patient create possibilities heretofore unimaginable. Nevertheless, Enactments and mutually inductive identifications are not only inevitable, but they also can be critical to the movement of an analysis, since they provide a special experiential circumstance for the ultimate illumination and interpretation of certain implicit transference–countertransference processes. They embody what Stern refers to as the "interpersonalization of dissociation" (2010).

In what manner does the collaborative effort of improvisation distinguish itself from the original sine qua non of psychoanalysis (i.e., interpretation) as well as from the contemporary psychoanalytic position regarding empathic understanding?

Improvisational principles draw from such performance arts as theater and jazz, and like these collaborative art forms psychoanalysis is an unscripted process. It relies on and attempts to "play" with the joint contributions of the coparticipants. The outcome of the process, however, is not an art piece per se but about the personal transformation leading to the growth and healing of the patient (as well as frequently that of the analyst). Therapy, nevertheless, is an inherently intense, intimate, and risky business. We get drawn into inevitable transference and countertransference enactments on a continuum of seriousness under the sway of nonconscious internal working models, unresolved developmental trauma, and mutual dissociation. Such enactments can be a force for therapeutic change or a vehicle for retraumatization. The outcome depends crucially on how the enactment is worked with in the therapeutic relationship—being contained and collaboratively explored, thereby validating the patient's subjective reality. This then lends to a shared, coconstructed emotional experience in which the rupture of the working alliance is repaired. When this does not occur, it risks replicating past abusive relationships as well as retraumatizing the patient.

All of this requires efforts at *collaboration* and *negotiation*, of which, as Donnell Stern wrote during the May 2010 IARRP Online Colloquium:

> ...Developing the sense of collaboration is more important than whatever understanding comes about as a result of it. Once you and the patient can collaborate about some part of experience that has been off limits, in other words, new understanding often seems to fall into place on its own. The analyst doesn't have to supply it by acts of interpretation. It is the new freedom that seems the most important accomplishment here; new understanding often seems to me to be the outcome of new freedom, and memorializes it.

Finally, as a mode of play, how does improvisation distinguish itself from other modes of play that might—with rare exception—be seen as less desirable in psychoanalysis?

Improvisation as a form of human play distinguishes itself from another version of play and that is about competition. This latter version of play is in evidence in a host of adversarial gaming situations such as Scrabble, tennis, debate, and any form of play that is constituted by winning versus losing. For the most part, I do not see a competitive mode of play as germane to psychoanalysis, with the possible exception of what Wolf (1988) refers to as the "adversarial selfobject function." In that form of play, the patient engages his analyst in a kind of argumentative to and fro that was absent in his development. From a Winnicottian perspective, this may facilitate the discovery that his aggression does not destroy the other—as his omnipotent fantasies might have led him to believe. But even in this case, if the analyst is "hell-bent" on winning, the results of such a "win" will likely represent the repetition of something domineering in the patient's life. Thus, to the degree to which the topic of improvisational play is sometimes mistakenly conflated with competitive versions of play, understandable concerns about the usurpation of the patient most certainly are bound to surface.

Improvisation, by contrast, cultivates a quality of "win–win"—that is, that the subjectivities of both parties are enlarged as a result. Indeed, the analyst comes to learn something about herself of which she might not have otherwise realized. And, of course, this is often discovered in the course of unraveling Enactments and episodes of mutually inductive identifications that enable her to move beyond her own prejudices and constraints that are a part of constraining the unconscious play between them.

References

Aron, L. (2003). The paradoxical place of enactment in psychoanalysis: Introduction. *Psychoanalytic Dialogues, 13*(5), 623–632.

Bass, A. (2003). "E" enactments in psychoanalysis: Another medium, another message. *Psychoanalytic Dialogues, 13*(5), 657–676.

Black, M. (2003). Enactment: Analytic musings on energy, language, and personal growth. *Psychoanalytic Dialogues, 13*(5), 633–656.

Coburn, W. (1999). Attitudes of embeddedness and transcendence in psychoanalysis: Subjectivity, self-experience, and countertransference. *Journal of the American Psychoanalytic Association, 27*, 101–119.

Phillips, A. (1993). *On kissing, tickling and being bored: Psychoanalytic essays on the unexamined life.* Cambridge MA: Harvard University Press.

Renik, O. (1993). Analytic interaction: Conceptualizing technique in light of the analyst's irreducible subjectivity. *Psychoanalytic Quarterly, 62*, 553–571.

Schafer, R. (1983). *The analytic attitude.* New York: Basic Books.

Wolf, E. (1988). *Treating the self: Elements of clinical self psychology.* New York: Guilford Press.

Author Index

479

Subject Index